GILLES DELEUZE AND THE FABULATION OF PHILOSOPHY

Powers of the False

1. *Gilles Deleuze and the Fabulation of Philosophy*
2. *Gilles Deleuze and the Filming of Philosophy*

GILLES DELEUZE AND THE FABULATION OF PHILOSOPHY

Powers of the False, Volume 1

GREGORY FLAXMAN

University of Minnesota Press

Minneapolis

London

Portions of this book were previously published as "Philosophy," in *Gilles Deleuze: Key Concepts*, 2nd ed., ed. Charles J. Stivale (London: Acumen, 2011), 216–25; "The Subject of Chaos," in *Deleuze, Science, and the Force of the Virtual*, ed. Peter Gaffney (Minneapolis: University of Minnesota Press, 2010), 191–209; "Deleuze's Platonism," in *The Deleuze Heritage Collection*, ed. Graham Jones and John Roffe (Edinburgh: University of Edinburgh Press, 2009), 8–26; "Sci Phi," in *Producing the New: Deleuze, Guattari, and Contemporary Life*, ed. Simon O'Sullivan and Stephen Zepke (London: Continuum, 2008), 11–21; "Losing Face" (with Elena Oxman), in *Deleuze and the Schizoanalysis of Cinema*, ed. Ian Buchanan and Patricia MacCormack (Edinburgh: University of Edinburgh Press, 2008), 39–51; "The Politics of Non-Being," in *Deleuzian Encounters: Studies in Contemporary Social Issues*, ed. Peta Malins and Anna Hickey-Moody (London: Palgrave, 2007), 27–39; "The Future of Utopia," *Symploke* 14 (2006): 197–215; "Transcendental Aesthetics: Gilles Deleuze and the Philosophy of Space," in *Deleuze and Space*, ed. Ian Buchanan and Gregg Lambert (Edinburgh: University of Edinburgh Press, 2005), 176–88.

Published by the University of Minnesota Press
111 Third Avenue South, Suite 290
Minneapolis, MN 55401-2520
http://www.upress.umn.edu

Library of Congress Cataloging in Publication Data

Flaxman, Gregory.
    Gilles Deleuze and the fabulation of philosophy / Gregory Flaxman
        p.   cm.
    Includes bibliographical references and index.
    ISBN 978-0-8166-6549-5 (hc : alk. paper).
    ISBN 978-0-8166-6550-1 (pb : alk. paper)
    1. Deleuze, Gilles, 1925–1995. 2. Philosophy. 3. Truthfulness and falsehood.
    4. Nietzsche, Friedrich Wilhelm, 1844–1900.   I. Title.
    B2430.D454F53 2012
    194–dc23
    2011017142

Printed in the United States of America on acid-free paper

The University of Minnesota is an equal-opportunity educator and employer.

18 17 16 15 14 13 12   10 9 8 7 6 5 4 3 2 1

FOR EMA—A PARADOX

CONTENTS

Abbreviations   ix

Preface   *The False to the Power of Two*   xiii

Introduction   *The Elements of Style*   1

1 Friendship and Philosophy, Nietzsche and Deleuze   22

2 From Genealogy to Geophilosophy   72

3 Deleuze among the Sophists   115

4 The Philosophy of Fiction and the Fiction of Philosophy   181

5 Philosophy in an Inhospitable Age   237

Coda   *Sci-Phi*   292

Acknowledgments   325

Notes   329

Index   375

ABBREVIATIONS

IN WRITING THIS BOOK, I chose to default to the English-language translations of Deleuze's works, no less to those editions produced in the United States as opposed to the U.K.; wherever I provide the original French text, the reader will find the reference in a note. But if the sense of an English-language Deleuze has become (for better or worse) fairly standardized, the same cannot be said for other authors whose writings are sufficiently represented in this book to demand the ease of abbreviations. In the case of Nietzsche, I opted to stick to Walter Kaufmann's editions. As much as I eagerly await the complete editions of Nietzsche's works that Stanford University Press has undertaken, this project is far from finished, and so I refer to what remain the most widely available editions. The same principle motivates my decision to refer to Edith Hamilton and Huntington Cairns's version of *The Collected Dialogues of Plato*. More recent translations of individual dialogues suggest considerable technical improvement, but none of these outweighs the advantage of a comprehensive and standardized collection. Finally, with respect to Kant, all references are made to the recent Cambridge translations under the supervision of Paul Guyer.

Works by Gilles Deleuze

CC	*Essays Critical and Clinical*
DI	*Desert Islands and Other Texts*
DR	*Difference and Repetition*
F	*Foucault*
Fold	*The Fold: Leibniz and the Baroque*
KCP	*Kant's Critical Philosophy*

LS	*Logic of Sense*
MI	*Cinema 1: The Movement-Image*
Neg	*Negotiations*
NP	*Nietzsche and Philosophy*
PI	*Pure Immanence*
PS	*Proust and Signs*
TI	*Cinema 2: The Time-Image*
TRM	*Two Regimes of Madness*

Works by Gilles Deleuze and Félix Guattari

AO	*Anti-Oedipus*
ATP	*A Thousand Plateaus*
K	*Kafka: Toward a Minor Literature*
WIP	*What Is Philosophy?*

Works by Gilles Deleuze and Claire Parnet

| Dia | *Dialogues II* |

Works by Immanuel Kant

| CPJ | *Critique of the Power of Judgment* |
| CPR | *Critique of Pure Reason* |

Works by Friedrich Nietzsche

BGE	*Beyond Good and Evil*
BOT	*Birth of Tragedy*
EH	*Ecce Homo*
GM	*On the Genealogy of Morals*
GS	*Gay Science*
PTG	*Philosophy in the Tragic Age of the Greeks*
TSZ	*Thus Spoke Zarathustra*

Platonic Dialogues

Gor.	*Gorgias*
Men.	*Menexenus*
Pha.	*Phaedrus*
Rep.	*Republic*
Sop.	*Sophist*
Tim.	*Timaeus*

PREFACE

The False to the Power of Two

> The world is neither true nor real but living. And the living world is the will to power, will to falsehood, which is actualized in many different powers.
>
> **GILLES DELEUZE,** *NIETZSCHE AND PHILOSOPHY*

WE OWE "THE POWERS OF THE FALSE" to Friedrich Nietzsche, for whom the phrase described the paradox and problem of philosophy itself. In Nietzsche's writings—and has any philosopher ever wrestled with the consequences of fiction in better faith?—the false designates the cynical end of a world lost to empty truths and rank deceitfulness, as well as the joyful possibility of creating the world anew. The false is the substance of the basest will and the highest one, but the appearance of contradiction is only the superficial rendering of a problem that remains to be evaluated apart from the opposition of Truth and falsehood. The false must become the subject of "extra-moral" (*außermoralisch*) evaluation, and if we begin here by returning to Nietzsche's critical and creative response to the task, we do so in order to augur its resumption and redoubling in Gilles Deleuze's philosophy.[1] We raise the false, so to speak, to the power of two.

In *Difference and Repetition*, where he declares his desire to reckon with the powers of the false, Deleuze insists that this problem entails the search for "new means of philosophical expression" and that this search was "begun by Nietzsche."[2] The critique of the true and the false demands the creation of a perspective, beyond truth and falsehood, corresponding to the creation of a new *style*; and as Deleuze duly notes, this problem inspires Nietzsche's fabulous experiments, most notably, the creation of the aphorism. Needless to say, no one can be expected to reproduce this remarkable and notorious style, and Deleuze does not try (this would hardly be the way to create new concepts).[3]

But his own series of expressive experiments, ranging from the subtlety of his commentaries to his collaborative efforts in schizoanalysis to the sovereign clarity of his late work, can be understood according to the self-same task—*to think and write differently.*

In the course of this book, I continually return to this phrase to describe how Deleuze follows Nietzsche's resolution—not according to letter, but in *spirit of letters,* or what we might call literature—to write against the grain of the most deeply engraved presuppositions of philosophy. As Nietzsche claims, the nature of knowledge qua science (*Wissenschaft*) has been dominated by a "will to Truth" that determines the basis for metaphysical representation and moral judgment by consigning the false to abnormality, immorality, and error.[4] To this will, Nietzsche responds by declaring that even the most truthful man (or woman) has never ceased to lie—and this is no simple statement. In a different context, the sentiment might seem to provide the opening to a familiar religious refrain, as if Nietzsche were no better than a preacher decrying the inescapable condition of original sin: "We are liars, every one of us, liars in the hands of an angry God." Of course, nothing could be further from Nietzsche's philosophy: inasmuch as we never cease to lie, he insists, this is because even the Truth constitutes a matter of invention. Lying isn't the fall from which we seek redemption, the Truth of God's grace, but the "truth" that there is no God, Man, or World apart from fabulation.[5] "There's no truth that doesn't 'falsify' established ideas" because the powers of the false designate the powers to create (*faire faux*).[6]

Among his most singular accounts of falsification, Nietzsche's parable "How the True World at Last Became a Myth" provides a brief and stunning account of this eponymous eventuality—the "history of an error" (*Die Geschicte eines Irrtums*).[7] Over the course of six aphorisms, the parable traces the metamorphosis of the True World from classical naiveté (the awesome innocence of the ancients) to contemporary nihilism (the bad conscience of the history of consciousness). In Nietzsche's writing, nowhere is this devolution more strikingly symptomatized than in the distance we feel from the ancient world: seemingly so "at home in the universe,"[8] the Greeks inspire an image of unquestioned vitality and unyielding instincts (*Treiben*) that seem to mock our doubts and disbeliefs. In our "twilight of the idols" (*Götzendämmerung*), Nietzsche suggests, the True World has become the subject of despondent, existential reckoning. What has happened? On the face of it,

Nietzsche's parable narrates the exodus of the World itself from immediate reality into the increasingly far-flung regions of skepticism, idealism, and positivism. But this eventuality actually comprises two movements, for the loss of the True World is redoubled by the reactive will that internalizes what we no longer externally apprehend, much less believe. While he describes the emigration of the real world from experience, Nietzsche also describes the immigration of an ideal one: truth takes up residence inside the subject, perhaps *as* the subject, the moral animal entitled to make promises and obligated to keep them.[9]

Thus, Nietzsche's parable follows the "history of an error" from the assurance of the True World to its endocolonization in a Truthful subject and, finally, to the collapse of both regimes. Once within the grasp of the sages, then promised to the faithful, and then mobilized as "Science," the True World has become unattainable, unknown, and useless.[10] "The 'true' world— an idea which is no longer good for anything, not even obligating—an idea which has become useless and superfluous" (*Portable Nietzsche*, 485). It may be that the only thing worse than the True World and the overarching regime of judgment (Platonic, Christian, Kantian, etc.) to which it gives rise is the loss of belief in any world.[11] Morality, Nietzsche once said, "is a long, audacious falsification,"[12] but the realization of this derealization, the truth of lying, no longer promises enlightenment. Knowledge is neither progressively acquired nor dialectically conquered but dissolves into disbelief. For this reason, "the end of the longest error" (*Portable Nietzsche*, 485) is not only the end of Truth but also of *illusion*: the loss of the real world is accompanied by the loss of the ideal one. Whether we've delegated the world to reference or to representation, to Truth or to appearance, the noonday of philosophy swallows any such outlines in shadowless immanence—in Deleuze's words, the "terrifying models of the pseudos in which the powers of the false unfold" (DR, 128).

What is to be done? How can we restore the world or, better still, revolutionize it? How can we refashion the false, which seems to have cost us the world, as the powers with which we might believe in the world again? These questions belong to Nietzsche's philosophy as to no other because, far from marginalizing or demonizing fabulation, he inscribes its powers at the heart of thinking and writing. As Deleuze argues, Nietzsche's singular genius does not consist in having pointed out the existence of the false but rather in having *affirmed* the false as the basis for all existence, as the power to *make exist*.

The audacity of this affirmation remains—when we stop to think about it—extraordinary. Even today, Nietzsche's resolution to enlist fabulation as the very practice of philosophy defies our sense of imagination, resisting assimilation to the common sense of a given "image of thought" and demanding, instead, that we "think without an image." In the powers of the false, Nietzsche gives rise to a new kind of critique and a new mode of creation that deterritorialize the ground of philosophy as we know it. "And if Nietzsche does not belong to philosophy," Deleuze explains, "perhaps it is because he was the first to conceive of another kind of discourse, counter-philosophy."[13]

Among Nietzsche's many gifts to philosophy, then, we should hardly be surprised that the powers of the false have not been received more warmly. The false entails profound risks that, Nietzsche says, are liable to be rejected or misunderstood. Thus, whenever Nietzsche says that his time has not come and that his philosophy must await the hospitality of future generations, we should think about the powers of the false. Whenever he says that the philosopher is a rare being, fated to wander like a stranger and appear like a comet ("incalculable, and therefore terror-inspiring"), we should think about the powers of the false.[14] Both the philosopher and the false are unrecognizable to contemporaries, antagonistic to any image of thought, and so both appeal to a future in which the contingencies of reception might be otherwise. Without an audience in the present, the philosopher is "born posthumously" and the concept addressed proleptically.[15] Therefore, and doubtless with his own fortune in mind, Nietzsche envisions the philosopher as an archer who fashions concepts into arrows and launches them into the future—all in the hope that someday someone will discover his projectiles. There could be no better image with which to begin this book than that of Gilles Deleuze surveying the landscapes of Nietzsche's philosophy, pausing to collect the arrows he comes across, depositing so many stray "aerolites" in his quiver.[16]

Beyond his commentaries, essays, reflections, and allusions, Deleuze's affinity for Nietzsche consists in having adopted the powers of the false, raising the orphan concept as his own and thereby raising it to a properly philosophical problem. Why? Because this concept designates the power of invention that conditions all concepts and all conceptualization. "To say that 'truth is created,'" Deleuze writes, "implies that the production of truth involves a series of operations that amount to working on a material—strictly speaking, a series of falsifications" (Neg, 126). No contemporary philosopher has pursued the problem of the false more relentlessly or affirmed its powers more scrupulously than Deleuze, and we should pause here at the outset of this book to understand the sense of this claim. Undoubtedly, Deleuze would be the first to acknowledge the litany of Nietzsche's commentators whom he read and admired: Pierre Klossowski, Maurice Blanchot, Jean Wahl, Michel Foucault, and Sarah Kofman, to name but a few.[17] And it could be argued that, beyond these names, the generation (or two) of French philosophers and theorists whom we associate with poststructuralism owed more to Nietzsche than any other philosopher.[18] Deleuze was one of a number of thinkers in the 1960s and 1970s for whom Nietzsche offered a way out of the malaise of phenomenology and existentialism that had settled into French philosophy, but his insistence on fabulation remains singular. Deleuze's flight from the proverbial "three H's" of phenomenology (Hegel, Husserl, Heidegger) is the affirmative "line of flight" (*ligne de fuite*) that returns to Nietzsche's philosophy, as we have briefly done here, to ramify the false and redouble its power to create.

Thus, in *Gilles Deleuze and the Fabulation of Philosophy*, I have sought to restore Nietzsche's legacy to Deleuze's philosophy and, thereby, to consider the latter in the framework of the false. But if the justifications for this book—the first of two volumes devoted to Deleuze's powers of the false—are ample, they are by no means obvious. With the significant exception of *Cinema 2*, which includes a chapter called "Powers of the False," Deleuze appeals to the phrase selectively, even sparingly. Such is the paradox of the fabulation, which is evoked so frugally because its powers are so ubiquitous, suffusing virtually everything Deleuze writes: the false outstrips any signifier and thereby demands the perpetual creation of a new language of concepts, at once "rigorous and anexact."[19] Indeed, the vitality of the false dwells in its endless plasticity (*vis elastica*), the power to assume countless different guises[20]; if the false can be said to exist, it "ex-ists" in-between (*au milieu*). Never strictly individuated, the false enters Deleuze's philosophy under the auspices of innumerable aliases and in countless different disguises: like Melville's Confidence Man or Nietzsche's Zarathustra, the false "appears" in the series of masks that, far from disclosing the face of truth, prolongs the variable sur-faces into a delirium.[21] In Deleuze's words, "fabulation—the fabulating function—does not consist in imagining or projecting an ego. Rather, it attains these visions, it raises itself to these becomings and powers" (CC, 3). What would it possibly mean to represent the false as fixed, unitary, determined, except to relegate its "becomings and powers" once more to the regime of Truth and to make the false yet again the object of sedentary knowledge? The false takes so many shapes and wears so many masks because its "essence" is to become, to dwell in the "being of becoming" (NP, 24).[22] The nature of the false is *metamorphosis*.

This avowal forms the point of departure for *Gilles Deleuze and the Fabulation of Philosophy*, which follows the powers of the false, as if it were Ariadne's thread, through the labyrinth of Deleuze's writings, subtly stitching together the disparate regions of his philosophy—from his friendship with Nietzsche to his critique of Plato, from his affirmation of classical philosophy to his experiments in rhizomatic expression, from his elaboration of Kant's aesthetics to his imagination of Kafka's minor literature, from his reflections of our control society to his engagements with chaos. If not the cause, fabulation is something like the fate to which Deleuze's philosophy eternally returns so as to resume Nietzsche's question: how can we affirm the false, apart from its basest inclinations, as the highest power of creation, of life? While it might otherwise usher in the most lamentable relativism, this question instigates the response which Deleuze's philosophy, pace Nietzsche, passes from the worst (or most truthful) instincts of the false to its vital expression. In his own terms, and according to his own tastes, Deleuze grapples with the end of the world and the genesis of a new one (*pars destruens, pars construens*), and by briefly describing these two tasks, which redouble Nietzsche's own philosophical project, we can anticipate the structure that underwrites the two volumes of *Powers of the False*.

In the first place, and with respect to the process of critique, Deleuze returns to Nietzsche's unyielding imperative to "philosophize with a hammer,"[23] to destroy the idols that have traditionally grounded philosophy. "There is no truth of the world as it is thought, no reality of the sensible world, all is evaluation," Deleuze writes, "Being, truth, and reality are themselves only valid as evaluations, that is to say as lies" (NP, 184). As we know, this conclusion is all too frequently met with a species of deliberate stupidity whereby we say that, in a world bereft of truth, we lack the exigency to mount a critique and the resources to discern distinctions: without transcendent criteria, what difference can we possibly make? To this question we should respond by adapting Nietzsche's maxim: beyond truth and lying does not mean beyond good and bad.[24] Rather, good and bad must become the expression of *immanent evaluation*. "Evaluation is defined as the differential element of corresponding values, an element which is both critical and creative," Deleuze explains (NP, 1). In other words, values are evaluated on the basis of the difference or distance that characterizes their perspective and, thereby, their expression. We evaluate values insofar as they are the product of evaluations, but in so doing, our evaluations invent corresponding values. "The problem of critique is that of the value of values, of the evaluation from which their value arises, thus the problem of their creation" (ibid.).

Therefore, in the second place, Deleuze returns to Nietzsche's avowal that critical evaluation marshals the powers of false. "To actualize the will to falsehood under any power whatever, to actualize the will to power under any quality whatever is always to evaluate," he says (NP, 184). More than a method, evaluation consists in an ethos, a style, a mode of thinking and living: "To live is to evaluate" (ibid.). This is why "we always have the beliefs, feelings, and thoughts that we deserve given our way of being or our style of life" (ibid., 1). This conclusion is all too frequently met with a second species of stupidity whereby the style of evaluation is conflated with the symptom, or *Stimmung*, of nihilism, as if critique were invariably, irredeemably negative. To this we should respond that, while critique destroys the idols of transcendence, it does so affirmatively, even joyfully, because it *creates* an evaluation and corresponding values. For Deleuze, critique razes transcendent values in order to proffer a vital rejoinder—perhaps the only rejoinder—to our abject cynicism and implacable pessimism. Only the powers of the false are capable of confronting nihilism with a philosophical "creationism," of submitting values to a transformation with which we can enchant a world.

In this light, the ostensible opposition with which we began—the opposition between a base exercise of the false and a noble one—actually discloses the far more profound problem of *transvaluation*. In relation to the Truth, we know that the false always gets a bad name, always gets pegged as deception or error. But when Nietzsche undertakes transvaluation, and when Deleuze returns to this task, each affirms the false as the highest value—the value of creation. Philosophy remains stillborn if we don't muster this higher power of the false to transform expression and create new concepts: "the power of falsehood must be selected, redoubled, or repeated and thus elevated to a higher power" (NP, 102). Indeed, "our highest thoughts take falsehood into account," and to this we should add that our highest thoughts invariably turn "falsehood into a higher power" (ibid., 105).

> The power of falsehood must be taken as far as a *will* to deceive, an artistic will which alone is capable of competing with the ascetic ideal and successfully opposing it. It is art which invents the lies that raise falsehood to this highest affirmative power, that turns the will to deceive into something which is affirmed in the power of falsehood. (Ibid., 102)

For Deleuze, as for Nietzsche, the highest powers of the false are realized in the work of art, but the relations that philosophy enjoys with the arts invariably give rise to its own novel expressions. Historically, the first part of this equation, or what we call aesthetics, has been more easily grasped than the second. Deleuze's voluminous writings on art are generally divided among particular arts and media, each of which undertakes its respective fabulation on the basis of its own materials—and each of which gives rise to the taxonomy of signs and, thence, to the creation of concepts. Indeed, when it comes to the arts, we tend to rely on the formula "Deleuze and . . ."—as if in each case (literature, cinema, painting, music, etc.) we were dealing with a different domain that the self-same philosopher engages. And, no doubt, readers may be tempted to conclude that the two volumes of *Powers of the False* follow suit: after all, these books are roughly organized around particular arts, literature, and cinema that preoccupy Deleuze and provoke his vast creations of concepts. Literature draws on writing to deterritorialize the ordinary imposition of "order-words" (*mots d'ordre*) and to express the inexpressible becoming of "a life," whereas cinema formulates images that deterritorialize the inscription of a "sensory-motor schema" and express "time in the pure state."[25]

Nevertheless, to regard literature and cinema as mere objects of conceptualization is to misconstrue these two books as much as to misunderstand the nature of Deleuze's own philosophy. Notwithstanding the profound role that these arts play in Deleuze's work as conceptual provocateurs, *Powers of the False* concerns the means with which Deleuze devises a *philosophical* assemblage with literature on the one hand and with cinema on the other. These are very different "machines," and they give rise to the very different tasks of these two volumes. In the first place, we turn to literature (or, more accurately, writing) in order to dramatize the philosophical expression that defines Deleuze's creation of concepts. In the second place, we turn to cinema in order to consider the cosmos of concepts themselves. In other words, where *Gilles Deleuze and the Fabulation of Philosophy* revolves around the development of Deleuze's *style*, which we will endeavor to understand as the variable expression of thinking and writing, its sequel revolves around the *fabulation* of particular (particulated, "parti-colored") concepts. In both cases, we turn to art in order to grasp the ways that Deleuze enlists the false, first as the fabulation of philosophy, then as a philosophy of fabulation.[26]

INTRODUCTION

The Elements of Style

> Publish each healer that in city lives
> Or country houses at the end of drives;
> Harrow the house of the dead; look shining at
> New styles of architecture, a change of heart.
>
> **W. H. AUDEN,** "PETITION" (1929)

The Philosophical Novel

AS MUCH AS HE LOVED LITERATURE, engaging a remarkable range of
writers for the purposes of philosophy, Gilles Deleuze doesn't seem to have
had much affinity for the "philosophical novel." Of *A Thousand Plateaus,* for
instance, he bristles when an interviewer suggests that it might be a work of
fiction:[1] the book, Deleuze says, is "philosophy, nothing but philosophy."[2]
What explains this reaction? Notwithstanding significant exceptions, above
all Nietzsche's *Zarathustra,* the philosophical novel risks the very presuppositions and methods against which Deleuze's work is waged:[3] the worst
instances of the genre prolong the duality of its disciplines into a mode of
representation and a model of recognition. From the predictable didacticism
of characters made into mouthpieces for ideas, to the reductive resemblance
that submits events to correspondence, to the overarching allegory imposed
on the narrative design, the crudest species of the philosophical novel constitute a kind of novelization of philosophy, the abstraction of both disciplines
to an "image of thought."

From one end of his work to the other, Deleuze invokes this "image"
to describe the assumptions that tacitly determine thought in advance
of thinking. Unlike objective presuppositions, which are explicitly stated,
the image of thought derives from subjective, unspoken, and what he calls

"pre-philosophical" presuppositions that underwrite even the initial premises of philosophy with a kind of "upright nature," *Eudoxus* and *Epistemon* (DR, 131). Thus, when Descartes clears the ground of everything but the surest thing, the brute fact of cogitation ("I think"), in order to secure existence ("I am"), Deleuze notes: "it is presumed that everyone knows, independently of concepts, what is meant by self, thinking, and being" (ibid., 129). Before it has even begun, thinking presupposes a thoroughgoing common sense and an abundant goodwill that relegate its direst eventualities to exception and error. Safeguarded from stuttering idiocy, unapologetic malice, and outright madness, Deleuze writes, "Philosophy is like the expression of a Universal Mind that is in agreement with itself in order to determine explicit and communicable significations so long as they are based in the goodwill of thinking."[4]

It is no coincidence that this passage, one of his earliest elaborations of the image of thought, appears in a book principally concerned with a novelist.[5] In *Proust and Signs*, Deleuze explicitly contests the traditional model of philosophical investigation "based on 'premeditated decision'" (PS, 95) by invoking a nonphilosophical and literary image, namely, *A la recherche du temps perdu*. Dispatching these very decisions and presuppositions, Proust revels in the creation of signs and series that are never determined in advance of experience; rather, his image of thought takes flight from the vagaries and contingencies of the search (*recherche*). As Proust writes, "The truths that intelligence grasps directly in the open light of day have something less profound, less *necessary* about them than those that life has communicated to us *in spite of ourselves* in an impression, a material impression" (ibid., 95–96). Deleuze dubs this narrative an "adventure of the involuntary," and it is precisely on the basis of this *reasonless reason* that a new and rival image of thought appears. "Thereby is manifested the 'philosophical' bearing of Proust's work," Deleuze maintains: "it vies with philosophy. Proust sets up an image of thought in opposition to that of philosophy" (ibid., 94).

Whether this is a new image or, perhaps more accurately, the creation of thought in the absence of an image, Deleuze refuses the conventional claims of the "philosophical novel" in order to affiliate philosophy even more closely with literature. But how or, for that matter, why? Let us recall Deleuze's avowal, in *Difference and Repetition*, that the problem of philosophy today lies in creating "new means of expression" (DR, xxi): while he specifically mentions both cinema and theater as ready resources for this transformation, Deleuze's own philosophical expression remains more deeply indebted to literature than to any other art. The reason is so obvious that we're liable to overlook it, for among the arts and nonphilosophical domains with which Deleuze felt affinity, philosophy and literature share an intimacy based on their common medium—writing. The complex theoretical history of the term notwithstanding, Deleuze affirms *l'écriture* as a metamorphosis that, by definition, eludes disciplinary precincts: "Writing is inseparable from becoming" (CC, 1).[6] In literature, he discovers unprecedented experiments in expression, lines of flight that evade determinate identity and sedentary territory, but we might say that Deleuze also discovers the avatar of the corresponding transformation of philosophy into an expressive experiment, a writing machine. To write is to create, no less to create concepts.

The revelations of writing reverberate throughout Deleuze's philosophy, but precisely because this vital ethos underwrites the multiplicity of his concepts and because it hides (so to speak) in plain sight, we're liable to ignore it or, worse still, mistake it for something like the philosophical novel. But nothing could be further from the spirit of his turn to literature. Where Deleuze engages so many writers ("nonphilosophers") in the name of philosophy, the philosophical novel achieves something like the inverse, importing a well-worn cognitive model onto the literary "plane of composition."[7] We need not invoke the name of Ayn Rand to grasp why the genre potentially promises the worst of both its disciplinary worlds, grafting a philosophical image of thought onto the horizon of fictive possibility. It bears repeating that this is not the fate of every philosophical novel, but as far as Deleuze is concerned, it's the most lamentable one because the genre consigns literature to the cause of recognition and the task of representation. Whatever the nature of the correspondence between its disciplines, the philosophical novel ultimately rests on the *factum brutum* of the correspondence itself—the *analogy*—which reigns over both literature and philosophy, providing the presupposition of their common rule or proportion. And this is not just any presupposition. The "essence of judgment" (DR, 33), analogy "essentially belongs to the world of representation" (ibid., 302), organizing the conformity between particular and general, matter and form, before which all becoming ceases.

Therefore, Deleuze concludes, "You'll get nowhere by latching onto some parallel movement": rather than recourse to analogy, "you have to make a move yourself" (Neg, 125).[8] The book before you is nothing if not an attempt to consider how Deleuze *makes his own move*, how he creates the means of thinking and writing that, philosophically speaking, *gets us somewhere new*. To think differently or otherwise—this is Deleuze's refrain, and while he makes it the task of philosophy, the writers to whom he looks are by no means philosophers. With Proust and Kafka as much as Nietzsche and Kierkegaard, Deleuze conducts experiments that rebuff even our most enduring presuppositions. No matter what their discipline, his precursors are those who stray into frontiers where the image of thought dissolves and where problems are posed in the absence of expectations. Hence, in contrast to Descartes's enduring dictum, "Cogito ergo sum," we might recall Kafka's singular protagonist, Gregor Samsa, whose eponymous metamorphosis could be expressed as follows: "I think, but I don't know what I am." What is the thing that thinks and what is thought?

Of Kafka's "minor literature," no less all literature (the minor provides "the conditions for every literature"[9]), Deleuze affirms the powers of fiction to outstrip (*dépasser*) our most calcified opinions and encrusted habits of thought. To write is to fabulate new modes of existence that carry us "off the rails."[10] This is why Deleuze says that, "among those who make books with a literary intent, even among the mad, there are very few who can call themselves writers" (CC, 6). We find authors everywhere, but writers are rare beings whose deliriums "pass through peoples, races, and tribes" and thereby attain a "universal history" in the sense that identity itself is displaced, at least potentially, into "all the names of history" (ibid., 4).[11] After all, what does it mean to attribute thinking to the identity of an "I" when the latter becomes a beetle ("The Metamorphosis"), or stands for a collective population of mice ("Josephine, the Mouse Singer"), or comes from the mouth of an ape ("A Report to an Academy")? In writing, at least as we are describing it here, the question of "being" or "essence" (what is . . . ?), which is so typical in the tradition of philosophy, gives way to an experiment in experience and existence, which is pursued to the most improbable ends (what if . . . ?). The writer, Deleuze says, is "someone who creates their own impossibilities, and thereby creates possibilities" (Neg, 133).

Between Fiction and Philosophy

The nature of this claim—to create the possible as well as the impossible— may well strike us as the height of arrogance or naiveté. Even if we do admit the fabulous nature of literature, we could well argue that "the arts" constitute something like the socially and even legally sanctioned sphere in which the false can be exercised, as if an artwork always came to us in scare quotes that marked its existence apart from the world. By contrast, Deleuze takes the arts to be something like the most contracted expression of all expression, and in this respect he refuses the traditional precincts that segregate the arts or, for that matter, distinguish them a priori from philosophy. "Writers, painters, directors, architects, musicians are as much 'thinkers' as they are philosophers," he insists (TI, 172), but this broad characterization invariably gives rise to "finer articulations."[12] While all of the arts, no less than philosophy, partake in thinking, the distinctions between these disciplines "should be sought at the level of their material creation" (ibid., 172). Each discipline undertakes its own creative task, according to its resources and predilections, in its own (*propre*) sphere.[13]

Broadly construed, Deleuze asserts that artists create signs on a plane of composition, while philosophers create concepts on a plane of immanence. These are different topoi, different materials, and different practices. But rather than preclude any possible relation, this distinction forms the conditions with which philosophy engages the arts. Deleuze formulates assemblages with literature, cinema, painting, and music on the basis of the singular means of expression that each develops. Insofar as a work of art is a machine for creating and emitting signs, Deleuze effectively divides the arts according to the kinds of signs each creates and the kinds of conceptual engagement that each inspires on the part of philosophy. The sign is a collection of intensities—a "sensible aggregate"—that bears no relation to structuralism.[14] Far from designating an internal duality (signifier and signified) or referring to an external world, the sign finds no preordained place in the order of things and resists any possible recognition. There is no common sense that we can make of the sign, no good sense that we can we can ascribe to its existence, because the sign is that which defies the image of thought on which such sense is based.[15] To lift a formula from Deleuze, and with a view toward his formulation of literature, we should affirm that a sign is that which cannot be thought as well as that which can only be thought. The material differences among the arts are always cashed out at the specific level of the sign, but no matter what its type, the sign induces philosophy to "think differently" (*penser autrement*).

In this respect, it is worth recalling (as Deleuze does) the moment in Witold Gombrowicz's *Cosmos* when the narrator stumbles across the sight of something "peculiar and strange," a sparrow hanging from a wire noose in the middle of a thicket. Suddenly, the indifferent scattering of images gives way to a "shrieking eccentricity," a sign, before which the world genuflects in astonishment.[16] The sign is the "object of an encounter" (PS, 16): precisely because it was not anticipated, cannot be recognized, and will not be assimilated, it compels us to think.

> It is precisely the contingency of the encounter that guarantees the necessity of what leads us to think. The act of thinking does not proceed from a simple natural possibility; on the contrary, it is the only true creation. Creation is the genesis of the act of thinking within thought itself. This genesis implicates something that does violence to thought, which wrests it from its natural stupor and its merely abstract possibilities. (Ibid., 97)

Whenever Deleuze writes about art, whatever the art, he insists that signs defy conditions of possibility. In all the arts, the powers of the false consist in the capacity to create impossible sign-events—and this is especially true in relation to literature. "There is no literature without fabulation," Deleuze declares (CC, 3), and in his countless encounters with different writers, he describes a fabulative line that extends from the impersonal and indefinite sense of "a life" to the creation of a collective people whose "possibility of life" constitutes the work of a vital, literary politics (ibid., 4). "To write is certainly not to impose a form (of expression) on the matter of lived experience," Deleuze maintains in "Literature and Life" (ibid., 1). "Writing is a question of becoming, always incomplete, always in the midst of being formed, and goes beyond the matter of any livable or lived experience. It is a process, that is, a passage of Life that traverses both the livable and the lived" (ibid.). This "passage" begins what is, arguably, Deleuze's most systematic and synthetic account of literature, but far from subjecting the latter to an analogy with philosophy, he makes it the avatar of philosophical renovation. Literature rivals philosophy, but as we have already said, in so doing it precipitates the creation of new modes of thinking and writing—of a new image of thought. We need only consider the categories of the "livable and the lived," which constitute what Deleuze elsewhere defines as the two aspects of the "science of the sensible" (DR, 56). In this well-nigh Kantian formulation, the livable and the lived designate, respectively, the conditions of possibility for experience and experience as such. But in light of the "passage" of writing, these prototypically philosophical coordinates are invoked to underscore the irrelevance of transcendental determination and to demand the creation of a new language of philosophy.

The scope of this thesis should convince us to begin modestly by understanding the nature of Deleuze's encounters with literature and by "cashing out" the consequences.[17] Indeed, we generally take these encounters to be a species of Deleuze's engagement with nonphilosophy: in other words, he makes literature the object of a singular affinity because its flights and experiments become his philosophy's agent (provocateur). This is a common conceit in Deleuze's philosophy, and it is commonly repeated by his readers, but we are suggesting here that, in the shared context of writing, *something uncommon happens between fiction and philosophy*. Only by virtue of the division between philosophy and literature, on which we have lingered to this point, do we grasp the ambiguous frontiers into which they occasionally merge and the creative affinities they share. In Deleuze's terms, the very distinction between disciplines opens up the "zone of indiscernibility" into which both plunge: their encounter becomes the occasion for an exchange of forces. "The plane of composition of art and the plane of immanence of philosophy can slip into each other to the degree that parts of one may be occupied by entities of the other" (WIP, 66).

In *What Is Philosophy?* Deleuze and Guattari invoke a number of "hybrid geniuses"—Nietzsche and Kierkegaard, but also Hölderlin, Kleist, Rimbaud, Mallarmé, Kafka, Michaux, Pessoa, Artaud, Melville, Lawrence, and Henry Miller—whose experiments bring literature and philosophy into fantastic proximity (66).[18] These writers do not flee from categories so much as they engage a becoming that opens up degrees of freedom and creates new possibilities. Therefore, Deleuze says, writing fashions a "line of flight" that resists any form, and this conclusion gives rise to the inevitable question to which this book will repeatedly return (CC, 1–2): how can we understand Deleuze's own style, his means of expression, his mode of writing? More than virtually any philosopher of his generation (the exception, arguably, would be Derrida), Deleuze affirms philosophy as a matter of expression, of writing. It is surprising, then, that the question of expression remains relatively little discussed among his readers, as if it were marginal to the "content" of his philosophy and not, as we will affirm, the very sense and sensibility from which concepts are effectively inextricable.[19] "The concept's baptism calls for a specifically philosophical *taste* [*goût*] that proceeds with violence or by insinuation," Deleuze and Guattari write (WIP, 8). Taste "constitutes a philosophical language within language—not just a vocabulary but a syntax that attains the sublime or a great beauty" (ibid.). The ramifications of this assertion find no better expression than in Deleuze's own expression, in the taste he cultivates, the style he formulates, and the philosophy he fabulates. How else could we hope to understand Deleuze's own perverse imperatives—creation without negation, multiplicity without unity, thinking without transcendence—if we did not understand his work, even in its most metaphysical instances, as a matter of a style that draws philosophy and fiction into strange and subtle alliance? Is there really any philosophy, at least in Deleuze's sense of the term, without fabulation?

The "Deleuze Problem"

Deleuze defines philosophy as constructivism, as the construction and creation of concepts. Dispatching the presupposition of ideal or ground, a priori or origin—a Truth—that would orient philosophy, he maintains that even Truth is created.[20] In this light, perhaps we can recast the concept of the philosophical novel in the context of Deleuze's work, where the term should not refer to a generic distinction (e.g., *le roman*) so much as a genetic one—the determination to realize novelty, to create new concepts. We can do no better, and we might do much worse, than to characterize Deleuze's profusion of concepts by recalling Ezra Pound's modernist ethos: *make it new.*

This is the mantra of a perpetual fabulation, which Deleuze openly affirms in the realm of literature and tacitly makes the task of philosophy (CC, 5). No, Deleuze never writes a philosophical novel, but he draws on fiction to furnish the constituents of a new image of thought. "When I learned that there were such things as concepts," he once said, "the effect on me was something like the effect of fictional characters on others. They seemed just as alive and lively."[21] While a book of philosophy should never be written as a novel, then, perhaps Deleuze's philosophy should be *read* this way, approached in view of the characters and voices it aggregates, the countless encounters and events it elaborates, the repetitions and motifs it unfurls. "Philosophy's like a novel:

you have to ask 'What's going to happen?' 'What's happened?'" Deleuze explains. "Except the characters are concepts, and the settings, the scenes, are space-times" (Neg, 141).

But what kind of novel is this? A baroque one, no doubt: Deleuze's philosophical novel is composed of many distinct volumes, each of which constitutes a possible world, consistent and coherent unto itself, but not entirely reconcilable with or amenable to the others. In one world, Deleuze's philosophy reads as a kind of *Bildungsroman* that begins with a period of apprenticeships, particularly to Nietzsche and Spinoza, from which the young philosopher releases himself ("I had paid off my debts, Nietzsche and Spinoza had released me" [Dia, 16]) in order to write his "own" philosophy, namely, *Difference and Repetition* and *The Logic of Sense*. But in another world, in the wake of the events of 1968, the heretofore "pure philosopher" encounters the psychoanalyst Félix Guattari and undergoes a radical transformation that will set him off on a materialist philosophy and politics in *Anti-Oedipus*. In still another world, the elaboration of schizoanalysis becomes the precedent for the even more complex composition of *A Thousand Plateaus*, where the pretense of philosophical and historical teleology is exchanged for a thoroughgoing rhizomatics. In an altogether different world, Deleuze's turn to aesthetic questions, most notably in his two volumes on the cinema, gives rise to a remarkable creation of concepts in the service of ontology and even cosmology, the world as a meta-cinema. In yet another world, Deleuze's subsequent return to Leibniz reveals the inclination of a self-proclaimed "classical philosopher" (TRM, 365), whose devotion to a topology of thought reaches a point of clarification in *The Fold* as well as in *Foucault*. Then again, in his late and possibly last world, Deleuze's approach assumes a kind of luminous sobriety, the resolution to speak concretely about concepts, which imposes the question: *What Is Philosophy?*

In view of these worlds, and others that we have surely overlooked, to what does the proper name "Deleuze" refer if not something like the multiplicity of worlds, populated by countless thinkers, folded again and again (literally, com-plicated)? Confronted by this vast multiverse, how does one begin to unfold the philosopher? In a sense, the resolution to write a book about Deleuze is preposterous, as if we could hope to convey a philosophical life (*une vie philosophique*) comprised of so many lives, as if we could hope to convey the complexity of this labyrinth in the course of a book, or two, or ten. The remarkable scope of his work once provoked his friend Jean-François Lyotard to dub Deleuze a "library of Babel"[22]—and the reference, recalling Borges's story of the same title, marks something more than a measure of erudition.[23] We're liable to get lost in a library that contains virtually everything, to wander the labyrinth of Deleuze's philosophy without ever finding our way out, or ever grasping the shape of things, or ever making sense of it all. How do we navigate this profusion?

Let us begin by envisioning the labyrinth from above, as if the chaos of conceptual worlds were to give way, like one of Jackson Pollack's canvases, to a sense of complex design—the filigree of vectors intersecting and running askance, forking and converging again in the neighborhood (*voisinage*) of singular points that coagulate.[24] While each vector is composed of a series of events and unfolds a possible world, the endless ensemble of world-series has been scattered on the plane of immanence, cast across the virtual landscape. Faced with this nomadic distribution, where "worlds collide," let us affirm the mode of writing and thinking that threads its way through these worlds. Faced with so many versions of Deleuze (*milles Gilles*), we affirm the style that connects, embraces, and weaves together this "chaosmos" (DR, 57). Style is this supplest of lines, the one that passes through every series, that traverses the surface of concepts, and that draws together the philosophical plane, the plane of immanence, as a plane of *consistency*.[25] Finally, then, let's be clear about the stakes of this book, which is neither about literature, nor about the philosophy of literature, nor even about aesthetics sensu stricto. Rather, this book concerns Deleuze's style of thinking and writing—the "fabulation of philosophy."

Hence, in the five chapters that follow, the "literal" turn to literature is unique but not aberrant with respect to the different problems, questions, and experiments that we pursue in order to elaborate the elements of Deleuze's style. The first chapter considers his relationship with Nietzsche and the resulting formulation of a philosophical friendship (*philia-sophia*), from which Deleuze launches his own experiments in expression. The second chapter unfolds the particular sense in which Deleuze envisions thinking as an affair of the earth and situates its mythic and fabulous powers (*autochthony*) in relation to the creation of Greek philosophy. The third chapter returns to Deleuze's project to "overturn" (*renverser*) Platonism, making the philosopher indiscernible from the sophist and affirming the simulacrum (nonbeing) as the power of the false. The fourth chapter examines Deleuze's explicitly literary encounters in order to pose his own writing as the expression of a "minor philosophy." The fifth chapter reflects on the problem of philosophy qua expression in an age of marketing, communication, and opinion, when Deleuze resolves to affirm the power of creation and recover the faculty of utopia in order to confront our "society of control." Finally, the book's coda inverts the dubious question of the future of the philosophy to pose Deleuze as a philosopher devoted to thinking the future, or what he calls the Outside.

In every chapter, then, this book frames Deleuze's writings according to the subtle contours of a style, both modus operandi and modus vivendi, that draws together the entirety of his plane of immanence. In his own words, style constitutes "the line of flight, the exit that is a creation, the power of falsity that is truth" (Neg, 133). In tracing this line, however, we should also beware the ways in which Deleuze's style has provoked so much resistance. Among Anglo-American critics, Deleuze has been deemed a postmodernist, a nihilist, even an anarchist, his style dismissed as sophistic, solipsistic, and obfuscatory. While these labels bear witness to a variety of (arguably deliberate) misreadings, each of which would demand our analysis, they share a common inclination—to condemn the philosopher to giddy indifference and glib desire. In the words of a recent commentary, Deleuze is "out of this world," and this sentiment can be dated back to the earliest receptions of his work in English.[26] From the beginning, Deleuze was accused of dangerous liberation as much as profound abstraction, reductive monism as much as impossible complexity. Even today, Deleuze's corpse qua corpus is brought before the authorities, whether political, psychoanalytic, scientific, etc., and charged with "reckless endangerment," with thrusting philosophy into falsehood and plunging knowledge into chaos.

There is a great deal to be said on this score, as readers of this book will discover, but I've invoked this species of antagonism here not to address Deleuze's enemies but rather to contextualize his "friends." The hostility with which Deleuze was met, especially when his work first appeared in the Anglo-American world, has had lasting implications for what is now called "Deleuze Studies": inevitably, the animosity he attracted (and continues to attract, albeit in less obvious and more reactive manifestations) has inspired the corresponding mission to provide an explanation of—and defense for—his philosophy. Anyone who has ever picked up one of his books can attest that

Deleuze demands a measure of exposition, but beyond this obligation, he has long inspired the labor of *legitimation*. There are manifold historical and institutional reasons that explain this tendency, but my point is that, in the Anglo-American context, where the antagonism of Deleuze's reception has been matched at times by an equally zealous admiration, the task of befriending the philosopher seems to have demanded a well-nigh hermeneutic effort.[27] Introductions had to be made, arguments set straight, concepts elucidated, situated in traditional terms and recognizable trajectories.

The fact remains that, when it comes to Deleuze, we'll never be done with the pedagogy of concepts, but he would be the first to add that this pedagogy should never be conflated with common sense. In turning to Spinoza, Nietzsche, and Bergson, among others, Deleuze actually relishes a taste for the violence they do to common sense. These "minor philosophers" prolong philosophy to the point at which it becomes "something which cannot be assimilated" (Dia, 15), and shouldn't we affirm this tendency in Deleuze? The project to render Deleuze legitimate and legible has run its course, and as we will argue in the first chapter, this eventuality effectively dramatizes the problem of beginning and the concept of emergence to which he repeatedly returns. Deleuze often remarked that we never know anything at its beginning, when "things and people are always forced to conceal themselves, have to conceal themselves."[28] But shouldn't the same be said of his own philosophy and the logic of its reception? At the beginning, it was necessary to make Deleuze's work conform to dominant forces, to extract the "characteristics" he had "in common with the set" of philosophy, in order "not to be rejected" (MI, 3). At the beginning, Deleuze's work demanded a kind of fidelity, at once interpretive and introductory, that would make it comprehensible and credible. Thus, in many circles, Deleuze has been cast as a pure philosopher: the vicissitudes and complexities of his style, which have relied to no small degree on nonphilosophy, tend to be diminished or subsumed into a background from which concepts can be detached.

Perhaps the sense of this suggestion emerges when we consider Deleuze in light of what he called "the Nietzsche problem." Nietzsche's lamentable fate—to have been misunderstood or, worse, betrayed by the worst species of misreading—conferred on his philosophical friends the duty to return to the text in order to clarify misunderstandings and to correct errors: in other words, to "show how Nietzsche was used, twisted, and completely distorted by the fascists" (DI, 96). The ingenuity of Deleuze's commentaries on Nietzsche should not prevent us from discerning that he was no less bound by this duty—and yet, in the early 1970s, at the moment of *Anti-Oedipus,* Deleuze contends that the task posed by Nietzsche has changed. While the misinterpretation and abuse of Nietzsche persist, Deleuze avers that "this is perhaps no longer the problem. It is not at the level of the text that we must fight. Not because we are incapable of fighting at this level, but because such a fight is no longer *useful*" (ibid., 256; emphasis added). Do we not face a similar challenge in relation to Deleuze? Today we have reached the moment when the problem of Deleuze has changed, when he no longer demands justification and demands something more than explication. Whatever he is becoming, we are no longer at the beginning of Deleuze's reception but "in the middle" (*au milieu*)—and this is the milieu in which *Gilles Deleuze and the Fabulation of Philosophy* intervenes. We have reached the moment to ask—once more, or as if it had never been asked—how we can formulate a new relation to Deleuze. What can we *do* with Deleuze or, better still, what does his philosophy make possible? What are the forces that his philosophy inspires and which forces are capable, in turn, of ramifying his singular style?

The Fabulation of Philosophy

It is no accident that these questions are the same ones with which Deleuze himself returned to Nietzsche, and we can find no better place to begin to grasp the former's style of thinking and writing than by understanding his relation to the latter. Nietzsche is the gift that keeps on giving, inflecting Deleuze's philosophy with a vitality that runs from his early and explicit commentaries on the dangerous philosopher, to the inspirations of "capitalism and schizophrenia," to the subtle inflections of his later work. Hence, this book properly begins by elaborating the development of Deleuze's philosophy in the context of his apprenticeship to Nietzsche, about whom he writes and *through* whom, paradoxically, he says he learned to write for himself (Neg, 6).

Deleuze's thought is unthinkable without Nietzsche—but this is also why it must be thought here and now, when their friendship has been subject to recrimination and revision. What has happened? It was not so long ago that Deleuze's affinity for Nietzsche was at once so intimate, their affection so publicly displayed, as to need no affirmation. In France, the resurgence of

Nietzsche in the 1960s and 1970s was all but inextricable from Deleuze's philosophy. "Some of Nietzsche's French readers came to the texts directly; others came through Heidegger, and still others through Bataille," Alan Schrift admits, only to add: "All were profoundly influenced by Deleuze's groundbreaking 1962 study *Nietzsche et la philosophie.*"[29] Nonetheless, if the development of a "New Nietzsche" has become a truism in the history of theory, and especially in the "high theory" of structuralism and poststructuralism, this is arguably because this history, at least as it is now written, consists in having been overcome.[30] Today, Nietzsche seems to symbolize the kind of youthful excess that, like the theoretical counterculture with which he is often identified, we have disowned as the measure of our adulthood and propriety. The critical moment in which Nietzsche's *Grande Politique* could be entertained has given way in our current moment to something like a Realpolitik, and this transformation has doubtless influenced Deleuze's reception as well.

Broadly construed, the criticism to which Deleuze (qua Nietzsche) is subject can be divided into two categories: the begrudging and the unremitting. Among some critics, the affinity between the two is the subject of regret, as if Deleuze could still be salvaged by prying him away from this bad influence or as if he could be read in spite of Nietzsche, whom we are asked to ignore as a lapse in judgment. Consequently, Nietzsche is dispatched from Deleuze's affections in favor of other philosophers. In Alain Badiou's *Deleuze: The Clamor of Being* (2000), for instance, Plato is brought onstage in order to supplant Nietzsche from Deleuze's sentiments and thereby affirm the latter's somber asceticism, while in Slavoj Žižek's *Organs without Bodies: On Deleuze and Consequences* (2003), Hegel plays the part of the friend who steals the scene from Nietzsche or, rather, introduces an "other scene" where Lacan lies in wait. On other occasions, though, Deleuze's relationship to Nietzsche is subject to retribution, as if the former had been made a surrogate for an enduring battle waged against the latter. In *Arguments within English Marxism,* to take a particularly noteworthy instance, Perry Anderson berates *Anti-Oedipus* as the embodiment of a post-1968 romanticism whose overarching slogan, politicized "desire," has given rise to "the expression of a dejected post-lapsarian anarchism."[31] The great danger of this "subjectivist *Schwärmerei,*" Anderson adds, is that it "can legitimate the desire for death and destruction, just as much as the desire for life and liberty, as its origins in Nietzsche make clear."[32]

Let us be clear on this point: nothing could be further from Deleuze's affinity for Nietzsche. Far from the "beautiful soul" he is made out to be, Deleuze ramifies Nietzsche's most revolutionary forces to deterritorialize any pretense of *transcendental narcissism*: as he insists, Dionysus names not a god, nor even Nietzsche,[33] but the affirmation "of all that appears, 'even the most bitter suffering,' and appears in all that is affirmed. Multiple and pluralist affirmation—this is the essence of the tragic" (NP, 17). In Nietzsche's tragic philosophy, Deleuze affirms the power of an unrelenting "yes" with which we traverse negation and partake "the aesthetic form of joy" (ibid.). Thus, the first chapter considers Deleuze's "friendship" with Nietzsche, beginning with *Nietzsche and Philosophy* (1962), insofar as this early text anticipates the creation of subsequent modes of writing. In effect, Deleuze extracts a sense of expression from Nietzsche that describes his own expressive experiments, most significantly *Anti-Oedipus*. The chapter concludes, then, by arguing that Deleuze and Guattari's revolutionary schizoanalysis, which we typically read under the sign of Marxism or against that of Freudianism, remains unimaginable outside Nietzsche's own writing machine.

The second chapter returns to this "friendship" in order to demonstrate how Nietzsche's concept of genealogy gives rise to Deleuze's geophilosophy. In the wake of *Anti-Oedipus*, Nietzsche's proper name tends to recede, but his "conceptual persona" continues to inhabit Deleuze's philosophical plane of immanence, deterritorializing the pretense of fixed identities ("molarities") and opening up the drama of a strange posthumanism, both geological and geographical. If "Nietzsche founds geophilosophy" (WIP, 102), this is because at the furthest extremes of his critique we discover the suggestion of a philosophy equal to the earth itself. But this is only a suggestion, the intimation of a possibility that, for his part, Deleuze pursues from his earliest meditation on desert islands (1954) to his final collaboration with Guattari, *What Is Philosophy?* (1991).[34] It is in the latter, though, that the two explicitly define thinking in relation to the Earth (*la Terre*): neither an abstract practice nor an ideal sphere that could be imagined in the absence of matter, philosophy begins on the basis of terrestrial contingencies that augur the development of a truly "superior empiricism" (DR, 57).

In this respect, geophilosophy never refers to a general enterprise but rather concerns the emergence of the Greek world and the inauguration of its philosophical plane. Both the second and third chapters revolve around the invention of philosophy in Attica, where the vagaries of land and sea, the currents of colonizers and immigrants, the flows of goods and ideas give rise to an unprecedented conjunction—that of the philosophical plane of immanence and the philosopher. On the one hand, Deleuze and Guattari write, the milieu of philosophy is Greek because it derives from the contingent conditions of the earth, which shaped ancient Greece and its collection of *polei*. *What Is Philosophy?* stages this drama of mind and matter, *nous* and *physis*, in the context of Athens. Here, as nowhere else in the ancient world, the earth nurtured a particular social formation, conditioning the milieu of philosophy. But on the other hand, they insist that while philosophy is Greek, the philosopher is a foreigner or, better still, a stranger (*un étranger*) who arrives by virtue of the same contingent conditions of land and sea, surface and depth. In relation to the earth we discover the milieu of philosophy and the personage of the philosopher, drawn together by mutual and reciprocal determination, each realizing the possibilities of the other.

With respect to Athens, Deleuze traces a series of singular traits—*autochthony, philia, doxa*—whose combination catalyzes the formation of philosophy in the ancient world and anticipates the conditions of philosophy (as he suggests) in any world. Thus, chapter 2 analyzes the "origins of Greek thought" (Vernant) in the transformation of the polis, which redoubles the absolute deterritorialization of the earth in the relative deterritorialization of the Socius. To begin with, *autochthony* constitutes the myth of having been "born from the earth,"[35] a myth that bestows common origins on its citizens and thereby conditions an immanent "sociability." In the second place, and as a result, Athens develops a complex concept and practice of *philia*, the pleasure afforded by friendship and rivalry, which gradually dispenses with aristocratic privilege in favor of a democratic equality. Whence the third trait, *doxa*, for the polis increasingly affords a discursive sphere, open to the expression of opinion, within which even foreigners (*metics*) find their place. None born above another, friends measured and expressed their differences on the basis of a kind of competition, or "agonism," which came to characterize the domains of politics and law, athletics and war, rhetoric and philosophy.

Far from being destined, philosophy emerges on the basis of many contingencies, and in this respect geophilosophy resumes what Deleuze and Guattari call, in the context of capitalism, "universal history"[36]: in both cases— and, as Deleuze acknowledges, philosophy and capitalism are profoundly related[37]—the eventuality must be affirmed precisely because it might have been otherwise. Philosophy emerges not as a cultural miracle, nor as the result of a "chosen land," but as the contingent combination of contingencies.[38] Only when we appreciate the game of chance can we grasp why Platonism marks the awful advent of the reactive forces of philosophy. In Deleuze's words, Plato presents us with the "poisoned gift" (CC, 137) of transcendence, and chapter 3 takes this betrayal as its point of departure. While Platonism owes its emergence to the formation of a discursive and conceptual plane, its "taste" for Ideas imposes a vertical image of thought wholly at odds with what Deleuze and Guattari call the "horizontal" orientation of immanence (WIP, 89). Therefore, we return here to the remarkable episode in which Deleuze attempts to overturn Platonism: forgoing straightforward critique, Deleuze treats Plato as he does any enemy, namely, with the kind of uncanny intimacy that will make them the subject of philosophical buggery (*enculage*).

A commentary, Deleuze once said, ought to consist in making a philosopher give birth to something monstrous, but as he is quick to add, the trick is that the commentary must inspire (grudging) recognition, as if not even the feelings of repulsion could prevent the parent from owning up to the perverse offspring (Neg, 6). Nowhere is this method, genre, or means of expression more clearly undertaken than in Deleuze's treatment of Plato. Far from anything like denigration, Deleuze enacts his critique in the spirit of thoroughgoing fidelity in order to extend Platonism to unsuspected frontiers. For Deleuze, the great drama of Platonism consists in having consummated the agonistic diagram of philosophy: thinking as combat. But if this diagram forms the conditions for the emergence of Platonism and the retention of a kind of Heraclitan strife, it also introduces the problem—of chaotic contestation, of unregulated opinion, sophistry—against which Platonism reacts. Above all, this reaction consists in the recourse to Ideas, which provide the criteria to adjudicate among the contestants and thereby discern the real "suitor" and the right (*juste*) opinion from its pretension. For Plato, the philosopher lays claim to the Idea on the basis of his idealism, the divine power of an *anamnesis* to see beyond the mutable world of copies to eternal forms. And yet, as the chapter suggests, Deleuze responds by following Platonism to its most precarious dialogic juncture, the *Sophist*, where the protagonist (the Eleatic Stranger) cannot produce a "true" Idea of the sophist and, thus, cannot produce the Idea of the philosopher. Pursuing his double, the philosopher is hoisted by his own petard, his position and privilege lost according to his own logic; Platonism finally induces the profusion of simulacra it had sought to hold at bay. In this respect, the chapter concludes by considering Alain Badiou's charge that Deleuze is a Platonist *malgré lui-même*, to which we might respond that he is a Platonist *selon lui-même*—a Platonist according to his own reading, a Platonist who preserves a taste for fabulation, a Platonist who goes beyond Plato.

Inasmuch as this is the case, though, Deleuze is no sophist either. In its ancient form as much as its modern incarnation, the "idea-man" (*le concepteur*) contrives means of persuasion and deceit with which we might be tempted to confuse the powers of the false (WIP, 10). But these techniques rarely achieve the creative and genetic powers of affirmation that Deleuze discovers in literature and aspires to in philosophy. No false philosopher, Deleuze is a philosopher of the false. Hence, the fourth chapter cashes out the question of fabulation in terms of Deleuze's means of expression. While previous chapters have revolved around fabulation to a greater or lesser degree—as a meditation on critique, as a creation of concepts, as a practice of commentary—the fourth chapter explicitly dwells on Deleuze's style of thinking and writing in relation to literature. We have already suggested that Deleuze entertains a seemingly endless series of encounters with novelists, poets, and dramatists, who occupy his plane of immanence no less than philosophers. And we know that writers of all kinds become the provocateurs for Deleuze's own constructivism. But what remains in some sense to be understood is that literature, more than inspiring the creation of philosophical concepts, inspires Deleuze's own style of thinking and writing.

For Deleuze, "philosophical concepts are also 'sensibilia'" (WIP, 5), and it is this sensible sense of philosophy, or what we have called expression, that draws him to literature and, more precisely, to what we have called writing. Inasmuch as "writing is becoming," Deleuze looks to literature to formulate the philosophical means with which to resist the metaphysical, moral, and institutional prerogatives of philosophy. As he and Guattari ask in *Kafka: Toward a Minor Literature*, and as we will ask again here, "Is there a hope for philosophy, which for a long time has been an official, referential genre?" (K, 27). The answer arrives in the concept of "minor literature" itself: as much as it induces the question, minor literature also anticipates our response. Like the history of literature, especially in the formation of "great" national literatures, philosophy is traditionally determined by the state-form, which provides a bureaucratic image of thought and a correlative series of genres. In Kafka's writing and elsewhere, then, Deleuze and Guattari extract the characteristics of a minor literature, but in this chapter we will endeavor to produce, or reproduce, the sense of a "minor philosophy." Turning to Kafka's literary machine—to his deterritorialization of the dominant language, his creation of a collective assemblage of enunciation, and his production of an immanent politics—we pose these traits mutatis mutandis, as the constituents of Deleuze's writing machine and the "hope for philosophy."

"There is hope," Kafka once wrote, "but not for us." While this epigram seems to suggest the paradox of an even greater pessimism, we might instead understand it, in the context of Deleuze's philosophy, as the paradox of a great impersonalism: there is hope only when we cease to be ourselves and become something else. This conceit is particularly critical in the fifth and final chapter, which considers Deleuze in light of the antagonism to philosophy that characterizes the present. The prospect of thinking and writing differently is liable to seem unlikely, even utopian, today when philosophy faces rivals and enemies that, as Deleuze and Guattari write, not even Plato could have imagined. The most recent rivals to philosophy, the disciplines of communication are potentially the most dangerous inasmuch as they unapologetically transform the marketplace of ideas into a marketable form of the idea, the concept as advertising. Today we confront two intimately related problems. On the one hand, as we have just said, philosophy is besieged by new rivals: advertisers, designers, programmers, and marketers now claim to be the true creators of concepts. But on the other hand, this climate is such that the critical power that Deleuze once attached to the simulacrum has been subsumed and colonized by those same disciplines of communication, which have reduced its creation to a "packet of noodles," an exhibition, a slogan (WIP, 10).

These remarks form the challenge that ultimately defines Deleuze's late work and this last chapter. Toward the end of their lives, Deleuze and Guattari seem to find themselves in a Platonic bind, compelled to defend the privilege of philosophy and to define the philosopher apart from his or her rivals. But this momentary affinity quickly gives way in *What Is Philosophy?* to the affirmation of expression itself. In the face of what might otherwise be the source of overwhelming nihilism, Deleuze's late work aspires to a remarkable vitalism, revisiting the problem of *doxa* and affirming, once more, the creation of a style of thinking and writing. Hence, in relation to their doxographic rivals, Deleuze reprises the analysis of common and good sense that he had already established as the two sides of *Urdoxa* and the two aspects of the image of thought. In Deleuze's writings, especially in his meditations on the philosophy of science, common sense and good sense belong, respectively, to the mechanistic and the thermodynamic regimes, but as I argue here, his late work envisions the development of a new or imageless image of thought—namely, "chaos theory." From the nature of self-governing systems and dissipative structures, Deleuze extracts the sense of a becoming that renews the power of fabulation.

The chapter concludes, then, by cashing out chaos theory in terms of the unprecedented recourse to utopia, which Deleuze and Guattari elaborate in their last book to displace the promise of a future and better place (*eutopos*) in favor of the production of bifurcations within the present (*outopos*). To the suggestion that Deleuze's "hope"—to think differently or otherwise—remains hopelessly romantic, even utopian, we respond by insisting on the transvaluation of utopia itself. Drawing on the science of chaos and complexity, Deleuze defines utopia according to the singular moments in history that raise themselves from the certainty of chronometric time (*Chronos*) to something like a virtual sphere (*Aion*): in such an untimely interval—and Deleuze is thinking of the events of 1968—we can divagate the present into other worlds or introduce unprecedented possibilities into our own. In this light, perhaps the book's Coda describes the framework in which to grasp this process. The title "Sci Phi" refers to Deleuze's suggestion that a book of philosophy ought to be read as "a kind of science fiction" (DR, xx), and this exhortation should be grasped with all due precision—not to imagine the future of philosophy but, rather, to invent a philosophy of the future. The future is outside, unknown, but Deleuze folds this problem into the interval of the present, such that the most interiorized and exteriorized of surfaces are joined by the supple crease of a transversal line, a becoming, a flight.

We have called this line of flight, this singular becoming, "style" inasmuch as it traverses the entirety of Deleuze's philosophy, passing through countless expressions and situating them all on the same plane of immanence. Hence, while the previous five chapters elaborate a sequence that carries us from Deleuze's earliest writings to his last, from ancient philosophy to a "people to come," these chapters reflect so many autonomous worlds whose consistency remains a matter of style. This is the "Deleuze problem," the perverse consistency that accommodates the inconsistent, that induces the impossible and unthought, and that refuses to be assimilated. Deleuze is not the kind of problem that we labor to correct but a challenge to which we strive to be equal. Deleuze's problem is finally ours as well: how can we create a style commensurate to the power of the false?

1 FRIENDSHIP AND PHILOSOPHY, NIETZSCHE AND DELEUZE

Truth or Dare

Selective Affinities

> We must await the arrival of a new breed [*neuen Gattung*] of philosophers, ones whose taste and inclination are somehow the reverse of those we have seen so far—philosophers of the dangerous "Perhaps" [*Vielleicht*] in every sense.
>
> **FRIEDRICH NIETZSCHE**, *Beyond Good and Evil*

AN INCORRIGIBLY PROMISCUOUS THINKER, Gilles Deleuze entertained relationships with countless philosophers, "friends" and "enemies" alike, over the course of his life. But among the subjects of his many commentaries, he remained passionately, unwaveringly, and incomparably committed to Friedrich Nietzsche. Even in light of his relationship to Spinoza, whom he regarded as the other half of the "equation" that distinguished his early work (Neg, 125), Deleuze seems to have found in Nietzsche the friend with whom he could formulate his own philosophy. Where Spinoza demanded his most conventionally academic work, "according to the norms of the history of philosophy" (Dia, 15), Deleuze says that Nietzsche demanded a new means of *doing* philosophy.[1] It was Nietzsche from whom he learned, paradoxically, to "speak for himself" (Neg, 6).[2]

The beginning of Deleuze's apprenticeship to Nietzsche is typically identified with the appearance of *Nietzsche and Philosophy* in 1962, but the significance of the book also consists in having broken a hiatus during which Deleuze published almost nothing. "If you want to apply biobibliographical criteria to me," he says, "I confess I wrote my first book [on Hume, in 1953] fairly early on and then produced nothing more for eight years" (Neg, 138). Instead, the young philosopher seems to have undergone a kind of gestation, measuring the academic "horizon of expectations" and dreaming of a means of escape. This explains the beginning of Deleuze's attraction to Nietzsche, who offered the possibility of straying from the deep furrows of brow-beaten traditions.[3] As Pierre Bourdieu once suggested, and as we should affirm here, nothing made Nietzsche "an acceptable philosophical sponsor" for a generation of young French intellectuals as much as his vexed status in the very academic tradition that Deleuze, in particular, found so suffocating.[4] "It was Nietzsche who extricated me from all this," Deleuze explains, because Nietzsche "gives you a perverse taste—certainly something neither Marx nor Freud ever gave anyone—for saying simple things in your own way [*en son propre nom*], in affects, intensities, experiences, experiments" (Neg, 6).[5] Deleuze frees himself from the claims of a dominant or "majoritartian" philosophy by laying claim to Nietzsche, and it is this paradoxical operation—the procedures of an apprenticeship that become, in turn, the source of liberation—with which we must come to grips here. Only by understanding the nature of Deleuze's relationship with Nietzsche can we elaborate the practice of critique and the emergence of a properly philosophical "creationism" that their friendship avails.

In this respect, we might be tempted to say that Deleuze makes his friendship with Nietzsche into a method, and while this is no doubt true, the simple conclusion goes too far and not far enough. In relation to Nietzsche, Deleuze does not aspire to construct fixed procedures but to fashion a kind of hospitality to his friend and to the encounters, however unexpected, that they share. Far from assuming a priori principles, then, we can understand this friendship in terms of three intimately related movements, or phases, that trace the development of his philosophical style. In the first place, we can elaborate Deleuze's movement from apprenticeship to something like affection, namely, the resolution to abandon fidelity to word or text in favor of the measure of forces that Nietzsche inspires ("the Outside"). In the second place, we can elaborate Deleuze's movement from an interpretation of Nietzsche to the creation of a collective assemblage of enunciation that is as much aesthetic as epistemic (*sensibilia*). And in the third place, we can elaborate Deleuze's movement from the analysis of a delirious decoding, which he identifies with Nietzsche's aphorisms, to the formulation of his "own" writing machine, *en son propre nom*, or what he calls "schizoanalysis." The three parts of this chapter correspond to these three movements, according to which we'll seek to analyze the profound and subtle emergence of Deleuze's means of expression.

For Deleuze, as for Nietzsche, the question of style is as elusive as it is complex, but we might begin to approach it here, altogether simply, by averring that Deleuze's style of thinking and writing is virtually unimaginable without Nietzsche. While other philosophers may inspire his affinities, Deleuze treats Nietzsche with the kind of intimacy that suggests a deeper affection, "a perverse taste," which they share like the secret of a strange apostasy. What is this secret? Traditionally, we define philosophy as the love of wisdom (*philosophia*) and the philosopher as the lover of wisdom, but perhaps philosophy is also an exercise undertaken according to the concept of the friend (*philos*) that lies at its heart. "*Philosophos* does not mean 'wise man' but 'friend to wisdom' (*ami de la sagesse*)" (NP, 5), Deleuze writes in *Nietzsche and Philosophy*, and this is no small emendation. The prepossession of the philosopher, for whom wisdom is the singular and defining predicate, cedes to a preposition—"to" the potentially uncertain relation of friend and wisdom. Hence, "the friend who appears in philosophy no longer stands for an extrinsic persona, an example or empirical circumstance, but rather for a presence that is intrinsic to thought, a condition of possibility for thought itself, a living category, a transcendental lived reality (*un vécu transcendantal*)" (WIP, 3). We naturally think of the friend as otherwise and external, as another person in relation to the thinker and (just) another concept in relation to philosophy. But when we understand philosophy as a drama of relations, the friend will be cast as the intrinsic element, or "conceptual persona," whose role is to bear thought beyond its habits and conventions. The question of friendship, as Deleuze says, "goes to the heart of thought" (Neg, 162), but what is the nature of the friend? What would it mean to befriend wisdom? *What is philosophy?*

Over the course of his writings, from his earliest commentaries to his last book with Félix Guattari, Deleuze never fails to return to Nietzsche in the context of these questions. Inasmuch as Nietzsche "wants wisdom to overcome itself and to be overcome" (NP, 6), he befriends wisdom by sloughing off the solemnity with which thinking too often proceeds and embracing a spirit of bottomless irreverence.[6] In the face of all the demands made by wisdom (an unrelentingly judgmental friend, truly a pain in the ass), Nietzsche declares: "I wished to conquer the feeling of full irresponsibility" (ibid., 21).[7] And has any philosopher ever laid bare the system of metaphysical-moral responsibility as savagely? Most notably in *On the Genealogy of Morals,* but also elsewhere, Nietzsche traces morality back to a profound system of cruelty from which consciousness emerges as the inscription of debt ("the use of the cruelest mnemotechnics, in naked flesh, to impose a memory of words founded on the ancient biocosmic memory" [AO, 185]).[8] Whether divine or mundane, debt impresses itself on us in the form of a promise—to pay up, to fulfill one's end of the bargain, to be true to one's word. This is what it means to be a "moral animal": to have been made regular and predictable. "To breed an animal with the right to make promises (Ein Thier heranzüchten, das versprechen darf)," Nietzsche writes, "is this not the paradoxical task that nature has set itself in the case of man?" (GM, II §1).

In response to this task, Nietzsche announces that he will have done with debt in favor of an entirely different sense of relation—or what we have called friendship. As Deleuze says, Nietzsche makes *philos* "the one who appeals to wisdom, but in a way that one appeals to a mask without which one could not survive, the one who makes use of wisdom for new, bizarre and dangerous ends—ends which are hardly wise at all" (NP, 6).[9] In *On the Genealogy of Morals,* Nietzsche traces this unwise wisdom back to a daimonic instinct that first visited him in his childhood, when he began to experience a preternatural misgiving or, better yet, dubiousness (*Bedenklichkeit*) in the presence of those values whose origin seemed to exist *behind the world.* This daimon, he writes, "entered my life so early, so uninvited, so irresistibly, so much in contradiction with my environment, age, precedents, and descent |*Herkunft*| that I might almost have the right to call it my 'a priori'" (GM, I §3; translation modified). The singular nature of this impulse strikes us most distinctly when we recall Nietzsche's early critique of Socrates, who famously claimed to have been possessed by a daimonic instinct of his own, an *inner voice,* which intervened to forestall ill-advised action. "The favor of the gods has given me a marvelous gift, which has never left me since my childhood," he is reported to have said. "It is a voice which, when it makes itself heard, deters me from what I am about to do and never urges me on."[10] But if Socrates introduces instinct into thought, Nietzsche says, he does so only to purge thought of its tragic-orphic spirit, its Dionysian flights, and to consign it to the inhibitions of reason. "While in all productive men it is the instinct that is the creative-affirmative force [*schöpferisch-affirmative Kraft*], and consciousness acts critically and dissuasively," Nietzsche says that Socrates makes instinct into a critical faculty and consciousness into the lamentable agent of its own impotence—a "monstrosity *per defectum!*" (BOT, §13). Having internalized the daimonic instinct, Socrates consecrates the reactive formation of conscience and the emergence of a new, priestly morality: the Hellenic superego.

By contrast, Nietzsche's daimon transforms this sad idealism into an affirmative instinct and a joyous passion. "The use of philosophy is to sadden," Deleuze writes of Nietzsche, but even the most tragic sadness is already and immanently joyous because it liberates us from what has hitherto been the source of mystification (NP, 106). Never in the interest of higher values, Nietzsche's daimon acts with an unappeasable suspicion in the face of all values. His only a priori is to distrust the a priori. The reluctance of philosophers to question particular values gives way to a countervailing tendency—a disbelief, both genuine and profoundly disingenuous, of all values. For Nietzsche, Deleuze writes, "The notion of value loses all meaning if values are not seen as receptacles to be pierced, statues to be broken to find out what they contain, whether it is the most noble or the most base" (NP, 55). After all, what makes values valuable? Is there anything behind values? And might what we call "good values" derive from the basest of instincts? "It could even be possible that whatever gives value [*Werth*] to those good and honorable things has an incriminating link, bond, or tie to the very things that look like their evil opposites," Nietzsche writes; "perhaps they are even essentially the same. Perhaps!" (BGE, I §2) Nietzsche consummates this famous passage from *Beyond Good and Evil* with the very question that concerns us here: "But who is willing to take charge of such a dangerous Perhaps!" (ibid.).

The answer that we are proposing—the friend—reflects the paradoxical promise that brings Deleuze to Nietzsche. What is a friend if not the one with whom we dare to "think otherwise" (*penser autrement*)? This suggestion may help to explain why Deleuze affirms Nietzsche as the greatest friend of philosophy, the one who aspires to be the most *unwise*. Consider this aspiration in light of the French expression "be wise" (*soyez sage*), the literal sense of which is subtended by a more colloquial sense: to behave. Philosophically speaking, to be wise is to be well behaved, but against this tendency Nietzsche offers the rejoinder of a "gay science" that unsparingly seeks to destroy every pretense to higher wisdom. Perhaps the most dangerous philosopher, and the greatest friend, is precisely the philosopher of the dangerous perhaps (*des gefährlichen Vielleichts*). In this spirit, Nietzsche turns wisdom around on itself, recasting its most sacred truths—*gnothi seauton, cogito ergo sum, sapere aude*—into all manner of perversion: perhaps we are strangers to ourselves; perhaps we are unconscious; perhaps we should dare to be unwise. These mantras form the unprincipled principles of Nietzsche's friendship with philosophy, but they also constitute the unprecedented concept of friendship that he proffers to the future. And did he have a choice? Inasmuch as his achievement was to have made himself the end of a long metaphysical-moral tradition—to have "finally learn[ed] from the Sphinx to ask questions, too" (BGE, I §1)— Nietzsche's fate was to find himself a riddle to his contemporaries. Like the madman who appears in the marketplace to announce the death of God, Nietzsche arrives at the realization that he has come too early (GS, §125).[11] "The time hasn't come for me yet," he admits in *Ecce Homo;* "some are born posthumously" (EH, §1 "Why I Write Such Good Books"). Knowing as much, reckoning his own "untimely meditations" against an oblivious and self-satisfied present, he is compelled to address himself to the future. Whether or not this address is explicit, we should always hear in Nietzsche's words a provocation for philosophers to come: *Follow me if you dare, but know that, as a dare, my friendship entails risks and dangers that my own time could not accept.*

The premise of this chapter, and the gambit of this book, is that Gilles Deleuze accepts Nietzsche's dare and that this decision to enter into a friendship—with Nietzsche, with wisdom—defines a philosophical life like no other. Today, I have suggested, "the Nietzsche problem" seems to have been increasingly exorcised from Deleuze's philosophy, but what if we were to choose to affirm this problem, to situate it once more at the heart of Deleuze's work, and to see Deleuze himself as a philosopher of the "dangerous perhaps"? Isn't it time that we made Deleuze a problem rather than making him amenable to the security of so many commonplaces and codes, so many introductions and explanations?[12] Admittedly, this is no easy task, since it demands that we approach Deleuze's philosophy, as he did Nietzsche's, by submitting all higher values—even and especially the value of Truth—to critique. Critique "has done nothing insofar as it has not been brought to bear on truth itself, on true morality, on true religion" (NP, 90). In his long essay on Nietzsche from 1965, where he dwells on this sense of critique, Deleuze suggests that the power of truth lies as much in its consecration (above other values) as in its adjectivalization (in relation to other values). Indeed, we discover precisely these operations in Kant's philosophy, where critique is cashed out in the assurance of metaphysics and morals. "Kant denounces false claims to knowledge, but he doesn't question the ideal of knowledge; he denounces false morality, but he doesn't question the claims of morality or the nature and origin of its value," Deleuze writes. "He blames us for having confused domains and interests; but the domains remain intact, and the interests of reason, sacred (*true* knowledge, *true* morals, *true* religion)" (emphasis added).[13]

In other words, Truth acts to guarantee—to verify—other "interests" on the condition that Truth itself remains implicit, taken for granted, *beyond* critique. Nietzsche explains: "Truth was posited as being, as God, as the highest court of appeal" (GM, III §24). While it may refer to many things, then, this Truth refers above all things to an extra or supplementary dimension that ensures other values as valuable. Behind all our daily habits and illusions, Nietzsche suggests, Truth lingers like a distant star in whose vast and invisible gravitational field all our values are oriented: to be "all too human" is perhaps, and above all else, to be confined to the regularity and predictability of metaphysical-moral orbits. Of course, Nietzsche adds, the truthful man has never ceased to lie, but even our most blatant hypocrisies and outright fabrications seem to consolidate a higher ideal, an even more transcendent Truth. What is metaphysics if not this game of one-upsmanship, of Truth corrected and thereby raised once more to a new frame of transcendence? This is why Nietzsche imposes the paradox of an a priori misgiving: in the face of all the claims to truth, we must become incredulous. Truth will have to be submitted to critique like any other value, but it will also have to be submitted to critique *before* any other value since the Truth is what renders those values not only possible but, finally, credible—"*true* knowledge, *true* morals, *true* religion."

While Nietzsche mounts the great critique of Truth, it is Deleuze who, among recent philosophers, has pursued his friend's critical impulse to its most singular, its most remarkable, its most *incredible* ends—"ends which are hardly wise at all!" For this reason, our return to Deleuze must be made under the auspices of his own return to Nietzsche, whom he befriends without any promise of fidelity. Quite the contrary: when Deleuze befriends Nietzsche in the spirit of his unwisdom and apart from transcendent categories—on the basis of the forces he assembles and the affects he provokes, of his singular taste and style—he ensures that Nietzsche will always have been *misunderstood*. In fact, "the only thing we can really explain is how Nietzsche reserved for himself and for his readers, both contemporary and future generations, a particular right to misinterpret," Deleuze insists (DI, 252). What does this mean? The basic difficulty here concerns the "right" of misinterpretation, which one assumes to be the exclusive right, or liability, of the reader. We may bemoan difficult works, we may complain about the interpretive labor they exact, but we generally take misinterpretation to indicate our (readerly) failure. But Nietzsche's philosophy is an entirely different matter. He appropriates the right of misinterpretation *for himself and for his readers;* a philosophy that dissolves the pretense of Truth and the True World demands a reception that does likewise. Insofar as he unleashes "movements, bursts of extraordinary speed and slowness (here again we can see the role of the aphorism, with its variable speeds and its projectile-like movements)," Deleuze writes, "Nietzsche snatches thought from the element of truth and falsity" (NP, xiii).

Therefore, we might conclude this discussion by invoking of what are called "false friends" (or *faux amis*). Typically, the phrase designates false cognates between French and English, namely, those countless instances when the same word or an approximate identity between two words conceals discrete meanings in each language (e.g., in English, the signifier "chair" denotes a piece of furniture, but in French the same word means flesh). In our discussion, though, *faux amis* would define those who pretend to be Nietzsche's friend, provided that we understand "pretend" itself to be a false friend. In English, the verb "pretend" denotes fakery, masquerade, and (of course) pretense, but in French, *prétendre* also means to stake a claim. The friend is the one who lays claim to Nietzsche, or rather who claims an affinity with him, but *faux amis* do this on the basis of purported truth, which betrays Nietzsche's great unwisdom in favor of metaphysical-moral certainty. Hence, in relation to Nietzsche, Deleuze makes a crucial distinction between false friends and those whom we might call the "friends of the false"—those who refuse the designation of the true and the false in order to affirm the "powers of the false," those who undertake a perpetual fabulation and self-perpetuating metamorphosis (*faire faux*). Even as Truth seems to bring friends together, to secure their fidelity, and to underwrite their contracts, Nietzsche and Deleuze insist that friendship constitutes the means with which Truth becomes "conscious of itself as a problem." Inversely, then, perhaps the problem of Truth can be posed only " 'between friends,' as a secret [*confidence*] or a confidence [*confiance*], or as a challenge when confronting an enemy, and at the same time to reach that twilight when one distrusts even the friend" (WIP, 2).[14] Perhaps the problem of Truth is posed between friends because only in such a relationship, which is precisely a matter of mutual trust (*confiance*), can we introduce distrust. Perhaps only among friends can we risk the risk.

Toward an Aesthetics of Nietzsche's Reception

> Nietzsche remains inseparable, at every moment, from forces of the future [*de forces de l'avenir*], from the forces yet to come [*de forces encore à venir*] that his prayers invoke, that his thought outlines, that his art prefigures.
>
> **GILLES DELEUZE**, PREFACE TO THE ENGLISH TRANSLATION OF
> *NIETZSCHE AND PHILOSOPHY*

In his later years, as he moved from one rented room to another, assuming a strange and vital nomadism, Nietzsche wrote with an ever greater sense that his work would go ignored. He steadily lost friends and readers (often one and the same) over the course of his life; but as his audience dwindled, his mode of address grew more exaggerated, theatrical, and ironic ("one day the memory of something extraordinary will be linked to my name"; "it is only thanks to me that there are great politics on earth"; "I am the first Greek").[15] Indeed, Nietzsche fashions a persona that is overarching, global, even cosmological, but he does this in *response* to his disappearing readership as much as in spite of it.

Northrop Frye famously said that lyric poetry turns its back on it audience,[16] but in the absence of an audience, Nietzsche's lyric philosophy actually turns toward a not-yet-existent one. In the final book of *On the Genealogy of Morals,* for instance, he invokes friends at the moment of his greatest solitude. "And yet here again I touch on my problem, on our problem, my unknown friends [*meine unbekannten Freunde*] (for as yet I *know* of no friend)," Nietzsche writes, "what meaning would our whole being possess if it were not this, that in us the will to truth [*Wille zur Wahrheit*] becomes conscious of itself as a *problem?*" (GM III §27).[17] This rhetorical question cannot help but provoke countless more "sincere" questions. What is this will to truth? In what sense are we its vehicles? What does it mean to be, or to define being as, a "problem"? But beyond or before all these inquiries we might remark, as Nietzsche does, why it is that the friend should usher in such problems and should bring philosophy to such strange ends. Even if we say that the problem of truth is Nietzsche's own, that it belongs to his philosophy as to no other, we would have to admit that it is a problem he insists on addressing to others, to friends.

It is almost impossible to imagine that, when he posed the question, Nietzsche didn't have in mind the famous apostrophe attributed to Aristotle and later popularized by Montaigne: "O my friends, there is no friend" (O mes amis, il n'y a nul ami).[18] Nietzsche was thoroughly acquainted with Montaigne's works, having received the gift of his *Essais* from Cosima Wagner in 1870. Among these essays, he surely knew "On Friendship" ("De l'amitié"), where Montaigne cites this singular utterance in the course of condemning "vulgar and customary friendships." Still, the apostrophe seems to express a more fundamental lament (as, for instance, Jacques Derrida has argued) about the existential possibility of friendship.[19] Inasmuch as the aspirated desire of the address is contradicted by the declaration itself, the apostrophe holds the affirmation and negation of friendship—that pregnant comma!— in curious abeyance. "O my friends, there is no friend" marks a kind of logical suspension: the statement consists in the paradoxical relation between an invocation ("O my friends"), which exists in the here and how, and a generalization ("there is no friend"), which exists for all time. The paradox derives from the *contretemps,* and it is in this context that we discern the novelty of Nietzsche's address.[20] While it marks the absence of friendship in the present, his apostrophe—"my unknown friends (for as yet I *know* of no friend)"— holds out its promise against the threat of negation. Friends are never written off, not even paradoxically, since Nietzsche's paradox consists in the capacity to affirm friends despite all evidence to the contrary. The adverbial clause "as yet" (*dennoch*) bestows on friendship the hope of a discovery: Nietzsche displaces the failure to know (of) friends into a future when, for all we know, friends may yet be found.[21]

In his self-proclaimed "Prelude to a Philosophy of the Future," *Beyond Good and Evil,* Nietzsche seems to suggest that the arrival of such friends is pending. "And in all seriousness," he writes, "I see these new philosophers approaching" (BGE, I §2). While the emergence of these philosophers, presumably "Overmen" (*Übermenschen*), remains virtually impossible in the climate of modernity, Nietzsche renders nihilism propadeutic to the appearance of a "new breed of philosopher." This appearance demands the patient metamorphosis of a "race" whose genetic constituents the self-proclaimed "physician of culture" (*Arzt der Kultur*) diagnoses in the reactive forces of the present and envisions in the full-blooded transformation of the future. How does this occur? In his essay "Nietzsche," Deleuze traces the stages in the triumph of nihilism, each of which is successively grimmer, to the destruction of nihilism itself. Beyond the death of God, in the "twilight of the idols," when we cannot even muster the will to nothingness, the will to nothingness wants only its own destruction. But at this juncture a new philosopher and a new philosophy arise, since nihilism becomes the condition (or, rather, the unconditioning) under which values can be subject to absolute disbelief and, thence, to creation *ex nihilismus*. "And at this moment of the completion of nihilism (midnight)," Deleuze explains, "everything is ready—ready for a transmutation" (NP, 173).

Who can say at which stage of nihilism we find ourselves today? The only thing we can say with certainty is that, in the roughly hundred years since his death, Nietzsche has inspired and acquired more philosophical "friends" than he could have imagined. In its sheer, unremitting intensity, so strangely disproportionate to the relative indifference of his contemporary audience, Nietzsche's afterlife bears witness to a nearly endless series of claimants and counterclaimants. His *prétendants* run from vitalism to nihilism, from fascism to existentialism, from poststructuralism to posthumanism, from deconstruction to constructivism. It may well be that we can tell a philosopher by the company he keeps, by the friends he claims or, rather, who claim him; but even by these standards, Nietzsche's case is unique. Recruited by a host of diverse philosophical and theoretical enterprises and seemingly refuted by the rest, Nietzsche has suffered a reception that, in its worst moments, recalls the fate of Pentheus, torn to pieces by the Maenads, or of Dionysus, dismembered and crucified. Of course, the mistreatment of Nietzsche's philosophy—the occasions of false friendship—began with his sister's notorious misappropriations ("she tried to place Nietzsche in the service of National Socialism," Deleuze writes [PI, 65]), but the subsequent cases of injury have been so numerous that we wouldn't be the first to wonder at Nietzsche's fate. "It is clear that modern philosophy has largely lived off [*a vécu et vit encore*] Nietzsche," Deleuze once declared, but "not in the way he would have wished" (NP, 1). After the war, he explains, French philosophy expropriated the language of value from Nietzsche as well as Marx. "Everyone was talking about values, and they wanted 'axiology' to replace both ontology and the theory of knowledge," but as Deleuze adds, this operation effectively blunted the "critical and creative sense" of value (DI, 136). "What they made of it was an instrument of established values. It was pure anti-Nietzscheanism—even worse, it was Nietzsche hijacked, suppressed, it was Nietzsche brought back to Sunday Mass" (ibid., 136). But why is Nietzsche subject to so many misappropriations? Why is he betrayed more than any other philosopher?[22]

The answer goes to the heart of what it means to be Nietzsche's friend, for the abuse he suffered—the charges of virulent anti-Semitism and pure relativism, of complicit totalitarianism and apolitical aestheticism—should be traced back to the singular style he devises and the "dangerous perhaps" he unleashes. Of course, Nietzsche is inseparable from his own remarkable reception history, but as Deleuze suggests, this history attests to something in Nietzsche's own mode of expression. His writing functions like a kind of strange attractor, inducing countless interpretations, provoking "diabolical forces of the future" (Kafka), which threaten to steal him along different, and often dangerous, trajectories. We all know by now that Nietzsche's posthumous admirers include real tyrants and real murderers, that whenever we propose to know the truth of Nietzsche, he "will appear a nihilist, or worse a fascist; at best, he will seem an obscure or terrifying prophet" (NP, xii). And yet, the most horrific interpretations of his philosophy and the worst acts accomplished in his name compel us to confront the forces he assembles and the affects he provokes. The notorious instances of Nietzschean inspiration bear witness to a quality of expression that has no equivalent in philosophy because *it extends outside philosophy*. The Nietzsche question, Deleuze declares, involves more than "conceptual analysis"; it involves practical evaluations that evoke a whole atmosphere, all kinds of emotional dispositions in the reader" (ibid.).

To understand this assertion, which goes to the heart of not only Nietzsche's philosophy but Deleuze's as well, we must consider once more the rigors of friendship apart from its stereotypical obligations. In his preface to the English-language edition of *Nietzsche and Philosophy,* Deleuze argues that the very nature of Nietzsche's writing demands that we slough off a number of tendencies that would otherwise preclude any "positive relationship [*rapport positif*] between Nietzsche and his reader" (NP, xii). Perhaps symptomatically, this statement implies two discrete meanings, two approaches, that concern the ethics of interpretation. In the first place, the prospect of a "positive relationship" seems to suggest that a kind of unimpeded interpretive clarity exists between sender and receiver, writer and reader. If Deleuze naturally rejects this kind of relationship, it is because (in reading Nietzsche) he affirms the radical derealization of all communicative (or "inter-subjective") illusions. Philosophy finds no "final refuge in communication, which only works under the sway of opinions in order to create 'consensus and not concepts'" (WIP, 6). A positive relationship is impossible or, rather, its possibility rests on the apotheosis of the fantasy of universal communication that haunts philosophy with the promise of democratic discussion—of misunderstandings annulled and consensus achieved. Late in his life, one feels Deleuze's mounting contempt for the Habermasian promise of an updated public sphere, a new "communications society." His notorious allergy to discussion and debate, which informs his own method and style, likewise explains his hostility to the disciplines of communications, which insist on a model of "perpetual discussion" that subordinates the construction of concepts to "communicative rationality," to "universal democratic conversation" (WIP, 28). Communication does not create so much as it is "content to defend the vanished concept that defines its very condition," the "marketplace of ideas," as the fantasmatic vanishing point where capitalism and democracy are ostensibly reconciled.

It is against the prospect of a communications society that we might envision a different sense of the "positive relationship" to Nietzsche. "As long as the reader persists in" holding to certain preconceptions, Deleuze says that "there can be no positive relationship to Nietzsche" (TRM, 207). The conditional nature of this avowal underwrites the hope that a positive relationship *could* exist in the absence of an overarching model of thinking, when we dispense with the requirements of truth and experience the forces that Nietzsche assembles and the affects he induces. Positive should be understood to mean affirmative and affirming; beyond the question of "what does it mean?" we should ask: "what does it do—what forces is it able to provoke?"[23] The destiny of the aphorism, as Deleuze describes it, is no less fitting for Nietzsche himself, "whose sense changes—whose sense must change—according to the new forces which it is 'able' (has the power) to elicit" (TRM, 208).[24] The aphorism always encounters new forces, inspires new interpretations (and what is interpretation if not the application of force?), but what concerns us here is not the history of reception but a reception that detaches itself from the determinations of the present. At perhaps the most profound and enigmatic moment in all of his writings on Nietzsche, Deleuze insists that, in relation to the latter, something unusual and even philosophically unprecedented happens. "Something leaps from the book, making contact with a pure outside," Deleuze explains (DI, 256). What does this mean?

Though he dwells on a great many aphorisms, Deleuze consistently returns to the form of the aphorism as a matter of expression—an aggregate of intensities—which we can understand in terms of two features that characterize Nietzsche's singular and signatory style. In the first place, an aphorism is composed of a "delivery of intensities" that move us, affect us, beyond the determination of signifier or the sense of a proposition. "Nietzsche always maintained that there is the deepest relationship between concept and affect," Deleuze writes (NP, xii), because Nietzsche's concepts comprise sensible ordinates (*sensibilia*) that provoke and disorient us. In the second place, an aphorism forges an "immediate relation to the outside," which displaces thinking from the "interior [*l'intériorité*] of the soul or consciousness, the interior of essence or the concept" (DI, 255) into an immediate and unmediated relation to the Outside. "What constitutes the [traditional] style of philosophy is that the relation to the exterior is always mediated and dissolved by an interior, in an interior," Deleuze maintains (ibid.), but this is what Nietzsche leaves behind.

Forget the rigid division between the internal and the external (*Innenwelt* and *Umwelt*), the pitiable sequestration of consciousness from the world, or the predictable opposition between subject and object: for Nietzsche, the Outside unfolds the exteriority where forces emerge in the absence of any conditions of possibility. Rather, the reality of the possible derives from the clashes and contestation of forces themselves: "Nietzsche grounds thought, and writing, in an immediate relation to the Outside" (ibid.). Like Blanchot and Foucault, its other great *évocateurs,* Deleuze envisions the Outside beyond the offer of any image of thought—the Outside (*le Dehors*) is outside (*en dehors*) any model of what it means to think. But this is also why, Deleuze suggests, Nietzsche is the first philosopher of the Outside. Inasmuch as the aphorism leaps from the page, creating a "line of flight" beyond the frame of the text, the two features of the aphorism are not only inseparable: they are mutually inclusive. In relation to lived experiences, the aphorism "must be treated as flows which carry us always farther out, even further than the exterior; this is precisely intensity, or intensities" (DI, 257). An aphorism establishes a frame (*cadre*) within which we distinguish lines and movements, but only insofar as the frame, which ostensibly separates the interior from the exterior, gives way to a line that "comes from elsewhere" (ibid.). Not simply outside the frame but from *the Outside*, this line of flight dissolves the imposition of an overarching image in order to introduce thought into an impersonal field of forces.

Perhaps, now, we can return to the dangers and betrayals that characterize Nietzsche's reception. Of course, as we have already seen, Nietzsche anticipates the vagaries of his own reception in the intimate knowledge that his writing assembles forces that will provoke yet other forces, other interpretations. Misinterpretation cannot be reduced to misreading, to misunderstanding, to *error,* as if an intrinsic meaning had been deranged, because misinterpretation forms the condition of reading Nietzsche. The worst misinterpretations of Nietzsche are precisely those that insist on the possibility of an interpretation that does not miss, when in fact the "experience and movements" of his writing elude truthful interpretation and determinative judgment. For this reason, when Deleuze writes that "something leaps from the book, making contact with a pure outside," he is quick to add: *"It is this, I believe, which for Nietzsche's work is the right to misinterpret [le droit au contresens pour toute l'oeuvre de Nietzsche]"* (DI, 256; emphasis added).[25] Hence, the event of Nietzsche lies in the eventuality of his reception: "he" must be sought in the forces he inspires, however mistaken and perhaps even because they are mistaken. The aphorism leaps from the page, creating a line beyond the frame (*hors cadre*) of the text and, thereby, beyond any traditional sense of hermeneutics. Nietzsche formulates an assemblage of forces that inspires the creation of a "final force, the nth power," which in turn will reformulate the assemblage. With the Outside, which is at once *the field of forces and the fulguration of the future*, we finally pass from the question of what Nietzsche means to what he becomes: what affects does he produce, what forces does he "preflect," what thinking does he provoke?

We might conclude, then, by affirming these questions in terms of the dimension that characterizes the Outside. If the Outside remains so elusive, this is because it alludes to the different temporal registers that, for Deleuze, broadly define Nietzsche's writing. Nothing could be further from the model of hermeneutics, which insists on the interiority of the text, its essence or meaning, than the relation to the Outside, which traces the improbable torsion of a line of flight that leads to the most *exterior* ripple of reception, the expanding crest of a circumference that stretches into the frontiers of thought itself. An aphorism leaps from the page, propelling itself into a future where, Nietzsche hopes, it will find the hospitality of forces to ramify its own. In the first place, there is resistance to the *present*, to the common sense of our current opinions and habitual abstractions: the aphorism aggregates intensities that we cannot recognize, introducing thinking into a direct relation to the Outside. In the second place, though, there is also the opening to the *future*: the aphorism comprises an intensive "history of reception," the assemblage of forces, that opens like an aperture onto the creation of possibilities. "Emergence, change, and mutation affect composing forces, not composed forms," Deleuze explains (F, 87).[26] "In this way the Outside is always an opening on to a future: nothing ends, since nothing has begun, but everything is transformed [*se métamorphose*]" (F, 89). Ultimately, the risks and possibilities that accompany Nietzche's writings, and particularly his aphorisms, corresponds to his peculiar temporal sensibility, which spans past (history), present (resistance), and future (possibility) but which always marks the intervention of that which is *untimely* (*unzeitgemäß*).

From Apprenticeship to Expression

The Collective Assemblage of Interpretation

> I don't really do textual commentary. For me, a text is nothing but a cog in a larger extra-textual practice. It's not about using deconstruction, or any other textual practice, to do textual commentary; it's about seeing what one can do with an extra-textual practice that extends the text. You ask me whether I believe in the nomad as an answer [Vous me demandez si je crois à la réponse des nomades]. Yes, I do.
>
> GILLES DELEUZE, "NOMAD THOUGHT"

Ten years after he published *Nietzsche and Philosophy*, Deleuze returned to the subject of Nietzsche in the context of what we have been describing here as a theory of reception. In "Nomad Thought" (*Pensée nomade*) a short talk he wrote for the famous conference held at Cerisy-La-Salle in 1972, Deleuze begins by dwelling on Nietzsche's relation to "the most recent, most actual, most provisional-ultimate" forces (DI, 256). These forces are especially germane to the essay in question, which was written in the aftermath of the events of May '68 and which anticipates a political turn in Deleuze's philosophy that characterizes much of his subsequent work, especially with Félix Guattari. "Nomad Thought" was delivered the year after Deleuze and Guattari published *Anti-Oedipus,* their "introduction to nonfascist living," and the essay shares a vital desire to consider Nietzsche's philosophy as nothing less than an experiment in the art of living.[27] "How is it that musicians today feel some connection with Nietzsche in their music, although they do not at all make music in any Nietzschean sense that Nietzsche would understand? How is it that young painters, young filmmakers feel some connection with Nietzsche? What is going on?" (DI, 252).

These questions presage what we might take to be the underlying problem of the essay: how should we read Nietzsche today? In "Nomad Thought," Deleuze explains that there was a time "when it was important to show how Nietzsche was used, twisted, and completely distorted by the fascists" (DI, 256). But today, he adds, "this is perhaps no longer the problem. It is not at the level of the text that we must fight. Not because we are incapable of fighting at this level, but because such a fight is no longer *useful*" (ibid.; emphasis added). Consider for a moment the more traditional reading practice, namely, showing how Nietzsche has been "used, twisted, and completely distorted" (DI, 255). The necessity of this practice is belied by an implicit moral imperative, the duty of a kind of reading, which is at issue here. Historically, the fact that Nietzsche "inspired and inspires still many a young fascist" (DI, 256) has given rise to a broad, hermeneutic enterprise: the obligation to rescue Nietzsche from his most egregious readers. In Anglo-American circles, of course, Walter Kaufmann was largely responsible for this labor, and Deleuze notes the French figures ("Jean Wahl, Bataille, and Klossowski") who performed their own means of salvation (ibid.). The tremendous novelty of these thinkers notwithstanding, Deleuze's point is that the obligation to defend and justify Nietzsche promotes the "level of the text" as a field of reference and, thence, of evidence to which philosophy returns in the broad interest of "doing justice" to the original.

At first glance, Deleuze's early commentaries seem to belong to precisely the tradition of faithful interpretation. While he chooses to write about minor, disparaged, or disregarded philosophers (Hume, Bergson, Spinoza, etc.), his readings of these "infamous men" also consist, at least ostensibly, in restoring their philosophical enterprise.[28] This is especially true of Deleuze's treatment of Nietzsche, whose reputation as a figure of philosophical ill repute demanded the rehabilitation of his great, and misunderstood, rigor. "Nietzsche's posthumous fate" is beset by questions, problems, and enigmas with which we are never really finished (NP, ix). "This is why a book about Nietzsche must try hard to correct the practical or emotional misunderstanding [*l'incompréhension*] as well as re-establishing the conceptual analysis," Deleuze says (NP, xxii). Hence, when he was still relatively young, Deleuze collaborated with Michel Foucault to help organize Nietzsche's notes (*Nachlass*), which would form a crucial part of the project to publish the philosopher's *Complete Philosophical Works*. Under the auspices of two Italians, Giorgio Colli and Mazzino Montinari, the new edition of Nietzsche sought to redress the abuses that Elisabeth Förster-Nietzsche wrought on her brother's writings, the result of which had been (and, in English, remains) the misleading amalgamation called *The Will to Power*. "She didn't falsify the texts," Deleuze explains, "but we know that there are other ways to distort an author's thinking, even if by a merely arbitrary selection from among his papers" (DI, 128).[29]

In their editorial capacities, then, Deleuze and Foucault worked to remedy the chronology and provenance of Nietzsche's writings, but the nature of their friendship extended well beyond this service, this "good turn." For his part, Foucault readily acknowledged Nietzsche to be the inspiration for his great histories of modern discursive formations (madness, punishment, sexuality, etc.). No doubt, Deleuze remains altogether sympathetic to this approach, but he responds to "the Nietzsche question" on his own *philosophical* terms.[30] In *Nietzsche and Philosophy* and his essay "Nietzsche," Deleuze produces an elegant account of the philosopher's major concepts, conflicts, and critiques: the Nietzsche we discover there is almost systematic, as if Deleuze felt compelled to demonstrate his friend's philosophical legitimacy as well as his own. Here and elsewhere, Deleuze never ceases to elaborate Nietzsche's great philosophical concepts (sense and value, force and will, power and the eternal return, etc.), but given all that we have said about interpretation to this point, we might wonder: what distinguishes Deleuze's interpretation? Insofar as he develops a wholly different concept and mode of friendship, we have argued that Deleuze casts off the pretense of "what Nietzsche meant" in order to affirm, rather, what he is able to inspire, what forces he is capable of catalyzing. Nietzsche's writing machine does not exist apart from its reception, but we have also insisted that the paradoxical legitimacy of misinterpretation, the "right to misinterpret," lies in mobilizing the forces and powers that ramify the flows of intensities and enhance the complexity of connections. Nietzsche makes misinterpretation a "right" because his writing extends beyond the bounds of the text, to the Outside, where forces act on other forces, and reception always remain to be determined by the prospect of a final force—the future.

Therefore, in relation to Nietzsche, but also according to Nietzsche's concept of relation, Deleuze develops a suitably perverse ethos of interpretation. "Nietzsche posits it quite clearly," he writes, but what follows is neither a direct quotation of Nietzsche, nor an indirect report of what he said, so much as a kind of free-indirect discourse in which they commingle (DI, 256). As if inhabited by a spirit, Deleuze momentarily channels Nietzsche's own voice:

> If you want to know what I mean, find the force that gives what I say meaning, and a new meaning if need be. Hook up the text to this force. In this way, there are no problems of interpretation for Nietzsche, there are only problems of machining: to machine Nietzsche's text, to find out which actual external force will get something through, like a current of energy. (Ibid.)[31]

Neither exchanged nor alternately inhabited, as we might expect in the flow of discourse, the "I" in this passage is effectively, paradoxically shared (*partagé*): it "refers" to Nietzsche, or so we naturally assume, but in the absence of quotations, and in view of the proper name "Nietzsche" that appears in the next sentence, it is no less Deleuze's. However briefly, Deleuze and Nietzsche plunge into a "zone of indiscernibility" wherein we cannot distinguish one from the other. In effect, Deleuze has accomplished precisely what "he" advocates—to plug himself into the Nietzsche machine, to enter into an assemblage of forces. "This is a good way to read: all mistranslations [*contrasens*] are good—always provided that they do not consist in interpretations, but relate to the use of the book, that they multiply its use, that they create yet another language inside its language" (Dia, 5).

It is in this respect that we might consider the sense in which we have invoked Deleuze's "friendship" with Nietzsche, for this is no rhetorical flourish, no mere metaphor. To the contrary, we affirm that this friendship is absolutely and indubitably "real" but that this reality remains *internal to thinking*. Separated by roughly a hundred years, Deleuze nevertheless encounters his friend in the context of philosophy, on the plane of immanence. "This is not two friends who engage in thought," Deleuze and Guattari write. "Rather, it is thought itself which requires this division of thought between friends" (WIP, 69).[32] The friend does not refer to an actual person, nor even to the concept of a person, but to what we have previously called the "conceptual persona." As Deleuze and Guattari explain, "The conceptual persona with its personalized features intervenes between chaos and the diagrammatic features of the plane of immanence and also between the plane and the intensive features of the concepts that happen to populate it" (ibid.). Between the plane and its concepts, conceptual personae constitute a kind of "third thing" that effectuates their relation.[33] The sense of such an intermediary is doubtless lifted from Kant, who describes the mysterious operations of the schematism that relates the empirical and the transcendental; but where Kant treats the schemata as the rules of "determination" (CPR, A145), Deleuze eschews any such rules in favor of the process of friendship that entrusts conceptual personae with the task of mediating the quasi-chaos of the plane of immanence and the creation of concepts (Neg, 125). Thus, Kant defines the concept in relation to a unity of apperception, such that it must always be reducible to the form of "I think . . . ," Deleuze organizes thinking around an impersonal form that can accommodate countless personae: "one thinks with   "

This operation takes place as if the personae were so many divers, descending from the plane of immanence into the sea below, where singularities lie scattered like so many stray pearls. Braving the depths, they collect these shimmering ordinates (*chiffres*) and then return to the surface, where the singularities will be thrown on a table of immanence like a "handful of dice from chance-chaos" (WIP, 75). With each throw, we induce the features that will be arrayed, collected, and diagrammed in the concept. Moving silently, often unannounced, conceptual personae may be situated in particular territories of philosophy or may deterritorialize others, but philosophy could not take place without them. Indeed, the friend introduces a manner of sharing (*partage*) and a means of nomadic distribution (*répartition*) without which thinking, at least as Deleuze defines it, would not happen. Deleuze explains this process, especially in relation to "the friend," on a number of occasions, but perhaps nowhere as succinctly as in a letter to Dionysis Masculo. To the latter's supposition that the secret of thinking takes place between friends, Deleuze says: "Friendship comes first" because it entails "an internal condition of thought as such" (TRM, 334). Friendship forms the circumstance within which the experience and experiment of thinking arise apart from all our anticipatory opinions and habits.

If the friend is the "condition for pure thought," this is because this persona introduces the prospect of distrust and distress, wariness and anxiety. No one needs to be told that, precisely insofar as they demand our trust and inspire our affirmation, friends bear us into trials and adventures that we'd never venture on our own. Therefore, in this letter, as in Deleuze's work more generally, the vicissitudes of the intrinsic relation we have called "the friend" traverse all manner of affects, inclinations, and problems that lead the philosopher beyond the presupposition and precincts of thinking that belong to a self-same subject. In relation to the personal features of the conceptual persona, philosophy accedes to an impersonalism—not the apperceptive unity of "I think" but the becoming-imperceptible of "one thinks"—which sloughs off any determinable identity by virtue of passing through so many avatars, friends, with whom one's identity becomes the becoming of the one (*l'on*).[34] "I am no longer myself but thought's aptitude for finding itself and spreading across a plane that passes through me at several places" (WIP, 64).[35]

Perhaps now we can return to Deleuze's friendship with Nietzsche in the hope of understanding the relations and affections they share. In *Nietzsche and Philosophy*, as well as his other monographs on philosophers and his "own" books of philosophy, Deleuze's style of "interpretation" is frequently determined by the task and genre of commentary, which may well strike us as the most conservative and sacrosanct of forms. But as commentary, Deleuze's philosophy is no less an experiment, and often more so. Famously or infamously, Deleuze compares the labor of philosophical commentary to an unwelcome act of coupling, as if interpretation took the form, in every sense of the word, of *penetration*. Of the professional compulsion he felt early in his career to "do" the history of philosophy, Deleuze explains: "I suppose the main way I coped with it at the time was to see the history of philosophy as a sort of buggery [*enculage*] or (it comes to the same thing) immaculate conception" (Neg, 6.). Indeed, the rhetoric of "apprenticeship" naturally seems to evoke the image of a young philosopher willingly submitting himself to the aggressions of so many mentors (fill me with your wisdom!). But nothing could be further from Deleuze's method. The trope of buggery actually inverts this model of authority in order to make the great philosopher the unwitting victim forced to submit to the violent imposition of another. "I saw myself as taking an author from behind and giving him a child that would be his own offspring, yet monstrous," he says (ibid.). With respect to the task of commentary, Deleuze makes his own writing a secret violation, since it is the commentator who mounts the great philosopher in the spirit of perverse *jouissance* that will bear away all classical inhibitions. The task of commentary amounts to turning the tables on the history of philosophy, inseminating our father figures with all manner of different problems and questions.

On this score, friendship must be distinguished once more from the lineage to which Aristotle's apostrophe ("O my friends, there is no friend") gives rise. When Montaigne famously introduces this statement in "On Friendship," he reads it as an exhortation not to mistake the nobility of friendship for its "ordinary and customary" varieties—among which, he adds, we must include friendship with or among women.[36] "Besides, to tell the truth, the ordinary capacity of women is inadequate for that communion and fellowship which is the nurse of that sacred bond," Montaigne explains, "nor does their soul seem firm enough to endure the strain of so tight and durable a knot."[37] But where we are concerned, the occasion of friendship and especially the philosophical friendships that take place "among men" demands nothing less than a kind of *unmanning* (becoming-woman). Is it possible, Deleuze wonders, to impregnate the "great men" of philosophy to induce an unprecedented gestation in the hope that new concepts can be generated? The scope of Deleuze's own work attests precisely to the possibility of making friends with reluctant thinkers and of making such thinkers give rise to new concepts. This manner of buggering remains most obvious in Deleuze's commentaries on Plato and Kant, who constitute both his greatest enemies and, as we will see, the most significant "targets of opportunity" for critique. And we would have to add that even those philosophers to whom Deleuze is ostensibly sympathetic—Bergson, Hume, Spinoza, Leibniz—are likewise subjected to a kind of aggression, as if they had been lured by the courting rituals of a respectful commentary only to have to surrender to an unexpected intrusion.

The only exception to this logic, or the philosopher who provokes an exceptional logic, is Nietzsche. As Deleuze explains, their friendship must be distinguished from the business of buggering that he had previously undertaken. "Because it's impossible to make him submit to such a treatment," he writes of Nietzsche. "Children from behind, it's he who gives them to you" (Neg, 6; translation mine).[38] Is Deleuze speaking though Nietzsche or Nietzsche through Deleuze? Is Deleuze buggering Nietzsche or vice versa? And how would we know the difference? Because this is a friendship that cannot be assimilated to the dominance of either philosopher, Deleuze's is no longer a buggering-commentary but something else entirely—an ambiguous assemblage from which no certain truth, no definitive subject, no sure identity can be extracted. Theirs is a collective assemblage of enunciation to which our traditional questions find no clear answer: Who is speaking here? Who is in charge? Which one is the *sujet d'énoncé* and which one *sujet d'énonciation?* Surely both Deleuze and Nietzsche retain their proper names, but those names no longer refer to a person, an author, or an origin so much as a capacity for a "becoming" that happens *between* the two. "Becomings are not phenomena of imitation or assimilation, but of a double-capture, of nonparallel evolution, of nuptials between two reigns," Deleuze once explained, appropriately enough, in a conversation with Claire Parnet. "Nuptials are always against nature. Nuptials are the opposite of a couple. They are no longer binary machines: question-answer, masculine-feminine, man-animal, etc." (Dia, 2).

Notably, the Latin source of nuptials (*les noces*), *nubere,* signifies marriage to a woman, and so Deleuze's appropriation of the term and his deviation of the concept ought to be understood as a deliberate perversion. The nuptials in which Deleuze and Nietzsche engage make the distinction between man and woman, top and bottom, front and behind, sender and receiver ultimately indiscernible.[39] "There are two types of genius: one that fundamentally begets and wants to beget, and another that is impregnated and happy to give birth," Nietzsche once said, without adding what we must affirm here, namely: that it is possible in certain relationships and under certain circumstances to be both (BGE, 8 §248).[40] On this point, we should be clear about Deleuze's characterization of commentary as an "immaculate conception," which might otherwise suggest a divine origin or miraculation, when in fact he complicates the lines of philosophical parentage beyond the point of any clear attribution. Naturally, we are accustomed to the metaphor of paternity and the figure of fathering a text, but with Nietzsche, Deleuze engages in a perversion of parentage and production so bizarre that we cannot finally assign the labor to either but only to both. An encounter takes place, but of what kind? A child is born, but to whom? This is a bastard philosophy, bereft of any father because it suffers from too many: *pater semper incertus est* (paternity is always in doubt).

For this reason, it is never enough to declare the death of God or to commit to kill the father, since it is precisely the myth of this primordial patricide that gives birth to more profound discipline. In *Anti-Oedipus*, Deleuze and Guattari write:

> Nietzsche is exceedingly tired of all these stories revolving around the death of the father, the death of God, and wants to put an end to the interminable discourses of this nature, discourses already in vogue in his Hegelian epoch. . . . And he explains that strictly speaking this event has no importance whatsoever, that it merely concerns the latest Pope: God is dead or not dead, the father dead or not dead, it amounts to the same thing, since the same psychic repression (*refoulement*) and the same social repression (*répression*) continue unabated, here in the name of God or living father, there in the name of man or the dead father. (106)[41]

In this sense, the problem of the "god/father" is precisely that his death does not prevent his return, if not as a new daddy-divinity, then as the "name of man or the dead father." Every father is a dead father, Lacan famously avered, but this eventuality bears witness to the "name of the father" (*nom-du-père*) that has displaced the real thing with its representation.[42] The signifier possesses a mortifying power—the Greek word *sēma* meant both sign and tomb—insofar as it amounts to a prohibition, the "no" or *non-du-père* to which all subjects are subjected. Only when we renounce the authority over life and writing that the paternal metaphor imposes can we enter into a new relation—that of the son who is "the son of nothing, or of everyone, a brother" (CC, 84). Only this operation, Deleuze avows, can create a "fraternity that no longer passes through the father, but is built on the ruins of the paternal function, a function that presupposes the dissolution of all images of the father, following an autonomous line of alliance or proximity [*voisinage*] that makes the woman a sister, and the other man, a brother" (CC, 78). In other words, only this operation conditions the creation of friendship, but it remains to be seen how, for both Nietzsche and Deleuze, friendship is no less the condition for the foreclosure of the paternal metaphor and the production of a new kind of writing.

The Philosopher's Song

> It was Schopenhauer who defined architecture in terms of two forces, that of bearing and being borne, support and load, even if the two tend to merge together. But music appears to be the opposite of this, when Nietzsche separates himself more and more from the old forger, Wagner the magician: music is lightness [*la Légèreté*], pure weightlessness [*apesanteur*].
>
> **GILLES DELEUZE**, "THE MYSTERY OF ARIADNE ACCORDING TO NIETZSCHE"

Deleuze often said that we do not know anything—or any "thing"—at the beginning. Introduced into a given field of affairs, we're compelled to approximate the status quo, to blend into the given state of forces, to disguise our nature. Beginnings, openings, overtures, prefaces: these are not to be trusted. "The essence of a thing never appears at the outset, but in the middle, when its strength is assured" (MI, 3).[43] Perhaps Deleuze's philosophical career, and especially his relationship to Nietzsche, is determined by the same logic—by the pretense of conformity within which the power of claimancy is secretly nurtured. Between his early and explicit commentaries and the elusive returns to Nietzsche that characterize his later work, Deleuze seems to undertake (or undergo) a remarkable transformation. This much is clear when we compare *Nietzsche and Philosophy*, which remains broadly confined by "the bounds of traditional philosophical discourse," to Deleuze's subsequent writings on Nietzsche.[44] "It is in his later texts," Alan Schrift writes, "where Deleuze moves from an interpretation of Nietzsche to an experimentation *with* Nietzsche, that we see him begin to operate outside the 'official language' of philosophy, outside of those organizing rules that govern what can and cannot be said within philosophy."[45]

One could argue that this metamorphosis is already presaged by the very title of *Nietzsche and Philosophy*, which seems on first gloss to formulate Deleuze's relationship to Nietzsche as a matter of "philosophy, nothing but philosophy." After the question of fascism, with which it is surely linked, Deleuze argues that the overarching "ambiguity" of Nietzsche's thought concerns this very relation to philosophy. "And was this thought itself really philosophy," Deleuze asks. "Or was it over-violent poetry, made up of capricious aphorisms and pathological fragments, all of it too excessive?" (TRM, 203).[46] While this question might otherwise invoke the litany of denunciations that the discipline of philosophy has brought to bear against Nietzsche, Deleuze makes the object of condemnation—his sensibility, his *style*—the subject of affirmation. Nietzsche formulates philosophy by virtue of affirming what is outside philosophy or, rather, by affirming a relation to the Outside that he will make proper to philosophy. "Any thinkable or thought-sense is only brought into effect insofar as the forces that correspond to it in thought also take hold of something, appropriate something outside thought" (NP, 104). No systematization, no recoding, no philosophy can transmit Nietzsche's writing because his "problem lies elsewhere," namely, in "an immediate relation with the Outside" (DI, 255).

Thus, the title of Deleuze's monograph acquires a second and more subversive sense. Far from writing "Nietzsche's Philosophy," which would impute a possessive relationship or even some kind of equivalence, Deleuze formulates Nietzsche "and" philosophy as if their coexistence remains undecided, uncomfortable, problematic—as if the title consisted in a question. "And if Nietzsche does not belong to philosophy," Deleuze suggests, "perhaps it is because he was the first to conceive of another kind of discourse, counter-philosophy" (DI, 259). But what is this "counter-philosophy"? In what sense is Nietzsche's style of philosophy also a challenge to philosophy? Among his most enduring convictions, Deleuze insists that "what is called thinking" (Heidegger) is neither a natural "state of mind" nor a natural response to the "state of the world." When he says that "something in the world forces us to think" (DR, 139), Deleuze means that thinking exists only in relation to an outside, an unthought, that startles thought from a kind of slumber. We begin to think only in relation to a provocation, to a kind of *violence,* that comes from outside and that thereby eludes the categories, codes, and clichés that would otherwise determine experience.

Like Nietzsche, Deleuze suggests that the work of art is uniquely suited to producing this sensible violence and, what's more, that this is its fundamental avocation. Hence, "the true object of art is to create sensory aggregates [*agrégats sensibles*]," he says, whereas "the object of philosophy is to create concepts" (Neg, 123). Nevertheless, the uniqueness of Nietzsche's counter-philosophy is to have drawn these "objects" into propinquity by drawing on the resources of art in order to produce concepts. The procedures of Nietzsche's writing appropriate the elements of a literary and even an operatic style in the service of philosophy. In marked proximity to the work of art, which he defines as a machine devised to produce signs, Deleuze defines Nietzsche's singular genre, the aphorism, as "a sense-producing machine, in that order specific to thought" (DI, 137). While signs induce sensations, aphorisms induces sense. Of *Thus Spoke Zarathustra*, his most poetic and experimental work, Nietzsche declares: "I do not allow that anyone knows that book who has not at some time been profoundly wounded and at some time profoundly delighted" (GM, Preface §8).[47] In other words, Nietzsche measures the success of his writing in terms of the kinds of affects it is capable of generating—to *wound*, to *delight*—because this is what compels us to think. "It is no objection to say that creation is the prerogative of the sensory and the arts," Deleuze and Guattari write of Nietzsche, "since art brings spiritual entities into existence while philosophical concepts are also 'sensibilia'" (WIP, 5).

This fine point demands the greatest care, for the relationship that philosophy undertakes with art runs the risk of sacrificing the respective tasks of both. Indeed, Deleuze renounces the vulgar combination of philosophy and literature, because it tends to produce the worst species of either genre. We have already dwelled on this eventuality in the introduction, but we return to it here insofar as the risks and challenges can be dramatized in the context of Nietzsche's first book, *The Birth of Tragedy* (1872). The circumstances surrounding the text are well-known. Having recently assumed a chaired professorship in Basel, the young philologist embarked on an analysis of Greek tragedy, from its divine birth to its mundane death, which sought to rekindle the embers of the tragic spirit in the modern, and especially German, world. In this context, then, Nietzsche inevitably came to see this book as his most deeply flawed and immature. In his "Attempt at Self-Criticism" (1886), which he composed to accompany the text's republication, Nietzsche scorns the "length in excess," the *Sturm und Drang* of a project "constructed from a lot of immature, overgreen personal experiences, all of them close to the limits of communication" (BOT, "Attempt" §2). Published when he was only twenty-seven, *The Birth of Tragedy* was (in Nietzsche's words) "badly written, ponderous, embarrassing, image-mad and image-confused, sentimental, in places saccharine to the point of effeminacy" (ibid., §3). This appraisal might otherwise seem the expression of a reactionary maturity, or even a higher wisdom, were it not for the acknowledgement of the "task" that lies at the book's center and explains its very failure. At once confessional and critical, demanding and strangely forgiving, Nietzsche writes:

> I do not want to suppress entirely how disagreeable it now seems to me, how strange it appears now, after sixteen years—before a much older, a hundred times more demanding, but by no means colder eye which has not become a stranger to the task which this audacious book dared to tackle for the first time: *to look at science in the perspective of the artist, but at art in that of life* (die Wissenschaft unter der Optik des Künstlers zu sehn, die Kunst aber unter der des Lebens). (ibid., §2)

Nowhere are the stakes of this task—the creation of an aesthetic and vitalistic philosophy—more clearly dramatized than in *The Birth of Tragedy,* which recognizes the mission to write differently and then stages the failure to do so. The "youthful courage and suspicion" of the book notwithstanding, the mission to dispatch the "metaphysical comforts [*de*[*n*] *metaphysischen Tros*[*t*]]" (ibid., §7) of knowledge demanded a reorientation for which Nietzsche was not yet ready. With a "colder eye," the older "physician of culture" looks on his youthful book as if it were riven between hope and execution, promise and expression: the younger Nietzsche was "of two minds," at once boldly announcing the task but also unable to realize it. "Is it clear what task I first dared to touch with this book? How I regret now that I still lacked the courage (or immodesty?) to permit myself in every way an opinion, a venture [or risk: *Wagnisse*], and also an individual language of my own" (ibid.; translation modified).[48]

In a sense, Nietzsche came to regard this state of affairs as the very quandary of philosophy itself, which remains divided between its status as a "scientific" discipline and its "artistic" instinct. "Great dilemma," he writes elsewhere, "is philosophy an art or a science? Both in its purposes and its results it is an art. But it uses the same means as science—conceptual representation. Philosophy is a form of artistic invention."[49] In other words, philosophy draws on the constituents of *Wissenschaft,* of science qua knowledge, but Nietzsche regards the creation of concepts as a matter of *taste.* We always begin by *savoring* sensations, by selecting certain forces, according to our particular inclinations and tendencies. "The philosopher is not intelligent, if one calls 'intellegent' the man who looks for successes [*das Gute*] in his own affairs; Aristotle correctly said: 'That which Thales and Anaragoras know, one would call unusual, astonishing, difficult, divine, but also useless, because it had nothing to do with the successes/commodities of man'" (PTG, 43; translation modified).[50]

For Nietzsche, philosophy is distinguished from *Wissenschaft* by its taste for the "unusual" and its penchant for the "useless" (ibid., 3). Philosophy requires a sensibility that selects singular sensations (affects, passions) and, thereby, formulates a mode of expression, a style, that cannot be recruited into programmatic utility or common sense. In *Thus Spoke Zarathustra,* he explains:

> All my progress has been an attempting and a questioning—and truly, one has to *learn* how to answer such questioning! That however—is to my taste [*Geschmack*]: not good taste, not bad taste, but my taste, which I no longer conceal and of which I am no longer ashamed. (TSZ, "Of the Spirit of Gravity," III §2)

In view of the sensibility and style that he "no longer conceals," the worst that Nietzsche can say about his first book is that it is "badly written"—that it lacks a sense of style. The effort to assume the perspective of art and, indeed, of life demands not a logical program but an expressive one, and it is on this score that *The Birth of Tragedy* falls short. Of course, the older Nietzsche objected to the stench of Hegelianism that clung to the characterization of Apollo and Dionysus, but he finally denounces *The Birth of Tragedy* because it never really undertook the aesthetic task that was demanded. Instead, the book thrusts the responsibility to create a new or operatic philosophy onto opera itself: dedicated to Richard Wagner, the text concludes with a meditation on the composer, whom Nietzsche credits as the monumental expression of a modern tragic spirit. Subsequently, Nietzsche would regret the hopelessly romantic naiveté of this contention, but the "Attempt at Self-Criticism" suggests that this recourse to Wagner was contrived as a substitute, or excuse, for the failure to develop a musical spirit of his own. "What spoke here—as was admitted, not without suspicion—was something like a mystical, almost maenadic soul that stammered with difficulty, a feat of the will, as in a strange tongue, almost undecided whether it should communicate or conceal itself,"

Nietzsche writes (BOT, "Attempt" §3). "It *should have sung, this 'new soul'—and not spoken.* What I had to say then—too bad that I did not dare say it as a poet: perhaps I had the ability" (ibid.; emphasis added).

In the aftermath of *The Birth of Tragedy,* Nietzsche seems to have both learned to sing and to have let himself do so. Leaving behind his professorship, his debt to both discipline and institution, he embarked on a kind philosophical experimentation that is not metaphorically but *literally* operatic—a drama of voices and images, of auditions and visions, that "can only be read as a modern opera and seen and heard as such." Deleuze continues: "It is not that Nietzsche produces a philosophical opera or a piece of allegorical theater, but he creates a piece of theater or an opera which directly expresses thought as experience and movement" (NP, xiii). What does this mean? In order to create concepts, Deleuze avers, we must learn to bring aesthetic principles to bear on the process of philosophical expression. "Style in philosophy strains [*est tendu*] toward three different poles," he writes: "concepts, or new ways of thinking; percepts, or new ways of seeing and hearing; and affects, or new ways of feeling. They're the philosophical trinity, philosophy as opera: you need all three to *get things moving [faire le mouvement]*" (Neg, 164–65). In other words, we make thought move by creating concepts that bring to bear the very percepts and affects that we typically associate with the work of art. As Deleuze notes—and as the reference to opera confirms—no philosopher experimented with the possibilities of style more profoundly than Nietzsche, whose genius consists in an expression that mingles sense and sensibilia, thought and sensation. Nietzsche formulates countless voices through which he stages neither individuals nor subjects, but impersonal individuations and preindividual singularities. His "theater of philosophy" is populated by a grand cast of characters, but the drama consists in the play of sensations, intensities, and singularities that escape the determination of any subject or the reference to any object. "He dreams of putting Zarathustra to Bizet's music, as a form of derisive Wagnerian theater," Deleuze says. "He dreams of a music, as he does of a mask, for 'his own' philosophical theater" (DI, 127).

At this point, we could say, our discussion has come full circle. In tracing Deleuze's development—"considered in terms of its beginning, a thing is always poorly judged" (AO, 91)[51]—we have discovered the same logic at work in Nietzsche's development: in both cases, the philosopher's early work conceals his will to power, the forces he favors, which are still "making ready, in the shadows," until those forces can be expressed and affirmed. "We know that things and people are always forced to conceal themselves, have to conceal themselves when they begin. What else could they do?" Deleuze asks (MI, 3). "They come into being within a set which no longer includes them and, in order not to be rejected, have to project the characteristics which they retain in common with the set" (ibid.). In this respect, Deleuze follows Nietzsche's trajectory, as if only "in the middle" (*au milieu*) of his becoming could he come to terms with Nietzsche's metamorphisis. Neither philosopher can be understood on the basis of his beginning but must be grasped in the moment when his forces can be given voice. In both cases, we might say, what concerns us is a transformation of philosophy from a mode of representation, even the representation of aesthetics, to a mode of expression that accedes to creation—aesthetics—in its own right.

This transformation can be grasped in terms of the "two irreducible domains" that Deleuze discovers in Kant's critical philosophy, namely, "that of the theory of the sensible which captures only the real's conformity with possible experience; and that of the theory of the beautiful, which deals with the reality of the real in so far as it is thought" (DR, 68).[52] But in *Kant's Critical Philosophy* and the even more far-reaching "The Idea of Genesis in Kant's Esthetics," both published in 1963, Deleuze seems to refine the question of aesthetics, at least as concerns the creation of philosophy. In Kant's third *Critique,* the theory of the beautiful yields to an ostensibly fundamental dualism within the reality of the real itself, namely, the distinction between reception and creation. "The difficulties of Kantian esthetics in the first part of the *Critique of Judgment* have to do with the diversity of points of view," Deleuze writes (DI, 56). "On the one hand, Kant proposes an esthetics of the spectator, as in the theory of the judgment of taste; on the other hand, an esthetics or meta-esthetics of the creator, as in the theory of genius" (ibid.). The former, which defines the beautiful in terms of its experience, or aesthetic judgment, is by far the better known, but in *Nietzsche and Philosophy*, Deleuze already indicates that this constitutes the receptive and ultimately *reactive* formation of aesthetics. "When Kant distinguished beauty from all other interests, even moral ones, he was still putting himself in the position of the spectator, but of a less and less gifted spectator who now has only a disinterested regard for beauty" (NP, 102). In other words, the problem with Kant's deduction of the beautiful lies in the perspective with which aesthetics is framed, that of the ordinary spectator, the least distinguished sense of common sense, when Nietzsche raises the question of the vital creator and the singular act of creation. Thus, the consideration of the beautiful in Kant's philosophy gives way to the affirmative problem of creation, of genesis and genius, which Deleuze follows to the point at which it finally becomes *Nietzschean*.

As a matter of judgment, the beautiful is typically taken to concern a particular kind of aesthetic feeling that denotes the free indeterminate accord of the faculties (in this instance, understanding and imagination). In other words, the beautiful emerges in the absence of the subject, defined per the legislative organization of faculties whereby one governs the others, and the absence of the object, defined per the legislative organization as that which provokes and receives determination.[53] But what the judgment of the beautiful tosses away with one hand it retrieves, surreptitiously, with the other. Insofar as beautiful describes a subjective feeling, Kant insists that this sensation remains umbilically linked to an external world—to nature. The beautiful expresses the "aptitude of *nature* for producing objects that are reflected formally in the imagination" (DI, 63) because beauty consists in the feeling of harmony that our faculties enjoy with nature. In the experience of the beautiful, the indeterminate relation between the faculties bears witness to the "adequation" (*adequatio*) of subject and object, but when Deleuze turns to the question of genius, he affirms a process that eludes any point of reference. Above all, this transformation concerns what we have called the Outside, for if the beautiful retains the relation, however implicit, of the subject to nature, genius consists in a "subjective disposition" capable of creating "another nature" that goes beyond nature—even human nature (CPJ, §57/344). "The aesthetic goes beyond every concept because it produces the intuition of another nature than the nature given to us," Deleuze writes. "Thus invisible beings, the kingdom of the blessed, hell acquire a body; and love, death, acquire a dimension to make them adequate to their spiritual sense" (DI, 67). Adequation here does not refer to the relation between an internal judgment and an external referent but to the "spiritual sense" itself, which demands that creation go beyond nature and accede to the function of a pure fabulation.

It is one thing to say that genius creates a concept to which no intuition is adequate, but Deleuze's point is that genius goes "beyond all concepts because it creates the intuition of a nature other than that which is given to us: another nature whose phenomena would be true spiritual events, and whose events of the spirit, immediate natural determinations" (KCP, 56–57). Genius exists in the genesis of this sensibility, the creation of a mode of feeling, thinking, of life, which is outside reference or representation. Indeed, *genius develops a relation to the Outside* inasmuch as this experience, however improbable, difficult, and dangerous, or perhaps because of this, is by definition *unmediated.* Only in this respect can we understand what Deleuze means by Nietzsche's "literary genius," which might otherwise be understood as a matter of adornment, of so many tropes and allusions, not affects but affectations. Of course, Nietzsche deploys an astonishing array of literary techniques and a vast inventory of genres ("I have many stylistic possibilities—the most multifarious art of style that has ever been at the disposal of one man"[54]), but in so doing Niethezsche affirms philosophy as an aesthetic enterprise that, in Deleuze's terms, derives its rigor in relation to the Outside. In "Nomad Thought," Deleuze explains that

> Nietzsche grounds thought, and writing, in an immediate relation to the Outside. What is this: a beautiful painting or a beautiful drawing? There is a frame. An aphorism has a frame, too. But whatever is in the frame, at what point does it become beautiful? At the moment that one knows and feels that the movement, that the line that is framed comes from elsewhere, that it does not begin with the limits of the frame. (DI, 255).[55]

Neither simply accidental nor merely metaphorical, the invocation here of the beautiful should be taken seriously and literally insofar as Deleuze unfolds Nietzsche's philosophy as an aesthetic enterprise—*the creation of concepts as affective assemblages.* Inasmuch as the beautiful augurs the development of Nietzsche's philosophy, it will have to be carried beyond representation, to the practice of creating lines and movement that traverse the frame (*cadre*) and carry us outside the frame (*hors cadre*) or to the Outside (*le Dehors*). This is the sense in which we should appreciate Nietzsche's aphorisms, which trigger "a play of forces, a state of forces which are always exterior to one another. An aphorism doesn't mean anything; it signifies nothing and no more has a signifier than a signified. Those would be ways of restoring a text's interiority" (ibid., 256). In Nietzsche's philosophy, finally, Deleuze discovers the song that will convey thought beyond representation, beyond philosophy itself, to the Outside—and it remains for us to grasp how Deleuze carries this tune himself.

Après Nietzsche: Schizoanalysis avant la Lettre

The Art of Decoding

> Félix sees writing as a schizoid flow drawing in all sorts of things. I'm
> interested in the way a page of writing flies off in all directions and at the
> same time closes right up on itself like an egg. And in the reticences, the
> resonances, the lurches, and all the larvae you can find in a book. Then we
> really started writing together, it wasn't any problem.
>
> —GILLES DELEUZE, *NEGOTIATIONS*

In "Nomad Thought," Deleuze asks of today's readers: "What we want to know
is how *they* have received Nietzsche?" (DI, 252). But what we are asking here is
how *Deleuze* has received Nietzsche. We know that Nietzsche inspires enduring affection, but what does Deleuze do with Nietzsche's affects? How does he
take, or make, flight (*faire fuir*)? We can begin to formulate an answer in view
of the book that is often said to mark Deleuze's "liberation" from traditional
philosophy, namely, *Anti-Oedipus* (1972). Most commentators on Deleuze's
work have treated this text, his first collaboration with Félix Guattari, as a turn
away from his apprenticeship to so many philosophers and a turn toward the
creation of a new politics. Beyond even *Difference and Repetition* (1968)—
ostensibly the first book of philosophy that was his own and, in any case, the
first book he wrote whose title lacked a proper name—*Anti-Oedipus* claims a
notorious place in Deleuze's oeuvre, sometimes lauded, sometimes regretted,
but always acknowledged.[56]

Deleuze and Guattari's collaboration formulates its revolutionary politics,
or what the authors will call schizoanalysis, under the auspices of a materialist
psychiatry that emerges from and insists on the "relationship between desire
and the social field" (AO, 118). Refusing any essential distinction between the
two, materialist psychiatry presupposes the "insertion of desire into the economic infrastructure itself" (*l'insertion des pulsions dans la production soci-
ale*) (ibid.).[57] In other words, we construct the sense of social organizations
on the basis of a plane of production within which mind and matter, man and
nature, *noesis* and *physis* are immanent. Hence, it should be of little surprise
that *Anti-Oedipus* brings together Freud and Marx, since these thinkers represent, respectively, the great modern analyses of psychical-libidinal economy and material-capitalist economy. Nevertheless, as we will contend here,
the expropriation of these critiques into the operations of schizoanalysis,

understood as an evaluation of codes and an experiment in decoding, bears witness to a style of thinking and writing that reaches beyond Marx, beyond Freud—to Nietzsche. Though he appears fleetingly, it is Nietzsche who occupies the most significant place in *Anti-Oedipus*—as its amateur ethnologist, its primitive economist, its profound psychologist, and above all else, the patron saint of its style. We know that Deleuze credits Nietzsche with having formulated "the notion of style as politics," but in *Anti-Oedipus* he and Guattari undertake this task on their own terms.

Broadly construed, the style and politics of *Anti-Oedipus* emerge from Nietzsche's prior "inscriptions," which we can understand in two discrete, though intimately related, senses. In the first place, we have already alluded to Nietzsche's remarkable analysis of mnemotechnics, the system whereby morals and memories are written in the flesh.[58] To promise is to be indebted, but one can assume a debt, and thereby commit oneself to the expectation of the future, only inasmuch as a memory has been "burned" (*eingebrannt*) into the body and preserved in or as consciousness; the remainder of a trauma ("only that which never ceases to hurt stays in the memory") is also a reminder (always pay your debts on time) (GM, II §3). The transformation of this trauma into guilt, conscience, and morality forms the long "story of how responsibility originated [*die Geschichte von der Herkunft der Verantwortlichkeit*]," which Nietzsche writes in *On the Genealogy of Morals* and which Deleuze and Guattari rewrite in *Anti-Oedipus* (GM, II §2).[59] At the heart of the human, at the mythic and memorial point where we extract our nature apart from nature, Deleuze and Guattari transform Nietzsche's thesis into the constituents of a concept and an operation they call "coding." Inscription constitutes the most primitive expression of coding, namely, the process of organizing matter into bodies, of brute determination. Codes function both individually (e.g., in the case of a genome) and collectively (e.g., in the case of a social formation), but in any case, they are defined insofar as they order life, determining its forms, boundaries, and significance. Indeed, the work of coding and recoding is so thoroughgoing that we are apt to mistake life for its codes—say, for the structures of psychoanalysis (or, nowadays, the designations of the DSM) or for the abstraction of labor power (or, nowadays, the biopolitical calculations of risk and reward on which states and corporations collaborate).

Therefore, in contrast to the logic of exchange that has dominated considerations of primitive societies, *Anti-Oedipus* defines the very existence of the socius, of human desire qua social production, according to the logic of debt and the painful application of its codes. Primitive societies are but the most overt and "savage" instances of this logic whereby bodies are tattooed, inscribed with debts, then those same bodies are territorialized onto the body of the earth. (The nature of debt is conspicuously revealed in the French verb *devoir*, which means "to owe" but which also signifies, in its modal form, "should, ought, or must.") From this perspective, *Anti-Oedipus* seeks to describe the epistemic or epochal organization of the socius in terms of violent changes (i.e., the territorial system of the promise will be reterritorialized on the body of the despot, who possesses the right to decide over life and death), and even violent dissolutions (i.e., the system of codes will be decoded by the body of organs of capitalism, whose flows and leakages continually threaten to deterritorialize the socius). But whether we owe the deity, the despot, or "the man," debt endures as the disparity or distance that marks any relation of power. Even in the era of late capitalism, when the codes of modernity are subject to a "twilight of the idols," the current financial crisis, spinning out of the mortgage industry, reminds us that debts are still recorded—in statistics and actuarial tables that assess the risks and contingencies of countless eventualities, in a digital universe that tracks our predilections and purchases in order to incite further purchases ("readers who bought. . . ."), and in the sphere of a "control society" which nurtures new habits, neuroses, and addictions. Indeed, debt continually assumes and acquires new techno-cultural means with which to inscribe itself: the subject and soul have given way to the identity or niche, but even in the marketplace of personality, the prospect of coding returns like a savage atavism adapted to new practices of power and new means of indebtedness. "Control is short-term and rapidly shifting, but at the same time continuous and unbounded," Deleuze writes: "A man is no longer confined but a man in debt" (Neg, 181).

Nevertheless, if schizoanalysis follows Nietzsche's own analysis of codes, it does so by virtue of realizing a second sense of inscription, namely, the process of *writing*. While codes exist in order to "translate, convert, cash in" the intensities of lived experience, we are just as much concerned with the manner of decoding that Nietzsche unleashes and that Deleuze renews: "but Nietzsche, with his writing of intensities, tells us: don't exchange intensity for representations" (DI, 257; translation modified).[60] In "Nomad Thought," Deleuze outlines the three predominant means of this "exchange," which is to say, three different (though related) means of coding: "laws, contracts, and institutions" (ibid., 257). We know that philosophy is often developed along these very lines, as a bureaucracy that defines thinking according to the protocols of administration and management; but—and this is Deleuze's point—Nietzsche's thought escapes the sovereign forms of philosophy by creating a style of writing and thinking that decodes the inscription of codes at the same time that it inscribes itself as a perpetual decoding. "We read an aphorism or a poem from *Thus Spoke Zarathustra*," Deleuze writes, "but materially and formally, texts like that cannot be understood by the establishment or the application of a *law*, or by the offer of a *contractual relation*, or by the foundation of an *institution*" (ibid., 255; emphasis added).

Nothing could be further from the "republic of letters" and its sovereign form of judgment, the maxim, than the transmission of what Deleuze calls intensities Nietzsche creates. Thus, when Deleuze and Guattari describe their desire to "transmit something that resists coding [[*fait*] *passer quelque chose qui échappe aux codes*]" (Neg, 22), we must understand the undertaking of a project that resumes Nietzsche's revolutionary writing and makes that writing the precursor to schizoanalysis. Recall the affirmation with which we began this chapter: in Deleuze's words, Nietzsche "gives you a perverse taste—certainly something neither Marx nor Freud ever gave anyone—for saying simple things in your own way, in affects, intensities, experiences, experiments" (Neg, 6). In fact, Deleuze elaborates Nietzsche's unique status as a critic of codes and purveyor of decoding precisely by considering him in relation to Marx and Freud. In "Nomad Thought," he refers to the "trinity of Marx, Nietzsche, Freud" as an established critical conceit—notably, Foucault delivered his well-known essay "Nietzsche, Freud, Marx" at the same colloquium that Deleuze organized in 1964—but Deleuze makes the reference in order to mark an integral difference.[61] For his generation, which came of age in the 1960s and early 1970s, the figure of this ménage-à-trois promised not only a return to a monumental series of modern critiques but also a departure from an earlier triumvirate, the so-called three H's (Hegel, Husserl, and Heidegger), who hitherto dominated French philosophy. "At the Liberation we were still strangely stuck in the history of philosophy," Deleuze says. "We simply plunged into Hegel, Husserl, Heidegger; we threw ourselves like puppies into a scholasticism worse than that of the Middle Ages" (Dia, 12). In the wake of these devotions, Deleuze's generation can be characterized by the genre and spirit of "the return," whereby Marx, Nietzsche, and Freud are resurrected for the purposes of critiquing the present. And we would be remiss if we didn't admit that each of these "masters of suspicion"[62] has been associated with the concerted labor of critical retrieval that sought to resurrect their respective writings: we speak of Althusser's Marx, Deleuze's Nietzsche, and Lacan's Freud.

Marx, Nietzsche, and Freud represent the three great critiques in response to modernity, but their recovery comes, so to speak, at the end of modernity, when they seem to offer the promise of a critical renewal. Doubtless this reflects the respective orientations of these three critiques, each of which develops the procedures to analyze a body that suffers from so many modern maladies—from exploitation, from nihilism, from discontent. Surely this is why all three figures are drafted into the delirious decoding of *Anti-Oedipus,* but in the framework of schizoanalysis, Nietzsche's contribution should not be underestimated. Compared to Marx and Freud, Deleuze says, Nietzsche goes further, tries to "get something through" (DI, 253). Nietzsche "gives you a perverse taste"—but a taste for what? After all, doesn't Freud analyze the way that lived experience is determined by social forces into a "universal neurosis"? And doesn't Marx analyze the way that lived experience is converted into labor power under the pretense of the "universality of capitalism"? In what sense should we distinguish Nietzsche's writing from these critiques? At first glance, Deleuze responds by displacing the eventualities suffered by Marx and Freud onto their respective readers. Thus, "if one examines not the letter of Marx and Freud, but the becoming of Marxism and of Freudianism, we see, paradoxically, Marxists and Freudians engaged in an attempt to recode Marx and Freud" (ibid., 253). In other words, Deleuze suggests, the proper name has been appropriated in the name of a program, a school, a party, a coding, an *orthodoxy.*

And yet, Deleuze continues, if Marxism and Freudianism reflect the triumph of reactive forces, this is because the inclination already exists, respectively, in Marx and Freud themselves. The masters of discourse give rise to "discourses of the master." Freud decodes the private and unconscious aspect of culture to reveal the logic of modernity and the drives, but this logic is recoded by the family: "'you fall ill through the family and recover through the family'—this is not the same family" (DI, 253). Marx decodes the public and politico-economic aspects of culture to reveal the logic of modernity and capital, but this logic is recoded by the state: "'the state has made you ill and the state will cure you'—this cannot be the same state" (ibid.). The point here is not to diminish Deleuze's appreciation for Marxism, or even for psychoanalysis, but to understand how he disavows these discourses in the spirit of a decoding that takes Marx and Freud beyond their discursive limits and their tendency to become recoded. Even as "enemies of the state," Marxism and psychoanalysis remain "fundamental bureaucracies" (ibid.) that cannot be thought apart from the state. Their decodings never fail to draw a limit— the presentiment of a law, contract, or institution—beyond which they do not venture and according to which they will be recoded. The utopianism of Marxism and of Freudianism consists in redressing disparity or lack, in imagining a more equal distribution or a better form of governance (whether this is the state or the correlative state of the family). Because of and beyond the inequities of our socius, we retain a phantasm, a pastoral idyll (in Marx's words, "to hunt in the morning, fish in the afternoon, rear cattle in the evening, and criticize after dinner"[63]) that claims to cast off codes only in order to insinuate them just as thoroughly. "What at the horizon of our culture in fact constitutes Marxism and psychoanalysis as those two fundamental bureaucracies, the one public, the other private," Deleuze writes, "is their effort to recode as best they can precisely that which on the horizon ceaselessly tends to come uncoded" (ibid., 253).

"*This is not at all what Nietzsche is about,*" Deleuze maintains. "His problem is elsewhere. For Nietzsche, it is about getting something through in every past, present, and future code, something which does not and will not let itself be recoded" (DI, 253; emphasis added). In the course of this chapter, we have described this "problem" in terms of a kind of writing distinguished by the emanation of intensities and an immediate relation to the Outside. Nietzsche's aphorisms produce intensities and affects that refuse to be recoded by any element of the state: instead, they launch a line of flight that places us in direct and immediate relation to the exteriority of forces. The aphorism expresses "the form of exteriority of thought," but as Deleuze and Guattari insist, this form "is not at all *another image* in opposition to the image inspired by the state apparatus" (ATP, 377). We will return to the "state apparatus" at length in the context of Deleuze's own relation to literature (chapter 4), but this undertaking is already presaged in *Anti-Oedipus*, where the brief and explicit turn to Nietzsche provokes the affirmation of writing as a profound and joyous resistance. The force or forces of the Outside, which are always emergent, always becoming, always in the process of creating, are (by definition) at war with the values and codes of the state-form and the determination of the metaphysical, moral, and well-nigh molar order Deleuze calls representation. Far from consisting in a representation, then, the aphorism draws on the very forces of the Outside, the power of fabulation and becoming, to deterritorialize representation itself. Like the simulacrum, with which Deleuze overturns Plato's republic of philosophy, the aphorism delivers a "force that destroys both the image *and* its copies, the model *and* its reproductions, every possibility of subordinating thought to a model of the True, the Just, the Right" (ibid.). Nietzsche does not replace one world with another (or better) one but takes decoding to its virtual limit, releasing it from the latent promise of future codes and the explicit threat of its savage recoding. "Faced with the way in which our societies come uncoded, codes leaking away on every side, Nietzsche does not try to perform a recoding. He says: this hasn't yet gone far enough, you're nothing but children" (DI, 254).

Deleuze calls this operation "uncoding" (*décodage*) (ibid., 253), but he is quick to distinguish it from the reactive impulse to negate or delimit forces. Unlike Marx and Freud, Nietzsche creates a counterphilosophy that constitutes a perpetual critique of modernity: assembling forces in the absence of a master code, the paternal metaphor, he devises a writing machine with which to unfold a kind of plane (*plan)* of exteriority, before which the state-apparatus and its regime of representation would be powerless. As Deleuze writes, "It is the Nietzschean method that makes Nietzsche's text not something about which we have to ask: 'is this fascist, bourgeois, or revolutionary in itself?'—but a field of exteriority where fascist, bourgeois, or revolutionary forces confront one another" (DI, 256). In other words, Nietzsche's writing opens thought to the agonism of forces we have called the Outside. Hence, whereas Marx and Freud formulate a relative decoding, or what Deleuze deems "the dawn of modern culture," Nietzsche alone takes the "emancipation of European man," the process of modern decodification, to its virtual limit or nth degree, where the state machine breaks down. Far from producing a critique of modern culture that remains thoroughly modern, Nietzsche unleashes "untimely meditations" that usher us into "the dawn of counterculture" (DI, 252).

While Deleuze discovers the possibilities of uncoding in Nietzsche's writing, he and Guattari undertake their own radical uncoding in the context of

Anti-Oedipus. It is no secret that the first volume of *Capitalism and Schizo-phrenia* is a difficult book: a departure in style from Deleuze's earlier and more academic works, even the baroque *Logic of Sense*, Deleuze and Guattari's collaboration is bent on enacting the decoding process that it also describes. *Anti-Oedipus* is, as Deleuze says elsewhere, both "agent and object" of deterritorialization (DI, 256). One need look no further than the book's opening page for confirmation of this new mode of writing, which dispenses with the pretense of introduction, of writing "before" writing, in order to hurl us into its becoming. We might pause here, on the subject of introductions, to cash out the style of schizoanalysis. Deleuze has never been one for preambles: for the most part, his introductions are either too short to provide a genuine introduction (the parabolic and aphoristic introductions of most of his works, and even the prefaces he writes for new editions) or, occasionally, too long not to be considered a work in its own right (the "Introduction: Rhizome" of *A Thousand Plateaus*). But perhaps this is how it ought to be, since a "successful" introduction would be either redundant or disingenuous. It would be redundant insofar as an introduction claims to transcribe and synthesize what is already *in* the book, to redouble and properly introduce what is to come. For the reader, a properly successful introduction would have to be, in the context of the book of which it is a part, superfluous. But inasmuch as an introduction is not redundant, inasmuch as it seeks to be original, the claim of introduction (to introduce) would be disingenuous. In other words, this kind of introduction betrays its sense of purpose by virtue of detaching itself from the text—it speaks as if it did not belong to the text, as if it exists *avant la lettre*. No doubt this is why, as Deleuze says, beginning is always a problem for philosophy, for the introduction constitutes precisely the opportunity to provide the conditions, presuppositions, and codes that are part of the book but also stand apart from it.

In *Anti-Oedipus*, then, one could say that Deleuze and Guattari dispense with the pretense of introduction and even intention. Rather, the book begins *in media res*, insinuating us without warning into the workings of schizoanalysis: "It is at work everywhere, functioning smoothly at times, at other times in fits and starts. It breathes, it heats, it eats. It shits and fucks. What a mistake to have ever called it *the* id" (Ça fonctionne partout, tantôt sans arrêt, tantôt discontinu. Ça respire, ça chauffe, ça mange. Ça chie, ça baise. Quelle erreur d'avoir dit le ça) (AO, 1). In the original French, the passage consists in a far richer evocation of the mechanism within which the schizo writes and is written. The word *ça,* for which we have substituted "it," is also the French translation of Freud's "Id" (*das Ich*). Hence, in the final sentence of this passage, which implicitly differentiates *ça* from le *ça,* the text expresses straightaway the desire to produce a different kind of unconscious and a different kind of writing—not based on the private fantasies of its psychoanalytic manifestation but rather on an impersonal desire "at work everywhere." Deleuze and Guattari are not playing on words but rather decoding the dominant sense of the unconscious qua language by appealing to a different, schizoanalytic expression. In short, they return the unconscious to the status of an indeterminate noun that, far from concealing itself, writes itself everywhere and all the time.

Interestingly, this sentiment echoes a famous piece of graffiti that emerged during the events of May 1968: *Les structures ne marchent pas dans la rue.* The antistructuralist slogan plays on the verb *marcher,* which denotes marching as well as the more figurative sense of working or functioning. Thus, we could say that structures do not march, do not take to the streets because they do not materialize a politics but rather symptomatize the failure of social and material conditions: the failure of modern institutions that lead from the nuclear family to organized religion to systems of education and health and the institution of psychoanalysis itself. In contradistinction to an unconscious based on the repression of certain signifiers, which inevitably remains to be analyzed by a new regime of scholars and priests, Deleuze and Guattari engage a machinic unconscious (*ça*) that is always working and always already political: its machinations, far from being neurotically coded (as the universal subject), consist in schizophrenic decoding and deterritorialization. Indeed, the model of the schizo does not derive from the nuclear family but from the field of (later) capitalism, which unleashes its own wild wave of decoding that the schizo surfs, riding the crestline as it sweeps across the earth. "Schizophrenia as a process is desiring-production, but it is this production as it functions as the end, as the limits of social production determined by the conditions of capitalism" (AO, 130).

Unlike the social machines of earlier historical formations (epochs), whether territorial or despotic, Deleuze avouches that our capitalist "society does not function according to codes" (DI, 253).[64] "The decoding of flows and the deterritorialization of the socius thus constitutes the most characteristic and most important tendency of capitalism. It continually draws near its limit, which is a genuinely schizophrenic limit," they explain. Indeed, this process "tends, with all the strength at its command, to produce the schizo as the subject of the decoded flows on the body without organs—more capitalist than the capitalist and more proletarian than the proletariat" (AO, 34). The codes that had formerly inscribed humans on the body of the earth or the body of the despot are dissolved into so many flows: flows of money and goods, of property and production, of populations and libido, flows of speech and writing.[65] As they add, "The tendency is being carried further and further to the point that capitalism with all its flows may dispatch itself straight to the moon: we really haven't seen anything yet" (ibid.).[66]

Style as Politics (Schizoanalysis)

> [Nietzsche] compares the thinker to an arrow shot by nature that another thinker picks up where it has fallen so that he can shoot it somewhere else.
>
> **GILLES DELEUZE,** "PREFACE TO THE ENGLISH TRANSLATION"
> OF *NIETZSCHE AND PHILOSOPHY*

Once more we should affirm Nietzsche's philosophy as a kind of schizo-analysis *avant la lettre:* if *Anti-Oedipus* calls on the unholy alliance of Marx and Freud, the coupling itself entails an operation of delirious uncoding that is "neither Marxist nor Freudian. Deleuze realized that in order for anything to emerge, Marxism and Freudianism would require a little jostling," Vincent Descombes writes. "The vocabulary of the *Anti-Oedipus* is sometimes Marxist, sometimes Freudian, but the critical strand is Nietzschean, from start to finish."[67] Notably, for Descombes, as for recent thinkers like Alain Badiou who have repeated the sentiment, Deleuze's Nietzscheanism is not exactly a good thing. But what does it mean to be "Nietzschean"?

While it is possible to transform the proper name of Marx into Marxism, and of Freud into Freudianism, Nietzsche's institutionalization tends to the tragic—or the comic. The instances of the former—from the appropriations of National Socialism to the inspirations of Leopold and Loeb—are renowned, but the latter is both more common and, arguably, more telling. We all know the picture of corduroyed, collegiate pretense for which a copy of *The Portable*

Nietzsche seems standard issue. As if Nietzsche could be reduced to an identification, worn as an affectation, whether fascist or bohemian. As if Nietzsche represented a lifestyle—a niche, a market—as opposed to an experimentation in the arts of living. How could one adhere to "Nietzscheanism," except at the cost of an "appalling synthesis"? What does the proper name "Nietzsche" signify if not, beyond the always-questionable body of texts (which do we include, and which are to be omitted as stray notes, ephemera, or the work of madness?), the trajectory of a becoming that eludes any fixed identity or sure predicates? "There is no Nietzsche-the-self [*le moi Nietzsche*], professor of philology, who suddenly loses his mind and supposedly identifies with all sorts of strange people," Deleuze and Guattari conclude; "rather, there is the Nietzschean subject who passes through a series of states, and who identifies these states with the names of history: 'every name in history is I . . . ' " (AO, 21). Even in the midst of growing madness, Nietzsche's late writings, signed as they are with so many names ("Zarathustra," "the Crucified," etc.), suggest the process into which schizoanalysis will enter, namely, what Deleuze calls the "method of And" (TI, 180).

In the context of *Anti-Oedipus,* which describes a series of three syntheses, this method assumes a particular importance, providing as it does the imperative of a perpetual production, which Deleuze and Guattari deem the eventuality of capitalism and its limit.[68] Moving between "this and then that," schizoanalysis constitutes a proliferation of syntheses, a self-perpetuating connectivism. "The productive synthesis, the production of production, is inherently connective in nature: 'and . . . ' 'and then . . . ' " (ibid., 5). The "method of And" is a "method of Between," which inhabits an interstice or interval and thereby refuses to lapse into determination: schizoanlysis is at once synthetic and intervallic. "The schizophrenic is the universal producer," Deleuze and Guattari say (ibid., 7), and inasmuch as this is the case, the process of production is tantamount to the mandate of becoming: the connective synthesis means that that schizo is not a subject, is not subjectivized, but ex-ists as a perpetual caesura and con-sists in a prolific bricolage from which no overarching "I" can be extracted. We no longer speak of an author, a philosopher, a subject—how could we?—but of a writing machine that produces intensities and that, in the case of Nietzsche, invests particular names with "zones of intensity" (ibid., 21). In *Anti-Oedipus,* where the question of the schizo turns to the loss of the subject, Deleuze and Guattari describe how

Nietzsche's mad writing "spreads itself out along the entire circumference of the circle [of the subject], the center of which has been abandoned by the ego. At the center is the desiring machine," which spins out a kind of schizo history on the basis of its own remarkable decoding and deterritorialization: "*every name in history is I . . .* " (ibid.).

In this light, we should recall the interpretations and betrayals to which Nietzsche has been subject. We began this chapter by evoking the long reception history that has produced so many different and often degraded versions of the philosopher, but at the end of this chapter, we might well say that Nietzsche's radical style of thinking and writing provokes, perhaps even *necessitates,* the reactive forces of his own recoding. The paradox, no doubt implicit in many philosophers, marks Nietzsche apart from all other philosophers: he projects a revolutionary aggregate of forces into the future, but those forces are liable to be reterritorialized, stitched and sewn into the ground of a sedentary regime. Of the "dangers lying in wait for us," Deleuze outlines three different travesties of codification with which Nietzsche is met: "A demagogic danger ('young people are on our side . . . '). A paternalistic danger (advice to the young reader of Nietzsche). And above all, the danger of an appalling synthesis" (DI, 252). In each of these dangers, we experience the overarching urge to determine an authoritative reading, whether populist, paternal, or "paranoid." Isn't the demagogic danger precisely that of Marxism, which insists on the fraternity of the people or the party or the school, without which Nietzsche cannot be understood and properly enacted? And isn't the paternalistic danger precisely that of psychoanalysis, which insists on the presence of a father-figure, author and authority, whether we remake Nietzsche in this image or make other mediators claim the right to speak for Nietzsche as one would a dead father? Indeed, these specific dangers augur what might be called the fundamental danger that haunts Nietzsche's writing, since both are species of an "appalling synthesis" whereby Nietzsche is submitted to the accounting of philosophical legibility and legitimacy—an overarching recoding.

We have already considered the endless appropriations to which Nietzsche is subjected, no less his betrayal at the hands of so many critics, but in light of our discussion of *Anti-Oedipus,* we might take this opportunity to note Deleuze's similar fate. It is hardly surprising that the criticism leveled against Deleuze—the condemnation of wild style, the dismissal of subjective fragmentation, the suggestion of nihilism—recalls Nietzsche's reception. Indeed, these sentiments form the basis for a recoding to which both philosophers have been submitted, but this repetition is no less a matter of their relation, since Deleuze has been condemned on the basis of his Nietzscheanism. The proxy war into which Deleuze and, by extension, Guattari are recruited is perhaps most clearly demonstrated in Fredric Jameson's monumental text, *The Political Unconscious* (1981), which effectively established the strategy of recoding that has continually characterized the Anglo-American reception of Deleuze's work. In fact, Jameson's critique of Deleuze constitutes the resumption of an earlier critique of Nietzsche, this one launched by Lukács. In *The Historical Novel,* to which Jameson's own "transcoding" and "totalizing" project is duly indebted, Lukács says that Nietzsche "takes aim against academic history writing" at the cost of reducing this enterprise to no more than the "philosophical justification of the apologetic falsification of history" —the cynical capitulation to a world of privatized experiences, scattered perspectives, and isolated subjectivism.[69] *The Political Unconscious* not only revisits this criticism but effectively renews it in the framework of Nietzsche's "poststructuralist" and "postmodern" epigones:

> It is, for instance, increasingly clear that hermeneutic or interpretative activity has become one of the basic, polemical targets of contemporary poststructuralism in France, which—powerfully buttressed by the authority of Nietzsche—has tended to identify such operations with historicism, and in particular with the dialectic and its valorization of absence and the negative, its assertion of the necessity and priority of totalizing thought. I will agree with the identification, with this description of the ideological affinities and implication of the ideal of the interpretive or hermeneutic act; but I will argue that this critique is misplaced.[70]

Significantly, this passage is immediately followed by an invocation of "one of the most dramatic of such recent attacks on interpretation: *The Anti-Oedipus,* by Gilles Deleuze and Félix Guattari."[71] Jameson's analysis of the book, which emerges in the context of a complex meditation on the critical possibilities of contemporary Marxism, can hardly be called hostile; *The Political Unconscious* suggests that Deleuze and Guattari's work is "very much in the spirit of the present work," which also claims to critique the sequestration of "fantasy-experience" from the domain of material production.[72] If

Anti-Oedipus primarily constitutes an attack on Freudian interpretation, as Jameson suggests, this is because his reading renders psychoanalysis the very species of overcoding that Deleuze and Guattari nominate as their overarching enemy. Psychoanalysis constitutes a kind of experiential condensation, "a reduction and a rewriting of the whole rich and random multiple realities of concrete everyday experience into the contained, strategically pre-limited terms of the family narrative."[73] Ultimately, Jameson continues, Deleuze and Guattari wage war against the "system of allegorical interpretations in which the data of one narrative line are radically impoverished by their rewriting according to the paradigm of another narrative."[74]

But if he readily acknowledges that the project of *Anti-Oedipus* constitutes a critique of codes and the operations of coding, Jameson nevertheless undertakes an interpretation of the book that enacts a broadly Marxian recodification of Deleuze and Guattari: the imposition of dualism and even dialectic onto their "immanent analysis."[75] "If such perceptions are to be celebrated in their intensity," he writes of schizoanalysis, "they must be accompanied by some initial appearance of continuity, some ideology of unification already in place, which it is their mission to rebuke or shatter. The value of the molecular in Deleuze, for instance, depends structurally on the preexisting molar or unifying impulse against which its truth is read."[76] In a more recent essay, "Marxism and Dualism in Deleuze," Jameson prolongs this necessity into the contention that Deleuze's thought is effectively structured by dualisms. Ostensibly, these dualisms represent Deleuze's inexorable attempt to translate an overpopulated conceptual milieu, to organize thinking (*pace* Hegel) into strategic oppositions: territorialization and deterritorialization, coding and decoding, molar and molecular, etc.[77] In the language of Marxism, we could call this process mediation, but Jameson adds: "If a more modern characterization of mediation is wanted, we will say that this operation is understood as a process of transcoding: as the invention of a set of terms, the strategic choice of a particular code or language, such that the same terminology can be used to analyze two quite distinct types of objects or 'texts,' or two very different structural levels of reality."[78]

Never mind that *Anti-Oedipus* explicitly affirms its project of *decoding* against the dialectical mechanisms and mediations of Marxism as much as those of psychoanalysis: inasmuch as we understand Jameson's to be a profound and deliberate misinterpretation, we do so in view of Deleuze and

Guattari's contention that misinterpretation always conceals "a political motive" (ibid., 23). What, then, is the motive to make the decoding of desire the justification for the enterprise of recoding, a transcoding, or (as we will see) an overcoding? In light of *Anti-Oedipus,* and the clinical or diagnostic spirit in which it is written ("Lacan himself says 'I'm not getting much help,' " Deleuze says, "We thought we'd give him some schizophrenic help" [Neg, 14]), we might understand Jameson's response *symptomatically*—as a species of paranoia. In their materialist psychiatry, Deleuze and Guattari oppose the intensities and flows of schizoanalysis to the overcodings of paranoia and a paranoid regime, but this opposition only assumes its critical and ethical dimension on the basis of what could be called the "style of psychosis"—the paranoid and the schizo designate different expressions of psychosis: not different structures, as psychoanalysis would have it, but an overarching meta-structure (paranoia) and an astructured and asignifying assemblage (schizophrenia). The psychoanalytic formulation of psychosis is, in a sense, produced from the aspect of a "universal neurosis," but it nonetheless describes the eventuality within which schizoanalysis can be grasped. As Lacan contends, the psychotic suffers from the "foreclosure" (*Verwerfung*) of the paternal metaphor, the Name-of-the-Father (*le Nom du Père*), which provides the empty signifier that coheres the semiotic-social field and without which it dissolves into heterogeneity and happenstance. In fact, as Deleuze and Guattari write, "the role of the paternal metaphor or signifier corresponds to despotic overcoding."[79] In the simplest sense, the name is the "no" (le *Non du Père*), the prohibitive form of the signifier, which detours us from the immanence of *jouissance* and into the delimitations and detours of the drives.[80] The "centralizing or unifying automaton" (ATP, 17), the Name-of-the-Father coheres all other dimensions of the machinic assemblage and determines the presentiment of their totality. Deleuze and Guattari's respect for Lacan notwithstanding, there's more than a little patricide in *Anti-Oedipus:* inasmuch as the name or paternal metaphor constitutes the means of cohering the semiotic field, psychosis constitutes a crisis of belief, the *derealization* of all identities. In the language of *Anti-Oedipus,* Deleuze and Guattari refer to this as the elimination of the "overcoding dimension," but in so doing they effectively revalue this process.

The psychotic "break," or foreclosure, induces two distinct epistemological responses or, better yet, two distinct styles of thinking in relation to their common condition: the paranoid and the schizo. In the case of paranoia, as Freud noted, we tend to confuse aetiology with symptomatology, to mistake cause for effect: the symptoms of paranoia, the remarkable delusions and conspiracies with which the world is remade, actually conceal their cause, namely, a prior "apocalypse" of meaning.[81] The disease is psychosis, but the cure is paranoia, which reconstructs meaning all the more hermetically and globally on the ground of this wasteland. No one recodes like a paranoid, whose tyrannical and totalizing creation we would not be wrong to dub a "geopolitical aesthetic." But if the paranoid flight from psychosis is sublime, as Jameson's work on conspiracy attests, Deleuze and Guattari never cease to affirm a different style of psychosis. Whereas the paranoid style (in American politics and elsewhere) imposes an overcoding organization—a plot—on the world, the schizo relishes the delirium of a wandering line that never stops decoding. The irony of the paranoid reading—of Jameson's reading—is that, when Deleuze and Guattari appropriate the discourse of Marx and Freud, they do so not to recode them, nor to use them to recode culture, but to deterritorialize these codes into all kinds of schizoid flows. Schizoanalysis traverses the inscriptions of codes by devising its own wandering line of writing, "passing from one code to another," *even from Marxism to Freudianism,* but always taking them to new uncoded extremes. The schizo "deliberately scrambles all the codes, by quickly shifting from one to another, according to the question asked him, never giving the same explanation from one day to the next, never invoking the same genealogy, never recording the same event in the same way" (AO, 15). Schizophrenia is etymologically and sometime diagnostically confused with what's now called "multiple personality disorder," but the complex partitioning with which we associate the latter, the formation of so many semistable centers of equilibrium, ought to be distinguished from the schizo's sense of becoming.

In this respect, we might refer once more to the paternal metaphor, for in the "name" (*le Nom du Père*), which we have already described as a "no" (*le Non du Père*), there is buried another aural pun (*les non-dupes errent*). For Lacan, of course, this phrase suggests that those who are not duped by the signifier, who are not metaphorically interpellated by the Name of the Father, are most in error. But insofar as Deleuze abandons the notion of error and misinterpretations (all interpretations are misinterpretations), we might say that the phrase acquires a different sense: those who are not duped are destined to errantry, to the erratic line of flight with which we describe the questing and quixotic knight as much as the wandering stroll of the schizophrenic. Indeed, Deleuze and Guattari begin by describing the schizophrenic line— the schizo "out for a walk" (AO, 2) or, just as surely, the schizophrenic out for a write—according to the concept of the *bal(l)ade*. In French, *se balader* means to stroll; a *balade* is a kind of meandering line, or ramble, but the noun form, especially in its alternate spelling, *ballade,* also signifies a narrative song or a particularly lengthy genre of verse. Thus, Deleuze's neologism invokes an astructured and improvisatory experience at the same time it suggests a mode of meandering expression, a perpetual and perpetuating line of deterritorialization. The *bal(l)ade* consists in the verse with which philosophy *sings* the song of the Outside, the fabulous line of flight that we follow to the exteriority of forces. In this sense, to write is to trace a line that makes language itself take flight, but Deleuze is careful to distinguish this from any common sense of evasion. It would be a mistake, finally, to regard this flight as an attempt to run away, to flee, as if we were taking a vacation or dodging out on bail, for the line takes flight only as an active principle and an affirmation: *fuir = faire fuir.*[82] Inasmuch as they displace the neurotic staging of fantasy for the reality of the real—not a detour through the drives but rather a "detour through the direct" (MI, 206)—Deleuze and Guattari undertake schizoanalysis as a kind of critical and creative *delirium,* an improvisatory line of flight. This line must be made—not as a reaction in relation to an organization that would remain intact, but as a line of improvisation and an emission of intensities that cuts across the rigid organization and opens us to a pure Outside. Perhaps, finally, this is what it means to be Nietzschean, for as Deleuze explains in "Nomad Thought":

It is about getting something through in every past, present, and future code, something which does not and will not let itself be recoded. Getting it through on a new body, inventing a body on which it can pass or flow: a body that would be ours, the body of Earth, the body of writing. (DI, 253)

2 FROM GENEALOGY TO GEOPHILOSOPHY

The Ends of Origin

What Is Genealogy?

> Genealogy does not oppose itself to history as the lofty and profound gaze of the philosopher might compare to the mole-like perspective of the scholar; on the contrary, it rejects the metahistorical deployment of ideal signification and indefinite teleologies. It opposes itself to the search for "origins."
>
> **MICHEL FOUCAULT,** "NIETZSCHE, GENEALOGY, HISTORY"

IF WE KNOW A PHILOSOPHER according to the friends he or she chooses, this is because we appraise and evaluate the philosopher on the basis of the mad cast of characters assembled for the drama at hand—"the idiosyncrasy of his [or her] conceptual personae" (WIP, 64). By this measure, Deleuze must be counted among the most idiosyncratic of philosophers. Few have populated the plane of immanence with the variety and multiplicity of conceptual personae, both named (Plato, Spinoza, Leibniz, Bergson, etc.) and generic (the stranger, the schizo, the jurist, the walker [*promeneur*], etc.), that we find in Deleuze's writing. No doubt this makes understanding him an often baffling affair: after all, we can always ask, *which* Deleuze? Perhaps there are as many versions of Deleuze as he invents conceptual personae, or as many as there are phases in his career, or books he writes, but this is precisely why we have oriented Deleuze's plane of immanence around two conceptual personae, "the friend" and "Nietzsche." While the former evokes the unique sense of hospitality that characterizes Deleuze's philosophy and initiates his *invitation* to Nietzsche, the latter entails a unique sense of taste with which Deleuze transforms philosophy into a contest of friends and rivals.

This transformation is obvious enough in the very nature of Deleuze's friendship with Nietzsche, which undergoes a remarkable shift from his early commentaries to the later works that will concern us here. In the wake of *Anti-Oedipus*, the proper name "Nietzsche" becomes more elusive but no less vital in Deleuze's philosophy. The fluctuations of their relationship, the passage from apprenticeship to friendship, give rise to a new sense of relation and a different modality of thinking. "I had paid off my debts" to Nietzsche, Deleuze says, but this is what makes him *free* to engage Nietzsche on new grounds, namely, as the persona with which to invent a kind of thinking commensurate to the earth (Dia, 16). Hence, in *What Is Philosophy?* Deleuze and Guattari declare that "Nietzsche founded geophilosophy" (WP, 102), and we should understand this to mean that, both with Guattari and alone, Deleuze lays down a plane of immanence on which the conceptual persona "Nietzsche" intercedes to anticipate geophilosophy. As such, the chapter to follow elaborates the tortuous line that, beginning with Nietzsche's genealogy, we will trace to the concept and practice of geophilosophy, and this line leads us straightaway to the knotty paradox of our thesis: etymologically speaking, we propose to lay down a course that leads from *gene-* qua genealogy to *geo-* qua geophilosophy—from familial and human lineages to the inhuman milieu of the earth. Insofar as genealogy describes our "all too human" descent, in what sense could it possibly anticipate the movement outside humanity, to "a world without others" (*un monde sans autrui*)—to the earth?[1] How does genealogy, the study of ancestry, presage a geophilosophical practice in which "paternity does not exist" and the subject dissolves in the slow passage of geological time?

After the death of God and in the aftermath of his alibi, the Man-form, Deleuze redoubles Nietzsche's philosophical problem, namely: to enter on philosophy without assuming a priori conditions, to engage the power of critique without respect to Truth (God or Man). In a sense, this paradox helps us to formulate the very definition of genealogy—a critique of origins that proceeds by foreclosing origins. In "Nietzsche, Genealogy, History," Michel Foucault brilliantly demonstrates that Nietzsche's concept of "origin" entails three distinct, albeit related, definitions.[2] To begin with, an origin refers to that first instance that exists before all the subsequent events of history.

Second, an origin refers to a grand and solemn essence that corresponds to the most precious of moments. The third and "final postulate," Foucault says, "is linked to the previous two: it would be the site of *truth*."[3] Indeed, the offer of origins constitutes the promise of continuity and causality, of coherence and logic, of beginning and ends, and ultimately of Truth. The irony, then, is that the concept of origin ought "by rights" to imply a stable and truthful point of departure, an *origin*, but Nietzsche revokes any such promise. It is as if, at the very point when an origin is miraculously provided for the grounding of history, genealogy suggests that the origin is but a mask beneath which we peer to find—another mask. It is as if, at the very point that genealogy is drawn toward the ground of metaphysics, it also draws its distinction from the pretense of Truth: in Nietzsche's words, "under all foundations, under every ground, a subsoil still more profound" (BGE, §289).[4]

Nietzsche accomplishes this double movement by deploying a remarkably complex semantics of origin, and an equally sophisticated conceptual field, around three different terms: *Ursprung*, or "springing forth"; *Herkunft*, or "whence coming," related to *Ankuft*, or "arrival"; and *Entstehung*, or "rising out of." As Foucault explains, Nietzsche submits "origin" to a kind of serialization that progressively deterritorializes any certain and solid sense of beginning, of essence, of truth. In contrast to the ascent along the ladder of origins, Nietzsche formulates a countervailing tendency according to which the notion of an origin is hollowed out from its "self-same" origin. Hence, the series of these terms, which suggests a kind of triumphalism of Truth, actually indicates the rebellious operations of genealogy, which analyzes the disparate field of forces and the correlative "will to power" that belie the offer of origins.

Genealogy begins to reveal itself to us when we realize that Nietzsche's most grandiose deployments of "origin" are also, generally speaking, his most parodic. By the time of his mature critiques of morality, Nietzsche tends to reserve the pomp and circumstance of *Ursprung*, the pretense of a great beginning, for moments of great irony. At the outset of *On the Genealogy of Morals*, for instance, he endeavors to distinguish his own critical method from other "historians" who typically explain the invention of morals by virtue of habit or utility. "Originally," Nietzsche writes, as if he were precisely such a historian, "one approved unegoistic actions and called them good from the point of view of those to whom they were useful" (ibid., GM, 1 §2). In describing this "English" tendency, Nietzsche ironically adopts the rhetoric of *Ursprung*

(Man hat ursprünglich—so dekretieren sie—unegoistische Handlungen von Seiten Derer gelobt und gut genannt, denen sie erwiesen wurden, also denen sie nützlich waren) to mark the utilitarian taste for origins at the same time that he marks his own distance from this tendency. Indeed, Nietzsche undertakes the subversion of origin and truth at those very moments when a transcendent *Ursprung* is divested of its solemnity and even innocence—when we no longer believe in truth "in itself."

Notably, in the very sentence before he mockingly adopts the English historians' appeal to origin, Nietzsche describes their failure as follows: "The way they have bungled their moral genealogy comes to light at the very beginning, where the task is to investigate the origin [*Hekunft*] of the concept and judgment 'good'" (GM, 1 §2). In this case, where he effectively characterizes the general project of "moral genealogy," and even as he prepares for the failure of this project in the following sentence, Nietzsche formulates a critical and conceptual distinction: the word "beginning" does not refer to *Ursprung* but rather to a new term, *Herkunft*. Interestingly, the moral tendency that Nietzsche underscores in what follows ("Originally, one approved unegoistic actions and called them good from the point of view of those to whom they were useful. . . ."[GM, 1 §2]) seems to consist in precisely the absence of irony that we have heretofore identified with *Ursprung,* as if the very failure of the concept of origin derived from its sincerity or, perhaps, its truthfulness. The distinction we are marking here is crucial, for if *Ursprung* clings to a sense of transcendent and unitary origin, then *Herkunft* signifies a typological notion of descent, a sense of origin that implies a national or even ethnographic designation with which *Ursprung* itself will be framed in turn. Doubtless, in the context of the English historians and German Idealists to whom the early pages of *On the Genealogy of Morals* are devoted, the analysis of origin qua descent (*Herkunft*) is especially important ("The great book of modern ethnology is not so much Mauss's *The Gift* as Nietzsche's *On the Genealogy of Morals,*" Deleuze and Guattari proclaim [AO, 190]). On the one hand, as we have already seen, the English tradition of moral history consists in a *Herkunft* characterized by consummate common sense: the predilection of the English is expressed in a taste for a utilitarian *Ursprung.* But on the other hand, the German tradition of moral critique, symbolized by Kant, consists in a *Herkunft* characterized by the insistence on a transcendental system of judgment: the Kantian predilection lies in a taste for an ideal *Ursprung.*

Perhaps the greatest conceit of Deleuze's analysis of genealogy is to have grasped its practice in light of a kind of idealism that he situates in Kant's transcendental philosophy. As Deleuze avers, "Kant is the first philosopher who understood critique as having to be total and positive as critique" (NP, 89). But if Kant claims the virtue of having openly introduced a practice of immanent self-scrutiny into philosophy, he also claims the vice of having tacitly introduced limits to that practice. Genealogy pursues critique beyond the Kantian framework, beyond metaphysical-moral limits, since as Kant concedes, there are things—e.g., God, freedom, immortality—that critique must not consider (*noli me tangere*) (CPR, Bxxx). But beyond even the sacred categories that Kant avows, Deleuze insists that the very problem of critique must be located in its premise, in a critique of reason based on reason, since this work will invariably leave reason itself untouched. "Kant lacked a method which permitted reason to be judged from inside [*du dedans*] without giving it the task of being its own judge": as a result, critique ends up affirming the "rights of the criticized" (NP, 89).[5] Kant never gets to the point of evaluating the genesis of reason, the relation of forces and the disposition of the will that bring its particular requirements into existence. After all, what would be the *reason of reason, the will to reason?*[6] "Transcendental philosophy discovers conditions which still remain external to the conditioned" (ibid., 91), but this is why genealogy eliminates every case of exceptionalism.[7] In contrast to both the utilitarian and the idealist tendencies, Nietzsche devises a critique that spares no one and nothing. This is what it means to "philosophize with a hammer": to enjoin an absolute critique in the sense, say, that von Clausewitz alludes to "absolute warfare"—unlimited and unyielding, beyond laws, contracts, institutions.[8] Genealogy is a "war machine"—but we must always insist that the destruction of ideals, morals, and higher values does not mean the end of evaluation. To the contrary, the end of ideals means the terrible urgency to bring evaluation to bear on all values as well as the joyful responsibility to create new values. This double movement defines genealogy, and we can only hope to grasp Nietzsche's "gay science" in light of the pursuit and dissolution of origins with which we began. Thus, in the opening section of *On the Genealogy of Morals,* where he refers to "the origin of *agathos,*" Nietzsche specifically uses *Herkunft* not only to discuss the etymology of the Greek word, typically understood to signify "the good," but also because its origin is "susceptible of several interpretations" (GM, I §5).[9] Genealogy begins by evaluating the significance (*valeur*) of particular words, tracing back altogether common denominations through the tendrils of association and the tangles of sense, though never with an eye toward an ultimate meaning, an origin. Inasmuch as origin itself is "susceptible of several interpretations," genealogy undertakes its work in the absence of beginnings or ends, linearity or causality. The genealogist invariably discovers that

> the entire history of a "thing," an organ, a custom can in this way be a continuous sign-chain of ever new interpretations and adaptations whose causes do not even have to be related to one another but, on the contrary, in some cases succeed and alternate with one another in a purely chance fashion. The "evolution" [*Entwicklung*] of a thing, a custom, an organ is thus by no means its progress toward a goal, even less a logical progress by the shortest route and with the smallest expenditure of force—but a succession of more or less profound, more or less mutually independent processes of subduing, plus the resistances they encounter, the attempts at transformation for the purpose of defense and reaction, and the results of successful counteractions. The form is fluid, but the "meaning" is even more so. (GM, II §12)

The suspicion with which the genealogist treats all phenomena, even facts ("there are no facts," Nietzsche asserts, "only interpretations!"[10]), is rewarded by the perverse realization that their sense does not correspond to anything essential. Rather, what's essential is the variability of interpretation and the multiplication of sense. In other words, even as we are tempted to understand something (say, an object) as that solidity or substance which different forces alternately capture or lose, as if words and things, sense and event, were ultimately discrete, this is the very dualism against which Nietzsche rails. "Nietzsche substitutes the correlation of sense and phenomenon for the metaphysical duality of appearance and essence and for the scientific relation of cause and effect," Deleuze insists (NP, 3). The sense of any given "thing" must be sought in relation to the forces that capture it because they *create* it. The genealogist rejects once and for all the "innocence" which we attribute to semantic drift, as if the changing shape of words were buoyed along by an impassive ocean under which the sea-bed remains terra firma, in order to affirm the divagations of etymology as the expression of real forces (notably, in its verb form, the French *dériver* indicates both the action of deriving something, of obtaining an origin, as well as that of drifting).[11] "There is no object (phenomenon) which is not already possessed since in itself it is not an appearance but the apparition of a force," Deleuze explains. In fact, "the object itself is the force, expression of a force" (NP, 6).

In this spirit, Nietzsche introduces a final term into the conceptual neighborhood (*voisinage*) of origin we have been analyzing. Where *Ursprung* designates the innocence of originary unity, and where *Herkunft* suggests the promising ends of etymological descent, Nietzsche invokes *Entstehung* to indicate "the moment of arising." Needless to say, there is no "thing in itself" (*Ding an sich*) for Nietzsche, but we should always follow his critique, his genealogy, to its absolute end: there is "no thing," nothing at all, no object as such, no substance to speak of, only the emergence (*Entstehung*) of forces and the exteriority of their relations. "There is therefore an emergence [*devenir*] of forces which remains distinct from the history of forms, since it operates in a different dimension" (ibid.), Deleuze writes. To this "moment," which is forever untimely, and to this "emergence," which is always beyond us, we have given the name "the Outside." As Deleuze adds, "the outside concerns force: if force is always in relation with other forces, forces necessarily refer to an irreducible outside which no longer even has any form and is made up of distances that cannot be broken down through which one force acts on another or is acted upon another" (F, 86). Indeed, the emergence (*Entstehung*) of forces supplants both the parody of *Ursprung* and the plurality of *Herkunft* with the genetic relations that constitute the field of contention from which values are created—or, as Nietzsche will say, *legislated*. But what is legislation?

The origin—however silent, because it is silent—always denotes a sphere of conflict or *agonism*. In the remarkable second section of the *Genealogy*, for instance, Nietzsche describes how the "sphere of legal obligations" actually emerges from violence and dominations: "the moral conceptual world of 'guilt,' 'conscience,' 'duty,' 'sacredness of duty' had its origin [*Entstehungsheerd*]," he writes, adding that "its origin—its beginning [*Anfrang*], has been, as with the beginning of all great things on earth, thoroughly and for a long time doused with blood" (GM, II §6). The disinterested Kantian code of morality, the categorical imperative, "smells of blood and torture" (ibid.). Far from consisting in a wondrous and mythic beginning, then, *Entstehung* characterizes the struggle according to which a dominant interpretation comes to the fore. Interpretation is always a subduing; nothing (no "thing") is separable from the multiplicity of senses with which it is determined and the plurality of forces that take hold of it, but in every given case there is a sense which expresses the greatest affinity with the thing and its predominant force. "There is no event, no phenomenon, word or thought which does not have a multiple sense" (NP, 4), Deleuze maintains, but the multiple entails the predominance of one sense among others and the dominance of certain forces over others.

Therefore, while we affirm that all interpretation is misinterpretation, we should always remember: not all misinterpretations are created equal. Indeed, the assumption of equality is among the worst misinterpretations of Nietzsche, since it effectively ignores the predominance of one sense and the domination of particular values (say, equality) over others. This is why Nietzsche evokes the concept of value as the correlative of sense. "The sense of something is its relation to the force that takes possession of it," Deleuze writes. "The value of something is the hierarchy of forces which are expressed in it as a complex phenomenon" (NP, 8). What determines a given value is not a point of transcendent origin but rather what Nietzsche calls the "pathos of distance" (GM, III §14), which defines the relationship among forces, for the preeminence of one force is just as much the distance between forces (i.e., dominating and dominated). "It was from the height of this pathos of distance that they first seized the right to create values and to coin names for them; what did utility matter?" (ibid., I §2). The difference of distance is value. In Deleuze's words, genealogy entails "the referring back of all things and any kind of origin to values, but also the referring back of these values to something which is, as it were, their origin and determines their value" (ibid.NP, 2), namely, the differential and synthetic relation between forces—the will to power.[12] The origin does not yield an ultimate and overcoded truth but, instead, a field of agonism and origination, of struggle and creation, that can only be surveyed by and measured according to the principle of will. "The origin is the difference in the origin," Deleuze explains, but "difference in the origin is *hierarchy,* that is to say the relation of a dominant to a dominated force, of an obeyed to an obeying will" (ibid., 8). Whereas the promise of origin ostensibly lies in the offer of Truth, of a metaphysical and moral ground, genealogy ultimately dissolves the ground beneath our feet in order to affirm the contestation of forces and the synthesis of will.

Genealogy beyond Genealogy

> If it is true that the triumph of reactive forces constitutes man, then the whole method of dramatization aims to discover other types of expression, other relations of forces, to discover another reality of the will to power capable of transmuting its too-human nuances. According to Nietzsche the unhuman and the superhuman—a thing, an animal or a god—are no less capable of dramatisation than a man or his determinations. They too express a type, a type of forces unknown to man. The method of dramatization surpasses man on every side. A will of the earth, what would a will capable of affirming the earth be like? What does it want, this will without which the earth itself remains meaningless? What is its quality, a quality which also becomes the quality of the earth? Nietzsche replies: "The weightless."
>
> **GILLES DELEUZE,** *NIETZSCHE AND PHILOSOPHY*

In *What Is Philosophy?* Deleuze and Guattari suggest that the practice of genealogy augurs the invention of geophilosophy by relinquishing the "history of consciousness," of subjects and the subject-form, in favor of the creation of national characterologies (WIP, 102). "Nietzsche founded geophilosophy by seeking to determine the national characteristics [*characteristiques nationaux*] of French, English, and German philosophy," they write, adding that the "history of philosophy is therefore marked by national characteristics or rather by nationalitarianisms [*nationalitaires*], which are like philosophical 'opinions'" (ibid., 104). We have briefly noted Nietzsche's sense of "nationalitarianisms" in the previous section, and we will have occasion to return to this predilection, but the real challenge of geophilosophy consists in making all such affiliations (even and especially national ones) a matter of the earth.

This task, which is by no means an easy one, entails what we might call the "genealogy of genealogy." The etymology of genealogy typically describes the study of lineages (*genoi*) dating back to the aristocratic families of archaic Greece and the designation of hereditary lines, or races, but also denoting, more abstractly, the field of familial resemblances or categories. In the consecration of blood ties and kinship, the Greeks presage the emergence of a sovereign form of thinking that determines the various nationalisms of philosophy. But beyond or before these meanings, we might still wonder what links genealogy to geophilosophy—or, in the Greek lexicon, what links descent (*gen-*) to the earth (*ge, geo-*)? The surprising absence of any discernible relation between these two etymological lines is a matter of a complex partition among the Greeks, for whom *ge* (γη) and its more poetic form, gaia (γαια), were definitively distinguished from the world of humans. In Hesiod's myth *gaia* emerges from chaos and, in conjunction with *eros,* sows the seeds of gods and men; *gaia* gives rise to generation, but what is generated grows apart from *gaia,* on a different ground. Thus, Greek mythology differentiates between two lineages of the earth, *gaia* and *kthon.* The primordial earth (*ge*) denotes a cosmic being to which even "those who live on the earth" (*epikhthonioi*) have no claim; human relations, which we ascribe to families and familial lineages, belong to *kthon.* As Nicole Loraux writes, "*kthon* is not the primordial earth (*ge*) but the earth on which homes and cities of men are situated, firmly established between the sky of the Olympian gods and the depths of Hades."[13] At the heart of autochthony, the Greek myth of having been born of the earth (*kthon*), there remains the distance that separates humans from the "other" earth. Even in myth, Loraux adds, "men are *mortal* (*brotoi, thnetoi anthropoi*) before they are characterized as terrestrial," since as mortals they cannot claim to inhabit *gaia,* the earth beyond the earth, the virtual earth that redoubles our plane of actualizations, the socio-physics of the world, the history of civilization, life and death.

Geophilosophy consists in nothing less that the resolution to situate philosophy in relation to inhuman *gaia* as opposed to inhabited *kthon*—in other words, to make thinking a matter of the earth rather than a measure of the ground. Geophilosophy begins by deterritorializing thought from the habitas of a transcendental ego, the unity of apperception that represents itself to itself. We are "strangers to ourselves" or, rather, "unknown to ourselves" (*Wir sind uns unbekannt*), Nietzsche says in the preface to *On the Genealogy of Morals,* and we would do well to take this as both a diagnosis and a prescription (GM, Preface §1). In the first place, and most obviously, Nietzsche bemoans our failure to understand ourselves—our passions, our drives. We do not know the constituents of what we are, of the will we embody and the forces that compose that will. This diagnosis immediately suggests the project of innumerable therapies, even psychoanalysis, which hold out the promise of repairing our psychic alienation and "getting us in touch with our feelings." But nothing could be further from the sense of "health" that Nietzsche and Deleuze develop, since it is precisely the pathological constraints of the

Man-form—the sniveling neuroticism, the detoured drives, the pathetic conformism, the fugitive fantasies, the lingering *ressentiment*—that they reject as the reactive therapies of modern society, "discipline the gentle way" (Foucault). In the second place, then, when Nietzsche urges us to become strangers to ourselves, he seems to suggest that critique can begin only by virtue of an ineluctable estrangement whereby we look at ourselves with stranger's eyes. The aim of genealogy—to disclose the constituents of the will and the corresponding values that define this mode of living—succeeds by evacuating the very subject that we associate with traditional models of health and our "clinic of control."[14] What is genealogy if not the critical avatar of a strange, new vitality that overleaps our "all too human" humanity?

Genealogy does not aim to overcome our estrangement but extends it into yet stranger realms, returning us to the desert, the starkness of the earth, from whence we came; as Nietzsche says, we must "discover this land for the first time" (GM, Preface §7). Genealogy is an ascesis, a deterritorialization so thorough that we lose the coordinates that made us, however strange, nevertheless "ourselves." Inasmuch as the self, cogito, ego, or subject remain the effect of reactive forces, genealogy undertakes an act of critical imagination that is nothing less than *catastrophic* because it means our extinction, as if a metaphysical meltdown reduced the *décalage* of consciousness to the chaotic play of differences and intensities. The perspective of genealogy is not only extramoral but *extrahuman,* beyond conscience and consciousness. The Man-form yields to an appraisal of forces and a measure of the will to power that carry us beyond the human and into the derealization of identities—the play of molecules—that we invoked in the context of schizoanalysis: "It may well be that these peregrinations are the schizo's own particular way of rediscovering the earth" (AO, 35).[15] And like the schizo, who rides the wave of a tremendous deterritorialization of all fixed values, genealogy assumes the rigor of a critical demystification whereby we submit ourselves to disbelief. "We can already foresee that the forces within do not necessarily contribute to the composition of the Man-form," Deleuze writes, "but may be otherwise invested in another compound or form: even over a short period of time Man has not always existed, and will not exist for ever" (F, 124).

The second sight to which genealogy leads us—the vision of a "world without others"[16]—demands a remarkable effort of aesthetic imagination. No doubt this is why we typically entrust its undertaking to fiction, or even science-fiction, which explores the most dire prospects of our extinction. But what would it mean for philosophy to extend itself beyond our own existence? Perhaps this is what Nietzsche means when he writes, near the end of *On the Genealogy of Morals,* that "the value of truth must for once be *called experimentally into question"* (GM, III §24), for critique enlists a power of destruction that is no less a power of invention: *pars detruens, pars construens.* To produce a critique of the "value of values," Deleuze says, is just as much the "problem of their creation" (NP, 1). Only in this way does philosophy become a form of perpetual critique and critique in turn become a form of perpetual innovation. In "On Truth and Lying in a Non-Moral Sense," the astonishing short essay he composed in 1873, Nietzsche enacts this experiment by posing humanity in the context of a universe so vast as to render our precious and self-important sense of Truth all but irrelevant.[17] "In some remote corner of the universe that is poured out in countless flickering solar systems, there once was a star on which clever animals invented knowledge," he writes, only to add that "after nature had taken a few breaths, the star froze and the clever animals [*die klugen Tiere*] had to die."[18] Whereas the "world-historical" perspective of philosophy grants the invention of truth an august and originary place, Nietzsche evokes this event on a scale so vast as to divest us, the "clever animals," of the metaphysical-moral narrative that organizes the universe and places us at its center. The assumption of our feeble insignificance, which Nietzsche compares to that of an insect ("if we could communicate with the gnat, we would learn that it too swims through the air with the same pathos and feels within itself the flying center of the world"[19]), introduces a perspective ("the pathos of distance") from which to measure our knowledge, our sacred sense of truth, since it is precisely this sense of miserable vulnerability, relativism, and nihilism that *provokes* the will to truth. The universe so outstrips our "contemptible and insignificant" humanity as to incarnate the reaction formation according to which we have built the "enormous structure of beams and boards of the concepts, to which the poor man clings for dear life," and with which "the proud man, the philosopher, believes he sees the eyes of the universe focused telescopically from all directions upon his actions and thoughts."[20]

But what if we did not exist or if existence included us only contingently? If "a truthful world presupposes a truthful man," as Deleuze writes, what would happen if philosophy effaced man, however hypothetically or temporarily, and made itself an *affair of the earth?* In *Beyond Good and Evil,* the book that precedes and in some sense inspires *On the Genealogy of Morals,* Nietzsche suggests that the operation of genealogy approximates that of "natural history." Because the subjects of history tend to be naturalized, accepted as a priori and treated with causal indifference (*laissez aller*), the purpose of a natural history is to deterritorialize philosophy onto a vastly different milieu. "Could it be that moralists harbor a hatred of the primeval forests and the tropics?" Nietzsche asks (BGE, V §197). Inversely, could it be that amorality harbors a love of those same forests and tropics, of the strangeness of the earth itself? "Whether *you* like them, these fruits of ours? But what is that to the trees? What is that to *us*, us philosophers?" (GM, Preface §2), Or as Deleuze writes, "Our situation in relation to existence is such that we have not even recognized the will which is capable of evaluating the earth (of 'weighing' it), nor the force capable of interpreting existence" (NP, 23). Whereas if moralists "look for something 'pathological' [*krankhaftig*] at the bottom of all tropical monsters and growths" (BGE, V §197), as Nietzsche says, "philosophers of the dangerous 'Perhaps'" (ibid., I §2) arrive from outside, divesting thought of its codes in order to merge with the powers of the earth. This is the challenge to which Deleuze and Guattari respond in the name of geophilosophy, which we can define as the extension of genealogy into the depths of the earth (geology) and onto the surfaces of the earth (geography). Genealogy presages this geo-dynamic enterprise because the lineage of signs and the history of forces are written on the earth itself—in the mineralization from which we emerged as vertebrates, on the landscape which we have transformed over millennia, to the vast fossil record to which we will return, perhaps some day to be recovered by a future species. We write on and are written on the geolandscape, in innumerable layers and strata. Indeed, geophilosophy analyzes the "dynamic elements (energy flow, non-linear causality)" that, as Manuel Delanda explains, "we have in common with other nonliving historical structures."[21]

Deleuze's affinity for the earth, not just as a concept but as the milieu within which concepts must be created, dates back to his earliest published work. His little essay "Desert Islands" (1953) might otherwise seem a species of juvenilia (until relatively recently, it was neither collected nor translated into English) were it not for his precocious insistence that philosophy must be understood as a geographical practice. The problem, as Deleuze writes, is that this view does not square with our sense of common sense, and nowhere do we experience the disjunction between the predilection of the imagination and eventualities of the earth more forcefully than in the context of islands. We tend to imagine islands by virtue of imposing our human motives, locating them in the leaving behind of one world or the founding of another, but always envisioning them on the model of sovereign ground. In other words, we ignore the geological and geographical movements of the earth, and Deleuze adds, this is the point: "humans can live on an island only by forgetting what an island represented" (DI, 9). In point of fact, all islands are deserted or, inversely, only on the condition of its desertion is an island really an island, and this proposition immediately deterritorializes ground and subject alike. When we really think about it, the very existence of islands, which are either "from before or from after humankind," recalls us to our own lamentable mortality, inducing a kind of memento mori (ibid.).

Deleuze invokes the earth qua island to displace humanity from its transcendent assumptions. The thought of living on an island is literally unbearable and perhaps, at some level, inconceivable, but this is all the more reason that it must be thought. In this spirit, Deleuze begins his short essay by explaining that, according to geographers, "there are two kinds of islands": while some are "accidental, derived islands" that endure the inundation or erosion of larger bodies, even if at the cost of watery isolation, others are "originary, essential islands" that emerge from the eruptions and convulsions of the earth below the sea (ibid.). Islands are either continental or oceanic, but whatever the case, an island consists in movements and deterritorializations within which human societies appear provisional, even irrelevant. "That England is populated will always come as a surprise," Deleuze remarks, but what really surprises its inhabitants is that *England is an island,* since this brute fact must be perpetually forgotten (ibid.).

For this reason, the great modern myth of the deserted island, *Robinson Crusoe,* depicts its eponymous English hero, the victim of a shipwreck, as a colonizer who resolves to remake "his island" in the image of his own civilization. Free to live however he chooses, to invent any habitas he can imagine, Crusoe sets up the island as the bureau office of a "true-born Briton," as Marx famously put it.[22] Has anyone embodied the Protestant work ethic more thoroughly than Crusoe, who rediscovers his cultural inheritance, the virtue of God and industry, in the place where we would least expect to find it? Over the course of twenty-eight years, the castaway becomes—even more European!

"The mythical recreation of the world from a deserted island gives way to the reconstitution of everyday bourgeois life," Deleuze writes of Defoe's novel (DI, 12). We say that no man is an island, but Crusoe makes clear that the "man form" territorializes the island, making it the ground for subject and object.

By contrast, Deleuze asks us to envision a people who, far from grafting civilization on the island, enter into relations with the earth that create a kind of mutual resonance. Were these people "sufficiently separate, sufficiently creative, they would give the island only a dynamic image of itself, a consciousness of the movement which produced the island," he writes (ibid., DI, 10). *"Then geography and the imagination will be one"* (ibid., 11; emphasis mine). This affirmation, rendered in the future tense rather than the conditional mood, assumes a kind of geographic imagination that in some sense describes Deleuze's own philosophical development. After this early invocation of Crusoe, Deleuze ventured to return to the island and to reenchant geography once again in a remarkable essay that he published roughly fifteen years later: "Michel Tournier, or the World without Others."[23] Tournier and Deleuze had been friends since childhood, and this may explain the vibrant conceptual affinity that existed between the novelist and the philosopher; in a sense, Tournier seems to have anticipated the philosophical landscape that we are elaborating here. No doubt Deleuze thought as much: his essay turns to his friend's luminous novel *Friday* not only as a way to reprise the Crusoe myth but, also, to pursue Tournier's revolutionary retelling. Beyond altering the dates and circumstances of Defoe's novel, *Friday* makes "the isle as much the hero of the novel as Robinson or Friday" (LS, 302). Where the first Crusoe suffers from the incapacity to think in relation to the island and, thereby, to imagine thinking as an affair of the earth, Tournier's same-named protagonist enters into a series of experiments on, and with, the island whereby his self-same subjectivity dissolves. Slipping into the swampy mire in the middle of the island or burrowing into the cave below it or languishing on the lush surface of its combs, this Crusoe eventually loses the regularity of perception, the credibility of language, and the very presentiment of other people that had heretofore sustained his being. When a recalcitrant and dreamy Friday appears, eventually destroying his erstwhile master's store of goods, the reservoir of his objects and history recovered from the shipwreck, the last vestiges of "his" past, Crusoe passes into a new and ethereal existence that, as Deleuze suggests, is commensurate to the earth.

At the end of Tournier's novel, then, Crusoe refuses the opportunity to leave the island that his earlier namesake had so happily accepted: his "rescue" would only serve to return him to a society of others and to the organization of the Man-form from which he has progressively detached himself in a profound becoming with the island. The geographical imagination is such that Crusoe can no more leave than the island can be transported. Hence, Deleuze extends genealogy beyond the Man-form, but we might say that this development augurs the invention of geophilosophy without yet realizing it. For if we have deterritorialized the subject in relation to the earth—if, in the language of *Anti-Oedipus,* we have discovered the decoded limit of the subject, the schizo, *homo natura*—it remains for us to follow the deterritorializations of the earth and to make these movements the condition of thinking itself. Hence, we conclude here, at the limits of genealogy, by envisioning a philosophy of the earth that "brings together all the elements"—man and nature, mind and matter—"within a single embrace" (WIP, 85).

The End of the World as We Know It

What Is Geophilosophy?

> Geography is not confined to providing historical form with a substance and variable places. It is not merely physical and human but mental, like the landscape.
>
> **GILLES DELEUZE** AND **FÉLIX GUATTARI**, *WHAT IS PHILOSOPHY?*

In *What Is Philosophy?* Deleuze and Guattari invoke Kant's self-proclaimed Copernican Revolution as a precursor to their own geophilosophy. Like the astronomer, who calculated the movement of celestial bodies by displacing the earth from its epicentric presupposition, Kant displaces philosophy from the premises of a divine regime. "This would be just like the first thoughts of Copernicus," Kant writes, for when the astronomer "did not make good progress in the explanations of the celestial motions if he assumed that the entire celestial host revolves around the observer, [he]tried to see if he might not have greater success if he made the observer revolve around the stars at rest" (CPR, Bxvi). In other words, Copernicus effectively decenters the subject from its traditional coordinates, but if Kant repeats this gesture in his own philosophy, if he revokes the transcendent assurances that define our fundamental place in the cosmos, he does so by establishing a transcendental system in the subject-form. In a critical footnote, Kant refines his analogy to Copernicus by explaining that the latter dared, "in a manner contradictory of the senses yet true, to seek for the observed movements not in the objects of the heavens but in their observer" (ibid., Bxxii). Thus, the anthropocentrism that had organized the structure of the *cosmos* gives way, in the *Critique of Pure Reason,* to a *universal* structure of reason and judgment. As Kant makes clear on any number of occasions, the metaphysical-moral order he attributes to the subject would be no less applicable (mutatis mutandis) anywhere else and among any other intelligent species.

Therefore, Kant's perspectival shift merely replaces a divine vantage with an (extra) terrestrial one, but as Deleuze often suggests, the death of God remains utterly meaningless unless we pursue it to its logical ends. Typically, what we call the death of God is really a trade-off: the latter is absented, but this knowledge bestows on humans the consciousness of his mortality, which is both anticipatory and memorial: *unüberholbar* (Heidegger). Hence, the real problem posed by God's death lies in the fate of the "Man-form," which has no more claim to existence than its transcendent predecessor: as Deleuze writes, even the forces within man—"the force to imagine, remember, conceive, wish, and so on"—do not presuppose the "Man-form" (F, 124). Hence, inasmuch as Deleuze and Guattari repeat Kant's Copernican turn, they do so in order to carry the impulse beyond its Kantian conclusions, to the plane of absolute deterritorialization. In *What Is Philosophy?* Deleuze and Guattari detach philosophy from its anthropocentric moorings in order to put thought in "direct relationship with the earth" (WIP, 85). In discussing geophilosophy, then, we should bear in mind that the prefix "geo" (derived from *ge*) signifies precisely the deterritorialization of thinking from its human regime (*gene*)— the "categories of subject and object" (ibid., 85)—onto the earth.

Broadly construed, Deleuze and Guattari elaborate the relation between thought and the earth in the course of three collaborations—*Anti-Oedipus, A Thousand Plateaus,* and *What Is Philosophy?*—that transform and refine what we have broadly called geophilosophy. In *Anti-Oedipus,* the earth appears as the great "body without organs" on which the primitive socius is inscribed like the complex and ritualistic symbolism of a tattoo. The development of civilization partitions and territorializes the earth, rendering it the "multiple and divided object of labor," but even these forces—the leveling of forests and wetlands, the building of cities and strip malls, the materialization of sub-urbs and neighborhoods—testify to "the unique indivisible entity" of the earth itself, "the full body that falls back on [*se rabat sur*] the forces of pro-duction and appropriates them for its own as the natural or divine precondi-tion" (AO, 140-41).[24] Later, in *A Thousand Plateaus,* the analysis of the earth is resumed as a "geology of morals" that diagrams the bands of intensities with which each successive socius territorializes the earth. The bodies that traverse the ground, that build on it or reduce it to rubble, are not separable from the earth but rather constitute the infinite surface movements that will be folded into its strata.[25] Finally, in *What Is Philosophy?* Deleuze and Guattari seem to return from the depths of geology to the surfaces of geography, on which the dramas of the earth unfold in a kind of *longue durée* that includes humans only contingently, secondarily.

When Deleuze and Guattari ask *who the earth thinks it is?* we should understand them to mean: what would it mean to make thinking an affair of the earth? What if, no longer defining it in terms of "a line drawn between subject and object nor a revolving of one around the other," we were to under-stand thinking in terms of the "relationship that takes place between territory [*territoires*] and the earth [*la terre*]"? (WIP, 86). The proximity of these terms—*territories, terre*—suggests the slippage to which they are prone and, thence, the imperative to insist on their vital distinction. In French, we normally dis-tinguish between two meanings of *terre,* one related to the soil, the other to the planet, but Deleuze stresses the sense in which the former becomes ter-ritorialized as territory (as, say, homeland or fatherland), whereas the lat-ter deterritorializes these coordinates. The territory and the earth constitute the "components" of a broad spectrum characterized by reterritorialization ("from earth to territory") on one side and deterritorialization ("from territory to earth") on the other (ibid., 86). Whereas territories have been imposed on the earth under the auspices of so many codes that capture and shape mat-ter, the earth "constantly carries out a movement of deterritorialization on the spot, by which it goes beyond any territory," unleashing all kinds of inten-sities, flows, becomings (ibid., 86). But if the earth is "deterritorialized and deterritorializing," designating as it does the virtual limit that dissolves the actualizations of even the most stubborn ("molar") of formations, Deleuze and Guattari never cease to measure this tendency against that of territories and (re)territorialization. "The earth is certainly not the same thing as the territory," they write of romantic music and art. Rather, the earth "is the intense point at the deepest [*profond*] level of the territory or is projected outside it like a focal point, where all the forces draw together in a close embrace [*corps-à-corps*]" (ATP, 339-40).

In the language of *A Thousand Plateaus*, then, we could say that the territory is determined stratigraphically, according to the encrustation of cultures and civilizations. Each new territory asserts its supremacy in relation not only to what preceded it but, we might say, to the earth itself, but eventually its monuments will crumble and even the most advanced of civilizations will be reduced to sediment, compacted into strata, on which the next civilization and every one thereafter will unwittingly dance. Thus, we follow the contours of the strata, coiled in bands, like seams in leading us deeper and deeper into the earth—and yet, Deleuze and Guattari insist, the earth constitutes the most profound point of this series, the limit or inside, which projects the most exterior surface. In other words, the virtual point at the heart of the earth emanates a pure field of forces that redoubles the interior outside all strata. In this respect, we might imagine the earth topologically, as if each of us were a pleat in the supple *super-fold* that traverses thought and matter, tracing the imperceptible line that relates the inside and the Outside. In his luminous book on Foucault, Deleuze describes the topology with which we can imagine this well-nigh "ontological" folding. Across the great span of Foucault's work, Deleuze argues, we find the analysis of a fold that relates inside and outside: "in all his work Foucault seems haunted by this theme of an inside which is merely the fold of the outside" (F, 97). The trajectory of this folding concludes (prematurely) in *The Use of Pleasure*, where Foucault resolves to "go back to the Greeks" and describe the emergence of a new diagram of power. The agonic sphere into which the Greeks entered, even and especially in the name of democracy, entailed a relation of the self to the self, a fold of force on force, an auto-affection of force, which redoubles the epistemically unique interiority in an outside. "Far from ignoring interiority, individuality or subjectivity," Deleuze explains, the Greeks "invented the subject, but only as a derivative or the product of a 'subjectivization' [*subjectivation*]" (ibid., 101).

This description is no less applicable to Foucault himself inasmuch as he sought to develop a "dimension of subjectivity derived from power and knowledge [*pouvoir et savoir*] without being dependent on them" (ibid.). Indeed,

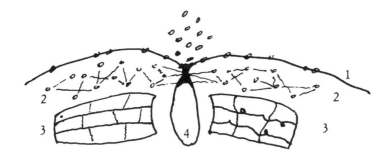

1. Line of the outside
2. Strategic zone
3. Strata
4. Fold (zone of subjectivation)

Deleuze's diagram of Foucault

this is the very definition of subjectivization; this is what sets its "derivation" (the folding of the Outside) apart from the determination (the conditions of an existence) of subjection. Hence, Deleuze folds and unfolds his map of sub-jectivization on the basis of supple lining that draws together the fundamental elements of Foucault's thinking. In their more abstract form, we might simply refer to these elements as "knowledge, power, self," but in the context of Fou-cault's work, Deleuze argues, each takes on a specific, topological function—strata, outside, and subjectivization (respectively). "The three agencies are at once relatively independent and constantly replacing one another," Deleuze maintains (ibid.). While each of these "agencies of topology" produces its own (*propre*) map according to which the other agencies will be organized, they are all topologically implicated and complicated, immanently and intricately folded. "The strata have the task of continually producing levels [*couches*] that force something new to be seen or said," he adds. "But equally the relation to the outside has the task of reassessing the forces established, while, last of all, the relation to oneself has the task of calling up and producing new modes of subjectivization" (ibid.). Deleuze's topology is really a topology of topologies, a map that emplots Foucault's three maps along the fabulous folding of a line between inside and outside.

We have lingered on the trajectory of Foucault's *pliage* because, in a sense, Deleuze and Guattari redouble the formulation of this diagram in the development of geophilosophy, which likewise takes up the Greek world in order to consider the torsion of a fold that is unfolded along an exteriority where forces relate to and affect other forces. The line of the Outside is a "floating line with no contours which is the only element that makes two forms in battle communicate" (F, 113): there is always something "Heraclitean" about the Outside, for the Earth itself has become a furious field of combat, of rival forces that deterritorialize the pretense of any ground. Perhaps only in this sense can we understand Deleuze and Guattari's contention that "the territory is German, the Earth Greek" (ATP, 374), for these designations actually describe different means of geographical relation and, one might say, *imagination*: the territorial ground and the deterritorialized outside. Of course, the complication to which this distinction invariably leads is that the German Romantics frequently laid claim to the territory on the basis of the Greeks, the imputed precursors to the revival of a mythic and philosophical spirit in German culture. "Modern philosophy is reterritorialized on Greece as a form of its own past," Deleuze and Guattari write, adding that:

> German philosophers especially have lived the relationship with Greece as a personal relationship. But they indeed lived it as the reverse or contrary of the Greeks, the symmetrical inverse: the Greeks kept the plane of immanence that they constructed in enthusiasm and drunkenness, but they had to search for the concepts with which to fill it so as to avoid falling back into the figures of the east. As for us, we possess concepts—after so many centuries of Western thought we think we possess them—but we hardly know where to put them because we lack a genuine plane, misled as we are by Christian transcendence. (WIP, 101)

Among the great romantics, the Greeks provided not only a mythic model but also mythic predecessors. "For intellectuals like Goethe, Schiller, and Wilhelm von Humboldt, Greek art represented an absolute standard of beauty, as well as the foundation of self-cultivation."[26] Nourished by this earlier generation of romantic thinkers, even Nietzsche's early writings on the "tragic age of the Greeks" still envision the spell of a mythic resurrection: while Greece remains the only milieu in human history where the philosopher and poet (both "tragic" beings) were at home, the singular event of the Greeks reveals a profound kinship with the contemporary German cultural renaissance. In the later stages of *The Birth of Tragedy*, Nietzsche announces: "I shall also name those forces which seem to me to guarantee a *rebirth of tragedy*—and perhaps other blessed hopes for the German genius!" (BOT, §16)

For the young Nietzsche, the avatars of this new "tragic culture" (ibid., §18) in opera (Wagner) and philosophy (Schopenhauer) provided evidence that modernity could still tap an ancient "Dionysian root" (ibid., § 19), that the Greek miracle could be resurrected and possessed by a similarly chosen people.[27] As George Williamson has written, Nietzsche's first book "sought to trace the roots of German Protestantism to the spirit of Greek Dionysianism, now reborn in a German tradition of absolute music that promised to overturn the optimistic foundations of modern culture and give rise to a 'new' cult of genius."[28] Drafts of *The Birth of Tragedy* allude to a kind of Hellenicized Christianity that, forgoing the femininity of Judaism, appeal to an earlier reverence for "pity" (*Mitleid*) whose emblem was the "Gospel of John born from the Greek atmosphere, from the soil of the Dionysian."[29] References to this "Greek gospel" were finally effaced from the printed edition, but what we find in this published version of the text, perhaps as a result, is stranger still: the absence of virtually any reference to Christianity. In effect, Nietzsche has yet to realize the latter as his great enemy; he remains enrapt by what might be termed "the miracle of the Greeks," which yokes antiquity and contemporary Germany in spite of differences that would subsequently become the subject of his own unapologetic indictments of modernity. As he averred in subsequent years, and always with greater ferocity, "My aim is to generate open enmity between our contemporary 'culture' and antiquity. Whoever wishes to serve the former must *hate* the latter" (as quoted in PTG, 6).

Nothing situates the question of Greece as the "birthplace of philosophy" more poorly than its miraculous anointment, since this explanation not only stamps Greece with a Christian conceit but, in so doing, misconstrues the *emergence* of philosophy itself. "What the Greeks did was not a miracle," Deleuze writes (F, 113). Returning to the distinction between the Greek Earth and German Ground, then, we might say that the latter imposed an image of Christianity onto the Greek world, baptizing it with a kind of divine blessing that renders it the singular basis for the efflorescence of its own culture. Greece is Germanicized, but as Nietzsche asks and Deleuze repeats, what could be worse "than to find oneself facing a German when one was expecting a Greek?" (WIP, 108-9). Hence, when Deleuze and Guattari avow that "the territory is German, the Earth Greek," we should understand that the romantic tendency of the Germans was precisely to graft a territory on the earth, subjecting surfaces and movements to the "grouping of powers [*groupements de puissance*]" (ATP, 341).[30] German philosophy "wants to reconquer the Greek plane of immanence," they say, but to do so it will reterritorialize the earth, lay down foundations, efface the contingencies that had made the Greek world possible (WIP, 104).

In the context of the Romantic imagination, then, Deleuze and Guattari declare, "The territory has become desert earth, but a celestial Stranger arrives to reestablish [*re-fonder*] the territory or to reterritorialize the earth" (WIP, 86). Indeed, the "disjunction" between territory and earth "is precisely what determines the status of the romantic artist in that she or he no longer confronts the gaping of chaos but the pull of the Ground (*Fond*)" (ATP, 339)[31] The romantics resurrect the Ground, confirming once more the form of the subject and the transcendental imagination, even in the midst of a deserted sphere; but as we will see, the constituents of the Greek world return us to the earth, affirming before all else the plane of immanence. Among the German Idealists, Deleuze and Guattari write, "A mania for founding, for conquering, inspires this philosophy: what the Greeks possessed Autochthonously, German philosophy would have through conquest and foundation, so that it would make immanence immanent to something, to its own Act of philosophizing, to its own philosophizing subjectivity" (WIP, 104-5).

The Greek Milieu

> Philosophy appears in Greece as a result of contingency rather than necessity, as a result of ambience or milieu rather than an origin, of a becoming rather than a history, of a geography rather than a historiography, of a grace rather than a nature.
> **GILLES DELEUZE** AND **FÉLIX GUATTARI**, *WHAT IS PHILOSOPHY?*

The founding or grounding of philosophy inevitably returns us to the "cult of origins" which we have sought to dispatch, first in Nietzsche's writing and now in Deleuze's, and so it remains for us to accede to the deterritorialization that both philosophers discern in the emergence of ancient Greece—to "affirm the power of a 'milieu'" (WIP, 96). The innovation of geophilosophy consists, perhaps above all else, in grasping the uniqueness of the Greek milieu as the product of circumstances that conjoin and ramify each other. Indeed, geophilosophy is first and foremost the geophilosophy of the Greeks and the emergence of philosophy itself, but the contingent conditions that characterize this process provide, in turn, the indices with which we understand Deleuze and Guattari's philosophy of the earth. There is nothing inevitable or even necessary that underwrites the conjunction of these contingencies, but perhaps that is why we ought to embrace philosophy as the necessary outcome of their unique combination. "The principle of reason such as it appears in philosophy is a principle of contingent reason and is put like this," Deleuze and Guattari maintain: "there is no good reason but contingent reason; there is no universal history except of contingency" (ibid., 93).

Therefore, when Deleuze and Guattari ask "why philosophy in Greece at that moment?" we should understand the question, simply and literally, to mean: why not elsewhere, at other times and in other milieux? Why should we begin in Ancient Greece even in the face of evidence that, as Émile Bréhier once noted, mythico-philosophical texts were being produced in the East at the same time if not before?[32] Why begin with a western tradition and not with an eastern one? These questions might otherwise be the source of endless debate if we do not define philosophy as the creation of concepts and define the task of philosophy in relation to the earth. "Thinking consists in stretching [tendre] out a plane of immanence that absorbs the earth," Deleuze and Guattari explain (WIP, 88), and it is on this basis that we can extract the geographical features—the contingences—that condition the appearance of the philosophical plane. The sense of this process recalls Nietzsche's great exhortation to love our fate (amor fati!), which affirms the arbitrary circumstances of our existence as the necessary conditions of the life we experience and the fate we deserve. Fate does not rescue us from chance but rather affirms chance as causa sui, and this ought to be kept in mind as we unfold the Greek plane of immanence. The eventuality of Greece is absolutely singular insofar as each of these contingences "could have been different" (ibid., 93), but to admit as much is to affirm contingency itself, the contingent combination of contingencies, as our own conditions.

Naturally, we are transfixed by the surface effects of the earth, the frenetic and scattershot developments of a given land or another, but the speed with which things take place at one level is conditioned by a slowness that takes place in the depths. If humans are slow beings composed of fantastic speeds, as Malraux suggested and Deleuze approvingly quotes, then the earth is the inverse: the appearance of fantastic speeds, of frantic surface activity, is really the result of astonishing geological sluggishness. No doubt this is why, in the two volumes of *Capitalism and Schizophrenia,* Deleuze and Guattari refer to the earth as a "great unengendered stasis" (AO, 141), but we might say that this pronouncement is still made from the perspective of humans, if not as subjects then as a socius. By contrast, in *What Is Philosophy?* Deleuze and Guattari aspire to the perspective of the earth and to what we have called geophilosophy. Deleuze and Guattari's account of Greek philosophy can be situated in the broader trajectory of the Mediterranean world with which we associate the historian Fernand Braudel. In *What Is Philosophy?* they specifically refer to Braudel's great history of the Italian city-states in view of the commercial and conceptual relations that the Greeks realized: the resonance between these historical eventualities bespeaks a new critical perspective that spreads itself over the earth. "Philosophy is a geophilosophy in precisely the same way that history is a geohistory from Braudel's point of view" (WIP, 95).

In *The Mediterranean in the Ancient World* (1998), published after both Deleuze and Guattari had died, Braudel approaches "the origins of Greek thought" from a perspective that we might simply call geophilosophical.[33] In this, his last book, Braudel extends the span of modern Mediterranean history that had constituted his life project into a *longue durée* that will envision a world before man. If human civilization were to be figured into the geological and geographical history of the Mediterranean, Braudel says, it would constitute nothing but the last two minutes of the last day of the first year. Thus, we might imagine the geophilosophy of Greece as if from the perspective of a satellite, as old as the world itself, which has trained a camera on the planet. A cosmic long take begins in something like the Paleozoia era, when the camera initiates an infinitely gradual zoom (think of Michael Snow) that takes us from the plodding focus on the globe to the vast area that would eventually become the Mediterranean, to the vicinity of the Aegean, and finally to the hub of Athens.

From this perspective, and according to this duration of millions upon millions of years, we can imagine how life in the Mediterranean was shaped by a series of geological eventualities and geographical transformations.

Broadly construed, then, we might extract three different geodynamic contingencies—(1) the "fractal" design of Greece, (2) the relatively poor quality of the Greek soil, and (3) the relative distance of Greece from the empires of the east—that combined to give rise to the Greek city. In Athens, above all, the philosophy that took shape, the civic structure that conditioned its efflorescence, the "precapitalist" economy that conditioned exchange—all of this takes place in the "deep time" of the earth. In Braudel's words:

> The many violent foldings of the Tertiary era took place at the expense of this very ancient Mediterranean, much larger than the present one. All the mountains, from the Baltic Cordillera to the Rif, the Atlas, the Alps and the Apennines, the Balkans, the Taurus and the Caucasus, were heaved out of the ancient sea. They reduced its area, raising from the great sea bed not only sedimentary rocks—sands, clays, sandstones, thick layers of limestone—but also deeply buried primitive rocks. The mountains surrounding, strangling, barricading and compartmentalizing the long coastline are the flesh and bones of the ancestral Tethys.[34]

Within a range of variables, the people who took up life at the edge of the Mediterranean—especially in the vicinity of what we call Greece—were confined by both sea and mountains, which made inhabiting the narrow strips of arable land a difficult task. While these coastal plains were easily flooded, the mountains conditioned "the most primitive ways of life."

The evolution of cities in the Mediterranean emerged against these and other conditions—the desert Sahel impinging on the sea across modern-day Egypt and Tunisia, the shallow, navigable waters that run southward from Sicily, the climactic changes and, consequently, the sustained erosion from increasing water. Unlike Mesopotamia and Egypt, which had long been settled, "the less populous areas, which covered much wider areas than these privileged regions, were more open to migrations or indeed invasion. They yielded to incomers, without necessarily noticing what was happening: Asia Minor in the broad sense and archaic Greece were both examples of such regions."[35] The invitation that Greece extended to those beyond its shores derived, in large part, from the sheer extent of its shoreline. "Greece seems to have a fractal structure insofar as each point of the peninsula is close to the sea and its sides have great length" (WIP, 87). Indeed, Greece extends a kind of geographical hospitality to foreigners, strangers, and immigrants that will be redoubled, as we will see, by political hospitality. The gradual development of the Greek world is characterized, comparatively, by a kind of "power vacuum" into which not only people but, also, goods, customs, and even knowledge will flood, giving rise to numerous cities and settlements along the coastline.

If the first contingency of geophilosophy draws people to Greece, the second contingency concerns the conditions that, reciprocally, forced the Greek *polei* to look beyond their shores, to establish relations with other cities and other peoples, exercising sovereignty and engaging in vigorous trade. Inasmuch as the Greeks transform the Aegean into this "bath of immanence," the very plane on which geography and philosophy merge, this dynamism derives in part from the relative scarcity of arable land and, especially in the case of Athens, the relatively poor quality of that land. In *The History of the Peloponnesian War,* for instance, Thucydides argues that the development and stability of Athens should be attributed, among other things, to the paradoxical blessing of inhospitable soil, "which made her unattractive to invaders (and less prone to civil strife)."[36] Attica is an arid land, a pebble without history, but if this general circumstance discourages its enemies, it also demands of its people an engagement with the outside. "Everything conspired with the process of pauperization to drive men to distant shores," Braudel concludes.[37] In Ancient Greece, cities invariably took to the sea, the result of which was feverish competition. "All round the Aegean, the Greek cities began to grow: tiny independent worlds, basically similar but competing with each other as rivals."[38]

Far from debilitating or destroying each other, the rivalry between *polei* catalyzed increasingly complex and heretofore unimaginable systems, but this was only possible in view of the third and final geophilosophical contingency. For if the design of the Mediterranean drove populations into the Greek "cyclonic zone," and if the fractal nature of Greece drove its settlers into relations of trade and exchange, we must finally understand that the intense competition—the agonism—of the *polei* was possible only by virtue of the geographical distance that the Greeks enjoyed with respect to the empires to the East. As Deleuze and Guattari write, the Greek cities

are the first to be at once near enough to and far enough away from the archaic eastern empires to be able to benefit from them without following their model. Rather than establish themselves in the pores of the empires, they are steeped in a new component; they develop a particular mode of deterritorialization that proceeds by immanence; they form a *milieu of immanence.* It is like an "international market" organized along the borders of the Orient between a multiplicity of independent cities or distinct societies that are nevertheless attached to one another and within which artisans and merchants find a freedom and mobility denied to them in empires. (WIP, 87)

The powers to the east predominantly organized themselves according to tyrannical, oracular, and ultimately imperial forms, but the Greek city-states emerged on the edge of these vast orders: without having to submit to their authority, appearing beyond their periphery or in their wake, the Greek cities entered into an unprecedented zone of mercantilism and a sphere of exchange.[39] "It was then that the network of Greek cities, both ancient and modern, really 'went live,'" Braudel writes.[40]

The logic of geophilosophy that we have adumbrated here consists in the conjunction of the Mediterranean and the Greek city, of the geographical and the social, of the Earth and the territory, which we should imagine like two facets of the plane of immanence that relate to and ramify each other. While the earth constitutes the field of absolute deterritorialization which "goes beyond any territory" and that "brings together all the elements within a single embrace" (WIP, 85), Deleuze and Guattari nevertheless insist that the earth does not exist apart from the territory. "Territory and earth are two components with two zones of indiscernibility: deterritorialization (from territory to the earth) and reterritorialization (from earth to the territory). We cannot say which comes first" (ibid., 86). Far from asserting the priority or causality of its components, geophilosophy bids us to measure the *relationship* between territory and earth. What does this mean?

What Is Philosophy? lingers on two social formations, the imperial state and the Greek city, which characterize two distinct modes of deterritorialization in the ancient world. In the empires to the east, such as Persia, "deterritorialization takes place through transcendence: it tends to develop vertically from on high, according to a celestial component of the earth" (ibid.). Philosophy is destined to remain stillborn under the vertical conditions of this *Urstaat,* given over as it is to the higher power of "wisdom or religion" (WIP, 89). By contrast, in the Greek cities in general, and Athens in particular, deterritorialization takes place *horizontally.* Where imperial states appeal to transcendence, the city adapts "the territory to the geometrical extensiveness [*étendue*] that can be continued in commercial circuits" (ibid.). We must be careful to understand this point without overstating its conclusion. As Deleuze and Guattari write, "the originality of the Greeks should rather be sought in the relation between the relative and the absolute" (ibid., 90), in the ways that the polis adapts to and ramifies the earth. Naturally, the Greek cities reterritorialize the earth and its commercial networks on the *agora,* the marketplace that forms the nexus of economic, political, and ultimately rhetorical life. And yet, even as it reterritorializes, the "originality" of the polis consists in having eschewed "projection in a figure"—the tracings of transcendent shadows, of wisdom and religion—for an immanent plane (ibid.). The relative deterritorialization of the polis unfurls in relation to the earth, not in opposition to it, the result of which will be the formulation of the horizontal "connections" along the surface of this plane and thence the creation of philosophy.

In the words of Jean-Pierre Vernant, the great structural anthropologist of the ancient world, "Philosophy is a creature of the city" because what the Greek city defined was not only a topographical milieu but a mental one: the polis "opened up a new spiritual horizon."[41] Shaped by the conditions of land and sea, of resources and climate, the city creates a unique *topos* and thereby gives rise to what might be called a *topos noêtos.* What does this mean? In his "Allegory of the Divided Line," Plato famously distinguishes between the sensible world (*topos aistêthos*) and the intelligible one (*topos noêtos*), but in the context of geophilosophy, Deleuze describes the way that the polis unfolds a philosophical plane that redoubles the earth.[42] Philosophy finds its home in the city because the city develops a distinct and altogether complex relation to the earth that we will unfold in the remainder of this chapter. In Athens, Deleuze and Guattari write, "thinking consists in stretching out a plane of immanence that absorbs the earth (or rather, 'adsorbs' it)" (WIP, 88). Let us conclude this section, then, by dwelling on this phrase once more, especially inasmuch as the transitive verb here, *tendre,* is associated with various procedures—of stretching, spreading—but also, adjectivally, with a sense of tenderness or even love. With *tendre* we suggest the paradoxical tightening produced by an embrace: to open one's arms (*tendre les bras*) to another, to reach out (*tendre la main*) to the land. The plane of immanence is inclusive: unfurled, the plane extends over the vastness of social, economic, and political exchanges in relation to the absolute deterritorialization of the earth. This is the drama of geophilosophy.

The Emergence of Philosophy

Autochthony

> And the country which brought them up is not like other countries, a stepmother to her children, but their own true mother: she bore them and nourished them and received them, and in her bosom they now repose. It is meet and right, therefore, that we should begin by praising the land which is their mother, and that will be a way of praising their noble birth.
>
> **PLATO,** *MENEXENUS*

Having traced the geographic constituents of the Greek world, we are now in a position to inquire into philosophy itself. After all, how does philosophy emerge on the Greek plane of immanence? The logic of our answer, as Deleuze writes, becomes "particularly clear in the case of Athens and its democracy," since in Attica the city effectively extends the deterritorialization of the earth into the social field (CC, 136). "When relative deterritorialization is itself horizontal, or immanent," Deleuze and Guattari write, "it combines [*elle se conjugue*] with the absolute deterritorialization of the plane of immanence that carries the movements of relative deterritorialization to infinity, by transforming them (milieu, friend, opinion)" (WIP, 90).

In "Plato, the Greeks," a short essay he published in 1992, Deleuze traces the development of this combination according to these parenthetical terms, which are no less the indices of philosophy itself. Thus, Deleuze sketches the development of Greek philosophy according to three discrete though related characteristics that define the polis: a "milieu of immanence" (*autochthony*), a "pleasure in forming association" (*philia*), and a "certain taste for opinion" (*doxa*) (WIP, 87–88). These traits "constitute the conditions under which philosophy was born and developed" (CC, 136), and yet we would have to admit that the relation between them—the ways in which they effect and ramify each other, the sense in which they constitute a complex series—remains vague, as if the lineaments of geophilosophy still waited to be cashed out in the diagram of Athens.

Geophilosophy is among Deleuze and Guattari's most enigmatic concepts because it is no more than sketched in the spare and suggestive pages of *What Is Philosophy?* Hence, in order to elaborate the concept, we might conclude this chapter by pursuing the path they suggest, if only to recover their sense of the Greek world. In both "Plato, the Greeks" and *What Is Philosophy?* Deleuze conceives of geophilosophy in terms that recall the Paris School of French classical structuralists who came of age in the 1960s, and we return to this school here in order to express this material–mental practice. Jean-Pierre Vernant was among the most renowned of a cadre of anthropologists and historians—including Marcel Detienne, Pierre Vidal-Naquet, and Nicole Loraux—whom Deleuze read and admired. Above all else, Deleuze seems to have absorbed the school's singular conviction that, far from being inimical to philosophy, the persistence of a mythic sphere in classical Greece enabled its creation as a rigorous practice of thinking. In the spirit of Louis Gernet, who served as their mentor and model, the Paris School sought to integrate the unreason of myth into the rational discourse of philosophy. In the mystical Greek sects, for instance, Gernet discovers the elements of philosophy making ready in the shadows—"not only a vocabulary and some of its metaphors but, from the beginning, a direction of thought."[43] The mythical flavor of philosophy, clear enough in Empedocles and Heraclitus, continues to infuse the development of the discourse well into its Platonic enunciation. "When Plato wants to make the concept of his knowledge present and vivid, he has recourse to comparisons from the Mysteries," Gernet writes. "Truth is perceived in a kind of *epopteia,* that is, in a vision analogous to the one reserved for those initiated into the higher Mysteries."[44]

Nowhere does the strange relation of myth and philosophy confront us more forcefully and more counterintuitively than in autochthony, the myth of having been born of the earth. And no mythic conceit dominated the iconography and rhetoric of classical Athens as completely as autochthony, which effectively provided its citizens with a story of their origin and, thence, the ground of their common identity. Athens entertained a remarkably vast array of autochthonous myths, each of which was subject to just as many variations, but the most famous mythical premise ascribed the naissance of city and citizens to divine origins: chasing the virginal Athena, the lusty god Hephaistos "fertilizes" the earth in a moment of *eros* and *eris,* of sexuality and strife. This stray seed gives rise to Erechtheonios, the first Athenian, whose origins are both autochthonous and divine, born as he is of the earth and the gods. But how can we reconcile the origins that the myth ostensibly institutes with the critique of origins that we undertook in the exercise of genealogy and that we are undertaking now in the name of geophilosophy? In what sense does autochthony, which seems to partake in the logic of reterritorialization, if not to provide its paradigmatic instance, actually unleash a deterritorialization of the earth from which philosophy emerges?

In the apparent contradiction between geography and mythos, we are tempted to regard autochthony as nothing less than a kind of Athenian ideology. But while it constitutes the expression of a kind of nationalism, the complexity of the myth is to have conditioned, at the same time, another logic with which the relative deterritorialization of the *demos* takes shape. The "mordant irony" (Detienne) of autochthony does not escape the Athenians or their chroniclers. "What is now called Greece was not formerly inhabited with any stability," Thucydides writes; rather, "there was emigration from the earliest times, and everyone left their homes easily under pressure."[45] The convoluted story of the Erechtheum duly expresses the conjunction of land and sea in the divine origins of autochthonous Athens. According to one of their most popular myths, the Athenians gained their name and sponsorship at the time when the immortals themselves were dividing the *timai* (gifts or prizes) of the earth. Poseidon is the first god on the scene, but Athena arrives thereafter to make her claim to the territory. As a result, either Zeus, the people of Athens, or both undertake a process of adjudication whereby Athena is finally awarded the honor. Vanquished here as he was elsewhere, Poseidon returns later, under the aegis of Emolpians, to seek vengeance. In the events that follow, the Athenian king Erechtheonios is killed by Poseidon's trident and deposited within the earth, whereupon Athena declares that a temple, the Erechtheum, be built in his honor. Given as much, one would expect the structure to bear witness to the "founder" of the city, Pallas Athena, who is credited with providing both the divine substance for her namesake as well as its divine protection. But inasmuch as the Erectheum is graced by her symbolism, in particular by the olive tree that was said to have sprouted from the point at which Athena's spear struck the earth, her presence is offset by the saltwater well, or "little sea," that embodies the spirit of Poseidon. "The Erechtheum, the temple of Athena and Poseidon" (WIP, 86), Deleuze and Guattari add, as if to intimate what we have sought to articulate: autochthony characterizes a "power of the earth" that follows the immanence of the sea as much as the rootedness of the tree.[46]

Indeed, the paradox of autochthony lies in the ostensible opposition between movement and stasis, between geography and myth, and even between the sea and the land—but we can hope to understand this paradox by paring away the uninhibitedly arrogant proclamations made in the name of the myth itself. When Athenians referred to themselves as Erectheions, the children of Erechtheionos, they engaged in a complex operation that invoked the earth for purposes that, in mythically establishing the city, deterritorialize the territory. As Detienne writes: "Praise of the pure autochthony, of the Athenians of (peasant) stock, who no longer hear any of these rumors of the historian about who knows what arid land, dump for exiles, for fugitives, for those landless peoples."[47] Instead, the paradox can be comprehended only when we grasp that the deterritorialization of the earth, far from inhibiting Greek autochthony, actually inspires its nationalistic claims and coheres its citizenry as a body politic. The proclamations of autochthony are, as Detienne and Loraux have shown, expression and evidence of profound narcissism: the myth of having been born from the earth and of descending from the gods announces the identity which Athens promoted and with which it distinguished itself from other *polei*. To be a citizen of Athens was to belong to the earth, which coursed through one's blood and calcified itself in one's bones. (It should hardly surprise us that autochthony was regularly invoked in the genre of the funeral orations, the *epitaphios:* descended from the earth, the dead must be returned to it.) From the perspective of autochthony, the Athenians come to regard all others foreigners as uncivilized—as barbarians (*xenoi*)—because they do not belong to Athens and, therefore, belong nowhere on earth. Indeed, the mythic origins of Athens bestow on its people a purity in relation to which all other people are judged. "We have a natural hatred of the Barbarian," Plato explains, "because we are purely Greek and without barbarian admixture" (Men., 245c–d).[48] Not just citizens, the Athenians are, logically, the *only* citizens.

Among Athenians, autochthony was invoked rhetorically and exercised politically, but the complicated connotations and operations of the myth yield three distinct, albeit related, claims. In the first place, autochthony is tantamount to uniformity: inasmuch as its people descended from the earth, Athens claimed homogeneity based on shared "good birth" (*eugeneia*). As Lysias explains in Plato's eponymous dialogue: "The origin of our existence is based on right; our ancestors were not, like most nations, an assembly of peoples of every origin, nor did they have to expel others in order to inhabit a foreign land; rather, as autochthones, they acquired in one instant a mother and a fatherland.[49]" In the second place, autochthony is tantamount to genealogy: inasmuch as the citizens traced their origin to the earth, Athens claimed to be the oldest of *polei*. While others were still wandering, the Athenians ostensibly occupied the same place from time immemorial. As Pericles famously declares: "Our land, always the same people having lived here generation upon generation, our ancestors handed down to us by their own merit, until now."[50] In the third place, autochthony is tantamount to stability: inasmuch as the city belongs to the earth, inasmuch as it ostensibly established civilization long before others, Athens claimed a kind of privileged political stability. The "always"(*aei*) to which Athenians appeal—as a noun, *aiôn* connotes both the force of life and of time, which Aristotle deems the "span of existence"— is finally cashed out in the belief in an enduring civic order. When cities are "constituted by populations of every origin and formed of unequal elements," their governments are subject to disruption and distress, but autochthonous Athens advertised its imperturbable continuity.[51] "We are the good autochthones, born from the earth on which the inhabitants have remained the same since the beginning, without break. A land that our ancestors have transmitted to us."[52]

Each of these three claims is clearly demonstrable in Herodotus's account of the Greco-Persian wars. In response to the Syracusans offer to divide command, the Athenian envoy recalls the myth of autochthony in order to claim military pride of place:

> Where would be the advantage of our having raised up a naval force greater than that of any other Greek people, if nevertheless we should suffer Syracusans to take the command away from us?—from us, I say, who are Athenians, the most ancient nation in Greece, the only Greeks who have never changed their abode—the people who are said by the poet Homer to have sent to Troy the man best able of all the Greeks to array and marshal an army—so that we may be allowed to boast somewhat.[53]

Here as elsewhere, autochthony forms the mythic core of a kind of patriotism: not only are the Athenians born from the earth, not only are they the oldest and purest of people, but as such they are the most able to organize, to lead, to *govern*. The only true citizens of the only true nation, Athenians claimed preeminence among other "nations," which they regarded as *prétendants*—false claimants to that which belonged to Athens alone. But if the claims of autochthony naturally extend to relations that we might call external, especially insofar as the city declares its imperial sovereignty and its superiority in relation to others (barbarian cities), these claims also define the internal relations of Athens and its citizen-autochthones. The pretense of Athenian narcissism ("to boast somewhat") promulgates a mythic identity that is belied by an interiorization of that same myth, which determines the people (*demos*) as autochthonous inhabitants and, thence, as citizens. Indeed, while many *polei* possessed autochthonous myths (*Spartoi* actually means "the Sewn"), and while the Arcadians in particular claimed an autochthonous heritage that explicitly competed with that of Athens, only in Athens does autochthony formulate the conditions for the radical social relations from which democracy and, thence, philosophy emerge.

Both because of and beyond the self-aggrandizement of autochthony, Deleuze contends that the implications of the myth cannot be reduced to Greek nationalism or its subsequent (and vulgar) romanticism. The ideological labor of autochthony yields to the contours of a supple logic within which myth translates the geographic contingencies of the earth into the geometrical *topos* of the city. Indeed, autochthony opens up a complex negotiation with the real ("machinic") relations of geophilosophy, the modulation of matter and thought, that concerns us here. Consider the relation between thought and the earth in light of the Erechtheum, which was built to commemorate the "first autochthon," Erechtheonios. One of the several structures that rest on the Acropolis, the Erechtheum boasts a singular architectural conceit: whereas the neighboring Parthenon is built on a broad limestone foundation that imposed a level surface on the mount, the Erechtheum follows the slope of the terrain as it descends from the east and north (the temple walls are significantly lower on the other sides). The Erechtheum is not "grounded" on Doric lines but rather traces the wandering line of the landscape from which the geometry of surfaces arise. In Deleuze and Guattari's words, the earth adapts "the territory to geometrical extensiveness" (WIP, 86). In other words, the myth of autochthony gives rise to the logic of a particular social diagram, the polis—but how?

In *Menexenus,* where he is asked to demonstrate the genre of the *epitaphio,* Socrates sketches the broad outline of our response: "equality of origin established by nature obliges us to seek political equality established by law" (238e-239a). In other words, equality of origin (*isogonia*) gives rise in Athens to political equality (*isonomia*), and this complex operation demands careful consideration. Because they are autochthones, because they are born of the earth and, thereafter, descended from it, the Athenians are all related: in Plato's words, "We who are citizens are brethren, the children all of one mother" (ibid., 238c-d). Autochthony inspires the image of a common maternity and, thence, the imagination of the city itself as a family in which, among the "brothers," no one enjoys natural superiority. Athens confers on all of its citizens (*Andres Athênaioi*) common prestige. Beloved by the gods (*theophilês*) and children of the earth (*autochthones*), Athenians "draw from this communal birth unequaled nobility."[54] In this respect, however, autochthony actually indicates two different senses of origin, since the myth effectively transforms the earth from the womb of Athenians into a "civic soil which, instead of a mother, was the land of their fathers."[55] The earth is both mother and father but it is, more accurately, mother and *then* father—a place of nativity qua nativism and *then* a patriarchal qua political inheritance.

While the presuppositions of a fatherland (*patria*) will be affirmed in the consecration of Athenian democracy, the development of a social diagram based on friendship among equals—or what Deleuze calls *philia*—is already visible in the early or "prepolitical" formations of community. In archaic Greece, where aristocratic families (*genoi*) shared and competed for power, the incipient constituents of a political sphere were established in vast assemblies. Detienne locates the formation of this sphere in the warrior rituals and funerary games that, preceding the emergence of the city, nonetheless provided the initial and enduring diagram for organizing its political geometry. After Achilles had been buried, for instance, "Thetis personally organized the funeral games. She set down in the middle of the assembly (*theke mesôi en agôni*) the beautiful prizes for the best of the Acheans."[56] Once something is set *en meson,* in the center, it becomes "common property" and thereby confers on its participants a common status. As Detienne explains, the assembly becomes a "common space, hardly suitable for personal digressions but entirely suitable for public, i.e., political, concerns."[57] Indeed, the image of warriors equidistantly situated around this booty, along the circumference of a perfect circle, presages the geometry of the polis itself. "The circular, symmetrical space favored by such [warrior] institutions found its purely political expression in the social space of the city, centered on the *Agora*."[58]

Initially identified with the marketplace, the *agora* constitutes the milieu that came to define a new sphere of "association." The "international marketplace" into which the Greeks enter, and which they internalize, conditions the transformation of association on the basis of exchange and competition. In Athens, Deleuze and Guattari write, we discover "a pure sociability as milieu of immanence, the 'intrinsic nature of association,' which is opposed to imperial sovereignty and implies no prior interest because, on the contrary, competing interests presuppose it" (WIP, 87). Where once social relations had been hierarchically organized by the prerogatives of aristocracy and lineage (*gene*), the spirit of competition that sustained these filial relations gradually passed into new ways of distributing power. "We do not think it right to be one another's masters or servants," Plato explains of autochthonous Athens (Men., 239a). Rather, citizens were understood to be naturally alike, no matter the difference in their "origin, rank, and function." As Vernant adds, "This likeness laid the foundation for the unity of the polis, since for the Greeks only those who were alike could be mutually united by *philia*, joined in the same community."[59] No citizen could claim inherent privilege: instead, the citizenry came to be characterized as equal and alike, bound by reciprocal bonds of friendship.[60]

Philia, Doxa, Philosophia...

> The history of philosophy must not hide the fact that in every case the Greeks had to become philosophers in the first place, just as philosophers had to become Greek.
>
> **GILLES DELEUZE** AND **FÉLIX GUATTARI**, *WHAT IS PHILOSOPHY?*

In light of geophilosophy we have lingered on autochthony because it describes a real relation to the earth as a field of material and mental deterritorialization. Indeed, the mythic logic of autochthony augurs the complex development of a social sphere, characterized no less by *philia* and *doxa*, within which we have endeavored to understand the emergence of philosophy as an affair of the earth. How does this happen? In what sense does autochthony usher in the constituents of this *topos noêtos*?

In the *Menexenus,* Socrates refers to Athens as an aristocracy as well as a democracy, and in the context of autochthony the reason should be obvious. The nobility conferred on citizens by autochthony gradually came to underwrite equal and identical relations among them: Athens is a democracy because its people, the *demos,* ostensibly enjoy an aristocracy of the earth. Historically, this eventuality is associated with the reforms introduced by Cleisthenes in the sixth century B.C.E., when the right to participation and claimancy that had characterized the clans of the warrior theater (the *agôn*) came to determine the wider sphere of political and civic discourse (the *agora*) where a collective sovereignty took shape.[61] In Athens, "all citizens participated equally in civil rights which distinguished them *en bloc* from resident foreigners, integrated socially but not politically."[62] The democracy of Athens rested on a belief, repeatedly expressed and represented, that its autochthonous origins ordained a privileged and enduring socio-political organization defined by "equal participation of all citizens in the exercise of power."[63] Bestowed on every citizen—and let us be clear, this meant only men who were neither foreign residents nor slaves—*isonomia* is writ large in the organization of the polis, in the geometrical and proportional parameters within which the citizen moved, discoursed, loved, and fought. The city-state "was organized as a homogeneous entity in which the center alone had a privileged position, precisely because, in relation to it, all the various points occupied by the citizens appear symmetrical and reversible"[64]

Just as in an earlier era the booty had been set down *es to menon* (in the middle) of the warrior-aristocrats, so now the laws, knowledge, and writing (for instance, the inscriptions on stone called *parapegmata*) were situated *es to menon*—as shared property of the city, at once disclosed to all and applying to all. "In the framework of the city, the tie that bound one man to another thus became reciprocal, replacing the hierarchical relations of submission and dominance," Vernant writes. "All those who shared in the state were defined as *homoioi*—men who were alike—and later, more abstractly, as *isoi,* or equals."[65] All born of the earth, all endowed with nobility, the Athenians participated as equals and in a spirit of *philia,* provided we recall the sense we have previously given to the term. Relations of *philia* formulate bonds of love that are inseparable from rivalry. For Deleuze as for Nietzsche, the most profound sign of the "health" enjoyed by the polis, and the sign with which we pass to the final condition of geophilosophy, is that *philia* induces a sphere of contestation, even strife (*eris*). Only when a relationship among equals (*isoi*) engenders competition between them can we speak of *philia*. "If we really want to say that philosophy originates with the Greeks," Deleuze and Guattari write, "it is because the city, unlike the empire or the state, invents the *agôn* as the rule of a society of 'friends,' of the community of free men as rivals (citizens)" (WIP, 9). *Philia* prolongs the diagram of the *agôn* into the sphere of the city, where the pursuits of athletic prowess, love, and politics are organized along the lines of a warrior theater in which friends vie as equals for supremacy.

The spirit of the *agôn* infuses the fields and forums of Greek life, but insofar as we are following this agonism to the political sphere and ultimately to the philosophical plane of immanence, we should mark the critical transformation of civic contestation, namely, the way it came to characterize *speech*. "The system of the polis implied, first of all, the extraordinary preeminence of speech over all other instruments of power," Vernant writes.[66] In effect, the development of democratic Athens entails the transformation of discourse, the great power of which had formerly belonged to those whom Detienne calls the "masters of truth"—to the diviner, the bard, the king. Whereas these masters sought to illuminate "what has been, what is, and what will be," to formulate an overarching truth that left no room for response, debate, or disagreement, the polis increasingly renders speech the province of the *demos*, of citizen–friends, each of whom claimed equal right and power to speak.[67] The nature of speech is transformed, the oracular and mystical pronouncement of truth (*aletheia*) giving way to persuasion. In a democracy like Athens, Deleuze writes, "opinion obviously assumes a decisive importance" because the principle of equality and relations of *philia* ultimately demand the form of free exchange and the forum of rhetorical combat (CC, 136).

Hence, just as we have passed from *autochthony* to *philia*, so now we pass from *philia* to *doxa*, the last of the three indices of philosophy. "The Greek city puts forward the friend or rival as social relation, and it lays out the plane of immanence," Deleuze and Guattari write, "but it also makes *free opinion* (*doxa*) prevail" (WIP, 79). The city countenances an exchange of opinion, which is no less an exchange among equals and a contestation among rivals. Speech in the polis "presupposed a public to which it was addressed, as to a judge whose ruling could not be appealed, who decided with hands upraised between two parties who came before him," Vernant writes.[68] "It was this purely human choice that measured the persuasive victory of the two addresses, ensuring the victory of one speaker over his adversary." Opinions are solutions to which philosophy seeks the respective problems: indeed philosophy begins when *autochthony* and *philia* are ramified by and exercised as *doxa*. There is no overarching principle that grounds philosophy unless we understand it to be a "synthetic and contingent principle—an encounter, a conjunction," Deleuze and Guattari maintain (WIP, 93); philosophy "is not insufficient by itself but contingent in itself." The contingencies that we have traced to this point (*autochthony, philia, doxa*) are no less contingently combined, synthesized, to create the condition for philosophy; but even here, on the eve of this strange philosophical Sabbath, a kind of contingency remains to be realized.

In this regard, perhaps we can finally understand Nietzsche as the precursor to geophilosophy and the latter, in the hands of Deleuze and Guattari, as a matter of reconciling Nietzsche to autochthony. Often criticized for misappropriating the Greeks and misconstruing the origins of philosophy, Nietzsche nevertheless provides the broad and paradoxical constituents of the philosophy of the earth that we have analyzed to this point. In *Philosophy in the Tragic Age of the Greeks,* he offers two descriptions of the nature of Greek philosophy that, while seeming to be mutually exclusive, condition philosophy as the conjunction of absolute and relative deterritorialization.[69] On the one hand, as we have seen, Nietzsche rejects the nativist claim whereby Greek philosophy emerges autochthonously as the possession of a particular chosen people who belong to the land. "On the contrary," he writes of the Greeks, "they invariably absorbed other living cultures" (PTG, 30). Hence, Nietzsche derides autochthony as a potential "explanation" of the Greek world, regarding its significance among his contemporaries as a historical fantasy—the belief in a people who, suffering from no alienation, belong to the land as a homeland (*Heimat*). "Nothing would be sillier than to claim an autochthonous development for the Greeks," he concludes (ibid.). Indeed, Nietzsche's description of the Greek world recalls the contingencies we have elaborated at the heart of geophilosophy—how conditions of land and sea made Greece into a kind of "cyclonic zone" attracting immigrants and travelers, how the poor quality of the soil compelled Greeks to leave their own shores, and finally how the relative distance of *polei* from imperial influence conditioned their competition and, thence, their collective development, their *coevolution*.

But on the other hand, Nietzsche argues that Greece provides the only genuinely hospitable milieu that the philosopher has ever known. "In other times and places, the philosopher is a chance wanderer, lonely in a totally hostile environment which he either creeps past or attacks with a clenched fist," Nietzsche writes. "Among the Greeks alone, he is not an accident" (ibid., 33). In other words, the philosopher belongs to Greece as to no other place: while schools of philosophy may begin elsewhere (the Ionians, the Pythagorans, the Eleatics) they all came to Athens. What are we to make of this paradox? These principles—broadly construed, the denial of a Greek philosophical homeland and the affirmation of a Greek philosophical homeland—might strike us as contradictory were we not to understand geophilosophy on the basis of the relation between absolute deterritorialization and relative deterritorialization, between the philosopher qua the stranger and philosophy qua milieu, between *typos* and *topos*. As Deleuze and Guattari write, "It took a century for the name *philosopher,* no doubt invented by Heraclitus of Ephesus, to find its correlate in the word *philosophy,* no doubt invented by Plato the Athenian" (WIP, 87). In the words of Jean-Pierre Faye, which they quote, "Asia, Italy, and Africa are the odyssean phases of the journey connecting *philosophos* to philosophy" (ibid.). The relative deterritorialization of Athens—the way that it also *reterritorializes* the earth on the agora—nonetheless opens the city to vagaries and currents of the sea, which brings philosophers to its shores. Thus, Deleuze and Guattari hold that, in Athens, "deterritorialization takes place through immanence: it frees an autochthon, that is to say, a power of the earth that follows a maritime component that goes under the sea to reestablish the territory" (ibid., 86).

While Athens reserved the rights of democratic participation for citizens, it attracted strangers from all over the Mediterranean to participate in its rhetorical and philosophical *agôn*. Even as it reinforced the requirements of citizenship and even as it maintained slavery, ancient Athens welcomed strangers to the city and counted this hospitality as a virtue. In his renowned eulogy for those who had fallen in the Peloponnesian War, Pericles hails the openness of Athens, which effectively created the category of *metics* (*metoikountas, metokoi*)—of resident foreigners—by making quasi-legal provisions for their habitation in the city. Without political rights or direct legal recourse, unable to possess land and required to pay a personal tax, *metics* were strictly distinguished from the citizens of Athens; and yet, *metics* were welcomed and integrated into the city as Hoplites, tenant farmers, craftsmen, traders, and ultimately artists and intellectuals (the orator Lysis was said to be the "richest of *metics*"[70]). The irony of Athenian autochthony is that, while it conditions the emergence of the ancient plane of immanence, this milieu is realized only inasmuch as it establishes conjunctions with strangers, aliens, and immigrants who come from afar. "These types come from the borderland of the Greek world, strangers in flight, breaking with the empire and colonized by the peoples of Apollo—not only artisans and merchants but philosophers," write Deleuze and Guattari (WIP, 87).

We began this section by invoking geophilosophy in terms of the relation between the absolute deterritorialization of the earth and the relative deterritorialization of the polis, and we can now affirm that this relation materializes in the encounter between strangers and the city, philosophers and philosophy. "Philosophers are strangers, but philosophy is Greek" (ibid.). Ultimately, what makes philosophy possible is the connection established between Athens (the immanent milieu to which autochthons belong) and the stranger (whom the plane of immanence carries, like a great wave, to the city). Hence, while we say that the philosopher must encounter philosophy, what we really mean is that the conjunction of immigrant and city, sea and land, earth and territory, deterritorialization and reterritorialization, *produces* the philosopher and philosophy. The Athenian milieu welcomes strangers, those who are not autochthonous, but these strangers will inhabit the plane of immanence that autochthony conditions: they will make the *topos* of the city a *topos noêtos—a thinking place*. Whence Detienne's extraordinary statement that "between autochthony and foundation, there is something like an antipathy,"[71] for the myth of belonging to the earth inaugurates the socio-logic at whose end we find the contestation of forces and the geometry (*isonomia*) of strife (*eris*). At bottom, autochthony has no bottom, no base, no ground, since it gives way to a kind of Heraclitan rivalry of forces. On this plane of immanence strangers and citizens come together as friends and combatants.

As we conclude this chapter, and in view of the one to follow, we might acknowledge the agonistic "diagram" that runs through a seemingly endless series of Athenian venues, for this is both the bare possibility of philosophy as well as, in Plato's terms, its enduring problem. Indeed, Plato casts his own philosophy in opposition to the free exchange of opinion which the city conditions: "what Plato criticizes in the Athenian democracy is the fact that anyone can lay claim to anything" (CC, 137). In other words, what Plato criticizes is that no transcendent criteria exist in order to render a judgment among claimants, to distinguish the real suitor from the fake pretenders. "Far from belonging to the order of Episteme," Detienne writes, "*doxa* was associated with *kairos*, 'the time of possible human action,' that is, the time of contingency and ambiguity."[72] Pragmatic and occasional, dialogical and unstable, *doxai* "are of the same nature as the statues of Daedelus: 'they run away and escape.'"[73] To this crisis, Plato responds by creating Ideas as the very criteria with which to make distinctions, to provide an instance of transcendence within the field of immanence. The Idea provides the means to adjudicate between rivals, to discern the true from the false. In Platonism, "universals of contemplation are supposed to gauge the respective value of rival opinions so as to raise them to the level of knowledge" (WIP, 79). Unlike the myth of autochthony, which catalyzed the formation of *philia* and *doxa*, unleashing the chain reaction of "contingent contingencies" that condition the philosophical plane of immanence, Plato invents a transcendent myth. The first or founding myth of autochthony is replaced by a myth that, having been introduced onto the plane of immanence, constructs the myth of a higher reality and the ground for judgment itself. One myth gives way to another, immanence gives way to transcendence.

3 DELEUZE AMONG THE SOPHISTS

The Gift of Transcendence and the Measure of Immanence

The Problem with Plato

> But, if it is true that the *Theaetetus* is a foundation of error, does not Plato hold in reserve the rights of other rival determinations, like the delirium of the *Phaedrus*, so that it seems to us that the image of thought in Plato plots many other tracks?
>
> **GILLES DELEUZE** AND **FÉLIX GUATTARI**, *WHAT IS PHILOSOPHY?*

FOR DELEUZE, LIKE NIETZSCHE BEFORE HIM, Platonism names the most reactive and regrettable moment in the history of philosophy—the moment when philosophy submits itself to transcendence. "The poisoned gift of Platonism is to have introduced transcendence into philosophy," Deleuze writes, "to have given transcendence a plausible philosophical meaning (the triumph of the judgment of God)" (CC, 136). But inasmuch as this is the case—inasmuch as Platonism, the presumptive origin of philosophy, also designates its enduring problem—why is it that Deleuze's engagement with the subject comprises a bare fraction of his work?

The author of countless commentaries, on friends and enemies alike, Deleuze never devoted a book to Plato, endeavoring instead to condense his critique into the space of a couple of dozen pages. This critique began in earnest with the composition of an essay, "Reversing Platonism," which he published in 1966 and which thereafter formed the basis for his most concerted meditations on the subject.[1] In *Difference and Repetition* and the first appendix to the *Logic of Sense* (published in 1968 and 1969, respectively), Deleuze recasts the language and sentiments of the earlier essay into the pivotal movements of a philosophy of difference. And yet, as we have suggested, these spare pages seem strangely incommensurate to the task of reversing Platonism: limited to dense textual episodes and then relegated to a smattering of references in his later writings, the reversal of Platonism is liable to leave us feeling let down. Deleuze's commentary on Plato approximates the perverse disappointment of an old Jewish joke (most famously told by Woody Allen) in which two diners complain about a meal: "The food's not very good," says one, to which the other responds, "and such small portions." Admittedly, in the case of Deleuze's critique, the logic of this joke is reversed—"such small portions," we say to ourselves, "and the food's not very good"—but the double sense of dissatisfaction is no less present. *Is that all there is?*

This reaction is as good a point of departure as any, since it demands that, in returning to Deleuze's reading of Plato, we understand its "finer articulations," the delicate divagation of his thinking. At this point in his career—poised between his previous "apprenticeships" to philosophers (Hume, Nietzsche, Spinoza, Bergson, Kant, etc.) and his subsequent excursions "outside" philosophy (into geography, political economy, cinema, the baroque)—the overturning of Plato constitutes a critical moment in Deleuze's *vie philosophique.* Speaking of *Difference and Repetition* and *The Logic of Sense,* Deleuze says that he had finally paid off his debts to his philosophical precursors (most notably, for our purposes, Nietzsche) and had begun to write "for himself." No doubt he continues to write through others, such as Plato, but in so doing Deleuze seems to have become himself. While commentary persists, it takes on the strange suppleness of a critique that, far from opposing Platonism, adopts its logic and carries it to its absolute limits, plunging us into the unsuspected and bottomless depths, the reasonless reason, of its mad dialectic.[2]

"This is how Nietzsche defined the task of philosophy," Deleuze declares, but as I have suggested, the same should be said of Deleuze, who (in his own words) pursues Plato "the way that Plato tracks down the sophist" (LS, 253). The sense of this double or redoubled pursuit, to which this chapter adds yet another iteration, begins by taking Platonism to its own limits. In other words, we will pursue Platonism by prolonging it to the point where its grounding distinction between original and copy relents to a pluralism of differences. The overturning of Platonism cannot settle for anything less than the destruction of this great dualism, and this cannot occur on the basis of a new dualism (Kant), nor can it be dialecticized in a movement that perpetually returns us to the figure of an opposition (Hegel), nor can it be inverted in the spirit of a materialist history (Marx). Rather, Deleuze insists that the task of reversing Platonism must be sought in Plato himself insofar as he alights on the concept of the simulacrum—a *copy without a model*—with which both transcendent Ideas and subsequent idealisms are dispatched. In the dialectical pursuit of the sophist, we are finally compelled to encounter the appearance qua apparition (*apparaître*) of something that cannot be distinguished "from originals or from models." As Deleuze writes, "We are reminded of the grand finale of the *Sophist:* difference is displaced, division turns back on itself and begins to function in reverse" (DR, 68).

When we say that Deleuze prolongs Plato's own method to delirious ends, we mean that Deleuze enacts his critique by virtue of a kind of writing and thinking that becomes Platonic so that Platonism itself becomes something else. Hence, beyond adumbrating Deleuze's critique of Platonism, or even in order to do so, we find ourselves faced with the task of producing an exegesis equal to Deleuze's own particular mode of expression. After all, how does Deleuze formulate a critique of representation that does not consist in representation? And how do we repeat Deleuze's critique without availing ourselves of a notion of the "original"? The overturning of Platonism, Deleuze writes, "can only occur by virtue of denying the primacy of original over copy, of model over image, glorifying the reign of simulacra and reflections" (DR, 66). To be "true" to Deleuze, then, one must affirm the powers of the false, but only insofar as we refuse to confuse these powers with the baseness of petty lies. We have previously quoted Nietzsche to the effect that even the most truthful man never ceases to lie, but if we insist on the difference that distinguishes the powers of the false from mere deceit, it is because these powers create an excess of truths, a plurality of possible worlds, that bear the world beyond the precincts of truth and lying. In this spirit, the discussion to follow aims to produce the "full text" of Deleuze's critique—provided we understand that such an unamended and unedited version does not exist and never did. In other words, what follows should be understood as a simulacrum of Deleuze's Platonism, a counterfeit of the critique "in its entirety"— but in reproducing the nonexistent original, we will aspire to affirm the rigor of Deleuze's method. The simulacrum constitutes the furthest reach of critique, the ends of which finally compel us to give up on the pretense of ends or beginnings, truth or transcendence.

Recalling the elaboration of "geophilosophy" that concluded the previous chapter, we can already anticipate that Deleuze is concerned with two modes of transcendence—one "external" and one "internal." While we will ultimately turn to the latter, or Platonic, introduction of transcendence within philosophy ("to have given transcendence a plausible philosophical meaning"), we might begin here by revisiting the more preliminary or "nonphilosophical" sense of transcendence with which we are already familiar. In the empires to the east, the imperial and oracular formations of transcendence effectively preclude the emergence of philosophy. The development of "wisdom or religion" projects a celestial order of symbols over and above the earth, but this transcendence remains profoundly at odds with the philosophical creation of concepts. Indeed, Deleuze defines philosophy as precisely the creation of concepts, as a constructivism, which demands a horizonal milieu unmediated by the vertical interventions of an "imperial unity or spiritual empire." In short, the emergence of philosophy does not lie with transcendence but with *immanence* (WIP, 89).

As we've seen, Deleuze's elaboration of "the origins of Greek thought" never ceases to affirm the great French tradition of classical anthropology—a tradition for which the birth of philosophy is inseparable from, and incomprehensible without, the terrestrial relations of the Greek city-state (polis). As Pierre Vidal-Naquet neatly summarizes, philosophy "arose within a specific political, economic, and social framework, namely, that of the city-state, which itself appeared only through a decisive crisis of sovereignty and within a social space unencumbered by the dominating presence of a Minoan or Mycenaean monarch modeled after Eastern 'despots.' "[3] Likewise, to his own question— "In what sense, we ask, is Greece the philosopher's territory or philosophy's earth?" (WIP, 88)[4]—Deleuze responds by underscoring the contingent features whereby the polis unfolds a plane of immanence for the creation of concepts. "This is particularly clear in the case of Athens and its democracy," he writes: "*autochthonia, philia, doxa* are its three fundamental traits and constitute the conditions under which philosophy was born and developed" (CC, 136). While we have already discussed these features at length, we might recapitulate their combinatorial logic here in view of the (active) appearance of philosophy that they anticipate and the Platonic (reactive) forces they engender.

In Athens, we discover not only the convergence of these contingencies (*authochthony*, the principle of equality; *philia*, the development of both friendship and rivalry; and *doxa*, the efflorescence of opinion and exchange) but, as a process, the development of a sphere of intellectual rivalry. The polis is characterized by "societies of friends, that is, by free rivals whose claims in each case enter into a competitive *agôn*" (CC, 136), Deleuze writes, but how does philosophy become a kind of agonism? Among the Greeks, the *agôn* denoted an assembly of warriors as well as the contests that took place among them. In both cases, the term described a particular assemblage, a spatial arrangement, organized around relations of equality and rivalry: equidistantly spaced along the periphery of a circle, the warriors enjoy an equal opportunity with respect to whatever is placed, or takes place, in the center (*mesôi en agôni*). Deleuze's intervention consists in prolonging the *agôn* into an abstract diagram, an assemblage of forces, which he reads across the entire social field of Athens.[5] The *agôn* becomes a kind of "warrior theater" whose features can be traced through the city's various domains—"love, athletics, politics, the magistratures" (ibid.). In ancient Athens, for instance, the *agôn* characterized virtually every aspect of the city, from the Panathenaic games in which warriors vied, to the dramatic festivals in which tragedians competed, to the political *agora* in which statesmen contended. If philosophy consummates this series, as Deleuze suggests, this is because it deploys the diagram of rivalry as the form and forum for the exercise of thought: the *agôn* is realized in a heretofore impossible context, namely, an intelligible place (*topos noêtos*). The civic space of claimants and rivals is redoubled by a philosophical sphere: Athens induces an unprecedented *agôn* of Ideas, an agonism of the Idea.[6]

Only in the context of this new sphere, where thinking becomes a form of combat and the thinker a combatant, can we begin to understand why Platonism marks both the first instance of philosophical transcendence and, arguably, the worst. Only in this context can we understand why Platonism constitutes a reaction against its own conditions; as Jean-Pierre Vernant once said, Platonism is "both the destroyer and the heir."[7] Whence the double movement of immanence and transcendence, of deterritorialization and reterritorialization, that we must follow if we are to grasp Deleuze's own operation. On the one hand, the city makes possible the emergence of philosophy as the space of opinion (*doxa*) and the philosopher as the one who "sets out to 'rectify' or secure the opinion of men" (CC, 137). Neither a sage nor a mystic, the philosopher "presents himself as a friend to wisdom" (*philo-sophia*) or, rather, as the one who befriends Ideas as both an intimate and a petitioner. How could we fail to count peripatetic Socrates among this new class of philosophers unleashed by democratic Athens? How could we imagine the dialectical advent of Platonism in the absence of the city's field of immanence? But on the other hand, Platonism constitutes an astonishing reaction against the sphere of opinion and, more broadly, against the opportunities for thinking opened up by the polis. Not only does Athens progressively unfold equal relations among citizens whose autochthonous origins qualify them to enjoy the equal rights of political claimancy; but the history of the city bears witness to an ever-increasing hospitality to travelers, visitors, and alien residents (*metoikoi*)—to strangers—who will participate in the vast, and at times unruly, space of philosophical contestation.[8] Thus "what Plato criticizes in the Athenian democracy," Deleuze writes, "is that anyone can lay claim to anything" (ibid.)—that no firm and fixed criteria exist to adjudicate among claimants, much less to guarantee that philosophers can be distinguished, or can distinguish themselves, from their rivals.

Plato denounces his own rivals, or sophists, as a class of rhetoricians whom he describes as claiming to speak about (or lay claim to) every art. If democracy makes possible a universal claimancy, then the sophist appears on the scene as a claimant to the universal—the one who "professes to be able, by a single form of skill, to produce all things."[9] Rising to prominence in the second half of the fifth century B.C.E., when Athens enjoyed unprecedented prosperity, the sophists responded to both the democratic institutions that nurtured the exercise of *doxa* and the financial conditions that rewarded the teaching of doxology, that is, the art of rhetoric (*rhêtorikê technê*) and the art of politics (*politikê technê*). Whereas Athenian education had been essentially aristocratic, determined as it was by nobility and inherited wealth, the sophists "introduced an intellectual education that would enable anyone with the means to pay for it to play a distinguished part in city life."[10] Their skills found an eager marketplace in the city, where young men, having finished their schooling at the age of fourteen, apprenticed under these masters in order to prepare for a career in politics. In this context, Socrates critiques the sophists as purveyors of the art of flattery to "young men of wealth and rank" (Sop., 223a–b), as instructors in the art of argumentation (*eristikê technê*), and as tutors in the discipline of statesmanship—but the denigrations also inspire comparison.[11] No less a rhetorician, an intellectual, and a teacher, Socrates enjoyed affinities with the sophists that are duly noted in Plato's own dialogues and elsewhere[12]: in *Protagoras*, he is mistaken for a sophist, in *Lesser Hippias*, he all but acts the parts of one; and in Aristophanes' *Clouds*, he is explicitly named one.[13]

While the relationship between Socrates and the sophists entails all kinds of complications, the relationship between Platonism and sophistry is more tangled still, extending as it does beyond the dialogic adventures of its great protagonist to implicate the practice and profession of philosophy itself. Inasmuch as philosophy *and* sophistry concern the nature of wisdom (*sophia*), Plato suggests, both draw on a common genealogy to which the former will lay claim as the true representative, "the sophistry that is of a noble lineage" (Sop., 231b).[14] Whereas the sophist contrives so many masks and thereby dwells in obscurity, the philosopher is endowed with a god's keen eye: he sees past the ambiguity (*lêthê*) of images to the shining outlines of Ideas. Whereas the sophist is the ignoble maker of resemblances, the creator of false simulacra, the philosopher is the diviner of truth. But "even here," Deleuze asks, "do we not encounter all kinds of claimants who say, 'I am the true philosopher, the friend of Wisdom or the well-founded'"? (WIP, 9). In other words, if "anyone can lay claim to anything" in democratic Athens, the predicament posed by the sophist is that this particular democrat lays claim to the status of the philosopher. The problem with the distinction between sophist and philosopher is that the talent of the former, however ignoble, lies in his very ability to counterfeit the nobility of the latter. After all, were the sophist merely a bad copy of the philosopher, then there would be no problem—a distinction could be easily drawn. But as Plato acknowledges, even when we encounter the noblest definition of the philosopher, that of the "physician" of the soul, we are forced to admit that this "description has some resemblance" to the sophist (Sop., 230e–231a). The sophist's obfuscation lies in nothing less than his peculiar ability to pull off the philosophical disguise beyond the philosopher's best estimation. The sophist inhabits the gloaming in which the copy becomes indiscernible from the original—or, rather, in which the original gives way to a double, and then another, unto infinity. Deleuze deems this the agonism of "the simulator and the friend," for the warrior theater appeals to no higher authority to decide between its actors, between its claimants. Who is the real friend to the concept? Who is the genuine or "well-founded" philosopher as opposed to the fake?

Tracking Down Platonism

> The Sophist leads us to the point where we can no longer distinguish him from Socrates himself—the ironist working in private by means of brief arguments.
>
> **GILLES DELEUZE,** "PLATO AND THE SIMULACRUM"

In a sense, the fatal moment for philosophy arrives in the wake of these questions, if not in response to them, when the Idea appears on the scene to distinguish among the players. The fatal moment for philosophy arrives when Platonism resolves not only to rectify opinion but to impose the criteria for its verification. As Deleuze writes, this explains "the necessity for Plato to put things in order and to create authorities for judging the validity of these claims: the Ideas of philosophical concepts" (WIP, 9). The transcendent intervenes to rescue philosophy from the pure competition of claims and to revise the discourse of truth itself in order to enable a power of judgment over all claims. Transcendence ("the triumph of the judgment of God") lies in the recourse to a metaphysical-moral narrative that circumscribes the plane of immanence and domesticates its differences: in response to the agonistic sphere of philosophy, which is its very condition, the reactive turn of Platonism proffers transcendent pieties that will stifle its forces. Platonism introduces a new problem with respect to transcendence. Where the vertical formation of imperial wisdom withheld the horizontal formulation of philosophy and the immanent creation of concepts, what we are beginning to grasp here is that the reactive trope of Platonism consists in the contrivance of a "transcendence that can be exercised and situated *within* the field of immanence itself" (CC, 137; emphasis added). As Deleuze summarizes, "This is the meaning of the theory of Ideas."

The lamentable ingenuity of the Platonic Idea (*Eidos*) rests with the creation of a labor that is at once properly philosophical (i.e., not external to the field of philosophy) but that nevertheless brings to bear a power of transcendence that will reign over the philosophical plane. Under the auspices of Platonism, the Idea that had heretofore acted as the basis for claimancy and for the pluralism of sense becomes the point of reference for adjudicating between claims and claimants. Yes, Plato participates in the warrior theater of philosophy, but in so doing he summons transcendent Ideas with which to bring judgment to bear on the combatants and even the combat itself.

Hence the subtlety of Platonic *ressentiment:* while it "differs from imperial or mythical transcendence" (CC, 137), the Platonic Idea nevertheless manages to smuggle a little bit of despotism and a certain kind of myth onto the plane of immanence. Platonism develops its own, altogether particular relationship to Ideas, which will allow the philosopher to intervene in the world of images and to distinguish among them. In Deleuze's words, Plato battles the Sophists "over the remains of an ancient Sage," but we should add that Plato's "victory" consists in laying claim to the Idea as a divine source of wisdom and the quasi-divine right to make judgments (WIP, 9).

This recourse was common enough among the Pre-Socratics, for whom philosophy was still under the spell of a mythic (or, as Nietzsche says, "tragic") tradition. The Pre-Socratics regularly professed to retain a "divine portion" (*theia moira*) of wisdom that, in Louis Gernet's words, "is at once the consequence and the guarantee of eminent dignity. . . . It designates a kind of divine election of the philosopher."[15] The Greeks called this philosophical gift *anamnêsis,* and it did not simply disappear with the emergence of Socratic reason: as Gernet and others have amply noted, "What lasted up to Plato's time, at least on a mythical level, was the ideal of a vision of 'another world.' "[16] Particularly in the *Phaedrus,* but also in other dialogues, the philosopher appears to enjoy a gift of memory that separates the soul from the body—he is the one who drinks "the water of Mnemosyne."[17] Thus, in response to Phaedrus's demands (he wants better examples than his own reported discourse on love), Socrates remarks:

> Good sir, there is something welling up within my breast which makes me feel that I could find something different, and something better, to say. I am of course well aware it can't be anything originating in my own mind, for I know my own ignorance: so, I can only suppose that it has been poured into me, through my ears, as into a vessel, from some external source.[18]

In a single stroke the philosopher is debunked of originality only to be raised by the gods to new heights of authority. In Plato's famous image, the philosopher leaves the cave seeking divine knowledge, but he returns to the obscurity of terrestrial (and subterranean) relations bearing that knowledge, as if he could shed heavenly light on the depths of human problems. But what distinguishes Platonic wisdom from its sagacious predecessors?

Nietzsche suggests that we can distinguish among appeals to the sage in light of the genealogy of the term itself: "The Greek word designating 'sage' is etymologically related to *sapio*, I taste, *sapiens*, he who tastes, *sisyphos*, the man of keenest taste" (PTG, 43). The philosopher is the man of taste, he who samples and savors: philosophy is not an intellectual endeavor, Nietzsche insists, unless we understand even the intellect to be a matter of discrimination—for example, a preference for "the unusual, the astonishing, the difficult and the divine" (ibid.). But if the sagacity of the philosopher expresses itself in a taste for such problems, we would have to admit that in Platonism the appeal to the sages also comes to represent a taste for solutions. It is often said that Socrates brings philosophy from the heavens into the marketplace, but it is no less the case that the marketplace is subjected by Platonism to heavenly (i.e, "last") judgment. Indeed, as we have already begun to understand, Platonic transcendence determines and delimits the exercise of active forces by virtue of a fiction, or myth, on the basis of which reactive forces "place themselves up on high and entice active forces into a trap" (NP, 58). But in what sense, we have asked, can we evaluate the quality of Platonism itself, the forces it brings to bear? When Deleuze analyzes the "measure of forces" in *Nietzsche and Philosophy*, he explicitly evokes an episode from Plato's *Gorgias* to describe and demonstrate their reactive quality. At one point in the dialogue, after the eponymous sophist and Socrates have argued over "the good," Callicles steps in to offer a distinction between nature and law that Deleuze will adopt in turn: if strong forces are those which extend themselves to the limits of their power, to the nth degree, then reactive forces are those which "separate a force from what it can do. Law, in this sense, expresses the triumph of the weak over the strong" (ibid.). The nature of reactive forces—and shouldn't we take Socrates to be both representative and arbiter of these forces?—consists in separating force from its exercise, from its active exertion and immanent differentiation.

For this reason, the rise of reactive forces and their corresponding values does not signify that those forces in turn become active or dominant: *the reactive triumphs as dominated,* without in the least bit relinquishing its bad conscience or asceticism (NP, 59).[19] Weak forces are reactive insofar as their weakness neither prevents their triumph nor alters their qualitative state. "The slave does not cease being a slave by being triumphant," Deleuze writes; "when the weak triumph, it is not by forming a greater force but by separating force from what it can do" (ibid.). Though opposed, then, there is no antithesis between active and reactive forces because their qualitative difference derives from wholly different motives: active forces prolong themselves by virtue of a perpetual differentiation that takes them to the limits of the power, whereas reactive forces are those that seduce their active counterparts into forms of slavishness, transforming the active into stunted versions of their former selves (the typology of the weak). In this context, finally, Socrates' response to Callicles (initially he misunderstands the latter's distinction between the strong and the weak, then he simply changes the subject) marks the reactive spirit of Platonism itself. Socrates, "the wisest of men," does not wish to understand: he refuses to take the measure of transcendence, preferring instead to make the myth of transcendence his measurement.

The history of philosophy bears witness to the nearly uninterrupted appeal to transcendence. The imperial and oracular forms of transcendence that prevent the conditions of philosophy are redoubled by the philosophical lineage of statesmen and saints—but Deleuze's point is that Platonism provides the first instance, the model, for this series. If Socrates is first saint of philosophy, Plato is its first statesman. Platonism is responsible for having introduced, in embryo, the principle of transcendence that would mature into the regime of representation. This is the "poisoned gift" of Platonism, the gift that keeps on giving: "And modern philosophy will follow Plato in this regard, encountering a transcendence at the heart of immanence as such" (CC, 137). For this reason, philosophy must return to the moment when it first acquired its pious character, assuming the mission of a "will to truth" that *betrays* its own contingent, combative, and immanent origins. At a fundamental level, Deleuze's philosophy takes its point of departure as the repudiation of the enduring Platonic legacy of transcendence. His reaction to Platonism constitutes nothing less than a reaction against the reactive—a declaration of war made in the name of the warrior theater of philosophy. This is why, as Deleuze avows, philosophy has never had any other task than the overturning (*renversement*) of Platonism. "Every reaction against Platonism," he writes, "is a restoration of immanence in its full extension and in its purity, which forbids the return of any transcendence" (ibid.).

Nevertheless, Deleuze's critique—no small critique!—provides the basis for a reading that will seek to make of Plato, the first enemy of a philosophy of immanence, an uncanny ally.[20] How can we possibly reconcile the image of enduring enmity with that of positive friendship? However counterintuitive, or because it is counterintuitive, the logic of our answer begins to emerge only when we see Deleuze's relationship to Platonism in light of the legacy of failed critique to which Platonism so often gives rise. As Michel Foucault remarked in "Theatricum Philosophicum," his admiring essay on Deleuze, "Overturn Platonism: what philosophy has not tried?"[21] While the question attests to the repeated attempts to effect an overturning, it also acknowledges that this task is destined to be repeated because we always and unwittingly return to the same modus operandi wherein overturning = transcendence. Surely this is why, in response to the suggestion that Platonism "seems to mean the abolition of the world of essences and of the world of appearances," Deleuze is quick to add that, were this the case, overturning would "date back to Hegel or, better yet, to Kant" (LS, 253). No remark could be more telling, for in the stroke of a single sentence Deleuze forecloses the traditional sense of overturning, which belongs to idealism, in favor of a wholly different operation. "Transcendental idealism" makes overturning an overcoming, an *Aufhebung,* thereby repeating the movement of transcendence it seeks to replace. But as Deleuze duly cautions, "One dialectician cannot accuse another of standing on his head—it is the fundamental character of the dialectic itself" (NP, 158). In other words, the logic of inverting inversion, of transcending transcendence, leads us inexorably into a stale or lifeless repetition: in this dialectic, which we will ultimately distinguish from Platonism, transcendence begets more transcendence. Indeed, transcendence always hails itself as "new and improved," but it is neither able to induce novelty nor to shake loose of the autism of the same.

So what do we mean by "overturning Platonism"? Deleuze lifts both the terms and the task from Nietzsche, whose own battle against Socrates suggests the constituents of an entirely different procedure. Nietzsche's is an immanent critique that foregoes all external perspectives, all presuppositions of transcendence, for an unmediated engagement with Platonism— its forces, its values, and what Deleuze will call its "motivations." Inasmuch as the "denunciation of essences and appearance has the disadvantage of being abstract," failing as it does to illuminate the *reason of its reason,* both Nietzsche and Deleuze suggest that the overturning of Platonism "must mean to bring this motivation into the light of day, to 'track it down'—the way that Plato tracks down the Sophist" (LS, 256). We might take the opportunity here to linger on this formulation, which circumscribes the immediate locus of the counterintuitive logic, or paradox, which will guide the discussion to follow. The exhortation to track down Platonism is qualified by an example drawn from Platonism, and at first glance this would hardly seem to provide the basis for a novel overturning. Are we really to track down Platonism *as Platonists?* But this is precisely what Deleuze has in mind, provided we grasp that the injunction entails not just any sort of Platonism but rather the singular episode that Deleuze will call "the most extraordinary adventure of Platonism"—the attempt to track down the sophist (ibid.).

The story of "Plato among the sophists," which we have briefly described, may well strike us as heroic or even Homeric. When Plato appears among the sophists in order to preserve the truth of the Idea, Foucault writes, it is as if "with the abrupt appearance of Ulysses, the eternal husband, the false suitors disappear. *Exeunt* simulacra."[22] It goes without saying that Plato himself is largely responsible for this narrative: for so much of what we know of these rhetoricians, "we are dependent upon Plato's profoundly hostile treatment of them, presented with all the power of his literary genius and driven home with a philosophical impact that is little short of overwhelming."[23] The surprise of Deleuze's approach, then, is that he should turn to the sophist in the spirit of Plato's hostile genius, not in spite of it. The first sign of this approach is the choice of the *Sophist* itself. Rather than evoke any one of the numerous eponymous dialogues in which a sophist actually appears (e.g., *Protagoras, Gorgias, Euthydemus,* either *Hippias*), Deleuze frames his critique of Platonism around the singular dialogue in which the sophist, though the subject in question, never subjectively materializes. Why? The dialogues named after particular sophists tend to revolve around the specific problems that arise in the course of discussion or debate, but in the *Sophist,* where he is absent, we could say that the eponymous type emerges as the *problem* of philosophy itself. Inasmuch as it revolves around the question "what or who is the sophist?" the dialogue transforms this figure into an Idea, but this gesture will transform the Idea from a solution into an even more profound, and perhaps unfathomable, question.[24]

In the *Sophist,* Plato embarks on a dialectical pursuit that remains unique among his dialogues: instead of seeking the true claimant in accordance with the Idea, "Plato proposes to isolate the false claimant *par excellence*" (DR, 61). But for this reason, we might say that Plato's wager is lost before the game has begun because its motivation ("what is a sophist?" or "who is the real sophist?") is already a perversion of the traditional Platonic question. After all, what Idea could possibly correspond to the sophist if this figure consists in simulation and deception, in arts that defy truth-telling? What would be the truth of the sophist? On the one hand, as an imitator and maker of images, the sophist cannot possibly be identified with a correlative Idea—unless the Idea exists to justify the inauthentic itself (i.e., "the true sophist is the false claimant"). On the other hand, in the absence of such an Idea, the pursuit and condemnation of the sophist cannot possibly succeed, and so the sophist will have to be affirmed qua the inauthentic, thereby casting doubt on the ground of philosophy (i.e., "the false sophist speaks the truth"). How can we possibly define the sophist, the shapeshifter, the chameleon, or the con artist? Worse still, as Plato's dialogue dramatizes, the philosopher who resolves to hunt down the sophist discovers that the more zealous his efforts, the more his own identity as "the real thing" is thrown into doubt. This is the fine point of Deleuze's critique, for only by faithfully following Plato do we realize that the divinely authored distinction between the philosopher and the sophist— the model and the copy—no longer holds sway.

In this light, Deleuze's effort to overturn Platonism arguably goes beyond even that of Nietzsche himself. In his aphorisms and *Nachlass*, Nietzsche often complained of feeling suspiciously and uncomfortably near to Socrates, even though he regarded the "wisest of men" as his greatest enemy. Socrates "is so close to me," Nietzsche admits, "that I am almost constantly doing battle with him" (PTG, 13). The question that concerns us here is how to undertake such a battle, and it is on this score that Deleuze arguably becomes *even more Nietzschean than Nietzsche*. For Deleuze invents a method that effectively transforms Nietzsche's proximity into the very basis of his critical procedure. Deleuze dubs this procedure "counter-utilization" (*contre-effectuation*) in order to underscore the sense in which it runs against the grain of common critique (LS, 264).[25] Donning the mask of the sophist—and what is the sophist beyond a mask, a guise?—Deleuze unleashes a phantom Platonism that will strip the original of its privilege, its originality, its Truth. His is the method of a saboteur who steals inside the state of philosophy, who enacts his violence by producing those peculiar signs, or simulacra, which will appear at the very limit of Platonism, where it "confronts sophism as its enemy, but also as its limit or double" (CC, 136).[26]

It is no secret that the simulacrum has become a commonplace of critical theory and continental philosophy, but if Deleuze's treatment of the concept remains the most profound and the most unforgiving, as we will argue, this is because it remains the most thoroughly Platonic. The key to Deleuze's critique of Platonism lies in affirming that this very critique "conserve[s] many Platonic characteristics" (DR, 59), and we might go so far as to say that there would be no reason for his turn to Platonism had he not discovered the procedures for its overturning within Platonism itself. Deleuze's method of commentary never opposes Platonism from beyond its precincts but rather slips into those precincts undetected in order "to construct, by way of this small lateral leap, a dethroned para-Platonism." Or, as Foucault adds, Deleuze's method lies in "displacing himself within" Platonism.[27] Like the sophist, Deleuze insinuates himself into the Platonic republic in order to induce an altogether perverse difference within Platonism itself. Far from transcending the world of essences and appearances, Deleuze accomplished the "overturning of Platonism" by returning to its dialectic in order to effect its turning inward. Inasmuch as we hope to elaborate this *détournement,* our exposition follows Deleuze's own method, eschewing all external or transcendent perspectives in favor of an immanent critique: we can only hope to overturn Platonism *from the inside,* by wheedling ourselves within its logic in order to press its own methods to delirious and even dangerous conclusions.

The Drama of Ideas

> It is necessary to know that war is common and that right is strife and that all things happen by strife and necessity.
> **HERACLITUS**

Deleuze's is a Platonism without piety, not the precursor of a metaphysical-moral narrative (as in Nietzsche's description of Christianity as "Platonism for the masses"), but the vestigial expression of a profound agonism. Even as Platonism augurs the tradition of philosophy founded on transcendence, no less the domestication of difference as that which is determined by transcendence, Deleuze insists that its procedures have not yet calcified into the rigid structure—"the powers of the One, the Analogous, the Similar and even the Negative" (DR, 59)—that constitutes representation in its mature form. On the one hand, then, Platonism constitutes the expression of reactive forces insofar as it founds the philosophical basis for the subordination of difference, namely, the transcendence of the Idea. But on the other hand, as Deleuze argues, Platonism establishes the Idea in such a way that its subordinate differences cannot be subordinated *in toto*—or, rather, Platonism secretly establishes the possibility for the *insubordination of differences*. Like "an animal in the process of being tamed, whose final resistant movements bear witness better than they would in a state of freedom to a nature soon to be lost" (ibid.), Platonism marks a moment of transition when difference has yet to be domesticated and identities consolidated. As Deleuze sums up, "The Heraclitan world still growls in Platonism" (ibid.).

The invocation—or resurrection—of Heraclitus was among Nietzsche's most enduring labors, and it is surely "his" Heraclitus whom Deleuze summons here. In *Philosophy in the Tragic Age of the Greeks,* where he offers his most extensive consideration of the philosopher from Ephesus, Nietzsche describes how Heraclitus imagines becoming, "the impermanence of everything actual," as the division of forces into "qualitatively different, opposed activities" (PTG, 54). This division distributes forces in opposing directions which are condemned to be resolved by most minds into the indelicate and overarching guise of fixed and rigid qualities: "light and dark, bitter and sweet are attached to each other and interlocked at any given moment like wrestlers of whom sometimes the one, sometimes the other is on top." Thus, as Heraclitus is reported to have said, "The real constitution of things is accustomed to hide itself."[28] But to the keen eye, he adds, the impression of permanence gives way to the intuition that this is only the momentary victory of particular forces, the brief triumph of a particular quality of force in a battle that endures eternally. This combat is one in which Ideas, far from forming the last recourse of judgment or the ground within which all differences are mollified, serve instead as the basis for the battle. As Nietzsche explains of Heraclitus,

> the apparent permanence we see in things is by no means the end of the war; the contest endures in all eternity. Everything that happens, happens in accordance with this strife, and it is just in the strife that eternal justice is revealed. It is a wonderful idea, welling up from the purest strings of Hellenism, the idea that strife embodies the everlasting sovereignty of strict justice, bound to everlasting laws. Only a Greek was capable of finding such an idea to be the fundament of

a cosmology; it is Hesiod's good Eris transformed into the cosmic principle; it is the contest-idea of the Greek individual and the Greek state, taken from the gymnasium and the palaestra, from the artist's *agôn,* from the contest between political parties and between cities—all transformed into universal application so that now the wheels of the cosmos turn on it (PTG, 55–56).

The Heraclitan legacy, which Nietzsche and Deleuze resume, bestows on the philosopher a perverted anamnesis, the capacity to peer beneath the integument of representation, beneath the identities and resemblances into which difference is superficially resolved, and into the various forms of contestation that organize virtually every sphere of the polis. From the perspective that Heraclitus avails, strife (*eris*) is not placated in the Greek world but rather provides the diagrammatic contours for a rivalry that will be carried out into so many civic spaces in Athens—in the marketplace where merchants compete, the warrior theater where athletes do battle, and finally the rhetorical sphere that we define as the basis of philosophy. As Nietzsche writes, for the Greeks, "the goal of agonal education was the welfare of the whole or of the civic state. Every Athenian, for example, had to develop himself in contest, so much so as to be the highest benefit to Athens and bring it the least harm."[29] But what we must understand here is that these contests carry us beyond any possible "victory," for the appearance of an individual who rises above the mass of men, the unparalleled genius or incomparable warrior, would exhaust the very source of Greek life. "That is the core of the Hellenic concept of contest: it abhors sovereign mastery, and fears its dangers; it desires, as *protection* against one genius—a second genius."[30] Indeed, the nature of agonism resides in the perpetuation of agonism itself, for the health of the city relied on the affirmation of the contest rather than a conclusive triumph of final judgment. As Nietzsche explained of his own "Greek" intuition, one can "no longer see the contesting pairs and their referees as separate; the judges themselves seemed to be striving in the contest and the contestants seemed to be judging them" (PTG, 57).

Deleuze follows the intuition that the "pure justice" of this struggle submits everything, even judgment itself, to strife by prolonging this sense of contestation into the realm of sophistry and even Platonism. "Heraclitus and the sophists make an infernal racket. It is as though there were a strange double that dogs Socrates' footsteps and haunts even Plato's style, inserting itself into the repetitions and variations of that style" (DR, 127). In pursuit of the sophist, the philosopher is brought to the point of impeaching his own transcendent authority: the Platonic dialectic undergoes an involution that will swallow both the judge and the process of judgment in the expression of an enduring and indefatigable strife—the clamor of being and the combat of difference. "The struggle of the many is pure justice itself! In fact, the one is the many" (PTG, 59), Heraclitus writes, but how is it possible that the Heraclitan world still lurks beneath the placid surface of Platonism? How do we square the Heraclitan one with the Platonic One? Recently, the answer to this question has been dominated by Alain Badiou's *Deleuze and the Clamor of Being,* which maintains that Deleuze's Pre-Socratic penchant actually conceals a well-nigh Platonic commitment to the totalizing set (One). But as we will argue, what Deleuze retains from Heraclitus and what he rediscovers once more in Plato is the sense of an agonism that envelops even the Idea of justice in the drama of difference: the figure of the sophist retains the Pre-Socratic spirit of rivalry.

In order to understand as much, we might begin here by inquiring whether Deleuze's reading of Platonism is really so far afield from the critical compromise-formation to which Platonism itself famously lays claim. In the *Sophist,* for instance, we are told that between "the giants and the gods"—between the competing traditions of dynamic materialism and enduring idealism—a kind of "interminable battle is being fought." Platonism negotiates between those philosophers who "drag everything down to earth out of heaven and the unseen, literally grasping rocks and trees in their hands," and those who are "very wary in defending their position somewhere in the heights of the unseen, maintaining with all their force that true reality consists in certain intelligible and bodiless forms" (Sop., 246ab). Ostensibly, this epic contest is resolved in the divine myth of the world offered by the *Timaeus,* where Plato acknowledges that "the father and creator" contrived eternal Ideas qua Forms (*Eidê*) and, from these forms, copies of "moving and living" creatures: "Now the nature of the ideal being was everlasting, but to bestow this attribute in its fullness on a creature was impossible. Wherefore he resolved to have a moving image of eternity."[31] By introducing Ideas, then, Plato seems to have struck on the means to square the chaos of images and the certitude of eternal verities: the empirical vicissitudes here seem to testify to an eternal Idea that "rests in unity" (ibid.).[32]

Inversely, we could say that images, which after all compose *this* world, *our* world, are destined to be regarded as little more than empirical afterthoughts, projections cast by the divine *lumen,* the play of shadows on the wall of a cave. The tradition of Platonism unleashes remarkable ladders and lineages, a vast caste system or "chain of Being," but these gradations rest on a primary differentiation—the segregation of the noble Idea from the mongrel differences of the image. By definition all images (*eidôla*) are "images of" something, imitations made with reference to and in deference to Ideas (*Eidê*). Thus, images are always already relegated to the status of resemblance: next to the real thing, the model or Idea, an imitation bears the stain or impurity of that nonbeing that is really unreal (*ouk on ouk ontos estin ontos*). Nevertheless, as Deleuze has suggested of Platonism, "The great manifest duality of Idea and image is present only in this goal: to assure the latent distinction between two sorts of images and to give a concrete criterion" (LS, 257).

The overarching distinction between Ideas and images, between *Eidê* and *eidôla,* begets the mechanism to make this distinction. The Idea that constitutes the model for the image also furnishes the criteria to distinguish between images. At the most fundamental level, the distinction among images concerns the nature of imitation itself, namely, whether it is a matter of fabrications that claim a kind of "use-value" or whether it contrives a kind of nonproductive mimesis. In the *Republic,* to take the most notable example, Socrates distinguishes between the demiurgic labor of a carpenter who makes a bed and the imitative play of the artist who paints a bed. The bed itself is the work of an artisan for whom the material conditions of use will draw its production into a relation of internal resemblance to its model or essence: though he lacks true knowledge of the Idea, the craftsman's labor is directed by a sense of good judgment and right opinion. But the painting of the bed consists in a copy of the carpenter's production, a copy one more time removed from a model, a reality *secundum quid.* What is an image, Plato asks, if not "a second such object [*heteron toiouton*] made in the likeness of a true one?" (Sop., 240a).

If reference to the Idea seems the last word on Platonic difference, however, it is also the first word on Deleuze's procedures for producing a difference within Platonism. In effect, what he will find at the base of Platonism is that the Idea, which reigns over images, also participates in the immanent differentiation of images. In "The Method of Dramatization," which constitutes the text of his dissertation defense, Deleuze lays out the constituents of this intuition by evoking the common expectation we bring to the Idea in order to lay bare his own sense of Platonic possibilities:

The Idea, the discovery of the Idea, is inseparable from a certain type of question. The Idea is first and foremost an "objectality" [*objectité*] that corresponds, as such, to a certain way of asking questions. Platonism has determined the Idea's form as *what is X?* This noble question is supposed to concern the essence and is opposed to vulgar questions which point merely to the example of the accident. (DI, 95)

We might say that before the grand question of "what is . . . ?" Platonism displaces all other questions as incidental—as matters of opinion (*doxa*). Typically, we do not ask where or when justice emerges, but rather "what is the just?" since this question alone seems to take us to the heart of the matter, to get to the "thing itself." But in asking this question, Platonism often propels us into logical detours that draw us further away from anything like the determination of essences and, instead, into all manner of other considerations. Not surprisingly, then, Deleuze gravitates toward a number of later Platonic dialogues, sometimes called "aporetic," in which the essential issue, once raised, remains unresolved. In these works, the very question of "what is . . . ?" constitutes something closer to a pretense or ruse under which wholly different concerns are smuggled into thought. "Is it possible that the question of essence is the question of contradiction, that it leads us into inextricable contradictions?" Deleuze asks. "But when the Platonic dialectic becomes something serious and positive, it takes on other forms: who? in the *Republic;* how much? in the *Philebus;* where and when? in the *Sophist;* and in which case? in the *Parmenides*" (ibid., 95).

Despite its eternal and universal pretensions, then, the Idea is liable to give way to the question of the case, the circumstance, the instance. In the legal terms on which Deleuze occasionally draws, we could say that the principle or right accorded the Idea (*quid juris?*) no longer designates an absolute opposition to contingent features, to the facts of the case (*quid facti?*), but now designates the imperative to formulate those contingencies as obligatory.[33] By no means mere subsidiaries to or derivatives of the Idea, these new questions—"*who? how? how much? where and when? in which case?*"—constitute an entirely different framework for the Idea, the "sketch for the genuine spatio-temporal coordinates of the Idea" (DI, 96). The world is no longer the moving picture of eternity: rather, eternity has come to disclose a vast "subrepresentational" drama. The transcendence of the Platonic Idea gives way at a deeper level to a remarkable mise-en-scène, to the dynamisms that lie beneath the Idea and constitute the intensive field of differences from which it emerges. Far from securing itself beyond the bounds of chance, the Idea unfolds according to contingent coordinates: it mobilizes the very singularities that might otherwise have been denigrated as accidental or incidental but that acquire their rights in this new noetic landscape. The Idea folds the here and now, space and time, into a problem that, by no means "representing" them, expresses those singularities along a line of action: this is its drama.

Deleuze's theory of immanent Ideas develops most clearly in the context of his engagement with Kant's philosophy. In part, this is because Kant explicitly renders a distinction between a priori concepts, or categories, which define the conditions of possible experience, and those Ideas that exceed the conditions of possible experience. But if the latter (e.g., God) is afforded a transcendent status (CPR, Bxxix-Bxxx), it is the "transcendental" exercise of Ideas that interests Deleuze: while we cannot possibly know God in any transcendent sense, the Idea of God nonetheless designates the event horizon where knowledge becomes indeterminate with respect to the concepts of representation. For Deleuze, transcendental means *problematic,* since Ideas mark out the field of problems that, rather than being understood according to the rules of representation, demand to be thought because they constitute aporias in thought itself. Hence, even as God remains eternally unknowable and strictly speaking outside knowledge itself, the status of God as a problem defines an immanent relationship to thought that we can transpose from Kant's terms (that which "we can think about but never know") to Deleuze's (that which we can never know but which, for that reason, lies at the very heart of thought—as the unthought, as the problem that *must* be thought).

These remarks should already indicate the anticipatory role that Platonism assumes in the development of Deleuze's theory of the Idea, for the nature of the Platonic Idea, even as it develops the criteria for adjudicating between and among different images, also acquires this power by virtue of profound differences—or what we have called the drama of spatio-temporal dynamisms. The peculiar inversion to which Deleuze submits the Kantian Idea has been prepared by an earlier, and perhaps even more astonishing, inversion of the Platonic Idea. It is as if we had suddenly found ourselves approaching the Idea from beneath or behind—as if the ascendant aspirations of the Idea had suddenly given way to a perilous descent. Consider for a moment the remarkable semantic shift that characterizes *eidos* in the centuries prior to its more strictly philosophical deployment. Long before Plato and then Aristotle latched onto the term, *eidos* underwent an uncanny reversal—a reversal befitting "the uncanny" (*das Unheimliche*). In the Pre-Socratics, *eidos* typically designated the visible shapes and the substance of what we see, and this significance dominates well beyond the precincts of philosophy (in the *Poetics*, Aristotle discusses a passage from Homer describing Dolon, *hos rh'ê toi eidos men eên kakos,* in which *eidos* refers to the appearance of deformity or ugliness).[34] The history of subsequent usage progressively linked the term to a more general notion of "characteristic" or "type," and this sense still clings to Socrates' occasional invocation of *eidos* to distinguish ethical qualities.

In this light, the paradox of our proposal consists in inverting the orientation of divine gift with which the philosopher is associated. In other words, while Platonism claims the unique capacity to look behind the world, the capacity to see through ambiguity, ignorance, and forgetfulness, Deleuze's commentary on Plato suggests that this *anamnêsis* assumes an ironic aspect. Even when Plato seems to consummate the transformation of *eidos* from outward manifestation to intelligible place (*topos noêtos*), the presence of the former remains, if only mythically, in the soul's dim recollection of its communion with such forms. Instead of recalling the noetic Idea from which appearances are derived and according to which they will be measured, the philosopher encounters the Idea only to glimpse, beneath its divine and Apollonian surface, the intoxicated vertigo of differences below. It is as if our perspective had been turned around; we look at the problem "through a glass, darkly," through the privilege of the Idea and into the confusion of rival claims, the combat of competing forces, the chaos of differences. Deleuze's is an inverted *anamnêsis:* he peers beneath the overarching design of Ideas and into the heterogenesis of differences percolating below—"the mad element that subsists and occurs on the other side of the order that Ideas impose and that things receive" (LS, 2).

The Dialectic of Rivals

The Platonic Procedure

And the modern man dislikes in an artist nothing so much as the personal battle-feeling, whereas the Greek recognizes the artist only in such a personal struggle. There where the modern suspects weakness of the work of art, the Hellene seeks the source of his highest strength! That, which by way of example in Plato is of special artistic importance in his dialogues, is usually the result of an emulation with the art of the orators, of the sophists, of the dramatists of his time, invented deliberately in order that at the end he could say: "Behold, I can also do what my great rivals can; yea I can do it even better than they. No Protagoras has composed such beautiful myths as I, no dramatist such a spirited and fascinating whole as the *Symposium,* no orator penned such an oration as I put up in the *Gorgias*—and now I reject all that together and condemn all imitative art! Only the contest made me a poet, a sophist, an orator!" What a problem unfolds itself there before us, if we ask about the relationship between the contest and the conception of the work of art!

FRIEDRICH NIETZSCHE, "HOMER'S CONTEST"

The proliferation of differences at which we've arrived may well constitute the most singularly surprising aspect of Deleuze's Platonism. Deleuze turns to Plato's Ideas—the very same Ideas that seem to cost philosophy its cruelty, its ecstasy, its vitality—in order to rekindle the very spirit of Dionysus! The Idea constitutes "that zone of obscure distinction which it preserves within itself, that undifferentiation which is no less perfectly determined," Deleuze insists: "*this is its drunkenness*" (DI, 101; emphasis added). Surely this is why Deleuze's return to Platonism begins by recovering the latter from Aristotle's subsequent critiques and correctives, which invariably dampen Plato's own flights of intoxication. Our "mistake lies in trying to understand Platonic division on the basis of Aristotelian requirements," Deleuze writes, for in so doing we subject Plato's experiments to Aristotle's regular regime of representation—to epistemological categories and to logical demonstrations (DR, 59). The legacy of this approach is no less with us today: above all, Heidegger codified the contemporary practice of reading Platonism through Aristotle's interpretations. "We wish to strike out in the opposite direction, from Aristotle back to Plato," Heidegger announces in *Platon: Sophistes,* the text of his 1924–25 lectures. "This way is not unprecedented. It follows from the old principle of hermeneutics, namely, that interpretation should proceed from the clear to the obscure. Even those who have only a rough acquaintance with Aristotle will see from the level of his work that it is no bold assertion to maintain that Aristotle understood Plato."[35]

By contrast, we are arguing that Deleuze's "bold assertion" amounts to a wholly inverted perspective, namely, that Aristotle misreads Plato by imposing his own ordered "image of thought" on the operation of Ideas. Perhaps the only thing worse than the "poison gift" of Platonism, which in any case we are in the process of "re-gifting," is the interpretation of Platonism that Aristotle bequeaths. The common sense of Aristotle's approach all too easily corrects the idiosyncrasy of Platonism. Naturally, then, as Stanley Rosen insists in the context of the *Sophist,* "The first step in reading Plato is to put aside our Aristotelian spectacles,"[36] but Deleuze actually controverts this logic: perhaps Aristotle's scientific (*epistêmonikon*) explanation unwittingly underscores something unassimilable in Plato. Hence, while we do not want to judge Platonism on the basis of Aristotle's requirements, perhaps the latter reveal the ingenuity and originality of Platonic division. "Aristotle indeed saw what is irreplaceable in Platonism," Deleuze writes, but the problem is that "he made it precisely the basis of a criticism of Plato" (DR, 59). Deleuze does not avoid the Aristotelian reading so much as he makes the object of its criticism—Plato's unreasonable sense of reason, his strange refusal of mediation, and his unique elaboration of the Idea—the source of a joyous reclamation.

In particular, Deleuze dwells on Aristotle's unyielding inclination to graft the regime of specification onto a philosophy that has yet to resign itself to any such regimented sense of difference. "Here we find the principle which lies behind a confusion disastrous for the entire philosophy of difference," Deleuze declares of specification, "assigning a distinctive [*propre*] concept of difference is confused with the inscription of difference within concepts in general—the determination of the concept of difference is confused with the inscription of difference in the identity of an undetermined concept" (DR, 32). The principle is disastrous because, by submitting difference to species and to the method of specification, Aristotle reduces it to a mere predicate of the concept rather than entertaining the possibility that Platonism avails, namely, a concept of difference itself and, therefore, an entirely different sense of the concept. No matter how granular specification renders concepts, right down to the *infima species* itself, this procedure fails to create a *concept of difference.* As Deleuze writes of Aristotle, "Specific difference refers only to an entirely relative maximum, a point of accommodation for the Greek eye— in particular for the Greek eye which sees the mean, and has lost the sense of Dionysian transports and metamorphoses" (ibid.).

The opposition between this measured, modest eye and its delirious, drunken precedent provides the basis for understanding the broad machinations of Aristotle's corrections—and their undoing. Notably, Aristotle uses the same word, *eidos,* to designate "species" that Plato deploys to designate divine Ideas, but this convergence already indicates the remarkable differences that open up between these two philosophical methods. For Aristotle, we reach the definition of a species by providing the genus (*genos*) under which it falls and the differentia (*diaphora*) that characterizes its specificity within that larger category. While Aristotle occasionally praises and even practices something like Platonic division, he finally assimilates division to his own method of demonstration (*apodeixis*)—an account based on an overarching structure of reason that signifies what it is to be something. Not surprisingly, then, Aristotle objects to the nature of reason in Platonic division because it fails to operate systematically. Whereas Aristotelian reason aspires toward a kind of knowledge that consists in deductions from necessary premises, or causes, to specific definitions, Platonism defies the most basic dictate of specification, namely, that the *diaphora* must be necessary. As opposed to syllogism, the reason of Platonic division is, in a word, unreasonable. Arguably the most famous instance of this lapse of reason made in the name of reason consists in Plato's definition of the essence of man, "a biped without feathers." The elements here demonstrate the "failure" of Plato's method, for the accuracy of these predicates—a man does walk, does not have feathers—never raises them to the level of necessity. Rather, the predicates are, according to the overarching dictates of Aristotelian reason, wholly accidental (*kata sumbebêkos*), allowing as they do other creatures to be smuggled into the definition. As Edgar Allan Poe wrote, following Diogenes Laertius, "Very pertinently it was demanded of Plato, why a picked chicken, which was clearly a 'biped without feathers,' was not, according to his own definition, a man?"[37]

The absurdity of the riposte exposes the idiosyncratic ends to which division leads, and it is from this perspective, already so out of sympathy with the peculiarities of Platonism, that Aristotle launches his correctives. For Aristotle, the reason which should operate division is doubly absent; beyond even the failure to decide "whether something falls into one species rather than another," the reason for division itself remains murky, as if we weren't really sure that something should be a genus or a species, or why a genus should have a claim on reason. While Platonism wears the mask of an inchoate form of specification, the Idea is neither organized according to the structure of genera and species, nor does it produce its definition, à la Aristotle, in such a way that the subject and its predicates are absolutely reversible (i.e., "X is this collection of predicates" and "this collection of predicates is X").[38] The result of this strange Platonic process, as Poe clearly understood, is *humor.* In the *Sophist,* for instance, the discussion eventually lands on the distinction between the arts of medicine and the labor of the bath-man: as we are told, both address the purification of the body—the former inwardly and the latter outwardly. The absurdity of this distinction is by no means inimical to the dialectic because the Platonic dialectic does not privilege arts but, instead, "counts one of them not a whit more ridiculous than another" (Sop., 227c).[39] As Socrates admits elsewhere, division "is not without interest for the comedians,"[40] and this is at once the reason for its condemnation (in Aristotle) and the reason for its recovery (in Deleuze).

In Aristotle's estimation, as we have already seen, Plato fails to provide the overarching assurance that division will reach the "appropriate" definition or conclusion, since "when conclusions are drawn without their appropriate middles, the alleged necessity by which the inference follows from the premises is open to a question as to the reason for it."[41] In other words, as Deleuze explains, we would have to say that what is ultimately missing in the Platonic process of division is mediation, or the so-called "middle term" (*meson*), which forms the hinge on which the syllogism swings (DR, 59). For instance, in the famous syllogism that concludes "Socrates is mortal," we find that this proposition is deduced from the premise that "all men are mortal" by virtue of another proposition that provides the reason or explanation, namely, that "Socrates is a man." While the middle term, "man," does not appear in the conclusion, it conditions that conclusion by providing the identity of a concept that brings together Plato with the predicate of mortality. This simple example provides the basis for educing how Aristotle defines man as a "two-footed, rational animal": man belongs to the genus "animal" and is specified according to the predicates "bipedal" and "rational." But in the Platonic definition of man that we previously considered, a "biped without feathers," we are compelled to ask what brings together this subject and these predicates. Without the overarching genus "animal," which functions as the middle term in Aristotle's definition, Plato reaches his conclusion by a haphazard, unregulated sort of division.[42]

Nevertheless, this is precisely the point at which Deleuze promotes the Platonic dialectic, arguing as he does that the absence of the middle term characterizes a kind of remarkable innocence—a mode of philosophy that has not yet given itself over to the representation, a style of thought that preserves the immanent possibility for invention. In Plato, Deleuze says:

> mediation has not yet found its ready-made movement. The Idea is not yet the concept of an object which submits the world to the requirements of representation, but rather a brute presence which can be invoked in the world only in function of that which is not "representable" in things. The idea has therefore not yet chosen to relate difference to the identity of a concept in general: it has not given up hope of finding a pure concept of difference in itself. (DR, 59)

The absence of the middle term actually constitutes the great ingenuity of Platonism, signaling as it does a kind of fugitive resistance to the demands of representation. In effect, Plato has "not yet chosen to relate difference to the identity of a concept in general" (ibid.). In Platonism, rather, the dialectical method consists in a process of division that never takes its bearing according to the genus, that never makes itself the inverse of generalization, and that never amounts to the determination of species.[43] In the absence of mediation, Platonic division amounts to a "bad and illicit syllogism." And yet, Deleuze adds, the Aristotelian "objection clearly fails if Platonic division in no way proposes to determine the species of a genus—or if, rather, it proposes to do so, but superficially and even ironically, the better to hide under this mask its true secret" (DR, 59). What Aristotle criticizes in the Platonic method, what he takes to be the immaturity or the naïveté according to which it lacks sufficient reason, actually consists in its subversive "secret." Precisely because it has yet to assume the overarching sense of "the concept of an object which submits the world to the requirements of representation," the Platonic Idea constitutes a kind of "brute presence" that is not yet resigned to specific difference but that still holds out the hope for difference in itself (ibid.). The Idea may well invoke transcendence, but it does so in order to undertake the task of division that conducts an immanent differentiation, that differentiates immanently, and surveys the differential plane of immanence. How does this happen?

Let us return to the question of "what is X?" Despite its superficial promise of specification, the importance of this question is that it potentially leads to an entirely different process—what we have heretofore called dramatization.

"It is in no way a question of dividing a determinate genus into definite species," Deleuze explains of the Platonic dialectic, "but of dividing a confused
species into pure lines of descent, or of selecting a pure line from material
which is not" (DR, 59–60). The dialectic pursues the "pure line" by assembling the pretenders to the Idea, by demanding that each account for itself
before the Idea, and finally by anointing the "true pretender" according to
criteria provided by the Idea. In other words, the dialectic does not specify
but *selects;* the method of Platonic division "has to do with selecting among
the pretenders, distinguishing good and bad copies or, rather, copies (always
well-founded) and simulacra (always engulfed in dissimilarity [*toujours abî-
més dans la dissemblance*])" (LS, 257).[44] Notably, Deleuze invokes *prétendants* to designate those who lay claim to the idea, and while the English word
"claimants" seems the most appropriate translation, it tends to deprive us of
the connotation of "pretending" or, better yet, "pretension." Claimancy cannot convey the sense of deceptive posturing and posturing self-importance
to which pretension calls our attention.[45] Indeed, Deleuze treats the pretension to Ideas, and the dramatic distinction among images, in the framework
of what the neo-Platonists defined as participation. "To participate means to
have a part in, to have after, to have in the second place," Deleuze writes (DR,
62), but the object of its claim is the "ground itself," the Idea, or essence, that
is identical to itself (*auto kath' hauto*).[46] All claims pretend to the Idea, for only
the Idea posseses the quality firsthand (in Plato's formulation, for instance,
"only justice is just"). Only according to that which is unparticipated, or the
Idea, can we speak of the participated ("the quality of being just") and the
participants ("the just man"). Thus, all participants to the pure quality of justice, to the Idea, will be graded along a chain of degradations: "As for those
whom we call just, they possess the quality of being just in the second, third,
or fourth place" (ibid.).

Under the auspices of pretension, then, the Platonic question "what
is . . . ?" is displaced by "which one?" In the *Statesman,* for instance, the philosopher's task is to determine the genuine shepherd of men, but as Deleuze
explains, "all sorts of rivals spring up, the doctor, the merchant, the laborer,
and say: 'I am the shepherd of men'" (LS, 254). Likewise, in the *Phaedrus,*
the philosopher's task is to determine the bona fide lover or, more precisely,
to discern the true love that grounds such delirium, but in the same way, so
many rivals step forward to say: "I am the inspired one, the lover." Hence, if

the dialectic consists in those procedures whereby rivals are assembled, organized, and finally *selected,* it is the last of these procedures on which Deleuze places the greatest stress. "The Platonic dialectic is neither a dialectic of contradiction nor of contrariety," explains Deleuze, "but a dialectic of rivalry (*amphisbêtêsis*), a dialectic of rivals and suitors [*prétendants*]" that explicitly places the philosopher in the position to choose the right or real one (ibid.). Because pretenders make claims that are contested, the philosopher assumes an honored place: insofar as he has access to the Idea, he can bring to bear the testing, analysis, and measurement in order to carry out a selection. In other words, we could say that transcendence exercises itself proximally in the philosopher, who judges in its name and by virtue of its powers. The power of the Idea, to which the philosopher claims privileged access, consists in bestowing on him the privilege of adjudicating among litigants. Rather than being simply opposed to copies and images, then, the Platonic Idea actually has as its motive the process of distinguishing between them and selecting from among them.

The Grounding Myth

> Height is the properly Platonic Orient. The philosopher's work is always determined as an ascent and conversion, that is, as the movement of turning toward the high principle [*principle d'en haut*] from which the movement proceeds, and also of being determined, fulfilled, and known [*se connaître*] in the guise of such a motion.
> **GILLES DELEUZE,** *LOGIC OF SENSE*

Everywhere in Platonism the Idea serves as a principle of selection that induces but also intervenes in the dialectical process, cordoning off good images from bad images, genuine images from false ones. There is no claimancy without the ground (the unparticipated, the Idea), and in turn no ground without the appeals made by claimants who must be tested. This testing we call division, the procedure whereby claimants appeal to the Idea and, reciprocally, the Idea "measures and makes a difference" (DR, 62). This is why, Deleuze says, Platonism constitutes a "philosophical *Odyssey*," since we are bound at its conclusion to look out among rivals, among suitors, and ask: which is the real one—the "eternal husband"? (LS, 254).

Therefore, to Aristotle's denigration that "it is neither possible to refute a statement by this method of division, nor to draw a conclusion about an accident or property of a thing, nor about its genus," Deleuze offers no objections. Perhaps the dialectic of division is superficially or ironically concerned with such matters, but its profound operation ought to be understood according to "series or lines of descent in depth which mark the operation of a selective foundation or an elective participation" (DR, 62). It is in this light that Alain Badiou's characterization of Deleuze, to which we might briefly return, ought to strike us as so out of character. Of division in general, and specifically the division "used, in the *Sophist,* to define the angler," Badiou contends that it amounts to a "sedentary *nomos*" against which Deleuze's entire work is opposed[47]—and yet, as we have just seen, nothing could be further from Deleuze's sense of this dialectic or of difference. Badiou renders Platonic division a thoroughly predictable method that, drawing on analogy, passes through a series of binaries on its way to a conclusion, but it is precisely because it fails to measure up to the Aristotelian model (the real sedentary *nomos*) that Deleuze values division. Far from fixed, Platonic division looks to the Idea to mobilize a remarkably active (perhaps even hyperactive) process: even as it suggests the constituents of a pure *logos,* of rules of representation, division actually constitutes a *logos tomeus* (word knife), the philosopher's concealed weapon, with which he slashes up "an undifferenciated logical matter" in order to carve a pure line of descent (DR, 60).

The difference between Platonic division and Aristotelian definition appears most clearly in view of the respective "images of thought" to which each gives rise. The Aristotelian definition, especially as we have become accustomed to it, aims to account for everything ranging from the broadest genera to the most particularized species. Indeed, the design of Aristotelianism is, in the language of Deleuze and Guattari, thoroughly "aborescent"— "a sad image of thought that is forever imitating the multiple on the basis of a centered or segmented higher unity" (ATP, 16). Aristotle's system develops the multiple on the basis of a "One that becomes two," of an ordered series of dichotomies, that attest to the model of the Tree and all of its permutations ("the root-foundation, *Grund, racine, fondement*" [ATP, 18]). The third-century logician Porphyry famously depicted the Aristotelian system as a tree leading from the overarching category of substance all the way to "logical species." In the illustration of the Porphyrian tree depicted here, for instance, we

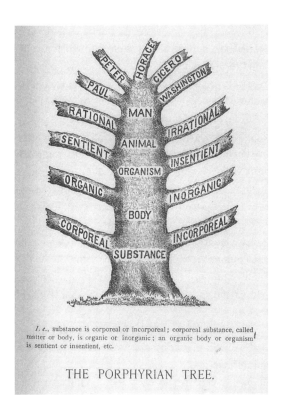

I. e., substance is corporeal or incorporeal; corporeal substance, called matter or body, is organic or inorganic; an organic body or organism is sentient or insentient, etc.

The Porphyrian Tree

THE PORPHYRIAN TREE.

can define "man" (the species *homo*) according to the hierarchical series of predicates (material, living, sentient, rational) derived from a corresponding series of hierarchical genera (substance, body, organism, animal). The definition of man bespeaks the organization of Aristotle's regime of representation, which "runs through and covers the entire domain, extending from the highest genera to the smallest species" (LS, 259).[48]

By contrast, Plato's dialectic leads to the production of lines of separation and division that, were we to imagine the unspooling of all its strands, would appear more like the makeshift filigree of a spider's web than any geometrical design. The dialectical method in Plato engenders potentially endless divisions, unwinding in ever more idiosyncratic and improvisational lines. Precisely because it lacks the overarching rule of reason, the particular pursuit of reason in every dialectical-juridical case elaborates a singularly torturous path. In this respect, we might briefly consider the question that begins the *Sophist,* since it marks the degree to which recent critics, like Badiou, have failed to understand Deleuze's Platonism. Inasmuch as the dialogue opens by posing the question "what or who is the angler?" this example of dialectic is chosen because it is comprehensible, relatively small, and preliminary to the more difficult question that will concern us shortly—"what or who is the sophist?" But if the subject is simple, it immediately elicits what will seem, by Aristotelian standards, the irrational decision to divide the genus of angling into two species, the arts of production and the arts of acquisition. The former includes both farming and mimetic art, whereas the latter includes all kinds of learning, as well as moneymaking, hunting, and angling. But why is fishing among the arts of acquisition? And why should acquisition be divided into exchange and mastery, and the latter, to which the angler belongs, divided into competitive and hunting, and so on? If we were to trace out the dialogue's initial definition of the angler, as Seth Benardete has done, we would find ourselves facing a vast series of divisions that lead us from the art of angling to sophistry.[49]

Though the shape of the Platonic dialectic initially appears regular, guided as it is by division, division itself proceeds without overarching constraints, uninhibited and unguided by the "schematism" afforded by a middle term. Along a swift line of descent, and into the chasm below, the philosopher rappels in search of a definition (say, "what or who is the angler?"). But in the absence of mediation, this dialectic assumes a vertiginous quality: the orderly division that gives way to selection, and so on, is also a perilous slope. Deleuze never ceases to emphasize the hazards of Platonism, likening the dialectic of rivalry to the risk, always assumed by pretenders, of death. "It is a dangerous trial without thread and without net" (*sans fil et sans filet*) (DR, 60).

If we are to understand and even embrace Platonism, as Deleuze does, then we must begin to appreciate the sense in which its most peculiar and idiosyncratic moments in no way undermine division so much as they drive it. Neither orderly nor analogical, dialectical division "is a capricious, incoherent procedure which jumps from one singularity to another" (ibid.). The wonder of the process, we might say, is that it ever lights on any means of closure at all. "The labyrinth of chaos is untangled," Deleuze writes of Platonism, "but without thread or the assistance of thread" (ibid.). The dialectical design recalls the Borgesian formula, frequently cited by Deleuze, that the greatest

```
                          art
                         /  \
                  poetic   acquisitive
                           /  \
                   exchange   mastery
                             /  \
                 competitive   hunting
                             /  \
                     lifeless   living
                               /  \
                   in-liquid   pedestrial
                                /  \
                         wild   tame
                                 /  \
                     violent   persuasive
                                  /  \
                          public   private
                                   /  \
                      erotics   wage-earning
                                    /  \
                          flattery   sophistics
```

**Plato's dialectic:
the initial pursuit
of the sophist**

labyrinth is a straight line: "I know of a Greek labyrinth which is a straight line . . . which is invisible and everlasting."[50] Of course, the peculiar "line" refers to Xeno's spatio-logical paradoxes, but the surprise is that Deleuze manages to make Platonic dialectic assume a labyrinthine quality. Surveying the shape to which division gives rise, we see that its complexity does not consist in multiple lineages but rather in the multiplicity of a single lineage that pitches us into inestimable and perhaps even infinite depths. Indeed, Plato's lines of descent could conceivably extend into endless exercises, and the selection of the real might never come to fruition, were it not for some kind of intervention in the last instance. This point cannot be emphasized enough: the procedures of selection always require some form of deus ex machina, the contrivance of a ground without which we would plunge into chaos.

It is in this respect that we must evaluate the status of the Idea once more. For if the Idea conditions the dialectic of division, providing the mise-en-scène within which all manner of different (or "rival") dramatizations will be staged, we must recognize that in so doing it also provides the conditions for the judgment of those dramatizations. While the Idea initially inspires the dialectical search for the real, the so-called true pretender, the Idea also intervenes in order to delimit this search, to resolve the endless series of divisions. From the perspective of these two poles, of foundation and selection, the function of the Idea in the Platonic dialectic acquires a circular structure, forming as it does the basis for the dialectical problem ("what?" or "who?" or "which?") and, at the same time, the ground according to which the problem can be resolved. The Idea constitutes both the beginning and the end of the dialogue: if it carves out the dialogical and dialectical space within which the drama of rival claims will play out, those claims are no less in need of adjudication if the question of "which one?" is to be resolved. How does this happen? Like so much of his commentary on Platonism, Deleuze's answer to this question returns to the tradition of Greek anthropology on which we have dwelled. Ranging from the early writings of Louis Gernet and Jean-Pierre Vernant to the most recent forays of Marcel Detienne and Nicole Loraux, this tradition has consistently resisted the opposition between reason and fabulation—or, more precisely, between *logos* and *mythos*. In the words of Pierre Vidal-Naquet, which could well be taken as the mantra of this school, we might say that with the emergence of reason in the ancient world, "myth was not left behind, and what we call 'reason' for the Greeks is often myth."[51] Even in Platonism the concept of reason never exists in a relationship of "mere" antithesis or antagonism to myth. Despite the apparent opposition of these forces—in the *Phaedo*, for instance, *logos* not only stands for rational and truthful accounting but also stands against the fanciful and false possibilities afforded by *mythos*—myth is by no means incompatible with or outside of Plato's dialectical process, as if all of a sudden a voice from on high were to announce "enough of this division—let's get down to the real thing." Rather: "It is as though division, once it abandons the mask of determining species and discloses its true goal, nevertheless renounces the realization of this goal and is instead relayed by the simple 'play' of myth" (DR, 60).[52]

Far from marking the passage from myth to reason, the Platonic dialectic retains the function of myth as the very ground of reason. Division looks to myth to provide a foundation that will be integrated into its procedures in order to operate and justify selection itself. In other words, when Plato establishes his method of dialectic and division, he makes the ground function as both the object of the claim and the test of the claimant. The claimant does not lay claim to the ground by putting down stakes in order to say, "This is mine—I own it." The Platonic claim will never be decided according to who arrived first, to whose claim was filed first, for the claim does not appeal to the domain of human law, susceptible as it is to the foibles of opinion, but rather to a quasi-divine authority. The homesteader and miner test the ground for its value, but in Platonism the ground tests its claimants, as if one were to put down stakes only to be deemed a trespasser who has strayed onto lands for which he or she is deemed unworthy. To this end, Plato endows the Idea with a mythic status, effectively providing a story of foundation according to which transcendent criteria are introduced onto the philosophical plane: or, as Deleuze writes, myth "permits the construction of a model according to which the different pretenders can be judged" (LS, 255). In the *Phaedrus*, for instance, the authentification of the real lover takes place according to the myth of the circulation of souls who still bear the pale memory of Ideas. Likewise, in the *Statesman* the selection of this figure takes place according to the myth of an ancient God who ruled the world of men. In both cases, the process of division, which could conceivably extend indefinitely, folds the myth into its very structure in order make possible an immanent measurement. In Deleuze's words, which we must be careful not to misconstrue, division takes place "according to the ontological measure afforded by the myth" (DR, 61).

And yet, if myth seems to offer the dialectic recourse to a ground, this ground should not be mistaken for what philosophers traditionally call *Grund,* since the Platonic foundation "relates difference to the One" (ibid., 62) in such a way that we never reach the point of transcendental abstraction that this process entails in subsequent idealisms. As Deleuze writes, myth provides "*an imaginary equivalent to mediation*" (ibid., 61; emphasis added), since it only *appears* to operate according to, say, the Aristotelian middle term. Myth offers the pretense of ontology and the guise of mediation, but it is neither truly ontological nor effectively mediatory. Rather, it is in the absence of ontology and mediation that Plato resorts to myth as the ultimate adjudicator to ground the dialectic and thereby settle once and for all the line of inquiry. "Division demands such a foundation as the ground capable of making a difference," Deleuze explains. "Conversely, the foundation demands division as the state of difference in that which must be grounded" (ibid., 62). Myth is the "story of a foundation" of the Ideas as well as the model for the Idea "according to which the different pretenders can be judged" (LS, 255). In light of Deleuze's comparison of Platonism to the "philosophical *Odyssey,*" we might understand this circular motion in the context of the conclusion to Homer's epic. After ten years of wandering, Odysseus finally returns to Ithaca to find his wife and home besieged by suitors. In order to survey the situation, he draws on Athena's powers to disguise himself as an old vagrant. But before his wife, Penelope, is able to see through the ruse, his old nurse Eurycleia recognizes her long-absent master:

> the old woman took up the shining basin she used for foot washing, and poured in a great deal of water, the cold first, and then she added the hot to it. Now Odysseus was sitting close by the fire, but suddenly turned to the dark side; for presently he thought in his heart that, as she handled him, she might be aware of his scar, and all his story might come out. She came up close and washed her lord, and at once she recognized that scar, which once the boar with his white tusk had inflicted on him, when he went to Parnassus, to Autolykos and his children.[53]

Insofar as the famous scar serves as the mark that reveals Odysseus's identity, we might expect this sign to have been anticipated in the epic text. But nowhere prior to this scene is the scar mentioned, and the story of its acquisition only arrives *after* its recognition. Eric Auerbach's famous exegesis of this

Homeric logic, in the opening chapter of *Mimesis,* dwells on precisely this peculiar narrative moment by noting that what follows the recognition—the story of the scar, told in almost seventy verses—does not abide by the structure of any kind of recollection. Homer "knows no background," Auerbach writes. "What he narrates is for the time being the only present, and fills both the stage and the reader's mind completely."[54] Far from being already in place in the past, even in the mind of either Odysseus or Eurycleia, the myth seems to issue from the wound, as if the scar had unleashed the very narrative that should by all rights have presupposed it. The wound precedes and produces its own myth even as it appears to inscribe the moment of its production, and while this seems to contradict our sense of myth as that which is, or ought to be, in that past, Deleuze's point is that myths never really come from the past as if out of nowhere. The pretension to a claim conjures the myth itself, fabulating the very ground beneath our feet: *"What needs a foundation is, in fact, always a pretension or a claim. It is the pretender who appeals to a foundation"* (LS, 255; emphasis added).

The Mythic Ground

> The good birth (*Eugeneia*) is in the first place founded on the origin of our ancestors, who, instead of being immigrants and making their descendents Metics in the country to which they themselves came as outsiders, were authochthones, really and truly inhabiting their fatherland, raised not as others by a stepmother, but by the earth, their mother.
>
> **PLATO,** *MENEXENUS*

From his earliest commentaries to his last philosophical breath in "Immanence: A Life," Deleuze eschewed the temptation to ground philosophy, preferring instead to begin from the point of view of a groundless ground or ungrounded ground, which he will call many things including, notably, the Earth. Indeed, Deleuze admits a taste for apocalypse because, among other things, the cataclysmic images it unleashes remind us of the pure retort of the earth—of a groundlessness that mocks the pretension of our metaphysical structures. At these moments, it is as if our anthropocentric narcissism provoked the profound and sublime power of the earth: we philosophical "colonizers" impose ourselves so thoroughly and ruthlessly as to forget the earth, which rises up in turn, launching its subterranean powers toward the surface. When this does happen, at least in our cultural imaginary, the reaction of the earth tends to consist in a regression to some more primitive and ultimately unimpeachable Law: for instance, in Peter Weir's film *The Last Wave,* the claims of civilization are forced to confront the prerogatives of the earth, whose catastrophic prophecy has heretofore remained the secret province of the aboriginal "people of the land." Such examples bear witness to a higher or supernatural power, which rejects its claimants *on the very ground* that they are interlopers, pretenders who do not effectively participate in the spirit of the earth. The ground is territorialized on the earth, but the earth constitutes a field of absolute deterritorialization within which the claims of possession and ownership are apt to be ignored, even mocked: the earth trembles and quakes with laughter at the arrogance of a ground that, in the span of an instant, can suffer obliteration. To befriend the earth in the name of its essence, of one's participation in the ground or on such grounds, is surely the quickest way to have one's claim go unrewarded, since the earth responds to an entirely different logic. Anthropologists note that aboriginal peoples rarely if ever speak of ownership in relation to the earth because it is to this plane of immanence that they *belong:* they are not (ontological) possessors but rather partakers in a profound ecology of immanence.

But what happens when the ground of Platonism, of Ideas, relents to the groundlessness of the earth? If the purpose of myth is to ground the idea, what are we to make of those myths, called autochthonous, which invoke a power that extends beneath any solid ground to embrace the earth itself? In the previous chapter we considered how the Athenians called on autochthony in order to define themselves in relation to the land—as the original Greeks, the authentic inheritors of its natural law—and against other city states. "They alone inhabited the soil in which they were born and which they left to their descendants," Demosthenes says of Athenians. While virtually every Greek polis claimed some version of autochthony, Athens placed this myth at the heart of its existence and its identity, which is to say, as the basis of its aristocracy. As Nicole Loraux writes, "autochthony is *the Athenian myth par excellence:* reference to it is always intended to diminish the other Greeks in an imaginary victory of the one over the others, the true over the false."[55] The advantages of autochthony were numerous, providing as it did a sense of age and endurance, of land and lineage, provenance and privilege, which Athenians lorded over other cities. But in the same stroke that this myth established the narcissistic privilege enjoyed by Athens as opposed to its Greek rivals, autochthony also established the basis for equality and rivalry within the city itself. Because citizens were defined by virtue of a noble lineage that derived from the soil itself, no Athenian was inherently better than another. All were endowed with equal rights and privileges to be exercised within the political sphere of the city. "Thus democracy, the rule of law, is a consequence of the legitimate—and therefore noble—origin of the Athenians," Loraux explains, adding that this occurs by virtue of "an implicit reasoning, brought out by Plato in the *Menexenus,* that deduces political equality from equality of origin."

Indeed, the *Menexenus* suggests the problem that autochthony provokes in Platonism, for in this unique dialogue Socrates is compelled by circumstances to rehearse the constituents of an oratorical genre, the eulogy or *epitaphios,* which effectively demands the invocation of the myth. The titular interlocutor asks Socrates to recite the funeral oration he had heard Aspasia, a "mistress in the art of rhetoric" (Men., 235e), deliver the day before. In so doing, Socrates must follow the generic protocols of this altogether well-governed form, which invokes the dead in the context of the living citizens who, likewise, enjoy the noble imprimatur of the polis. Of the dead, then, he begins by proclaiming: "Their ancestors were not strangers nor are these their descendants sojourners only, whose fathers have come from another country, but they are the children of the soil, dwelling and living in their own land" (ibid., 237b).[56] Autochthony conditions a common bond among the people of Athens, whom the myth makes out to be children of the same mother—"children of the soil." All born of the earth, all related, none above the other, citizens enjoy a mythic relationship to the land that will be codified in the political relations defined by equality. Indeed, the logic of autochthony is so frequently recited and represented in the life of Athens that its reiteration in the *Menexenus,* however ironic, nonetheless serves as a perfectly clear distillation of the myth:

> We and our kind, all brothers born of the same mother, believe ourselves to be neither masters nor slaves of each other; rather equality of origin [*isogonia*] established by nature obliges us to seek political equality [*isonomia*] established by law. (Ibid., 238e–239a)

The *epitaphios* demands an appeal to autochthony, which Socrates is honor-bound to deliver but for which he harbors genuine contempt. Why? Because the funeral oration follows the serial logic (*authochthony, philia, doxa*) we have heretofore described as the basis for the emergence of philosophy, namely, the way that a myth of having been born from the soil gives rise to relations of equality and to a doxological field of claimancy. "Natural equality of birth compels us to seek for legal equality," Socrates explains of Athens, "and to recognize no superiority except in the reputation of virtue and wisdom" (ibid., 239a). Nevertheless, in so describing the consequences that autochthony sets going, Socrates enacts a logic contrary to his own philosophical predilections. For myth in this of all instances—the autochthonous myth of Athens—does not confirm the grounding of the Idea but rather unfolds a plane of immanence whereby relations of equality and reciprocity underwrite the combat of competing claims. How else can we possibly understand the dilemma that autochthony poses for Socrates, for Platonism, except insofar as the earth assumes the prospect of a selection that, as we have already seen in the previous chapter, does not ground philosophy so much as it utterly deterritorializes it? While the doctrine of mythic judgment effectively introduces transcendence onto the plane of immanence, autochthony is unique—aberrant. It anoints the status of noble citizenship to Athenians, relegating all others to the status of foreigners, strangers, or slaves, but autochthony also eliminates a doctrine of privilege among Athenians: the common origin of the earth ungrounds hierarchies, submitting all such determinations to a "subsoil more profound" (BGE, 289). For this reason, we could say that autochthony consists in the very myth which, by virtue of its unique deterritorialization, necessitates all subsequent Platonic myths. For Plato, the mythical groundlessness of the earth will demand the introduction of a mythic ground.

Doubtless it is in this light that we should finally understand Socrates' invocation of his "own" autochthonous myth. In the course of the *Republic*, Socrates confesses that a myth will have to be contrived to justify the apportionment of citizens into different castes and the allocation of their different tasks. The entire polis—rulers, warriors, artisans, all citizens—must be persuaded that their "training and education" is not something undertaken in the pragmatic political sphere of the Republic but rather consists in the natural order of things. The myth promulgates an illusion that the citizens dreamed "at the time they were down within the earth being molded and fostered themselves" (Rep., 414de). Such is the "noble lie" that Socrates invents—the lie enacted with a noble purpose in view and with the noble caste in mind:

> And when they were quite finished the earth being their mother delivered them, and now as if the land were their mother and their nurse they ought to take thought for her and defend her against attack and regard the other citizens as their brothers and children of the selfsame earth. (Ibid.)

If we return to this well-worn episode, it is not simply because here, of all places, Socrates discloses the truth of myth as a lie but because he does so by revising the myth of autochthony itself. Insofar as Platonism undertakes to construct the ground of the *Republic*—let us say, the "republic of philosophy"—it must be laid down over and against the immanence of the earth. For Plato, the myth must form the ground, even at the cost of exposing the myth as a lie.

Only this explains the modified autochthony that Socrates elaborates. On the one hand, the passage above suggests the basis of a myth that would compel citizens, in the tradition of autochthony, to see each other as brothers and children—as members of the same family, all born of the earth. On the other hand, though, Socrates goes on to adumbrate the myth in such a way as to preclude the spirit of equality and claimancy to which autochthony traditionally gives rise. This myth does not condition the democracy of claims but justifies their natural hierarchy. As Socrates explains, the ruler must convey to the people of the Republic that the God who fashioned them from the earth "mingled" different metals (gold, silver, bronze, iron) with their souls, the result of which is that transcendent means—criteria—have been provided for distinguishing castes and apportioning tasks. Unlike the myth of autochthony, which conditions the formulation of the plane of immanence, Plato devises his own myth of autochthony to validate transcendence. The first or founding myth of autochthony is replaced by a myth that, having been introduced onto the plane of immanence, constructs the myth of a higher reality and the grounds with which to judge our reality. One myth gives way to another, immanence gives way to transcendence.

Overturning Platonism

The Sophist at Last

> The point is that in this text, by a paradoxical utilization of the method, a counter-utilization, Plato proposes to isolate the false claimant [prétendant] par excellence, the one who lays claim [prétend] to everything without any right: the sophist.
>
> **GILLES DELEUZE,** *DIFFERENCE AND REPETITION*

It should now be obvious why Deleuze calls the *Sophist* "the most extraordinary adventure of Platonism" (LS, 256), for this dialogue conducts an experiment like no other—an experiment in which the dialectic effectively undertakes the task of division in the absence of any myth to secure the Idea. The sophist is pursued without recourse to transcendence, and as we will see, this is both the problem that Platonism ultimately confronts with respect to the Idea and the beginning of a new mode of considering the Idea *as a problem*. Indeed, only when we have grasped the problem posed by the sophist can we understand the peculiar path taken by the dialogue, which compels the philosopher to make a difference within a field of immanence. What happens when a distinction must be made "on the ground" (as military tacticians might say) but without any ground?

In the *Sophist*, the philosopher's response consists for the most part in making a distinction within images "as if" his operation were still attached to the Idea. Like Wile E. Coyote, whose pursuits of the Road Runner often seem to defy gravity until he recognizes that no ground exists beneath his feet, the Stranger proceeds as if the transcendent guarantee will be obtained in the last instance only to discover that his operation is ungrounded. Nowhere else does Platonism more closely approach this groundless ground—and, thence, the overturning of Platonism—than in this dialogue. While it begins in the common spirit of determining the lineage of a particular entity ("what is a sophist?"), the *Sophist* operates in the absence of any grounding myth, as if the promise of dialectical denouement had been withheld. Notably, in those dialogues with which Deleuze compares the *Sophist*—namely, the *Phaedrus* and the *Statesman*—the pursuit of a question determines a kind of progressive rarefaction whereby the search for truth (the "true lover," the "true statesman") raises us into a mythical realm that will provide the pure model of the

Idea. "The popular and technical images of the philosopher seem to have been set by Platonism," Deleuze writes: "The philosopher is a being of ascents; he is the one who leaves the cave and rises up [*s'élève et se purifie d'autant plus qu'il s'élève*]" (LS, 127).[57] But as we are beginning to see, the *Sophist* reorients the Platonic dialectic; the ascent so characteristic of other dialogues gives way here to a dangerous descent. The reason for this inverted trajectory is not difficult to grasp. "In the *Sophist*," Deleuze writes, "the method of division is employed paradoxically, not in order to evaluate the just pretenders, but, on the contrary, in order to define [*traquer*] the false pretender as such" (ibid., 256).[58]

Far from seeking a world behind the world, which would simply consist in yet another foundation, we glimpse here the "ungrounding" (*effondement*) of foundations whereby the rule of representation is annihilated by the vertigo of simulacrum. In his great aphorism from *Beyond Good and Evil*, to which we have alluded, Nietzsche suggests that the overturning of Platonism would entail a vast reorientation of philosophy. Indeed, the *Sophist* makes us doubt:

> whether a philosopher could have "final and real" opinions at all, whether behind each of his caves there does not and must not lie another, deeper cave— a stranger, more comprehensive world, an abyss [*Abgrund*] behind every ground [*Grund*], beneath every "foundation" [*Begründung*]. (BGE, 289)

Without the assumption of the Idea to ground the dialectic—the Idea which has heretofore assured the determination of images and the hierarchical differentiation between them—the Stranger descends into the cavernous world of images without any link to the world above and, thence, without any assurance of finding footing on the ground below. As a result, the logical trajectory of division is inverted: rather than descending into difference on the basis of transcendence, this dialogue descends into difference in order, ostensibly, to induce transcendence. As we have already argued of Platonism in general, so in the *Sophist* the philosopher assumes the task of discernment, of "making a difference," and yet here the philosopher finds himself on new and unfamiliar ground. In this most uncanny of dialogues, the philosopher's task is no longer to anoint the real pretender, the true lineage, but to seek out the false pretender. The *Sophist* is perverted by virtue of having his or her task inverted, the selection of the truth having given way to the process of ferreting out the untruth, of hunting down the sophist.

And so we return to the point with which we began: in Deleuze's words, "'to reverse Platonism' must mean to bring this motivation out into the light of day, to 'track it down'—the way Plato tracks down the Sophist" (LS, 253). The peripatetic inclinations so evident and available in other Platonic dialogues finally give way here to a new mission: *search and destroy*. Without the overarching function of reason to tame difference and domesticate images to the Idea, the philosopher is like a bounty-hunter: both judge and executioner. His authority, derived from the Ideas to which he lays claim, works in the absence of the universal mediator and so always tends toward an independent dialectical logic following its own singular line. As the dialogue exhorts: "Come then, it is now for us to see that we do not again relax the pursuit of our quarry" (Sop., 235ab). In the *Sophist,* the dramatic diegesis of this pursuit takes shape around an encounter between Socrates and a Stranger from Elea, whom the former lightheartedly solicits to expose the Greek "weakness in philosophical discourse, like a spirit of refutation" (ibid., 216b). The jest leads to Socrates' ironic suggestion that today we struggle to discern philosophers. As he adds, philosophers are

> hardly easier to discern than a God. Such men—the genuine, not the sham philosophers—as they go from city to city surveying from a height the life beneath them, appear, owing to the world's blindness, to wear all sorts of shapes. To some they seem of no account, to others above all worth: now they wear the guise of statesmen, now of Sophists, and sometimes they might give the impression of simply being mad. (Ibid., 216c)

While this confession will form the basis for the dialectic to follow, it does so by virtue of an allusion to the very episode in the *Odyssey* on which we have previously dwelled. As Stanley Rosen has noted, the indiscernibility of the philosopher, like that of a god, recalls the eponymous hero's return to Ithaca.[59] His identity disguised, Odysseus is accosted by suitors, one of whom unwittingly says: "gods looking like strangers from afar become all things and wander about the cities, viewing human hubris and righteousness."[60] Accordingly, the "genuine" philosophers to whom Socrates refers find themselves in the position of Odysseus among the suitors—not only hidden in plain sight but, we might say, in need of a myth to verify their status apart from these counterfeiters. Remember that, initially, we drew on the drama of the hero's return to define Odysseus as the "eternal husband" who vanquishes the suitors, the counterfeit husbands. Subsequently we returned to this episode in order to qualify the nature of the hero's claim, contra his rivals, as a matter of his mythic verification. But now we are in a position to suggest that the drama of Odysseus's return to Ithaca, far from exposing the falseness of the suitors, potentially exposes the hero to risk. Disguised as a vagrant, Odysseus is as much a "false suitor" as the "true husband," and in the context of the *Sophist*—a dialogue that, after all, undertakes the search for a mythic Idea without a corresponding myth—even the truth of Odysseus becomes suspect. His disguise is disclosed by the discovery of the scar, from which the myth issues like fresh blood, but what if no scar and no myth existed to distinguish the Greek hero from his rivals? What if Odysseus returned unable to authenticate himself, unable to identify himself apart from his rivals, so that he became a "true" rival? What if all the suitors bore such a scar, so that neither Eurycleia nor Penelope could finally tell the difference? What if the "eternal husband" were suddenly to become the perpetually indiscernible sophist?

Inasmuch as the *Sophist* is often regarded as the central part of a trilogy, framed on the one side by the *Theaetetus* and on the other by the *Statesman,* it is worth noting at this point that all three dialogues concern the claims of philosophy and the philosopher. The *Sophist* appears to respond to the *Theaetetus,* which has already raised the very possibility that Socrates is no different from the sophist Protagoras. "It is this apparent convergence that makes it necessary to appeal to the Eleatic stranger," Seth Benardete writes. "He is there to show whether or not Socrates really is a sophist."[61] But in this particular dialogue the philosopher is potentially rendered a pretender because his pursuit of the sophist necessarily implicates the philosopher in a rivalry; he is no less a claimant to the gift of wisdom, and his claim is no less subject to doubt. For this reason, among others, scholars have speculated that these extant dialogues suggest the existence of another, missing, or unrecorded dialogue, the *Philosopher*—perhaps the text of the philosopher's myth or the mythic text of the philosopher? In any case, if a myth were to pertain to the *Sophist,* it would surely consist in the belief that the philosopher has been bathed in the *lumen* of the gods, that he does in fact enjoy some access to the heavens, that he is the true friend of the Idea. In other words, the myth would pertain to *anamnêsis,* the divine gift that sustains the philosopher's privileged status in relation to myth itself, namely, as the one who accedes to a pure vision of the Idea.

In the absence of such a myth, the *Sophist* confers the dialectical mission on the Stranger, who is "elected" to undertake this task because his background suits him to deal with precisely the confusion into which the title figure drags philosophers. Having been schooled in the Eleatic tradition, which was beset by sophists, he is a kind of philosophical veteran trained in counterinsurgency, well-versed in the Parmenidean practice of combating this scourge.[62] What may surprise us, then, is that the Stranger, far from following Parmenides' own fondness for lengthy disquisition, accepts Socrates' suggestion to follow "the method of asking questions, as Parmenides himself did on one occasion in developing some magnificent arguments in my presence" (Sop., 217c). In other words, the Stranger actually begins in Platonic fashion. Taking on young Theaetetus as his interlocutor, he accepts the invitation to hunt down the sophist by following the very path of division that we have heretofore examined, namely, the pursuit of the angler. But this initial gambit, intended as it is to introduce the dialectical practice and thereby pave a path to the sophist, quickly becomes complicated. Like the angler, the sophist is also a "hunter," the difference being that he hunts his prey in "land and water of another sort—rivers of wealth and broad meadows of generous youth" (ibid., 222b). While the analogy between angler and sophist is intended to expose the latter as a mercenary, it ends up opening up sophistry itself to a mercurial multiplicity. In the guise of "hunter," for instance, the sophist can be (1) "a hired hunter of young men"; (2) "a merchant of learning as nourishment of the soul"; (3) "a retail dealer in the same wares [i.e., learning]"; (4) a seller of "products of his own manufacture"; (5) "an athlete in debate, appropriating the subdivision of contention which consists in the art of eristic"; 6) "a purifier of the soul from conceits that block understanding" (ibid., 231de).

The "single" series of the sophist opens up a garden of forking paths within which the dialectician is liable to become hopelessly lost. As Theatetus concludes, "By this time the Sophist has appeared in so many guises that for my part I am puzzled to see what description one is to maintain as truly expressing his real nature" (ibid., 231bc). Because he claims to be able to argue about any subject whatever, whether on heaven or earth, the sophist's art of disputation (and the fact that he is paid for it) must derive from the belief that he possesses knowledge of all subjects.[63] "The pretensions of this art of controversy amount, it seems, to a capacity for disputation on any subject whatever" (ibid., 232e). The sophist Hippias, for instance, famously bragged of having composed epics, poems, and essays; of having mastered grammar, rhythm, and mnemonics; of having made his rings, his seal, his clothes—in short, the sophist brags of a "universal genius" (Rep., 598d). Inasmuch as no single definition can account for such "genius," however, the Stranger suggests that we can define the sophist as he who partakes in every category but also, and for this reason, eludes them all: "the Sophist possesses a sort of reputed and apparent knowledge on all subjects, but not the reality" (Sop., 233c). By definition, or the absence of definition, the Sophist lays claim to every Idea but participates in none of them. Paradoxically, we could define the sophist as the one who is incompatible with the Platonic One, the being who cannot be assimilated to Being.

The Simulacrum

Understood in this broad sense, the image not only comes to be integrated into the domain of *doxa* in respect of that which makes it the opposite of *episteme*, but it also seems to be introduced into the heart itself of *doxa*, whose boundaries and whose field of application it reveals at one and the same time. Of *doxa* it can be said that, unlike science, it is just 'opinion', as uncertain and fluctuating as the objects on which it has bearing. But the connection of *doxa* with the universe of the image is far more intimate and direct.

JEAN-PIERRE VERNANT, *MORTALS AND IMMORTALS*

Perhaps we can understand both the problem of the sophist and the Stranger's subsequent response by considering the former in terms of the category into which Platonism draws him: the artist or imitator. Among image-makers, Plato makes a fundamental distinction according to the ends to which the image is put. In the *Sophist,* as in the *Republic,* the artisan is affirmed because he makes his imitation by fixing his eyes on the use of his creation, which endows the object with a kind of "right opinion" that preserves its resemblance to the original Idea or Form. But the artist is the producer detached from any use-value, twice removed from the original, and so his production is automatically degraded. Not surprisingly, then, Plato associates the artist with the sophist, who is likewise an imitator (*mimêtês*) and a maker of images (*eidôlou poiêtês*). Not only does the artist create a potentially infinite variety of images but, in so doing, he or she assumes the bearing of an infinite number of characters. In other words, the sophist qua artist is as multiple as his or her art is differentiated. As Vernant notes, "The best poet (for Plato, the worst one) is the one who has the talent for representing all the characters with their various traits and thus appears like a monster who is likely to assume all forms, a magician of metamorphoses—a Proteus."[64]

And yet, this attribute, this becoming, also seems to provide an end-game in which the sophist is sure to be caught. The Stranger resolves to make a distinction within imitation (*mimesis*) that will allow him to formulate a corresponding distinction between the sophist and the philosopher. "Agreed then that we should at once quarter the ground by dividing the art of image-making," the Stranger unwittingly urges, "and if, as soon as we descend into that enclosure, we meet with the Sophist at bay, we should arrest him on the royal order of reason, report the capture, and hand him over to the sovereign" (Sop., 235bc). In the *Sophist,* the question of the image ranges across a variety of domains and media, and it is primarily in response to this diversity that the Stranger calls for a common definition to account for all those examples on which Theaetetus "bestows the single name of image [*eidôlon*], a name you extend to all of these as if they were just one thing" (ibid., 240a). This endeavor leads, as it does in the *Republic,* to the acknowledgement that imitations refer to a single Idea, which we can copy but which belongs to a kind of divine creation. In this context, we might recall Deleuze's insistence that "the great manifest duality of Idea and image is present only in this goal: to assure the latent distinction between two sorts of images and to give a concrete criterion" (LS, 257). The fundamental difference between Ideas and images provides the criteria—"the reality and the truth" (Rep., 596e)—to make distinctions among images. But if Plato defines the image in a more technical light than his philosophical predecessors, he does so by virtue of making the image qua imitation "the common and characteristic feature of all figurative or representational activities."[65] Images are always already degraded by virtue of being copies of the Idea, but a distinction can be drawn between images according to their *technê,* to their means of expression. Some pay homage to the Idea, while others degrade it.

In the *Republic,* Socrates begins to "make the difference" between images by distinguishing between the work of the artisan and the artwork of the artist. Whereas the former creates useful images, the latter—the sophist, the (con) artist (*mimêtês*)—produces useless fabrications "of or for image-making [*eidôlou poiêtês*]" (Sop., 235b). Indeed, these fabrications include all the different means and media of the mimetic arts that strive for resemblance between copy and model even as they create copies twice removed from the Idea. Likewise, in the *Sophist*, the Stranger initially seems to suggest that the image-simulacrum is "bad" because it is a copy of a copy, the beginning of a chain of degradations that will lead us increasingly further away from the Idea. But we would be mistaken to understand the simulacrum simply along these lines. Such degradations invariably pay heed to the fantasy of the original, for the differences marked by the corruption of the image inevitably sustain the ideal perfection of the model itself. By regarding the simulacrum merely as a copy of a copy, as a copy twice (or however many times) removed from the original, we pay tribute to an original, when in fact the genetic power of the simulacrum lies, as the Stranger already intuits, in its capacity to dethrone the model and to distort the relation of resemblance. Hence, the Stranger refines the distinction within imitation and between images by arguing that an image can either be faithful to its model or can only *appear* to be so. It is worth quoting the dialogue at length:

STRANGER: Following, then, the same method as before, I seem once more to make out two forms of imitation, but as yet I do not feel able to discover in which of the two the type we are seeking is found.

THEAETETUS: Make your division first, at any rate, and tell us what two forms you mean.

STRANGER: One art that I see contained in it is the making of likenesses. The perfect example of this consists in creating a copy that conforms to the proportions of the original in all dimensions and giving moreover the proper color to every part.

THEAETETUS: Why, is not that what all imitations try to do?

STRANGER: Not those sculptors or painters whose works are of colossal size. If they were to reproduce the true proportions of a well-made figure, as you know, the upper parts would look too small, and the lower too large, because we see the one at a distance, the other close at hand.

THEAETETUS: That is true.

STRANGER: So artists, leaving the truth to take care of itself, do in fact put into the images they make, not the real proportions, but those that will appear beautiful.

THEAETETUS: Quite so.

STRANGER: The first kind of image, then, being like the original, may fairly be called a likeness [*eikôn*].

THEAETETUS: Yes.

STRANGER: Now, what are we to call the kind which only appears to be a likeness of a well-made figure because it is not seen from a satisfactory point of view, but to a spectator with eyes that could fully take in so large an object would not be even like the original it professes to resemble? Since it seems to be a likeness, but is not really so, may we not call it a semblance [*phantasma*]?

THEAETETUS: By all means.

STRANGER: And this is a very extensive class, in painting and in imitation of all sorts.

THEAETETUS: True.

STRANGER: So the best name for the art which created, not a likeness, but a semblance will be semblance-making.

THEAETETUS: Quite so.

STRANGER: These, then, are the two forms of image-making I meant—the making of likenesses and the making of semblances.

(Sop., 235c–236c)

In effect, this discussion rests on the critical distinction that refines the terms of our analysis further still. Whereas certain images, or icon-copies (*eikones*), faithfully resemble their models, conforming to their original size and proportion, other images, or simulacra (*phantasmata*), forego any such fidelity in favor of introducing distortion and disproportion that convey the *illusion* of resemblance. In returning to the *Sophist*, then, Deleuze stresses that we can no longer make a distinction between model and copy, copy and simulacrum, on the basis of tried and true assurances. After all, what is the true, the good? The difference between good and bad images, which ostensibly establishes the task that philosophy undertakes (by divining the good) and sophistry obfuscates (by proliferating the bad), is invariably perverted, since the substance of the sophist's simulacrification—his own (self?) image—lies in his peculiar ability to pull off the con, to don the pretense of philosophy (or anything else) beyond the philosopher's best estimation. We cannot judge bad images merely by virtue of what they lack, by virtue of a perceptible degradation, when their ostensible immorality lies in their capacity to deceive the observer and to *appear* moral.

In this respect, the *Sophist* marks a distinction that, while by no means contradictory to the one contrived in the *Republic,* introduces a wrinkle that allows Deleuze to unfold the concept of the simulacrum. On the one hand, as the Stranger suggests, particular images qua copies (*eikones*) are "well-founded" imitations "endowed with resemblance" (LS, 257). Resemblance "goes less from one thing to another than from one thing to an Idea, since it is the Idea which comprehends the relations and proportions constitutive of the internal essence," Deleuze writes. "Being both internal and spiritual, resemblance is the measure of any pretension. The copy truly resembles something to the degree that it resembles the Idea of that thing" (ibid.) On the other hand, however, the simulacrum confronts the Stranger with a problem that, far from being the obverse of the copy, threatens to collapse the integrity of the very distinctions on which the status of the Idea and image are predicated. Whatever their pretense, simulacra "pretend to [it] underhandedly, under cover of an aggression, an insinuation, a subversion, 'against the father,' and without passing through the Idea," Deleuze writes. "Theirs is an unfounded pretension, concealing a dissimilarity [*dissemblance*] which is an internal unbalance" (ibid., 256). Inasmuch as the Platonic distinction lies in the "internal" fidelity that a likeness bears to its original, the simulacrum maintains a purely "external" similarity—a similarity that only *appears* to be faithful.[66] The power of the simulacrum is, as Deleuze suggests, far more perverse than that of mere corruption along a chain of being, since the simulacrum unfastens the links of the chain itself.

Plato's treatment of simulacra tends to begin with those plastic arts that concern the image in purely perceptual and visible terms, namely, painting and sculpture. The former works in the same way as does a mirror turned now to the sun and stars, now to the earth and animals: reflecting "visible objects [*phainomena*], but without any true reality" (Rep., 596de). As the Stranger explains, in terms that virtually mimic Socrates' own warnings in the *Republic,* the artist is "able to deceive the innocent minds of children, if he shows them his drawings at a distance, into thinking that he is capable of creating, in full reality, anything he chooses to make" (Sop., 234b). The unreal image of the painting is "really a likeness" (Sop., 240a)—it does not "represent something as it is," but "represents that which seems as it is" (Rep., 598b). So how do the plastic arts give rise to this pretense? The Stranger's initial description of the simulacrum suggests that "in works either of sculpture or of painting, which are of any magnitude, there is a certain degree of deception," and Socrates echoes this sentiment in the *Republic*, where he condemns imitations of colossal size. More to the point, Deleuze writes, "Plato specifies that the simulacrum implies huge dimensions, depths, and distances that the observer cannot master" (LS, 258). When we are faced with such enormity, it is precisely the sense of comparison, of proportion, that gets lost: gargantuan images outstrip the power of perception, giving rise to all kinds of false impressions. Of course, perception is always given to glitches and mistakes, but, as Plato argues, the work of art, or simulacrum, plays on the unfortunate nature of human nature. "The simulacrum seizes upon a *constituent disparity* in the thing from which it strips the rank of model," Deleuze writes (DR, 67; emphasis added). In this regard, paradoxically, we define the simulacrum as a copy without a model, an image without a referent.

Consider the example of Michelangelo's *David*, which is often upheld as a paragon of realism but which, on closer inspection, demonstrates the basis of Plato's concerns. As the artist realized, the size of the sculpture (more than thirteen feet tall) introduced perspectival problems that would have to be addressed. The scope of the figure and its placement atop a pedestal already meant that it would be viewed from a much greater distance than if, say, the statue had been made to scale. But this distance invariably distorts one's sense of perception. Based on one's vantage point, the depiction of a properly proportioned *David* would seem disproportionate, since certain appendages would appear strangely diminished in relation to the towering body. Therefore, Michelangelo achieves the effect of resemblance by disfiguring select features—in particular, the statue's right hand, which he will make abnormally large. In other words, the artist achieves the perception of proportionality by virtue of a "constituent disparity" between two different spatial registers that are only (or apparently) reconciled along a perspectival line: from a distance, the disproportionate "David" appears altogether proportionate. The closer we approach the statue, the more we are liable to recognize its curious dimensions, but the further away we stray from the statue, the more our perception of it will hew to a sense of strict resemblance.

In this respect, the internal or spiritual resemblance, which ostensibly guarantees a relation between the Idea and the copy, undergoes a mutation such that we are now borne along by the external relation (or nonrelation) between an image and a perception. In the case of the simulacrum, our perception of the object, far from begetting an objective sense of judgment, is folded into the object itself. In Deleuze's words, simulacra "include the differential point of view; and the observer becomes part of the simulacrum itself, which is transformed and deformed by his point of view" (LS, 258). What appears to be a faithful representation is in fact an image without a likeness, an image bearing no internal similarity. "Placing disparates in communication, resonance, forced movement, would thus be the characteristics of the simulacrum."[67] Not incidentally, Michelangelo's technical inspiration for the *David* draws on the tradition of Greek statuary that had grown to prominence during Plato's own lifetime. Unlike their archaic predecessors, the classical sculptors of ancient Greece began to experiment with human forms, gradually contorting the constraints of proportionality in order to express physical motion and even emotion. As Howard Hibbard explains:

> The figure Michelangelo carved stands in a pose hallowed by Greco-Roman statuary—neither walking nor still, it is a version of the *contrapposto* pose that had become the norm for standing statues in the later fifth century B.C. By *contrapposto* is meant the asymmetrical arrangement of limbs, with the weight borne chiefly by one leg, which gives a sense of the normal action of gravity and movement. The result looks natural, a unified pose rather than an accumulation of observed detail. It is, however, an artifact, a simulation of nature.[68]

We might go a step further here and say that the simulacrum is not even a "simulation of nature," since its dissymmetry and disproportion constitute a copy of that which does not exist in nature even though it seems utterly natural. For Plato, the danger posed by such works of art is that, on the basis of ostensibly representing nature, they draw spectators, especially ignorant ones, increasingly away from the transcendent model and into the world of perverse copies. The simulacrum exerts the persuasive force of reality when looked on in a certain way and, especially, by certain "unwise" people; it draws weaker minds away from the Idea and into appearances (*phantasiai*). In short, the simulacrum appeals to "that part of us that is remote from intelligence" (Rep., 603b), and as Plato suggests, the threat of immorality is even more pronounced in the context of the "spoken images" (*eidôla legomena*).

"Abgrundung" (Response to Badiou)

> Simulation is the phantasm itself, that is, the effect of the functioning of the simulacrum as machinery—a Dionysian machine. It involves the false as power [*puissance*], *Pseudos*, in the sense in which Nietzsche speaks of the highest power of the false. By rising to the surface, the simulacrum makes the Same and the Similar, the model and the copy, fall under the power of the false [*phantasm*]. It renders the order of participation, the fixity of distribution, the determination of the hierarchy impossible. It establishes the world of nomadic distributions and crowned anarchies. Far from being a new foundation [*fondement*], it engulfs all foundations, it assures a universal breakdown [*effondrement*], but as a joyful and positive event, as an unfounding [*effondement*].
>
> **GILLES DELEUZE**, "PLATO AND THE SIMULACRUM"

Inasmuch as Plato associates the sophist with artistic mimesis, the specific production of the sophist is identified with the medium of speech. The sophist is a linguistic *mimêtês*. Having treated visual arts and images, the Stranger explains:

> Then must we not expect to find a corresponding form of skill in the region of discourse, making it possible to impose upon the young who are still far removed from the reality of things, by means of words that cheat the ear, exhibiting images of all things in the shadow play of discourse, so as to make them believe that they are hearing the truth and that the speaker is in all matters the wisest of men? (Sop., 234cd)

Just as we should mistrust the painter who holds his mirror up to nature, we should distrust the sophist who contrives this "painterly technique" (ibid., 234b) in language: both create phantoms, images of amusement (*paignion*), and in so doing both lead us astray from the metaphysical-moral certainty of the Idea. Nevertheless, the dangers posed by the sophist (or poet) extend far beyond the threat posed by the painter and sculptor, since the latter are limited to those with this technical aptitude. The sophist, however, revels in a medium in which we all participate and to which we are subject all the time. The sophist's disease is infectious, repeatable, endlessly transmissible; it is capable not only of being passed along a chain of speakers but, moreover, of being transmitted to very nearly the entire citizenry of Athens at once.

In this light, the analysis of the sophist's spoken image returns us, however briefly, to the genre of the *epitaphios*. Beyond the ritualistic problems that this manner of eulogy presented, Plato indicates that the *epitaphios* draws on the persuasive power of sophistry. Indeed, such funerary orations subject their listeners to a kind of narcosis, a "waking dream," that steals them away from rational thought. For Plato, Loraux explains:

> No Athenian could resist this oration, so expert were the orators, described from the outset as *sophoi*, in spellbinding the souls of their listeners. The funeral oration, then, is a piece of sorcery (*goêteia*), that is, deception, which relates it to the speeches of the Sophist, so skilled at "pouring bewitching words into one's ears [*dia tôn ôtôn tois logois goêteuein*], at presenting fictions [*eidôla legomena*] and thus giving an impression of the true."[69]

In the first place, Plato argues, the *epitaphios* achieves its effects by a rhetorical sleight of hand, for under the guise of commemorating the dead, the speech addresses the living citizenry: under the auspices of a discourse about the departed that duly returns to the past, to the origins of the polis, the eulogy works to influence its present listeners, subjecting them to its mythic language. For Plato, this epideictic force can be felt most distinctly in the inflation of the individual and collective Athenian ego, for the heroic oration, the description of the dead, exerts its influence on the living listener who imagines himself "to have become greater and nobler and finer" (Men., 235b). Indeed, the sophist maintains what Plato will call "an association, contact, and friendship" with the inconsistent part of the soul, appealing to the very becoming which those less "temperate and intelligent" individuals harbor (Rep., 603b and 604ab).

In this respect, notably, the *epitaphios* shares with *anamnêsis* a kind of ecstasy beneath which, Loraux writes, we discover "a profound opposition: it is not enough to escape time, for one must also know how to unite one's soul with the divine and not with the deified simulacrum that is the Athenian ideal."[70] The *epitaphios* introduces a kind of sophistic *anamnêsis* that, far from opening up the Truth to which the philosopher lays claim, instead creates "fantasies in speech" that will seduce its listeners into ecstatic flights. Its oration transforms the very reality that, according to Plato, one should seek to "rigidly designate." In short, the *epitaphios* accomplishes a kind of fabulation, transporting its audience, bearing them away on its mythic discourse—the "revelation of internal and immutable being."[71] No longer the privilege of the philosopher, *anamnêsis* spreads among the people. It is a vision, Detienne writes, that "induces or promotes *enthousiasmos*."[72] Effacing the very distinction between reality and fantasy, the *epitaphios* magically conjures a sense of the polis that "ends by displacing Athens from itself and substituting for the real city the phantom of an ideal polis, a utopia."[73] We will have occasion to return to the question of utopia in the following chapter, when the ethical question raised by the genre can be adumbrated at length. But in the present context we might simply consider how the sophist is capable of producing this profound and ecstatic effect—in Socrates' words, to carry one off to the "Islands of the Blessed" (Men., 235c). What is the quality of speaking images that achieves this remarkable *anamnêsis*, which transports souls from this earth or, rather, makes a new earth?

As if in response to this question, Deleuze begins *The Logic of Sense* by declaring that "Plato invites us to distinguish between two dimensions," which we can henceforth pose in terms of language (LS, 2). In the first, language operates in the dimension of "limited and measured things, of fixed qualities," whereas in the second, language opens up "a pure becoming without measure, a veritable becoming-mad, which never rests" (ibid., 2–3). In the first case, we proceed according to "good sense" along a series of present moments and particularized subjects, such that the movement of language seems to exist between so many fixed points. By contrast, the second dimension of language "moves in both directions at once," shuttling into the past and the future: in Plato's own words, " 'hotter' never stops where it is but is always going a point further, and the same applies to colder."[74] For Deleuze, this opposition goes beyond (or beneath) that of the ideal and the empirical, the intelligible and the sensible, or even the Idea and the copy, for it expresses a "subterranean dualism between that which receives the action of the Idea and that which eludes this action" (LS, 2). The distinction Deleuze draws here in the field of language is the very one we have drawn in the field of visual images between copies and simulacra. In the discursive realm, like the visual one, we refine the broad category of images (*eidôla*) to accommodate "finer articulations" that make a difference within images. Whereas copies still bear a relation of resemblance to the Idea, "designating the pauses and rests which receive the action of the Idea," simulacra detach themselves from this relation at the cost of both the Idea and the copy, "expressing the movements of rebel becomings" (ibid.). If the former fixes the limits of the present as that which exists, then the latter displaces and divides itself into past and future, before and after, more and less, giving rise to a language that "overrides the limits and restores them to the infinite equivalence of an unlimited becoming" (ibid., 3; translation modified).[75]

Therefore, we have reached the point at which the problem initially posed by the sophist—the problem that compelled the Stranger to try to define the sophist by virtue of his images, or simulacra—has been duplicated by the simulacra themselves. The becoming-imperceptible with which the sophist eludes the Platonic dialectic is redoubled at the level of the image, and especially the speaking image, which Plato likewise acknowledges to consist in a perpetual becoming that eludes the present. In both cases, paradoxically, the distinction is made only to be effaced according to its own criteria: we discern good copies from bad simulacra because the latter elude the distinction we want to make between copies and simulacra. Indeed, the simulacrum confutes the criteria of selection, confounding the basis on which the overarching Idea authenticates. The simulacrum cannot be hunted down and differentiated in any traditional sense because it is difference itself. Isn't this finally the very definition of sophistry, namely, the image of Platonism that bears no real resemblance to Platonism, the image that strips Platonism of its rank once and for all?

Whence the conclusion to the *Sophist* in which the Stranger is hoisted by his own petard, subverted by the very mechanisms and distinctions he had brought to bear in the first place. The pursuit he undertakes in order to rescue philosophy *inevitably* induces the apotheosis of bewilderment from which Platonism had sought to deliver philosophy. At the very point when the sophist has been chased into his "lurking place," into the dwelling of imitation, when the division of imitation has been cast according to good and bad copies, the Platonic mission loses its bearings. Why? If the stranger identifies the sophist with fantastic images, he will have already tacitly granted the being of those images because "the audacity of the statement lies in its implication that 'what is not' has being, for in no other way could a falsehood come to have being" (Sop., 237a). In other words, the Stranger must choose between identifying the sophist with likenesses, which is not the case and which threatens a patent contradiction in the course of the dialectic; or identifying the sophist with resemblances, which resolves the dialectical contradiction but also condemns the presentiment of truth itself. Ultimately, the aim of preserving the philosopher's position over and against the sophist leads Platonism to confront its own demise. In Deleuze's words, "as a consequence of searching in the direction of the simulacrum and of leaning over its abyss, Plato discovers, in the flash of an instant, that the simulacrum is not simply a false copy, but that it places in question the very notations [*notions*] of copy and model" (LS, 256).

Only in this light, after we have traced Deleuze's remarkable procedures for overturning Platonism, do we see that overturning is accomplished by Platonism itself. But how does Deleuze finally extract a Platonic line of flight that extends beyond Platonism? What is the nature, however denatured, of *Deleuze's Platonism?* At the conclusion of the *Sophist,* the Stranger labors to resolve the questions raised in the dialogue according to his own Eleatic training. Having been thwarted in his dialectical pursuit of the sophist, having determined no sound criteria to adjudicate between pretenders, having found himself unable to distinguish himself from simulacra, the philosopher seems to "head home," withdrawing into the logic of Being (*to on*) and nonbeing (*to mê on*) for which his teacher, Parmenides, was renowned. The revival of this distinction, especially as a kind of deus ex machina, suggests something closer to the Stranger's last refuge, as if he hoped to rescue some measure of certainty by retreating to native soil. As Deleuze admits, among the Greeks who formulated the distinction between Being and nonbeing, the latter tended to lead to two alternatives: "either there is no non-being, and negation is illusory and ungrounded, or there is non-being, which puts the negative in being and grounds the negation" (DR, 63). The first position belongs, above all, to Parmenides, who denies the existence of nonbeing tout court; the second belongs, in various forms, to the sophists, who launch their assault on Parmenides by reducing potentially everything to nonbeing.

But in the context of the *Sophist,* where the battle between these foes seems to be staged anew, a third sense of nonbeing emerges in which the concept is tacitly affirmed without lapsing into negation.[76] The aim of preserving the philosopher's position over and against the sophist leads Platonism to confront nonbeing as the failure of "common sense" that cannot, for all that, be reduced to the negative, the nonexistent: *nihil* (LS, 256). For Deleuze, "it is precisely not the negative which plays this role" of nonbeing, and insofar as this is the case, "we must consider whether or not the celebrated thesis of the sophist, despite certain ambiguities, should be understood as follows: 'non' in the expression 'non-being' expresses *something other than the negative*" (DR, 63). In the context of Platonism, then, Deleuze articulates both being and nonbeing in the form of a problem. There is neither Being nor nonbeing but rather an enigma that he will call "(non)-being" or "?-being" (ibid., 64). The question of being has never been anything but that of the simulacrum, which deterritorializes being and nonbeing alike, swallowing both into the problem of being or, as Deleuze will say, "the being of the problem." In fact, we have already anticipated this conclusion in our own elaboration of the *Sophist,* where the Platonic pursuit leads us to anoint both the sophist and the simulacrum as a copy without a model—a copy that dethrones the supposition of the model.

If there is any reason to speak of a "Judeo-Platonic tradition," as Nietzsche suggested, it lies in the fact that in both cases the metaphysical-moral universe is conditioned by a Law prohibiting images and that this Law is essentially apodictic, without qualifications or stipulations, deaf to all questions, beyond the scope of debate, impervious to reason because it founds reason. To represent means to "re-present *as . . .* "—to insist that every image follows from the Idea qua Being and, therefore, that there can be no image in itself. The real danger of the simulacrum does not lie in its status as a representation or likeness, not even a very bad one, but in the creation of an image that cannot be elucidated according to the logic of representation. Nothing is negated in nonbeing but rather *nonbeing indicates the presence of something that should not "be" according to reason.* Perhaps we can attribute this paradox to a kind of design flaw in the metaphysical-moral universe, a gap or fissure in the tissue of the world through which something enters that is not of this world. Indeed, the simulacrum could be defined as that which should not exist but nevertheless does, that which should not be but nevertheless is. After all, what does a simulacrum *do?* Plato defines it as useless, and we may be likewise tempted, especially in the context of modern aesthetics, to relate the uselessness of this image to the modern sense in which art is hailed as its own justification, as *l'art pour l'art.* But this is neither what Plato suggests nor what our critique to this point implies. If the simulacrum represents a threat to the republic of philosophy, this is not because it is absolutely unproductive, as if we were to say to the artist, "what's your painting of a bed good for? I can't sleep on it." Rather, the simulacrum produces—confusion. In

Masters of Truth in Archaic Greece, Marcel Detienne considers the avocation of the sophist in precisely this context. "Both sophistry and rhetoric, which appeared with the advent of the Greek city, were forms of thought founded on ambiguity," he writes, adding that "no one more carefully noted their ambiguous aspect than Plato. He remarked that *philodoxoi* were people 'who loved and regarded tones and beautiful colors and the like,' people concerned with intermediate things that partook of both being and non-being."[77] The ambition of sophistry is not the Being of Truth nor even the Truth of Being, but persuasion (*peithô*) and trickery (*apatê*). "In a fundamentally ambiguous world, these mental techniques allowed the domination of men through the power of ambiguity itself," Detienne declares. "Both sophists and orators were thus very much men of *doxa.*"[78]

The importance of *doxa* consists not only in its relation to the sophist, who dwells in its milieu, but in its relation to the simulacrum, to the ambiguous signs that the practice of doxography potentially induces. Indeed, the image of the simulacrum, which is also the simulacrum of an image, is intimately and even etymologically related to *doxa. "Doxa* comes from *dokein,* which signifies 'to seem, to appear,' " Jean-Pierre Vernant has argued. "The field of *doxa* is that of appearances, of those semblances best expressed by the image."[79] In this light, notably, the *Sophist* recapitulates the serial conditions of philosophy with which we began: *authochtonia, philia, doxa.* In the first place, the dialogue begins in the absence of a correlative myth, which is to say, by the ungrounding (let us say, the *Ab-grundung*) of the ground of Platonism. In the second place, given this deterritorialization, the Idea no longer provides the divine criteria for dealing with "conditions of the ground," and so the philosopher returns from the heights of judgment to the drama of friendship and rivalry—to the *agôn* of Ideas. "With the creation of philosophy," Deleuze writes, "the Greeks violently force the friend into a relationship that is no longer a relationship with an other but one with an Entity, an Objectality [*Objectité*], an Essence" (WIP, 3). Finally, as we can now see, the philosopher's agonism is defined by opinion, for both philosopher and sophist (and how would we tell them apart?) must participate in the contest of claims, of pretensions, which always begin in the midst of *doxa.* For Deleuze, as for the anthropological tradition on which he draws, the Greek philosopher is the creature of the city because philosophy emerges within the doxological sphere of the city where, again, "anyone can lay claim to anything," where even Being is made a matter of claimancy. In short, the milieu of philosophy is not ontological but *doxological.*

No doubt, it is under the sign of the simulacrum that Deleuze's philosophy has suffered the most grievous misunderstandings, from accusations of outright relativism to more recent charges of unsuspected piety. The antithesis between these charges notwithstanding—and shouldn't we always be wary when a philosopher inspires perfectly contradictory reactions?—these two perspectives or "claims" to the name of Deleuze share an equally absolutist logic: either Deleuze absolutely refuses all structure, distinction, and determination in favor of the pure chaos of differences, or he absolutely redeems the specter of chaos by submitting difference to the overarching One. The former reading, as Alain Badiou has come to characterize it, "naively" imagines Deleuze to have added "his contribution to the ruin of metaphysics, to the 'overturning of Platonism,' by promoting, against the sedentary *nomos* of Essences, the nomadic *nomos* of precarious actualizations, divergent series, and unpredictable creations."[80] Inasmuch as it ever really existed, this caricature seems to have been largely indebted to the reception of *Capitalism and Schizophrenia,* which earned Deleuze and Félix Guattari the reputation, "in the whispering of fan clubs or sectlike groups," of being theoretical revolutionaries. "What is of greatest interest to us about *Anti-Oedipus,*" Manfred Frank characteristically wrote, "is that it is a symptom and, indeed, a particularly glaring one, which, due to the resonance it found in the younger generation, has shown us that one cannot simply shrug one's shoulders or laugh and return to the normal academic agenda."[81] Especially in Anglo-American circles, we are told, Deleuze was recruited by those who settled on an image of the philosopher as a kind of giddy nihilist for whom, like Nietzsche, everything was fair game now that transcendent principles had been eliminated. In Badiou's words, Deleuze inspired the "superficial doxa of an anarcho-desiring Deleuzianism,"[82] and it is against this reception, against the ostensible delusion of Deleuzians, that his own critique is broadly aimed. Only under the guise of Deleuze's presumed anarchy, only under the presentiment of his apostasy, does Badiou's own "sober" treatment acquire its air of absolute redemption: in a word, Deleuze must be *saved.*

Admittedly, this counterintuitive approach may well strike us as a faithful approximation of Deleuze's own means of commentary: doesn't Badiou befriend Deleuze in order to turn the latter to new and unexpected ends?

Still we might wonder whether the nature of this "friendship" follows the dictates of Deleuze's own scrupulous fidelity or merely draws on its name in the interest of its own self-interest. Consider how Deleuze unfolds the practice of commentary, for the guiding principle of his writing on other philosophers could be summed up with one phrase: "keep your friends close, but keep your enemies closer." While Deleuze often treats his philosophical friends in an unexpected and occasionally mischievous manner, as if they were actually strangers ("a *philosophically* clean shaven-Marx . . . "), he treats his enemies with an equally unexpected hospitality, proffering a kind of intimacy, immediacy, and even *immanence* that will make of them familiars and fellow-thinkers (DR, xxi). His commentaries unfailingly demonstrate a loving attention to detail because, in each case, he *enacts* the philosophy in question, as if Deleuze had resolved to play the part of the philosopher in question—of Nietzsche, of Bergson, of Hume, of Spinoza, of Kant, and even of Plato. In Platonic terms, the rigor of commentary derives from the fidelity of the philosopher-actor and the conformity of his mimesis, the creation of an image that, however much it may raise an eyebrow or a doubt, cannot be disowned in the name of the original. Of his manner of commentary, Deleuze insists that "the author had to actually say all that I had him saying": the perversity of commentary amounts to nothing less than its faithful adherence to the original—not in order to effect a stale repetition but rather to induce difference itself (Neg, 6). The experience of dipping into Deleuze's excursuses about both his friends and enemies always provokes a moment of astonishment, as if a queer kind of ventriloquism had been contrived. How is it possible, we ask ourselves, that this philosopher has been made to speak these words, which are his, but which sound as though he had never uttered them before?

The remarkable care with which Deleuze mounts his commentaries—even and especially in the case of Plato, as we have seen—seems strangely at odds with the careless intimacies of his own commentators, who are so determined to make Deleuze into someone or something else, to embrace or capture his philosophy in the name of another school of thought. The irony of the commentaries Deleuze has inspired is that his own critique of transcendence should give way to so many attempts to restore transcendence, whether by means of an enduring structure, an inevitable negation, or an ultimate ground. Thus we are told that Deleuze is a grand dualist (Jameson), an unwitting dialectician (Žižek), or a devout ontologist (Badiou). The last of these cases, which concerns us here, is arguably the most seductive, since its chain of presumptive associations and scattered references has been stitched together into the alluring image of Deleuze as a Platonist. As Badiou declares, "Deleuzianism is fundamentally a Platonism with a different accentuation."[83] This conclusion is even more surprising in light of the fact that Badiou initially hails Deleuze as a philosopher fashioned in quintessentially pre-Socratic style, a philosopher concerned with multiplicity as opposed to unity, with animal becoming as opposed to numerical being. In Peter Hallward's words, "Deleuze is the presocratic to Badiou's Plato,"[84] but Badiou's commentary establishes this distinction only in order to revise it, to disabuse us of this delusional reading by virtue of another that appears to know better.

Thus, at the very juncture where we might be tempted to align Badiou's commentary on Deleuze with the latter's own means of commentary, we can mark a critical—and one might say Platonic—difference. While Deleuze slips into the discourse of another, the apparent effect of this mimesis is merely the external aspect of a commentary that conceals an internal, or spiritual, difference. For Deleuze, commentary itself is a kind of sophistry insofar as the critic imperceptibly insinuates himself or herself into the discourse of another, speaking in the other's voice and with the other's own words, and yet also divagating his or her statements and concepts along unexpected lines of flight. By contrast, Badiou assumes an external perspective, approaching Deleuze from the assumptions of his own philosophy, but this vantage forms the pretense for a reading that will insist on its internal, or psychological, fidelity. Unlike Deleuze's method of commentary, which we have understood in the milieu of sophistry, Badiou's method is hermeneutic: he places his (bad) faith in a process of interpretation which claims to know Deleuze better than he knows himself, as if at every turn we were confronted by the suggestion of what Deleuze "really" meant.[85] Where Deleuze affirms sophistry as the most faithful and even *literal* form of commentary, Badiou religiously advocates interpretation in order to go behind Deleuze's own statements and retrieve their true meaning.

In this light, Badiou's most fundamental interpretation—the interpretation from which all others follow—consists in translating Deleuze's important (albeit relatively early and fairly localized) formulation that "Being is univocal" into an assertion that his entire philosophy is predicated on "an ontological precomprehension of Being as one." Indeed, Badiou argues that "it is the occurrence of the One—renamed by Deleuze the One-All—that forms the supreme destination of thought and to which thought is accordingly *conse-crated"* (emphasis added).[86] Of course, the transposition of these terms is not a product of Deleuze's consecration but of Badiou's: the theological opera-tion he attributes to Deleuze is wholly his own. This sleight of hand conceals the profound difference that separates the two philosophers, since Deleuze develops the notion of univocity (also called "One-all" or "Omnitudo") pre-cisely in order to insist on a field of differences that precedes and resists any totalizing impulse. With respect to Deleuze, then, *Badiou subtracts the clamor from being,* thereby enacting the very logic that he claims to have extracted, that is, making the One-all into a totalized set of differences. "Badiou's entire critique rests on a conflation of the univocity of being with a Platonic con-ception of the One," writes Nathan Widder. "But univocity, far from being a Platonist doctrine, is in fact an Aristotelian one, even if it has been adapted to service a Platonist-Augustinian theology."[87]

Once this ontological "One" is installed, the very considerations to which Deleuze devotes so much thought—the emergence of the sophist, the pro-duction of the simulacrum, the overturning of Platonism—can be written off as testaments to Platonism itself: if the One conditions the phenomenal world and all the equivocal instantiations of being, then even the ostensi-bly subversive simulacra only exist to verify the One-Being.[88] For Badiou, the multiple consists in the formal or modal character of the One: if the latter is tantamount to a plane of univocity, its multiplicities of material differences (or what Deleuze would call "differenciations") consist in a plane of equiv-ocity. "The world of beings," Badiou concludes, "is the theater of the simula-crum of Being."[89] Hence, Badiou claims that "Deleuze's philosophy is in no way a critical philosophy" because, according to his own reading, the over-turning of Platonism ends by bearing witness to the enduring and intractable premise of a holy Platonism.[90] Badiou redeems Deleuze, the crowned-prince of "crowned-anarchy," by making him rigorous, monkish, *pious*—but in the context of the sophist and the simulacrum we might wonder whether this is not in fact the *appearance* of piety. Badiou maintains that Deleuze resem-bles Plato more than he ever wishes to admit, but perhaps this is merely an impression of resemblance, the pretense of the simulacrum to which Badiou unwittingly falls prey. Indeed, Badiou's inclination ought to be met with the Stranger's caution in the *Sophist:* to the suggestion that his description of the philosopher "has some resemblance with the sophist," he responds that "the cautious man should above all be on his guard against resemblances" (Sop., 231a). Isn't resemblance the very "effect" that Deleuze wishes to produce, namely, to engage in a critique so faithful as to be virtually indistinguishable from its object and yet a critique whose internal difference diverts its object into the most improbable ends?

The overturning of Platonism consists in the art of producing simulacra—*beginning with the simulacrum of Platonism itself.* The strangeness of Deleuze's critique takes its method and measure from Platonism in order to overturn Platonism. "Was it not Plato himself who pointed out the direction for the reversal of Platonism?" (LS, 256). This is the paradox that Badiou seems to have glossed, the paradox of piety that conceals a war machine, the paradox of a friendship that countenances rivalry, the paradox of an ontology that hides a profound agonism, the paradox of the sophist who produces *doxa.*[91] While Badiou focuses almost exclusively on Deleuze's engagement with Platonism in *Difference and Repetition* and the *Logic of Sense,* the lineage of Deleuze's Platonism, especially as regards *doxa,* actually surfaces most clearly in Deleuze's fairly late excursion into the Greek world, when the questions raised in his earlier books had remained fallow for many years. As we've seen, in *What Is Philosophy?* as well as his short essay "Plato and the Greeks," Deleuze eventually revisits the question of Platonism, but these texts forego any consideration of Being in favor of a consideration of the claims of philosophy and the philosopher as a claimant.[92] And even if we were to make a case that these are related spheres (for instance, in the context of medieval philosophy, where ontology initially and more often than not refers to matters of rhetoric), we must insist that the return to Plato is not undertaken under the auspices of the comprehension of eternal Being but rather the problem of *doxa.* For Plato, of course, *doxa* is opposed to Being, but *doxa* also defines the field in which one (such as the sophist) can lay claim to Being or, for that matter, fabulate it. What Badiou takes to be Deleuze's Platonism, the evocation of a grand ontology, constitutes the very sense in which Deleuze transforms even ontology into a matter of *doxa* and of *paradoxa.* Once more: the ground becomes an abyss.

In this respect, finally, Badiou's rendering—a Platonic Deleuze—seems to compound one misunderstanding (that Deleuze's philosophy is ontological, through and through) with another (that, as an ontologically inspired philosophy, it falls short of properly constituting its univocal field). In other words, as Peter Hallward has pointed out, the accusation that Deleuze's is a philosophy of Being is only preliminary to Badiou's real critique of Deleuze, that this quasi-mystical "Substance or the One" preserves a kind of mystical relationship to God. By submitting all difference to the One-All, Badiou argues, Deleuze situates himself in a philosophical tradition that affirms a well-nigh theological substance, a plane of immanence, which fails to undertake the secular and mathematical subtraction of "every truth from the ordinary and everyday."[93] Notably, Badiou's argument recalls an old Jewish joke in which a man, orphaned at birth and raised in a secular world, is approached by rabbinical authorities who have discovered him to be the blood child of orthodox parents. "The good news is that you are in fact Jewish," they explain. "The bad news is that, as a Jew, you've been a total failure." The logic of this joke, or the joke of this logic, is that Deleuze is called before the "philosophical authorities" to be authenticated as a Platonist, an ontologist, and then informed that, regrettably, he has not been a very good one. If we disregard the second judgment, the bad news, it is because our entire discussion to this point has situated its condition, the good news, in an entirely different light. Yes, we could say, Deleuze is a Platonist, but he is a Platonist in an entirely different and radical sense: no "philosopher of being," Deleuze makes Platonism emerge from the problem of *doxa* and the being of the simulacrum—the powers of the false. Once more, and after all, who is the "real" sophist? What is the "true" simulacrum?

4

THE PHILOSOPHY OF FICTION
AND THE FICTION OF PHILOSOPHY

Style and the State-Form

The Philandering of Philosophy: A Literary Affair

> Great philosophers are great stylists too.
>
> **GILLES DELEUZE,** *NEGOTIATIONS*

WE HAVE ASKED IT BEFORE, but the question bears repeating: was there ever a more *promiscuous* philosopher than Gilles Deleuze? While other philosophers remain faithful to a particular thinker or school, to a method or a presupposition, Deleuze declares no abiding loyalties: not only does he mingle with countless philosophers, but he flirts with just as many writers, filmmakers, and artists.[1] Deleuze's style is guided by passion, desire, or what might simply be called love (*philia*), which does not lie in an external person but an immanent imperative: in E. M. Forster's words, "only connect."[2] If we define philosophy as the art of creating concepts, then we must also appreciate that, for Deleuze, concepts never emerge in isolation but must be created in amorous relations with other domains. Far from extolling the immaculate conception of the concept, Deleuze insists that philosophy is connective, conjugal. Far from marrying the concept to a single partner in perpetuity, Deleuze follows a profligate line, forming new associations, experimenting here and there, and always returning—fondly, but without promises—to those associations that have produced the most conceptual joy ("Joy emerges as the sole motivation for philosophizing" [PI, 84]).

To all a priori claims, to all conceptual virginities, to all philosophies that proudly declare their solitude, severity, and purity, Deleuze affirms: *Have intercourse!* But to this we should add, *don't just fuck anyone.* We should always remember: promiscuity demands that we cultivate tastes and develop a sensibility (where, when, how, how many?) that the ascetic anchorite will never know. For Deleuze, the task of philosophy consists in formulating alliances with other means of expression, with the sensations and intensities that affect us, disorient us, move us. "Something in the world forces us to think," Deleuze writes. "This something is the object not of recognition but of a fundamental *encounter*" (DR, 140). In *Difference and Repetition,* Deleuze illuminates the distinction between recognition and the encounter on the basis of Socrates' contention that there are two kinds of perception—one common, the other confounding. On the one hand, "some reports of our perceptions do not provoke thought to reconsideration because the judgment of them by sensation seems adequate" (DR, 138; Rep. VII 523b); but on the other hand, some perceptions "invite the intellect to reflection because the sensation yields to nothing that can be trusted" (il y en a d'autres qui l'engagent tout à fait dans cet examen, en tant que la perception ne donne rien de sain).[3]

The first kind of perception we call recognition, namely, the process whereby thought discovers its own self-image in the image of something else. When Deleuze refers to a dogmatic image of thought, we should always recall the mechanism of recognition whereby thinking is "filled with no more than an image of itself, one in which it recognizes itself the more it recognizes things" (DR, 138). But where recognition appeals to preexistent memories, habits, and opinions with which we are always rediscovering what we already know, the encounter outstrips the adequacy of this determinative judgment and the "adequation" (*adequatio*) that it traditionally actualizes (say, as the relation of subject and object). An encounter constitutes that which we cannot re-cognize, cannot subsume to a preordained opinion, cannot gloss as a habit of mind. Needless to say, it is not as if such events happen all the time. In the course of life, caught up as we are in the "hundred visions and revisions" (Eliot) of a day, we're overwhelmed by the compulsion to recognize, to communicate, to make sense: the concerted organization of clichés is no less the threshold of comprehension beyond which we only rarely find occasions to venture.[4] This is why encounters, however rare, because they are rare, are of such importance: they detour thought from avenues of recognition into non-sense, novelty and invention. Not surprisingly, Deleuze associates the encounter with the signs and images of art, understood in the broadest sense, but this doesn't tell us very much. Deleuze is hardly the first to have responded to the labor of recognition and the communication of opinion (*doxa*) by turning to aesthetics: the recourse goes back to the modernists, if not the romantics. But perhaps we can come to terms with the uniqueness of Deleuze's solution by understanding it in light of the Platonic logic that we considered in the last chapter.

For Plato the freedom of expression introduces the unbridled right to express opinion, to make claims, even to claim the right of philosophy itself. The city is given over to *prétendants,* sophists and artists alike, whom he regards as the most dangerous eventuality of democracy: by producing simulacra, these claimants threaten metaphysical authenticity and moral order alike. Plato responds to this "crowned anarchy" (DR, 37) by appealing to the ideal Forms (*Eidê*), which provide the criteria to organize and adjudicate the chaos of human discourse, the sphere of claimancy as well as artistic creation. The Forms provide something like the divine criteria for judgment, the means with which to discern the true from the false, to distinguish the morally sound from the morally suspect. But when Deleuze analyzes the philosophical history of recognition, beginning as it does in Platonism and running through Hegel to its contemporary formation in "societies of control," he never poses it as a solution to *doxa* but as the other side of its problematic. Opinion does not exist without expressing recognition and being recognized in turn: "This is a table, this is an apple, this the piece of wax, Good morning Theatetus" (DR, 35). How do we escape the model of recognition and the determination of *doxa*?

Deleuze turns to the work of art because, especially in its literary formation, it musters the powers of the false to create the "impossible." Art is not privileged before all instances (*quid juris*) but is exceptional on the basis of each and every creative instance (*quid facti*). Put differently, we could say that the work of art creates "signs," provided we grasp the sign apart from the sense of reference or representation with which the term is typically identified. As we have said on previous occasions, Deleuze defines the sign as an assemblage of intensities—of percepts and affects—that we encounter in the absence of recognition: but what does this mean? The nature of the sign can be summarized in two seemingly antithetical formulations. In the first place, what forces us to think is not an object at all, since there is no "sign of" something: the sign does not have a model, refers to no Idea. Hence, we say that *the sign can only be sensed.* But if we admit that signs cannot be grasped from the perspective of a determinative judgment on behalf of a subject, nor can they be grasped as an indeterminate representation on the side of an object, the sign has no referent to which it can be assigned. Hence, we would also have to say that *the sign cannot be sensed.* The relation between these two formulas constitutes the very paradox that defines the sign—"not a sensible being but the being of the sensible" (ibid.,140). We encounter the sign only insofar as it confounds us, "moves the soul, 'perplexes it'—forces it to pose a problem . . . " (DR, 140).[5] The categories and clichés, schemas and habits that constitute the structure of recognition are *in absentia* here: inasmuch as there is sense, there is no given or common sense.

No wonder that Plato would just as soon dispatch the poets from the Republic: they trouble the sedentary organization of knowledge (*nomos*), the sense in which Ideas adjudicate particular claims, the sense in which philosophers ought to be kings. Nor should it surprise us that the object of condemnation in Platonism becomes, in Deleuze's philosophy, the subject of enduring appreciation, even love, for the poets—artists of any kind—produce signs that jilt us, disturb us, force us to think differently. It is in this light that Deleuze formulates his relationships to the arts, particularly to literature, which produces the very signs that compel philosophy to devise the mise-en-scène of new problems and thereby create new concepts. Literature remains, above all else, a machine for the production of signs, to which Deleuze's philosophy responds by devising new connections, a new machinism, which selects sensations and ordinates singularities in the interest of creating new concepts. In the world of Proust's *A la recherche du temps perdu,* Deleuze develops not only a vast taxonomy of signs but a typology of forces and passions within which the concept of character itself emerges. In the cosmos of Gombrowicz, Deleuze dwells on the ceaseless flood of singularities, events, and partial objects to extract a concept of a semi-aleatory series, a "chaosmos" of signs. In the context of Melville, Deleuze discovers a range of conceptual personae (the confidence man, the cosmopolitan, the idiot) who will undermine the very premise of truth and lying, demanding instead the affirmation of a new concept of the false. And in light of Kafka's writing, which imagines the framework for a "literature of small people" (*Schema zur Charakteristik kleiner Literaturen*), Deleuze creates the concept of minor literature and, more generally, of minorization, which will infuse his entire philosophico-political enterprise.

In each case, the writing machine consists in an emission of intensities that provoke us to think differently: this is why Deleuze plugs his philosophical machine into so many literary ones. But if Deleuze's philosophy formulates an assemblage with literature to produces concepts, we might venture beyond this conclusion to consider how the engagement with literature deterritorializes philosophy itself, setting it off on so many lines of flight. Deleuze's frequent affairs with literature acquire a unique distinction because, far from simply formulating so many "Platonic" friendships, he relishes what might more aptly be called "friends with benefits." This chapter concerns the ways that Deleuze's encounters with writers, especially writers of fiction, draws his own means of expression into a peculiar intimacy with literature and draws out his will to fabulation. Let's be clear: Deleuze does not write literature. As we have said, literature creates "percepts" and "affects," or what we have called signs, whereas philosophy creates concepts. And yet philosophy shares with literature the medium and experience of writing with which it forms a "zone of indiscernibility." Indeed, Deleuze dwells on a number of writers whose literary discourse is effectively philosophical (consider Tournier's notion of the "Other Person," Burroughs's notion of "control," etc.), but philosophy is no less capable of undertaking a kind of becoming-literary. Philosophy produces signs—yes, concepts have an affective intensity—that take us beyond philosophy. To write literature or philosophy, at least as Deleuze envisions it, is to invent expressions that escape the prescribed genres of exposition to which both are, in their own way, traditionally betrothed.

The nature of Deleuze's style of philosophy emerges in the course of his rejections, refusals, and rebuttals of the dominant generic traditions with which his own philosophy is confronted. "And neither is it enough to say, 'Down with genres,'" Deleuze urges, because "one must effectively write in such a way that there are no more 'genres,' etc." (Dia, 17). Genres prescribe the rules and regulations, the "horizon of expectations," against which the task of writing is waged.[6] Rather, the flight from genre—from dialogue, meditation, history, and finally critique—provides the occasion for an articulation of Deleuze's own style of philosophy, the genre of philosophy sui generis. Deleuze once said of Bergson that "in him there is something which cannot be assimilated, which enabled him to provide a shock" to thought. But shouldn't we say the same of Deleuze, that he too writes a philosophy that "cannot be assimilated"? (Dia, 15). The notorious difficulty of Deleuze's writing is never the result of semantic overdetermination or "syntactic cleverness" but, above all else, attests to "the search for new means of expression" (ibid., 8). What does this mean? Why do we need "new means of philosophical expression" when philosophers have managed to make do with a familiar set of standard forms and respectable styles? This skepticism is interesting for our purposes not because of its objections, which are almost to be expected, but because of the grounds of those objections, which effectively reduce expression to a superfluous adornment or empty affectation. "It's strange how people some-times say that philosophers have no style," Deleuze once remarked (Neg, 100), but what's stranger still is that philosophers themselves have conditioned this condemnation, as if style were merely the afterthought to a more authentic labor. Indeed, the philosophical denigration of philosophical style begins to make sense only when we see it as a matter of precedence: expression suf-fers whenever philosophy orients itself around the preexistence of presup-positions and the apriority of knowledge because, by rights, these form the ground next to which writing itself is secondary (i.e., mannerism).

The suppression or denial of style invariably designates the belief in that which is given in advance by that which exists beforehand. "The philosopher readily presupposes the mind as mind, the thinker as thinker, wants the truth, loves or desires the truth, naturally seeks out the truth," Deleuze laments. "He assumes in advance the good will of thinking; all his investigation is based on a 'premeditated decision'" (PS, 94). The great presupposition that reigns over classical philosophy, serving as its first and fundamental law, concerns this very insistence on the good will of thought and the thinker. All the more ubiq-uitous because it often goes undetected, the convictions of this *Eudoxus* con-stitute the enduring certainty with which philosophy so often begins, assuring us about what "everybody knows."[7] Traditionally, philosophy presupposes that we share a common sense, the constituents of which define us as "thinking beings" (*cogitas cogitans*) and the ends of which are lodged in the overarching sphere of representation. This common sense "consists only of the supposition that thought is the natural exercise of a faculty, of the presupposition that there is a natural capacity for thought endowed with a talent for truth or an affinity with the true, under the double aspect of a *good will on the part of the thinker* and an *upright nature [nature droite] on the part of thought*" (DR, 131). Only under these auspices do we arrive at "the harmonious exercise of all faculties upon a supposed same object" (ibid., 133). Not only does each faculty relate to the same object, but the identity of the object consists in the accord reached between faculties—a common sense. The agreement between faculties relies on "a subjective principle of collaboration of the faculties for 'everybody'—in other words, a common sense as a *concordia facultatum*" (ibid., 133).

Surely this is why Deleuze says that the prospect of "beginning" is always fraught for philosophy. Openings and outsets tend to inspire the propaedeutic innocence with which we claim to clean the slate and start afresh: the "style-lessness" of philosophy is no less a claim to guilessness, as if the philosopher could speak the Truth—whether by divine appointment (Plato), empirical artlessness (Descartes), rational critique (Kant), or communicative rational-ity (Habermas). "Philosophy takes the side of the idiot as though of a man without presupposition," Deleuze says (ibid., 130; translation modified), but this ostensibly honest accounting forms the source of our most subtle self-deceptions. No degree of idiocy or autism is sufficient to raze all our uncon-scious assumptions when it is precisely this state of mind, this good will, which determines the guiding principles of traditional philosophy. It is as if philosophy "had kept nothing back," Deleuze remarks, "except, of course, the essential—namely, the form of this discourse" (ibid.).

Inasmuch as the first presupposition of philosophy is also its first lie, *pro-ton pseudos,* we are left with the worry of how to begin and in what sense we can begin *otherwise.* How can philosophy slough off the methods and struc-tures of its "old style," the habits with which it has gone about thinking for so long? Rather than begin in so-called good faith—and what could be more dishonest, more unfaithful!—Deleuze wonders if we shouldn't begin in bad faith, with all the disrespect we can possibly muster. Why not nurture a state of ill will, raising "isolated and passionate cries" against all common sense and expectation? (ibid., 130). In *Difference and Repetition,* he writes:

> Such protest does not take place in the name of aristocratic prejudices: it is not a question of saying what few think and knowing what it means to think. On the contrary, it is a question of someone—if only one—with the necessary modesty of not managing to know what everybody knows, and modestly denying what everybody is supposed to recognize. Someone who neither allows himself to be represented nor wishes to represent anything. Not an individual endowed with good will and a natural capacity for thought, but an individual full of ill will who does not manage to think, either naturally or conceptually (ibid.).

In this immodest one, who passionately refuses to submit to even the most self-evident premises, we should immediately mark our distance from what we have heretofore called the idiot. The latter, the child of *Eudoxus,* remains tacitly but all the more determinately grounded in universal assumptions. Whenever we hear that something is "so obvious even an idiot could understand it," we know that idiocy has been mobilized for the purpose of relating thought to the universal: to say that even the idiot can understand something is to say anyone—or, rather, *everyone*—can understand it. The lowest common denominator, the idiot becomes the source of common sense and good sense, the Forrest Gump of philosophy for whom everything can be reduced to the superficial wisdom of clichés.

No doubt this explains Deleuze's advice: if you insist on being an idiot, at least do it in "the Russian manner" (DR, 130). Of course, we could say that every national idiocy has its virtues, but the Russian version is perhaps the most stubborn, the most defiant, and the most disagreeable. Consider Dostoyevsky's *Notes from Underground,* in which the narrator famously (or infamously) refuses to be bound by any form of common sense. Misanthrope, hermit, and fledgling anti-Christ, the "underground man" begins his text by avowing: "I am a wicked man. An unattractive man," only to admit: "And I lied about myself just now when I said I was a wicked official. I lied out of wickedness."[8] At a purely logical level, we could say that this contradiction amounts to an instance of the liar's paradox: the singular assertion "I am lying" disables the very system of truthful (or provable) propositions. But if no credibility can be formally attached to this discourse, its strange sense nevertheless insists in the resolution to "have done with judgment" (CC, 126). To all truth claims, the underground man responds: "My God, but what do I care about the laws of nature and arithmetic if for some reason these laws and two times two is four are not to my liking?"[9] This question, this cry, remarks the superior innocence of the idiot who will not consent to what everybody knows, who will not even consent to a universal form of knowing. This idiocy does not submit to the legislation of reason and the governance of common sense but achieves a kind of sublime non-sense.[10] Perhaps, finally, this is what it means to "go underground"—not to retreat, to withdraw, or to bury one's head in the sand, but to prepare an even more profound deterritorialization than if we had stayed above ground. While the terrain can be parsed and parceled out on the surface, the subterranean world dissolves any sense of delineations;

in going underground, Dostoyevsky says, we become "like a man who has 'renounced the soil and popular root.' "[11]

The State of Philosophy: A Bureaucratic Affair

> Philosophy is shot through with the project of becoming the official language of a Pure State. The exercise of thought thus conforms to the goals of a real State, to the dominant meanings and to the requirements of an established order.
>
> **GILLES DELEUZE,** *DIALOGUES II*

Still—still!—the style of thinking, writing, and ultimately living that we are evoking here entails more than merely raising our voices against what "everyone knows," since that form of protest threatens merely to exalt the stability and sanity of the powers that be. The renovation of philosophy cannot be sought in a simple detachment from the institution of the state when philosophy is always already so saturated with the mechanisms of the state (of language, of code, of contract) that, no matter how isolated, we tend to remake thinking along the lines of the state and to organize our own private fascisms. As Foucault asks in the preface to *Anti-Oedipus*: How "does one keep from being fascist, even (especially) when one believes oneself to be a revolutionary militant? How do we rid our speech and our acts, our hearts and our pleasures, of fascism?" (xv) Or, to put it more simply still, how do we think apart from the state?

We need look no further than our own state-form to understand the dilemmas of raising our voice against the state, for the lineage of modern philosophy and modern democracy share a common denominator, *representation*. Ostensibly partitioned between the two domains, representation is at once an epistemological process that conditions each person as a subject and a political process that emerges from the people as subjects. While philosophy never ceases to confirm the subjective faculties we share and with which we determine the world, democracy always reminds us that the power to represent is, among subjects, liable to be inverted. Representation consists as much in being "represented" as it does in "representing": in the democratic last instance, we submit to the majority, such that no mere avowal of opposition— "not my president," "not my policy," "not my war"—is sufficient to perform the derangement of sense and the liberation of style. However virulently they are posed, our conventional forms of dissent nevertheless consist in representation, the representation of dissent, because they take the measure of their difference from that which is the same; as Deleuze writes, "The prefix RE- in the word representation signifies the conceptual form of the identical which subordinates differences" (DR, 56).

Representation tolerates difference insofar as it refers to identity, but we are appealing here to the formulation of a style that inhabits difference in itself, a difference that "eludes the majority [ce qui se soustrait toujours de la majorité]" (WIP, 108).[12] As Deleuze explains: "It is the same every time there is mediation or representation. The representant says: 'Everyone recognizes that . . .', but there is always an unrepresented singularity who does not recognize precisely because it is not everyone or universal" (DR, 52). This occasion, so to speak, emerges most distinctly in "What Is a Minor Literature?"—the signature chapter of Deleuze and Guattari's book *Kafka*. There they elaborate Kafka's vision of an aesthetic and political sociology. At the end of the chapter, once they have analyzed the procedures for deterritorializing the sovereign order of representation, for constructing a collective assemblage of enunciation, and finally for affirming a new politics Deleuze and Guattari ask whether philosophy can achieve its own minorization. "Is there a hope for philosophy, which for a long time has been an official, referential genre?" (Y a-t-il une chance pour la philosophie, elle qui forma longtemps un genre official et référentiaire?) (K, 27).[13] Perhaps the answer already lies in the question itself, since the grammatically inessential clause ("which . . . ") forecasts the essential task that we will consider here, namely, how to create a philosophical expression that is neither official nor referential—*a philosophy neither governed by the form of the state nor determined by the order of representation.*

While no one will be surprised to learn that philosophy is beholden to the state, the full extent of this compromised formation must be grasped if we are to envision the new politics to which Deleuze finally points. Traditionally, and to a remarkable degree, the state has financed the institutions and furnished the resources on which philosophy relies in order to "produce" knowledge. Not simply an academic discipline, philosophy remains a state-sponsored discipline; and the notable exceptions to this scholarly citizenship—Spinoza's passionate apostasy, Kierkegaard's elusive pseudonymity, Nietzsche's delirious multiplicity—only confirm that, as a rule, philosophers exist as the stable elements of a sedentary state. Consider Leibniz's imperative to make new truths "without overthrowing established feelings": as Deleuze admits, especially in the idealist tradition ("from Kant to Hegel"), "we see the philosopher remaining, in the last resort, a thoroughly civil and pious character, loving to blend the aims of culture with the good of religion, morality of the State" (NP, 104). In his unremittingly critical account of the philosophical laborer, *Schopenhauer as Educator,* Nietzsche sought to lay bear the compromises that the state demands of its intellectual employees; "supported by the state," he writes, the philosopher "must also put up with being viewed by the state as someone who has given up pursuing truth in every nook and cranny."[14] Because the state effectively countenances their investigations, philosophers assume the status of functionaries who are not only responsible for knowledge but responsible *before* a vast and often unacknowledged bureaucracy. The philosopher pledges himself or herself to "everything the state demands for its own well-being: for example, a particular form of religion, social order, and military organization—on each of these is written *noli me tangere.* Has any university philosophy professor ever realized the full extent of his obligations and limitations?"[15]

No doubt, most professors would happily offer an accounting of their obligations, but Nietzsche's question augurs far less conspicuous and far more profound capitulations.[16] Beyond the concessions philosophy makes to the state, concessions that are routinely posed at the level of what can be said and that relegate speech, as a matter of law, to a kind of pure content—beyond these concessions, the "obligations and limits" of philosophy must be grasped at the level of what we have called *expression.* While "thought contents are sometimes criticized for being too conformist" (ATP, 374), Deleuze and Guattari write, the real question posed by the relation of philosophy and the state concerns "form itself." To what degree does philosophy presuppose the state-form and adopt it as an implicit model of what it means to think? Historically, Deleuze suggests, the logic, genre, syntax—the *style*—of philosophy has been circumscribed by the form of the state. Philosophy is largely determined by the various genres and the forms of language that the state validates, perpetuates, and disseminates. "Philosophical discourse has always maintained an essential relation to the law, the institution, and the contract," Deleuze declares, "all of which are the Sovereign's problem, traversing the ages of sedentary history from despotic formations to democracies" (DI, 259; translation modified).[17]

As we have suggested in previous chapters, so now we must grasp that the ensemble of "laws, institutions, and contracts" constitutes the codes that condition philosophy as a state-form, organizing its genres and determining its composition. "Thought as such is already in conformity with a model that it borrows from the State apparatus, which defines for it goals and paths, conduits, channels, organs, an entire *organon*. There is thus an image of thought covering all of thought" (ATP, 374). The conformism to the state-form stages the unconscious drama whereby philosophy endows itself with a sovereign image of thought, incarnating a state of mind or, better yet, *a state in mind* that replicates the state itself. As Deleuze explains, philosophy "invents a properly spiritual State, as an absolute state, which is by no means a dream, since it operates effectively in the mind. Hence the importance of notions such as universality, method, question and answer, judgment, or recognition, of just correct, always having correct ideas" (Dia, 13). The reciprocal ramification of the state and philosophy takes place through the production and reproduction of the subject, the citizen of the state and the state of the citizen. On the one hand, Deleuze and Guattari write, "The state gives thought a form of interiority," since the state introjects its own image into an internal landscape that will become the chambers of a vast administrative machinery divided among so many faculties (ibid.). "Hence the importance of themes like those of a republic of spirits, an enquiry of the understanding, a court of reason, a pure 'right' of thought, with ministers of the Interior and bureaucrats of pure thought" (ibid.). On the other hand, though, when they say that the state gives thought a form of interiority, an administrative and juridical image of thought, Deleuze and Guattari are quick to add that "thought gives interiority a form of universality" (ATP, 375), since the administration of thought conducts business in such a way as to expect that common sense obtains among all branch offices, among each and every subject, insofar as subjects find the source of their agreement in the state itself.

Thus, as Deleuze and Guattari write, "It is easy to see what thought gains from this: a gravity it would never have on its own, a center that makes everything, including the State, appear to exist by its own efficacy or its own sanction" (ibid.). But they add, "the State gains just as much. Indeed, by developing in thought in this way the State-form gains something essential—a whole consensus. Only thought is capable of inventing the fiction of a State that is universal by right [*universel en droit*], of elevating the State to the level of *de jure* universality [*l'État à l'universel de droit*]" (ATP, 375). The "old style" of philosophy always wears this Janus-face whereby the state reproduces the form of representation just as the latter reproduces the organizations and institutions of the state. The "official and referential" nature of philosophy ensures that thinking and its attendant politics will always amount to the conformism of common sense, since its very mechanism of re-presentation is effectively conditioned to recognize that which is "always already." It is as if the state franchises subjectivity, offering its philosophers a model plan to which they must adhere if they are to be recognized and to recognize the state in return.[18] Deleuze defines representation in terms of a "regime" precisely because representation always falls back on the model of the state-form, just as the state always falls back on the form of representation. The state-form cannot be severed from representation because representation effectively interiorizes the state in the subject, just as the state exteriorizes the subject in the universality of the state.

The sovereignty of philosophy is nowhere more clearly illustrated than in Kant's transcendental idealism, which installs the form of legislation and the determination of common sense in the architecture of the subject. Kant invents the bureaucracy of critique on the model of a tribunal of judgment, according to which reason is not only the object of investigation but also its instrument. Indeed, the genius of Kant's administration lies in the bureaucratic pretension of "separate spheres," such that the "critique of pure reason" by reason plays out "as if" these were discrete entities. "Is this not the Kantian contradiction, making reason both tribunal and accused; constituting it as judge and plaintiff, judging and judged?" (NP, 91). Indeed, the principle of this kind of critique recalls the disappointing inquiries into political power to which bureaucracies generally give rise, each new commission holding the promise of an investigation that will just as surely be compromised by alliances and allegiances with the institutions of power. Our democratic (and characteristically American) response to the problem of critique always seems to lie in the hope that a genuinely "independent prosecutor" can be found, one who can't be bought or sold and who, for this reason, will carry critique through to its end. When it comes to the viability of critique, we place our faith in a representative of the very system which is to be critiqued, in the jurist, in the friend of wisdom and justice, whose honesty (we hope) will procure an untouchable autonomy.

Deleuze argues that the Kantian tradition of judgment is always already cast in these terms—*and that it is precisely the claim to independence, to autonomy, to sovereignty, to the state-form, that compromises critique as such.* Kant picks up the philosopher's hammer only to exchange it for the judge's gavel.[19] This model of critique never reaches the highest echelons of power, since this would mean impeaching its own credibility as a representative of and devotee to reason. In fact, pure reason marks the conditions and limits of his first critique, just as the practical reason marks the conditions and limits of his second critique. "Critique has everything—a tribunal of justices of the peace, a registration room, a register," Deleuze writes of Kant, "except the power of a new politics which overturns the image of thought" (DR, 137). In this respect, Deleuze's reading of Kant aims to provide "a new politics" on the basis of the transformation of judgment. In Kant's first two critiques, the conviction of philosophy rests in the administration of a bureaucracy, the subjective constituents of which assume a state-form—a tribunal of judgment and, in the last instance, a particular faculty to assume the function of overarching determination. In the *Critique of Pure Reason* and the *Critique of Practical Reason,* a "transcendental" faculty governs the other faculties and legislates their common sense.

But Deleuze insists that in the *Critique of Judgment* Kant transforms the structure of determinative judgment into an aesthetic mode of judgment, a *free* and *indeterminate* agreement among the faculties. In determinative judgments, the faculty of understanding presides over judgment in order to be able to say, "I think X," but in the third *Critique* Kant argues that particular encounters give rise to a mode of reflective judgment that derives from a harmony among faculties, between the imagination and the understanding. Kant displaces thought from the labor of determinative judgment, which proceeds on the basis of a dominant faculty, onto an aesthetic judgment that occurs in the absence of any hierarchy. In effect, Deleuze pursues this reflective turn by taking Kant's internal conditions and tendencies to their furthest extreme—to the point where transcendental idealism, which determines the conditions of possibility for experience in advance of experience, gives way to a transcendental empiricism, where "the conditions of experience in general must become conditions of real experience" (LS, 260). How does this happen? In order to appreciate this complex transformation, let us take our bearings in terms of the fundamental assumptions of transcendental idealism, which we nominally assume to have been partitioned among Kant's three critiques. Ostensibly, each critique entails a sphere of operations (epistemology, ethics, and aesthetics) and a correlative mode of judgment (pure or speculative reason, practical reason, and taste). But the question of aesthetics itself ranges between the two modes of judgment that we have just defined, between determinative judgment and reflective judgment, and it's to this transformation that we turn.

In the first place, the *Critique of Pure Reason* relegates aesthetics, and sensation more generally, to the sphere of "transcendental aesthetics," namely, an exposition of the conditions of possible experience (CPR, A19–A22). The designation of aesthetics as a "science of the sensible" grafts a preordained form on sensation and a predetermined limit on the sensible (lived and livable, so to speak), but in the *Critique of Judgment,* where Kant returns to the question of aesthetics under different auspices, a new sense of the sensible emerges. "Is there a higher form of feeling?" Deleuze asks of Kant (KCP, 47). In view of this argument, we might respond by affirming that, in the third *Critique,* feeling achieves a higher form insofar as form itself is transformed.[20] "In fact, 'form' now means this: the reflection of a singular object in the imagination," but—and this is Deleuze's point—the judgment is detached from the object, which has given rise to a "higher form of feeling" (ibid.). The aesthetic judgment we discover here, especially in the context of the beautiful, is not determinative; rather, it entertains a reflected form wherein no autonomous faculty presides over the others. "It is Kant who finally turns the philosopher into the Judge at the same time that reason becomes a tribunal," Deleuze and Guattari write, only to ask: "but is this the legislative power of a determining judge, or the juridical power, the jurisprudence, of a reflecting judge" (WIP, 72).

If Deleuze insists that aesthetic (or reflective) judgment is the ultimate problem of Kant's philosophy, the point to which all three critiques finally lead, this is because the mystery of this judgment forms the genetic disposition for all judgment. "How could any faculty, which is legislative for a particular purpose, induce the other faculties to perform complementary, indispensable tasks, if all the faculties together were not, to begin with, capable of a free spontaneous agreement, without legislation, without purpose, without predominance?" (DI, 58) In other words, aesthetic judgment is *heautonomous* insofar as "it legislates over itself. The faculty of feeling has no *domain* (neither phenomena nor things in themselves); it does not express the conditions to which a kind of object must be subject, but solely the subjective conditions for the exercise of the faculties" (KCP, 48).[21] The indeterminate accord of the faculties diffuses the apperceptive unity of the subject into a kind of spontaneous self-organization whereby we reflect on the conditions of judgment itself. Inasmuch as the deduction of aesthetic judgment compels us to go beyond the analytic conclusion—"the imagination becomes free at the same time that the understanding becomes indeterminate" (DI, 66)—it concerns no object but judgment itself. The fact of the matter is that determinative judgment is no less an art of invention than reflective judgment, but the art remains hidden, shrouded in a "mystery" that prescribes conditions of possibility without acknowledging that even those conditions have been created. Whence the importance of reflective judgment. Never governed by a faculty, reflective judgment moves "in the direction of the category in which it is reflected" (TI, 276): thought takes as its "object" not an object at all but rather the category of judgment. Reflective judgment implies the capacity to disclose a "depth that remains hidden" (KCP, 60) in determinative judgment because it draws the diagram of the forced accord, the "diffuse world conspiracy" (MI, 210), which conditions determination itself.

At the furthest limit of Kant's philosophy, Deleuze discovers the suggestion of a species of critique and a modality of judgment that engages power immanently and differentially, without recourse to a priori categories—an analysis that traverses the material plane and envisions the diagram of power in a given social field. Deleuze defines the diagram as "a map, a cartography that is coextensive with the whole social field": composed of functions and matters, a diagram consists in a "spatio-temporal multiplicity," a map of forces and relations that reveals how power is arrayed across a variety of forms (F, 34.). In this respect, Deleuze recounts an episode in Rossellini's *Europa '51* (*The Greatest Love*) when the protagonist, a woman firmly entrenched in a bourgeois life, agrees to fill-in at a factory for a few days. In her new job, Irene catches herself at the end of a shift watching workers filing in. In that hallucinatory interval, her train of thought assumes the state of reflective judgment; the determination of the scene according to given categories—workers, factory, capital, etc.—reveals a different organization of lines and singularities: "*I thought I was seeing convicts:* the factory is a prison, school is a prison, literally, not metaphorically" (TI, 20). In Rossellini's film, then, we discover the expression of a reflective judgment that Deleuze likewise finds in Foucault's histories and Kafka's fictions: the creation of a diagram that discloses the differential forces from which determinative judgment takes rise, the organization of power that subtends the social formation, threading through so many seemingly disparate institutions and disciplines—education, health, law, politics, the military.

What concerns us here, at the end of this section and in view of those to follow, is that the development of a philosophy capable of detaching itself from the state-form and of critiquing the "order of things" finds its solution in the domain of aesthetics. To this point, we have largely dwelled on aesthetics in its philosophical, and largely Kantian, framework, but Deleuze suggests that inasmuch as philosophy realizes the promise of aesthetic critique and creation, it does so by following a literary path. This conceit has never been far from our considerations, but we underscore it here because we are in a position to understand, in the most explicit sense, how Deleuze himself transforms philosophy by virtue of a turn to fiction. Hence, in the remainder of this chapter, as we endeavor to escape the "official and referential" nature of philosophy and to produce what we will call a "minor philosophy," we might keep this formula in mind: *not Kant but Kafka*. The philosophical answer to the problem of the state and of representation should not be sought in Kant but in Kafka, in an expression that no longer suffers under the conditions of an administrative machinery and moral economy of the sedentary state but is displaced onto obscure frontiers and into labyrinthine streets where new movements and novel distributions become possible: a nomadic philosophy, a gypsy politics. If we are almost loathe to call this adventure philosophy, that's because it invokes forces of thought that invariably escape the regime of representation, finding its resources in the very means which philosophy traditionally seeks to prohibit—perversity, madness, deception, *writing*. . . .

How to Do Things with Words

Majority Rules and Minority Writes

> Becoming stranger to oneself, to one's language or nation, is not this the peculiarity [*le propre*] of the philosopher and philosophy, their "style," or what is called philosophical gobbledygook [*charabia philosophique*]?
> **GILLES DELEUZE** AND **FÉLIX GUATTARI,** *WHAT IS PHILOSOPHY?*

What does it mean to write? In *A Thousand Plateaus,* Deleuze and Guattari state that "when one writes, the only question is which other machine the literary machine can be plugged into, must be plugged into in order to work" (ATP, 4). Both with and without Guattari, Deleuze never ceases to invoke writing, apart from the homogenous image of language and the normative model of linguistics, in order to affirm a conjunctive and pragmatic imperative: the "method of AND" (TI, 180). The most basic definition we can give to writing is "just connect." This point, perhaps more available in French than English, could be rendered *pas une agencement juste, mais juste une agencement,* in the sense that when we evacuate the function of justice, of law, and finally of the state-form, the assemblage of writing becomes its own rationale: just connect. Of course, we connect words, clauses, sentences, paragraphs, but we should understand connection to consist in the establishment of relations that extend beyond the closed circuit of the signifier and the closed form of the subject. Far from belonging to a totality or unity, writing is connecting and, moreover, connecting across intervals (*heterogenesis*). The proliferation of syntheses never need be submitted to the judgment of sufficient reason because they are the sufficient reason of writing.

The question of writing is neither a matter of interpretation, nor of meaning, but of *measure*—"how it becomes, and what element is going to play the role of heterogeneity, a saturating body that makes the whole assembly flow away [*fait fuir l'ensemble*] and that breaks the symbolic structure, no less than it breaks hermeneutic interpretation, the ordinary association of ideas, the imaginary archetype" (K, 7).[22] Indeed, the procedure with which we engage a writing-assemblage is this: never synthesize the manifold, but always multiply the syntheses. In the absence of universal language, the logic of the signifier, or a deep structure, to write should mean to produce an assemblage, or what Deleuze and Guattari define as a multiplicity: "An assemblage is precisely this increase in the dimensions of a multiplicity that necessarily changes in nature as it expands its connections" (ATP, 8). Departing from the labor of hermeneutics, which establishes the primacy of a subject and an object to be worshiped ("our modern way of believing and being pious": the flesh and the word [AO, 171]), an assemblage demands *quantification.* To "quantify writing" is to create new "units of measure" (ATP, 4) that respond to what a book creates, its lines and singularities, connections and combinations. "There is no difference between what a book talks about and how it is made," Deleuze and

Guattari say (ibid.). A book is what it does, what it creates and induces, which is why we must pose it against the regime of representation.

This distinction can be cashed out in terms of linguistics itself, namely, between the theory of "pragmatics," which conceives of language as an assemblage of "inherent variation" (D, 34), and the theory of a "deep structure" that poses every linguistic instance according to universal and normative conditions. *A Thousand Plateaus* explicitly identifies the latter theory with Noam Chomsky, the avatar of a field that we now identify as cognitive or neurolinguistics.[23] But whatever we call it, Deleuze contends that the majoritarian image of linguistics trades the play of intensities for a unified, consistent, and homogeneous system. As we will see, Deleuze stakes out the very question of minorization in opposition to the dominant tendency of linguistics, of proper usage and comprehensibility, which formulates the image of a language system around the presupposition of all that is constant and invariable—norms, rules, standards, syntax, structures, etc. Most linguists "presuppose the existence of a system of language," he says, "and even if they claim not to, these other linguists still remain committed to universals like subject, object, message, *and* code, competence, etc." (TRM, 70). Indeed, the arborescent image of language bears witness to a tradition of linguistics based on the discovery of a grounded and normative structure. The codifications and limits to which this assemblage gives rise may explain why Deleuze and Guattari have always resisted the concept of ideology, of a world mediated by "imaginary relation" (Althusser), as the basis for understanding language. There is nothing imaginary about the power of language, which is expressed in an endless series of impositions, of "order-words" (*mots d'ordre*). The sense of the French phrase denotes slogans and clichés, but Deleuze and Guattari also draw on its literal meaning insofar as every instance of language is tantamount to a directive.[24] "Order-words do not concern commands only, but every act that is linked to statements by a 'social obligation.' Every statement displays this link, directly or indirectly. Questions, promises, are order-words," Deleuze and Guattari write (ATP, 79). "Language is made not to be believed but to be obeyed, and to compel obedience" (ibid., 76).

The hermeneutics of suspicion is such that we tend to think of the way language conceals and distorts the operation of power, but Deleuze contends that language should be measured in the direct application of oppression that we find in every speech act. In *A Thousand Plateaus*, he and Guattari begin their chapter on linguistics by foregrounding precisely the immanence of language and power.

> When the schoolmistress instructs her students on a rule of grammar or arithmetic, she is not informing them, any more than she is informing herself when she questions a student. She does not so much instruct as "insign" [*enseigne*], give orders or commands. A teacher's commands are not external or additional to what he or she teaches us. They do not flow from primary significations or result from information: an order always and already concerns prior orders, which is why ordering is a redundancy. The compulsory education machine does not communicate information; it imposes upon the child semiotic coordinates. (75–76)

With respect to language, we might recall Godard's dictum, quoted by Deleuze, that "all children are political prisoners" (Neg, 41). Children are always at the behest of a system of subjectification. We are accustomed to say that the name awaits the child, but what this means is that in every child the subtle inscription of subjectivity will be undertaken anew—discipline "the gentle way."[25] While the school organizes a disciplinary diagram, as Foucault has shown ("the school is a prison"), Deleuze's point is that language itself constitutes a collective machine of subjection; "it imposes upon the child semiotic coordinates possessing the dual foundations of grammar (masculine-feminine, singular-plural, noun-verb, subject of the statement-subject of enunciation, etc.)" (ATP, 75). Children are submitted to the codifications of order-words, forced to succumb to the rules and protocols of language, and only occasionally do we glimpse that what we call education might also consist in a kind of vast micropolitics: say this, recite that, speak properly, assume your rightful place, *behave* (*soyez sage!*). "Every order-word, even a father's to his son, carries a little death sentence—a Judgment, as Kafka put it" (ibid., 76).

As a collective assemblage of order-words, language does not exist distinct from bodies but is intermingled in (nondiscursive) matter. We see this most clearly in what J. L. Austin first termed "performative utterances," namely, those statements that do not describe or reflect a given state of affairs but immanently intervene to transform it: "to order, question, promise, or affirm is not to inform someone about a command, doubt, engagement, or assertion but to effectuate these specific, immanent, and necessarily implicit acts" (ibid., 77).[26] When a preacher pronounces two people married, the statement enacts a new state of affairs and transforms the bodies into a state that did not obtain before. But far from restricting this mode of discourse to an exceptional class of "nondiscursive presuppositions"—wedding vows, baptisms, legal decisions—Austin defines language itself by virtue of the "illocutionary force" that characterizes every utterance as much as every body.[27] Deleuze occasionally speaks of the "sayable and the seeable," of language and visibilities, but the collective assemblage of order-words consists in "the set of all *incorporeal transformations* current in a given society and *attributed* to the bodies of that society" (ibid., 81). Whereas corporeal transformations mark the development and maturity of bodies, most notably the human body, Deleuze invokes the incorporeal aspect of the socius, which expresses something that cannot be located in the body and yet will define the body itself: "majority, retirement, any given age category, are incorporeal transformations that are immediately attributed to bodies in a particular society" (ibid.). Subjects are invoked and actualized in the course of discourse, not according to predetermined grammatical constants but rather according to the pragmatics of linguistic variables, a vast and metamorphosizing assemblage.

William Burroughs said that "language is a virus,"[28] but what Deleuze teaches us is that the virus is precisely that of order and order-words, which produce a strange new malady: the "regular and predictable" human. The virus is *control,* the "nature and transmission of order-words in a given social field" (ibid., 79), which produce the organization of subjects (*subjectivation*) and the determination of meaning (*signifiance*). The machinic assemblage of order-words formulates the image of a proper and correct syntax, of a correct means of thinking and expression. By force of habit and forgetting, we tend to make ourselves at home in a language, becoming unconscious or insensate to the compulsory enterprise of order-words. But there are always a few who are in a position to feel the force of language. We have already referred to children, for whom the instantiation of grammar, which has not yet established a permanent foothold, often seems like a kind of merciless indoctrination. Likewise, we could refer to minorities, for whom the regime of another's language places them in the peculiar position to witness the power relations that mark what are, seemingly, the simplest of pleasantries. Finally, we could refer to certain schizophrenics and psychotics, who experience the feeling of language as an alien presence, a signifying machine that they sense has been implanted like a microchip in the brain or a radio transmitter in a molar. To what do these cases, and especially the case of the schizo, refer if not the nature of language as an "influencing machine"?[29] "There is no mother tongue," Deleuze and Guattari readily admit, but there is always "a power takeover by a dominant language within a political multiplicity. Language stabilizes around a parish, a bishopric, a capital" (ATP, 7).[30]

But if the imposition of language is always and invariably a kind of micropolitics, under what auspices can the incidents and events that compose language be synthesized? What is the image of language that promotes its stabilization and that constitutes a "language of power"? The latter phrase denotes the way that certain vernaculars historically arose as the means of codifying exchanges within growing commercial and state bureaucracies. In Europe, for instance, the industry of print capitalism in the fifteenth and then sixteenth centuries, having inundated the relatively small readership for Latin texts, turned to publishing particular vernaculars in order to create and address new markets. Beyond the wealth of religious publications that followed Luther's *Ninety-five Theses,* Benedict Anderson describes how the initial alliance between print capitalism and theological texts gradually gave way over the next several centuries to the "slow, geographically uneven spread of particular vernaculars as instruments of administrative centralization."[31] In other words, incipient languages of power at once attacked the hegemony of one language, Latin, in order to establish an even more profound hegemony over other languages, subsuming all the established and itinerant vernaculars, widespread sociolects, and particular ideolects under an overarching authority. The development of official languages effectively conditioned the modern state-form by determining the complexity of burgeoning bureaucracies, which in turn distributed literacy around an increasingly codified and contractualized vernacular.

Inevitably, then, the emergence of the modern nation-state relied in large part on the coincidence of national languages and increasingly distributed national literatures. If very nearly "all modern self-conceived nations—and also nation-states—have 'national print-languages,' "[32] as Anderson contends, this is because in forms and formality, in terminology and codes, literature came to facilitate and regulate all manner of discourse. Writing developed as a means of stabilizing language and, in the same stroke, evoking the image of a body-politic. Literature coincided with, but also codified and popularized, the standardization of language: in Great Britain, for instance, this process can be traced to the late eighteenth century, when the standardization of spelling, punctuation, and lexicography was overtly undertaken by the state and tacitly pursued by a national literature. As Deleuze and Guattari suggest, literary texts were quickly folded into the mechanisms of bureaucracy—embedded in the relations of the authority linked to the state ("the author function is linked to the juridical and institutional system that encompasses, determines, and articulates the universe of discourses"[33]), determined by the form of a mimetic activity governed by the state ("the law of the book is the law of reflection, the One that becomes two" [ibid.]), and redoubling the state itself ("noble, signifying, and subjective organic interiority" [ATP, 5]). Nothing consolidated the emergence of languages of power as much as the formation of the "state-apparatus book," which was inscribed in "state-sponsored" relations (of authorship, purchase, etc.) at the same time that it distributed the image of a state-language. In his diaries, notably, Kafka admits that his beloved Goethe epitomizes the great German representative of the state literary form inasmuch as he codified a particular syntax that continues to exert a kind of pressure on writing. "Goethe probably retards the development of the German language by the force of his writing," Kafka explains in his diaries.[34] "Even though prose style has often traveled away from him in the interim, still, in the end, as at present, it returns to him with strengthened yearning and even adopts obsolete idioms found in Goethe."[35]

It is in the context of the state-form and of the literature it underwrites that Kafka dares to imagine an altogether different kind of writing. In contrast to the image of a major language and a major literature, to a codified syntax and a belletristic tradition, Kafka sketches a literature of small peoples: minor literature is collective without being either "official or referential." In his remarkable diary entry from Christmas day of 1911, Kafka imagines a sociology on the basis of literature, a revolutionary assemblage of letters, that is not only minor but also *utopian*.[36] In the space of a few spare though brilliant pages, he describes a kind of literary society sufficient to reclaim the phrase from the banalities of privilege, stuffiness, and elitism to which it is so often consigned. For Kafka, this society reaches from the emergence of a thriving literary exchange, including magazines and a vigorous book trade as well as an "eagerness" for new texts; to the development of a literary culture, not only of writers but of readers, who draw on writing to enable the discussion "of the antithesis between father and sons" and catalyze "the assimilation of dissatisfied elements"[37]; and, finally, to the genesis of a popular and literary discourse—"a keeping of a diary by a nation which is something entirely different from historiography and results in a more rapid (and yet always closely scrutinized) development."[38]

It should be clear enough why the prospects of minor literature derive from the absence of a major literature. Sketched in his diary, enacted in his fiction, Kafka imagines this literary-political assemblage in contrast to the dominant language and the statuary of great books. In a minor literature, where "talents do not abound" or at least where greatness does not reign over the expression of talent, "the conditions are not given for an *individual enunciation*, which would be that of some 'master' and could be separated from the *collective enunciation*" (K, 17). The status and signifier of the master must be perpetually absented, since this is what frees enunciation to become collective: in a minor literature, every statement is a matter of struggle, of rivalry, but for that reason each statement is the expression of a multiplicity. Minor literature opens the sphere of what Kafka calls "genuine competition" and this point bears underscoring. Kafka describes a literary agonism that, in light of our discussion of Greek philosophy, we might imagine along the lines of a warrior theater: literature becomes not only the medium but the sphere of rivalries that cannot take place in the symbolic and sedentary spaces of major languages and literatures, where tradition conditions the individual talent. The competition to which Kafka alludes, however much it entails economics, is ultimately literary insofar as it describes an agonism of ideas as a competition between ideas that will be traded and exchanged, transformed and parlayed, developed or thrown away, but always in some measure *lived* (in the process of writing, Kafka says, he experiences "states during which I lived entirely in each idea, but also realized each one of them"[39]). Among such a small people, literature is life: it ceases to be bounded by transcendence and assumes the sense of an immanent politics. Far from existing at a great and exalted distance, the literary canon is a continual source of encounter and experience; "the writings themselves do not act independently upon the memory" (die Dichtungen selbständig die Erinnerung nicht beeinflussen],[40] Kafka says, because they are integrated in the present creation of memory, as rememoration, collective fabulation of past and future.

And yet, for all of his hopefulness, Kafka concludes his elucubration of minor literature on a note of sadness: as he wrote to Max Brod, "There is hope, but not for us" (Sinn ist da—nur nicht für uns).[41] Looking back over the diary entry, then, Kafka admits, "It is difficult to read—just when one has felt this useful, happy life in all one's being."[42] In other words, the usefulness of minor literature reproaches the conditions in which literature and life exist today. Minor literature must be imagined precisely because it does not exist, but inasmuch as this is the case, minor literature acquires the sense of a process, a kind of invention that aspires to a literary socio-politics. The literary and political life of a small people does not exist (or not yet) but must be created, virtually, in a kind of writing that commences by inventing a different use of language. For this reason, the concept of a minor literature begins not just with Kafka but with those writers (Deleuze names Beckett, Joyce, Luca, Bene) who live far from home in their "own" language or who choose to inhabit a foreign language—in any case, those who experience the displacement and dispossession that marks a different kind of writing. The intuition of the child, the immigrant, and the schizo, to which we have referred, is finally expressed in those writers who are strangers to, or estrange themselves from, their mother tongue.

This prospect recalls the humiliating moment in Joyce's *Portrait of an Artist as a Young Man* when Stephen Daedalus, a student at Trinity College, finds himself speaking to one of the English deans. In the midst of the conversation, which concerns the difference between literary language and the language of the marketplace, the dean directs Stephen to tend to the fire: "You must choose the pure oil and you must be careful when you pour it in not to overflow it, not to pour in more than the funnel can hold." Stephen responds with surprise: "Is that called a funnel? Is it not a tundish?"[43] The distinction between literary and commercial language thus gives way to a more profound disjunction: in the word "funnel" Stephen discovers the diminishment of his own vernacular and the dispossession of "English." The nonreferential space that opens up between the two terms, between "the Queen's English" and its Irish "bastardization," is not a matter of mere translation but of scarcely spoken prepossession. Soon enough, Stephen feels the slow growth of an embolism that constitutes something like a blockage in language itself:

> The language in which we are speaking is his before it is mine. How different are the words home, Christ, ale, master, on his lips and on mine! I cannot speak or write these words without unrest of spirit. His language, so familiar

and so foreign, will always be for me an acquired speech. I have not made or accepted its words. My voice holds them at bay. My soul frets in the shadow of his language.[44]

What Stephen realizes, and what Deleuze affirms, is that language and literature are always riven by power. The most mundane instance of language is political—or, rather, *micropolitical*—but this is also why Deleuze refuses to identify minor literature solely with the explicit politics of nation or exile. The colonial and postcolonial circumstances with which we often identify minor literature provide only the most exemplary and exploitative conditions for its creation. As Deleuze and Guattari ask: "How many people today live in a language that is not their own? Or no longer, or not yet, even know their own and know poorly the major language that they are forced to serve?" (K, 19).

Especially today, when colonization takes place as much at home as abroad, when the order-word has acquired new technological means of delivery, the task of minor literature is the task of all literature: to make this dispossession the condition of writing, not as victimization, nor as martyrdom, but as the power of an impersonalization. Only by virtue of making ourselves inscrutable minorities and elusive nomads do we realize a new politics and a new people. Far from propagating the myth of a dominant nation or given race, the minor exists only "in the name of the oppression it suffers: there is no race but inferior, minoritarian; there is no dominant race; a race is not defined by its purity but rather by the impurity conferred on it by the system of domination. Bastard and mixed-blood are the true names of race" (ATP, 379). Indeed, the becoming minor of literature is realized in a kind of becoming-scapegoat: under the auspices of Gregor Samsa, Kafka becomes the contemptible bug against whom (or which) the rest of the family vent their anger and frustration; in the guise of Bartleby, Melville transforms himself into the pitiable scrivener whom everyone comes to despise; in the figure of le Momo, Artaud makes himself the object of God's wrath, torture, and infinite condemnation. In each case, the expression of becoming evokes the forces of judgment, whether in the framework of the family, the police, or the clinic, but in the scope of minor literature perhaps this must be risked if we are "to have done with judgment." In other words, the judgment that the writer encounters must be made the promise of the last judgment—not in the sense of a consummating or total judgment ("the end of days") but rather the end of judgment itself, which leaves life thereafter to play out its own cruel and joyous theater of intensities. Minor literature adopts "this role and this function of collective and even revolutionary enunciation: it is literature that produces an active solidarity, despite skepticism" (K, 17).[45]

Deterritorializing Language

> To be a foreigner [un étranger], but in one's own language, and not simply as someone who speaks a language other than his or her own. To be bilingual, multilingual, but in a single and same language, without even dialect or patois.... One attains this result only by sobriety, creative subtraction. Continuous variation has only ascetic lines, a touch of herb and pure water.
>
> **GILLES DELEUZE** AND **FÉLIX GUATTARI,** *A THOUSAND PLATEAUS*

Is it possible to create a philosophy along the lines of a minor literature? "Is there a hope for philosophy, which for a long time has been an official, referential genre?" Our answer begins with Deleuze and Guattari's analysis of Kafka, who furnishes the three basic characteristics of minor literature that we will transpose, in the remainder of this chapter, into the characteristics of minor philosophy. First, in minor literatures "language is effected with a high coefficient of deterritorialization [la langue y est affectée d'un fort coefficient de déterritorialisation]"[46]; second, "everything in them is political [c'est que tout y est politique]"[47]; third, in minor literatures "everything takes on a collective value [une valeur collective]"[48] (K, 18, 19).

In "Nomad Thought" Deleuze suggests that Nietzsche's closest writerly relative is actually Kafka, with whom he shares a capacity for expressing intensities that, like nomadic tribes, come from beyond the frontiers of the state, from the Outside, "as both agent and object" of deterritorialization (DI, 257). But what of Deleuze? In the remainder of this chapter, we will argue that not only does Deleuze minorize philosophy but that his elaboration of minor literature ought to be taken as a description of his own writing. Each characteristic of minor literature can be understood, mutatis mutandis, as the characteristic of Deleuze's *minor philosophy*. Hence, we begin by considering the deterritorialization of language in light of the argument we have traced to this point—that both literature and philosophy pursue minorization—and in view of the countless misunderstandings to which this argument gives rise.

The most suggestive and enigmatic of the three characteristics, the contention that minor literature "is effected with a high coefficient of deterritorialization" (K, 16) is sufficiently vague to invite all kinds of claimants who say, "We are the true minor literature; we are the true minority." But nothing could be further from minorization, which deterritorializes the very transcendent elements with which major literatures are tacitly identified. Minor literature has nothing to do with romantic reminiscences of the homeland (*Heimat*), Deleuze says, but with dispossession, and this intuition can help to clarify the confusions that surround its deterritorialization. In *Kafka* and elsewhere, Deleuze and Guattari always insist on the distinction between a minor language and a minor literature. We know that there are countless minorities for whom the prospect of assimilation is at once the most personal and most political of problems. And we know that minor language may harbor whole populations who reject the dominant language, refusing to assimilate, preserving their own "memories of underdevelopment." But minor literature is something else—not an alternative but a becoming. Minor languages may well constitute the conditions for the creation of a minor literature, but by no means necessarily: while minor languages are ubiquitous, the creation of a minor literature designates something rare and singular, a language within language, a new syntax.

This sense of minor literature is prone to two kinds of confusion—what we might call linguistic contrivances and contrived languages—from which it must be detached if it is to deterritorialize the "official and referential" nature of language. In the first place, minor literature is potentially mistaken for linguistic playfulness, as if we could achieve deterritorialization on the basis of so many surreal gestures and ludic contrivances. But as Deleuze and Guattari write, "no typographical cleverness, no lexical agility, no blending of or creation of words, no syntactical boldness, can substitute" for the minor (ATP, 24).[49] These flights of fancy, they argue, are "more often than not merely mimetic procedures used to disseminate or disperse a unity"—and as a result, they only end up confirming "a different dimension for an image-book" (ibid, 22). In the second place, minor literature is potentially mistaken for contrived languages, as if we could achieve deterritorialization by virtue of creating a wholly original language. But nonnatural languages are no less apt to codify a unity of language or to give rise to such a unity: among linguists, in particular, invented languages enjoy a privileged (and, we might say, festishized) place insofar as they are said to attest to a universal "language instinct" and an equally universal "deep structure." But neither the deliberative invention of a language (e.g., Esperanto, Klingon) nor the accidental invention of one (e.g., pidgin languages created for trade, such as Russian–Norwegian *koiné* or the seafarers' language of *barese,* or the more controversial cases of twin-speak and the "made-up" languages of children raised in isolation) can undertake the becoming of the minor.

Both linguistic contrivances and contrived language actually sustain the dominance of a major language, and in this regard Deleuze and Guattari insist that minor literature demands the deterritorialization of language itself. In short, "minor literature doesn't come from a minor language [une littérature mineure n'est pas celle d'une langue mineure]."[50] Rather, it is "that which a minority constructs within a major language" (K, 16). Minorization does not report or represent this delirium but enacts it as so many expressive intensities that create a stammering new syntax within the dominant language. Minor literature "is neither another language nor a rediscovered patois, but a becoming-other of language, a minorization of this major language, a delirium that carries it off, a witch's line that escapes the dominant system" (CC, 5). In this light, the minor is less a matter of particular circumstances in which writers have the good or bad luck to be reared (which invites the absurdity of rejoicing in one's miserable circumstances, the good fortune of misfortune), than of the singular conditions that literature must assume, no matter what its circumstances. "We might as well say that minor no longer designates specific literatures but the revolutionary conditions for every literature within the heart of what is called great (of established) literature," Deleuze and Guattari admit (K, 18).[51] "Even he who has the misfortune of being born in the country of a great literature must write in its language, just as a Czech Jew writes in German, or an Ouzbekian writes in Russian" (ibid.). A minor literature always concerns a becoming-foreign, a becoming-strange beyond estrangement (*Verfremdungseffekt*), and in this regard we might refer to Kafka's anecdote of the swimming champion who paddles himself downstream, finally going ashore only to find that the language spoken, though his own, strikes him as utterly incomprehensible—that he is a foreigner in his native land and tongue. "I speak the same language as you, and yet I don't understand a word you're saying" (CC, 5).

The case of Kafka proves exemplary in the development of a minor literature because, with respect to his own circumstances, he lived this estrangement and experienced it as the "impossibility" of writing. Kafka was reared as
a German-speaking Jew in Prague, where the vast majority of residents were
speakers of Czech and the rest were comprised of a Jewish minority and an
even smaller faction of "well-to-do ethnic Germans."[52] While he learned to
speak Czech fluently, we would have to say that Kafka's native tongue was
German, though it was a German inflected by both Czech (*Mauscheldeutsch*)
and Yiddish (*Kuchelböhmisch*).[53] Among the Jewish minority, these linguistic
hybrids bear witness to a reaction against the "poverty" of Prague German,
which consisted in an empty and bureaucratic language—"a sort of ceremo-
nial language subsidized by the state."[54] As Klaus Wagenback adds, Prague
German was like a "foreign body, dry and colorless like paper": it lacked the
spirit of a living, speaking population to breathe life into its static and evac-
uated order-words. What had happened? In the interest of domination and
communication, of making the minor language the major or official language
of Prague, the semantic and syntactic possibilities of the German had been
dramatically diminished, generally reduced to simpler elements, specifically
suited to the predilections of Czech. Nothing characterized Prague German
so much as its profusion of "errors," of nonstandard usages, and of grammatical irregularities. "Separated from a naturalizing, integrating ethnic German
speech community," Ronald Bogue writes, German "had undergone numerous deformations through its proximity to Czech, and its impoverishment had
forced a limited vocabulary to assume multiple functions, each term taking
on an intensive and shifting polyvocality."[55]

While Kafka laments the problems of writing in so many contexts, we are
concerned here with the way the politics of language make it *impossible* for
him to write and how, in turn, Kafka invents a *possibility*. As Deleuze and
Guattari explain:

> The impossibility of writing other than in German is for the Prague Jews the
> feeling of an irreducible distance from their primitive Czech territoriality. And
> the impossibility of writing in German is the deterritorialization of the German
> population itself, an oppressive minority that speaks a language cut off from the
> masses, like a "paper language or an artificial language; this is all the more true
> for the Jews who are simultaneously a part of this minority and excluded from it,
> like 'gypsies who have stolen a German child from its crib.'" (K, 17)

Thus, Kafka's singular genius is to have pushed this impossibility to the point of a withering deterritorialization. But how does this happen? As a Jew living in Prague, a speaker of Czech conversant in Yiddish and, to a lesser extent, Hebrew, Kafka's choice to write in German, an official or "paper language," situates him irremediably as a stranger within language and thereby conditions his own strange treatment of language. The "impossibility" that defines minor literature will become its solution—adopt the stolen child and then, yes, gently starve it. Withhold the tropes, the borrowings, the substance that would otherwise nourish it: make yourself a "deterritorialized language, appropriate for strange and minor uses" (ibid.). Technically, Kafka's German is correct and proficient, but for all of its rigorous sobriety—or, rather, *by dint of its rigorous sobriety*—he detaches it from the major language. Kafka opts to write in the most stripped-down, technical, and seemingly least literary language, desiccating his idiom to the point of "a willed poverty" (ibid., 19). He deterritorializes language according to the most "sober revolutionary" procedures, stripping it of all affectations, such that the minimal emissions of words vibrate with remarkable intensity: as Deleuze says in another context, Kafka make words visible, makes them *shine*.[56]

We might imagine the anorexic project of developing a minor literature along the lines of Kafka's story "A Hunger Artist" (*Ein Hungerkünstler*) who revels in the intensities and deliriums of his own attenuation. If this story claims a singular place in Kafka's oeuvre, as is often suggested, this is because it provides something like the secret of his fiction, the emaciated experiment/experience with which he deterritorializes all of his writing. "Fasting is also a constant theme in Kafka's writings," Deleuze and Guattari suggest (K, 20). "His writings are a long history of fasts" (ibid.). In his inimitable and starving style, Kafka's nondescript narrator begins the story by explaining how the practice of "professional fasting," once the subject of great interest across Europe, evoking the fascination of crowds and the marvel of children, has become a kind of spectacular atavism, a bizarre holdover from another era.[57] This eventuality coincides with the sad lot of the story's eponymous and unnamed protagonist, who once enjoyed great popularity but has now outlived it: his talent still intact, if not better than ever (at what age, after all, does a hunger artist reach the height of his or her powers?), the artist faces the prospect of an indifferent audience and an anonymous existence. The subtlety and genius of Kafka's style here lies in moving *imperceptibly* from a description of the fate of an "art" to that of an "artist" who is never named, nor described, but reduced to the emptiness of a pronoun that appears, after a page and a half, as the most impersonal of singularities—*a* hunger artist.

Ironically, the more the hunger artist suffers from a "change in public interest," the more he is deserted by "the amusement seekers," the more he resolves to "astound the world by establishing a record never yet achieved."[58] Thus, the artist fires his manager-impresario and hires himself to a circus where no one can prevent him from performing a feat of incomprehensible fasting. As the story ends, and the hunger artist has attenuated himself to the point of all but disappearing, the circus overseer finally empties his cage out and installs a new attraction, a beautiful and muscular panther, a vision of "life." And yet, the vitalism expressed in the story takes flight from the anorexic artist, who literally disappears in a fabulous becoming, a nomadism *sur place*, that no mere physiology can possibly measure. The life to which Kafka gestures, and about which Deleuze writes, is vitalist without being organic—an intensity that cannot be located in bodies or states of affairs, but in a style that will invent them both. "Style, in a great writer, is always a style of life too," Deleuze maintains, "not anything at all personal, but inventing a possibility of life, a way of existing" (Neg, 100). We typically associate "lifestyle" with a kind of commercial and consumerist banality—"You've come a long way, baby!"— but nothing could be further from the sense of minor literature and its style of writing. Hence, as Deleuze explains to Claire Parnet, "I should like to say what a style is. It belongs to people of whom you normally say, 'They have no style'" (Dia, 4). This definition should not be confused with the claim of style-less objectivity, neutrality, and universality to which we alluded at the beginning of the chapter. This latter is all the more firmly conditioned by the tacit presuppositions of an image of thought, whereas Deleuze affirms nonstyle as the dissolution of those very presuppositions. Nonstyle is achieved by dint of displacement, dispossession, *subtraction*. In Kafka's writing, nonstyle entails what we have called a "willed poverty," a style that "proceeds by dryness and sobriety" in order to strip back all affectations, leaving nothing behind but intensities (K, 19). "The closer language approaches it, the more 'sober' style becomes" (TRM, 374). Hence, one could conclude that there is "no such thing as style," as Deleuze says, but only on the condition that we affirm nonstyle as the "purest expression of style" (ibid., 371). What would be the "elements of a style to come which does not exist?" (PS, 165).[59]

The answer, with which we conclude our discussion of the deterritorialization of language, lies in Deleuze's frequent, if cryptic, call for an end to metaphor. This exhortation may well strike us as surprising, even counter-intuitive, given Deleuze's panoply of colorful concepts, which are frequently designated by peculiar neologisms (e.g., faciality) or strange, borrowed expressions (e.g., the body without organs). But Deleuze constantly asserts that his concepts are not metaphors and that the creation of concepts is in no way metaphorical. Rather, concepts are expressive intensities. Especially in the context of what we have called minor philosophy, concepts are developed as part of a war machine turned against the method of regulating language and stabilizing words (LS, 287)—above all, with metaphor. In his own writings, on the spare occasions when he deals with metaphor, Deleuze dismisses the trope, saying that it "just confuses matters and has no real importance" (Neg, 29) or that "there are no metaphors, only combinations" (Dia, 117). But in his writings with Guattari, for reasons that will become clear, Deleuze wages an open attack on metaphor. In *Kafka*, for instance, they say that writing destroys metaphor and achieves its expression in the absence of metaphor. "Kafka deliberately kills all metaphor, all symbolism, all signification, no less all designation. Metamorphosis is the contrary of metaphor," they write (K, 22). "There is no longer any proper sense of figurative sense, but only a distribution of states that is part of the range of the word. The thing and other things are no longer anything but intensities overrun by deterritorialized sound or words" (ibid.).

There are no metaphors in Kafka's writing: Gregor Samsa wakes us to discover that he has turned into a bug, and *"this was no dream."* [60] Kafka "means" exactly what he writes, and his writing is what it does. There is no waking up from a dream, no recourse to another level of reality, no world behind the world. The man is a vermin, the father is a tyrant, the law is a broken and sadistic machine, children are political prisoners, the school is a prison. But what would it mean to write philosophy in the absence of metaphor and to develop a kind of nonstyle? Or, what amounts to the same thing, how can we deterritorialize philosophy? Inasmuch as philosophy traditionally redoubles the state-form, as we have seen, it does so by reproducing the metaphor of the state—the structure and sovereignty of the signifier—in each subject (of the signifier). Hence, the resolution to "kill metaphor" (K, 60) acquires its problem-structure when we understand metaphor to consist in a most fundamental expression of a dominant language, namely, the power to organize the social field. Indeed, the signifier consists in the automatism of a virtual system existing in each of us simultaneously and unconsciously. In Lacan's terms, with which Deleuze and Guattari duly wrestle and which they duly derange, the social field is organized around the imposition of the "Name-of-the-Father" (*Nom-du-Père*), the "paternal metaphor," which governs the distribution jouissance according to a prohibition (*Non-du-Père*) and, thence, the production of a lack of being (*manqué-à-être*) that defines the subject as the universalization of neurosis.

We might recall here our discussion of *Anti-Oedipus* in chapter 1, where we argued that schizoanalysis undertakes the foreclosure of the Name-of-the-Father in the interest of unleashing the errancy of thinking and writing otherwise (*les non-dupes-errent*). Likewise, Deleuze's minor philosophy begins on the basis of foreclosing the paternal metaphor and, thereby, unleashing language into all manner of becoming. If metaphor is the contrary and enemy of metamorphosis, underwriting the promise of *signifiance* and subjectivization, of regularity and predictability, then we must have done with this overcoding dimension. Like a minor literature, a minor philosophy always eliminates the transcendent dimension of metaphor. Only then can we affirm the indetermination of a substantial multiplicity. This is "the only way that one belongs to the multiple: always subtracted" (ATP, 7). For this reason, Deleuze and Guattari formulate the literary assemblage, the book as multiplicity, according to the principle of "n−1." If we take "n" to be "the number of dimensions one already has available," the art of subtraction consists in the removal of the unary trait (*traite unaire*) or overcoding dimension (ibid.). The one is the shadow or specter that determines and overdetermines the multiple, attributing it to a preliminary unity, and so the multiple is destined to remain still-born without the benefit of this subtraction: only by getting rid of the transcendent function, by foreclosing that which confers a form of "common sense" across all other dimensions, can writing unleash the becoming of the multiple.

But what does this mean in the context of philosophy? After all, philosophy is not a language, at least not a natural one, but Deleuze and Guattari insist that philosophy possesses a syntax that, like a language, takes on a dominant order and habitas. Consider for a moment that the grammatical sense of syntax—as an ordering of words according to the rules of connection and relation—is historically preceded by the use of the term to characterize the systematic constitution of minds and bodies. In the context of the history of philosophy, we might say that the dominant syntax is modeled on precisely such an image of thought, of mind and body. Based on the syntax of subject and object, the illusion of a homogenous set of conceptual constants, philosophy will have to be submitted to a derangement of a new syntax, a foreign language within its language. "The concept's baptism calls for a specifically philosophical taste that proceeds with violence or by insinuation and constitutes a philosophical language within language," Deleuze and Guattari conclude; "not just a vocabulary but a syntax that attains the sublime or a great beauty" (WIP, 8).

Minority Report

Free-Indirect Philosophy

> The proper name (*nom propre*) does not designate an individual: it is on the contrary when the individual opens up to the multiplicity pervading him or her [*traversant de part en part*], at the outcome of the most severe operation of depersonalization, that he or she acquires his or her true proper name. The proper name is an instant apprehension of a multiplicity. The proper name is the subject of a pure infinitive comprehended as such in a field of intensity.
>
> **GILLES DELEUZE** AND **FÉLIX GUATTARI,** *A THOUSAND PLATEAUS*

Whether as minor literature or minor philosophy, writing consists in making the dominant syntax stutter by inventing a "foreign language in language." Having considered what is, surely, the most prominent and debated aspect of writing—the deterritorialization of language—we are now in a position to conclude this chapter by analyzing the other two traits of minor literature: the creation of a collective assemblage of enunciation and the formulation of a people who are missing. It is worth noting that both of these characteristics introduce the possibility for resurrecting metaphor, offering new dimensions of transcendence, as the subject or as subjects ("*the* people"): thus, in elaborating both characteristics, we begin straightaway by affirming that each must *prolong* deterritorialization.

The collective assemblage of enunciation can be defined as nothing less than the deterritorialization of the subject. We traditionally define the state-apparatus book on the basis of a holy trinity of author, narrator, and character, for these are the means with which we "attribute the book to a subject" (ATP, 4). The god of the book is a "three person'd God" (Donne); but whichever god we choose to worship, and *because* we choose to worship, we "overlook the working of matters, and the exteriority of their relations" (ATP, 3). Whenever we return to any one of these gods, we miss the measure of the writing itself, the connections it makes possible, the virtual reality it invents. "It is to fabricate a beneficent God to explain geological movements," Deleuze and Guattari conclude (ibid.). Thus, the writing-assemblage only seems to open itself to us in all its complexity when we foreclose the subject of the signifier (or the signifier of the subject) that reigns over the book as its unique or transcendent dimension. Heretofore we have considered this process according to the foreclosure of the overarching dimension, metaphor, which codes all the other dimensions. Under the auspices of this paternal metaphor, language assumes the image of a stable system of subjectification and *signifiance,* but when we eliminate this overcoding dimension, writing becomes a nomad's art that, without home or habitas, dissolves the subject into singularities and lines, novel distributions and linkages—a collective assemblage of enunciation.

The task of making this assemblage, which describes the second characteristic of minor literature, is by no means particular to literature (in the cinema, for instance, we find fantastic collective assemblages of words and things, enunciations and visibilities). But in the context of writing, the literary assemblage and the philosophical assemblage undertake an experiment that will bear them into the most intimate of relationships. Deleuze sketches this relation in the context of a crucial distinction which we have effectively maintained but which we must now expressly mention: the author versus the writer. Broadly construed, Deleuze differentiates between *the function of authorship,* which remains linked to legal and juridical relations that designate the subject as an organizing and originating entity; *and the process of writing,* which annihilates the last vestiges of individuality and interiority. "The author is a subject of enunciation, but the writer—who is not an author— is not" (Dia, 51). Of course, the writer retains his or her proper name, but the name does not refer to the subject of a demonstrative (*this* man, *that* woman, *this* philosopher, *that* novelist). Rather, it designates "something which happens" (ibid.)—a singular and impersonal event.[61] If writing is becoming, even becoming-imperceptible, what does the writer become if not a collective assemblage, traversing so many different perspectives and voices? "There are no individual statements, there never are. Every statement is the product of a machinic assemblage, in other words, of collective agents of enunciation (take 'collective agents' to mean not peoples or societies but multiplicities)" (ATP, 37).

The construction of a collective assemblage of enunciation cannot be separated from the literary invention of "free-indirect discourse." Hence, in order to understand this aspect of minor literature, and to envision Deleuze's own free-indirect philosophy, we might begin by situating this discourse in its literary history. While language absolutely refuses any definitive point of departure, always going "from saying to saying" (ibid., 76), the irony of free-indirect discourse is to have been signed and dated in the history of the novel. The British novel began (quasi) autobiographically, with the recording of memoirs (*Robinson Crusoe*) and letters (*Pamela*), but the development of the genre in the eighteenth century constitutes, at least in some sense, the efflorescence of a third person form that allowed for an overarching and well-nigh divine perspective (*Tom Jones*) or a moralizing presence (*Belinda*). Broadly construed, these novelistic modes are dominated by the combination of direct discourse, which records the particularity of a statement (I said, " . . . "), and indirect discourse, which represents the generality of a sentiment (she said that . . .). But the development of the third person also catalyzes the development of a "free-indirect discourse," whereby the impersonal or third person expression accommodates the utterances or thoughts of a character without providing a "tag clause" to specify him/her.[62] Ostensibly operating as indirect discourse, the free-indirect is prototypically defined by virtue of the capacity of the narrator to slip into the perspective—the spirit—of a character. In *Cecelia* (1782), one of the earliest and most renowned examples of novelistic free-indirect discourse, Frances Burney frequently closes the distance between the third person and her taciturn heroine by drawing on the resources of the free-indirect to express Cecelia's sensibility in the midst of an endless series of social negotiations. As to whether Cecelia will secure "the best offices and best wishes" from Miss Belfield, Burney writes: "Would she obtain them? no; the most romantic generosity would revolt from such a demand, for however precarious was her own chance with Delvile, Miss Belfield she was sure could not have any."[63] Even in the last part of the sentence, where names appear as objects of speculation, we might ask: Whose speculations are these? Who is speaking here?

Direct and indirect discourse achieve a measure of certainty by virtue of the pronouns they provide, whether named or not, since these determine the statement according to a perspectival authority and linguistic propriety. Typically, then, direct and indirect speech subjectivize reportage, hitching writing to a signifying chain, to the subject of enunciation (the one who speaks) or the subject of the statement (the one who is spoken of). As such, language exists "only through the distinction and the complementarity of a subject of enunciation, who is in connection with sense, and a subject of the statement, who is in connection, directly or metaphorically, with the designated thing" (K, 20). But free-indirect discourse introduces a dimension of language within language that both mixes subjects and eludes any subject; in Deleuze's words, "It consists in slipping another expressing subject into a statement which already has an expressing subject" (TRM, 371).[64] How do we know when we are in the presence of the free-indirect, how can we codify its occurrence? Linguists and narratologists have enumerated a litany of rhetorical clues, instances of diction, and even grammatical indicators that mark the presence of another subject within the third person. Perhaps there's no more obvious marker of this discourse than the rhetorical question, as in Woolf's *Mrs. Dalloway*: "She would take her silks, her scissors, her—what was it?—her thimble, of course, down to the drawing room, for she must also write and see that things generally were more or less in order."[65]

But the countless rhetorical indices with which we labor to verify free-indirect already suggest the sense in which this discourse is not rhetorical at all. We labor to glean the markers of the free-indirect at the cost of grasping the writing machine—the collective assemblage of enunciation—that produces this discourse. Introducing the habits of thought and speech into the narrator's own, the free-indirect constitutes a language within language that is nothing less than a "unique syntactical form" (TRM, 371). The importance of this point cannot be overestimated, since it concerns not only free-indirect discourse but, more largely, the very project of a minor literature to write otherwise (*autrement*). The free-indirect opens up a kind of liminal space, what Deleuze elsewhere calls a "zone of indiscernibility" (ATP, 280) between speech and narration, between the idiomatic and the indirect. Surely this explains the debates it's inspired. While some characterize it according to a "dual-voice hypothesis" that claims to find the "markers of two discursive events," others argue that the free-indirect consists in "a speakerless (narratorless) representation of one subjectivity or self."[66] What these claims confirm, beyond their opposition, is that the problem of free-indirect discourse is the problem of *a syntax that defies the codification of a subject or speaker.* The efflorescence of free-indirect discourse constitutes the means to manipulate and, at its furthest extreme, elude the determination of subjectivity. The free-indirect does not report what "I" see, nor does is represent what "she" thinks: it simply—and not so simply—*presents.*

It is for this reason that indirect discourse, *especially "free" indirect discourse,* is of exemplary value: there are no clear, distinctive contours; what comes first is not an insertion of variously individuated statements, or an interlocking of different subjects of enunciation, but a collective assemblage resulting in the determination of relative subjectification proceedings, or assignations or individuality and their shifting distributions within discourse. Indirect discourse is not explained by the distinction between subjects; rather, it is the assemblage, as it freely appears in this discourse, that explains all the voices present within a single voice. (ATP, 80)

In this sense, Deleuze argues, the free-indirect "is the determinant element of syntax" (TRM, 371): far from consisting in an occasional instance, the discourse underwrites every instance of speech, which reports and will be reported, in an endless series of inflections. The question, then, concerns the use to which we put the free-indirect, the literary and philosophical ethos that animates the syntax. Burney's literary heir, Jane Austen, provides a particularly illuminating example of free-indirect discourse against which to measure the modern flights that Deleuze favors. In effect, Austen makes the free-indirect the mechanism of a moral syntax that reaffirms proper sense in relation to the proliferation of indirect speech that she seems to love but, also, fear. Austen read Burney with pleasure, sharing her fondness for the variety of idiolects that society conditions in its countless exchanges and collects in a vast assemblage of enunciation. At parties, in homes, on the street, Austen's characters engage in a version of what might otherwise be called civil society but what we might designate, in Deleuze's term, as a "machinic assemblage." To put it another way, Austen creates "a precise state of intermingling of bodies in a society, including all the attractions and repulsions, sympathies and antipathies, alterations, amalgamations, penetrations, and expansions that affect bodies of all kinds in their relations to one another" (ATP, 90). In her novels, this intermingling is expressed in and by language, in talking and reading and even writing, which carry characters along in their tides and wakes. Bodies are brought together and repelled in an endless series of linguistic encounters—always affective, usually polite, and more often than not *pointless.*

Far more than Burney, Austen relishes "the 'nothing-saying' of talk, the hum of ready-made, prefabricated language that smoothes everyday intercourse for good or ill and is almost communal."[67] Her novels and their societies traffic in triviality and nattering, innuendo and gossip, but this is precisely what interests us here, in the context of our discussion of free-indirect discourse and on the way to free-indirect philosophy. We generally take gossip ("talk") to be the most degraded genre of speech, but for this reason it is also something like its purest instance, the vanishing point where "talk becomes its own purpose." Gossip is speech so desperate for an object that it will take someone's word for it.[68] "In purely sociable conversation," Georg Simmel once wrote, "the topic is merely the indispensable medium through which the lively exchange of speech unfolds its attractions"[69]—but sociability winnows away the topic to virtually nothing ("nothing-saying"). This contention becomes clearer when we grasp that, for Deleuze and Guattari, there is no such thing as direct speech. Rather, language is that which "always goes from saying to saying" (ATP, 76). Because language claims no "non-linguistic origin," no first referent, its very *substance is repetition.* "Language is not content to go from a first party to a second party, from one who has seen to one who has not, but necessarily goes from a second party to a third party, neither of whom has seen" (ibid., 77).

Thus, even when reference is ostensibly restored in Austen's novels—when we learn what "really" happened, when the horrible misunderstanding, cruel deception, or awful truth is revealed—this happens by virtue of indirect speech. In the incestuous hamlets of Austen's fictions, where boredom stokes interest on the slightest pretext, we cannot even conceive of reference outside of the circulation of rumors, of "reports," which fly from one character to another, one gathering to another. "We believe that narrative consists not in communicating what one has seen but in transmitting what one has heard," Deleuze and Guattari write (ATP, 76), and they might as well be speaking of Austen. Insofar as a merest sliver of information "is only the strict minimum necessary for the emission, transmission, and observation of orders as commands" (ibid.), rumor, slander, bitchery, opinion—the "crudest" of speech acts—also constitute sublime instances of narrative. In other words, Deleuze and Guattari write, "Narrative is hearsay" (*Ouï-dire*) (ibid.).[70] For Austen, the moral order does not, cannot intervene between words and things but insinuates itself within and among the order of statements, the collective assemblage of enunciation, with which it is coterminous. "The order does not refer to prior significations or to a prior organization of distinctive units" (ibid.), but what this means, in Austen's novels, is the invention of a free-indirect discourse that provides the means of evaluating speech and speakers. We should think of Austen as a kind of Platonist who always insists on a distinction within opinion—or, rather, between bad opinions based on faulty judgment and "right opinions"—that her novels will stage, most notably in relation to their heroines but, also, to other characters, all of whom will be evaluated on the basis of their own capacity to evaluate, to interpret, to discern the true from the false.[71]

In Austen, faulty judgment is exercised and symptomatized by virtue of a predilection for hearsay, speculation, and gossip. To this "bad taste," her novels respond by developing a distinctive free-indirect discourse that accommodates the redundancy, politeness, and conventions of speech even as it proffers a sense of organization and moral authority—the ordering of orderwords. Take *Emma,* where the narrator slips into the free-indirect in the context of those characters whose moral and psychological foibles remain most suspect. The sensible inflections of the snide Mrs. Elton, the doddering Mr. Woodhouse, and of course "clever" Emma are filtered through the third-person narrative, whereas the moral center of the novelistic universe, Mr. Knightly, is all but exempt from the technique. Naturally, we could say that this is because Knightly is the least likely to entertain rumor, but the point only confirms our argument: because he is disinclined toward reports, the narrator gives Knightly to us "straight," without coloring, exaggeration, or (too much) irony. Knightly is capable of conveying the truth (apart from "news") because he embodies, more closely than anyone else, the ideal—"honest and open"—order of things. Here and elsewhere in Austen's novels, the politics of free-indirect discourse could be said to consist in the means of relinquishing the narrative voice in favor of so many other voices—only in order to return the metaphysical-moral subject to the stage that much more certainly. What her free-indirect discourse gives up in the way of pronouns it takes back in the form of judgment: the effects may be ironic, sympathetic, subtle, and complex, but we would almost never call them morally vague.[72] Austen deploys the free-indirect not just to reveal characters but to judge *character*.

Not unsurprisingly, Deleuze's investment in free-indirect discourse derives from its subsequent, and largely modernist, development. Where Austen had deployed it to preserve and consolidate a sensible hierarchy, the increasingly experimental development of free-indirect discourse makes it the means of exfoliating subjectivity—whether in a brilliant stream of consciousness or in a heterogenesis of sentiments that produce a kind of "anonymous murmur" (F, 9). Beyond Austen's novel, or even "the second Emma" (Bovary), whose consciousness Flaubert unfolds in a torrent of free-indirect discourse, we might say that Deleuze locates the precursor to his own philosophical technique in the modernism of Joyce, Woolf, Beckett, and Kafka. As a matter of taste and style, Deleuze effectively aligns the first two writers with a more decadent mode of minor literature that resolves to "artificially enrich" language, "to swell it up through all the resources of symbolism, or oneirism, of esoteric use, of a hidden signifier" (K, 19). Hence, Deleuze and Guattari add, Joyce "never stops operating by exhilaration and overdetermination and brings about all sorts of worldwide reterritorializations" (ibid.). But in the course of this chapter we have elaborated "the other way" of minor literature, which "proceeds by dryness and sobriety, a willed poverty, pushing deterritorialization to such an extreme that nothing remains but intensities." Kafka remains the avatar of this procedure because he pursues deterritorialization to the point where language relents all symbolism and signification, where the "paper language" of Prague German realizes a fleshless vitality. "Since the language is arid, make it vibrate with new intensity," Deleuze and Guattari advise (ibid.). "Arrive at a perfect and unformed expression, a materially intense expression" (ibid.).

Kafka does this by evacuating himself from expression in order to speak and see through others, with whom the friction of the free-indirect produces new intensities, new lines of flight. In "The Metamorphosis," for instance, Kafka's third-person narrator lives uncomfortably close to his characters, as if the cramped apartment they inhabit forces the narrator to share not only the space but also a voice. Here as elsewhere, the presence of an objective third-person voice, separable from and uninflected by characterological perspective, all but ceases to exist. In Dorrit Cohn's words, Kafka renders "the entire fictional world as an uninterrupted vision avec"[73]: he never gives us an event without sense, so to speak, because the free-indirect subtly and invariably renders the event through the perspectival sensibility of another. In the case of "The Metamorphosis," however, the focalization of this vision undergoes a remarkable shift: from the moment he wakes up to find himself changed, Gregor Samsa constitutes the source of a free-indirect discourse, one that operates with uncanny sobriety in relation to the events of the story. His first thought, after all, is to blame his transformation on the demands of his job: "Traveling about day in, day out. It is much more irritating work than doing the actual business of the office, and on top of that there's the trouble of constant traveling, of worrying about train connections, the bed and irregular meals, casual acquaintances that are always new and never become intimate friends. The devil take it all!"[74] From his initial denial until its final pages, the story is focalized through Gregor, who in turn informs the narrative with a rationality that, as the story progresses, lapses into spare questions and mute curiosity. When his sister Grete plays music one night, we are told, "Gregor crawled a little farther forward and lowered his head to the ground so that it might be possible for his eyes to meet hers. Was he an animal, that music had such an effect on him?"[75]

That same night, when the family goes to sleep, Gregor dies. But in the aftermath, the story expresses a "passage of life" that extends beyond even Gregor's terminated line of flight. The third-person narrative undergoes its own metamorphosis inasmuch as the story shifts from a collective assemblage organized primarily around the intensities of Gregor's becoming, to the remaining members of the family—his mother, father, and sister—who feel "as if a burden had been lifted from them."[76] In its conclusion, "The Metamorphosis" follows the drama from the discovery of the carcass, to the gradual development of familial "composure," to the confirmation of their scarcely spoken "new dreams and excellent intentions."[77] Together, a family once more, the three leave the apartment for a day in the country. On the tram ride, Kafka writes, "they canvassed their prospects for the future, and it appeared on closer inspection that these were not at all bad."[78] With this happily bourgeois scene, which draws toward the triangle in order to mark their distance from the dead vermin, we pass into a stifling and sedentary familial assemblage.

As they ponder the "immediate improvement in their condition"—they have jobs, their prospects are good—we can glimpse the "libidinal economy" of regulated subjects and recognizable relations, the awful "reconstitution of the familial block" (K, 87). Indeed, "The Metamorphosis" ends with the parents watching their daughter, who "sprang to her feet first and stretched her young body" in a moment that is nothing short of grotesque.[79] The slender image of the girl alive to the world is, as Maurice Blanchot once said, "the height of horror"[80]—a vision of life that seems to exist in the cruelest comparison to the inscrutable and inhuman transformation that has preceded it. Like "A Hunger Artist," this story seems to parade a demonstration of "bare life" before our eyes as if to shame its antecedent. The animal—the panther but, more frightening still, the human animal, this girl—appears to embody pure vitality, but as Deleuze and Guattari say, it is an image of "mortuary perfection" (K, 39). What does this mean?

While the family triangle draws together on the basis of the aura of death, the impersonal line of life (*Aion*) unfolds beyond the organization of subject and object, in the passage between "the livable and the lived"—the passage of writing itself. "There is always an indescribable joy that springs from great books," Deleuze once said, "even when they speak of ugly, desperate, or terrifying things" (DI, 258). In "The Metamorphosis," the joy lies in not only the unprecedented becoming of Gregor but, as such, in the becoming that traverses all subjects and leaves them all behind. Gregor becomes a bug, his sister becomes a panther (of sorts) and they are all, strangely, animals—but the story elaborates a becoming that, traversing the most hideous state of affairs and actualizing the most horrible possibilities, consists in *freely, indirectly* eluding all of them in a becoming-imperceptible. This is what it means to deterritorialize the subject: in the absence of centralizing, subjective authority, free-indirect discourse insinuates itself in an agglomeration of languages within languages, of speakers within speakers. "It is almost as if every expressing subject contained others, each of which speaks a diverse language, the one in the other" (TRM, 371).

While we have seen as much in Kafka's work, we can conclude here by understanding how Deleuze deterritorializes the subject in the course of creating a "free-indirect philosophy." The constituents of this philosophy should already be obvious in the course of Deleuze's numerous commentaries, each of which offers the possibility of writing with and through another. Readers of Deleuze will immediately attest to the countless conjunctions he inspires, the numberless voices he channels; in each case, he makes the encounter an occasion to think and write through another, and then another, and another, until his own voice attains its own impersonal singularity. We have already quoted Deleuze's admission that, in response to the crushing inertia of the academic tradition of philosophy, "the main way I coped with it at the time was to see the history of philosophy as a sort of buggery" (Neg, 6). But what's important here, and what brings to light Deleuze's method, is the explanation that follows:

> I saw myself as taking an author from behind and giving him a child that would be his own offspring, yet monstrous. It was really important for it to be his own child, because the author had to actually say all I had him saying. But the child was bound to be monstrous too, because it resulted from all sorts of shifting, slipping, dislocations, and hidden emissions that I really enjoyed. (Ibid., 6)

This is the work of free-indirect philosophy with which Deleuze engages other philosophers, no less the history of philosophy, reproducing it both faithfully and monstrously. The subject of each commentary "had to actually say all I had him saying" (Neg, 6), for only then will the philosopher own up, however reluctantly, to the child. In any case, the perverse nature of commentary deterritorializes both subject and object into an "anonymous murmur" (F, 47) of voices. This paradox is perhaps resolved when we grasp that Deleuze's commentary would reveal to its subject that there is no subject as such and that the proper name no longer designates the source of writing but its result. Ultimately, "the collective assemblage is always like a murmur [*rumeur*] from which I take my proper name, the constellation of voices, concordant or not, from which I draw my voice" (ATP, 84).

We might conclude our consideration of the collective assemblage by considering its process—and it is always "in process," becoming—along the lines of a kind of demonic possession. In *Dialogues* Deleuze explains that the Greeks forged a fundamental distinction between gods and demons: "Demons are different from gods, because gods have fixed attributes, properties and functions, territories and codes: they have to do with rails, boundaries, and surveys" (Dia, 40). Divinity involves the mythic distribution of *timai*, the partition of the prizes and rewards, of territories and even peoples. Among the gods, we speak of attributes, of "properties and functions," which territorialize the earth.

We know the vast mythography: Athena, the "gray-eyed" goddess of war who presides over the city that bears her name and its autochthonous myth; Poseidon, the resentful and irritable god of the sea who inhabits so many cities, including Athens, as a kind of secondary presence. By comparison, demons are never attached to attributes, to a fixed identity or sure epithet, because demonism is a mad process of connection across intervals, a helter-skelter of heterogenesis, a *nomadic nomos*. "Then there is a completely other distribution which must be called nomadic, a nomad nomos, without property, enclosure or measure," Deleuze writes in *Difference and Repetition* (36). "Here, there is no longer a division of that which is distributed but rather a division among those who distribute themselves in an open space" (ibid.). We have already spoken of Nietzsche's daimonism, of his instinctive suspicion of higher values and his determination to smash all remaining idols, but Deleuze's free-indirect philosophy constitutes a demonism that traverses the scattered fragments of the statuary, that selects names and voices, utterances and images, in a collective assemblage of enunciation. "Such a distribution is demonic rather than divine, since it is a peculiarity of demons to operate in the intervals between the gods' fields of action, as it is to leap over the barriers or the enclosures, thereby confounding the barriers between properties" (DR, 37). Of course, demons undertake a possession, but their being is the becoming between so many bodies and states of affairs—a passage of life. "What demons do is jump across intervals, and from one interval to another," Deleuze writes (Dia, 40), and he should know: what else is his philosophy but a demonism that passes between possessions, always forging connecting and relations in the collective assemblage of enunciation, auguring the presentiment of a people and a politics to come. "Nothing pertains or belongs to any person, but all persons here and there in such a manner as to cover the largest possible space" (DR, 36).

"Style as Politics"

And how could we not feel that our freedom and strength find their place, not in the divine universal nor in the human personality, but in these singularities which are more ours than we ourselves are, more divine than the gods, as they animate concretely poem and aphorism, permanent revolution and partial action? What is bureaucratic in these fantastic machines which are peoples and poems? It suffices that we dissipate ourselves a little, that we be able to be at the surface [*que nous sachions être à la surface*], that we stretch our skin like a drum, in order that the great politics begin.

—**GILLES DELEUZE**, *LOGIC OF SENSE* (TRANSLATION MODIFIED)

Much has been said about the politics of minor literature, but all of our conclusions take their measure from Deleuze's singular declaration that "*the people are missing*" (TI, 216). Adapted from Paul Klee's remark that "the people is essential yet lacking" (ATP, 346), analyzed in the context of Kafka's writings, and parlayed in a variety of other domains (cinema, but also history, science, and philosophy), this proposition has assumed the status of a mantra in Deleuze's work, often repeated but still enigmatic. After all, why do we say that "the people are missing"?

At first glance the statement seems to signify the sad capitulation to the pessimism of the present, to the impossibility of politics today, but perhaps we should understand something else entirely. For Deleuze, the paradoxical invocation of a "people who are missing" does not represent the negation of a people nor their totalization, but rather the affirmation of a people and politics to come: "the people no longer exist, or not yet" (TI, 126).[81] The people are *positively* missing and, therefore, must be *invented*. In this sense, the politics of minor literature consists neither in representing a determinate state of affairs, nor in raising the consciousness of given conditions, so much as in creating a new ensemble of relations and possibilities.[82] To Kafka, to all minor writers, the resources of a traditional or major literature are closed off; when we say that writing is impossible, we mean that the only possibility is to write—to create the conditions of possibility in writing that would make writing as such possible (*autocatalysis*). Minor literature must invent the possible, and this is no easy proposition. If "writing" takes place so rarely, as Deleuze suggests, this is because it emerges beyond our expectations, beyond representation, even beyond the Law with which we typically designate the limits of the possible. Writing "moves in the direction of the ill-formed or incomplete," traipsing into frontiers that are only imagined in the process of writing itself (CC, 1).[83]

Thus, when Deleuze and Guattari aver that "national consciousness, uncertain or oppressed, necessarily exists by means of literature" (K, 16), they suggest that literature assumes its most overtly political and revolutionary guise when it becomes the province of the "uncertain or oppressed"—those who claim no nation or land as their own, those who possess no autonomous state or sovereignty, those on whom a language is imposed or who become displaced within the dominant language. In these cases, the "invention of a people to come" is the only possibility. Indeed, minor literature emerges from its impossibility inasmuch as its obstacles, blockages, and prohibitions condition a rare and vital intimacy between the personal and the political. Far from having to dialectically develop a connection between the subject and the nation, the private and the public, minor literature renders even the most personal and intimate instances political. "What in great literature goes on down below, constituting a not indisputable cellar of the structure, here takes place in the full light of day," Kafka writes in his diaries; "what is there a matter of passing interest for a few, here absorbs everyone no less than as a matter of life or death."[84]

The juxtaposition here between major ("great") literature and minor literature recalls the distinction between the author and the writer that we have already discussed, as if the author were born of the right to privacy and "a room of one's own" and the writer were born from cramped, squalid communalism. But minor literature is not a question of one's subjectivity (race, gender, class) or circumstances (developed and developing world). Rather, it is a question of pursuing a kind of deterritorialization that makes room for populations and tribes, a collective assemblage of enunciation. Inasmuch as state literature suppresses politics, confining it in so many metaphors and displacements, finally stuffing what really "goes on" into a netherworld that will have to be retrieved, endlessly interpreted, by the masters, psychoanalysts and scholar-priests, minor literature embarks on a kind of writing that requires no interpretation: who can afford private, bourgeois neuroses in the midst of this collective where everyone already knows everyone else's business? The congestion of the minor needs no interpretation because if one's politics aren't already shared, then they are sure to be soon enough: searching desperately for any modicum of space, for any stray window to open or fire escape to duck out, for any possible escape, what need has minor literature to be *hermeneutically sealed*?

In light of this description, it is hardly surprising that the concept of minor literature has met with ample skepticism and, in certain circles, severe criticism, as if it traded on a kind of misery, romanticizing the experience of real poverty and real suffering. Doesn't Deleuze finally profit at the expense of minorities whose reality, both material and mental, he ostensibly colonizes? Don't concepts such as minorization and nomadism finally demarcate, to use Deleuze and Guattari's own term, the "capture" of particular features in the service of an entirely different, intellectual world—our so-called "first world"? These questions ought to return us to the essential strangeness of a minor literature, which Deleuze and Guattari define apart from both minor languages and minorities sensu stricto. The conditions for a minor literature may be more "available" among minorities and in the context of minor languages, but the fine-grained distinctions to which this gives rise—languages within languages, castes within minority-formations—cut across first and third world in ways that make those categories already archaic. The ostensible divisions of these "worlds" have become impossibly complicated (literally, "folded together and over one another") by the shuffling of global socioeconomic conditions. The second world, which referred to nations under the sway of Soviet influence and centralized ("communist") economies no longer exists, and the other two have become increasingly difficult to designate or justify. When Western nations face debt crises that we associate with what used to be called the third world, the landscape of power relations requires a new map, not topographical but topological, not longitudinal but transversal, to account for the curious proximities and distances of wealth and class, leisure and suffering.

Rather than demonizing the minor in the name of outworn concepts (like "minority") which are already the provenance of a linguistic and juridical dominance, we might recognize the minor as a response to these conceptual conditions. The notion of the minor does not entail a third world because it develops a concept based on singular traits that may just as well be located in any world—in our world. Language is riven by power, literature is always political: the conditions for minorization exist within every major language, but they must be extracted and created along singular lines of circumstance and improvisation. The conditions of the minor do not refer to any infinitely particularized attribute nor to any transcendental condition but to the multiplicity "of peoples, who remained to be united, or should not be united, for the problem to change" (TI, 220). The minor does not "belong" to a minority, to a people who have been ethnically or socioeconomically predetermined, because the minor designates a process of becoming, of minorization, that even minorities must undertake. Take the writer Frantz Fanon, who hails from the French colony of Martinique (where he is taught by Aimé Césaire) but emigrates to France (where he trains as a psychiatrist), and then relocates to Algeria (where he becomes a member of the FLN and the analyst par excellence of decolonization). In short, Fanon's life is a "becoming-minor" by dint of which he produces a collective assemblage of enunciation.

Perhaps what Deleuze so sparsely invokes—not the condition of strict socioeconomic, or political circumstance but the creation of new conditions, a people to come—should be phrased epigrammatically: *not the third world but the third person*. The remainder of our discussion is dedicated to understanding this formulation, but none of our analyses will make sense if we don't discern what the "third person" proffers or why Deleuze makes it the basis for pursuing "style as politics" (DI, 254). The logic of minor literature, arising as it does from the intuition that language is (mircro-) political, consists in developing what is at once a new style of expression and a new politics. This sense of this assertion—style as politics = syntax as politics—crystallizes in the context of linguistics, where the consideration of person and tense reveals a passage from the first person, to the third person, to the impersonality of a people to come. No doubt, this passage is anticipated by the great French linguist Emile Benveniste, who sought to analyze and complicate the "subject in language." As he argued, the question the self, subject, or person is unwittingly concealed by linguistics because its presence is assumed in order to explain the order of language rather than being posed as a problem. Hence, in lieu of this homogenous image of language, which presumes a consistent logic operating across all three singular pronouns (I, you, she), Benveniste poses the problem of the subject "in the widest possible sense," that is, in terms of what he calls discourse—"language in action."[85] In considering both "Relationships of Person in the Verb" and "The Nature of Pronouns," where the question of subjectivity in language is most clearly at stake, Benveniste comes to a singular and irrefutable conclusion: the discursive nature of the person shifts from the first and second person to the third. The first and second person are rendered meaningful in the moment of speaking insofar as "I" and "you" are deployed and defined according to each new speech-act ("I'll go to the store, while you watch the kids"; "no, I'll stay, you need the break"). Right now, I am evoking and embodying "I" in this disquisition, but were you to ask me a question, the pronominal roles would be reversed, and I would assume the position of the addressee—"I" would be your "you." Thus, the significance of "I" and "you" is always specified and actualized in the instance of their utterance: "I" is the one who says "I," and "you" is the one "designated by the 'I' and cannot be thought outside of a situation set up by starting with 'I.' "[86]

By contrast, the third person is displaced from the discursive dyad, reduced to the spectral existence of another to whom you and I refer but whose being remains elusive. If the third person does in fact say something about someone, that someone—the "personal" element of these denominations—is in absentia. Hence, the "third person is always treated differently and not as a real verbal 'person,' " Benveniste notes,[87] and it is perhaps no accident that at particularly remarkable moments Benveniste himself assumes the most impersonal form of third-person: "one should be fully aware of the peculiar fact that the 'third person' is the only one by which a *thing* is predicated verbally."[88] Inasmuch as he seeks to clarify this "*thing*," Benveniste redraws the question of the person on a new, and more finely grained, categorization. Because the "I" defines and differentiates itself discursively, as the transcendent and self-referential instance in relation to all others, Benveniste calls it the subjective person. Conversely, the "you" will always be defined by the "I," in relation to a statement to which it is external; for this reason, Benveniste calls "you" the "non-subjective person."[89] But both of these cases should be distinguished from the "he, she, it, one, etc.," which constitute something else. The third person is neither internal nor external to the statement but otherwise and absent. As Benveniste notes, the distinction between these terms is even more clearly expressed in Arabic, where grammarians define the first person as "the one who speaks," the second person as "the one who is addressed," and the third person, most significantly, as "the one who is absent." But how do we infuse that absence and give life to those who are missing?

Perhaps, finally, what Benveniste suggests is what Lawrence Ferlinghetti called "the fourth person singular,"[90] for the "one" (*l'on*) exists as an evanescent and impersonal instance that is as much the absence of one: accommodating potentially everyone, the one is plural but, for this reason, always intervallic, passing between and among. Both inclusive and exclusive, interior and exterior, the "one" should always be affirmed as a becoming *imperceptible*. The one is the "one who is missing," but what we are suggesting here is that only by virtue of acceding to this perverse condition, beyond and before the subject, does minor literature invent a "people to come." Why? In

"Literature and Life," the short and aphoristic piece that opens *Essays Critical and Clinical,* Deleuze identifies literature itself with "the power of the impersonal—which is not a generality but a singularity at the highest point: a man, a woman, a beast, a stomach, a child. It is not the first two persons that function as the condition for literary enunciation; literature begins only when the third person is born in us that strips us of the power to say 'I'" (CC, 3). For Deleuze, this description suits a number of writers, but the case of Kafka is almost paradigmatic. In his diaries, Kafka famously claims to have become a writer when he gave up the first person for the third. In *The Castle* (*Das Schloß*), his last and ultimately unfinished novel, Kafka began by writing in the first person, from the perspective of K. the land surveyor, only to rewrite the early portions of the text in a third person given over to free-indirect discourse. For Kafka, literature literally consists in the passage from I (*Ich*) to he (*er*), but the third person must be emptied out of its contents. The aim of a minor literature is to inhabit and perpetuate this absence, this becoming, by virtue of a kind of ventriloquism: always speaking through others, Kafka gives over his proper name to a becoming impersonal, to an anonymity and imperceptibility—"the one" (*l'on*)—which can accommodate a people to come.

The eventuality of the impersonal nonperson seems to have emerged, for Deleuze, from a kind of equation with which we can summarize the process of the minor and the production of a people to come. We began by considering the assertion that "minor literature possesses a high coefficient of deterritorialization," namely, the subtraction of the overcoding dimension of language and the transcendence of the paternal metaphor: n−1. Then, we considered the avowal that minor literature creates a collective assemblage of enunciation, which we identified with the population of the deterritorialized plane. The deterritorialization of language forecloses the transcendent or overcoding dimension in order to formulate a collective assemblage of languages within languages, of subjects within subjects: a multiplicity. This is "the only way that one belongs to the multiple: always subtracted." Finally, we are considering the imagination of a politics on the basis that "the people are missing," which we have identified with the expression of not only the third person but an impersonal nonperson. In other terms: n−1 = *l'on*. As opposed to what is traditionally called a multiple qua manifold, which remains attributable to a subject, the assemblage qua multiplicity constitutes a substantive inasmuch as it refers to no subject as a preliminary unity. Of the literary assemblage, at least as Deleuze and Guattari envision it, we would have to say that it "has neither subject nor object, only determinations, magnitudes, and dimensions that cannot increase in number without the multiplicity changing in nature" (ATP, 8).[91]

The logical or paralogical operation of "n–1 = *l'on*" designates the supple procedures of a style that subtracts in order to add. Always begin by deterritorializing the transcendent dimension: only then do we unmoor ourselves from that which defines the self or subject—only then do we conjure the hospitality sufficient to gather other peoples, tribes, and populations, "the polyphony of expressing subjects and the modulation of statements that constitute style" (TRM, 373). As Deleuze explains to Claire Parnet:

> In each of us there is, as it were, an ascesis, in part turned against ourselves. We are deserts, but populated by tribes, flora and fauna. We pass our time in ordering these tribes, arranging them in other ways, getting rid of some and encouraging others to prosper. And all these clans, all these crowds, do not undermine the desert, which is our very ascesis. On the contrary, they inhabit it, they pass through it, over it. (Dia, 11)

Inasmuch as a people exists, they exist (virtually, we might say) in the writer as a collective assemblage of enunciation. If the subject is merely the product of the habit of enunciation, the articulation and repetition of "order-words" according to which it acquires the semblance of identity, in free-indirect discourse we are "free" to become a pack, a crowd, a mass, a people. To produce a minor literature, then, the writer becomes a kind of nonentity, emptying himself or herself of all marks of unique personality, originality, and even "greatness" in order to slip into so many other voices, to become the murmur from which all voices are raised, to create the voice of "a people to come."

These populations inhabit us like a great murmur of voices through which we speak and which speak through us. Deleuze seems to anticipate this process in his more strictly philosophical writings, especially *Difference and Repetition,* where the problem of an impersonal assemblage of voices is elaborated in quasi-ontological terms. Traditionally, the question of Being has been posed analogically, in terms of the relation of genus and species, but Deleuze treats Being univocally, as a pure ontology of differences. "There has only ever been one ontological proposition: Being is Univocal," Deleuze says in *Difference and Repetition* (DR, 35). But univocity should never be confused with unity (the One), since as Deleuze adds: "A single voice raises the clamor of being" (ibid.). This last phrase, which is the subject of great contention and confusion, might seem to suggest that all species testify to the supra-genus of Being unless we heed the distinction that marks univocity: "In effect, the essential of univocity is not that Being is said in a single and same sense, but that it is said, in a single and same sense, of all its individuating differences and intrinsic modalities" (ibid., 36). It is worth noting that Deleuze takes his distance from ontology qua Being in his later works, a point to which we'll return, but what we are suggesting here is that univocity is resumed, and enacted, in Deleuze's work under the auspices of a collective assemblage of enunciation, which is no less the anonymous murmur that "raises the clamor" of voices. Before it is ever a matter of ontology, we might say, univocity is a matter of style, the impersonal ontogenesis from which even ontology emerges. What speaks in *l'on* is not the One (Unity) but univocity, since the impersonal form empties itself out to accommodate countless enunciations: n-1 = *l'on* ("One-All").[92]

For Deleuze, the becoming-imperceptible to which the writer aspires is no less the basis for a remarkable hospitality to populations with, through, and about whom one fabulates a new people—not a state of subjects but the vanishing point of the virtual lines of flight we unleash. Minor literature "expresses these assemblages, under conditions that are not given outside, and that exist solely as diabolical powers to come or as revolutionary forces to construct" (K, 18). Nothing is represented in minor literature, least of all a people: we're beyond that. Representation is conceived on the basis of a kind of expression that Deleuze and Guattari associate, in the framework of stratification, with the usurpation of contents of bodies extracted from matter. But minor literature detaches itself from contents. Beyond ideals, categories, and representation, minor literature hurtles us "towards a pure Form which sets itself up as an autonomous vision of the content" (MI, 74). This is what it means to displace metaphor with metamorphosis, namely, to create an "expression that outdistances or advances" the state of affairs we typically identify with content.

And so we reach the most elusive aspect of minor literature, the power of fabulation—the power of the false. What does this mean? In a diary entry that dates from the writing of "The Judgment," Kafka reflects on the strange task of writing, which consists in a kind of creationism that, even in the most mundane and modest of circumstances, strikes him as remarkable. "When I write without calculation a sentence like the following: 'He looked out the window,' this sentence is already perfect."[93] Resonating with a similar moment in "The Judgment" itself—" . . . and with his elbows propped on the writing table [he] was gazing out the window at the river, the bridge, the hills on the farther bank with their tender green"[94] —the sentence is "perfect" inasmuch as its five simple words realize a world of their own. Perfection consists in the power of the most banal expression to create a perspective, a frame, and the possibility of an event, which in a single stroke have set the "real world" ablaze, burning it to the ground, removing the ground, and then creating an entirely new one in its place. Of the composition of "The Judgment," which seized him in a frenzy, Kafka says: "The fearful strain and joy, how the story developed before me, as if I were advancing over water. Several times during this night I heaved my own weight on my back. How everything can be said, how for everything, for the strangest fancies, there waits a great fire in which they perish and rise up again."[95] *Pars destruens, pars construens.*

In this respect, the expression of minor literature outstrips determination, emanating intensities and unleashing lines of flight that leave the world behind. Minor literature invents "expression that precedes contents, either in order to prefigure the rigid forms into which they are going to flow, or in order to make them take off along a line of flight or of transformation" (K, 85).[96] By dismantling the rigid social assemblage, which amounts to nothing less than affirming that "the people do not exist," a minor literature invents a collective assemblage and creates, a "people to come." As Deleuze and Guattari write in *A Thousand Plateaus:*

> the problem of the artist is that the modern depopulation of the people results in an open earth, and by means of art, or by means to which art contributes. Instead of being bombarded from all sides by a limiting cosmos, the people and the earth must be like vectors of a cosmos that carries them off; then the cosmos will be art. From depopulation, make a cosmic people; from deterritorialization, a cosmic earth. (ATP, 346)

In this light, finally, we ought to hazard defining minor philosophy as the invention of precisely such a "cosmic people"—the invention of a people to come. The risk of such a philosophy is inestimable, for it will have to situate itself in a present devoid of people: in a sense, minor philosophy expressly begins when the world has ended, in the wake of an apocalypse, at the point when representation itself has been razed and the world must be created once more. "The transmutation already takes effect with every great book, and every great book constitutes a health of tomorrow [*Tout grand livre opère déjà la transmutation, et fait la santé de demain*]" (DI, 258).[97] This is the task that a new political philosophy, a minor philosophy, confronts today: the people are missing, but the real question is—will philosophy rise to the task of their invention?

5

PHILOSOPHY IN AN INHOSPITABLE AGE

The Problem of the Present

No Country for Old Men?

> He was too tough to experience disappointments and resentments—
> negative affections. In this nihilist *fin de siècle*, he was affirmation.
> Right through to illness and death. Why did I speak of him in the past?
> He laughed, he is laughing, he is here. It's your sadness, idiot, he'd say.
> **JEAN-FRANÇOIS LYOTARD,** *MISÈRE DE LA PHILOSOPHIE*
> (*ON THE OCCASION OF DELEUZE'S DEATH*)

IN THE PREVIOUS FOUR CHAPTERS, we have traced Deleuze's expressive
line of flight from his apprenticeship to philosophers, especially minor ones,
the creation of his own minor style. This trajectory might well suggest a kind of
triumphal narrative or *Bildungsroman*—the fulfillment, so to speak, of "great
expectations"—were we not to understand that his style never announces the
ascension of a subject (an author-form), nor reconciles that subject to a state-
form (a major philosophy), but deprives writing of these attributes. Indeed,
Deleuze increasingly undertakes what we have called an ascesis, the evacuation of entrenched regimes and encrusted opinions, in order to deterritorialize the plane of immanence and depersonalize its means of expression.

Thus, we have analyzed the emergence of Deleuze's own means of expression in light of his engagement with literature, but the real measure of his
style—what does philosophy *do*?—properly emerges in the context of the
rivals and enemies that confront philosophy today. In the introduction to
What Is Philosophy? (1991), for instance, Deleuze and Guattari pose the question of their own relevance in a world that sometimes seems reserved for

what we might call, with all due cynicism, a different "market," "niche," or "demographic." If anything, the intervening twenty-odd years since its publication have only made these concerns seem more prescient: today, more than ever, philosophy is under assault, besieged by all kinds of forces—commercial, communicative, social scientific—that lay claim to the concept at the same time that philosophy itself increasingly hews to the model of other disciplines—cognitivism, neuro-biology, political science, (bio- and business) ethics—that compromise its own concepts to the core. How can philosophy, Deleuze and Guattari wonder, "compete against young executives in a race for the universals of communication for determining the marketable form of the concept, *Merz?*" (WIP, 11). In a world dominated by commerce (*Commerz*), where thinking itself seems to have become the enterprise of the young and restless, how can an "old person"—an old philosopher—respond?

Besieged by the marketers and marketplace of philosophy, Deleuze and Guattari confess to feeling a little like Plato among the sophists. "In successive challenges," they write, modern philosophy has "confronted increasingly insolent and calamitous rivals that Plato himself would never have imagined in his most comic moments" (ibid., 10). It is as if the world, at least as we have sought to understand it in prior chapters, has been turned on its head—as if the philosopher of the false had found himself safeguarding philosophy against so many sophists. Having once defined the task of philosophy as the "overturning of Platonism," Deleuze—Deleuze!—expresses a kind of sympathy for his erstwhile enemy, whose plight seems to have become his own. After all, "what is philosophy?" is a perfectly Platonic question; and just as Plato struggled to formulate a reply, to secure philosophy apart from its many claimants, Deleuze and Guattari appear to find themselves providing an answer that is also a defense. What else can one do? Like Plato, Deleuze and Guattari write, "do we not encounter all kinds of claimants who say, 'I am the true philosopher, the friend of Wisdom or the Well-Founded?'" (ibid., 9). Like Plato, do we not feel the compulsion to introduce transcendence in order to determine the true philosopher and the true nature of philosophy? Do we not feel the desire to turn against *doxa* by appealing to the ideal in order to govern the field of immanence? In old age, we might be tempted to say, Deleuze acquires the sense of having become the father he rejected—a Platonist at last.

Broadly construed, the discussion to follow repudiates this suggestion by evoking the very different line of flight, neither Platonic nor doxological, that Deleuze formulates (both with Guattari and alone) in order to tackle the problem of our "communications society." In *What Is Philosophy?* the challenge posed by the present provokes a reconsideration of philosophy, no less art and science, which demands that we raise the false to new powers. But what distinguishes this reaction from the Platonic reaction formation we have previously considered? Far from resorting to a higher authority (an "Idea") or producing a social program (a "Republic"), Deleuze and Guattari reply *affectively*, according to a passage of feeling from sadness to joy, from regret to revaluation, and thence from negation to affirmation. "Certainly, it is painful to learn that *Concept* indicates a society of information services and engineering," they write. "But the more philosophy comes up against shameless and inane rivals and encounters them at its very core, the more it feels driven to fulfill the task of creating concepts that are aerolites rather than commercial products. It gets the giggles to wipe away the tears" (ibid., 11).[1] This reaction immediately recalls the sense of humor that Deleuze relishes in both Nietzsche and Kafka, for whom the most absurd and nihilistic conclusions are the source of uncontrollable laughter.[2] "Even Max Brod tells us how the audience would laugh hysterically when Kafka used to read *The Trial*," Deleuze writes (DI, 257).

This is surely how we should understand *What Is Philosophy?* Neither neurotic nor parodic, the giggles to which Deleuze and Guattari confess bear witness to a kind of conceptual vivacity that one might not otherwise expect. Written in old age—Guattari died the year following its publication, and Deleuze three years after that—the book never cedes to ill health, to pessimism, much less to Platonism, but makes those inclinations and bad affects cause for joyful creation. But how? Like Nietzsche, Deleuze often insists that the illnesses from which great writers, artists, and philosophers suffer are the sign of a singular health. "It is strange how great thinkers have a fragile personal life, an uncertain health, at the same time that they carry life to the state of absolute power [*puissances*] or of 'Great Health' " (Dia, 5). In certain cases, such as Nietzsche's own, the thinker endures all manner of ailments, "suffocating things whose passage exhausts him, while nonetheless giving him a becoming that a dominant and substantial health would render impossible" (CC, 3). To think, to write, is to live this strange logic. The writer ventures to the frontiers of experience, to the Outside, where he or she encounters the most outlandish visions and auditions. These intensities inscribe themselves on the body, scarring and somatizing the writer at the same time that they shape and modulate the brain. As a result, Deleuze says, "The artist or philosopher often has slender, frail health, a weak constitution, a shaky hold on things" (Neg, 143). "Yet it is not death that breaks them, but seeing, experiencing, thinking too much life" (ibid.). The physical frailty (*faiblesse*) and exhaustion (*épuisement*) from which the writer suffers are the cost and condition of a remarkable literary energy.

Whence the paradoxical "athleticism" that, Deleuze says, belongs to writing: "far from reconciling literature with sports or turning it into an Olympic event," he says, "this athleticism is exercised in flight and the breakdown [*défection*] of the organic body—an athlete in bed, as Michaux put it"(CC, 2). Deleuze was well acquainted with this fate. Suffering from tuberculosis and lung cancer, he was left in his later years "chained up like a dog"[3] to an oxygen machine—"an athlete in bed" (ibid.). But if *What Is Philosophy?* nevertheless achieves a kind of athleticism, this is because he and Guattari make old age the basis for an unadorned and vital reflection on philosophy. Only late in life, when sobriety has settled into one's bones, does one experience the "irresistible health" equal to the question of philosophy itself. "It was asked before; it was always being asked, but too indirectly or obliquely; the question was too artificial, too abstract" (WIP, 1). While the question has always existed, only in old age do Deleuze and Guattari attain the will (*amori fati!*) commensurate with the problem it raises.[4] Only when one attains the absolute sobriety of old age, when all of the affectations have been shorn away and one reaches a kind of nonstyle, can the question be posed: "What is it I have been doing all my life?" (ibid., 1).[5]

Ostensibly, the answer they provide here is no different than prior iterations—"the art of forming, inventing, and fabricating concepts" (WIP, 2)—but the style of *What Is Philosophy?* departs from any of their previous collaborations. The notorious difficulties of *Anti-Oedipus* (the schizoanalytic method), of *Kafka* (the disorienting elaboration of lines and intensities), and of *A Thousand Plateaus* (the machinic assemblage of plateaus), give way to an unprecedented clarity. Luminous yet sober, unrestrained yet rigorous, *What Is Philosophy?* announces its moment and purpose in "the time for speaking concretely" (WIP, 1). It is as if the late hour demanded the uncompromised formulation of a style determined to detach itself from affectation and personality. Poised "between life and death," *What Is Philosophy?* evokes the splendid impersonality of a style that becomes singular the more it becomes anonymous (ibid.).[6] Apart from imitation or aspiration, *nonstyle* consists in nothing less than the expression of a *vis elastica* that escapes metaphysical, moral, or even organic determination.[7]

Deleuze once said that everything he wrote was vitalistic ("or at least I hope it is" [Neg, 143]), but his is a peculiar vitalism. Neither physiological nor personal, vitality harkens to the "power of a nonorganic life" that Deleuze discovers in so many lines of expression—"a line that's drawn, a line of writing, a line of music," or even a conceptual line (ibid.). Whatever the mode, he situates this life line on a plane of immanence. In his last published essay, "Immanence: a Life," Deleuze alludes to a "life of pure immanence, neutral, beyond good and evil, since only the subject that incarnated it in the midst of things made it good or bad" (TRM, 384). Immanence means immediate and unmediated—beyond judgment. Life is an immanent expression of the passage through bodies and states of affairs, a fluidentity that constitutes an impersonal line of flight.[8] Life is never "immanent to" anything, since this formulation invariably presupposes a relation beyond the plane "to" something transcendent. "We will say of pure immanence that it is A LIFE, and nothing more," Deleuze writes. "It is not immanent to life, but the immanence that is in nothing else is itself a life. A life is the immanence of immanence, absolute immanence: it is complete power, complete beatitude" (ibid., 385–86).

Both here and elsewhere, Deleuze invokes Spinoza's sublime "plan" of immanence, but this nomination must be grasped in terms of Deleuze's own philosophy and his own revised Spinozism (WIP, 48). In *Difference and Repetition*, Deleuze elaborates this glorious philosophical immanence only to conclude by admitting that Spinoza stops short of a pure plane of pure immanence: "there still remains a difference between substance and the modes" (DR, 40). What does this mean? When Deleuze says that "substance must itself be said *of* the modes and only of the modes," the preposition should be understood to consist in the disclosure of a strange semi-autonomy. "Spinoza's substance appears independent" only inasmuch as it aspires to natural law and theological necessity on which the modes and functions are dependent (ibid.). For this reason, Deleuze suggests, the sliver of a mist—the mist of transcendence—still rises from this plane of immanence. And yet, in "Immanence: A Life," Deleuze names Spinoza as the singular philosopher for whom "immanence is not immanent to substance; on the contrary substance and its modes are in immanence" (TRM, 385). What has happened?

The transformation does not lie in Spinoza but in Deleuze's reading of Spinozistic substance, which exists in and as immanence only insofar as substance is submitted to deterritorialization. In classical philosophy, substance is "matter endowed with form" (ATP, 338), but Deleuze and Guattari reformulate the concept on the basis of extreme states, "far from equilibrium," when the plane of immanence gives way to pure difference and substance assumes an entirely new and unstable sense. In *A Thousand Plateaus,* for instance, Deleuze and Guattari declare that "the interval is substance" (ibid., 478): the unity we attribute to substance is dispersed into the differential undulations of immanence which "a life" traverses. As opposed to saying that "substance is interval," which maintains the priority of the former, they displace substance "in itself" by affirming the substantial nature of difference as the expression of an immanent and intervallic plane. When they say that "interval is substance," they mean that interval is *real* and that the line it draws consists in the "consistency itself of the real."[9] The plane of immanence and the *vis elastica* that traverses the plane are never imaginary, but Deleuze is always careful to distinguish their virtual reality—the event and the experience of thinking—from its actualization. Subject and object, bodies and states of affairs are actualized (differenciated) on the plane of immanence, but these are the after-effects of the virtual events (differentiations) that escape determinate space-time.[10] The event of a life does not exist in the past, present, or future but, as Deleuze writes, in the "immensity of an empty time where one sees the event to come and already past" (TRM, 387).

In "Immanence: A Life," Deleuze unfolds the concept of the event and the problem of life in the context of a brilliant episode from *Our Mutual Friend.* In Dickens's novel, the scoundrel Riderhood has suffered an accident of his own making, whereupon he is brought back to his boardinghouse. "Supple to twist and turn as the Rogue has ever been," the man has been reduced to "a flabby lump of mortality."[11] Dickens writes: "Doctor examines the dank carcase, and pronounces, not hopefully, that it is worth while trying to reanimate the same. All the best means are at once in action, and everybody present lends a hand, and a heart and soul."[12] Indeed, those who gather round this man as he lies on his deathbed demonstrate a loving attention previously unknown—*but not for the man himself.* "No one has the least regard for the man; with them all, he has been an object of avoidance, suspicion, and aversion."[13] Rather, the "rough men" hovering over the body wait for a sign of life, at once singular and impersonal, that no longer belongs to *this* man: "Neither Riderhood in this world, nor Riderhood in the other, could draw tears from them; but a striving human soul between the two can do it easily."[14] The interval between life and death, substance or soul, is detached from the scoundrel, who becomes "a *'homo tantum'* with whom everyone sympathizes and who attains a kind of beatitude" (TRM, 391). However briefly, the man becomes *a* man, *a* life. In Dickens' words, "the spark of life within him is curiously separable from himself now, and they have a deep interest in it, probably because it IS life, and they are living and must die."[15]

For Deleuze, then, the line of life opens up an in-between that eludes any time line in favor of a remarkable interval, an event. Forget about the cardinal points that mark the flight of Xeno's arrow: the events through which a life passes never follow the infinitely divisible instants of a given trajectory or the chronometric moments of so many years on earth. The event is happening, it has already happened, it has yet to happen—it belongs to no time but concerns that which Nietzsche called the "untimely" (*das Unzeitige, das Unzeitgemässe*). Consider once more the story of Odysseus's cicatrix, which we discussed in chapter 3. The hero has returned to Ithaca, disguised as a vagrant, to steal among the suitors who have descended on his estate, but his old nurse Eurycleia soon identifies her long-absent master. Holding his "scarred limb in her hands," she experiences a moment of profound recognition (*anagnorisis*): "at once she knew the scar."[16] Thus, Odysseus's worry—that "the whole truth would come out"—is realized, but not as we might imagine.[17] At no point in Homer's text has the scar been mentioned prior to its invocation, whereupon its story spills forth—how the young Odysseus had been injured in the act of killing a wild boar, and how the scar had effectively marked his first act of courage. In old age, when he has returned home after years at war and sea, when he must assemble the forces of guile and courage once more in order to dispatch the suitors, Odysseus discovers the scar as if for the first time, as if it had existed apart from his body, as if it were the event to which he must become equal: "My wound existed before me, I was born to embody it'" (LS, 148). Deleuze lifts this line from the poet Joe Bosquet to underscore that the event is above all virtual, an incorporeality detached from history, whose "neutral splendor" waits to be actualized and affirmed (ibid.).

Indeed, the contingency of the event—it might not have happened, it might have happened to someone else, it might have happened otherwise—is no argument against its affirmation. We always get the fate we deserve on the basis of our capacity to affirm *fortuna* as our fate (*amor fati!*). The only conceivable ethics, Deleuze says, is "not to be unworthy of what happens to us" (ne pas être indigne de ce qui nous arrive) (ibid., 149).[18]

Perhaps, finally, this is how we should understand the task of *What Is Philosophy?*—to be equal to the question that has been waiting all along. In old age, paradoxically, Deleuze and Guattari formulate a nonstyle commensurate to the question of philosophy today: the liability that might have haunted their last collaboration becomes the rigorous practice of a remarkable liberation. Take the impulses of old age to which Deleuze and Guattari allude in order to designate the singularity of their own line of flight. In the first place, they dwell on the ostensible *freedom* that the elderly enjoy—to do as they wish, to pursue their desires, without the weight of worrying what one ought to do. But in the second place, they note the *necessity* that grips the aged with a kind of responsibility to value the time that remains and not to cede it to insignificance or frivolity. We know the clichés of old age that these respective impulses seem to inspire, as if the image of the elderly oscillated between wild experimentation and overwrought reflection, between acting out and internalization. But Deleuze and Guattari suggest that in old age it is also possible to bring freedom and necessity together, to make them resonate and ramify each other, as the freedom to undertake that which is necessary and the necessity to bring one's freedom to bear. Old age introduces the freedom to ask the question that, however necessary, or perhaps because it was necessary, had proven too daunting or too elusive. "There are times when old age produces not eternal youth but a sovereign freedom [*liberté*]," they write, "a pure necessity in which one enjoys a moment of grace between life and death, and in which all the parts of the machine come together to send into the future a feature that cuts across all ages" (WIP, 2-3).

The Marketplace of Ideas

> Communication always comes too early or too late, and when it comes to creating, conversation is always superfluous.
> **GILLES DELEUZE** AND **FÉLIX GUATTARI,** *WHAT IS PHILOSOPHY?*

Given all we have said to this point, perhaps we can appreciate "the late Deleuze" by situating this work in the context of the rivals with whom he contends. *What Is Philosophy?* reviews a number of such challengers, those who claim to wrest the creation of concepts from the right (*quid juris*) of philosophy, and in a sense this series stands as an abbreviated genealogy of Deleuze and Guattari's own intellectual development. "Closer to our time, philosophy has encountered many new rivals," which they trace from the "human science, especially sociology," to the systems "of epistemology, of linguistics, or even of psychoanalysis and logic analysis," to the most recent of claimants, namely, the "disciplines of communication" (WIP, 10). In the early decades of the twentieth-century, philosophy (and we might think of Bergson here) battled sociological rivals, Neo-Kantians and positivists alike; but by the time Deleuze and Guattari began their careers, in the late 1950s and early 1960s, these rivals had been largely displaced by the rise of linguistics, psychoanalysis, anthropology, etc. Intellectually speaking, Deleuze and Guattari established themselves at the very moment that the science of structuralism reached is apogee, especially in France, and it shouldn't surprise us that both men initially expressed genuine affinity for these epistemologies.[19] "That was hardly surprising," Deleuze once explained, since both he and Guattari "owed so much to Lacan" (Neg, 13).

The radical reorientation that characterizes the assemblage "Deleuze-Guattari"—what makes structuralism an antagonist? what makes psychoanalysis an enemy?—remains a matter of debate, but above all else, the two seem to have been changed by virtue of their mutual encounter. "And then there was my meeting with Félix Guattari," Deleuze writes, "the way we understood and complemented, depersonalized and singularized—in short, loved—one another" (ibid., 7).[20] When Deleuze and Guattari first met, they recall, each thought the other had "gone further," only to discover that this intuition reflected their own sense of limitation. Deleuze remained lodged within a fairly academic logic—"I was working solely with concepts, rather timidly in fact"—while Guattari "was still talking in terms of structures, signifiers, the phallus, and so on (ibid., 13). The dissolution of this debt invariably and explicitly drives their early collaborations, in *Anti-Oedipus* and *Kafka,* which respond to psychoanalysis by constructing a "war machine" to battle the "structures, signifiers, the phallus" that had become so ubiquitous and fashionable, especially in Paris of the early 1970s (ibid.).[21] But in *A Thousand*

Plateaus, when the debt to structuralism has been paid off or paid back, Deleuze and Guattari begin a slow pan, so to speak, that will encompass new circumstances and rivals. Subject and structure are no less problems with which they wrestle in their later works, but these are cast as constituents of a sustained "plan sequence" that envisions the broad reconstitution of forces of a new *episteme.* The subject has given way to the subjectification of communication, the structure to a collective assemblage of enunciation, a society of opinion and "control."

The critique of "communications society," which is forecast in the second volume of *Capitalism and Schizophrenia,* is given full voice in *What Is Philosophy?* which confronts this society and its self-professed disciplines ("computer science, marketing, design, and advertising" [WIP, 10]) as rivals. The philosopher today finds himself or herself besieged by those who promote clichés, slogans, and opinion as concepts. "This is our concern," Deleuze and Guattari write in the voice of these marketing gurus: "we are the creative ones, we are the *ideas men [concepteurs]*! We are the friends of the concept, we put it in our computers" (ibid., 10). Today, the "idea man" (or woman) is everywhere and everywhere celebrated, for this ambitious executive, this young *apprentice*—ad man, mad-man, or idea man—transforms the concept into a form of immediate promotion and self-promotion.[22] A philosophy that discharges opinion does so at the expense of thinking. By laying claim to the concept, the idea man (*le concepteur*) effectively kills the concept (*tuer le concept*). In *What Is Philosophy?* Deleuze and Guattari admit that "it is understandable why marketing appropriates the concept and advertising puts itself forward as the conceiver par excellence, as the poet and thinker" (99). Still, they add, "What is most distressing is not this shameless appropriation but the conception of philosophy that made it possible in the first place." The most "shameless of rivals," these disciplines are also, arguably, the most dangerous because they lay claim to what philosophy creates, the concept, as province and *product.* As Deleuze and Guattari write, the concept "has become the set of product displays (historical, scientific, artistic, sexual, pragmatic)," and in the same stroke, "the event has become the exhibition that sets up various displays and the 'exchange of ideas' it is supposed to promote" (ibid., 10).

Late in life, when his "distress" can no longer be put off, when he determines to confront the society of communications, Deleuze seems to resolve to write precisely about those concepts that seem most elusive and, we might add, most liable to be reterritorialized on reactive grounds. (Is it really so hard to imagine Deleuze's posthumous recruitment into the uninhibited marketplace of capital and ideas, or the growing technologies of biopower and genetic engineering?) Much has been said about what Deleuze hoped to write had he lived longer, about the books he planned on Marx and on natural philosophy; but what's truly striking is the work he accomplished before his death, which returns to his most fundamental concepts—the virtual, the event, the plane immanence, a life—with a clarity and concreteness that is very nearly crystalline. At this late hour, and in the face of so many *concepteurs*, Deleuze responds by aspiring to nothing less than what we have called nonstyle. But in describing "the time for speaking concretely," he and Guattari also suggest that, at earlier moments, even when the question of philosophy was posed, they lacked resolution. *What Is Philosophy?* looks back on their previous works as if they were too auspicious, too caught up in the moment to realize philosophy as an untimely event. "There was too much desire to do philosophy to wonder what it was, except as a stylistic exercise" (1).[23]

As we know all too well, style is a tricky concept in Deleuze's philosophy, where it acquires the negative sense of pretense, affectation, and an overabundance of personality ("lifestyle") as well as the positive sense of subtraction, impersonality, and the becoming-imperceptible of the writer (nonstyle). But in light of *What Is Philosophy?* we might say that this very division is staged in Deleuze's own writing, between the busy, purposive philosopher seized with "too much desire" and the older, sober philosopher who selects and collects passions by dissipating himself. Perhaps this distinction can best be understood in light of an episode in Deleuze's life and writing that, though largely forgotten, unwittingly reveals the altered state of the late work. In 1977, Minuit published a pamphlet, "On the New Philosophers (plus a More General Problem)," in which Deleuze responded to what was already becoming an intellectual phenomenon in France and elsewhere. In a relatively short period of time, the New Philosophers (*Les Nouveaux Philosophes*) had achieved astonishing notoriety: in the late seventies and early eighties, the members of this loosely defined group were fixtures on the best-seller lists, no less radio and television, where they pitched a kind of popular, intellectual sentiment suited to a post-1968 generation.[24] A few months after the appearance of Deleuze's pamphlet, which was structured as an interview, *Time* magazine featured an article on the group that declared, "In the current context of French politics, the leitmotiv of the New Philosophers may well be the theme that many are yearning to hear."[25]

So great was the exposure generated by the New Philosophers that they inspired the phase *pub philosophie,* taken from *publicité philosophie,* in order to express the integration of marketing and concepts. Surely, this is what motivates Deleuze to undertake the interview: if he feels little more than contempt for the group, he nevertheless feels the need to respond to "a more general problem" they raise.[26] Indeed, the New Philosophers represent an early and unabashed "conception of philosophy" based on marketing and communications, and in a sense Deleuze's response constitutes a rehearsal for the confrontation with "the marketable form of the concept" that he and Guattari will mount later on (WIP, 11). The novelty of the New Philosopher does not in any way consist in creation, but in a "marketing enterprise [that] represents the submission of thought to the media" (TRM, 147).[27] Their moniker is at once wholly justified and totally unjust: "They are new, yes, but conformist in the highest degree," Deleuze says (ibid.). Indeed, they produce the most timely of books, suited to vicissitudes of taste and fashion, appealing to the appropriate forces, addictions, and desires of the market. "There is something new here," he admits: "marketing the philosophical book. It's a new idea. It had to occur to someone first" (*il 'fallait' l'avoir*) (ibid., 142).[28]

While the New Philosophers represent a wholly reactionary development in the history of contemporary French thought, appealing to the base instincts of "opinion-makers," Deleuze says that this "does not preclude a profound modernism, a watered down analysis of landscape and market place" (ibid.).[29] More entrepreneurial than philosophical, the New Philosophers are novel inasmuch as this generation of rivals and claimants has consolidated its power in light of the logic of new (mass) media. Hence, the adjective "new" should be understood in the context of communications, where it forms an assemblage with the forces of marketing: *new and improved!* The condemnation of *concepteurs* that Deleuze and Guattari undertake in *What Is Philosophy?* is no less suited to the New Philosophers, who already make the concept a "set of product displays" and the event "the exhibition that sets up the various displays and the 'exchange of ideas' it is supposed to promote" (WIP, 10). No one returns today to the New Philosophers in the name of the concepts they created, and the reason is clear: like a product whose shelf life expires or a fashion that becomes outdated, the movement ought to be understood as a commercial enterprise—a fad. Consider the name itself, which was bestowed by the title of a dossier that appeared in *Les Nouvelles Littéraires* in 1976 with the explicit purpose of creating a buzz, a sensation. Edited by Bernard-Henri Lévy, who would become their de facto leader and publicist, the dossier included articles, interviews, and exchanges featuring a number of those associated with the group, often in dialogue with established intellectual luminaries, all designed to demonstrate that the New Philosophers had been blessed with the "imprimatur of the philosophico-literary establishment."[30]

Inasmuch as they acquired a name, the New Philosophers acquired a brand name, which was publicized and marketed in turn.[31] But what does the name signify? If "we cannot say that these New Philosophers are a school" (TRM, 141), Deleuze insists that this is because they come from fields with no shared methodology. In other words, the name does not designate an epistemological consensus so much as the conversion of epistemology itself into a new regime of communication. The New Philosophers are not philosophical enemies but doxological ones—the avatars of a new communications society. This is the "more general problem" that Deleuze's interview promises, but we would also have to admit that it doesn't really deliver: this analysis remains framed generically (by the interview form) and, just as much, personally (by his obvious contempt). And, no doubt, the problem of the New Philosophers felt "personal" to Deleuze: Lévy's *Barbarism with a Human Face* not only excoriated Deleuze and Guattari but did so in the midst of a wholesale renunciation of the political events of May '68. "We know them well, these happy warriors, apostles of the drift and celebrators of diversity," he writes. "These sailors of a modern ship of fools have their helmsmen, Saint Gilles and Saint Félix, shepherds of the flock and authors of *Anti-Oedipus*."[32] The "fools" constitute the generation of '68, whom the New Philosophers unilaterally denounced as "an image of Evil," implicating Deleuze and Guattari as the perpetrators of the malignant fraud. In Deleuze's words, the New Philosophers "pissed on" the political and intellectual experience of '68, denigrating its profound hope and misunderstanding its dispiriting aftermath.

The severity of Deleuze's reaction derives from what we have previously called the ethics of the event, namely, "not to be unworthy of what happens to us" (LS, 149). In response to May '68, which remained the subject of disappointment, Deleuze never lapses into nihilism but rather passes through all the bad effects in order to produce a new politics. What else is schizoanalysis, which Deleuze says was written in response to May '68, if not this affirmative politics? By contrast, the New Philosophers not only identified as members of the "lost generation" but spoke on behalf of political pessimism. They suffered from a kind of "left melancholy" worse than leftist defeat—leftist disenchantment.[33] Once at the vanguard of a revolutionary uprising—they were among the "May Fools"—the New Philosophers congregated under the banner of an equally revolutionary renunciation that passed from Althusserian Marxism to Maoist *gauchisme* to fervent anti-Marxism.[34] In the span of less than ten years, they came to "subscribe to the idea that Marxism is an evil and obsolete ideology that leads inevitably to totalitarianism and terror."[35] Where others sought to distinguish between Marxism and Soviet communism, sometimes too apologetically, the New Philosophers followed their disenchantment straight from " 'bureaucratic phenomenon' to the 'Stalinist deviation,' from Stalin's 'crimes' to Lenin's 'faults,' " finally tracing the original sin back to "the founding-father himself, Karl Capital and the holy scripture."[36]

The New Philosophers advertised themselves as witnesses to history and spokesman for those who suffered its cruel fate (in particular, they spoke for the victims of the Gulag, but as they were quick to add, the Gulag was everywhere[37]). In Deleuze's words, they introduced a "sort of philosophy-as-marketing, often directed against the USSR," but even in the absence of the Soviet Union, their conjunctive chorus of economic liberalism and democratic liberalism has only grown louder in recent years (Neg, 152). While the genealogy of the New Philosophers remains distinctly French, they presage an image of thought whose fundamental constituents have become altogether familiar. The real (not "as advertised") Bush doctrine consisted in the consecration of economic liberalism (the right to own property, to buy and sell goods, to participate as agents in and of capitalism) as an element of, and condition for, political liberalism (human rights). In this sense, we should say, Deleuze's critique of the New Philosophers suggests the prospects and problems of contending with the discourse of neoliberalism that we confront today.

In his pamphlet, Deleuze ascribes two fundamental characteristics to the New Philosophers—the enunciation of universal concepts and the concomitant development of an author-function charged with enunciating those concepts. In the first place, he notes, these philosophers work exclusively with "big concepts, all puffed up like an abscess: THE Law, Power [*LE pouvoir*], Master, THE World, THE Revolution, Faith, etc." (TRM, 139). Inasmuch as the New Philosophers "have introduced France to literary and philosophical marketing," they make philosophy into an enterprise that, under the pretense of "pustulated" concepts, actually works against the prospects of invention (ibid.).[38] They produce all manner of pale and vacuous concepts that hardly deserve the name except insofar as they lay claim to it. In the second place, Deleuze adds, the New Philosophers induce the return (with a vengeance) of the author-function, which can be grasped in view of the marketing function that we are in the midst of describing here. In the absence of more finely grained concepts that would effectively do the work of expressing subtle differentiations, the New Philosophers shift the focus of thinking onto the "expressing subject" (*sujet d'énonciation*) who must "take itself all the more seriously in relation to empty propositions" (ibid.). For some time now, Deleuze says, modern philosophy has been trying to "create extremely differentiated concepts, to escape gross dualisms" by virtue of uncovering "creative functions which would no longer require an author-function for them to be active (in music, painting, audio-visual arts, film, and even philosophy)" (ibid.). Of course, this is Deleuze's own propensity, but the New Philosophers pursue a very nearly antithetical approach. They forsake the "fine articulations" of philosophy for the spectacle of the event and the creation of a grandiose author-function, or what we might call the celebrity-witness.[39] "It is not for nothing that they emphasize their youth and beauty in interviews," Gayatri Spivak once said of the New Philosophers; or as Henri-Lévy himself was reported to have said, "God is dead, but my hair is perfect."[40]

In "On the New Philosophers," Deleuze lambastes the group for having reduced philosophy to communication by mobilizing media and genres in the interest of marketing. Thus, the critique of the New Philosophy revolves around their transformation of writing and thinking into a commercial event, an exhibition, or promotion. "Marketing has its own particular logic," Deleuze says. "You have to talk about the book, or get the book talked about, rather than let the book do the talking. Theoretically, you could have all the newspaper articles, interviews, conferences, and radio shows replace the book altogether, it needn't exist at all" (TRM, 144). In this respect, it's worth recalling Deleuze's horror of discussion and debate. He religiously avoided attacks, arguments, and roundtables; even his "interviews" consist, more often than not, in written responses. Thus, in *Dialogues,* Deleuze begins by explaining:

It is very hard to "explain oneself"—an interview, a dialogue, a conversation. Most of the time, when someone asks me a question, even one which relates to me, I see that, strictly, I don't have anything to say. Questions are invented, like anything else. If you aren't allowed to invent your questions, with elements from all over the place, from never mind where, if people "pose" them to you, you haven't much to say. The art of constructing a problem is very important: you invent a problem, a problem-position, before finding a solution. None of this happens in an interview, a conversation, a discussion. Even reflection, whether it is alone, or between two or more, is not enough. Above all, not reflection. Objections are even worse. Every time someone puts an objection to me, I want to say, "OK, OK, let's go on to something else." It is the same thing when I am asked a general question. The aim is not to answer questions, it is to get out, to get out of it. (1)

If discussion is a forum for opinions, Deleuze insists that philosophy is something else—the formation of problems and the creation of concepts. "Of what concern is it to philosophy that someone has such a view, and thinks this or that, if the problems at stake are not stated?" Deleuze and Guattari write in *What Is Philosophy?* (WIP, 28). More often than not, discussion attests to the fact that we have given up on thinking in favor of opinion, the realm of discourse in which we can find the basis for agreement ("the society of those who love cheese," the authors jokingly offer [ibid., 145]) and thereby ignore the problems that might be at stake in even so superficial a consensus. If you want eliminate philosophy, to foreclose its mere possibility, Deleuze says, just start a discussion. Philosophy is overtaken by discussion, the book by paratexts and publicity. But insofar as interviews about the work replace the work itself, the wonder is that *this* interview takes place at all. In "On the New Philosopher," Deleuze is never asked to elaborate his own concepts but, instead, merely to respond to a kind of phenomenon. After an initial question, in which he is queried about what he thinks of the group ("Not much"), the interviewer asks if Deleuze isn't responding now because Lévy's *Barbarism with a Human Face* "violently attacked" him. "Don't be ridiculous," Deleuze responds (TRM, 140), but what seems ridiculous, in retrospect, is that Deleuze agreed to participate at all and, worse still, that he was forced to address philosophy in the context of gossip.

Indeed, a note of regret colors the interview, as if Deleuze found himself acting out his basest instincts *malgré soi.* The reluctance—the revulsion—we feel is confirmed by the disclosure that while Deleuze "wanted to discuss the New Philosophers for a while now," he "didn't know how" (ibid.). How can one avoid becoming part of the structure of debate and the mechanism of publicity? How can one respond to the New Philosophers without being drawn into their very machinations, into opinion and even gossip? "They devote their time and energy to attacks, counterattacks, and to counter-counterattacks," Deleuze says (ibid.). In short, the task of confronting the New Philosophers poses risks and problems that are inseparable from the model of philosophy they propose. Deleuze seems to anticipate the eventuality that even his critique will be misconstrued, will have been misconstrued: "They must be saying to themselves: look how jealous he is of our success" (ibid.).[41] And yet, inasmuch as Deleuze worries that his critique will be taken as *ressentiment* or, worse, the sign of his own desire for success, this fear already condemns the pamphlet to reactive instincts, the circuit of "attack and counter-attack." "A few philosophers may feel a certain curiosity and goodwill toward" the New Philosophers, Deleuze says (ibid. 142). "But my perspective is teratological: it is a horror show, and I'm fascinated in spite of myself."[42]

In this respect, however, the "More General Problem" of the title is never truly general enough: Deleuze never detaches thought from a kind of personalism. More critique than creation, the interview remains determined by its own time and timeliness. While "On the New Philosophers" diagnoses the reactive and commercialized elements of the group, Deleuze never completely passes through its own reactive passions; the mood of apocalyptic laughter and the creative modalities of "a life" are conspicuously lacking here. Of the New Philosopher, Deleuze says, "I don't have time to respond more than once," but once is probably more than enough (ibid., 140). From the perspective of *What Is Philosophy?* the event remains stillborn—a publication, marked by its time and place, that never liberates a line of flight. In view of our discussion of old age, we might say that Deleuze had not yet reached it, had not yet attained it, that he still lacked the vitality to traverse the moment and accede to the question of philosophy. Both with Guattari and alone, then, Deleuze's late writings attest to a profound effort to address problems that he had not sufficiently "explored," as if to elucidate the creative endeavor of philosophy in the face of forces that threaten to turn all concepts into products and opinions.[43] Philosophy "is neither reflective nor contemplative, but creative," Deleuze writes in a late fragment. "I believe this has always been the case with philosophy, but I have not yet been able to express myself on the matter. This is why the next book I write will be a short text on the question: *What Is Philosophy?*" (ibid., 366).

Chaos and Doxa

The Problem of Opinion

> We fall back into the most abject conditions that Nietzsche diagnosed as the art of the pleb or bad taste in philosophy: a reduction of the concept to propositions like simple opinions; false perceptions and bad feelings (illusions of transcendence or universals) engulfing the plane of immanence; the model of a form of knowledge that constitutes only a supposedly higher opinion, *Urdoxa*; a replacement of conceptual personae by teachers or leaders of schools.
>
> **GILLES DELEUZE** AND **FÉLIX GUATTARI**, *WHAT IS PHILOSOPHY?*

In *What Is Philosophy?* even as Deleuze and Guattari dwell on the dilemma of philosophy *today*, when it is besieged by opinion and "the marketable form of the concept" (WIP, 11), they do so in order to draw a line from the conditions and circumstances of the present to the history of philosophy itself ("all ages"). Beginning in the ancient world, where "rivalry culminates in the battle between philosopher and sophist" (ibid., 9), philosophy confronts all manner of adversaries who claim its name and rank. Platonism marks the first in a long and inevitable series of encounters between philosophy and its *prétendants*. Philosophy lives in a kind of "permanent crisis" (ibid., 82) of its own devising: its conditions of existence are also the possible conditions of its destruction. Inasmuch as it "makes *free opinion* [*doxa*] prevail" (ibid., 79), philosophy invariably countenances the efflorescence of its rivals.

For this reason, Deleuze and Guattari suggest that the history of philosophy can be recapitulated according to three predominant responses to the problem of *doxa*. In each case—whether as contemplation, reflection, or communication—philosophy introduces the "illusion of transcendence" (ibid., 49) in order to defend against opinion, to adjudicate its claims, and to organize its exchange. In the first place, contemplation is identified with Platonism, or what Deleuze and Guattari describe as an "eidetic" framework, which provides the criteria to adjudicate among claimants; as we have seen, Plato establishes "universals of contemplation" in order to "gauge the respective value of rival opinions so as to raise them to the level of knowledge" (WIP, 79). Contemplation is "the transcendence of a Something, or of a One higher than everything," rising from the plane of immanence like a divine object that allows us to make distinctions with respect to the true claimant and the right opinion (ibid., 46). In the second place, reflection is identified with Kantianism, which Deleuze and Guattari define as a critique that replaces the eidetic with a new idealism. Kant submits eternal Ideas and Forms to critique only to contrive a new transcendence in the Subject, the site of representation. From the external and even mythic basis of contemplation we pass to the internal and suprasensible basis of reflection, which demands a "Subject to which the field of immanence is only attributed by belonging to a self that necessarily represents such a subject to itself" (ibid.).

The final stage of this brief history concerns communication, which Deleuze and Guattari identify, at least in its initial stages, with Husserl. Broadly construed, we could say that this eventuality is already anticipated by the previous modes of transcendence, by the movement from a divine "Something" to a representing "Subject": in the dialectic of contemplation and reflection, the Form redounds into the transcendental (and transcendent) ego, thereby inducing communication as a new dialectic, namely, between subjects. At the risk of great simplification, Deleuze regards this as the fundamental problem of phenomenology.[44] In *Cinema 1,* he insists on a radical opposition between his own (largely Bergsonian) sense of perception and Husserl's phenomenology, especially inasmuch as Husserl makes "natural perception" an anchored subject, "a being in the world, an opening to the world which will be expressed in the famous 'all consciousness is consciousness of something'" (MI, 59)—its condition. This famous slogan crystallizes the dialectical resolution of phenomenology insofar as consciousness consummates itself in relation to something or someone, *intersubjectively:* "thought depends on man's relations with the world" (WIP, 209). At last, "when immanence becomes immanent 'to' a transcendental subjectivity," this subject discovers that "the hallmark or figure [*chiffre*] of a transcendence must appear as action now referring to another self, to another consciousness" (ibid., 46). Transcendence does not lie in "Something" or even "Someone" but in "the privileged transcendence of an intersubjective world populated by other selves," and as

Deleuze and Guattari are quick to add, this "hardly gets us out of the sphere of opinions" (ibid., 210).

Indeed, the problem with intersubjectivity is that "an ideal world populated by cultural formations and the human community" does not simply adopt transcendence to govern the efflorescence of *doxa* but makes *doxa* itself transcendent. Intersubjectivity leads us to an "*Urdoxa* posited as original opinion, or meaning of meanings" (ibid., 210). But what do we mean by *doxa,* much less *Urdoxa*? Traditionally, Deleuze and Guattari say, philosophers lapse into opinion when they offer insights in the form of solutions that have no problem or whose problems remains poorly posed. "In short, solutions are reviewed without ever determining what the problem is (substance, in Aristotle, Descartes, Leibniz), since the problem is only copied from the propositions that serve as its answer" (ibid., 80). The result of all superficially or clumsily stated problems is doxographic—and this is no less true of the problem of *doxa* itself. Indeed, the task before us is to create the problem and concept of opinion without, for all that, lapsing into opinion. For this reason, Deleuze suggests, the formation of *doxa* should be grasped in its properly *reactive* spirit, which is to say, as a flight from another and prior problem—chaos. The very difficulty of approaching chaos demonstrates the allure of opinion, which displaces the molecular frenzy of "infinite variabilities" moving at "infinite speeds" and, thereby, provides the subjects and objects, habits and clichés, with which order is "won from chaos" (ibid., 201, 205). Take communication, which Deleuze and Guattari say is sometimes defined "by initial pieces of information, sometimes by large-scale pieces of information, which usually go from the elementary to the composite, or from the present to the future, or from the molecular to the molar" (ibid., 205): in this trajectory, we can already anticipate the broad contours of an image of thought that ranges from the inderminate to determination, from chaos to opinion, without regard to "finer articulations."

The relation between chaos and opinion (*doxa*) defines not only the problem of philosophy but of thinking itself, whatever its form or discipline, inasmuch as thinking today is in the midst (*au milieu*) of confronting a new task: how to wrestle with the problem of chaos without, for all that, taming chance. It is in this sense that we might understand Deleuze and Guattari's resolution in *What Is Philosophy?* to divide thinking among three domains—philosophy, science, art. "There's no order of priority among these disciplines," Deleuze says elsewhere. "Each is creative. The true object of science is to create functions, the true object of art is to create sensory aggregates, and the object of philosophy is to create concepts" (Neg, 123). Whatever they produce, though, these domains are situated between chaos and *doxa,* born of the former, drawn to the latter. What does this mean? As Deleuze writes, the ontogenesis of "what is called thinking" lies in mother chaos, which "has three daughters, depending on the plane that cuts through it: these are the *Chaoids*—art, science, and philosophy—as forms of thought or creation" (WIP, 208). Art, science, and philosophy exist only insofar as they take a "cross-section" of chaos, as if each one drew a secant traversing a common brain. Thus, the distinction between these planes, which Deleuze and Guattari insist on throughout *What Is Philosophy?* bears witness in the book's final pages to the grey matter of chaos as their *common non-denominator*: the brain is "the *junction* (not the unity) *of the three planes*" (ibid.).[45] Inasmuch as philosophical thought acquires its character and its consistency in relation to that which is nonphilosophical, to the Outside, the same would have to be affirmed of chaos's other daughters. "*Philosophy needs a nonphilosophy that comprehends it; it needs a nonphilosophical comprehension just as art needs nonart and science needs nonscience*" (ibid.).

Therefore, the three daughters of chaos constitute distinct planes only on the condition that each one exists "in an essential relationship with the No that concerns it" (ibid.)—but this relationship does not signify negation. Science, art, and philosophy do not negate chaos, nor even sublate it, so much as each affirms a relation to that which remains beyond its domain: the No designates the experience of an unthought—the Outside. Only in this view can we understand Deleuze's avowal in *The Fold* that "chaos does not exist," [46] which might otherwise strike us as a denial tout court. But in fact the claim ought to be regarded in the sense that the event, which ostensibly marks our encounter with chaos, is also the event that makes chaos itself emerge. Chaos does not exist apart from thinking and from being thought, even if this confrontation renders it unthought or Outside. In each case, then, chaos consists in the impossible and unthinkable that does not exist apart from being filtered through the membrane (*crible*: the "membrain") of thought. There is no chaos apart from the screen, no chaos "in itself," but neither is there a screen apart from chaos. So long as we speak of chaos, we speak of a kind of quasi-chaos, of a little bit of sense that (however minimal) we extract, because "we" are the filtration of chaos just as chaos is created by this filtration. Chaos "is an abstraction because it is inseparable from a screen that makes something—something rather than nothing—emerge from it," Deleuze writes. "Chaos would be a pure Many, a purely disjunctive diversity, while the something is a One, not a pregiven unity, but instead the indefinite article that designates a certain singularity" (ibid.).[47]

The conditional tense in which chaos is rendered here bears witness to the problem it entails, for when we encounter or experience chaos, we almost always tend to do too little or too much. On the one hand, when we refuse to recognize our need for sense, we supply too little order, as if we could simply slip into pure, untrammeled chaos. As Deleuze once commented, this eventuality would consist in the fantasy of "withdraw[ing] the pure sensible from representation" and, thereby, "determin[ing] it as that which remains once representation has been eliminated" a kind of "a contradictory flux" or "rhapsody of sensations" (DR, 56). When we approach chaos so closely, we cannot get a hold of our ideas, which slip through the sieve of our brain-plane without leaving any trace, any residue, any *sense* behind. "Nothing is more distressing than a thought that escapes itself, than ideas that fly off, that disappear hardly formed, already eroded by forgetfulness or precipitated into others that we no longer master," Deleuze and Guattari write (WIP, 201). On the other hand, and as a result, the threat of chaos makes us "want to hang on to fixed opinions so much. We ask only that our ideas are linked together according to a minimum of constant rules" (ibid.). When we muster the indelicate urge for order, we run the risk not of chaos but of the reaction (reactive) formation it induces. "We require a little order to protect us from chaos," Deleuze and Guattari admit (ibid.), but we almost always muster too much: the cure is far graver than the disease. "It is as if the *struggle against chaos* does not take place without an affinity with the enemy," Deleuze and Guattari write, "because another struggle develops and takes on more importance—the struggle *against opinion,* which claims to protect us from chaos itself."

The paradox and problem of chaos, then, is that it should give way to an even more troubled relationship with opinion (*doxa*), the foster parent who threatens to alienate philosophy, science, and art from its ontogenetic parent. The children fly from chaos to *doxa*, and it remains for us to understand both what this means for thinking and how we can think otherwise. In *Difference and Repetition,* where he embarks on a sustained analysis of *doxa*, Deleuze divides its operation into two discrete, though intimately related, orthodoxies—common sense and good sense—that we will consider in turn. We have already broached common sense in the previous chapter, where we analyzed its operation in terms of the labor of recognition, namely, the preexistence of categories and rules whereby experience is determined in advance—*re-cognized*—according to what we already know. Opinion is intimately related to recognition, but it formulates the operation of common sense on an inverse scale: whereas recognition moves from the abstract to the particular, *doxa* moves from the particular to the general. Indeed, *doxa* pertains to a kind of abstraction from our lived situation: we immediately pass from "this or that," "here and now," to a generalization that pertains to conditions that derive from or purport to cover all manner of situations. But as Deleuze and Guattari insist, the procedures of abstraction would be inconceivable if the one who stated the opinion did not, in turn, identify himself or herself with "a generic subject experiencing a common affection" (WIP, 145). Thus, like recognition, *doxa* presupposes an abstract enunciation that refers to an abstract subject.

Whence the double sense of common sense, which inevitably circulates between a universal subject (*Cogitatio natura universalis*) and a universe of subjects (*concordia facultatum*). Common sense prescribes not only what we know but, more importantly, the form of knowledge itself, which emerges as consensus—both within the individual (as, say, the agreement legislated between faculties) and among individuals (as, say, an agreement legislated among the people). The agreement of faculties within the subject is reflected in a broader agreement between subjects. *Doxa* extends the model of recognition into a discursive or communicative sphere, since it "gives to the recognition of truth an extension and criteria that are naturally those of an 'orthodoxy': a true opinion will be the one that coincides with that of the group to which one belongs by expressing it" (WIP, 146). The model of *doxa* is like a game show where we are openly or implicitly asked to reiterate what everyone knows—what the survey says, what the majority believes, what amounts to common sense.

But if philosophical common sense appeals to the regularity of the subject in an abstract and determinable present, how is this regularity distributed over time? In view of this question, Deleuze argues, common sense looks to good sense as its "faculty of distribution."[48] Whereas common sense imposes the presuppositions of the subject and object on difference, good sense sustains these presuppositions (or opinions) in time by distributing difference according to the assurance of progressive homogenization. "Difference is that by which the given is given as diverse," Deleuze writes, but good sense makes difference—or what we have called intensity—into diversity by introducing variables which agglomerate into measure and average, statistic and probability (DR, 222).[49] Whether we are determining "level, temperature, pressure, tension, potential" (ibid.), these measures already indicate the sense in which differential intensities will be overwritten by the surface effects they condition (differentiation).

This is the paradox of good sense: difference qua intensity constitutes the "reason of all phenomena, the condition of that which appears," but in good sense "we know intensity only . . . as covered over by qualities" (DR, 223).[50] The nature of good sense is such that, when we begin with a field of differences, even an ostensible chaos of differences, this state of affairs is immediately posited as the "origin = x of the diverse." Good sense rests on an irreversible synthesis of time: its arrow always shoots from the differences of the past to the homogenized diversity of the future, from "the particular to the general." Or, to put it another way, the faculty of distribution makes difference the precedent to its own equalization. "Perhaps good sense even presupposes madness in order to come after and correct what madness there is in any prior distribution," Deleuze writes (ibid., 224). In other words, "chaos" exists only as an antecedent to order, which inexorably subjects intensity to new distributions or to "repartitions" (ibid.). "In effect, since every partial system has its origin in a difference which individualizes its domain, how would an observer situated within the system grasp this difference except as past and highly 'improbable,' given that it is behind him?" Deleuze asks (ibid., 225). "On the other hand, at the heart of the same system, the future, the probable and the cancellation of difference are identified in the direction indicated by the arrow of time—in other words, the right direction" (ibid.).

In this respect, finally, the outlines of an *Urdoxa* take shape in the marriage of common sense and good sense. The two orthodoxies come together in this overarching formation insofar as both are means of domesticating chaos: common sense concerns what everyone knows, and good sense what everyone predicts. Common sense concerns the determination of elements according to universal presuppositions, while good sense concerns the determination of elements according to likely eventualities. More to the point, the presuppositions of common sense are redoubled by the probabilities of good sense. Collectively, they form what Deleuze calls an "image of thought," a model of what it means to think correctly and properly.[51]

The Coming Chaosmos

> The idea that truth isn't something already out there we have to discover, but has to be created in every domain, is obvious in the sciences, for instance.
>
> **GILLES DELEUZE,** *NEGOTIATIONS*

How, then, can we elude the constraints of the image of thought and begin, however modestly, to introduce chaos into thinking? Once more, we are left with the question of how to think otherwise, and if in the previous chapter we turned to literature to formulate our response, we turn here to the domain of science. Like the relationship between philosophy and the arts, the relationship between philosophy and science remains a matter of delicacy and discretion. Indeed, these divisions are justifiably the source of debate and disagreement—as if Deleuze, who once declared that the "only true criticism is comparative,"[52] had endeavored late in his life to define science, art, and philosophy as distinct and even disciplinary precincts. But while science, philosophy, and art lay claim to their own planes, each autonomous in its own domain, we have lingered on instances when the problems, procedures, or events posed in one domain resonate with another and provoke a strange proximity.

This is doubtless the case in *What Is Philosophy?* where the philosophical problem of chaos leads the authors to consider how the problem has been posed in the sciences, especially in struggles to formulate the sense of "non-equilibrium" systems. In such systems, Deleuze and Guattari note, scientists consider how chaotic states can give rise to astonishing and unprecedented complexity. Today, they write, "science takes a bit of chaos in a system of coordinates and forms a referenced chaos that becomes Nature, and from which it extracts an aleatory function and chaoid variables" (WIP, 206). This impulse, operating across an array of fields, has been called just as many things (chaos theory, complexity studies, self-organizing systems, Stochastic processes, etc.), but what concerns us here is how Deleuze and Guattari discover the resources with which to unfold the problem in philosophy—or, we could say, as *chaosophy*. On a number of occasions, Deleuze refers to the writings of Ilya Prigogine and Isabelle Stengers, whose work on nonequilibrium thermodynamics produces concepts that are, he says, "irreducibly philosophical, scientific, and artistic" (Neg, 29). But if the Nobel-winning scientist and the great philosopher of science inspire Deleuze's philosophy, it is worth noting that the feeling was mutual.[53] In their first book together, *La Nouvelle Alliance* (1986), Prigogine and Stengers pose the problem of chaos in an epistemological context that has remarkable affinity with Deleuze's work.[54] In particular, they refer to *Difference and Repetition* as a precursor to the work they are pursuing (notably, the English translation of the text, *Order Out of Chaos,* was abridged and does not include this discussion).

The extent to which Deleuze anticipates complexity becomes clear when we return to common sense and good sense. Prigogine and Stengers do not (in so many words) refer to these orthodoxies, but in *La Nouvelle Alliance* and elsewhere, common sense and good sense are clearly discernible in the prior paradigms of modern science. Among other things, *La Nouvelle Alliance* outlines its own genealogy, from the consolidation of classical physics to the turn to thermodynamics to the domain of the chemical and biological sciences today. For our purposes, this sequence describes a movement from the static and certain reversibility of mechanism, which we will align with common sense, to the irreversible distribution of thermodynamics, which we will align with good sense, to the science of complexity. The altogether unorthodox nature of this history lies not only in its obvious unwillingness to be bound by any one field but, moreover, its refusal to privilege physics as the science par excellence. Rather, Prigogine and Stengers suggest that physics has traditionally represented a determinable and calculable universe that, whether classical or even quantum, can be identified with an *Urdoxa*.[55]

In *What Is Philosophy?* Deleuze and Guattari define this *Urdoxa* on the basis of procedures that characterize the struggle of science to tame chaos. Inasmuch as it belongs to a plane of reference, science operates by slowing down chaos, reducing its measure to variables, but in so doing it runs a particular risk: by taking as its point of departure so many "centers of equilibrium," science determines "constants or limits" that it will assign to the entire system. Science subjects chaos to order whenever we select "only a small number of independent variables within coordinate axes," and this procedure has historically forecast two eventualities that Deleuze and Guattari duly note (WIP, 205). On the one hand, science has considered the relationships between those variables "whose future can be determined on the basis of the present (determinist calculus)," but on the other hand, science has introduced "so many variables at once that the state of affairs is only statistical (calculus of probabilities)" (ibid.). These two worldviews, the determinable and the probabilistic, loosely define the first two stages of the scientific genealogy on which we have embarked—the mechanistic and the thermodynamic, respectively—and it remains for us to pass through these paradigms in order to grasp the sense in which we can entertain a relation with chaos that eludes these orthodoxies.

In the world of classical science, defined as it was by the ascendancy of Newtonian physics, the invention of calculus bears witness to the "time reversible fundamental laws" that belie the workings of a divine, mathematic perfection—the mechanistic universe.[56] "The world of classical physics is an atemporal world which, if created, must have been created in one fell swoop, somewhat as an engineer creates a robot before letting it function alone."[57] In a sense, then, the move from classical physics to thermodynamics ought to be understood as the creation of something like a new God. In its consecrated, Laplacian guise, the God of classical physics constitutes a perfectly calculating divinity who presides over a perfectly reversible universe.

> For the science of Laplace which, in many respects, is still the classical conception of science today, a description is objective to the extent to which the observer is excluded and the description itself is made from a point lying *de jure* outside the world, that is, from the divine viewpoint to which the human soul, created as it was in God's image, had access from the beginning.[58]

Laplace's God represents the belief that, in a given system, we can "define all states as equivalent"[59]—no less that a single state ideally provides all the information we need to know about the past or future of the entire system.[60] As Edgar Allan aptly explained it: "It is not that the Deity *cannot* modify his laws, but that we insult him in imagining a possible necessity for modification. In their origin these laws were fashioned to embrace *all* contingencies which *could* lie in the Future. With God all is *Now*."[61]

As Prigogine and Stengers describe it, the trouble with this orthodoxy emerged at the beginning of the nineteenth century, when Fourier introduced "the first qualitative description of something inconceivable in classical dynamics—an irreversible process."[62] The very basis of thermodynamics, which would emerge over the course of the century, lay in the discovery of entropic processes, of inexorable differences or inequalities with respect to energy, that invariably entail irreversibility—time's arrow. But if the common sense of dynamics was, to some extent, displaced by thermodynamics, the latter was no less capable of proffering its own orthodoxy. Whereas classical physics defined itself by virtue of an overarching common sense, which promised a determinable universe, thermodynamics defines itself by an enduring good sense, a "faculty of distribution" that exists over time. As Deleuze writes:

> intensity defines an objective sense for a series of irreversible states which pass, like an "arrow of time," from more to less differenciated, from a productive to a reduced difference, and ultimately to a cancelled difference. We know how these themes of a reduction of difference, a uniformalization of identity, and an equalization of inequality stitched together for the last time a strange alliance at the end of the nineteenth century between science, good sense, and philosophy. Thermodynamics was the powerful furnace of that alloy. (DR, 223)

In linear thermodynamics, entropy is understood as a "natural process" that, once ascertained, allows us to predict the system as tending toward equilibrium (maximum entropy). Time is dissymmetrical insofar as, in a given system, entropy increases over time, but this dissymmetry will be progressively domesticated by probability. As Prigogine and Stengers write, entropy describes "evolution toward a 'disorder,' toward the most probable state."[63]

No Newtonian, the God of thermodynamics is an imprecise accountant who always leaves a remainder—and as Deleuze suggests, this difference is nothing less than the world itself. Neither inherently optimistic nor pessimistic, good sense assumes its patient posture on the basis of an enduring certainty that, "given world enough and time," we inexorably move from the proliferation of differences to their reduction. The God of entropy has all the time in the world because his time is commensurate with the world he corrects, slowly but inevitably eliminating chance, marching toward the certainty of "heat death." Like the common sense of physics, then, the good sense of (linear) thermodynamics is the means with which a God is invented to tame chance. As Prigogine and Stengers write, the "omniscient beings" of these sciences—"Laplace's or Maxwell's demon, or Einstein's God, beings that play such an important role in scientific reasoning"—ultimately "embody the kinds of extrapolation physicists thought they were allowed to make."[64] And what they extrapolate, in the last instance, is a kind of order with which to ward off chaos. It is in this sense that science can be called doxographic: it grafts/graphs order onto differences, finding zones of equilibrium and thereby abstracting the stable rules of the system. "God does not play dice with the universe," Einstein famously said,[65] and perhaps this statement, more than any other, allows us to grasp the sense in which, even today, science reinvents a new orthodoxy that "dreams of a unity, of unifying its laws, and that still searches today for a communion of the four forces" (WIP, 206).

In this light, Prigogine has consistently criticized contemporary, especially quantum, physics for its failure to cash out the consequences of nonlinear thermodynamics. While the discovery of the "uncertainty principle" (Heisenberg) famously foreclosed the possibility of quantum mechanical determinism, Prigogine contends that physics still hitches itself to this grand deterministic dream. In *A Brief History of Time*, for instance, Stephen Hawking writes, "Since the structure of molecules and their reactions with each other underlie all chemistry and biology, quantum mechanics allows us in principle to predict nearly everything we see around us, within the limits set by the uncertainty principle."[66] The point, of course, is that these limits have not precluded the principle of prediction, and this is surely why Hawking has been the subject of Prigogine's most persistent attack on quantum physics. Nevertheless, it is worth noting that recently Hawking has confessed that the aspirations to a "theory of everything" (say, string theory) have yet to truly confront the problem of chaos:

> In the standard positivist approach to the philosophy of science, physical theories live rent free in a Platonic heaven of ideal mathematical models. That is, a model can be arbitrarily detailed, and can contain an arbitrary amount of information, without affecting the universes they describe. But we are not angels, who view the universe from the outside. Instead, we and our models are both part of the universe we are describing.[67]

When Hawking says that models "don't live rent free," we should take this to mean that the creation of a model, no matter how much it presupposes its scientific detachment from the universe, is nonetheless part of the universe and, therefore, "costs energy" in that universe.[68] The energy expended and information acquired invariably implicate any theory in the system it aims to describe. In other words, there can be no "theory of everything" because such a theory cannot include its own description without suffering from either incompleteness or inconsistency. Thus, as Hawking admits, the problem of the universe gives rise to the conundrum that explicitly recalls Gödel's analysis of formal, arithmetical systems. Such systems can't be both consistent and complete, and Hawking seems to have concluded that cosmology must likewise confront this alternative. "The smart money is on the incomplete," he says, because this means that the universe is open to a future that cannot be predicted, that even all the time in the world to gather all possible information as to the history of a system is insufficient to predict the future because it must include us, we who predict and predicate, as "part of the universe we are describing."[69] The shortest possible description of the universe is—the universe itself.

Perhaps this realization can be cast in light of the appearance of "chaos" in ancient Greece, where the term did not designate disorder so much as an unbounded void. In his *Theogony*, for instance, Hesiod recounts the story whereby "Chaos came to be, but next wide-bosomed earth," which gives way in turn to the "starry Heaven."[70] Among the Greeks, chaos provides the womb of infinite undifferentiated depths from which the earth is given birth. In their inestimable "innocence" (Nietzsche), the Greeks understood that the becoming cosmos of chaos—or what we have called "chaosmos"—exists not only in the imagination of a myth but in the full extent to which the cosmos is no less a cosmogony. The cosmos is both *mythos* and *physis*, a "story of the universe" which the universe immanently engenders. Cosmos authors its own self-generation from chaos, and for this reason, its nature cannot be differentiated from its narrative: *its nature is narrative*. What is the cosmos if not the self-positing, self-referential, self-generating fabulation of particles, signs, and images according to which the universe spins its own story in real time? As cosmologists and the scientists of the nascent field of astrobiology have suggested, perhaps the cosmos is nothing else than this story, the perpetual and self-perpetuating auto-poesis of a universe whose self-consistency consists in particles giving rise to each other.[71]

Thus, beyond determinism and probability, beyond common sense and good sense, we can pose the problem of chaos once more. Chaos theory has discovered that systems existing far from equilibrium are capable of spontaneously generating unprecedented complexity. Prigogine and Stengers call these "dissipative structures" precisely because their order originates from chaos, from dissipative states, whose future we cannot predict.[72] But if we cannot predict the precipitation of future states, we can nevertheless entertain the eventualities to which they give rise as a range of possibilities that describe a given state of affairs ("phase space").[73] Hence, in the conclusion to *What Is Philosophy?* Deleuze and Guattari write: "One could conceive of a series of coordinates or phase spaces as a succession of filters, the earlier of which would be in each case a relatively chaotic state, and the latter a chaoid state, so that we would cross chaotic thresholds rather than go from the elementary to the composite" (WIP, 206). The nature of this conception recalls what mathematicians call a "Markov chain," a process whereby the next state of a given system is determined by the current state but without any reference to the past. In other words, the present includes all of the information that could affect the behavior of the system and the events that will characterize its next state—and yet, that information does not allow us to predict the future. The passage from one state to another is incalculable, but the current conditions define the statistical properties and describe its range of probabilities. Such systems are easily imagined on the basis of games of chance where the present, though the result of a previous draw, gives rise to the parameters within which chance and contingency operate. As Prigogine and Stengers write, "We are faced with chance events very similar to the fall of dice."[74] There are only so many possible outcomes, the selection of whichever one is random. As Deleuze reflects, "It is more like a successive drawing of cards, each one operating on chance but under external conditions determined by the previous draw. It is a combination of randomness and dependency like in a Markov chain" (TRM, 259).

For this reason, Markov chains are frequently used to describe systems that operate far from equilibrium, outstripping the conventional logic of determinism, pattern, and prediction and yielding to the invention of semi-aleatory series. The Markov process expresses an impulse that runs throughout Deleuze's work, from his earliest appreciations of stucturalist systems which introduce a kind of indeterminate remainder, to his consideration of games that eschew determinate contingency, to his evocation of conceptual personae who populate the plane of immanence and throw the dice on its shimmering surface. In each case, Deleuze gravitates toward a kind of quasi-chaos, namely, those series in which "the aleatory and the dependent" mingle (F, 86). In the feedback loop between what has been and what is to come, the eventuality of each new state retroactively changes the significance of the series—and yet, the present maintains an uncertainty, its parameters loosely distributed by relatively "extrinsic conditions laid down by the previous draw" (ibid., 87) and thereby open to so many degrees of freedom. As Nietzsche says, and Deleuze duly quotes, this is "the iron hand of necessity throwing the dice of chance" (ibid., 86).[75]

In *The Logic of Sense*, where the question of chance and the concept of the series are literally dramatized in the serial organization of the text, Deleuze analyzes the nature of these "semi-accidental series" by inventing what he calls "the ideal game" (LS, 59). In this game, which extends to the world itself, "there are no preexisting rules, but this does not mean that the game is without rules" (ibid.). When we revel in the lawless of random exercise, just as when we have recourse to a logic that eliminates chance tout court, we end any possibility of a game. In the ideal game, by contrast, rules exist—otherwise, the game would be a random and arbitrary exercise, not a game at all—but the rules themselves are created with each cast of the dice, which gives rise to a new state: "each move invents its own rules; it bears upon its own rule (ibid.)." Thus, Deleuze writes: "Far from dividing and apportioning chance in a really distinct number of throws, all throws affirm chance and endlessly ramify it with each throw" (ibid.). This is what Deleuze means by "crowned anarchy" (DR, 37): what if chance, instead of being determined within a predictable (and, should we not say, metaphysical-moral) structure, were unleashed as the very principle on which its fluid and self-synthesizing structure is contingent?[76]

Deleuze poses this question, perhaps most profoundly, in his remarkable excurses into the baroque, especially in Leibniz's strange philosophy, where the conditions for this delirium are already unwittingly in place. In Leibniz's "monadology," Deleuze discovers the madness with which the baroque flirts, the creation of countless possible worlds, and the rejoinder of a God who exercises the principle of sufficient reason to pick the best one, the most possible or "compossible," at the expense of the rest. Thus, Deleuze says, Leibniz saves truth at the price of damnation, but what if the baroque were to foreclose sufficient reason and to unleash possibility beyond any means of determination. In *The Fold*, Deleuze says that this question belongs to Borges, the greatest (and most

Chinese) of Leibnizians, who entertains this baroque eventuality in the creation of so many *incompossible* worlds (62-63). In "The Garden of the Forking Paths," Borges imagines this labyrinth emerging in the context of an incredible novel, by the Chinese philosopher Ts'ui Pên, which proceeds by an incomprehensible method. "In all fictions, each time a man meets diverse alternatives, he chooses one and eliminates the others," Borges writes, but in this fabulous novel, "the character chooses—simultaneously—all of them."[77] Only this, Deleuze says, can explain why Borges has recourse to a literary source: in formulating a problem on the order of Leibniz, he seeks "to have God pass into existence all incompossible worlds at once instead of choosing one of them, the best" (Fold, 63). In fiction the vein of the present potentially branches into countless capillaries, inducing "several futures, several times, which themselves proliferate and fork."[78] And yet, Borges will avow, the labyrinth is a straight line. The chronological line of time unfolds a perpetual present, but at each moment, at each cardinal point, the line opens onto a remarkable proliferation of possible worlds, the vertical and vertiginous multiplication of outcomes. The labyrinth is a line, but the line is not linear; in Borges's story, "*all* outcomes in fact occur; each is the starting point for other bifurcations."[79]

The universe of incompossibles, our multiverse, cannot be defined by the operations of an orthodoxy or the transcendence of an *Urdoxa*: it demands a new kind of thinking, supple and imageless, connective and improvisatory, which Deleuze discovers in the sciences and the arts but which he finally cashes out in philosophy. Once more, we could say, we need a new God, but Deleuze's *chaosophy* consists in having done with divine certainty in favor of introducing chance and contingency into thought. When science "turns against opinion, which lends to it a religious taste for unity or unification," Deleuze and Guattari say, it also "turns within itself against properly scientific opinion as *Urdoxa*, which consists sometimes in a determinist prediction (Laplace's God) and sometimes in probabilistic evaluation (Maxwell's demon)" (WIP, 206). To Einstein's contention that God does not play dice with the universe, then, we might respond: this is all God does. After all, Deleuze says, "what especially impedes God from making all possibles—even incompossibles—exist is that this would be a mendacious God, a trickster God, a deceiving God" (Fold, 63).

Jean-Jacques Lecercle has written that, like Nietzsche, Deleuze's philosophy ought to be reckoned as coherent but not systematic.[80] If we agree in principle with the distinction, we must also admit that its terms are not sufficiently fine-grained. In Deleuze's own terms—and this would be our revision of Lecercle's declaration—the plane of immanence is both consistent *and* inconsistent. This is not a matter of contradiction, Deleuze insists, because no single dimension adjudicates over and above the others: in the spirit of a perverse Leibniz, a Borges, we have imagined a cosmological and labyrinthine novel that embraces the profusion of possible worlds. Only when we affirm these worlds, not one above another (as "compossible"—the most possible) but in the pluralism of their impossible coexistence (as "incompossible"), do we realize the fullest extent of Deleuze's philosophical experiment.

Resistance to the Present

The History of Contingencies

> Greeks and democrats are strangely deformed in the mirror of the future.
>
> **GILLES DELEUZE** AND **FÉLIX GUATTARI**, *WHAT IS PHILOSOPHY?*

To this point, we have suggested that Deleuze's battle against doxography consists in having developed a new relation to chaos—and that this relation is inspired by the sciences of complexity. Especially late in life, the vitality of Deleuze's philosophy lies in following these sciences to a frontier defined by their respective proximity to chaos. "Chaos is not an inert or stationary state, nor is it a chance mixture," Deleuze and Guattari say (WIP, 42), but rather a "determinate chaos" that emerges between pure chance and absolute order, between chaos and *doxa*. Not only does chaos precipitate unsuspected complexity, but complexity itself exists in states that are far from equilibrium, where the "aleatory and the dependent" combine and where life takes flight. As Prigogine explains, "Life is only possible in open systems exchanging matter, energy and information with the outside world."[81]

But *what is life?* Needless to say, this is as formidable a question as we can imagine, but it must be posed, especially in the context of Deleuze's philosophy, if we are to grasp the curious nature of his vitalism and the complexity to which it gives rise. In his wonderful book *What Is Life?* the theoretical physicist Erwin Schrödinger ventured to consider how the question, "hover[ing] between biology and physics," escaped the faculties of contemporary science.[82] "How can the events in space and time which take place within the spatial boundaries of a living organism be accounted for by physics and chemistry?"[83] The question acquires even greater significance when we consider that, as Schrödinger admits, science has been enrapt by a theory of thermodynamics—the inevitable diminishment of available energy or information, *entropy*—that makes life seems unprecedented and miraculous. The "marvelous faculty of a living organism" resists the ostensibly inexorable tendency of systems to wind down, to gravitate toward disorder and inertia.[84] How is it that life endures, mutates, differentiates, grows ever more complex, and "evades the decay of equilibrium"?[85]

Anticipating the discovery of DNA, Schrödinger's answer was to look "within" the organism to smaller and smaller units that explain or contain this élan vital. But if science continues to peer inside, mapping the filigree of genome or calculating particle and wave functions in the subatomic world, Deleuze suggests that the problem of life is everywhere and immanent. The ghost is not in the machine; the ghost *is* the machine. Whatever we call life, whether we name it or attribute its enigma to other terms, the problem is the same: "What is it that breathes fire into the equations and makes a universe for them to describe?"[86] In the context of Deleuze's philosophy, as we have said, the suggestion of a kind of *vis elastica* should not lead us to regard life as an organic phenomenon, nor should we regard life as an individual or individuated phenomenon. "A life" is a becoming which draws together a collective assemblage in its passage through animal, vegetable, and mineral. The becoming of an indefinite and singular life implicates the immanent relations of a whole network, a society.

The expression of complexity that we have evoked to this point, of order at the edge of chaos, emerges on any number of different planes of matter, from the amalgamation of molecules to the organizations of birds in flight to the fluctuations of the stock market; but at whatever level, in whatever domain, the study of chaos insists on a kind of "macroscopic" perspective that embraces populations and systems. This is particularly true, Prigogine writes, in human societies, where "the condition of non-equilibrium is obviously satisfied." What does this mean? To begin with, and in the simplest possible terms, it means that "what one person does influences the actions of others."[87] When populations become sufficiently large to outgrow immediate coordination, we discover "complex collective structures that spontaneously emerge from simple autocatalytic interactions between numerous individuals and the environment."[88] Scientists describe such systems, where incidents can trigger large-scale effects, as nonlinear insofar as they perpetuate those particular conditions in which the system gives way to a range of possibilities, of bifurcations within the present. "A society is a nonlinear system," Prigogine says. The emergence of life ought to be sought in populations (or molecules, cells, individuals, etc.) that perpetuate these events with greater frequency, greater range of possibilities, and greater (global) effects. "This nonlinearity increases with the size of the society. Our present society is already full of possible bifurcations," Prigogine writes. "If I decide to take my umbrella because of uncertain weather, or leave it at home, I may consider this already as a kind of bifurcation."[89]

While we naturally want to distinguish "between trivial bifurcations and bifurcations which indeed lead to new historical systems,"[90] the "history" of any system consists in countless events, large or small, enduring or still-born. However we conceive of this event (the moment I take my umbrella, the crash of 1929, the Reformation), countless possibilities open up, forking paths where things might have been otherwise and perhaps, in another world, are. Of course, this is especially true today, when the world has been networked in so many ways that seemingly small-scale events are capable of catalyzing unforeseen eventualities. We see this with frightening clarity in the context of a global economy where incidental occurrences potentially trigger large-scale effects in the behavior of the entire system. Take the butterfly that we proverbially link with massive changes in the weather half-way around the world and imagine that the result is a tsunami, which wreaks havoc on shipping routes, causing a delay in the distribution of goods to the American consumer, which causes losses that will carry through the Asian markets, in which particular European banks are overinvested (say, in derivatives), which leads to a flood of bankruptcies that shake the world economy.

In order to grasp the cascade of events and effects, the historical study of macroscopic systems—of societies—demands a particular kind of duration and perspective that allows us to gauge broad shifts in population and organization, to extract the complex organization from what may seem, over the course of a year, a decade, or a century, like meaningless noise. Prigogine mentions Fernand Braudel and Immanuel Wallerstein as thinkers who have anticipated large-scale self-organization: in the former's penchant for the *longue durée* and the latter's elaboration of world-systems theory, we discover the constituents of complexity writ large. But to these names we should surely add those of Deleuze and Guattari. In geophilosophy and its earlier avatar, what they call "universal history," the two dwell on the contingencies of the earth and socius, the encounter of absolute and relative deterritorialization, that combine to crystallize unprecedented complexity. Theirs is a "history of contingencies, and not the history of necessity. Ruptures and limits, and not continuity," Deleuze and Guattari explain in *Anti-Oedipus* (AO, 140). Of capitalism as well as philosophy, they write: "Great accidents were necessary, and amazing encounters that could have happened elsewhere, or before, or might never have happened, in order for the flows to escape coding and, escaping, to nonetheless fashion a new machine bearing the determination of the capitalist socius" (ibid., 154).

Deleuze once said that he and Guattari "had remained Marxists, in our different ways" (Neg, 171), but in the context of our discussion to this point, we might qualify this Marxism. In effect, Deleuze and Guattari remain faithful to Marx by complexifying him. We have already witnessed something of this transformation in our discussion of *Anti-Oedipus* (chapter 1), but this process is redoubled in their subsequent collaborations. In the context of universal history and, then, geophilosophy, Marx undergoes a kind of transformation whereby: (1) capitalism, far from being inevitable, emerges in the combination of "contingent contingencies"; and (2) capitalism constitutes a complex system that, always operating far from equilibrium, exists in a kind of perpetual crisis. Both of these qualifications can be seen in Deleuze and Guattari's brief, though stunning, return to Marx in *What Is Philosophy?* There, they trace capitalism (*pace* Marx) to its basic cell, the encounter of "the two principle components," labor and wealth, whose contingent connection catalyzes a new socioeconomic organization (WIP, 97). Notably, they suggest, there is a critical difference between "wealth in general" and "labor tout court," on the one hand, and the combination of "naked labor and pure wealth," on the other (ibid.). Nothing in the discrete natures of wealth and labor can predict the eventuality of their conjunction—their "coming together as a commodity" (ibid.)—which far exceeds the sum of its parts. How can we understand this? Let's consider this "coming together" along the lines of an autocatalytic cell. The mixture of "naked labor and pure wealth" gives rise to the commodity, but in turn, the commodity-form fuels the efflorescence of "naked labor" (deterritorialized from the vestiges of a feudal economy into indus-trialism) and "pure wealth" (the accumulation of surplus capital and the all but total acquisition of the means of production). In the commodity, "naked labor and pure wealth" produce the conditions that redouble their conjunc-tion, in turn producing greater wealth and more available "biopower,"[91] the crisis which Marx analyzes but also symptomatizes (his critique corresponds to this crisis).[92]

This conjunction of naked labor and pure wealth has not ceased to drive capitalism, but in the context of the geophilosophy that Deleuze and Guattari adumbrate, it marks the singular event that we can trace from the more con-temporary formations of capitalism, or what we will call control, all the way back to ancient philosophy. Inasmuch as universal history is redoubled by geophilosophy, we might say, the analysis of the modern world is repeated in one sense and preceded in another by the ancient one. "Modern philosophy's link with capitalism is of the same kind as that of ancient philosophy with Greece," Deleuze and Guattari write: "*the connection of an absolute plane of immanence with a relative social milieu that functions through immanence*" (WIP, 98). This redoubling remains one of the more mysterious and misun-derstood aspects of *What Is Philosophy?* in large part because the resonance between ancient and modern does not simply correlate with philosophy and capitalism, respectively, but seems to suggest that each world concerns the relations between philosophy and capitalism. "Why philosophy in Greece at that moment? It is the same question for capitalism," Deleuze and Guat-tari explain: "why capitalism at these places and at these moments?" (ibid., 95). If the question makes us hesitate, this is because it seems to extend the notion of capitalism beyond the very historical framework with which Marx defines it: what is dialectical materialism if not the affirmation that capitalism is determined by specific conditions—let us say, to begin with, the emergence of "naked labor and pure wealth"?

Among the Greeks, then, Deleuze and Guattari never venture to speak of capitalism *sensu stricto* but rather of deterritorialization *lato sensu*, which links the ancient and the modern world, precapitalist Athens and modern Europe. In both cases, this deterritorialization implicates mind and matter, *nous* and *physis*, in a revolutionary becoming. "Why did philosophy survive in Greece? We cannot say that capitalism during the Middle Ages is the continu-ation of the Greek city (even the commercial forms are hardly comparable)," they write (ibid., 97). "But, for always contingent reasons, capitalism leads Europe into a fantastical relative deterritorialization that is due first of all to the city-town *and that itself takes place through immanence*" (ibid.). Even in the ancient world, where the invocation of capitalist production would be anachronistic, Deleuze and Guattari follow Fernand Braudel's intuition of a kind of pre-capitalism, the relations of a feverish international market-place that anticipates modern capitalism. Historians have "described these exchanges in terms of 'accumulation,' " Braudel writes, "in order to suggest that the economic take-off in the ancient world may already have involved a type of merchant 'capitalism,' with all the tension that implies."[93]

Let's put the problem more explicitly: why do certain milieus condition such "economic takeoff," when others, which appear to have the same basic constituents (markets, currency, even credit), remain stuck in "primitive" systems of exchange—savage coding and feudal debt?[94] The mystery of capitalism, of why it took place in certain times and places, is just as much the question of why it failed to emerge in others. As Deleuze and Guattari write, "Why not in China at some other moment, since so many of the components were already there? (WIP, 95-96). Consider either ancient China, which "for all its inventiveness in this domain (money, even paper money, was known there very early on), was very slow to make use of it"[95]; or early modern China, which "possessed material and technical knowledge that, in many cases, sur-passed its European counterparts," and yet remained under the sway of an imperial economy.[96] What explains this ostensible failure to launch? In the history of Marxism, this question has traditionally given rise to the vexed dis-cussion of the "Asiatic Mode of Production," and we might briefly rehearse this concept in order to grasp how Deleuze and Guattari envision an alternative. Beyond the differences that characterize even industrialized societies, Marx and Engels reflect on the even more profound differences between European capitalist states and the economic modes of production, whether sedentary or deferred, that they encountered in Asia. Prototypically, the Asiatic mode of production tends to refer to societies mired in a despotic state-form where the relative absence of private property characterizes self-sufficient villages dom-inated by agriculture.[97] Broadly construed, Marx and Engels avail themselves of two intimately related approaches to this mode of production. On the one hand, they underscore the idiosyncratic nature of Asian societies, their intran-sigence to capitalist logic, whereby they provide the negative means to verify the conditions of European feudalism that made capitalism possible. On the other hand, they envision such societies as perpetually delayed instances of the same European logic, thereby ascribing to a principle of uneven development that endorses the Occidental model (feudalism, mercantilism, capitalism) as the universal one. The inadequacy of both responses is immediately clear: the first allows for difference, but does so in the name of an entirely distinct and exotic mode that might well justify colonization; the second precludes socioeconomic differences and, as a result, blankly assimilates Asian societies to a Western standard. How, then, are we to grasp the difference that characterizes the so-called Asiatic mode of production?

Like Braudel, Deleuze and Guattari begin by formulating their answer on the basis of geographical and extrinsic circumstances. Literally "nothing intrinsic to Europe determined the outcome" of capitalism: geophilosophy concerns "a dynamics bearing no inherent relationship to any one culture" and, instead, reflects the vagaries of land and sea.[98] In this respect, we might recall our previous discussion of geophilosophy, where we considered the emergence of Greek philosophy in light of economy—and economy in light of the earth. In the second chapter, we argued that the Greek cities arise on the basis of a contingent combination of geographic contingencies, which we enumerated as (1) the "fractal" outline of Greece itself, the boundless coastline, which conditions travel and trade; (2) the poor quality of the soil, which drives the Greeks from the hinterlands to the sea; and (3) the relative distance that separates the Greek world from Imperial Formations, which enables trade but catalyzes the autonomous functions of the *polei* themselves. In the context of our current discussion, we would have to say that China "enjoys" none of these contingencies. Its ample coastline is overwhelmed by an interior so boundless that even the most inhospitable soil does not necessarily induce its inhabitants to venture to the sea. Rather than exist in relation to an Imperial Formation, China constitutes an *Urstaat* that either overwhelms its neighbors, which were "economies in their infancy (Japan, Indochina, the Malay Archipelago), easy to dominate and well-used to barter"[99]; or turns away from internationalism altogether, eventually moving the capital city from the coast to the interior.

Why does philosophy emerge in ancient Greece and not in China? Why does capitalism emerge in modern Europe and not to the east? In both cases, the answer lies in the imposition of a kind of imperial transcendence from which Greek philosophy and Western capitalism are (relatively) free. The Greek cities "are the first to be at once near enough to and far enough away from the archaic eastern empires to be able to benefit from them without following their model" (WIP, 87). Or, as Braudel writes, "Wherever it took place, the appearance of such autonomous urban centers is only conceivable in the absence of large-scale territorial states, which always have gargantuan appetites for conquest."[100] In this regard, we can begin to grasp the nature of the repetition that characterizes the ancient and the modern. In both cases, the formation of an "international marketplace" emerges from contingencies that combine to promote the large-scale behavior of the system toward complexity. In both, then, Braudel locates the development of capitalism in "cyclonic zones,"[101] or what we have called far from equilibrium conditions, where no *Urstaat* is present, where geographical circumstances induce a kind of hospitality to so many flows and forces. "The drama of the Greek city-states was rather like that of the cities of the Italian Renaissance," Braudel writes.[102] "This was logical enough, since the malaise of the Greek city-states had created—as could also be said of fifteenth century Italy—a cyclonic zone of low pressure, into which currents were drawn from all sides."[103] Bordering on the Mediterranean "bath of immanence," the Greek *polei* and, thereafter, the Italian city-states engaged in trade and competition that catalyze their co-evolution. In Braudel's words, "trade could be really profitable only if there was a vigorous and spontaneous electric current passing between high-voltage and low-voltage points . . . It was then that the network of Greek cities, both ancient and modern, really 'went live.' "[104]

In *What Is Philosophy?* Deleuze and Guattari reach the same conclusion. Far from equilibrium geographical systems can trigger fits and bouts of intense self-organization. This is precisely what happens in ancient Greece, where cities emerged, competed, and mutually ramified each other, and this process is no less characteristic of emergent capitalist systems.[105] To put it in the terms of nonlinear thermodynamics, capitalism emerges from large-scale nonequlibrium systems that create and ramify complex organization: "*the West extends and propagates its centers of immanence*" (WIP, 97). Thus, the logic of complexity should encourage us to realize the sense in which capitalism resumes and extends the eventualities that we analyzed in the Greek world (see chapter 2). "This is not the result of a Greek endeavor," Deleuze and Guattari insist, "but a resumption, in another form and with other means, on a scale hitherto unknown, which nonetheless relaunches the combination for which the Greeks took initiative" (ibid.). Between the ancient world and our own, we detect a resonance, as if capitalism emerges from a "contingent recommencement" (ibid., 98) of the very contingencies that had catalyzed the emergence of philosophy in ancient Athens: namely, the extension of a plane of immanence (*autochthony*), the emergence of a sphere of friendships and rivalries (*philia*), and the efflorescence of opinion (*doxa*).

Let us briefly recapitulate these contingencies, in their Athenian expression, in order to grasp their resumption in modern capitalism. To begin with, *autochthony* ought to be understood as the expression of a remarkable deterritorializing principle with which the Greeks made the Mediterranean a "bath of immanence" (WIP, 88).The Greek *polei* free themselves from the constraints of transcendent imperialism and enter into feverish competitions for markets, colonies, and prestige that redoubles the agonism that characterized its social diagram. [106] In this respect we have articulated the second condition of geophilosophy, for the network of Greek cities prepared the way for new kinds of relationship among its peoples. Indeed, the "international marketplace" into which the Greeks enter was conditioned by "a pure sociability as milieu of immanence, the 'intrinsic nature of association,' which is opposed to imperial sovereignty and implies no prior interest because, on the contrary, competing interests presuppose it" (ibid., 87). As we argued in the second chapter, only when a relationship of equality among equals (*isoi*) has been established do we find the emergence of genuine rivalry (*eris*), which extends from warrior games and athletic contests to the domain of speech and opinion (*doxa*). In Athens, the diagram of the *agôn* was prolonged into the spheres of love, politics, rhetoric, and—yes—philosophy. Ultimately, Greek philosophy derives from the contingencies of each characteristic, whereby immanence, friendship, and *doxa* ramify each other and thereby produce the possibility of the agonism of concepts.

Thus, we can begin to see how these traits are resumed under the auspices of capitalism, "even if they have taken on a new meaning, which explains the permanence of philosophy in the economy of our democratic world" (CC, 136–37). What we find in the Greek world will be renewed in the modern one—not just in the Italian city-states of the renaissance about which Braudel writes, but also in the broad extension of European (industrial) capitalism and, subsequently, in its global and informational organization. For its part, and "for always contingent reasons, capitalism leads Europe into a [similarly] fantastic relative deterritorialization that is due first of all to city-town and that itself takes place through immanence" (WIP, 97). In the first place, then, the immanence that *autochthony* evoked in Greece is resumed in the field of immanence of capital, where the "maritime component" linking cities is effectively transformed by the vast sea of commodity-exchange and the variable flows, or tributaries, that link its own markets (ibid., 102). In the second place, the sociability, or *philia,* that the Greeks enjoyed is resumed in the guise of "the society of brothers or comrades," which constitutes both the vast collective of workers as well as the promise of a new *demos* (ibid., 99). In the third place, the democratic taste for *doxa* is resumed in a new reign of opinion, which determines the shape of democratic institutions and the larger "public sphere" where a given society debates its problems and negotiates its future.[107]

Insofar as capitalism redoubles the contingencies of ancient philosophy, though, we know all too well that it has produced disappointments and miseries that are entirely its own. In the first place, the milieu, or plane of immanence, to which capitalism gives rise continues to sustain itself only by imposing relative, axiomatic limits (reterritorializations) which result in the development of liberal nation-states, whose investment almost always concerns markets more than actual democracy. As Deleuze and Guattari write, "Democratic States are so bound up with, and compromised by, dictatorial States that the defense of human right must necessarily take up the internal criticism of every democracy" (WIP, 106). In the second place, the society of brothers and friends, which made possible agonism and rivalry in the Greek world, now devolves into brute competitions of an uncivil society, a *bellum omnium contra omnes*, in which opinion and opinion-makers reign over the field of discourse. The "catastrophe" of democracy exists in each of us, in every "democrat" who confronts in the worst genocides as well as the most "insignificant conditions" what Deleuze and Guattari call "the meanness and vulgarity of existence that haunts democracies, before the propagation of these modes of existence and of thought-for-the-market, and before value ideals, and the opinions of our time" (ibid., 107). In short, the prospect of *philia* is transformed into the most shameful compromises: "We are no longer Greeks, and friendship is no longer the same" (ibid.). In the third and last place, the efflorescence of opinion, which challenged and even nurtured the development of philosophy, has been networked by a communications society, where marketing supplants philosophy and advertising slogans stand in for concepts. Free markets make free peoples; the time of the welfare state is over; God bless America—for everything else, there's MasterCard. In our communications society, where opinion flourishes under the auspices of new media and old genres, philosophy contends with doxographic disciplines that claim to be the real creators of concepts. And isn't this their very appeal? These disciplines promote what is, or at least what they lead us to believe is, the only rational response to the "brave new world" of globalization—conversation, cosmopolitanism, the public sphere, democracy, capitalism.

Not surprisingly, philosophies of communication frequently claim Socrates (and, by extension, the Platonic dialogue) as the avatar of their own philosophy of debate and consensus. As Deleuze and Guattari ask, tongue in cheek, "In Socrates was philosophy not a free discussion among friends? Is it not, as the conversation of free men, the summit of Greek sociability?" (WIP, 29). And to the careless eye, no doubt, the ancient world provides an image of exchange that anticipates the prospects of today's communication society. But inasmuch as the idea of communication "comes, perhaps, from the Greeks," Deleuze and Guattari write, "they distrusted it so much, and subjected it to such harsh treatment, that the concept was more like the ironical soliloquy bird that surveyed [*survolait*] the battlefield of destroyed rival opinions (the drunken guest at the banquet)" (ibid., 6).[108] The recourse to Plato is ironic—or, at least, it should be—in light of the fact that Plato himself looked on the democracy of opinion with more than ample contempt. For this reason, Deleuze and Guattari write, "it does no credit to philosophy for it to present itself as a new Athens by falling back on Universals of communication that would provide rules for the imaginary mastery of the markets and media (intersubjective idealism)" (ibid., 7). Whether in the guise of critical theory (the "perpetual discussion" and "communicative rationality" of Habermas [ibid., 28]) or contemporary pragmatism ("pleasant or aggressive dinner conversation at Mr. Rorty's" [ibid., 144]), the recourse to "Universals of communication" represents the very problem with which we must contend. We have seen a preview of this very problem in the short life of the "New Philosophers," but the threat of doxography continues apace. "Habermas is not the only one who would like to index philosophy on communication," Deleuze says. "Neither 'consensus' nor Rorty's 'rules of democratic conversation' are enough to create a concept" (TRM, 382), but they are more than enough to have hijacked the creation of concepts and to have reintroduced the presupposition and aspiration of orthodoxy into philosophy. What can philosophy, an "old man," do?

The Untimely (or, Utopia)

> Let us profit from this moment in which antiphilosophy is trying to be a language of power.
>
> **GILLES DELEUZE** AND **FÉLIX GUATTARI,** *KAFKA: TOWARD A MINOR LITERATURE*

Once more we have returned to the problem of the "communications society" with which we began this chapter and to the rivals with which philosophy contends today. In *What Is Philosophy?* as we noted, Deleuze and Guattari initially express a kind of sympathy for Plato: besieged by sophists, confronted by rivals at every turn, Plato seems to have anticipated the conditions of philosophy today. But if Deleuze and Guattari confront a kind of Platonic problem, this affinity is only the most superficial aspect of a philosophical response that remains to be grasped, in this final section, in the invention of a new politics—the means with which to resist the present. "We do not lack communication. On the contrary, we have too much of it," Deleuze and Guattari insist. "We lack creation. *We lack resistance to the present*" (WIP, 108).

The radical nature of *What Is Philosophy?*—its resistance—has not prevented critics from charging Deleuze with unrepentant conservativism. In an interview on the occasion of its publication, Didier Eribon begins by saying to Deleuze, "Your definition of philosophy is rather offensive. Aren't you concerned about being criticized for maintaining, or restoring, the traditional privilege granted to philosophy?" (TRM, 381). In so many words, Eribon charges Deleuze and Guattari with philosophical imperiousness, with having granted philosophy a "privilege" that goes back to Platonism itself. The more far-reaching and unspoken accusation, of course, indicts Deleuze on the basis of an aristocratic claim, familiar enough in the history of philosophy, to the orthodoxy of right thinking. How can one answer this criticism except to remark that perhaps this kind of aggressive misunderstanding is the cost of *believing* in philosophy today, since this is precisely what Deleuze means when he describes philosophy as having a "definite occupation": philosophy does not claim an ideal place but affirms a real task. Where Plato appeals to divine Ideas as the criteria with which to discern the true from the false, to organize the world of appearances, to make judgments, Deleuze and Guattari define philosophy as the creation of concepts—and as they are quick to add, "philosophy gains no privilege from that" (ibid., 381).

Roughly speaking, the problem is twofold. On the one hand, philosophy finds itself confronting a dogmatic image of thought—a communications society—that erodes past and future, memory and hope, in the habitas of a perpetual present. But on the other hand, inasmuch as we have resolved to resist the present, we are no less aware that philosophy cannot seek the remedy of the eternal or a priori, which only manages to displace *doxa* with *Urdoxa*. The task of creating concepts begins today when we resist "communication, exchange, consensus, and opinion" (WIP, 99). Perhaps the most damning thing Deleuze ever said about the philosophers of communication is that they have failed to find "a good concept, a truly critical concept" (TRM, 382) for communication itself because they never established it as a problem. Rather, these communicators presupposed the exchange of *doxa* and the pretense of democratic and universal *Urdoxa*. Where opinion inhabits a perpetual present in which "concepts" are marketed and consumed (think, for instance, of the "high concept" logic that defines the marketing of big-budget Hollywood films, especially bad ones[109]), philosophy must find ways to intervene in the present without, for all that, being "of" the present. As Deleuze and Guattari suggest, the mission of philosophy is to resonate with "its own epoch" without simply replying to the dominant determinations of that epoch, since such replies and reactions condemn philosophy to journalism, to current affairs, to *doxa* (WIP, 99).[110]

"If there is no universal democratic state," Deleuze and Guattari write, "it is because the market is the only thing that is universal in capitalism (ibid., 106). Hence, when Toni Negri asks him whether communism is still a viable option, perhaps now more than ever given the development of communication societies, Deleuze immediately retreats from any such promise. "The quest for 'universals of communication' ought to make us shudder," he says (Neg, 175). "We're definitely moving toward 'control' societies that no longer operate by confining people but through continuous control and instant communication" (ibid., 174). But what is "control" and what does Deleuze mean by "control societies"? Deleuze never used the term "neoliberalism," but if he had, he surely would have done so in the context of control, which describes the emergent, post-Fordist social diagram of contemporary Western societies. Whereas the prior episteme had already transformed the exercise of power into the vast disciplinary assemblage of modern socio-political institutions and the discursive fields to which they give rise, we might say that control societies invent a yet more "gentle" discipline. Deleuze credits Foucault with having unfolded this regime of power in the great waves of his histories. Foucault discerns the most contracted instance of the disciplinary diagram in the prison, and he traces this architecture of power—the organization of discourses (on criminality, madness, perversion, etc.), the array of lines (of sight and blindness), and the distribution of bodies (prisoners)—both historically and genealogically through so many institutional instances ("the school is a prison, the factory is a prison, literally, not metaphorically" [TI, 20]). But for both Deleuze and Foucault, this disciplinary episteme has given way to a new organization of power. The old disciplinary institutions and structures ("prisons, schools, hospitals") are steadily eroding, Deleuze says, and he adds that "they're breaking down because they're fighting a losing battle. New kinds of punishment, educations, health care are being stealthily introduced" (Neg, 174–75).

The transformation of our socius, which was still inchoate when Deleuze wrote his last works, entails the invention of a new critical enterprise. Whereas discipline still suggests a kind of interpretive retrieval, the diagram of control offers no experience of epiphany, raises no consciousness, because its diagram is never concealed—rather, it appears everywhere, guides every decision, becoming the very means of "decisionism." Not based on production but on marketing, the machinations of control are so cunning and its conspiracy so diffuse that it is difficult to appreciate the diagram of forces—the new biopolitical paradigm. Indeed, control outstrips any description of the technological transformation, however vast, that characterizes the reorganization of Western societies over the last half-century. These societies no doubt correspond to a new type of machine—the cybernetic machine or computer— but Deleuze says that "machines don't explain anything, you have to analyze the collective arrangement of which the machines are just one component" (Neg, 175). Even the introduction of new information systems remains to be grasped within a broader reorganization of power that, he adds, "is more deeply rooted in a mutation of capitalism" (ibid.,180). What is this mutation?

"We're definitely moving toward 'control' societies that are no longer exactly disciplinary," Deleuze says, by which he means that societies "no longer operate by confining people but through continuous control and instant communication" (ibid., 174). Where the diagram of disciplinary society, provided by the prison, found economic expression in the model of *factory*, the diagram of control society is provided by the model of *business*. The former mobilizes individuals into a body that can be managed and monitored, with the dim provision of course that they can conceivably mobilize themselves, forming unions and organizations. By contrast, businesses are "dispersive" to the degree that (1) they atomize individuals (or "dividuals") within communication networks that track their habits, consumption, addictions ("through continuous control and instant communication" [ibid.]); and (2) they establish an "inexorable rivalry presented as healthy competition, a wonderful motivation that sets individuals against one another and sets itself up in each of them, dividing each within himself" (ibid., 179). Consider the production of the commodity, which we described as the conjunction of "naked labor and pure wealth." Today, Deleuze says, production has given way to "meta-production": "What it seeks to sell is services, and what it seeks to buy, activities. It is a capitalism no longer directed toward production but toward products, that is, toward sales or markets. Thus it is essentially dispersive, with factories giving way to businesses," with products giving way to marketing, and with commodities giving way to advertisements (ibid., 181).

Philosophy cannot take refuge from control society because this kind of society, more than its epistemic predecessors, insinuates itself into the micro-movements of "what is called thinking": under the auspices of communication, it fills every last stray space and spare moment with a regime of clichés and slogans. Let us conclude this chapter by considering the possibilities of philosophy today, precisely when its prospects seem so dim. Or, inversely, perhaps we can understand the vitality of Deleuze's late philosophy only in view of the lamentable eventualities that thinking suffers today, in the endless loop of twenty-four-hour news cycles, when a relation beyond the present, to something like utopia, strikes us as thoroughly inconceivable. The "timeliness" of the communicative concept, its impoverished currency, cannot convey the richness of belief—of utopia—that once affirmed an "other" society, an "other" politics, an "other" history to be possible. Ironically, the postmodern anticipation that our master narratives were nearing extinction has gradually given way to the resignation that we are stuck with "this" sad society, "this" dismal politics, "this" irremediable history. In our worst moments, whether to ourselves or aloud, we're bound to ask: "What is to be done?" Of course, the history of this old Russian question, beginning with Chernyshevsky's social vision, then Tolstoy's moral one, and finally Lenin's revolutionary one, always consists in its conversion into a program concerning what *should* be done—but in our present context we might say that the question seems to have re-acquired the quality of a genuine, and perhaps genuinely unanswerable, appeal. What is to be done today, when the prospect of revolutionary politics seems impossibly antiquated? What is to be done when the figure of the philosopher has been thrust aside in favor of the new specialists, the avatars of communication?

"The media no longer needs intellectuals. I'm not saying that this reversal, this domestication of the intellectual, is a disaster," Deleuze once remarked, though we might as well add: it just feels that way (TRM, 143). However we traditionally define the figure of the intellectual, and god only knows how many ways this has been done, it seems that the intellectual today is defined primarily by virtue of discouragement. The causes of this discouragement have been elucidated by just as many commentators, but in view of our discussion here, we might remark on the condition itself—on what it means to have lost hope. The quietly devastating fact, so widespread that it often goes unspoken, is that in this world we seem unable to muster the peculiar optimism with which the intellectual laid claim to another, different, or better world.[111] Our cultural affinity for science fiction narratives in which humanity capitulates to vast extraterrestrial occupations seems, finally, to have been displaced by the sad revelation that we don't need any aliens to render our resistance futile, that we can no longer imagine the radical possibility of deviating from the present.

Thus, when we speak today of the future of utopia, we already anticipate the trouble with the genre in the the loss of the very aptitude on which hope traditionally rests. The power of utopia constituted one of the most enduring means of intellectual critique and political intervention because the capacity to imagine another place (*topos*), however different or because it is different (*outopos*), conditioned the means to intervene in the present, in the here and now. Far from being one narrative among others, utopia historically corresponds to something like our faculty of communal and political imagination.

But what happens when we can no longer invoke that faculty, when the trope of political hope is no longer available? Ironically, this is precisely the kind of bleak moment when we would be inclined to invoke utopia to conjure a hope for the future from the ashes of our despair—except for the fact that what makes this moment so depressing in the first place is that we no longer have recourse to utopianism. Whereas utopia traditionally concerned the fabulation of another world, we seem to have reached a point where or when we can no longer imagine the radical transformation of our own circumstances without a paroxysm of self-loathing, as though we should all know better by now than to indulge in impossible dreams. Today, we reach for utopia like an amputee reaching for a phantom limb: to discover there's no "there" there—and to feel stupid for having done so.

Of course, we have all heard the admonishments against utopia ("get over your far-flung hopes, stop fantasizing about a better world, and above all give up on all that Marxist blather"), but perhaps we should take these as the inducement to revalue utopia itself. Is it possible to reanimate the concept and what would this mean for political philosophy? If "we have lost the utopian function of criticism,"[112] as Hayden White has suggested, we ought to admit that the end has been a long time coming. For Deleuze, certainly, the locus of this problem can be traced back to the events of May '68, to which he returns intermittently throughout his writings. For instance: in a well-known conversation between Deleuze and Foucault, "Intellectuals and Power" (1972), both acknowledge that the events of '68 have exposed a completely different regime of power with which philosophers, and intellectuals in general, must wrestle. "For a long period," Foucault writes elsewhere, "the 'left' intellectual spoke, and was acknowledged the right of speaking, in the capacity of master of truth and justice"; but in the context of this conversation, he and Deleuze agree that this promise has been largely rescinded.[113] "It seems to me that the political involvement of the intellectual was traditionally the product of two different aspects of his activity," Foucault explains at the outset of the dialogue: "his position as an intellectual in bourgeois society, in the system of capitalist production and within the ideology it produces and imposes . . . and his proper discourse to the extent that it revealed a particular truth, that it disclosed political relationships where they were unsuspected" (DI, 207).

Notably, these "aspects" of the intellectual serve to locate our sense of the epistemic shift from discipline to control. Traditionally, the "left intellectual" undertakes critique on the basis of a claim to higher values and a better world—say, the utopianism of absolute social justice for universal human rights. But where the intellectual's function formerly relied on the conviction that the ignorant or ideologically blinded masses needed to be informed, today the intellectual has discovered that the masses "no longer need him to gain knowledge; they *know* perfectly well, without illusion; they know far better than he and they are certainly capable of expressing themselves" (ibid., 207). Naturally, in '68, certain philosophers and intellectuals tried to transcend these "series of amplified instabilities and fluctuations," to name its organs, to speak for its totality, but these same people are the ones who, Deleuze says, fail to perceive the event of May '68 qua an event (TRM, 233). "There were a lot of agitations, gesticulations, slogans, idiocies, illusions in '68," Deleuze admits, "but this is not what counts. What counts is what amounted to a visionary phenomenon, as if society suddenly saw what was intolerable in it and also saw the possibility for something else" (ibid., 233–34).

For Deleuze, this is surely the lesson of May '68, the promise of which was kindled not because of but *in spite of* the intervention of an intellectual class. The interesting thing about May 1968 is that it happened so spontaneously, that allegiances between constituencies and classes were not mediated by intellectuals but resulted from a kind of self-organization. When people ask, "Where was Foucault during these days?" or "what did Deleuze do?" they miss the point that what happened, or did not happen, is distinguished precisely by the absence of presiding figures—because in its most creative moments, the events of May '68 were those that escaped the determination of a professional intellectual structure (not only professional philosophers but professional politicians, etc.). Hence, unlike many for whom these events constituted the source of utter disappointment, *nihilism,* Deleuze looks back without recrimination. When he evokes the events of '68, he does so to extract a concept of the event itself.

> May '68 was a demonstration, an irruption, of a becoming in its pure state. It's fashionable these days to condemn the horrors of revolution. It's nothing new; English Romanticism is permeated by reflections on Cromwell very similar to present-day reflections on Stalin. They say revolutions turn out badly. But they're confusing two different things, the way revolutions turn out historically and people's revolutionary becoming. These relate to two different sets of

people. Men's only hope lies in a revolutionary becoming: the only way of casting off their shame or responding to what is intolerable. (Neg, 171)

Thus, when Deleuze and Guattari write that "May '68 did not happen," this
statement marks the division between the event and the representation or
reportage that surrounded the event, tried explain it. Those who strived to
represent the events of May '68, even and especially those who claimed in the
universal and utopian tradition to be the "subject who knows," only ensured
that, when all was said and done, its aftermath would be little different than
what had preceded it. Perhaps, in this way, the phrase "May '68 did not happen" takes on a second meaning. For the historical re-writing of the event, its
representation, ensures that May '68 cannot happen, which is to say, that the
residual and ineffaceable signs of the event, emanating as if from a distant star
we see years in the past, finds no hospitality, no understanding, in the present. "May '68 was not the result of a crisis, nor was it a reaction to a crisis. It
is rather the opposite. It is the current crisis, the impasses of the current crisis
in France that stem directly from the inability of French society to assimilate
May '68" (TRM, 234). In short, *May '68 did not take place, nor has it ceased
not to take place.*

Therefore, while "May '68" already determines a particular object within
historical conditions of possibility (it happened because of the workers,
because of the students, because of their brief alliance, etc.), the sense of the
event and the event of its sense escape historical causality, launching a line of
flight from the "present"—a line that, by its very nature, cannot be explained
from the perspective *of* the present. "Historians are not very fond of this
aspect" of the event, Deleuze and Guattari write. "They restore causality after
the face" (ibid., 233). By contrast, in "May '68 Did Not Take Place," Deleuze
and Guattari invoke chaos theory to describe the uniqueness of this political event:

> The event itself is a splitting off from, or a breaking with causality; it is a bifurca-
> tion, a deviation with respect to laws, an unstable condition which opens up a
> new field of the possible. Ilya Prigogine spoke of such states in which, even in
> physics, the slightest differences persist rather than cancel themselves out, and
> where completely independent phenomena resonate with each other. (ibid.)

Born of chance, precipitating unimaginable complexity, the aforementioned
event has been the subject of chaos theory, but Deleuze and Guattari situate

it at the heart of their political philosophy. This may explain why, in *What Is Philosophy?* Deleuze and Guattari take a curious (and virtually unprecedented) detour through the concept of utopia (WIP, 99–100). Very little of Deleuze's political philosophy explicitly anticipates this turn, and even here, the authors confess uneasiness about the term, which might normally suggest the displacement of one world by another or better one. But, instead, they transform utopia into the means to resist the logic of the present—to produce the event. This sense of utopia crystallizes when we consider the strange etymological history of the term. Soon after Sir Thomas More coined "utopia" in his eponymous satire, contemporaries began to suggest that the concept was better conveyed by an alternate spelling: "eutopia."[114] The brief existence of two different spellings suggests a critical conceptual juncture—a bifurcation—for More's original term "utopia" and its conversion (if not literally then at least figuratively) into "eutopia" reveal two very different notions. Of course, both consist in the modification of the Greek "place" or "*topos*," but the addition of "eu-" typically makes what follows it the subject of the good (e.g., euphemism, eudoxus, etc.). Thus, eutopia implies a "good place," and while the spelling of the term thereafter reverted to the original "utopia," the term retained this sense of a good place and a happy future. By contrast, Deleuze and Guattari invoke More's initial sense of the term—*utopia to the letter*—insofar as the prefix (*ou-* or *óú*) literally revokes the promise of an actual place. The prefix does not simply modify the sense of place but rather revokes its actualization in order to affirm a "no-place" or "non-place." Utopia is precisely the critical and conceptual operation that links the "now and here" to the "nowhere" (WIP, 100).

In this light, and by way of conclusion, we might distinguish between these two senses of utopia on the basis of their respective movements of deterritorialization. On the one hand, utopia qua eutopia displaces the real world onto another, and better, world, such that the initial deterritorialization gives way to the actualization of a new transcendence. On the other hand, utopia qua outopia intervenes in the actual world by means of another reality, a "virtual" reality, which opens up a disjunction in the space-time of the present. This may well explain why Deleuze and Guattari go so far as to suggest that the concept requires something like the invention of another word: the literal sense of utopia is so encrusted with connotations and assumptions that we lack any intuition of its potential power to open, within the present, a problem that is not of "this" world (ibid., 110).[115] Utopia, they write, "stands for absolute deterritorialization but always at the critical point at which it is connected with the present relative milieu, and especially with the forces that stifle this milieu" (ibid., 99–100). In other words, utopia does not designate a future world but an "absolute deterritorialization" of the present. Utopia "designates *that conjunction of philosophy, or of the concept, with the present milieu—* political philosophy" (ibid., 100).

Recalling the redoubling of absolute deterritorialization that we have traced in the ancient and modern world, we can understand why Deleuze and Guattari linger on these two geophilosophical epochs: "Actually, utopia is what links philosophy with its own epoch, with European capitalism, but also with the Greek city" (ibid., 99). But if philosophy makes utopia the means to intervene in the present, utopia also names the line that philosophy draws between the present time and something outside the present, something untimely. What does this mean? "Utopia does not split off from infinite movement," Deleuze and Guattari write (ibid.): rather, it insinuates itself into that movement in order to open up so many points where the contestation of forces resists determination and provokes the bifurcation of the present into possible worlds. In this regard, utopia bears the unmistakable traces of Deleuze's concept of nonbeing—though perhaps not as we might expect. Rather than linger on the term itself, to which Deleuze never really returns after *Difference and Repetition*, consider once more the alternatives into which nonbeing is typically drawn: "either there is no non-being, and negation is illusory and ungrounded, or there is non-being, which puts the negative in being and grounds the negation" (DR, 63). Deleuze's alternative, which is in fact the alternative to alternatives, introduces an entirely new and uncanny possibility, for as we have seen there might be "reasons to say *both* that there is non-being *and* that the negative is illusory" (ibid.). In other words, what concerns us here is the structure of a definition that releases us from the logic of exclusion ("either . . . or"), which is itself structured by negativity, in order to affirm the logic of a problem which by its very nature or denaturing nature ("both . . . and") cannot be pinned down. When Deleuze says that the "'non' in the expression 'non-being' expresses *something other than the negative*" (ibid.), we should apply the same supple logic to utopia: the "u" in utopia expresses something other than the negative.

Of course, standard utopias often define the good (*eu*) qua the future by virtue of a critique, or negation, of the present, but this is precisely where the genre has run aground. Inasmuch as we have defined utopia as a "non-place," we do not negate the world so much as we affirm what Nietzsche and then Deleuze call the untimely. Whereas the conceptualization of utopia qua eutopia effectively displaces us into a better future, utopia emerges strangely, unpredictably, and uncannily as a problem within the present. Confronted with our own nihilism, we can do no better, and we might do a lot worse, than to call on utopia "to work against the time and thereby have an effect on it, hopefully for the benefit of a future time."[116] The function of utopia doesn't refer to the actuality of revolution, for which we could (after all) wait indefinitely, but rather to the " 'enthusiasm' with which it is thought on the absolute plane of immanence, like the presentation of the infinite in the here and now, which includes nothing rational or even reasonable" (WIP, 100). This "event" draws a line of flight from what ostensibly happens (i.e., the actualizations of history) into the "unhistorical vapor" that envelops the various actors and spectators in a self-referential and self-positing self-affection.

This is the promise of utopia, which no longer offers another or better world but nourishes the instinct, the "enthusiasm" (*Schwärmerei*), with which we affirm the world as that which must be created. "What we most lack is a belief in the world, we have quite lost the world, it has been taken from us," Deleuze writes (Neg, 176). Perhaps the gift of old age is to have passed through the modern litany of degradations and devaluations, to have grasped finally that "Eros is sick," and to have resolved to believe in the world again and as if for the first time. To the question with which we began—"How could philosophy, an old person, compete against young executives in a race for the universals of communication for determining the marketable form of the concept, *Merz*?"—Deleuze offers not an answer but the rejoinder of a life and an innocence that, traversing the corrupt and capitalized field of philosophy, affirms the world as the perpetual commingling of grace and chance. When "you believe in the world you precipitate events, however conspicuous, that elude control, you engender new space-times, however small their surface or volume" (TI, 176). Paradoxically, we could say, utopia names this belief.

CODA

Sci-Phi

> It is the business of the future to be dangerous, and it is among the merits of science that it equips the future for its duties.
>
> **ALFRED NORTH WHITEHEAD,** *SCIENCE AND THE MODERN WORLD*

A Philosophy of the Future

IN THE COURSE OF THIS BOOK, we have returned again and again to Deleuze's declaration that the task of philosophy consists in the invention of new means of expression, but we have always done so by affirming that this constitutes his *own* task. Deleuze's abstract recommendation is also, and perhaps more importantly, his singular and self-imposed challenge to think and write differently: the powers of the false must be cashed out in the "fabulation of philosophy" itself. In each of the previous five chapters, then, we have endeavored to consider Deleuze's experiments in expression—in relation to Nietzsche (chapter 1), as the elaboration of geophilosophy (chapter 2), as the overturning of Platonism (chapter 3), on the basis of minor literature (chapter 4), and against the specter of our control society (chapter 5).

Nevertheless, as we look back, perhaps we can also discern the subtle contours of the line of flight that wends its way through the entirety of this book. Alighting on so many problems and questions, concepts and personae, we have traced the supple trajectory of Deleuze's philosophical life from his early commentaries to his late work, no less the history of philosophy he reads and revises, from its Greek avatars to its contemporary undertakings. In view of this "life-line," then, it remains for us to grapple with the question of philosophy in relation to the future. What does this mean? What is "the future" after all? A curious thing: whenever he was asked about the future of philosophy,

Deleuze responded with impatience. "It's very trying," he once admitted, and it's not hard to understand why (Dia, 1). We know that speculations of this sort—about the future of religion, democracy, the environment, or even philosophy—tend to be undertaken on behalf of the present, perhaps even as a symptom of the present, and so we are predisposed to speculate when things are least auspicious. Questions about the future of philosophy almost always entail the subtle suggestion that philosophy has no future: we ask after philosophy as if it were a wayward soul whose prospects have become the subject of increasingly dire prediction. What will become of it? Will it survive? Or, as Deleuze mocks, "Is it dead?" (ibid.).

This sentiment couldn't be further removed from Deleuze's own philosophical inclination, his style, which undertakes the joyous creation of concepts by refusing the common sense of what everyone knows and, by extension, the good sense of what everyone predicts. What is the future if not precisely that which surpasses all manner of speculation, giving way to "becomings which are silently at work, which are almost imperceptible"? (ibid., 2) Far from extending the present into the future, as perpetuation or prognostication, Deleuze summons the future in order to evacuate the very presence of the present. On the one hand, he defines the present as the order of *Chronos*, the measure of time that inhabits a perpetual *here and now*.[1] The malady of the present consists in having established an event horizon beyond which the future is constantly converted by this chronic logic from the possible to the determinable. In the present, ironically enough, "we have seen it all before" because events are always already re-presented. But, on the other hand, when Deleuze evokes the concept of the "event," he never ceases to affirm the becoming of another and untimely time, *Aion*, which eludes the representation of the present and resists the determinable and countable succession of instants. "Following Nietzsche, we discover, as more profound than time and eternity, the untimely," Deleuze writes, in other words, "acting counter to our time and thereby acting on our time and, let us hope, for the benefit of a time to come" (DR, xxi).

Doubtless Deleuze's untimely philosophy, his "nonphilosophy," crystallizes in no place more clearly than in the elaboration of utopia because, as he and Guattari conceive it, this concept literally affirms "no-place" (outopos) and "no-where" (Erehwon).[2] The literary and political formation of utopia describes the dissolution of the here and now, but in the scope of Deleuze's work, this untimely enterprise belongs to a much more enduring project. To this point, we have analyzed this project as a matter of style, the invention of new modes of thinking, writing, and living that suffuse his philosophy from end to end. Indeed, the embryo of this project gestates in Deleuze's earliest writings, even the uncollected miscellanea that precede "Desert Islands" (1953), but we have chosen to dwell here on *Difference and Repetition* (1968) inasmuch as it occasions the overt appeal for "new philosophical means of expression" (xxi).[3] This is no small occasion: as Deleuze suggests in the book's original (French) "Preface," something is happening that bears on the very nature of philosophy and implies its profound transformation. "The time is coming when it will hardly be possible to write a book of philosophy as it has been done for so long," he declares, and these circumstances—however lamentable, because they are lamentable, or perhaps because they must be made joyous—demand new means of expression (ibid.). Rather than render it his telos, then, Deleuze enlists the future to intervene in the present as both the diagnosis of the disappointing limits of philosophical style and the resolution to write differently, in the interest of a new style. The time is coming, he says, when we will speak of the traditional expression of philosophy as we do the ancien régime: "Ah! The old style . . . " (ibid.).

Over the course of the last five chapters, we have elaborated Deleuze's new style according to his relentless sense of critique and his perverse form of commentary, his minor philosophy and his geophilosophy, his exuberant schizoanalysis and his concrete sobriety. But as we draw to a close, we might aver that, no matter what his approach, Deleuze's style bears witness to a paradoxical provenance: not the result of the past, nor even the present, *his style derives from the future*. What does this mean? Typically, the future is understood as the sphere of consequences—as that which is caused—but Deleuze inverts this logic. "How else can one write but of those things which one doesn't know, or knows badly?" he asks in *Difference and Repetition*. "It is precisely there that we imagine having something to say. We write only at the frontiers of our knowledge, at the border which separates our knowledge from our ignorance and transforms the one into the other" (ibid.). To write is to perch oneself on a precipice, at the furthest reaches of the present, and to lean out over the mad pluralism of forces below—forces that are unknowable, impossible, and finally outside (*dehors*). In other words, we only wrestle with the problem of the future when we engage the emergence of the most exterior of forces. The future is outside, Deleuze says, but how do we think the Outside (*le Dehors*)?

Of course, this is a familiar refrain in Deleuze's philosophy, and we have returned to it repeatedly, but in the context of the problem that concerns us here, the problem of the future, we are in a position to reframe it. While Deleuze abjures any question as to the "future of philosophy," we might say that he does so in order to invert the terms of this formulation and affirm a "philosophy of the future." Taken from the subtitle of *Beyond Good and Evil, Philosophie der Zukunft*, this phrase is no less fitting a description of Deleuze's stylistic objective: the forces of the future—the forces of the Outside—must be virtualized in thinking and exercised in writing. This task is effectively signed and dated in *Difference and Repetition*. In the "Preface," to which we have referred, Deleuze contends that "a book of philosophy should be in part a very particular species of detective fiction, in part a kind of science fiction" (xx). Needless to say, the first of these genres is readily amenable to the methods of philosophy, and Deleuze is by no means alone in drawing on the "epistemological richness" (Jameson) of the detective, even as he does so according to his own tastes. ("By detective fiction we mean that concepts, with their zones of presence, should intervene to resolve local problems" [ibid.]) But the suggestion of science fiction is altogether singular. Why *this* genre for philosophy? If we are tempted to take this suggestion as a joke or jest (*blague*), that's probably because it seems to mark the distance between the privileged sphere of noble Ideas and the generic imagination of popular plots. But Deleuze adopts the principles of science fiction immanently, in the absence of parodic distance. Far from invoking the recitation of Klingon codes or the proffering of Jedi parables, his exhortation should be understood in the sense in which German sometimes (and somewhat archaically) renders science fiction as *Zukunftsroman*, a "future novel." What would it mean, *literally*, to create a *Zukunftsphilosophie*, a "future philosophy"?

Inasmuch as science fiction is devoted to the "not yet," the "otherwise," or the "Outside," Deleuze bids philosophy to follow suit. Whether heading off on a real voyage or an equally real *voyage sur place*, science fiction launches thought into those domains where, and dimensions in which, we can no longer quantify the world in terms of what we know but, instead, we must create concepts in response to that which "one doesn't know, or knows badly." This is no deficit or detriment but the rejoinder to the dominant image of thought and the prototypical question of philosophy: "what is . . . ?" The structure of this question inevitably tempts us to aspire to an essential and overarching common sense, but this is precisely why we turn to science fiction. We ought to look to the genre, Deleuze says, at the very point when the "weaknesses" of philosophy "become manifest" (DR, xxi), when it falls back on concepts of representation, "categories defined as the condition of possible experience" (ibid., 68). These "weaknesses" should not be confused with fragility (*faiblesse*) that characterizes the great health of particular philosophers: to the contrary, we are characterizing the reactive forces and the negative will mobilized in representation. Whenever experience is reduced to "what can be represented in the sensible," the vital appeal to think differently or otherwise is quashed (DR, 56).

This is why the recourse to science fiction strikes Deleuze with the force of an absolute exigency, for the genre pursues an experiment in experience that deterritorializes the concepts of representation. The signs and events of science fiction outstrip any measure, rendering epistemology mute and demanding new means of expression. To the question of "what is . . . ?" the genre insists on the fantastic exuberance of a new question: "what if . . . ?" We have reiterated this question, under various circumstances, in order to mark how philosophy might begin anew: rebuffing the pretense of reality, the "if" affirms the reality of pretense, the powers of the false, as the intrinsic element of thinking. The philosophy of the future begins by departing from the known world and setting out on errands, both physical and metaphysical, into the wilderness. Detoured from major thoroughfares, the philosopher wanders into labyrinths of his or her own devising, where unprecedented eventualities are realized. Estranged from its presuppositions and made strange in its exercise, philosophy "teaches us a strange [*étrange*: foreign, from the Outside] 'reason,' that of the multiple, chaos and difference" (ibid., 57). Whoever thought to make God into a kind supercomputer (Leibniz), time into the infinite feedback loop of an "eternal return" (Nietzsche), or the universe a kind of "metacinema" (MI, 59) of images (Bergson)? In these cases and countless others where a kind of science fiction has been ventured, we affirm the "if" that propels thinking and writing into new frontiers, "where no man has gone before" and where even the "Man-form" disperses into impossible new assemblages. This is the "splendor" of what Deleuze calls "the science fiction aspect" (DR, xx)—*sci-phi*.

The Ends of Representation (the "Science of the Sensible")

This is not your typical science fiction. If we are to understand both the problems and powers of sci-phi, Deleuze's evocation of the genre will have to be reckoned against its predominant sense, just as his mode of thinking (or what he initially calls superior empiricism) will have to be reckoned against the dominant sense of representation, or what we have called transcendental idealism. We begin, then, by revisiting aesthetics as both the locus of the problem at hand and the prospect of its revision. As Deleuze argues, aesthetics is traditionally divided between the commitment to render experience as the "being of the sensible" and the determination to produce the "conditions of possibility" for that experience; but as he adds, the distinction is almost always made to the benefit of the latter, namely, representation. "It is strange that aesthetics (as the science of the sensible) could be founded on what can be represented in the sensible" (DR, 56). We know by now how this fate plays out in Kant's critical philosophy, which is duly divided between the concepts of representation, or "the transcendental aesthetic," which he provides in the first *Critique,* and the domain of aesthetic experience, which he ventures in the third *Critique.* In this division, at least as it is traditionally construed, the loose scrim of the categories of space and time is cast over experience, leaving what escapes to inspire the free and indeterminate sense of aesthetic experience ("the beautiful").

Deleuze's remarkable reckoning with Kant—*Kant's Critical Philosophy,* he says, was "a book about an enemy" (Neg, 6)—ironically confirms what we are up against: the *Critique of Pure Reason* embarks on an exposition of the forms and an elaboration of conditions within which the "reality of the real" (DR, 211) is relegated to a kind of subplot. In Kant's transcendental idealism, the insistence on rendering aesthetics according to the concepts of representation ultimately defines experience abstractly, in advance of experience itself. In other words, these concepts are defined as a priori, and we should be clear about what this means. "The *a priori* is defined as being independent of experience, precisely because experience never 'gives' us anything which is universal and necessary," Deleuze explains (KCP, 11). As principles that have the status of right, then, the concepts of representation must be applied to experience, but at the same time, and reciprocally, experience must be subjected to these conditions. "Representation means the synthesis of that which is presented," Deleuze writes. "Synthesis therefore consists in the following: a diversity is represented, that is to say, posed as contained in a representation" (ibid., 14).[4] Thus, as Deleuze says, the tropes of representation that philosophers have enumerated—the resemblances among perceptions, the oppositions between predicates, the analogies amid judgments, etc.—condemn thought to a model of recognition whereby the subject ultimately grasps in each instance what it has put there to begin with.

Whether innocence, ignorance, or idiocy, representation is grounded on the promise that every encounter is subject to understanding because we represent the world only to discover—or re-discover—the "truth" that it conforms to our knowledge. "Thought is filled with no more than an image of itself, one in which it recognizes itself the more it recognizes things" (DR, 138). In this regard, the regime of representation has conditioned a longstanding affinity between philosophy and science fiction—an affinity with which we must contend if we are to affirm Deleuze's very different experiment. In the *Critique of Pure Reason*, Kant elaborates the conditions to account for any and every experiential possibility, and insofar as these conditions are prolonged beyond the earth and into the vastness of the cosmos, that's simply the logical extension of a metaphysical supposition: if representation accounts for anything under the sun, why not beyond it? Kant's early excursions into the question of extraterrestrial life, which might otherwise seem juvenile speculations, are actually belied by his certainty that the aptitudes and limits of reason are so entirely valid as to apply to intelligent beings on any planet.[5] From this vantage, the real labor of representation is not to imagine ourselves the center of the universe but to project our own image back into the stars. Despite Kant's Copernican turn, or rather as its correlative, we nurture a principle of sufficient arrogance to believe that our judgments apply anywhere and everywhere. "All the conformity to law, which impresses us so much about the movement of the stars and in chemical processes," Nietzsche writes of this delusion, "coincides at bottom with those properties which we bring to things. Thus it is we who impress ourselves in this way."[6]

In a cosmos potentially populated by an unimaginable variety of other beings, Kant maintains that all are subject to the faculty of reason and the structure of representation: the universal aspiration of philosophy is realized in the universe itself. This may well explain why, in science fiction, so many aliens look human, speak English, or suffer from our neuroses, but this laughable "coincidence" actually symptomatizes the illusion that the genre, no less philosophy itself, traditionally harbors. True to its terrestrial counterpart, the "next wave" of enlightenment all too often sets out for new worlds with the confidence that, anywhere in the universe, representation and reason (ought to) obtain. We cast representation into the furthest reaches of the cosmos in order to conclude that things are the same all over: as perpetual project and conventional assurance, then, science fiction has been (and often still is) conceived in the spirit of philosophical enlightenment (*Aufklärung*). Indeed, the rudiments of representation that we have sketched here are aptly consummated in Kant's "What is Enlightenment?" which describes the process whereby human nature attains it divine right.[7] The condition of this process, which concerns the progress of subjects and communities alike, is freedom; as Kant argues, the progressive realization of freedom is tantamount to the maturation of humanity and its independence from all the forms of tutelage that enslave reason. Conversely, any impingement on freedom effectively binds the future to the prejudices of the present and impedes enlightenment: "This would be a crime against human nature, whose original destiny lies precisely in such progress."[8] Historically, and somewhat prototypically, science fiction seems to unfold along the lines of "such progress," for in its avowedly enlightened utopias as much as in its negative examples and degraded dystopias, progress is affirmed under the auspices of metaphysical and especially moral reason. In the model of *Star Trek*, which depicts a universe largely characterized by "uneven development," disparities between civilizations are ultimately reconciled according to a common scale of progress (what is the "prime directive," the rule that Star Fleet must not intervene in societies that have not met a threshold of civilization, if not the very symbol of this enlightenment?). Insofar as science fiction is accused of being a cautionary and conservative genre as much as a liberating and liberal one, this is because its flights are liable to confirm transcendent values—the libidinal resilience of the family, the enduring symbol of democracy, the temperance of scientific rationality with moral wisdom, the metaphysical order of things.

It is against this tendency, or in the name of its violent destruction, that Deleuze bids us to envision a different sense of science fiction. No one need be reminded about the genre's corrective labor, its desire to salvage the present (Dick's "Minority Report") and to mend the very tears in the fabric of time (Bradbury's "A Sound of Thunder"), but perhaps these efforts constitute the last reactionary—and *reactive*—gasp in the face of the failure of representation. To this extent, the desperate attempts to rescue traditional values and recuperate the regime of representation actually condition the genre's experiments in experience. The vast epistemological machinery mobilized by the genre, the material and intellectual assemblage we call "science," paradoxically affirms those very encounters that outstrip any image of thought—the detection of a strange monolith on one of Jupiter's moons (*2001: A Space Odyssey*), the appearance of an astronaut's dead spouse on an orbiting space station (*Solaris*), the vertiginous proliferation of possible worlds (*Inception*). In this regard, sci-phi aspires to another, and very different, sense of aesthetics than the one we have described. Where Kant submits aesthetics to the architectonic of transcendental idealism in order to designate the field of the possible, Deleuze's transcendental empiricism recuperates aesthetics in relation to real experience—as that which cannot be represented. Metaphysical anomalies, baffling mutations, cracks in the time: science fiction delights in signs and images that "do not compute" according to the science of this or any other world, and Deleuze aspires to create a philosophy that follows suit.

If we don't know them already, we can easily imagine the risks that attend this thesis. Especially among Deleuze's critics, his philosophy has been the source of misunderstanding and hyperbole, providing as it does the pretext to discredit him as senseless, anarchic—the delusional Deleuze. But these distortions should always be read in light of the remarkable delicacy with which the philosopher actually treats the problem of the sensible: even and especially in view of sci-phi, the exigency of philosophy consists in bringing all due precision and sobriety to bear on the unthinkable. The dissolution of transcendence does not mean that we lapse into a "rhapsody of sensations" (DR, 56) or wallow in a sea of intensities. We always "require just a little bit of order to protect us from chaos," Deleuze and Guattari say (WIP, 201), because the desire to embrace chaos without any order at all is no less illusionary than the desire to ward it off entirely. Rejecting the detachment of idealism as well as the decadence of empiricism, Deleuze gestures toward a style of philosophy that moves beyond both and without regard for any dialectic between them. In *Difference and Repetition*, we know, he calls this philosophy transcendental empiricism, and he quotes the poet Blood to express "its profession of faith as a veritable aesthetic" (57). "Nature is contingent, excessive and mystical essentially," the poet explains. "Not unfortunately the universe is wild—game-flavored as a hawk's wing" (ibid.). Never establishing conditions beforehand, then, we affirm the untamed becoming of nature: because the sensible is fortunate enough to be wild, because it resists determination and expectation, and because it cannot be represented, transcendental empiricism bids us to think apart from conditions, to uncondition thought itself.

But if this were all, science fiction might no more than approximate something like surrealism, indulging arbitrary procedures and random effects, when what Deleuze envisions is a "logic of sensation" and "logic of sense." Thus, he continues to quote Blood: "The slow round of the engraver's lathe gains but the breadth of a hair, but the difference is distributed back over the whole curve, never an instant true—ever not quite" (ibid.). Difference defies identity, even if only by the "breadth of a hair," but in representation this difference is allocated over the trajectory of the lathe, as if in a series of instants, a chronometric arc, at each point a lie ("never an instant true") with respect to the event. Notably, this is precisely what mobilizes the transcendental aspect of empiricism. Because no overarching structure, preexistence schematism, or a priori concept exists to account for difference, sci-phi bids us to extract the features that would, in the case of each concept, define its singular conditions. The concept is never "exact" and does not aspire to be, but for all that, it remains profoundly "rigorous." In Deleuze's own terms, we could say that science fiction augurs the development of a "science of the sensible" (ibid., 56). While the phrase might otherwise conjure the exposition of the very conditions of possibility that we have heretofore analyzed, the "science of the sensible" undergoes a metamorphosis that carries us from transcendental idealism to transcendental empiricism, from Kant's implicit sense of science fiction to Deleuze's explicit pursuit of sci-phi.

In *Difference and Repetition*, Deleuze explains that empiricism itself becomes transcendental "only when we apprehend directly in the sensible that which can only be sensed, the very being of the sensible" (ibid., 56–57). Deleuze invokes science fiction because, in seeking to think the unthinkable, the ingenuity of the genre consists not only in having brought fiction to bear on science—that is, as the fabulation of new technologies, new societies, new forms of life—but also in having brought science to bear on fiction— as the mandate to render the sensible. The science may be fictionalized, but it underwrites the rigor with which the genre regards its otherworldly signs and extraterrestrial events. "SF takes off from a fictional ('literary') hypothesis," as Darko Suvin has written, "and develops it with totalizing ('scientific') rigor."[9]

The Three Deaths

If the eventualities of sci-phi are not "of this world," this is because, as Deleuze imagines it, the coherence of representation disintegrates under the onslaught of so many extraordinary signs and events. How else can one understand his aspiration, in *Difference and Repetition*, to write an "apocalyptic book" (xxi)? Deleuze determines to deterritorialize the *terra firma* of philosophy itself, to prolong thinking onto a plane of pure immanence and into a pluralism of absolute differences. And as he adds, the spirit of this endeavor was "manifestly in the air" (xix). Published in 1968, *Difference and Repetition* begins by characterizing "modern thought" as having been "born of the failure of representation, of the loss of identities, and the discovery of all the forces that act under the representation of the identical" (xiv). We have dwelled on the political and theoretical manifestations of this "failure," but Deleuze is concerned here with the larger stakes of a transformation—the deviation in the history of consciousness and the structure of representation to which it belongs. As he writes, philosophy "must leave the domain of representation in order to become 'experience,' transcendental empiricism" (ibid., 68). But how can we affirm the collapse of representation and the "intense world of differences" (ibid., 57) into which the world devolves?

While he never offers anything like a method, Deleuze nevertheless enumerates the challenges that describe the trajectory of sci-phi and augur its purpose—"the advent of a coherence which is no more our own, than that of mankind, than that of God or the world" (ibid., xix).[10] In other words, the philosophy of the future must traverse not one but three instances of apocalypse—the death of God, the death of Man, and the death of the World—if it is to think in the absence of representation. We pass from God, whose transcendent and "sufficient reason" organized existence ("we see all things in God," as Malebranche says[11]); to Man, in whom the transcendental faculty of reason legislates according to abstract Law (not God but the Good); and, finally, to the World, in which coherence resides as nature, substance, or being (the offer of ontology). Only at the end of this voyage through the catastrophic does philosophy think in the absence of an image; only then does it become sci-phi; only then does it become *dangerous*.

Hence, we begin with the death of God—but not as one might expect. At the conclusion of *Foucault*, in a section aptly titled "Towards a Formation of the Future,"[12] Deleuze says that though we tend to associate God's death with Nietzsche, Feuerbach "is the last thinker of the death of God: he shows that since man has never been anything but the unfold of man, man must fold and refold God" (F, 129–30). By contrast, Nietzsche already considers this an "old story, and as all old stories tend to multiply their versions, Nietzsche multiplies the death of God" (ibid.,130). In other words, Nietzsche carries out the execution so many times, and so comically, that the event remains dubious. Thus, *The Gay Science* famously describes how a madman runs into the marketplace one night to announce the death of God—only to be met with laughter. There are plenty of nonbelievers, atheists, in the audience, but these folks have not relinquished the divine so much as they have repressed it. "This tremendous event is still on its way, still wandering—it has not yet reached the ears of men. Lightning and thunder require time; the light of the stars requires time; deeds, though done, still require time to be seen and heard" (GS, §125).

If the event is delayed, the reason is that the coherence provided by God is not dead so much as it has passed on—to the Man-form. In a sense, we call "human" those who inherit coherence or, what amounts to the same thing, those for whom God has become "unconscious" (Lacan).[13] Thus, the immortality that belonged to God is resurrected in the Man-form: the source of our most tender vulnerability, "the mortality of the ego" (Freud) provokes the emergence of a transcendental ego that rescues us from the knowledge of our death (*sēma*).[14] The Man-form appears only when its divine predecessor expires because this begets the reckoning with finitude from which the human being takes shape as reaction formation—"secondary narcissism." "The force within man must begin by confronting and seizing hold of the forces of finitude as if they were forces from the outside: it is outside oneself that force must come up against finitude," Deleuze explains. "All this means is that when the forces within man enter into a relation with forces of finitude from the outside, then and only then does the set of forces compose the Man-form (and not the God-form). *Incipit Homo*" (F, 127). While Nietzsche is the first to have understood that the death of God must be coupled with the death of Man—that the former will have been botched unless the latter is carried out—it is surely Foucault, Deleuze says, who resumes and redoubles the mission to deterritorialize the Man-form. In his great histories of crime and punishment, madness and medicine, perversion and sexuality, Foucault dissolves the "human sciences" into the variable contours of *epistemoi*, historically contingent assemblages of force, which already anticipate human extinction—or, at least, our becoming otherwise. "We can already foresee that the forces within man do not necessarily contribute to the composition of a Man-form, but may be otherwise invested in another compound or form," Deleuze writes in *Foucault:* "Man has not always existed, and will not exist forever" (124).

Naturally, we are liable to think that, with this death, we have freed ourselves from coherence once and for all, but as Deleuze contends, we have only reached its most intransigent form: behind God and, then, beyond Man, there remains the coherence of the World and the promise of substance—or Being. In *Difference and Repetition* Deleuze argues that even the splendor of Spinozist substance (*Deus sive Natura*) detaches itself from the plane of immanence like a veil of the sheerest gossamer: "there still remains a difference between substance and its modes" (40). Even the unfolding of an immanent ontology retains the presentiment of a kind of transcendence, and perhaps there's no better current example of this illusion than the rise of "thing theory," which bestows ontological privilege on the brute presence, or thingness, of things.[15] The World, no less than God or Man, constitutes a kind of *theology* to which thinking is subjected, but if it is the last refuge of transcendence, it is also the most cunning and the most difficult to deterritorialize. Having gotten rid of the God and our "selves," how do we traverse the world of things, the world of substance, or even the world of being? In Spinozistic terms, how can substance "be said *of* the modes and only *of* the modes" (DR, 40).

It is at this juncture that Deleuze, heretofore our narrator, could be said to enter the scene. In the critical line that we have traced, leading us from God (Nietzsche) to Man (Foucault), we might say that the apocalypse of the World belongs to Deleuze. The uniqueness of his philosophy consists, in no small measure, in foreclosing the last haven of coherence. His sci-phi has no principle except this: we should never have recourse to the world of being, nor the being of the world, except insofar as these are subjected to absolute deterritorialization. As he notes, "difference is behind everything, but behind difference there is nothing" (DR, 57). In this respect, Deleuze's relationship with ontology, even what's been called the "ontology of the virtual," remains more deeply fraught than we are generally willing to admit. The late François Zourabichvili has provided arguably the most succinct and profound appraisal of this ontology: "If there is an attitude of Deleuze's philsophy, it is pretty much this: extinguishing the word being, and through this, ontology."[16] Indeed, Deleuze never ceases to articulate "in all of his letters—(exactly to the letter)—his agenda: the substitution of ET [AND] for EST [IS]"; or in what amounts to the same thing, the substitution of "becoming" for "being." The introduction of *A Thousand Plateaus* ends with these words: "Establish a logic of the AND, overthrow ontology."[17]

To do so, we should always begin by insisting on a fundamental distinction between the superficial aspect of difference (being) and the genetic aspect of difference (becoming). Of the former, Deleuze says that objects as much as subjects, things as much as people, Being as much as beings, do not explain anything so much as they must be explained. As "epiphenomena" (DR, 268), they dwell in molar differences that agglomerate and obscure the pluralism of molecular differences below. Where these superficial means render difference between and among identities, then, Deleuze affirms difference in itself, which is to say, as the vital and generative difference from which diversity is spawned. "Every phenomenon refers to an inequality by which it is conditioned": beneath the algorithmic pretense of any ordered, identifiable, and determinate world, we must always grasp the inequalities that "form the condition of our world" (ibid., 222). For Deleuze, we might say, ontology itself is always redoubled by ontogenesis—the mad play of differences and the emergence (*Entstehung*) of forces that provide the unreasonable reason of existence. As if both its cause and constituents, the fine grain of differences subtends the rough logic of opposing forces and determinate forms. As Deleuze writes in *Difference and Repetition*:

> There is a crucial experience of difference and a corresponding experiment: every time we find ourselves confronted or bound by a limitation or an opposition, we should ask what such a situation presupposes. It presupposes a swarm of differences, a pluralism of free, wild or untamed differences; a properly different and original space and time; all of which persist alongside the simplifications of limitation and opposition. A more profound real element must be defined in order for oppositions of forces or limitations of form to be drawn, one which is determined as an abstract [*informelle*] and potential multiplicity. (50)

In light of this description, we seem to have reached the point of grasping what Deleuze means, in *Difference and Repetition*, by the "splendor" of sci-phi. Under the spell of the genre, Deleuze says that he has come to "believe in a world in which the individuations are impersonal and the singularities are pre-individual" (ibid., xxi). And surely this belief makes what we are about to argue that much more difficult to believe: before the challenge to produce sci-phi, Deleuze says, *Difference and Repetition* fell short. In the "Preface," where he invokes the mission to write an "apocalyptic book," Deleuze also suggests that by this very standard the book cannot be considered a success. "What this book *should* therefore have made apparent," he writes, "is the advent of a coherence which is no more our own, that of mankind, than that of God or the world. *In this sense, it should have been an apocalyptic book*" (ibid.; emphasis added). This is a remarkable (and remarkably overlooked) admission, but it remains illegible unless we understand this failure and the subsequent resolve—to write sci-phi—it engenders. In later years, especially after meeting Guattari, Deleuze provided increasingly frank evaluations of *Difference and Repetition* as well as *The Logic of Sense*. But the distance we feel in these critiques is less a matter of time than of sensibility. As early as 1973, in his "Letter to a Harsh Critic," Deleuze says of these texts: "I know very well that they're still full of academic elements, they're heavy going, but they're an attempt to jolt, set in motion, something inside me, to treat writing as a flow, not a code." Though he "likes some passages," he says: "That's as far as it went" (Neg, 7).

The appraisal is striking not because Deleuze is so ungenerous but because he is so ungenerous with respect to his own *style*: his regrets pertain to the failure of expression (the "academic elements"). Thus, when we read this verdict—"it should have been an apocalyptic book"—it is impossible not to hear the echoes of Nietzsche's appraisal of *The Birth of Tragedy*: "it should have sung." In his "Attempt at Self-Criticism," we remember, Nietzsche says that his first book had hit on a problem to which he was not yet equal—"to look at knowledge in the perspective of art, and art in the perspective of life" (BOT, "Attempt at Self-Criticism §2). Looking back on the text years later, Nietzsche gives voice to a curious discrepancy, as if this early book had intuited the profound task of a future-philosophy—to invert the perspective of critique and thereby evaluate science aesthetically, on the basis of life—but had remained bound to the present, unable to realize the means adequate to the task. "What

I had to say then—too bad I did not say it as a poet: perhaps I had the ability" (ibid., "Attempt at Self-Criticism §3). If Deleuze issues a similar reaction in the course of looking back at *Difference and Repetition* (not his first book but the first in which, he says, he sought to do philosophy for himself), this is largely because, as we have argued, he sought to redouble Nietzsche's own critical inversion. He, too, had intuited the task of philosophy insofar as it moved from knowledge ("not the true nor the real but evaluation") to aesthetics ("not affirmation as acceptance but as creation") to ethics ("not man but the Over-man as the new form of life") (NP, 184–86)—but he, too, lacked the means of expression to carry out the project. More specifically, and in light of the writing he would subsequently undertake, we might say that the sense of science (*Wissenschaft*) had yet to be affirmed as fiction, produced in the spirit of a "sci-phi" that could cultivate "new form[s] of life." What Deleuze likes most in the book—those passages on "tiredness and contemplation" that exist, he says, as "living experiences" (Neg, 7)—are what the book lacks most. For all of its determination to think in relation to the reality of the real and write in the interest of new styles of life, *Difference and Repetition* still clings to the vestiges of an "old style."

The Ends of Ontology (the "Writing of Disaster")

In a sense, the dangers and misinterpretations to which the concept of style is subject are forecast in terms of the prototypical opposition between its "old" and "new" sense. In its most degraded aspects, style is liable to appear utterly anachronistic or entirely au courant: it either belongs to an antiquated world or suits the Zeitgeist. The older sense of style—what the romantics called "sensibility"—has withered over the last several centuries, in part because the subject on whom it rested, capable of transcendent feeling and creation, no longer holds sway. Once the province of select souls (Schlegel), and then of every subject (Kant), sensibility seems to have reached a tipping point in the apotheosis of aestheticism, the living of "life as a work of art" and the pursuit of "art for art's sake," that characterized its naturalist and modern efflorescence.

But if the aesthete represents the caricature of an old and outmoded sense style, the specter of decadence also anticipates the consolidation of a new style, altogether de rigueur, in which life is subject to fashion and faddishness, to commercialization and consumption. No one needs to be reminded of the clichés that surround the notion of "lifestyle" today. Saturated by capital, style has come to signify the vast marketplace in which every aspect of life— health care, schools, human service—has been privatized and submitted to a kind of decisionism; everything has become a purchase, and if this once meant that even taste or style could be bought, it now suggests something like the aggregate of our purchases, preferences, and even habits, which are submitted to so many algorithms that determine our niche and define our style ("customers who bought this book also purchased . . . "). The concept of style has been recruited and remade by the society of control; its vast appropriation is largely accomplished along the lines of the individual who is said to possess, in every sense of the word, a lifestyle. But the obverse side of our society of individualism, of the long-standing "culture of narcissism," is the winnowing of the subject beyond the range of "neurotic styles" or the designations of the DSM or even the codings of a given genome to the prospect of "dividuation."

In his astonishing "Postscript on Control Societies" (1990), Deleuze offers an analysis of the reorganization of power in contemporary societies that, now some twenty years old, seems more relevant than ever. "We are no longer dealing with a duality of mass and individual," he writes. "Individuals become '*dividuals*,' and masses become samples, data, markets of '*banks*'" (Neg, 180). The diagram of control has only multiplied in the era of globalization and age of terrorism, when the dense virtual fabric of communication networks covers the world so many times over. No longer a Western phenomenon, the socio-logic of control operates in the planning of new cities as well as the retrofitting of older ones, in the walling off of security zones and the gating of private communities (all "Green Zones"). The architecture of control and the production of the dividual stretches from Seoul to London to Jerusalem, from Dubai to Bombay to Toronto. As Deleuze writes: "We don't have to stray into science fiction to find a control mechanism that can fix the position of any given element at any given moment—an animal in a game reserve, a man in a business (electronic tagging)" (ibid, 120).

But in this context, we've suggested, science fiction is positioned to devise the means of expression commensurate to the problem of control. How—or, rather, how else—do we formulate the style with which to call on the future in order to resist the present? When Deleuze refers to style, as we have seen in previous chapters, he celebrates the sense in which one is said to suffer from stylelessness: in this "nonstyle," expression accedes to the vitality of impersonalism with which philosophy resists its own recruitment to communication. Instead, we might imagine that sci-phi undertakes a process of "counterutilization": philosophy appropriates the order-words, protocols, and even the technologies of control, perhaps by insinuating itself into the dominant languages, both verbal and informational, and thereby encoding a new syntax, a minor language for a digital age. Yes: even today—especially today—we believe that the abiding modesty of nonstyle is capable of catalyzing a fantastic deterritorialization whereby the "attributed" subject dissipates into all kinds of becomings, above all the becoming-imperceptible, of "a life." No longer a human life, not even an organic one, "a life" constitutes the prolongation of a metamorphosis, the improvisation of molecules, that passes through animal, vegetable, and mineral into materials not found in nature at all. Thus, at the end of *Foucault*, where Deleuze discusses this "posthumanism," he says that life has long since "enter[ed] into a relation with forces from the outside, those of silicon that supersede carbon, or genetic components that supersede the organism, or agrammaticalities which supersede the signifier" (F, 131–32). Of course, these relations immediately evoke so many works of science fiction insofar as the genre conducts its own experiments (deliberate or not) in cloning and mutation, artificial engineering and cyborg combinations. There is no subject here, only "a life" subject to becoming, but what's remarkable is that Deleuze describes these becomings in the same breath that he affirms new styles of expression. The fantastic pursuits of the "technologies of the self" do not minimize the question of style or extinguish the process of writing because, in both cases, the task is to lose our "selves" and discover new modes of living. The vicissitudes of "a life" are inextricable from the experiments in expression ("agrammaticalities which supersede the signifier") that propel us outside the rigid designations of representation. For this reason, as we have said, Deleuze rejoices in the indeterminate article—"a life," "a stomach," "a child"—that detaches experience from any possession, preposition, or prepossession. We are doubtless familiar with examples of these experiments from the laboratories, biospheres, and cryogenic chambers of science fiction, which preserve bodies (*Never Let Me Go*), genomes (*The Boys from Brazil*), and even noses (*Sleeper*). But where the function of the subject is still, or may yet be, attributed in these cases, the discovery of an organ without a body doesn't begin to account for the style to which sci-phi aspires and the body without organs it seeks to create.

In *Difference and Repetition*, the absolute deterritorialization and improvised connectivism that characterize this body are ventured in the insistence of the empirical apart from an individual and the exercise of the transcendental apart from a subject. Transcendental empiricism realizes the prospect of style by sloughing off the affectations of personality and dispersing the subject, ego, self into an anonymous "one," for only this fantastic anonymity is capable of accommodating unprecedented pluralism. Far from opposing itself to the many, or subsuming the many, or even enumerating the many in a set (*ensemble*), the impersonal and indefinite pronoun "one" is mobilized to create a multiplicity. Impersonalization is an ascesis, the evacuation of presuppositions with which we furnish a plane of immanence and amass its vast population, aggregate strange tribes and distribute nomadic tributaries. Only the nameless, sexless, indeterminate one is capable of assembling such a seemingly endless collection of thinkers, not only philosophers, but writers, painters, filmmakers, etc.—a virtual polyphony of voices. Thus, we find ourselves faced once more with the prospect of univocity—of a philosophy in which Being "is said, in a single and same sense, *of* all of its individuating differences and intrinsic modalities" (DR, 36). Both here and in chapter 4 we have effectively cashed out the concept of univocity in light of the question of style and the perpetual becoming-otherwise that achieves a kind of "anonymous murmur." In other words, when we affirm univocity as the "One-All" (ibid., 37), we do not do so in a numerical sense but in a syntactic–stylistic sense, as the impersonal one that persists by dint of writing, multiplying connections and relations. Univocity is the (not altogether somber) precursor to the collective assemblage of enunciation.

The nature of this claim—that univocity *bespeaks* Deleuze's impersonal style of creation and creation of style—ought to strike us most profoundly in the midst of *Difference and Repetition* itself, where the term seems well-nigh ontological. Preceding generic difference, and defying analogical difference, univocity refers to a "prior field," Deleuze explains, in which being is "immediately related to difference" (ibid., 38). For this reason, he immediately and inextricably links univocity to the concept of the simulacrum. "When the identity of things dissolves, being escapes to attain univocity, and begins to revolve around the different," Deleuze writes (ibid., 67). In a world where things are always already differential, the nature of being can only be affirmed in the absence of identity—as a copy without a model. "The simulacrum seizes on a constituent *disparity* in the thing from which it strips the rank of model" (ibid.). Of course, we have spoken at length of the simulacrum in the context of Deleuze's overturning of Platonism, but in the wake of *Difference and Repetition* and *The Logic of Sense*, where this overturning takes place, Deleuze largely abandons the simulacrum (and it is not incidental that univocity shares the same fate). Inasmuch as the simulacrum dethrones the pretense of an original, this critical enterprise seems to have lost not only Deleuze's favor but, we might say, his faith. Today, he and Guattari write, "The simulacrum, the simulation of a packet of noodles, has become the true concept, and the one who packages the product, commodity, or work of art has become the philosopher, conceptual personae, or artist" (WIP, 10). As Deleuze writes elsewhere, "it seems to me that I have totally abandoned the notion of the simulacrum, which is all but worthless" (TRM, 366).

Perhaps we are now in a position to better understand why the recourse to the logic of the simulacrum dooms *Difference and Repetition*, despite the offer of sci-phi, to persist in representation. On the face of it, this claim may well strike us as counterintuitive. On the opening page of the book's French "Preface," Deleuze declares, "The modern world is one of simulacra" (xix); and it would be hard to imagine a statement seemingly better suited to science fiction, where the uncanny discovery of the double returns with a vengeance—in feats of genetic engineering and organic robotics, from the no-wheres of wormholes and parallel universes. But in *Difference and Repetition*, where it is lent such singular importance, the concept of the simulacrum actually precludes the creation of what we have called sci-phi. In order to understand this abortion, it is worth noting that Deleuze's overture—to make philosophy "a kind of science fiction"—recalls nothing so much as a particular science fiction, namely, *The Invasion of the Body Snatchers*. Adopted from a pulp novel, the premise of the film, made in 1956 and then remade in 1978, is familiar enough: mysterious, extraterrestrial organisms have landed on earth and quickly insinuated their way into society. Whenever a human falls asleep in the presence of these extraterrestrial pods, the pods hatch a duplicate who (which?) takes on the form of the original human at the human's expense: the human "psyche" or "soul" dies so that the body can provide a host. In short order, our species stands at the brink of irrevocable transformation.

Notably, the "original" adaptation of *Invasion of the Body Snatchers,* directed by Don Siegel, was made during the second Red Scare, and it is frequently cast as a parable of cold war paranoia when Communism ostensibly threatened to insinuate itself into American minds, secretly brainwashing the citizenry in order to cultivate a new, quasi-Soviet strain of thought. The catch, of course, is that for this film's political analogy to "work," the body-snatching duplicates must be ideologically differentiated from their real (i.e., decent, free-thinking, American) counterparts. Without a firm distinction, the distinction with which we anoint "America" would be vacated. So how do we tell the real from the fake, how do we preserve the Truth? In Siegel's film, the duplicates are physically indistinguishable, but this external identity is belied at another level by a kind of spiritual vacancy, the absence of affect, which gives "real" humans pause. We glean something missing or different in the presence of the body snatchers, as if to say "it's her, but it's not *her!*" The italics underscore an internal mark that detaches the human from its double and draws a link or likeness to a higher value, the American myth of the true person—the individual. On the brink of simulacrification, the original is finally recuperated by the pretense of a moral prerogative that we might just as well call "human, all too human."

Against this backdrop we can appreciate the irony of Philip Kaufman's remake of *Invasion of the Body Snatchers*, which displaces the story's setting from the cold war paranoia of small-town America in the 1950s to the marijuana-laced malaise of San Francisco in the 1970s. In the aftermath of the city's hippie heyday, the film depicts its characters as if they suffered from something like widespread demystification—or what might simply be diffuse, drug-addled ennui. People are so stoned, pharma-colonized, psychiatricized, and finally deadened that when the affect-less aliens eventually hatch, they seem no different than their human counterparts. The old means of judgment have become impossible and, we might say, irrelevant: the spiritual distinction has been erased. The copy now expresses the evacuation of any originality, of any fixed identity, because the quality of "being human" is always already estranged, alienated: the copy has no model. The transcendent, moral order that governed the "original" *Invasion of the Body Snatchers* and upheld the pretense of originality "in the last instance" collapses into the drama of doubles. *Incipit simulacrum!*

It is in this same spirit that Deleuze celebrates the "reign of simulacra" in *Difference and Repetition*, where he hails the end of the world as we know it and the "advent of a new coherence." As we have said, it is tempting to regard this "advent" in the light of sci-phi, for Deleuze seems to have imagined a brave new world that "swallows up or destroys every ground which would function as an instance responsible for the difference between the original and the derived, between things and simulacra" (DR, 67). Of the process of this perpetual ungrounding, he avows, "Every thing, animal, or being assumes the status of the simulacrum" (ibid.). Why, then, is the "reign of the simulacra" so short lived? As we suggested in chapter 5, the gestation of the concept implies a problem and paradox with which Deleuze had yet to wrestle. Inasmuch as we define it as a copy without a model, the birth of the simulacrum is also the moment of its death, for its very existence renders the terms of its definition effectively meaningless: what would a "copy" mean anymore—and why invoke a language that remains beholden to the dead "model"? It is not just that the reference points are gone: we have entered into an infernal logic whereby (1) the existence of the simulacrum means that there is no simulacrum; but at the same time, and for the same reason, it also means (2) the existence of the simulacrum (re-)incarnates the aspect of identity and individuation once more; and finally, as a result, it means that (3) the exigency of the simulacrum itself, which had been destroyed and will have to be destroyed again, has been resurrected. The logic of the simulacrum, which overturns representation, also resurrects the dead as the condition of existence and the cost of its nonbeing.

Surely this is how we should understand Deleuze's assertion that *Difference and Repetition* failed to accede to the apocalypse that he advocated. His attempts to convey the essence of the simulacra as "?-being" or "(non)being"—that is, by dint of the very "typographical" cunning that he would later scorn (ATP, 22) —actually confirm what they are meant to deny, namely, the stubborn endurance of being, the obdurate intransigence of the world. Interestingly, in the context of Kaufman's version of *The Invasion of the Body Snatchers*, this odd logic appears at the film's end when the reign of doubles is seemingly complete: the protagonist (Donald Sutherland), perhaps the last real holdout, finally succumbs to the alien organisms. In the final shot, and now "transformed," he unleashes a terrifyingly inhuman scream that announces the extinction of the remaining vestiges of humanity and also, ironically, implies that such a distinction did in fact exist: in this awful utterance, we seem to discern the originality or authenticity that has been lost. It would be easy enough to understand this as the exceptional instance that finally and irrefutably provides proof of the human individual—but this misses the point. Once Sutherland yields and the last bastion of resistance has disappeared, we find ourselves among the doubles: it is from *their* perspective qua simulacra that we witness the scream and sense the intimation of something ineffably human. The problem with the simulacrum is that, even in the moment of triumph, it evokes what it had ostensibly destroyed— the model, the prospect of Being, and the whole regime of representation. Thus, in the final analysis, Deleuze's revolutionary affirmation that "things are simulacra themselves" retains an older style. Even as *Difference and Repetition* begins with a profound diagnosis of modern thought—"the failure of representation" (DR, xix) —the irony is that Deleuze's book shares the same fate. The collapse of representation does not prevent its perpetuation. The "writing of disaster," to lift Blanchot's title, has yet to be written, because the world is left intact.

Philosophy Postapocalypse

After Difference and Repetition, and even in the absence of its explicit evocation, the evolution of sci-phi grows more profound. The initial failure to incarnate an apocalyptic book seems, at first glance, to consign sci-phi to deferral—at least, until Deleuze can find the means of expression to carry it through. Only when we resolve to go beyond (dépasser) model and copy, original and simulacrum, do we accede to a style of thinking and writing sufficient to invent a new "syntax" of concepts (WIP, 8). Thus, sci-phi is announced only "to be continued," for Deleuze's writing over the next several decades returns to this problem under a variety of different guises—in the two volumes of Capitalism and Schizophrenia, where writing becomes a kind collaborative self-experiment to get "rid of oneself"; in his considerations of visual arts, such as cinema, where sensations of "time and space" unspool a cosmogenesis of images and signs; in his increasingly baroque commentaries on Leibniz and then Foucault, where perception becomes hallucinatory and experience "pre-individual"; and, finally, in his late writings, both alone and with Guattari, where thinking and writing open onto the landscapes of the brain.

But in view of this trajectory, which constitutes the last quarter century of his life, Deleuze also refines the mission of sci-phi. By the time he embarks on his late writings, the call for an apocalypse, with which he identified "transcendental empiricism," is no longer posed as the catastrophic origin—the nuclear propadeutic—that inaugurates philosophy; or, rather, the apocalypse is posed in so different a manner that the problem itself has changed. What has happened? Perhaps, in light of *Difference and Repetition*, we could say that we no longer need to induce the end of the world: representation has already failed, the present has already dissolved, and the future is already here. It is worth noting that, in some measure, this eventuality has been endorsed by science fiction itself. In *Pattern Recognition* (2003), William Gibson gives voice to a widespread sense of the problem that increasingly confronts the genre:

> We have no idea, now, of who, or what the inhabitants of our future might be. In that sense, we have no future. Not in the sense that our grandparents had a future, or thought they did. Fully imagined futures were the luxury of another day, one in which "now" was of some greater duration. For us, of course, things can change so abruptly, so violently, so profoundly, that futures like our grandparents' have insufficient "now" to stand on. We have no future because our present is too volatile.[18]

Not incidentally, Gibson's novel is the first in a trilogy that situates science fiction *in the present*, and one could argue that, mutatis mutandis, Deleuze's philosophy adopts a similar premise. The new style of philosophy will have to reckon with the apocalypse of representation not as a prospective outcome but as the circumstances of thought today. As Deleuze says, echoing Antonioni, Eros is sick (TI, 24). What is to be done? Bereft of transcendence, the modern world no longer claims our belief, its signifiers no longer inspire our investment (*Besetzung*). Where once libido took up residence, however symptomatically, in the objects of passion and faith, the substance of "a life" is now consigned to wander aimlessly, without preoccupations, in the absence of any sublime object.[19] We seem to have reached the dire moment when truth no longer compels our confidence or, worse still, doubles down as empty zealotry: "the best lack all conviction, while the worst /Are full of passionate intensity."[20] In *What Is Philosophy?* Deleuze and Guattari write: "it may be that believing in this world, in this life, has become our most difficult task, or the task of existence yet to be discovered on our plane of immanence today" (WIP, 75).

It is not inconceivable that we could mistake Deleuze's critical and clinical diagnosis—"we need reasons to believe in this world" (TI, 172)—for nihilism itself; but far from simply describing a shortfall, this statement affirms the exigency of learning to believe in the world again. By inventing concepts, we invent a world commensurate with the inspiration of belief. Creation is the autopoeisis of belief, but in the spirit of sci-phi, Deleuze also inverts this formulation: affirmation is no less creative because we affirm the auspices under which concepts are produced. Thus, he explains, "It was already a great turning point in philosophy, from Pascal to Nietzsche: to replace the model of knowledge with belief" (ibid.). Deleuze is no nihilist, but we'd be just as mistaken if we take him for an evangelist, as if his philosophy sought recourse in a call to religion and even a life of faith. Insofar as "we need an ethic or a faith," Deleuze says, it must outstrip faith as we have traditionally imagined it—"a faith that opposes religion" (MI, 116). Indeed, Deleuze defines the "turning point" in philosophy as the affirmation that knowledge is invented and that "truth is created" (Neg, 126). To believe is to affirm the powers of fabulation, for only when we affirm the power to "make-false" (*faire-faux*) do we surpass the true and the false and undertake the "whole transformation of belief" (TI, 172)—the foreclosure of the metaphysical, moral, and ultimately metaphorical dimension (*dit-mention*[21]) that organizes the structure of perception and recognition, memory and habit, passion and action.

Nothing less is sufficient to re-enchant the world—but this process has a price. The philosopher who accedes to science fiction has journeyed to the frontiers of sensation, has seen unfathomable events, and has survived, though not without having been changed by the experience. Consider the protagonist of *Close Encounters of the Third Kind,* whose literal and existential journey begins late one night when he catches sight of a UFO from his truck. Stopped at a railway crossing, he squints out the driver's side window at the blinding lights above until, quite suddenly, the craft disappears and it is as if nothing has happened. The following day, he'll discover the deep burn deposited on the exposed side of his face; thereafter, he'll begin to intuit the strange inclinations that have gripped his will—to draw an image that eludes him, to see the UFOs again, and finally to make his way to Devil's Tower where he'll finally experience an "encounter of the third kind." Likewise, Deleuze suggests, the philosopher bears witness to such encounters in the signs that have sculpted the flesh, the sensations that have resolved themselves in expression, the impressions that have shaped the delicate folds of gray matter. The rashes, blisters, scars of science fiction are only the most literal figurations of the relation to the Outside, which cannot be represented but which must nevertheless be thought.

Platonism tells us that the philosopher's soul touches the heavens, but the visionary flight of deterritorialization, whereby we dispense with representation in order to "think without an image," is also liable to lend the philosopher an air of insanity. "We head for the horizon, on the plane of immanence" (WIP, 41), and we return with "bloodshot eyes and pierced eardrums" (CC, 3). The wide-eyed seer of strange signs, the mad scientist laboring to invent fantastic machines, the intrepid explorer desperately searching for life elsewhere: the philosopher will become each in turn, and in turn he or she will be ridiculed for having become a stranger to his or her world. It is in this sense, after all, that we might allude to the *realism* of science fiction—not to return to a model of correspondence or correlationism but rather to insist on the reality of the real and the rigor of the event. As Deleuze writes in *Difference and Repetition*, empiricism itself becomes transcendental "only when we apprehend directly in the sensible that which can only be sensed, the very being of the sensible" (DR, 56–57). Sci-phi undertakes the invention of concepts in relation to that which, as we have said, cannot be sensed and can only be sensed: what we have called the "rigor" of sci-phi refers to the resolution to unfold a plane of consistency that includes the unthinkable, the impossible, the Outside. This is "the problem of writing: in order to designate something exactly, inexact expressions are unavoidable. Not at all because it is a necessary step, or because one can advance only by approximations; on the contrary, *it is the exact passage of that which is under way*" (ATP, 20; emphasis added). We can find no better definition of Deleuze's science of the sensible, not any better explanation of why, as he says, this is not science (*Wissenschaft*) as we know it. "We are therefore well aware, unfortunately, that we have spoken about science in a manner which was not scientific," he says in *Difference and Repetition* (xxi). But is there anything really unfortunate about this perversion, or is it rather Deleuze's good fortune to have recovered a sense of *fortuna*—of chance, becoming, "that which is under way"—and made it the substance of conceptualization?

This is among the most critical aspects of Deleuze's philosophy, but it is also among the least understood, especially in view of the profusion of works today that seek to introduce his admittedly difficult thought. The dilemma is that, in making Deleuze legible and even systematic, we assimilate the element of his philosophy "which cannot be assimilated" (Dia, 25). To the degree that Deleuze is represented, he is always misrepresented because we have failed to appreciate the expressive dimension of his philosophy that, in thinking and writing, goes beyond philosophy. As Deleuze and Guattari write, "The plane of consistency is also a plane of nonconsistency" (Le plan de consistance pourrait être nommé de non-consistance) (ATP, 266).[22] No doubt, there is a kind of Gödelian problem operating here inasmuch as, roughly speaking, we seem to affirm that Deleuze's philosophy cannot be both consistent and complete; but the mutual exclusivity of these terms, which implies the negation of one or the other, gives way in sci-phi to the queer logic of the Outside, from which philosophy draws the becomings of new forces, and toward which it vaults its own becomings and lines of flight. "The problem of philosophy is to acquire a consistency without losing anything of the infinite" (Le problème de la philosophie est d'acquérir une consistance, sans perdre l'infini dans lequel la pensée plonge) (WIP, 42), Deleuze and Guattari say.

We have posed sci-phi not as the solution to this problem so much as its means of expression, the imagination of all kinds of alternative realities, at once utopian and disarming, uncanny and familiar, *scientific and fictional*. Needless to say, no compound genre can be distilled into its component parts; science fiction is irreducible to the equation "science + fiction," but Deleuze's affinity for the genre emerges in light of the complex processes that philosophy undertakes with respect to these domains. Previously we defined philosophy, science, and art as the three "daughters of chaos," the three planes of thought, insofar as they share a common "brain." Deleuze's philosophy elaborates a complex neuronal network of lines and points, relations and singularities, and in the second half of this book we have effectively mapped out this brain, tracing the topology in relation to three planes—in relation to literature (chapter 4), then in relation to science (chapter 5), and now, in the midst of concluding, in relation to philosophy itself.

Nevertheless, in this series we would have to acknowledge that philosophy exists "in itself" only on the condition that it consists in drawing relations to each of these domains, confronting their signs and events, posing their problems and questions, appropriating their means and styles. To this extent, Deleuze's sense of philosophy invariably recalls Nietzsche's "great dilemma," namely, "is philosophy an art or a science? Both in its purposes and its results it is an art. But it uses the same means as science—conceptual representation. Philosophy is a form of artistic invention."[23] Deleuze's answer to this "dilemma" is no different. Philosophy is both science and art: it claims its integrity by drawing on the other domains in order to develop a task—the creation of concepts—that remains absolutely its own.

The Deleuzian Sublime (Toward a Philosophy of the Cinema)

Dissolve to: the first chapter of *What Is Philosophy?* where Deleuze and Guattari frame the expression of philosophy and stage the creation of concepts in a kind of apocalyptic aftermath. Like so many works of science fiction that begin in the wake of cataclysm—of nuclear holocaust (*A Boy and His Dog*), biological catastrophe (*Omega Man*), alien invasion (*They Live*), or evolutionary burnout (*Planet of the Apes*), etc.—we might understand the book's beginning as if in relation to a prior (not a priori) destruction. We begin not at the beginning, nor at the end, but in the middle (in medias res, au milieu), namely, with the one who witnesses, or has witnessed, the cataclysm. Heretofore we have cast the philosopher as the experimenter, explorer, visionary—the witness—and while we affirm the experience, we do so in order to evacuate the subject as such. In effect, this resolution is resumed in *What Is Philosophy?* where Deleuze and Guattari recast this encounter with the forces of the Outside, and thereby reconfigure philosophy itself, according to the concept-structure of "other person" (*l'autrui*).

Contrary to the traditional appeal to an overarching category of the Other, or a dialectic between self and other, the concept of the "other person" responds to an occasion. The scene is set, the drama established, by virtue of what would seem an innocuous kind of establishing shot:

> There is at some moment a calm and restful world. Suddenly a frightened face looms up that looks at something out of the field. The other person appears here

as neither subject nor object but as something that is very different: a possible world, the possibility of a frightening world. This possible world is not real, nor not yet, but it exists nonetheless: it is an expressed that exists only in its expression—the face or an equivalent of the face. (WIP, 17)

At first blush, these lines read more like directions in a script than they do a philosophical disquisition. It is as if the camera had been situated in the midst of an incomprehensible landscape: we find no structures, no points of reference, only the impersonal tense of the image—"there is"—in relation to a stray rectangle of space. The shot lingers until "a frightened face looms up that looks at something out of field" (ibid.). Though it appears without warning, the "other person" enters the scene gradually, as if the face—framed now in a tight close-up, choking out any stray space, depriving us of any depth—were detached from its body. Seemingly immobilized, the body has ceded all the power of movement to this "sur-flesh": in the place of an actual or actualized image of flight, the face takes flight along series of twitches, tremblings, and micro-movements. Something frightens the other person—perhaps something apocalyptic—but for now, all we see is the "affect-image," the surface of expression, the tortured landscape of features.

The other person represents nothing but expresses everything, however "intolerable" (TI, 18—but the face itself is no less intolerable. We keep hoping, expecting that something will break this long take—perhaps a sound, coming from off-screen or even issuing from the face itself; better still, a cut, presumably based on an eye-line match, to what the face has beheld, alternating between shot and reverse shot, seer and seen, subject and object. But in lieu of these eventualities, the frame stays firmly fixed and fixated on the face, to the point that any sense of space has been deterritorialized in the landscape of shifting features and virtual intensities. The image endures, the intensities continue to play on the face trapped in the frame, and we continue to watch. Never seeing what has been seen, we see only the immobile face, and if this makes us increasingly uneasy, the reason is that the face expresses our own conditions: we too are paralyzed, forced to watch this "reflective surface." But what is reflected? In this sense, the face is a kind of non-place (*non-lieu*) and non-space (*quelque-espace-quelconque*) that exists between that which we do not know and that which we can only imagine. Thus, the face constitutes a relay between the Outside, which it "wears" as an affect-image, and a possible world, which it projects. The face does not represent the real but unfolds an image of the affected, which is no less real, and thereby furnishes a source of imminent concern and conjecture. In other words, because it is not (yet) realized, the possible is inscribed as a *virtual reality*. Something has happened, is happening, will happen, but we do not see the cataclysm itself. The fright we see is never explained, never given reason or cause, but this contingency gives rise to unprecedented encounter.

Imagine that this frightened face is pressed up against the window of a spacecraft fleeing at full speed from a planet besieged by robots (*Battlestar Galactica*); or is the uncomprehending face of a salvage captain who happens on a terrifying, acid-based organism (*Alien*); or is the suffering grimace that confronts the image of human extinctions thousands of years in the past (*Planet of the Apes*). Of course, these cases anticipate the sense in which fright has been attributed to a source and in which the affection-image, the face, yields to a perception-image—in other words, what was off-screen is revealed. But precisely insofar as this off-screen (*hors cadre*) remains hidden and unexplained, we discover the dynamism of the other person, as the Outside (*le Dehors*). While the face confronts that which is unseen and off-screen, the reflective surface projects a possible world. Whether the frightened face registers the appearance of aliens, the inception of nuclear Holocaust, the dead husk of a planet ravaged by environmental entropy, these are not conditions of possibility but possible worlds. They do not exist in advance of experience but as its result: in a sense, experience itself has become the condition of the possible. The face before us, the repository of the sensible, demands the creation of the possible. Thus, whereas the Outside is reflected in the face, we might say that, under the auspices of a possible world, the future is *preflected* in the face. The face reflects that which we cannot see, expresses that which we can only see, and provokes the fabulation of that which we cannot yet see.

The paradox of the other person is, in this sense, the paradox that belongs to every concept: inspired by the Outside, the unrepresentable, the concept refers to nothing but itself. It is in light of this paradox that we can extend the elaboration of aesthetics on which we have embarked. We began by describing the division from which aesthetics traditionally suffers, and after laying out the dominant sense of aesthetics, the concepts of representation, we considered the minor sense of aesthetics, the reality of the real. In relation to the latter, which we have described as the science (or science fiction) of the sensible, we can now understand how the other person recalls and revises Kant's elaboration of aesthetic experience. For the post-apocalyptic scenario we have unfurled here immediately recalls the similarly catastrophic moment in the *Critique of Judgment* when the mechanism of representation breaks down. Kant calls "sublime" the experience whereby a sensation we encounter—a sensation that would normally be represented by the faculty of the imagination—provokes its collapse, only to be rescued by the faculty of reason. But what is it that we cannot imagine or represent to ourselves? "If nature is to be judged by us dynamically sublime, it must be represented as arousing fear" (CPJ, §28/260). In other words, Kant displaces the object-cause of the sensation in favor of the sensation itself, which precipitates the exhaustion of the imagination and, thence, the sublime intervention of reason. While the images to which Kant alludes—lofty waterfalls, threatening cliffs, boundless oceans, hurricanes, volcanoes—provoke the higher "end" (*Zweck/ Zweckmäßigkeit*) of the sublime, they are not the "thing itself." Indeed, "the wide ocean, enraged by storms, cannot be called sublime. Its visage is horrible," Kant writes; "and one must already have filled the mind with all sorts of ideas if by means of such an intuition it is to be put in the mood for a feeling which is itself sublime, in that the mind is incited to abandon sensibility and to occupy itself with ideas that contain a higher purposiveness [*Zweckmäßigkeit*]" (ibid., §23/245–46).

Like the other person, then, the sublime describes the creation of a concept without reference, but this conjunction ironically marks the pathos of distance between reactive and active concepts, between Kant and Deleuze. In the third *Critique*, the collapse of imagination begets the dialectical redemption of representation. The failure of one faculty ushers in the triumph of another, reason, which intervenes in the last instance to form a concept of the "inadequacy" of the imagination. The "properly sublime cannot be contained in any sensible form," Kant explains, "but concerns only ideas of reason, which, though no presentation adequate to them is possible, are provoked and called to mind precisely by this inadequacy, which does allow of sensible presentation" (ibid., §23/245). Whereas the experience of the beautiful—the free and indeterminate accord between faculties—effectively "schematizes without concepts" (DI, 59), the sublime conceptualizes in the absence of a schematism and without any "rules of determination" (CPR, A126). Whereas the form of the beautiful provokes the feeling of harmony between our faculties and nature, the sublime designates the power of reason to exist in the absence of nature and the world. Therefore, the feeling of the sublime, which began as fear, is transformed into that of *power* (CPJ, §23–25). Perhaps it took the vagaries of the French translations of Kant and Hegel to clarify the relation, hidden in the German terms *Erhabenen* and *Aufhebung*, between sublime and sublation. The former enacts the latter's "labor of the negative" *avant la lettre*; the sublime takes the faculty of imagination to its limit, its inadequacy, only to negate it in the interest of a higher concept of reason (sublation).

Inasmuch as he devises his own sense of the sublime, Deleuze duly transforms the transcendental organization—of discord, negation, and sublation—into a loose assemblage of the faculties, "each borne to the extreme point of its dissolution," which enter into a kind of "discordant harmony" (DR, 180). The transcendental exercise "in no way means that the faculty addresses itself to objects outside the world but, on the contrary, that it grasps that in the world which concerns it exclusively and brings it into the world" (ibid.). The contingency of the sensible, the singular circumstances (events) and appearances (signs) we encounter, must be affirmed as the real conditions for the "what is called thinking" (Heidegger). In *Difference and Repetition*, Deleuze says aesthetics becomes an "apodictic discipline" when that which could have been otherwise is affirmed as the exigency to create the concept itself. Between this early formulation and the late reflections of *What Is Philosophy?* we might say that Deleuze not only transforms these well-nigh Kantian constituents into the components of the other person but, in so doing, transforms the old style of philosophy into what we have risked calling his new one. In the other person, he and Guattari create the *mise-en-scène*—the supple distribution of relations and components—for their *mise-en-pensée*. The other person converts the dynamic mechanism of the sublime into the machinic assemblage of the concept.

What Is Philosophy? begins by considering the other person because, if not the "first" concept, it stages something like the problem of every concept. In the ordination of singularities and the assemblage of components, the other person dramatizes the very concept of the concept as the movement from affect to self-affection. The components of the other person—unseen off-screen, the affected face, and the possible world—enact the process whereby the forces of the Outside, though never represented, are expressed. Based in a sense without reference to an external world (*Umwelt*), folded into thought without designating an internal sphere (*Innenwelt*), the concept fashions a "fragmentary whole" that arrays a distribution of connections and relations. To think in relation to the Outside, to express the inexpressible: this is the task of sci-phi, and if we have pursued it in relation to writing, we might conclude here, under the sign of the face, by auguring its subsequent development. *Incipit cinema!*

ACKNOWLEDGMENTS

For Gilles Deleuze, the invention of new means of philosophical expression is almost invariably pursued in relation to friends, both philosophers and nonphilosophers, about whom he reflects, with whom he thinks, and through whom he writes. In the course of this book, which concerns Deleuze's sense of expression, I've come to appreciate the philosophy of friendship. So many conversations, arguments, texts, and contexts have underwritten *Gilles Deleuze and the Fabulation of Philosophy* that the offer of a proper name, no less a proprietary one (mine), seems to me now to risk the worst kind of fraudulence if "I" don't begin here by bearing witness to the collective assemblage of friends who made this work possible.

Naturally, I cannot account for every encounter and every relationship that influenced this book, but I extend my gratitude to those whose singular contributions, recorded here, I can only hope to have affirmed in the spirit in which they were given. Above all, I remain indebted to Peter Canning and Gregg Lambert, whose encouragement and insight have been of immeasurable value. Both helped me to grapple with the questions that lie at the heart of this book—the powers of the false, the possibility of friendship, the problem of style, and the prospects of "thinking differently." Their advice guided me as much as their rigor challenged me and their fellowship has buoyed me. Likewise, I wish to thank a number of friends whose continued support, both intellectual and emotional, sustained me in writing this book: Jeff Nealon, whose comments proved integral in producing the book's finished form; Elena Oxman, whose keenness of mind and judgment I have continually trusted; and Jean-Michel Rabaté, whose gentle mentoring I count on without ever having to ask for it.

No less important, I extend my enduring appreciation to Elise Harris and Anna Panszczyk, who helped me to put this book together. To say that they served as my readers, research assistants, and editors would be to vastly underestimate the degree to which I relied on their intelligence and knowledge, no less their patience and empathy. In matters of translation, conceptualization, and style, I ceaselessly sought Elise's rigor; in matters of organization, formulation, and format, I constantly depended on Anna's expertise. I also thank Bill Race and Will Washburn, both of whom I consulted on translations of ancient Greek. More generally, I was lucky enough to be able to call on a great many readers (Frida Beckman, Erin Branch, Scott Dill, Abe Geil, Jennifer Lange, Charlotte Lloyd, Matt Taylor, Tom Reinert, Eliza Richards, Lisa Trahair, Henry Veggian) without whose comments, queries, and criticisms this book would surely have been poorer. To this list I should add the names of Ron Bogue, Eleanor Kauffman, and Dan Smith, who fielded questions, or simply posed them, in ways that deeply shaped my thinking. Finally, the results of this thinking would have amounted to nothing were it not for the support, trust, and patience of the University of Minnesota Press: to my editor, Doug Armato, I extend my enduring thanks.

The process of writing this book was made a great deal easier, and doubtless shorter, by the generous provisions of two fellowships and the abiding support of the Department of English and Comparative Literature at the University of North Carolina. I am grateful to Bland Simpson, Beverly Taylor, and James Thompson, the department's most recent three chairs and my first three, for encouraging my work in ways large and small. At the University of North Carolina, the Institute of Arts and Humanities provided an important semester's leave during which much of the first two chapters were conceived. To the fellows with whom I shared that semester and to John McGowan, the institute's director and a source of genuinely pragmatic counsel, I express my gratitude. Similarly, I benefited from a year-long residency at Duke University's John Hope Franklin Institute, where I was part of a group brought together around the subject of "alternative political imaginaries." The last chapter of this book emerged in part from our discussions and arguments. To all my fellow participants, and especially to the seminar's conveners, Michael Hardt and Robyn Wiegman, I hope that what I have written conveys the rigor of our debates and the abiding fondness with which they were pursued. Finally, I was fortunate to benefit from two grants from the University Research Council that greatly aided my research.

This book bears the traces, however faint, of several preliminary publications and ventures. Nothing appears here as it did originally, and in most cases passages have been revised beyond recognition: still, the major theses of this book were first articulated "occasionally," and I would be remiss if I didn't thank those who made the occasions possible. In the first place, my gratitude goes to numerous book editors who offered the forum within which to pursue ideas or the impetus to embark on new ones: Ian Buchanan, Peter Gaffney, Anna Hickey-Moody, Graham Jones, Gregg Lambert, Patricia MacCormack, Peta Malins, Simon O'Sullivan, John Roffe, Charles Stivale, and Stephen Zepke. Likewise, I thank those who invited me to give lectures and thereby provided the audiences before whom this book was effectively rehearsed: Antonio Rodrigues Amorin, Sean Knierem, Hyon Joo Murphy, Angelo Restivo, and Patricia Pisters. Beyond these occasions, my students served as my constant (and often unwitting) audience: in classes, independent studies, and writing groups, I tested, revised, and refined many of the ideas that appear here. There are too many students to thank over the past few years, but I am compelled to mention Erin Allingham, Lynn Badia, Leslie Davison, Scott Dill, Nick Gaskill, Will Kaiser, Anna Lassiter, Charlotte Lloyd, Jessica Martell, Jason Maxwell, Will Nolan, Al Miller, Ben Rogerson, Emily O'Rourke, John Steen, and Elissa Zellinger.

Finally, this book about friendship is appropriately indebted to my friends and colleagues on whom I have called for advice, support, and (best of all) good humor. My thanks go out to Reid Barbour, Rita Barnard, Jen Bilik, Anne Bruder, Florence Dore, Eric Downing, Stefanie Fisher, Larry Grossberg, John Kirk, Dick Langston, Shayne Legassi, Jeff Maycock, Denis Mumby, Erin Nelson, Jeremy Packer, Andy Perrin, Ben Rhau, Joyce Rudinsky, Judith Sakowicz, Sarah Sharma, Christa Shusko, Randall Styers, Francesca Talenti, Asha Varadharajan, Mary Floyd Wilson, and Jessica Wolfe. As Sandra Bernhardt once said, "without you, I'm nothing"—and as Gilles Deleuze might have added, with you, I'm always becoming . . .

NOTES

Preface

1 In Nietzsche's writing, naturally, this project reaches its most sustained elaboration in *On the Genealogy of Morals and Ecce Homo*, trans. Walter Kaufmann (New York: Vintage, 1969), though the rudiments of this approach are already altogether evident in his early essay "The History of Moral Sensation." See *Human, All Too Human*, trans. Gary Handwerk (Stanford: Stanford University Press, 1995), 43–84.

2 Gilles Deleuze, *Difference and Repetition*, trans. Paul Patton (New York: Columbia University Press, 1994), xxi.

3 Deleuze is still stereotypically identified with the unique formulations that he and Guattari undertake in Gilles Deleuze and Félix Guattari, *Anti-Oedipus*, trans. Robert Hurley, Mark Seem, and Helen R. Lane (Minneapolis: University of Minnesota Press, 1986), and *A Thousand Plateaus*, trans. Brian Massumi (Minneapolis: University of Minnesota Press, 1987). Notwithstanding the great originality of these books, Deleuze's response to the challenge of philosophy, stretching out over roughly forty years, is abidingly complex.

4 See Friedrich Nietzsche, *The Birth of Tragedy*, trans. Walter Kaufmann (New York: Vintage, 1967), §19. Also see the "Attempt at Self-Criticism," which Nietzsche appended to this text on the occasion of its republication: there Nietzsche says that the critical evaluation of the "will to truth" must pass through aesthetics and, thence, life itself (§2).

5 These three terms—*God, Man,* and *the World* (substance)—are, as Deleuze says, the three illusions of transcendence through which philosophy passes on the road to immanence. I discuss this "triple murder" at length in this book's "Coda," but at this stage it is worth noting that, for Deleuze, Nietzsche remains virtually alone among philosophers who have effaced these specters of transcendence from the plane of immanence. See Deleuze, *Difference and Repetition*, 58.

6 Gilles Deleuze, *Negotiations 1972–1990*, trans. Martin Joughin (New York: Columbia University Press, 1995), 126.

7 Friedrich Nietzsche, *The Portable Nietzsche*, trans. Walter Kaufmann (New York: Penguin, 1977), 485. All references to *Twilight of the Idols* and, thence, "How the 'True

World' Finally Became a Fable," are rendered in terms of the *Portable Nietzsche* (Kaufmann never published a stand-alone edition of the text). Notably, Nietzsche's parable is among the sources for Gregg Lambert's superb study, *The Non-Philosophy of Gilles Deleuze* (London: Continuum, 2002), 90–113.

8 The phrase is taken from Stuart Kauffman, who uses it to describe the nature of life itself: far from consisting in a mere anomaly, Kauffman says, life is intimately and immanently bound up with the unfolding of the cosmos. See Stuart Kauffman, *At Home in the Universe: The Search for the Laws of Self-Organization and Complexity* (New York: Oxford University Press, 1995). I return to the question of complexity in chapter 5.

9 See, above all, the second part of the *Genealogy of Morals*, where Nietzsche outlines the emergence of the human (Man-form) according to the inscription of debt. I return to this subject in the first and second chapters.

10 See BOT, §15–16.

11 Doubtless, the True World was given over to judgment, guilt, and bad conscience, but we would be remiss if we didn't admit that this regime provided a sense of regularity and predictability that, however reactive, we miss.

12 Friedrich Nietzsche, *Beyond Good and Evil: Prelude to a Philosophy of the Future*, trans. Walter Kaufmann (New York: Vintage, 1989), §291.

13 See *Gilles Deleuze, Desert Island and Other Texts: 1953–1974*, ed. David Lapoujade, trans. Mike Taormina (New York: Semiotext[e], 2003), 259. The original title of this essay, "Pensée nomade," has been translated in this collection as "Nomadic Thought," but throughout this book I have employed the more elegant and supple "Nomad Thought."

14 Friedrich Nietzsche, *Philosophy in the Tragic Age of the Greeks*, trans. Marianne Cowan (Washington, D.C.: Regency Publishing, 1998), 34. Also see *Unfashionable Observations*, trans. Richard T. Gray (Stanford: Stanford University Press, 1995), "Schopenhauer as Educator," §7.

15 See Nietzsche, *Ecce Homo* in *On the Genealogy of Morals and Ecce Homo*, trans. Walter Kaufmann (New York: Vintage, 1967), "Why I Write Such Good Books" §1.

16 Gilles Deleuze and Félix Guattari, *What Is Philosophy?* trans. Hugh Tomlinson and Graham Burchell (New York: Columbia University Press, 1994), 11. The authors invent the "aerolite" to describe the sense in which concepts take flight and are composed, in turn, of movements and intensities along a line of flight.

17 Perhaps the singular moment of the singularly French reckoning with Nietzsche arrived in 1972, at the conference at Cerisy-La Salle, where Deleuze, Kofman, Nancy, Derrida, Lacoue-Labarth, Klossowski, Blanchot, and others gave papers. The results (over eight hundred pages) were published in *Nietzsche aujourd'hui* (Paris: Union Général d'Édition, 1973). Beyond reckoning with Nietzsche, this group of philosophers were engaged in a kind of extended conversation. In this regard, see Eleanor Kauffman, *Delirium of Praise: Bataille, Blanchot, Deleuze, Foucault, Klossowski* (Baltimore: Johns Hopkins University Press, 2001).

18 While far from approving, Vincent Descomes rightly situates Nietzsche at the heart of Deleuze's philosophy, no less the emergence of poststructuralism. See his *Modern French Philosophy*, trans. L. Scott Fox and J. M. Harding (Cambridge: Cambridge University Press, 1980).

19 The critical sense of "anexactitude" emerges most manifestly in *A Thousand Plateaus*, trans. Brian Massumi (Minneapolis: University of Minnesota Press, 1983). As Deleuze and Guattari say of writing: "in order to designate something exactly, anexact expressions are utterly unavoidable" (20). Significantly, the formulation of the rigorous and the anexact is lifted from Michel Serres. See *La naissance de la physique* (Paris: Éditions de Minuit, 1977), 29.

20 Gilles Deleuze, *Francis Bacon: The Logic of Sensation*, trans Daniel W. Smith (Minneapolis: University of Minnesota Press, 2003), 36.

21 See Gilles Deleuze, *Essays Critical and Clinical*, trans. Ariel Greco and Daniel W. Smith (Minneapolis: University of Minnesota Press, 1998), 101.

22 This forms part of the formula that Deleuze attributes to Nietzsche, namely, "*Return is the being of that which becomes*" (NP, 24). We cannot speak of being unless it refers to becoming, just as becoming must be referred to what Nietzsche calls the eternal return.

23 The subtitle of *Twilight of the Idols* is "How to Philosophize with a Hammer."

24 In the *Genealogy of Morals* and elsewhere Nietzsche insists that beyond good and evil does not mean beyond good and bad (Preface, I §4).

25 With respect to the literary problem, see "Literature and Life" in *Essays Critical and Clinical*, which offers the most condensed and aphoristic summation of writing per Deleuze. With respect to cinema, Deleuze's clearest and briefest summation probably lies in the brief and luminous interviews he gave in the wake of his cinema books. See "On the Movement-Image" and "On the Time-Image" in Deleuze, *Negotiations* (46–61).

26 Hence, while literature and cinema augur the shifting accent of our analysis, generating their respective tasks in light of Deleuze's philosophy, these tasks are no more separable, no more discrete than the duality of critique and creation from which, roughly speaking, they acquire their sense.

Introduction

1 Deleuze and Guattari, *A Thousand Plateaus*, 3–25.

2 Gilles Deleuze, "Eight Years Later: 1980 Interview in *Two Regimes of Madness: Texts and Interviews, 1975–1993*, trans. Ames Hodges and Mike Taorima (New York: Semiotext[e], 2007), 176. In this edition, the passage reads, "It's just plain old philosophy," but I have rendered it differently based on the original: "Philosophie, rien que de la philosophie, au sens traditionnel du mot." See Gilles Deleuze, *Deux régimes de fous* (Paris: Les Éditions de Minuit 2003), 163.

3 Friedrich Nietzsche, *Thus Spake Zarathustra*, trans. Walter Kaufmann (New York: Modern Library, 1995).

4 Gilles Deleuze, *Proust and Signs*, trans. Richard Howard (Minneapolis: University of Minnesota Press, 2000), 95.

5 *Proust and Signs* was originally published in 1964, but given Deleuze's significant additions to the text, its translation history is far more complicated. I am indebted to Gregg Lambert and Charles Stivale for having clarified this history.

6 Naturally, we associate the concept of *écriture* with a number of notable thinkers, including Roland Barthes, Jacques Lacan, Jean-Luc Nancy, Luce Irigarcy, and Jacques Derrida. Deleuze was well acquainted with these thinkers, but his notion of writing owed more to Proust and Kafka than to any of them. Of course, this shouldn't preclude questions about Deleuze's encounters with his contemporaries. In terms of Deleuze's relation to Derrida, about which a number of very thoughtful pieces have been written, see Paul Patton and John Protevi, eds., *Between Deleuze and Derrida* (London: Continuum, 2003), as well as Gabrielle Schwab, ed., *Derrida, Deleuze, Psychoanalysis* (New York: Columbia University Press, 2007).

7 For a description of this plane, which Deleuze distinguishes from the philosophical "plane of immanence," see *WIP* 65–67, 185–99.

8 Whenever we organize the relation between literature and philosophy on the basis of analogy, whenever we make this our image of thought, we do too little and too much—too little because we fail to describe the autonomy and intrinsic logic of each discipline, too much because we always already assume the nature of an engagement or that such an engagement is natural to begin with.

9 Gilles Deleuze and Félix Guattari, *Kafka: Toward a Minor Literature,* trans. Dona Polan (Minneapolis: University of Minnesota Press, 1986), 18. The sentiment, however, derives from Proust: "Great books are written in a kind of foreign language." See Proust's *Contre Saint Beauve* (Paris: Gallimard, 1987), 297.

10 Gilles Deleuze and Claire Parnet, *Dialogues II*, trans. Hugh Tomlinson and Barbara Habberjam (New York: Columbia University Press, 2007), 40.

11 The phrase comes from Nietzsche: in a late letter to Jacob Burckhardt (January 6, 1889), in the grips of impending madness, he writes: "At bottom I am all the names in history" (PN, 685–87).

12 Gilles Deleuze, *Cinema 2: The Time-Image*, trans. Hugh Tomlinson and Robert Galeta (Minneapolis: University of Minnesota Press, 1989), 172.

13 The importance of *propre* in this regard lies in its double adjectival significance, as the possessive "own" as well as attributative "clean"—that is, *cleanly*, distinctly.

14 See the third chapter of *Difference and Repetition*, where Deleuze displaces the image of thought by affirming philosophy on the basis of the encounter with signs.

15 Deleuze defines the "being of the sensible" as that which "cannot be sensed" and "can only be sensed" (DR, 236). I return to this paradox in chapter 4.

16 Witold Gombrowicz, *Cosmos and Pronographia: Two Novels*, trans. Eric Mosbacher and Alistair Hamilton (New York: Grove Press, 1985), 10.

17 This formulation, "to cash out," is one to which I frequently return in the course of this book as shorthand for considering the consequences—real, though not necessarily actual—of ideas. The phrase is derived, at least in my usage, from William James's resolution to seek the "cash-values" of truths in experiential terms, provided we understand that truth, far from being an eternal and essential attribute, is what "happens to an idea." See James's *Pragmatism and Other Writings*, ed. Giles Gunn (New York: Penguin, 2000), 88. James goes on to say that truth "will have to be *made*, made in relation incidental to the growth of a mass of verification-experience, to which the half-true ideas are all along contributing their quota" (98). This realization underwrites James's sense of a pragmatic ethos, or what approximates the action of cashing out. As he famously explains, "You must bring out of each word its practical cash-value, set it at work within the stream of your experience. It appears less as a solution, then, than as a program for more work, and more particularly as an indication of the ways in which existing realities may be *changed*" (28).

18 Like Foucault, Deleuze readily evacuates the traditional function of the author, because he preserves writing (and even, in a particular sense, the writer) as that which escapes the juridical, proprietary, or sovereign domain which the author-function determined. See, especially, "Literature and Life" (CC, 1–6), "What Is a Minor Literature?" (K, 16–27), and the "Introduction: Rhizome" to Deleuze and Guattari's *A Thousand Plateaus*, 3–25.

19 This tendency is by no means a rule: a number of Deleuze's commentators have begun to consider his philosophy in this light. See, for instance, Ronald Bogue's *Deleuze's Wakes: Tributes and Tributaries* (Albany: SUNY Press, 2004), which includes a section on "Deleuze's Style," as well as Charles Stivale's *Gilles Deleuze's ABC's: The Folds of Friendship* (Baltimore: Johns Hopkins University Press, 2008). More recently, Gregg Lambert's forthcoming book on Deleuze's image of thought, which returns to the subject of Proust, suggests that the question of style has arrived.

20 Philosophy is always already an aesthetic endeavor, but for this reason, divvying up philosophy on the basis of aesthetics, much less epistemology, ontology, and ethics, no longer suffices: these categories had been complicated beyond any confident measure. In this sense, Deleuze's work remains most closely related to Nietzsche's.

21 François Dosse, *Gilles Deleuze and Félix Guattari: Intersecting Lives,* trans. Deborah Glossman (New York: Columbia University Press, 2010), 90. Notably, Dosse quotes from an interview with novelist Michel Tournier, Deleuze's close friend since childhood.

22 See Jean-François Lyotard's text written on the occasion of Deleuze's death, *Liberation* (November 7, 1995), 36.

23 See "The Library of Babel," in Borges's *Collected Fictions*, trans. Andrew Hurley (New York: Penguin, 1998), 112–19. The library of Babel constitutes an archive in which every possible permutation of the elements of language and punctuation has been recorded within a virtually infinite collection of books (of no more than 410 pages). The vast

majority of books in this library are, naturally, total nonsense; but inasmuch as it is total, inasmuch as its volumes "encompass everything possible to express in all languages," Borges contends that the library necessarily contains every book that has ever been written in any language (118).

24 Pollack eventually began to paint by placing the canvas on the floor and standing over it in order to achieve his "drip" technique.

25 It is critical that we remember, going forward, that the plane of consistency is also a plane of inconsistency, in other words, that the plane resists totalization or completion. I return to this formulation more explicitly in the Coda.

26 For instance, see *The Political Unconscious*, where Fredric Jameson's behemoth of a first chapter offers an appreciative reading of *Anti-Oedipus* beneath which, and in a footnote, he expresses anxiety about the prospect of what effects the book might have outside of France, especially in the very different political history context of the United States. See Fredric Jameson, *The Political Unconscious: Narrative as a Socially Symbolic Act* (Ithaca, N.Y.: Cornell University Press, 1981), 41. Also see Gregg Lambert's incomparable analysis of Jameson's reading in *Who's Afraid of Deleuze and Guattari?* (London: Continuum, 2006).

27 See Lambert, *Who's Afraid of Deleuze and Guattari?* which provides by far the most far-reaching account of this reception. Of particular importance for our purposes, Lambert stresses the way in which the English translations of *Anti-Oedipus* and *A Thousand Plateaus* profoundly colored and characterized the broader reception of Deleuze's work.

28 Gilles Deleuze, *The Movement-Image*, trans. Hugh Tomlinson and Robert Galeta (Minneapolis: University of Minnesota Press, 1989), 3.

29 Alan D. Schrift, *Nietzsche's French Legacy: A Genealogy of Poststructualism* (London: Routledge, 1995), 2.

30 The "New Nietzsche" is also the title of an important collection of essays that helped to shape what might crudely be called a "poststructuralist Nietzsche." More accurately, though, the collection helped to introduce a largely "French Nietzsche" to Anglo-American audiences. Deleuze's essay "Nomad Thought," which I discuss at length in the first chapter, first appeared in this anthology. See David B. Allison, ed., *The New Nietzsche* (Cambridge, Mass.: MIT Press, 1977). Also see Schrift, *Nietzsche's French Legacy*.

31 Perry Anderson, *Arguments within English Marxism* (London: NLB, 1980), 178.

32 Ibid.

33 Nietzsche signs his letter to Overbeck (January 6, 1889) "Dionysus" (PN, 687).

34 As François Dosse writes, during the war Deleuze associated with others who shared the same nonacademic notion of philosophy. "Under Alain Clément's leadership, the group published a single issue of *Espace*, a philosophy journal, in which they openly expressed their hostility to the idea of interiority, illustrating the cover of this first and only issue with a toilet and the caption: 'a landscape is a state of mind' " (*Gilles Deleuze and Félix Guattari: Intersecting Lives*, 92).

35 This is, not incidentally, the title of Nicole Loraux's superb book on autochthony, to which I return in chapters 2 and 3. See *Born of the Earth: Myth and Politics in Athens,* trans. Selina Steward (Ithaca: Cornell University Press, 2000).

36 Deleuze and Guattari, *Anti-Oedipus,* 140.

37 "Modern philosophy's link with capitalism, therefore, is of the same kind as that of ancient philosophy with Greece: *the connection of an absolute plane of immanence with a relative social milieu that also functions through immanence*" (WIP, 98).

38 See WIP, 93.

1. Friendship and Philosophy, Nietzsche and Deleuze

1 At the conclusion of the only colloquium he ever organized, the renowned conference on Nietzsche held at the Abbey of Royamount (1964), Deleuze insists that Nietzsche's greatest contribution was to have created a "new means of expression to transform philosophy" (DI, 127).

2 In *Pourparlers,* the full quote reads: "Dire quelque chose en son propre nom, c'est très curieux ; car ce n'est pas du tout au moment où l'on se prend pour un moi, une personne ou un sujet qu'on parle en son nom" [To say something in one's own name, it is a curious thing; as it isn't at all the moment in which one takes oneself for a 'me', for a person or a subject who speaks in his own name] (15–16 ; translation mine). It is true that, for Deleuze, Spinoza and Nietzsche are nothing less than the apostates of immanence who lead philosophy into hitherto hidden and accursed areas: both elaborate a revolutionary plane of forces, a radical body of affects, and a riotous production of concepts with which Deleuze fashions the broad and unorthodox elements of his own philosophy. See Deleuze's filmed interview with Claire Parnet, *Abecedaire* ("H as in History of Philosophy"), dir. Pierre-André Boutang (1996).

3 During his years of formal education, Deleuze recalls, "no one talked about Nietzsche," and on the rare occasions when Nietzsche was called on to take part in the drama of the dominant philosophies of the 1950s (phenomenology, existentialism, even Kojève's Marxism), he was grossly miscast (DI, 136). "All the great philosophical ideas of the last century," Merleau-Ponty once declared, careful to include the philosophy of Nietzsche in the mix, "had their beginnings in Hegel." See Descombes, *Modern French Philosophy,* 11.

4 Pierre Bourdieu, *Homo Academicus,* trans. Peter Collier (Cambridge: Polity Press, 1990), xxiv.

5 For a description of Nietzsche's appeal in the wake of existentialism and structuralism, see Schrift, *Nietzsche's French Legacy,* 3ff.

6 In this instance, the French text goes a great deal further: "l'ami, dit Zarathoustra, est toujours un tiers entre je et moi, qui me pousse à me surmonter et à être surmonté pour vivre." See Gilles Deleuze, *Nietzsche et la philosophie* (Paris: PUF, 1970), 6. We might do

better to the translate this declaration as: "The friend . . . who pushes me to overcome myself and to be overcome by living."

7 Deleuze is quoting from sections in the *Will to Power* that do not appear in the abridged English edition. See the French edition, *La Volonté de puissance* (Paris: Librairie générale française, 1991), III 383.

8 Notably, the original reads: "Nietzsche dit : il s'agit de faire à l'homme une mémoire; et l'homme qui s'est constitué par une faculté active d'oubli, par un refoulement de la mémoire biologique, doit se faire une luire mémoire, qui soit collective, une mémoire des paroles et non plus des choses, une mémoire des signes et non plus des effets. Système de la cruauté, terrible alphabet, cette organisation qui trace des signes à même le corps: 'Peut-être n'y a-t-il même rien de plus terrible et de plus inquiétant dans la préhistoire de l'homme que sa mnémotechnique.'" Gilles Deleuze and Félix Guattari, *L'Anti-Œdipe* (Paris: Les Éditions de Minuit, 1972), 169.

9 "Philosophos ne veut pas dire sage, mais ami de la sagesse. Or, de quelle manière étrange il faut interpréter 'ami': l'ami, dit Zarathoustra, est toujours un tiers entre je et moi, qui me pousse à me surmonter et à être surmonté pour vivre. L'ami de la sagesse est celui qui se réclame de la sagesse, mais comme on se réclame d'un masque dans lequel on ne survivrait pas; celui qui fait servir la sagesse à de nouvelles fins, bizarres et dangereuses, fort peu sages en vérité" (*Nietzsche et la philosophie*, 6).

10 See Plato's *Apology*, in *Collected Dialogues of Plato*, ed. Edith Hamilton (Princeton, N.J.: Princeton University Press, 1963). Once Socrates is condemned to death, he addresses the judges who have voted to acquit him: "I think of you as my friends and I wish to show you the meaning of what has now happened to me. For to me, judges—and in calling you judges I am calling you rightly—something wonderful has taken place. For previously the familiar divinatory voice of the daimon always spoke to me quite frequently and opposed me even in very small things if I was about to do something I should not rightly do. And now there has happened to me that which might be considered and is generally thought to be the greatest of evils. But the divine sign opposed me neither when I left my home in the morning, nor when I was coming up here to the court, nor when I was about to say anything. And yet on other occasions it stopped me many times in the middle of speaking, but now, in this matter, it has opposed me in neither my deeds nor my words. What, then, do I suppose to be the cause of this? I will tell you. That which has happened to me seems to me to be good, and those of us do not conceive rightly who think that death is an evil. That which, to me, is a clear proof of this has occurred. For the familiar sign would surely have opposed me if I had not been about to do something good." See Plato's *Apology* (40 a-c).

11 Friedrich Nietzsche, *The Gay Science*, trans. Walter Kaufmann (New York: Vintage, 1974), #125.

12 Not that Deleuze is the "best" or "truest" or "most loyal" of friends, since these qualifications only serve to introduce the "old style" (DR, xxi) of respectful reading and faithful interpretation.

13 Gilles Deleuze, *Pure Immanence: Essays on a Life*, trans. Anne Boyman (New York: Zone, 2001), 70. As Deleuze writes of Kant, "there has never been a more conciliatory or respectful total critique" (NP, 89). "Nietzsche thinks the idea of critique is identical to philosophy," Deleuze writes, but he also thinks "that this is precisely the idea that Kant has missed, that he has compromised and spoilt, not only in its application but *in principle*" (ibid., 88; emphasis added). Kant ends up affirming the "rights of the criticized" (ibid., 89).

14 Two points must be made here. First, the French *confiance* ushers us into an interesting wordplay. The root *fi-* takes us to *foi* (faith), but also *se méfier* (to be wary of), *se fier* (to trust in/rely on), *fier* (adj.—proud, even conceited at times), *fiancer* (to betroth, to pledge—the English fiancé), *fidèle* (faithful). Second, the sense of what the English text renders as "twilight" remains, in the original French, a more complex and poetic evocation: "et tout à la fois atteindre à cette heure, entre chien et loup, où l'on se méfie même de l'ami." Gilles Deleuze and Félix Guarrari, *Qu'est-ce que la philosophie?* (Paris: Les Éditions de Minuit, 1991), 1. In other words, the distrust to which friendship gives rise plunges us into the interval between species, dog and wolf, wherein becoming occurs. I am indebted to Elise Harris for this insight.

15 These first two claims come from *Ecce Homo*, "Why Am I a Destiny?" §1.

16 Northrop Frye, *Antomy of Criticism*, ed. Robert Denham (Toronto: University of Toronto Press, 2006) 231.

17 In the original German, "unknown" (*unbekannten*) is in italics. "Und hier rühre ich wieder an mein Problem, an unser Problem, meine *unbekannten* Freunde (—denn noch weiss ich von keinem Freunde): welchen Sinn hätte unser ganzes Sein, wenn nicht den, dass in uns jener Wille zur Wahrheit sich selbst als Problem zum Bewusstsein gekommen wäre?"

18 Michel de Montaigne, *The Complete Essays of Montaigne*, trans. Donald M. Frame (Stanford: Stanford University Press, 1958), 135–44.

19 See Dudley M. Marchi, *Montaigne among the Moderns: Receptions of the Essais* (Providence, R.I.: Berghahn Books, 1994), 126.

20 As Jacques Derrida has written, Aristotle's contradictory statements "concatenate, they appear together, they are summoned to appear, in the present." It is notable, then, that Derrida's exhumation of Aristotle's phrase, despite lengthy discussion of Nietzsche, never alights on the address with which we are beginning here: "my unknown friends. . . ." See Derrida's *The Politics of Friendship*, trans. George Collins (London: Verso, 2005), 1.

21 "The secret of philosophy, because it was lost at the start, remains to be discovered in the future" (PI, 68).

22 Michel Haar, "Nietzsche and Metaphysical Language" in Allison, ed., *The New Nietzsche*, 5. Haar adds: "For about a decade now there has been a growing uneasiness with regard to Nietzsche: might he not be more inaccessible, more unapproachable, and more inevitably 'betrayed' than any philosopher before or since? Might he not be more veiled and

also more thoughtlessly read, and therefore more richly endowed with a future, than any other philosopher."

23 I have opted here to refer to an alternative translation of Deleuze's "Preface to the English Edition" of *Nietzsche and Philosophy*, xiii.

24 In Nietzsche's work, Deleuze adds, "typology begins with topology" because the Outside introduces a field of forces that demands to be characterized according to its variable dispositions, relations, and inclinations (NP, 115).

25 Gilles Deleuze, *L'île déserte et autres textes*, ed. David Lapoujade (Paris: Les Éditions de Minuit, 2002), 357.

26 Gilles Deleuze, *Foucault*, trans. Seán Hand (Minneapolis: University of Minnesota Press, 1988), 93. One should consult the original French here—"Le devenir, le changement, la mutation concernent les forces composantes, et non les formes composées"— inasmuch as it offers a more elegant, and ultimately far-reaching, conclusion. See Gilles Deleuze's *Foucault* (Paris: Les Éditions de Minuit, 1986), 93.

27 The phrase "introduction to nonfascist living" comes from Foucault's foreword to *Anti-Oedipus* (xv).

28 In this context, see Foucault, "Lives of Infamous Men," in *The Essential Works of Michel Foucault*, vol. 3: *Power*, trans. Robert Hurley (New York: New Press, 2000), 157–75.

29 Most famously, perhaps, Förster-Nietzsche eliminated the thirty-fifth aphorism of the *The Anti-Christ*, in which Nietzsche revised, or conflated, passages from the Bible.

30 Michel Foucault, "The Discourse of Language," in *The Archaeology of Knowledge* (New York: Pantheon, 1982), 218–19. In "Nietzsche, Genealogy, History," Foucault explains, no doubt with his own method in mind, that Nietzsche's genealogy "does not oppose itself to history as the lofty and profound gaze of the philosopher might compare to the mole-like perspective of the scholar; on the contrary, it rejects the metahistorical deployment of ideal signification and indefinite teleologies. It opposes itself to the search for 'origins.' " See Foucault, *The Essential Works of Michel Foucault*, vol. 2: *Aesthetics, Method, and Epistemology*, trans. Robert Hurley (New York: New Press, 1998), 370.

31 The French here is much more revealing: "si vous voulez savoir ce que je veux dire, trouvez la force qui donne un sens, au besoin un nouveau sens, à ce que je dis. Branchez ce texte sur cette force. De cette manière il n'y a pas de problème d'interprétation de Nietzsche, il n'y a que des problèmes de machination: machiner le texte de Nietzsche, chercher avec quelle force extérieure actuelle il fait passer quelque chose, un courant d'énergie" (Deleuze, *L'île déserte et autres textes*, 357).

32 The English translation here fails to capture the elegance of Deleuze's concept: "Ce ne sont pas deux amis qui s'exercent à penser, c'est la pensée qui exige que le penseur soit un ami, pour qu'elle se partage en elle-même et puisse s'exercer" (*Qu'est-ce que la philosophie?* 68).

33 Immanuel Kant, *Critique of Pure Reason*, ed. and trans. Paul Guyer and Allen W. Wood (Cambridge: Cambridge University Press, 1998), A155.

34 The importance of this pronoun, *l'on*, cannot be underestimated. We will return to this point at the conclusion of chapter 4, but even here, we would be remiss if we didn't remark that the "one" constitutes the pronoun par excellence of Deleuze's writing machine. For while the one (*l'on*) suggests an impersonal singularity, it is used as a pronoun to designate a plural group (as in the first person inclusive plural or "we"). When we say that "one is permitted" to do something, we really mean that anyone or everyone is permitted. Hence, in English, *l'on* is often rendered as "you"—in the sense, for instance, that the second person is used to speak of a general state of affairs ("you can't trust anyone these days"). In any case, Deleuze's use of the pronoun insits on a singularity that is no less, and always, a plurality.

35 Deleuze's sense here is not entirely captured by the English: "Je ne suis plus moi, mais une aptitude de la pensée à se voir et se développer à travers un plan qui me traverse en plusieurs endroits" (*Qu'est-ce que la philosophie?* 62).

36 Montaigne, *The Complete Essays of Montaigne*, 138 ff.

37 Ibid.

38 In French, the quote reads: "Car c'est impossible de lui faire subir à lui un pareil traitement. Des enfants dans le dos, c'est lui qui vous en fait" (*Pourparlers*, 15).

39 We immediately recognize the ambiguity of origins and authors to which becoming gives rise in the context of Nietzsche's own philosophy, which frequently embraces the metaphor of proud paternity only in order to make it flounder in favor of a feverish complexity of creation. In the preface to his first book, *The Birth of Tragedy*, Nietzsche provides a narrative of writing that veers from a story of paternal authorship into something else entirely. "While the thunder of the Battle of Wörth rolled across Europe," he writes, "the brooder and lover of riddles who fathered this book [*dem die Vaterschaft dieses Buches zu Theil ward*] was sitting in some corner of the Alps, utterly preoccupied with his ponderings and riddles and consequently very troubled and untroubled at the same time, writing down his thoughts about the Greeks." (BOT, §1). On the one hand, we are presented here with a father who watches over events as one watches children, oscillating from feeling worried [*bekümmert*] to feeling relatively unconcerned; on the other hand, the "child" in this scene is *The Birth of Tragedy* itself, as if to suggest that the war "rolling over Europe" was no distant conflict but one that had impressed itself on the author, subjecting him to its blows, inseminating him with "thoughts about the Greeks." In other words, the "father" of this book also suffers from a troubled pregnancy, for the very nature of becoming into which we enter with others lies in leaving our "self" (ego, cogito, subject) behind.

40 The German reads: "Es giebt zwei Arten des Genie's: eins, welches vor allem zeugt und zeugen will, und ein andres, welches sich gern befruchten lässt und gebiert." Also see Nietzsche, *The Gay Science:* "spiritual pregnancy produces the character of the contemplative type, to which the female character is related: these are male mothers" (§72).

41 The original reads: "Nietzsche est profondément las de toutes ces histoires faites autour de la mort du père, de la mort de Dieu, et veut mettre un terme aux discours

interminables à ce sujet, discours déjà à la mode en son temps hégelien. . . . Et il explique que cet événement n'a strictement aucune importance, qu'il n'intéresse vraiment que le dernier pape: Dieu mort ou pas mort, le père mort ou pas mort, ça revient au même, puisque la même répression et le même refoulement se poursuivent, ici au nom de Dieu ou d'un père vivant, là au nom de l'homme ou du père mort intériorisé" (L'Anti-Oedipe, 130).

42 As I explain later in this chapter, this phrase is pregnant with two other meanings that Lacan derives from a double pun. Notably, and perhaps fittingly, Lacan's seminar on the Name of the Father, scheduled for 1953, was cancelled: in effect, the father never arrives in name (i.e., of the seminar) but perseveres in the function of a signifier ("Je père-sévère," as Lacan writes). Hence, the Name of the Father remains one of the most enduring concepts in Lacan's oeuvre, appearing in his early, middle, and late work. But with an eye to our subsequent discussion, and especially with respect to Deleuze and Guattari's Anti-Oedipus, see Lacan's "On a Question Prior to Any Possible Treatment of Psychosis" in Écrits, trans. Bruce Fink (New York: W. W. Norton and Company, 2006), 445–88.

43 The translation here strangely omits a phrase in the original French. Deleuze writes: "L'essence d'une chose n'apparaît jamais au début, mais au milieu, dans le courant de son développement, quand ses forces sont affermies." With milieu, we know that the middle is no less an interval, an inexplicable place, such that its evocation as a current of development affirms a critical aspect of Deleuze's assertion: the strength of maturity lies in becoming (devenir). See Gilles Deleuze, L'Image-mouvement (Paris: Les Éditions des Minuits, 1983), 11. As Deleuze writes in Nietzsche and Philosophy (New York: Columbia University Press, 1983), "Interpretation reveals its complexity, when we realize that a new force can only appear and appropriate an object by first of all putting on the mask of the forces which are already in possession of the object" (5). If it is to survive, a new force is initially compelled to conceal its nature—and this bears as much on the force in question, which effectively interprets an object, as it does on the interpretation of that force, which effectively characterizes its differential relations to other forces. Only in the midday of philosophy do we discern the affirmative or negative will that has been disguised by so many masks: only then do we discover the "truth" of the mask itself.

44 Schrift, Nietzsche's French Legacy, 62.

45 Ibid.

46 The original reads: "Et cette pensée même, était-ce de la philosophie, n'était-ce pas plutôt une poésie violente, trop violente, des aphorismes trop capricieux, des fragments trop pathologiques?" (Deux régimes de fous, 187).

47 The original German reads: "so lasse ich Niemanden als dessen Kenner gelten, den nicht jedes seiner Worte irgendwann einmal tief verwundet und irgendwann einmal tief entzückt hat."

48 "Man versteht, an welche Aufgabe ich bereits mit diesem Buche zu rühren wagte? . . . Wie sehr bedauere ich es jetzt, dass ich damals noch nicht den Muth (oder die

Unbescheidenheit?) hatte, um mir in jedem Betrachte für so eigne Anschauung und Wagnisse auch eine eigne Sprache zu erlauben" (*"Versuch einer Selbstkritik"* §6).

49 "The Philosopher: Reflections on the Struggle between Art and Knowledge," *Philosophy and Truth: Selections from Nietzsche's Notebooks of the Early 1870's,* trans. and ed. Daniel Breazeale (Atlantic Highlands, N.J.: Humanities Press, 1979), 53.

50 Friedrich Nietzsche, *Philosophy in the Tragic Age of the Greeks,* trans. Marianne Cowan (Washington: Gateway Editions, 1996). The original reads: "Er ist nicht klug, wenn man klug den nennt, der in seinen eignen Angelegenheiten das Gute herausfindet; Aristoteles sagt mit Recht: 'Das, was Thales und Anaragoras wissen, wird man ungewöhnlich, erstaunlich, schwierig, göttlich nennen, aber unnütz, weil es ihnen nicht um die menschlichen Güter zu thun war'" (*Die Philosophie im Tragischen Zeitalter der Griechen,* §3).

51 In French: "Mais nous savons bien qu'une chose est toujours mal jugée d'après ses débuts" (*L'Anti-Oedipe,* 109).

52 Gilles Deleuze, *Kant's Critical Philosophy,* trans. Hugh Tomlinson and Barbara Habberjam (Minneapolis: University of Minnesota Press, 2003).

53 Immanuel Kant, *Critique of the Power of Judgment,* ed. Paul Guyer, trans. Paul Guyer and Eric Matthews (Cambridge: Cambridge University Press, 2000), §9/218.

54 See *Ecce Homo,* "Why Do I Write Such Good Books," §4.

55 Deleuze's original French is incomparably more expressive in terms of the relation between frame and the Outside: "Nietzsche au contraire fonde la pensée, l'écriture, sur une relation immédiate avec le dehors. Qu'est-ce que c'est, un très beau tableau ou un très beau dessin? Il y a un cadre. Un aphorisme aussi est encadré. Mais cela devient beau à partir du moment où l'on sait et où l'on sent que le mouvement, que la ligne qui est encadrée vient d'ailleurs, qu'elle ne commence pas dans la limite du cadre" (Deleuze, *L'île déserte et autres textes,* 356).

56 *Anti-Oedipus* marks what we have already called a pronounced change in style that Deleuze attributes to his collaboration. "Meeting Félix" was, he says, a decisive event in his philosophical life, the beginning of a beautiful friendship, but *Anti-Oedipus* also marks the resumption (as if it had ever been left off!) of a longstanding friendship with Nietzsche. François Dosse suggest as much in *Deleuze and Guattari: Intersecting Lives,* 13.

57 *L'Anti-Oedipe,* 141.

58 In Kafka's "In the Penal Colony," for instance, we find the most explicit rendering of this system in the depiction of an incredible inscription machine, an apparatus of punishment that kills the condemned by tatooing their crimes, pinprick by pinprick, along the parchment of the skin.

59 Note that in the German *Verantwortlichkeit* is italicized. As Nietzsche has already explained in the great second essay of *On the Genealogy of Morals:* "Man himself must first of all have become calculable, regular, necessary, even in his own image of himself, if he is to be able to stand securely for his own future, which is what one who promises

does [wie muss dazu der Mensch selbst vorerst berechenbar, regelmässig, nothwendig geworden sein, auch sich selbst für seine eigne Vorstellung, um endlich dergestalt, wie es ein Versprechender thut, für sich als Zukunft gut sagen zu können!]" (GM, II §1).

60 "Mais Nietzsche, avec son écriture d'intensités, nous dit: n'échangez pas l'intensité contre des representations" (Deleuze, *L'île déserte et autres textes*, 358).

61 See "Nietzsche, Freud, Marx" in *The Aesthetics, Method, and Epistemology, 2*: 269–78.

62 Descombes, *Modern French Philosophy*, 3.

63 Karl Marx and Friedrich Engels, *The German Ideology*, ed. Christopher Joan Arthur (New York: International Publishers, 1970), 53.

64 Far from reacting against this vast deterritorialization, schizoanalysis rides the crest of its wave: "the *capitalist machine,* insofar as it was built on the ruins of the despotic State more or less far removed in time, finds itself in a totally new situation: it is faced with the task of decoding and deterritorializing the flows" (DI, 253).

65 While the surface movements of this body are characterized by "experiences, intensities, becomings, transitions" (AO, 19), they arise from and fall back on [*se rebattent sur*] the degree zero of intensity that we have called the body without organs, the black hole of antiproduction at the heart of capitalism.

66 "One sometimes has the impression that the flows of capital would willingly dispatch themselves to the moon, if the capitalist state were not there to bring them back to the earth" (AO, 258).

67 Descombes, *Modern French Philosophy*, 173.

68 For a rigorous rendering of the three syntheses, see Joe Hughes, *Deleuze and the Genesis of Representation* (London: Continuum, 2008).

69 As Lukács writes, "it was not until Nietzsche that it [the philosophy of historical solipsism] is generalized in such cynical fashion. What it says in effect is that each unit, be it individual, race, or nation, can experience no more than itself. History exists only as a mirror to this ego, only as something to suit the special needs of the latter. History is a chaos, in itself is of no concern to us, but to which everyone may attribute a 'meaning' which suits him, according to his needs." See *The Historical Novel*, trans. Hannah and Stanley Mitchell (London: Merlin Press, 1982), 180.

70 Jameson, *The Political Unconscious*, 21.

71 Ibid.

72 Ibid.

73 Ibid., 21–22.

74 Ibid., 22.

75 In this framework, Jameson writes, "What is denounced is therefore a system of allegorical interpretation in which the data of one narrative line are radically impoverished by their rewriting according to the paradigm of another narrative, which is taken as the former's master code or Ur-narrative and proposed as the ultimate hidden or unconscious *meaning* of the first one" (ibid.).

76 Ibid., 53.

77 See Jameson, "Marxism and Dualism in Deleuze," *South Atlantic Quarterly* 96:3 (1997): 393–416.

78 Jameson, *The Political Unconscious*, 40.

79 Eugene Holland, *Deleuze and Guattari's* Anti-Oedipus: *Introduction to Schizoanalysis* (New York: Routledge, 1999), 90.

80 See Lacan's "On a Question Prior to Any Possible Treatment of Psychosis" in *Écrits*. Of course, this "dead" father haunts the entirety of Lacan's work, both as a return to Freud and an elaboration of the signifying structures, mathemes, and topologies of his own invention. As to the former, see Lacan's exemplary treatment of the dream of the dead father in *The Four Fundamental Concepts of Psychoanalysis: Seminar XI*, trans., Alan Sheridan, ed. Jacques-Alain Miller (New York: W. W. Norton and Company, 1998), 57–59; as to the latter, see *On Feminine Sexuality, the Limits of Love and Knowledge: Seminar XX, Encore*, trans. Bruce Fink, ed. Jacques-Alain Miller (New York: W. W. Norton and Company), 75–79.

81 As to Freud's elaboration of psychosis (and, thence, paranoia), see his analysis of Schreber in "Psychoanalytic Notes On an Autobiographical Account of A Case of Paranoia (Dementia Paranoides)" in *The Standard Edition of the Complete Psychological Works of Sigmund Freud*, vol. 12, trans. James Strachey (London: Hogarth Press, 1999), 3–82.

82 I owe François Zourabichvili for this formula. See *Le vocabulaire de Deleuze* (Paris: Ellipses, 2004), 40.

2. From Genealogy to Geophilosophy

1 Gilles Deleuze, *The Logic of Sense*, trans. Mark Lester and Charles Stivale (New York: Columbia University Press, 1990), 301.

2 See *The Essential Works of Michel Foucault*, vol. 3, 369–91.

3 Ibid., 372.

4 "Examining the history of reason," Foucault once wrote, the genealogist "learns that it was born in an altogether 'reasonable' fashion—from chance." If the genealogist "listens to history, he finds that there is 'something altogether different' behind things: not a timeless and essential secret but the secret that they have no essence, or that their essence was fabricated in a piecemeal fashion from alien forms" (ibid., 371).

5 As Deleuze writes, "there has never been a more conciliatory or respectful total critique" (NP, 89).

6 Even more broadly, we might say that Kant never reaches the point of situating reason as a value whose metaphysical distinction is always already moral. Like Truth, with which it is inextricably bound, reason is never understood with respect to the will and the question of the will.

7 "Transcendental principles are principles of conditioning and not of internal genesis. We require a genesis of reason itself, and also a genesis of the understanding and its

categories: what are the forces of reason and of the understanding? What is the will which hides itself and expresses itself in reason? What stands behind reason, in reason itself?" (NP, 91) .

8 See "Book IV: The Combat" in Carl von Clausewitz, *On War*, trans. J. J. Graham (Radford, Va.: Wilder Publishing, 2008). As Deleuze says, "Nietzsche notes that there has not yet been a 'great politics' " (NP, 91).

9 For an outline of the "Interpretation of Agathos," see F. E. Peters, *Greek Philosophical Terms: A Historical Lexicon* (New York: New York University Press, 1967), 4–6.

10 Friedrich Nietzsche, *Writings from the Late Notebooks*, trans. Kate Sturge (Cambridge: Cambridge University Press, 2003), Part 7 §60.

11 In our own time, for instance, we might take the gradual shifting of the value "liberal" to signal an overarching, even national, kind of political redistricting, such that we are often told that "the country has become more conservative in the last thirty years," etc. But in fact, if we were to trace the developments and deployments of "liberal" over this period, we would find a violent contestation whereby a particular, reactive force increasingly captures and determines what it meant to be liberal—overly tolerant, passive, effete, etc.

12 "The origin lies at a place of inevitable loss, the point where the truth of things is knotted to a truthful discourse, the site of a fleeting articulation that discourse has obscured and finally lost," Foucault writes of genealogy. "It is a new cruelty of history that now compels a reversal of this relationship and an abandonment of adolescent quests: behind the always recent, avaricious, and measured truth, it posits the ancient proliferation of errors" (Foucault, *Aesthetics, Method, and Epistemology*, 2:372).

13 Loraux, *Born of the Earth: Myth and Politics in Athens*, 4.

14 This phrase is borrowed from Peter Canning's work in progress, "The Clinic of Control."

15 "In the schizo, the two aspects of process are conjoined: the metaphysical process that puts us into contact with the 'demoniacal' element in nature or within the heart of the earth, and the historical process of social production that restores the autonomy of desiring-machines in relation to the deterritorialized social machine" (AO, 35).

16 The term is borrowed from Deleuze's essay "Michel Tournier, or the World without Others," which appears as an appendix to *The Logic of Sense*.

17 Friedrich Nietzsche, "On Truth and Lying in a Non-Moral Sense" in *The Nietzsche Reader*, ed. Keith Ansell-Pearson and Duncan Large (London: Blackwell, 2006).

18 Ibid., 114.

19 Ibid.

20 Ibid.

21 Manuel Delanda, *Intensive Science and Virtual Philosophy* (New York: Continuum, 2005), 20. The literature on Deleuze's theory of geophilosophy has been rapidly growing over the past several years, especially insofar as Delanda and others have begun the work of situating Deleuze's philosophy in the history of sciences. See section 1, "Lavas and Magmas," in Delanda's earlier book, *A Thousand Years of Nonlinear History*

(Cambridge: Zone, 2000). Also see Mark Bonta and John Protevi, *Deleuze and Geophilosophy: A Guide and Glossary* (Edinburgh: Edinburgh University Press, 2004).

22 See Karl Marx, *Capital: A Critique of Political Economy*, trans. David Fernbach (New York: Penguin, 1991), 170 (translation modified).

23 Deleuze, *Logic of Sense*, 301–21.

24 As Deleuze and Guattari add, "While the ground can be the productive element and the result of appropriation, the Earth is the great unengendered stasis, the element superior to production that conditions the common appropriation and utilization of the ground" (ATP, 140–41).

25 "Affirmation is the highest form of the will. But what is affirmed?" Deleuze writes. "The earth, life . . . But what form do the earth and life assume when they are objects of affirmation? A form unbeknownst to us who inhabit the desolate surface of the earth and who live in states close to zero" (PI, 83–84).

26 George Williamson, *The Longing for Myth in Germany: Religion and Aesthetic Culture from Romanticism to Nietzsche* (Chicago: University of Chicago Press, 2004), 7.

27 As Nietzsche writes in *The Birth of Tragedy*, "We have a feeling that the birth of a tragic age simply means a return to itself of the German spirit, a blessed self-discovery after powerful intrusive influences had for a long time compelled it, living as it did in helpless and unchaste barbarism, to servitude under their form. Now at last, on returning to the primitive source of its being, it may venture to stride along boldly and freely before the eyes of all nations without being attached to the lead string of a Romanic civilization; if only it can learn constantly from one people—the Greeks, from whom to be able to learn at all is itself a great honor and a rare distinction" (BOT, §19).

28 Williamson, *The Longing for Myth in Germany*, 249.

29 As quoted in ibid., 250.

30 *Mille plateaux*, 420.

31 The better translation for *fond* in this instance might be "background."

32 See Émile Bréhier's *The Hellenic Age*, trans. Joseph Thomas (Chicago: University of Chicago Press, 1965).

33 Fernand Braudel, *The Mediterranean in the Ancient World*, trans. Siân Reynolds (London: Penguin, 2007).

34 Ibid., 12.

35 Ibid., 135. In Braudel's words: "The natural fragmentation of the relief map of Greece, and the small size but the large number of plains (20 percent of the overall surface) seemed to preordain this political crystallization. . . . Greece was a pattern of islands whether real islands in the sea or 'islands on dry land.' Each of the Greek city-states occupied a limited terrain, with a few cultivated fields, two or three areas of grazing land for horses, enough vines and olive-groves to get by, some bare mountain slopes inhabited by herds of goats or sheep, an indented coastline with a harbor, and a city which would before long build ramparts—a little world cut off by mountains and sea.

Yes, Greece was indeed a pattern of islands" (see Fernand Braudel, *Memory and the Mediterranean* (New York: Vintage, 2002), 229).

36 Thucydides, *The History of the Peloponnesian War*, trans. Robert Crawley (Charleston, S.C.: Forgotten Books, 2008). As Thucydides writes, "The richest soils were always most subject to this change of masters; such as the district now called Thessaly, Boeotia, most of the Peloponnese, Arcadia excepted, and the most fertile parts of the rest of Hellas. The goodness of the land favoured the aggrandizement of particular individuals, and thus created faction which proved a fertile source of ruin. It also invited invasion. Accordingly Attica, from the poverty of its soil enjoying from a very remote period freedom from faction, never changed its inhabitants. And here is no inconsiderable exemplification of my assertion that the migrations were the cause of there being no correspondent growth in other parts. The most powerful victims of war or faction from the rest of Hellas took refuge with the Athenians as a safe retreat; and at an early period, becoming naturalized, swelled the already large population of the city to such a height that Attica became at last too small to hold them, and they had to send out colonies to Ionia" (I §2).

37 Braudel, *Memory and the Mediterranean,* 217. "Cities with less in the way of advantages tended to look outwards," Braudel writes elsewhere. "Sooner or later they had to sail the sea, to 'marry it' as Venice did in a later age, to enter into conflict with those who stood in their way, and to sail to the ends of the earth" (ibid., 230–31). And: "Almost from the first wave of emigration then, one must suppose the existence of merchants, commercial calculations, and even colonization motivated by commercial imperatives" (ibid., 218).

38 Ibid., 233.

39 Thus Braudel maintains: "Wherever it took place, the appearance of such autonomous urban centers is only conceivable in the absence of large-scale territorial states, which always have gargantuan appetites for conquest. The Italian cities in their prime in the fourteenth century A.D. would have been unimaginable without the great recessions of the Middle Ages, which dealt a mortal blow to those two political giants, the Germanic Holy Roman Empire and the Papacy as operated by Innocent III. It is my belief that the ancient Greek cities would not have seen the light of day if it had not been for the recession of the twelfth century B.C. They grew up during the dark ages following the Dorian invasion, since what had collapsed with the end of the Mycenaean civilization was the palace-centered state, with its mighty rulers and their all-powerful scribes, a greedy state as so many others were in the second millennium B.C." (*Memory and the Mediterranean*, 228–29).

40 Ibid., 216.

41 Jean-Pierre Vernant, *The Origins of Greek Thought* (Ithaca, N.Y.: Cornell University Press, 1984), 132, 148.

42 See "The Republic," Book VI, in *The Collected Dialogues of Plato*, ed. Hamilton.

43 Louis Gernet, *The Anthropology of Ancient Greece*, trans. John Hamilton and Blaise Nagy (Baltimore: Johns Hopkins University Press, 1981), 357.

44 Ibid., 358.

45 Thucydides, *History of the Peloponnesian War*, I §2.

46 The god of the sea, Poseidon himself inspired cults that paid tribute to the fertility of the soil. For the Greeks, as Detienne contends, "il y a en même temps, côte à côte, un Poséidon à col marin et un Poséidon bien terrien." See Marcel Detienne, *Comment être autochtone: Du pur Athénien au Français raciné* (Paris: Éditions Seuil, 2003), 46.

47 Ibid., 54. Translation mine. In the original, the quote reads: "Éloge du pur autochtone, de l'Athénien de souche que n'entend plus rien savoir ces ragots d'historien sur je ne sais quelle terre aride, dépotoir pour exiles, pour fugitifs, pour gens sans terre" (54).

48 See Plato's *Menexenus*, in *The Collected Dialogues of Plato*, ed. Hamilton.

49 As quoted in Loraux, *Born of the Earth*, 17.

50 Thucydides, *The History of the Peloponnesian War*, 2.36.1.

51 As quoted in Loraux , *Born of the Earth*, 22.

52 Detienne, *Comment être autochtone*, 22.

53 Herodotus, *Histories*, trans. George Rawlinson (London: Wordsworth Books, 1996), §161.

54 This quote comes from Hyperides' *Funeral Oration*, as quoted in Loraux, *Born of the Earth*, 19).

55 Ibid., 10–11.

56 Marcel Detienne, *Masters of Truth in Ancient Greece*, trans. Janet Lloyd (New York: Zone Books, 1996), 91.

57 Ibid., 96.

58 Ibid., 101.

59 Vernant, *The Origins of Greek Thought*, 60–61.

60 No development was more integral to the formation of Athens and its *isonomia* than the Hoplite Reform. In the course of the inevitable conflicts that arose from competing sovereignties, and especially in relation to Persia, Greek city-states developed a new class of warriors and a new means of warfare. Indeed, the Hoplite Reform is typically associated with the invention of a new form of military organization in which warriors were arrayed in a phalanx—a geometrical distribution of positions within which any individual could be replaced by any other. But this organization of collective combat was conditioned by an equally critical socioeconomic condition: where warriors previously came from particular families who enjoyed the military privilege of the *hippeis*, the reform effectively declared that "those who could bear the cost of the Hoplite equipment—that is, the small landowners who made up the demos, such as the *zeugitai* of Athens—were assigned the same level as those who owned horses" (Vernant, *The Origins of Greek Thought*, 62). In short, the reform helped to democratize the people, to make them a *demos*, by eradicating (within obvious limits) the prerogatives of the *genoi*. Thereafter, increasingly, citizens were organized according to a model of incipient *isonomia*. "The phalanx made of the hoplite, as the city made of the citizen, an interchangeable unit," Vernant writes (ibid.).

61 As Vernant writes, "The ideal of *isonomia* implies that the city resolves its problems, thanks to the normal functioning of its institutions, through respect for its *nomos.*" See his *Myth and Thought among the Greeks,* trans. Janet Lloyd and Jeff Fort (London: Routledge, 1983), 236. For a comprehensive analysis of this subject, see Pierre Lévêque and Pierre Vidal-Naquet, *Cleisthenes the Athenian: An Essay on the Representation of Space and Time in Greek Political Thought from the End of the Sixth Century to the Death of Plato,* trans. David Ames Cutis (Atlantic Highlands, N.J.: Humanities Press, 1996).

62 Loraux , *Born of the Earth,* 20.

63 Vernant, *The Origins of Greek Thought,* 61.

64 Vernant, *Myth and Thought Among the Greeks,* 214.

65 Vernant, *Origins of Greek Thought,* 61.

66 Ibid., 49.

67 Marcel Detienne, *The Greeks and Us,* trans. Janet Lloyd (Malden, Mass.: Polity Press, 2007), 61.

68 Vernant, *Origins of Greek Thought,* 50.

69 See Nietzsche, *Philosophy in the Tragic Age of the Greeks,* 29–34.

70 J. K. Davies, *Democracy and Classical Greece* (Cambridge: Harvard University Press, 1993), 92.

71 Detienne, *Comment être autochtone,* 56.

72 Detienne, *Masters of Truth,* 112.

73 Ibid.

3. Deleuze among the Sophists

1 The text of this essay can be found as an appendix in Leonard Lawlor's *Thinking through French Philosophy: The Being of the Question* (Bloomington: Indiana University Press, 2003). Lawlor's book remains one of the more important points of reference for understanding the tendencies of modern French philosophy, especially the relation of Deleuze and Derrida. Indeed, Deleuze's reading of Platonism brings him very close to what we might typically call deconstruction, though I think that it also brings Deleuze to the point that he is eventually compelled to "go beyond" deconstruction and, in a sense, to renounce the simulacrum. In this regard, see Eric Alliez's essay "Ontology and Logography: The Pharmacy, Plato and the Simulacrum" in *Between Deleuze and Derrida.*

2 Historically, this sentiment may explain why Deleuze's concept of the simulacrum has been eclipsed by subsequent iterations. Next to Jean Baudrillard's simulacrum, which imagines representation to have lapsed into the infinite degradation of copies that characterize our contemporary, infinitely mediated world—next to this, Deleuze's concept, which situates the simulacrum in the formation of the Greek polis and the emergence

of Platonism, seems perversely (and almost literally) archaic. But if Deleuze remains "old school" when it comes to the simulacrum, this is only in order to undertake a more revolutionary deterritorialization of representation than "the postmodern condition" could have imagined. Baudillard's simulacrum underscores the proliferation of copies and the disappearance of anything like an original, but the more distanced the copy, the more it remains beholden *ideally* to the very notion of the model on which Platonism itself is stereotypically predicated.

3 Vidal-Naquet's comments appear in the introduction to Detienne, *Masters of Truth in Archaic Greece*, 9.

4 As Nicole Loraux explains, "In the Greek world, in which oligarchy—the power of the few—dominates, in which mentalities are permanently imbued with aristocratic values, the Athenian Regime is the exception." See Loraux, *Born of the Earth*, 23.

5 For Deleuze, the diagram specifies the immanent and coextensive organization of power and knowledge. See the section "From the Archive to the Diagram" in his book *Foucault* for an elaboration of this concept.

6 "With the creation of philosophy," Deleuze writes, "the Greeks violently force the friend into a relationship that is no longer a relationship with an other but one with an Entity, an Objectality [*Objectité*], an Essence" (WIP, 3).

7 See Jean-Pierre Vernant's "The Birth of Images" in *Mortals and Immortals: Collected Essays*, ed. Froma Zeitlin (Princeton, N.J.: Princeton University Press, 1991).

8 As Nicole Loraux writes in *Born of the Earth*: "Not only was no crusade led by the Athenians in the name of autochthony, but xenophobia was essentially a Spartan practice, little prized in the democracy of Athens, where by all accounts strangers were better treated than in any other city" (20). With an eye to the sophists whom we will discuss, it should be pointed out that nearly all of the major figures—Protagoras, Gorgias, Prodicus, Hippias, Thrasymachus—were foreigners who came to Athens. As Jacqueline de Romilly has written, "Were it not for Athens, we should probably not even know the name 'Sophist'" See Jaqueline de Romilly, *The Great Sophists in Periclean Athens*, trans. Janet Lloyd (Oxford: Clarendon Press, 1992), 18.

9 See *Sophist* in *The Collected Dialogues of Plato*, ed. Hamilton, 234b.

10 de Romilly, *The Great Sophists in Periclean Athens*, 4.

11 After considerable debate, Socrates comes to the conclusion that "the activity as a whole [. . .] is not an art, but the occupation of a shrewd and enterprising spirit, and one naturally skilled in its dealings with men, and in sum and substance I call it flattery." See *Gorgias* in *Collected Dialogues of Plato*, ed. Hamilton, 245–46. Admittedly, Platonism gave voice to a kind of hostility characteristic of a fairly widespread reaction to the sophists. At various junctures, Aristophanes, Euripides, Isocrates, Aristotle, and Xenophon (among others) condemned these masters of rhetoric, but the task of battling the sophists, precisely because they resembled philosophers, belonged to Platonism.

12 Most notably, Diogenes Laertius suggests that the sophists were the originators of dialectic.

13 Socrates encountered the most famous of sophists, Protagoras, at a fairly young age, and the experience seems to have both inspired and fired the budding dialectician. No doubt Socrates feels something of the enthusiasm (*enthusiasmos*) that the sophists were said to conjure in their audience, but this excitement and esteem is thereafter undercut with irony and even disdain.

14 According to Plato, sophists confuse truth for phenomenal consequences, the result of which is that "they elevated half the truth to the whole": in short, they never reach the sphere of Ideas. See G. B. Kerferd, *The Sophistic Movement* (Cambridge: Cambridge University Press, 1981), 67.

15 Gernet, *The Anthropology of Ancient Greece*, 358.

16 "The more he rises the more he is purified," Deleuze writes of the Platonist. "Height is the properly Platonic Orient. The philosopher's work is always determined as an ascent and conversion, that is, as the movement of turning toward the high principle (*principle d'en haut)"* (LS, 127).

17 Detienne, *Masters of Truth in Archaic Greece,*123. For a philosophical consideration of Platonic transcendence, see John Sallis's magisterial *Being and Logos: The Way of Platonic Dialogues* (Atlantic Highlands, N.J.: Humanities Press International, 1986).

18 See the *Phaedrus* in *The Collected Dialogues of Plato,* ed. Hamilton, 235c–d.

19 "We can see here what happens between the sophist and the dialectician," Deleuze concludes, "on which side the good faith and the rigorous reasoning is." As he adds, Socrates "is too full of dialectical *ressentiment* and the spirit of revenge" (NP, 59).

20 Indeed, what makes such commentaries so ingenious is that, as Deleuze explains, he never seeks to debate his enemies' basic concepts or refuse the terms of their discourse: the task of commentary lies in having learned to speak a philosopher's idiom, but to speak it in a way that detours its regimented and regular framework into unanticipated eventualities.

21 Foucault, "Theatricum Philosophicum" in *The Essential Works of Michel Foucault,* vol. 2, 344. Foucault's response to this cynicism, a response in which he famously anoints Deleuze *the* philosopher of the twentieth century, bears witness to the latter's distinct methodology.

22 Ibid., 345. As Foucault elsewhere explains, between the sixth and fifth centuries B.C.E. a tremendous discursive shift occurred, for it came to pass that "the highest truth no longer resided in what discourse *was,* nor in what it *did:* it lay in what was *said.* The day dawned when truth moved over from ritualized act—potent and just—of enunciation to settle on what was enunciated itself: its meaning, its form, its object and its relation to what it referred to." See Foucault's "Discourse on Language," which is included in *The Archaeology of Knowledge,* 218. There, Foucault concludes, "and so the sophists were routed."

23 Kerferd, *The Sophistic Movement,* 1.

24 This may explain why Deleuze does not spend a great deal of time or space analyzing Plato's singular dialogue: the overturning of Platonism is not only anticipated but, to a certain degree, accomplished by Plato himself.

25 Gilles Deleuze, *Logique du sens* (Paris: 1969, Les Éditions de Minuit), 176.

26 Deleuze's notion of counterutilization and, more generally, of a counterthinking, shares numerous affinities with Foucault. See the second section of his book on *Foucault,* "Topology: 'Thinking Otherwise.' "

27 Foucault, *The Essential Works of Michel Foucault*, vol. 2, 344.

28 See G. S. Kirk, J. E. Raven, and M. Schofield, eds., *The Presocratic Philosophers* (Camridge: Cambridge University Press, 1984), 181–212.

29 "Homer's Contest," 40.

30 Ibid., 40.

31 See the *Timaeus* in *The Collected Dialogues of Plato,* ed. Hamilton, 37d.

32 The full quote reads: "When the father and creator saw the creature which he had made moving and living, the created image of the eternal gods, he rejoiced, and in his joy determined to make the copy still more like the original; and as this was eternal, he sought to make the universe eternal, so far as might be. Now the nature of the ideal being was everlasting, but to bestow this attribute in its fullness on a creature was impossible. Wherefore he resolved to have a moving image of eternity, and when he set in order the heaven, he made this image eternal but moving according to number, while eternity itself rests in unity; and this image we call time" (Tim., 37ce).

33 This is a distinction on which Deleuze occasionally calls in order to differentiate between laws based on overarching principles and those derived from empirical circumstances. In some sense, however, the import of this distinction might be cashed out in comparisons between Kant and Leibniz.

34 Aristotle, *Poetics*, trans. Richard Janko (Indianapolis: Hackett Publishing, 1987), 25.9.

35 Martin Heidegger, *Plato's Sophist,* trans. Richard Rojcewicz and André Schuwer (Bloomington: Indiana University Press, 1997), 8.

36 Stanley Rosen, *The Sophist: The Drama of Original and Image* (New Haven: Yale University Press, 1983), 7.

37 See Poe's "Diddling" in *The Complete Tales and Poems of Edgar Allan Poe* (Edison, N.J.: Castle Books, 2002), 315. For the original recounting of the episode, see Diogenes Laertius, *The Lives and Opinions of Eminent Philosophers,* trans. C. D. Yonge (Whitefish, Mont.: Kessinger Publishing, 2006), 231 (§40): "Plato defined man thus: 'Man is a two-footed, featherless animal,' and was much praised for this definition; so Diogenes plucked a cock and brought it to his school, and said, 'This is Plato's man.' On which account this addition was made to the definition, 'With broad, flat nails.' "

38 For a comprehensive explanation of these questions in Aristotle vis-à-vis Deleuze, see Nathan Widder, "Singularly Aristotle" in *Theory & Event* 1, no. 3 (1997).

39 In short, "the dialectical art never considers whether the benefit to be derived from the purge is greater or less than that to be derived from the sponge, and has not more interest in the one than the other; her endeavor is to know what is and what is not kindred in all arts, with a view to the acquisition of intelligence; and having this in view, she honors them all alike" (Soph., 227ab).

40 See *Statesman* in *The Collected Dialogues of Plato*, ed. Hamilton, 266c.

41 Aristotle, *Posterior Analytics*, trans. G. R. G. Mure Kessinger (Whitefish, Mont.: Hackett Publishing, 2004), 55.

42 As Aristotle writes, "For why should not the whole of this formula be true of man, and yet not exhibit his essential nature or definable form? Let 'animal' be the term signified by A, 'mortal' by B, and 'immortal' by C, and let 'man,' whose definition is to be got, be signified by D.

    A = animal
    B = mortal
    C = immortal
    D = man

The man who divides assumes that every animal is either mortal or immortal: i.e., whatever is A is all either B or C. Again, always dividing, he lays it down that man is an animal, so he assumes A of D as belonging to it. Now the true conclusion is that every D is either B or C, consequently man must be either mortal or immortal, but it is not necessary that man should be a mortal animal—this is begged: and this is what ought to have been proved syllogistically. And again, taking A as mortal animal, B as footed, C as footless, and D as man, he assumes in the same way that A inheres either in B or in C (for every mortal animal is either footed or footless), and he assumes A of D (for he assumed man, as we saw, to be a mortal animal); consequently it is necessary that man should be either a footed or a footless animal." See Aristotle, *Posterior Analytics*, 49 (A31).

43 Neither abstraction nor synthesis characterize the Idea in Platonism, and while Aristotle saw this as a weakness or immaturity in dire need of correction, Deleuze hails this as the opening for other philosophical possibilities and other philosophical worlds.

44 Deleuze, *Logique du sens*, 296.

45 See Daniel W. Smith, "The Concept of the Simulacrum: Deleuze and the Overturning of Platonism" in *Continental Philosophy Review* 38, no. 1–2 (April 2005): 118 (note 19).

46 Deleuze, *Logique du sens*, 294.

47 Alain Badiou, *Deleuze: The Clamor of Being*, trans. Louise Burchill (Minneapolis: University of Minnesota Press, 2000), 31.

48 For a more sustained treatment of the Porphyrian tree in the context of Deleuze's work, see Daniel W. Smith's essay "The Doctrine of Univocity: Deleuze's Ontology of Immanence" in *Deleuze and Religion*, ed. Mary Bryden (London: Routledge, 2000), 175–76.

49 Seth Benardete, *Plato's Sophist: The Drama of Original and Image* (Chicago: University of Chicago Press, 1986), 170.

50 Jorge-Luis Borges, "Death and the Compass" in *Collected Fictions*, 156.

51 Pierre Vidal-Naquet, *The Black Hunter: Forms of Thought and Forms of Society in the Greek World*, trans. Andrew Szegedy-Maszak (Baltimore: Johns Hopkins University Press, 1986), 253.

52 Notably, Deleuze is careful to caution us not to regard the myth as "an imaginary equivalent of mediation" (DR, 61). While myth and dialectic appear distinct, "this

distinction no longer matters once dialectic discovers its true method of division. Division demands such a foundation as the ground capable of making a difference. Conversely, the foundation demands division as the state of difference in that which must be grounded. Division is the true unity of dialectic and mythology, of the myth as foundation and of the logos as *logos tomeus*" (DR, 62).

53 Homer, *The Odyssey of Homer*, trans. Richmond Lattimore (New York: Harper & Row, 1975), 292 (original pagination, Book 19, 386–94). At this point, Odysseus has already been "scented out" by his dog Argos. But the scar marks a moment of recognition (*anagnorisis*). Notably, in the *Logic of Sense,* Deleuze reflects on the way the scar or wound preexists even the one who suffers it. We will return to this moment in chapter 4. Meanwhile see "The Twenty-First Series of the Event" (LS, 148–53).

54 Erich Auerbach, *Mimesis: The Representation of Reality in Western Literature* (Princeton: Princeton University Press, 2003), 4. Of this episode, Auerbach writes that the "first thought of the modern reader—that this is a device to increase suspense—is, if not wholly wrong, at least not the essential explanation of this Homeric procedure. . . . Here is the scar, which comes up in the course of the narrative; and Homer's feeling simply will not permit him to see it appear out of the darkness of an unilluminated past; it must be set up in full light." This setup, as Auerbach goes on to argue, cannot possibly be grasped as the effect of recollection on the part of any character: "To be sure, in the case of such long episodes as the one we are considering, a purely syntactical connection with the principal theme would hardly have been possible; but a connection with it through perspective would have been all the easier had the content been arranged with that end in view; if, that is, the entire story of the scar had been presented as a recollection which awakens in Odysseus's mind at this particular moment. It would have been perfectly easy to do. . . . But any such subjectivistic-perspectivistic procedure, creating a foreground and a background, resulting in the present lying open to the depths of the past, is entirely foreign to the Homeric style."

55 Nicole Loraux, *The Invention of Athens: The Funeral Oration in the Classical City,* trans. Alan Sheridan (New York: Zone Books, 2006), 211, 245.

56 "And the country which brought them up is not like other countries, a stepmother to her children, but their own true mother: she bore them and nourished them and received them, and in her bosom they now repose. It is meet and right, therefore, that we should begin by praising the land which is their mother, and that will be a way of praising their noble birth" (Men., 237bc).

57 Deleuze, *Logique du sens*, 152. Daniel Smith has written: "Platonic irony is, in this sense, a technique of ascent, a movement toward the principle on high, the ascetic ideal. The Sophist, by contrast, follows a descending movement of humor, a technique of descent that moves downward toward the vanity of the false copy, the self-contradicting sophist." See "The Concept of the Simulacrum: Deleuze and the Overturning of Platonism," 98.

58 As Deleuze explains, along the same lines, in *Difference and Repetition:* "The point is that in this text, by a paradoxical utilization of the [dialectical] method, a counter-utilization, Plato proposes to isolate the false claimant par excellence, the one who lays claim to everything without any right: the sophist" (61).

59 Rosen, *Plato's Sophist: The Drama of Original and Image,* 165.

60 Homer, *The Odyssey of Homer,* 17.485–86.

61 Benardete, *Plato's Sophist: The Drama of Original and Image,* xi.

62 Plato's earlier dialogue, *Parmenides,* records the young Socrates' admiring encounter with the older Eleatic and his famous student, Xeno, whose battles with the sophists— a battle between the logic of being and nonbeing—were renowned. See *Parmenides* in *The Collected Dialogues of Plato,* ed. Hamilton.

63 As the Stranger explains to Theaetetus, "How can they ever create a belief in the minds of young men that they are the wisest of men on all subjects? For clearly if they were not in the right in their controversies or did not appear to be so in the young men's eyes, and if the appearance did not enhance the belief that they are wise because they can dispute, then, to quote your own remark, it is hard to see why anyone should want to pay their fees and be taught the art of disputation" (Soph., 233b).

64 Vernant, *Mortals and Immortals,* 75.

65 Ibid., 165.

66 The distortion that befalls resemblance and that makes resemblance an external illusion is, of course, present in certain natural images to which Plato draws our attention— in dreams, for instance, but also in reflections glimpsed through water or shadow, where we seem to see something that does not in fact exist. "These *eidôla,* these images, are related to the true objects by resemblance and by comparative reality," Vernant explains, "just as are the creations of human art" (ibid.,166).

67 See "Reversing Platonism" in Lawlor, *Thinking through French Philosophy,* 171.

68 Howard Hibbard, *Michelangelo* (New York: Harper and Row, 1974), 56.

69 Loraux, *The Invention of Athens,* 333. The quote within the quote is taken from *Phaedrus* (264c); as Loraux notes, it refers explicitly to the theory of *logos* enunciated by Gorgias.

70 Ibid., 335.

71 Dienne, *Masters of Truth,* 122.

72 Ibid., 122.

73 Loraux, *The Invention of Athens,* 336.

74 See Plato, *Philebus* in *Collected Dialogues of Plato,* 24d.

75 The key here consists in the French verb *outrepasser,* which the English translation renders as "transcend"; but given Deleuze's general distaste for transcendence and the specific context here ("qui outrepasse les limites et les restitue à l'équivalence infinie d'un devenir illimité"), I have chosen to use "override." See Deleuze, *Logique du sens,* 11.

76 Indeed, *Sophist* resumes the very problem with which Parmenides (and his student, Xeno) were confronted.

77 Dienne, *Masters of Truth,* 116, 113–14.

78 Ibid., 179. In light of the question of persuasion, which one can trace beyond the sophists to Homer, see Michael Naas, *Turning: From Persuasion to Philosophy* (Atlantic Highlands, N.J.: Humanities Press, 1995).

79 Ibid., 179. The sophist's agonism, which he contrives everywhere he goes (a mobile milieu), finds its source and substance in the insubstantiality of the image, which is no less the instability of *doxa*.

80 As quoted in the "Translator's Preface" to *Deleuze: The Clamor of Being*, x.

81 Badiou, *Deleuze: The Clamor of Being*, 8.

82 Manfred Frank, *What Is Neostructuralism?* trans. Richard Gray (Minneapolis: University of Minnesota Press, 1989), 317.

83 Badiou, *Deleuze: The Clamor of Being*, 24.

84 Peter Hallward, *Badiou: A Subject to Truth* (Minneapolis: University of Minnesota Press, 2003), 76.

85 Deleuze aptly described this way of reading in a short piece, "Letter to a Harsh Critic": "You either see it as a box with something inside and start looking for what it signifies, and then if you're even more perverse or depraved you set off after signifiers. And you treat the next box like a box contained in the first or containing it. And you annotate and interpret and question, and write a book about the book, and so on" (Neg, 7). Hence, the surprise of Badiou's interpretation is not that he makes Deleuze a Platonist but that, in order to do so, he is forced to disregard, diminish, or denigrate Deleuze's own statements to the contrary.

86 Badiou, *Deleuze: The Clamor of Being*, 9.

87 Nathan Widder, "The Rights of the Simulacra: Deleuze and the Univocity of Being," *Continental Philosophy Review* 34 (2001): 439.

88 Ibid., 437–39. Like so much of the recent criticism Deleuze has incited, Badiou harps on the organization of dualisms, of "two names," that seems to dominate Deleuze's thought—virtual/actual, nomadic/sedentary, deterritorialized/reterritorialized. And as he says, "the nominal pair proceeds from one of these names." See *Deleuze: The Clamor of Being*, 43.

89 Badiou, *Deleuze: The Clamor of Being*, 25. Notably, Badiou seems to misconstrue the nature of differentiation, which Deleuze devises to describe what he otherwise calls "actualization." But the hierarchy on which Badiou insists in Deleuze's work, as if the virtual is the privileged term and the actual the diminished one, simply overrides the sense in which virtual and actual are immanent and, in a sense, inseparable.

90 Ibid., 20.

91 In some sense, the boldness with which Badiou would seduce us, moving from the first proposition to the second, from a classification (Deleuze is an ontologist/Platonist) to a qualification (Deleuze is a *bad* ontologist/Platonist), is also his most cunning stroke, since the qualification overwhelms and retroactively confirms its own tenuous presupposition. And yet this presupposition is precisely what we ought to address. Never mind, then, that Deleuze explicitly appeals to subtraction (the foreclosure of the

transcendent dimension) as the basis for writing and the writing of philosophy; never mind that Deleuze explicitly defines the plane of immanence as both consistent and inconsistent; and never mind that after the death of God and man, Deleuze will insist that philosophy pass through the death of substance: Badiou makes his arguments in spite of these points.

92 To a large degree, the very question of univocity drops out of Deleuze's writing after *The Logic of Sense*, replaced as it is by the plane of immanence.

93 Hallward, *Badiou: A Subject to Truth*, 176.

4. The Philosophy of Fiction and the Fiction of Philosophy

1 "Every philosophy must achieve its own manner of speaking about the arts and sciences," Deleuze writes (DR, xvi), adding that "a philosophical concept can never be confused with a scientific function or an artistic construction, but finds itself in affinity with these in this or that domain of science or style of art." Insofar as this chapter is devoted to Deleuze's relationship with literature, it has been catalyzed in no small part by a number of important works in the field. Among others, see Ronald Bogue, *Deleuze on Literature* (London: Routledge, 2003), Gregg Lambert, *The Non-Philosophy of Gilles Deleuze*, and Daniel W. Smith's introduction to the English translation of Deleuze, *Essays Critical and Clinical*.

2 This is the epigraph to E. M. Forster's novel *Howards End* (New York: Signet Classic, 1998).

3 Deleuze, *Différence et répétition*, 180.

4 Deleuze elaborates the organization of clichés in the last chapter of *The Movement-Image* and the first chapter of *The Time-Image*. As I have argued in the past, his rejoinder to this "conspiracy" turns on the appearance of signs that approximate the sublime—which is to say, signs that are "intolerable." Faced with that which is "too powerful, or too unjust, but sometimes also too beautiful," we resort to clichés (TI, 18). See *The Brain Is the Screen: Deleuze and the Philosophy of Cinema*, ed. Gregory Flaxman (Minneapolis: University of Minnesota Press, 2000), 37–38.

5 In French, the passage reads: "ce qui ne peut être que senti (le sentiendum ou l'être du sensible) émeut l'âme, la rend 'perplexe', c'est-à-dire la force à poser un problem." See Deleuze, *Différence et repetition*, 182.

6 See Hans Robert Jauss, *Towards an Aesthetics of Reception*, trans. Timothy Bahti (Minneapolis: University of Minnesota Press, 1982).

7 I have discussed this point in the "Introduction." To reiterate: even when philosophers introduce a rational method in order to get to the bottom of things, to validate reality or ensure truth, this method is always already underwritten by certain convictions. For instance, Descartes avoids defining man as a "rational animal," thereby escaping certain presuppositions (what is rationality? what is animality?), only to introduce subjec-

tive or implicit presuppositions of a different kind (what is the cogito? why does this form have a "natural" relationship with thinking?).

8 Fyodor Dostoyevsky, *Notes from Underground*, trans. Richard Pevear and Larissa Volokhonsky (New York: Vintage, 1993), 4.

9 Ibid., 13.

10 "The misfortune in speaking is not speaking, but speaking for others or representing something. The sensitive conscience (that is, the particular, difference, or *ta alla*) refuses" (DR, 52).

11 Dostoyevsky, *Notes from Underground*, 15.

12 Deleuze, *Qu'est-ce que la philosophie?* 104. On the one hand, the notion that self-consciously novelistic intellection could assume the role of philosophy, as some have argued, threatens to induce the studious and ponderous books that drain literature of what Deleuze describes as its unique vitality. On the other hand, the reciprocal notion that by dint of its own creativity philosophy could assume the role of literature, as some have claimed, threatens to induce the kind of "typographical, lexical, or even syntactical cleverness" (ATP, 6) that draws us away from what Deleuze describes as the 356 of fashioning concepts. "When someone asks what painting is, the answer is relatively simple. A painter is someone who creates on the order of lines and colors," Deleuze writes, whereas the philosopher "is someone who invents new concepts" (TRM, 176).

13 The original quotations refer to Gilles Deleuze and Félix Guattari, *Kafka: Pour une littérature mineure* (Paris: Les Éditions de Minuit, 1974), 50.

14 Nietzsche, *Unfashionable Observations*, 244.

15 Ibid., 244.

16 For instance: Kant's submission to political authority, Hegel's avowal of Prussia as the model of right (*Recht*), Heidegger's erstwhile commitment to National Socialism.

17 The original passage reads: "Le discours philosophique a toujours été dans un rapport essentiel avec la loi, l'institution, le contrat qui constituent le problème du Souverain, et qui traversent l'histoire sédentaire des formations despotiques aux démocraties" (Deleuze, *L'île déserte*, 361). Perhaps this is the sense in which to read Deleuze's avowal that "the 'signifier' is really the last philosophical metamorphosis of the despot" (DI, 259).

18 "The form of recognition has never sanctioned anything but the recognizable and the recognized; form will never inspire anything but conformities" (DR, 134).

19 "Nietzsche thinks the idea of critique is identical to philosophy," Deleuze writes, but he also thinks "that this is precisely the idea that Kant has missed, that he has compromised and spoilt, not only in its application but *in principle*" (NP, 88; emphasis mine).

20 Kant, *Critique of Pure Reason*, 46.

21 "The powers of cognitions that are set into play by this representation are hereby in free play, since no determinate concept restricts them to a particular state of cognition" (CPJ, §9/217).

22 Deleuze and Guattari, *Kafka: Pour une littérature mineure*, 14.

23 On this point, and for perhaps the most far-reaching elaboration of Deleuze vis-à-vis linguistics, see Jean-Jacques Lecercle, *Deleuze and Language* (New York: Palgrave Macmillan, 2002).

24 "We call order-words, not a particular category of explicit statements (for example, in the imperative), but the relation of every word or every statement to implicit presuppositions, in other words, to speech acts that are, and can only be, accomplished in the statement," Deleuze and Guattari write (ATP, 79).

25 See Michel Foucault's chapter "The Gentle Way in Punishment" in *Discipline and Punish* (New York: Vintage, 1997), 104–31.

26 See J. L. Austin, *How to Do Things with Words* (Oxford: Oxford University Press, 1976).

27 Ibid., 100 and 133ff. Likewise, Deleuze and Guattari write: "And the illocutionary is in turn explained by the collective assemblage of enunciation, by juridical acts or equivalents of juridical acts, which, far from depending on subjectification proceedings or assignations of subjects in language, in fact determine their distribution" (ATP, 78).

28 See *Word Virus: The William S. Burroughs Reader*, ed. James Grauerholz and Ira Silverberg (New York: Grove Press, 1998), 305ff.

29 My sense of psychosis here is largely indebted to the work of Willy Apollon, Lucie Cantin, and Danille Bergerson. The best English-language introduction to their work can be found in *After Lacan*, ed. Robert Hughes and Kathleen Ror Malone (Albany: SUNY Press, 2002).

30 "Chomsky's grammaticality, the categorical S symbol that dominates every sentence, is more fundamentally a marker of power than a syntactic marker: you will construct grammatically correct sentences, you will divide each statement into a noun phrase and a verb phrase" (ATP, 7). As Deleuze and Guattari respond, "Our criticism of these linguistic models is not that they are too abstract but, on the contrary, that they are not abstract enough, that they do not reach the *abstract machine*" (ibid.).

31 Benedict Anderson, *Imagined Communities: Reflections on the Origin and Spread of Nationalism* (London: Verso, 1991), 40.

32 Ibid., 46.

33 Foucault, "What Is an Author?" in *The Essential Works of Michel Foucault*, vol. 2, 216.

34 Franz Kafka, *Diaries of Franz Kafka*, trans. Joseph Kresh and Martin Greenberg (New York: Schocken, 1948–49), 197.

35 Ibid. The original German reads, "Goethe hält durch die Macht seiner Werke die Entwicklung der deutschen Sprache wahrscheinlich zurück. . . . Wenn sich auch die Prosa in der Zwischenzeit öfters von ihm entfernt, so ist sie doch schließlich, wie gerade gegenwärtig mit verstärkter Sehnsucht zu ihm zurückgekehrt und hat sich selbst alte bei Goethe vorfindliche sonst aber mit ihm nicht zusammenhängende Wendungen angeeignet, um sich an dem vervollständigten Anblick ihrer grenzenlosen Abhängigkeit zu erfreuen." See Franz Kafka, *Tagebücher* (Frankfurt: Fischer Taschenbuch Verlag, 1994), 318. Hence, a more accurate translation might read: "Even when the prose style has meanwhile often distanced itself from him, it [prose] always returned to him in the

end, as at present, with a strengthened yearning, and it has acquired in old Goethe certain documentable turning points [*Wendungen*]—though independent of Goethe himself—in order to rejoice in the panoramic vision of its limitless dependence."

36 See Ritchie Robertson, *Kafka: Judaism, Politics, Literature* (Oxford: Oxford University Press, 1987), 24.

37 Kafka, *Diaries of Franz Kafka*, 191.

38 Ibid., 191. The original reads: "Dieses Tagebuchführen einer Nation, das etwas ganz anderes ist als Geschichtsschreibung und als Folge dessen, eine schnellere und doch immer vielseitig überprüfte Entwicklung" (Kafka, *Tagebücher*, 313).

39 Quoted in Maurice Blanchot, *The Work of Fire*, trans. Charlotte Mandell (Stanford: Stanford University Press, 1995), 19.

40 Kafka, *Diaries of Franz Kafka*, 193. Kafka, *Tagebücher*, 315.

41 Ibid., 195.

42 Ibid., 195. Kafka, *Tagebücher*, 326.

43 James Joyce, *The Portable James Joyce*, ed. Harry Levin (New York: Penguin, 1976), 452.

44 Ibid., 453.

45 In the original, the passage reads: "C'est la littérature qui se trouve chargée positivement de ce rôle et de cette fonction d'énonciation collective, et même révolutionnaire: c'est la littérature qui produit une solidarité active, malgré le scepticisme" (Deleuze and Guattari, *Kafka: Pour une littérature mineure,* 31).

46 Ibid., 29.

47 Ibid., 30.

48 Ibid., 31.

49 The delicate enterprise should not be confused with the slip-ups, screw-ups, aporias, and misunderstandings that a minor language often unleashes within a major language—the peculiar bugs, hiccups, and glitches that provoke native speakers to wince, as if hearing a musician hit a wrong note. The instrumentalization, so to speak, of this tendency is the basis of parody, not minor literature, and we would do well to recall the hilarious episode in Pynchon, *Gravity's Rainbow,* in which the Soviets plan to regularize the diverse Arabic vernaculars that were inherited after the revolution. The historical essentials of the subplot are fairly accurate: having realized that the Cyrillic alphabet could not be imposed on the various Arabic populations and equally various dialects in one swift blow, the Soviet authorities formed the NTA (New Turkic Alphabet) in order to codify existing tribal languages into national languages under the rubric of a Latin alphabet, and thence to establish Russian as the "second native language." Into this great transliteration program Pynchon introduces a kind of battle between ne'er-do-wells assigned to various committees, each responsible for one letter, engaged in a ludicrous battle to assert the supremacy of their own letter and to bring the others down. When a representative of the "G" Committee resolves to steal letters from other committees and change them into his own letter by "using loan words as an entering wedge," he triggers a chain of reactions that culminates with "fistfights in the hallway

with unreconstructed Cyrillicists, and whispers of a campaign to boycott, throughout the Islamic world, any Latin alphabet." While the "official" regulation of languages, such as the Soviets embarked on or the French government pretends to conduct today, is apt to induce the most arbitrary of manipulations, we have to admit that the possibility of frenetically stealing words and letters offers little promise for the creation of a minor literature. See Pynchon, *Gravity's Rainbow,* 359.

50 Deleuze and Guattari, *Kafka: Pour une littérature mineure,* 29.

51 Ibid., 33.

52 Bogue, *Deleuze on Literature,* 95.

53 Note that I do not mean to suggest here a one-to-one relationship between its dominant province and its German-inspired distortion: the mélange of languages to which Kafka (above all) bears witness is far more complicated than that.

54 Klaus Wagenbach, *Franz Kafka: Pictures of a Life* (New York: Pantheon, 1984), 87.

55 Bogue, *Deleuze on Literature,* 96.

56 See Deleuze's chapter, "Strata or Historical Formations: The Visible and the Articulable (Knowledge)," in *Foucault.*

57 Franz Kafka, *Franz Kafka: The Complete Stories,* ed. Nahum N. Glatzer (New York: Schocken Books, 1995), 268.

58 Ibid., 274.

59 As Deleuze says, in an entirely different way, Proust achieves his own nonstyle by straining language to the point that it "reaches the limit" (PS, 113). He adds: "Can we not say that Proust, too, has no style? Is it possible to say that Proust's sentence, inimitable or too readily imitable, in any case immediately recognizable, endowed with a syntax and a vocabulary that are extremely idiosyncratic, producing effects that must be designated by Proust's own name, is nonetheless without style?" (ibid., 165).

60 Kafka's case is exemplary in this respect; his name has been transposed into an adjective, "Kafkaesque," which does not refer to a person but—often mistakenly, almost always stereotypically—a style of expression and experience.

61 Kafka, *The Complete Stories,* 89.

62 Gerald Prince, *A Dictionary of Narratology* (Lincoln: University of Nebraska Press, 2003), 34.

63 Frances Burney, *Cecelia; or, Memoirs of an Heiress* (New York: BiblioLife, 2008), 336.

64 The facility of Deleuze's French deserves to be marked here: "il consiste, dans un énoncé qui dépend d'un sujet d'énonciation donné, à glisser un autre sujet d'énonciation." See Deleuze, *Deux régimes des fous,* 344.

65 Virginia Woolf, *Mrs. Dalloway* (Herstfordshire: Wordsworth Editions, 1996), 28.

66 Prince, *A Dictionary of Narratology,* 34.

67 Janet Todd, *Cambridge Introduction to Jane Austen* (Cambridge: Cambridge University Press, 2006), 30.

68 Hence, when we consider "the minimal condition for the transmission of order-words" (ATP, 88), we should immediately think of gossip, which forms the barest justification

for speech. Gossip exists merely to be repeated, passed on under the auspices of an earlier utterance, and another, and yet another.

69 Georg Simmel, *The Sociology of Georg Simmel*, trans. Kurt H. Wolff (New York: Free Press, 1964), 52.

70 Language is risky business in these fictions: descriptions of secrets and reports, mercenaries and spies, deception and treachery bear witness to the dangers of discourse.

71 Austen's heroines are roughly separable into those who possess sense and those who lack it. In the case of the latter, for whom the gift is not innate or has not been properly taught, her protagonists must suffer a kind of education because their own judgment is immature—too sentimental (*Sense and Sensibility*), too headstrong (*Pride and Prejudice*), or too enamored with its own cleverness (*Emma*).

72 We could say that one of the singular and brilliant exceptions to this rule is Emma's own anagnorisis, namely, the realization that Knightly is her destiny: "It darted through her, with the speed of an arrow, that Mr. Knightly must marry no one but herself!" The metaphor of the arrow, the rhetoric of negation, and the insistence of the punctuation give this realization an air of misgiving. See Jane Austen, *Emma*, ed. Alistair Duckworth (New York: Palgrave, 2002), 324.

73 Dorrit Cohn, *Transparent Minds: Narrative Modes for Presenting Consciousness in Fiction* (Princeton, N.J.: Princeton University Press, 1983), 111–12.

74 Kafka, *Franz Kafka: The Complete Stories*, 90.

75 Ibid., 130.

76 Ibid., 138.

77 Ibid., 139.

78 Ibid.

79 Ibid.

80 Blanchot, *Work of Fire*, 10.

81 In this light we might compare Deleuze's statement to the kinds of "quasi-negation" to which structuralism and poststructuralism have made us accustomed. For instance, when Baudrillard says that "the gulf war did not happen," we are led to understand that the real was so mediated by images, copies, and recordings as to have existed by virtue of representation, not "in itself." Or when Lacan says that "Woman does not exist," we are led to grasp that the nature of Woman consists in a fantasy promoted in order to repress the trauma of sexual difference. In both cases, the phrase gives way not to a paradox so much as a stipulation: neither the gulf war nor Woman exist according to our common sense of them. But when Deleuze says that the people are missing he does not hedge the meaning of the statement, nor does he provide an equally plausible, though antinomical, response to the cliché that the people do indeed exist (i.e., they exist, but not as we think). For Deleuze, the people do not exist, which means that they must be made to exist—they must be created. See Jean Baudrillard, *The Gulf War Did Not Take Place*, trans. Paul Patton (Bloomington: Indiana University Press, 1995) and Jacques Lacan's *Seminar XX, Encore: On Feminine Sexuality, the Limits of Love and Knowledge*.

82 Note that the logic here inevitably recalls our discussion of Nietzsche, who addressed his own philosophy to the future. We recall the lines from *On the Genealogy of Morals* on which we dwelled in the first chapter: "And yet here again I touch on my problem, on our problem, my unknown friends [*meine unbekannten Freunde*] (for as yet I *know* of no friend)" (GM, III 27). In other words, Nietzsche addresses himself to a future, which cannot be known but which philosophy nonetheless endeavors to create.

83 The original reads: "Écrire est une affaire de devenir, toujours inachevé . . . " (*Critique et clinique*, 10).

84 Kafka, *Diaries of Franz Kafka*, 17. The original reads: "Was innerhalb großer Litteraturen unten sich abspielt und einen nicht unentbehrlichen Keller des Gebäudes bildet, geschieht hier im vollen Licht, was dort einen augenblicksweisen Zusammenlauf entstehen läßt, führt hier nichts weniger als die Entscheidung über Leben und Tod aller herbei" (Kafka, *Tagebücher*, 203).

85 See Emile Benveniste's *Problems in General Linguistics* (Miami: University of Miami Press, 1973). By discourse, Benveniste means "every variety of oral discourse of every nature and every level, from trivial conversation to the most elaborate oration"—in other words, "all the genres in which someone addresses himself to someone, proclaims himself as a speaker, and organizes what he says in the category of person" (209).

86 Ibid., 197.

87 Ibid., 198.

88 Ibid., 199.

89 Ibid., 201.

90 See, for instance, Ferlinghetti's poem "He" in *Starting from San Francisco* (New York: New Directions Publishing, 1967), 26: "And he is the eye of the fourth person singular/ of which nobody speaks."

91 For Lacanian psychoanalysis and, thereafter, the politico-semiotic analysis it inspired, the "master signifier" is that signifier to which others look to orient themselves in a given semiotic field. The key aspect of the master signifier, as Žižek has pointed out so brilliantly, is that its transcendence derives from what is, in effect, the absence of meaning: other signifiers and speakers look to the master signifiers insofar as the latter reflect and ramify various and even opposed constituencies (e.g., the signifier "liberal"). See, for instance, Lacan's "Subversion of the Subject and the Dialectic of Desire in the Freudian Unconscious" in *Écrits*, 671–702. Also see Ernesto Laclau and Chantal Mouffe's *Hegemony and Socialist Strategy* (London: Verso, 1985) and Slavoj Žižek, *The Subline Object of Ideology* (London: Verso, 1989), especially chapter 3.

92 "When the identity of a thing dissolves, being escapes to attain univocity, and begins to revolve around the different" (DR, 67). Univocity is not unity but rather the collective assemblage in which philosophy ceases to conceive of Being on the basis of the One (i.e., as an equivocal concept).

93 Kafka, *Diaries of Franz Kafka*, 212–13. Kafka's original reads: "Wenn ich wahllos einen Satz hinschreibe z.B. Er schaute aus dem Fenster so ist er schon vollkommen" (Kafka,

Tagebüche, 16). I am indebted to J. Hillis Miller's article, "A Defense of Literature and Literary Study in a Time of Globalization and the New Tele-technologies," for this insight into Kafka. See *Neohelicon 34* (2007) 2, 13–22.

94 Kafka, *Franz Kafka: The Complete Stories,* 77. The original reads: "Er hatte gerade einen Brief an einen sich im Ausland befindenden Jugendfreund beendet, verschloß ihn in spielerischer Langsamkeit und sah dann, den Ellbogen auf den Schreibtisch gestützt, aus dem Fenster auf den Fluß, die Brücke und die Anhöhen am anderen Ufer mit ihrem schwachen Grün." See Franz Kafka, "Das Urteil" (Norderstedt, Germany: GRIN Verlag, 2008), 3.

95 Kafka, *Diaries of Franz Kafka,* 212–13. The German reads: "Die fürchterliche Anstrengung und Freude, wie sich die Geschichte vor mir entwickelte wie ich in einem Gewässer vorwärtskam. Mehrmals in dieser Nacht trug ich mein Gewicht auf dem Rücken. Wie alles gewagt werden kann, wie für alle, für die fremdesten Einfälle ein großes Feuer bereitet ist, in dem sie vergehn und auferstehn" (Kafka, *Tagebücher,* 291).

96 For Deleuze and Guattari, "the statement is individuated, and enunciation subjectified, only to the extent that an impersonal collective assemblage requires it and determines it to be so" (ATP, 80).

97 Deleuze, *L'île déserte et autres texts,* 359.5.

5. Philosophy in an Inhospitable Age

1 The suggestion in French is even more explicit. When Deleuze and Guattari write, "Elle a des fous rires qui emportent ses larmes" (Deleuze, *Qu'est-ce que la philosophie?,* 16), laughter *itself* bears away the tears in a passage from one affective state to another.

2 While critics have tended to associate Kafka and Nietzsche with the burden of existentialism—with "the spirit of seriousness, the spirit of gravity" (DI, 258)—Deleuze insists that this interpretation fails to appreciate the humor that traverses their writings. In their texts, we experience a constant play of "high and low intensities," buoyed along by so many paradoxes, humors, and ironies. Consider the magnificent and meticulous punishment reserved for prisoners in Kafka's "The Penal Colony," or the awful conclusion ("never to have been born!") to which the Greeks are led in Nietzsche's *Birth of Tragedy*: in both cases, the worst of fates ought to bring us to unthrottled and full-throated laughter. Nietzsche's aphorisms are no less hysterical: "I have canonized laughter," Zarathustra exclaims; "you Higher Men, learn—to laugh!" (TSZ, "Of the Higher Man"). See Charles Stivale's *Gilles Deleuze's ABCs: The Folds of Friendship* for an extended analysis of laughter in Deleuze's work.

3 Philip Goodchild, *Deleuze and Guattari: An Introduction to the Politics of Desire* (Thousand Oaks, Calif.: Sage, 1996), 1.

4 Deleuze and Guattari forego *doing* philosophy for a hiatus, the opening of an interval in the sensory-motor schema of perceptions and actions, when philosophy turns to the problem of thought and affection becomes *self-affection.*

5　As Deleuze and Guattari say, "the answer not only had to take note of the question, it had to determine its moment, its occasions and circumstances, its landscape and personae, its conditions and unknowns" (WIP, 2).

6　This nonstyle constitutes a mode of experience and expression that, heretofore, Deleuze reserves for the characterization of literature. In Kafka's prose, we've spoken of a kind of "willed poverty" that "proceeds by dryness and sobriety" in order to strip back the affectations of style, leaving nothing behind but intensities (K, 19). In an entirely different way, Proust strains language to the point that "*language in its entirety reaches the limit*" (CC, 113). As Deleuze adds, "Should we instead speak with Proust of a nonstyle, that is, of 'the elements of a style to come which does not exist'?" (*PS*, 165). And then: "Can we not say that Proust, too, has no style?" (ibid.). And then: "Style here does not propose to describe nor to suggest: as in Balzac, it is explicative, it explicates with images. It is nonstyle because it is identified with 'interpreting,' pure and without subject, and multiplies the viewpoints toward the sentence, within the sentence" (ibid., 166).

7　As Deleuze writes in the context of paining, "Movement does not explain sensation; on the contrary it is explained by the elasticity of sensation, its *vis elastica*." See Deleuze, *Francis Bacon*, 36.

8　See Peter Canning's "Fluidentity" in *Substance* 44 (1984): 34–45.

9　François Zoutrabichvili, *Le Vocabulaire de Deleuze* (Paris: Ellipsis, 2003), 30.

10　Deleuze unfolds this distinction in *Difference and Repetition*, 207–21, 245–47.

11　Charles Dickens, *Our Mutual Friend* (New York: Modern Library, 2002), 432, 433.

12　Ibid., 432.

13　Ibid.

14　Ibid., 433.

15　Ibid., 432.

16　Homer, *The Odyssey*, 292 (original pagination, Book 19, 386–94).

17　Ibid.

18　Deleuze, *Logique du sens*, 149

19　While Deleuze's affection for systems and series underwrites the development of his own early "games-theory," Guattari's apprenticeship to Lacan and to the institution of psychoanalysis testifies to his own education in structural linguistics.

20　It is fair to say that *Gilles Deleuze and the Fabulation of Philosophy* short shrifts Deleuze's relationship with Guattari, which ought by rights to constitute a book of its own. Indeed, in the last few years, Guattari's contribution to their conceptual assemblage has been given increasingly serious consideration, perhaps nowhere as persuasively as in Dosse, *Gilles Deleuze and Félix Guattari: Intersecting Lives*.

21　See *Who's Afraid of Deleuze and Guattari*, 67–101.

22　It need not be said that the commercial figure of the apprentice has nothing whatsoever to do with Deleuze's apprenticeship to a legion of minor philosophers. The latter are not masters but experimenters, in whose mad laboratories Deleuze bounces about.

23 "On avait trop envie de faire de la philosophie, on ne se demandait pas ce qu'elle était, sauf par exercice de style" (*Qu'est-ce que la philosophie?* 7).

24 See Dosse, *Gilles Deleuze and Félix Guattari: Intersecting Lives*, 374–78. Dosse's criticisms of the group are duly redoubled here, especially considering the way that, long after New Philosophy was forgotten, its members have continued to achieve success and power. This is most obviously the case with Bernard Henri-Lévy (BHL), whose controversial book *Who Killed Daniel Pearl?* trans James X. Mitchell (London: Duckworth Publishers, 2004) actually emerged from a trip he took as Jacques Chirac's special envoy to Afghanistan. Like BHL, André Glucksmann has also veered to the right, supporting military intervention in the Middle East and endorsing Nicolas Sarkozy for president. See "Porquoi je choisi Nicolas Sarkozy," *Le Monde*, January 29, 2007. For an assessment of the afterlife of the New Philosophers, see Danielle Salvatore Schiffer, *Critique de la déraison pure: La faillite intellectuelle des "nouveaux philosophes" et de leurs epigones* (Paris: François Bourin Editeur, 2010). Schiffer's critique affirms the sense in which BHL "ne comprend toujours par Nietzsche" and why he fails to grasp Deleuze (80–82).

25 *Time* magazine, September 12, 1977.

26 In *Gilles Deleuze and Félix Guattari: Intersecting Lives*, Dosse recounts the circumstances surrounding Deleuze's decision to respond (374–78). His reason is that while the New Philosophers are, at the level of their thought, the height of silliness, they nevertheless represent something altogether serious. As Deleuze is reported to have said: "We are in a samizdat situation. We are in the minority. I need to tell you who these people are. They are always on the side of whoever is in power, no matter what" (376).

27 This conclusion clearly emerges in light of *Barbarism with a Human Face* (New York: Harper and Row, 1979), which Lévy confessed to writing hastily in response to the market demand. Having been preceded by a kind of commercial campaign, the New Philosophy had been branded and advertised, the public primed, but the product was still missing. See Gayatri Chakravorty Spivak and Michael Ryan's review essay on the New Philosophers, "Anarchism Revisited: A New Philosophy" in *Diacritics* 8, no. 2 (Summer, 1978): 66–79. As they write of Lévy: "A book had to be written fast; it did not particularly matter on what, as long as it was ready for the FNAC shelves by the Spring" (72).

28 Deleuze, *Deux régimes de fous*, 129.

29 "This is why, if we pursue this line of argument to its limit, a book is worth less than the newspaper article written about it or the interview that comes after it. Intellectuals and writers, even artists, are thus forced to become journalists if they want to conform to the norm. This is a new type of thought, the interview-thought, the sound-bite thought. We can imagine a book that would be about a newspaper article, and not the reverse" (TRM, 142–43).

30 As Fatos Tarifa has noted, the letters cannily featured these young turks in dialogue with famous intellectuals, such as Claude Lévi-Strauss and Roland Barthes, in order to provide the impression of an imprimatur that "was granted to the 'new movement,' which the dossier purported to herald. Lévy's introduction of the dossier aimed at producing

maximum impact in public, giving the impression that something truly new, original, unusual, ground-breaking, and exciting was happening in French thought." See Tarifa's "The Poverty of the 'New Philosophy' " in *Modern Age* 50 (June 22, 2008): 228. A month after the dossier appeared, the marketing campaign was resumed in *Le Nouvel Observateur*, where Gérard Petijean branded a number of other thinkers New Philosophers, including André Glucksmann, Guy Hochquenhem, and even Jean Baudrillard.

31 "They dominated public perception of the day, creating the impression that a moment of philosophical adventure was happening in contemporary French thought," Tarifa explains ("The Poverty of the 'New Philosophy,' " 229). The New Philosophers appeared on television and graced the covers of glossy magazines, quickly becoming intellectual celebrities.

32 Lévy, *Barbarism with a Human Face*, 6.

33 Nothing confirmed this sentiment as profoundly and publicly as the appearance of Aleksandr Solzhenitsyn's narrative of the Soviet labor camp system, *The Gulag Archipelago*, which was published in France in 1974. For the New Philosophers, the text confirmed what the events of '68 had already suggested, namely, the possibility of a terror of the left (communism) that was every bit as dangerous as the terror of the right (fascism).

34 As Oskar Negt explains: "One must keep in mind that many of these intellectuals were bitterly disillusioned more than once in less than ten years. First, they were inspired by the May Revolution and blamed the French Communist Party for not having carried it far enough. Then, some of them tried to channel their energies into Maoist Leninism and were again bitterly disappointed by the shift of power in China. And, when rumors leaked out about deportations and mass executions in Cambodia, the basic equation 'Socialism equals Gulag equals Marxism' became an *idée fixe* for several of them." See Negt's "Reflections on France's 'Nouveaux Philosophes' and the Crisis of Marxism." *SubStance* 11, no. 4, 58.

35 Tarifa, "The Poverty of the 'New Philosophy,' " 230.

36 Henri-Lévy, *Barbarism with a Human Face*, 180–81. As André Glucksmann put it, there would be "No Russian camps without Marxism." See *La cuisiniere et le mangeur d'hommes: Essai sur L'etat, le marxisme, les camps de concentration* (Paris: Éditions du Seuil, 1975), 40.

37 This sentiment is given expression in André Glucksmann's *The Master Thinkers* (New York: HarperCollins, 1980).

38 As Deleuze explains, this kind of philosopher most closely approximates the politician, "who is above all concerned to deny that which 'differs', so as to conserve or prolong an established historical order, or to establish a historical order which already calls forth in the world the forms of its representation" (DR, 53).

39 Deleuze was among a number of writers, including Régis Debray and Jacques Rancière, who argued that the celebrity enjoyed by the New Philosophers existed in proportion

to the dead and forgotten, whose suffering they resurrected and marketed to suit a diet of European guilt and a taste for opinion. The "New Philosophers are writing a martyrology: the Gulag and the victims of history. They live off corpses" (TRM, 144). Indeed, the New Philosophers were the entrepreneurs of the camps, of all camps, because they figured out how to put their own pretty faces on misery.

40 "Anarchism Revisited: A New Philosophy," 79; Tarifa, "The Poverty of the 'New Philosophy,'" 226.

41 This sentiment is confirmed by François Aubral, who, along with Xavir Delacourt, produced the first major response to the New Philosophers: *Contre la nouvelle philosophie* (Paris: Gallimard, 1977). Inspired by this response, and encouraged to formulate a response of his own, Deleuze sat down with the authors in 1977 to discuss possible courses of action. Aubral averred that a brief piece by Deleuze would crush the group; Deleuze responded, "but you know, they'd just say I was jealous of the younger generation. And I don't want to speak to the media, you know I don't go in for that, it's not my sort of thing" (Dosse, *Deleuze and Guattari: Intersecting Lives*, 376).

42 The original French here is revealing: "Du coup, je crois que certains d'entre nous peuvent même éprouver une curiosité bienveillante pour cette opération, d'un point de vue purement naturaliste ou entomologique. Moi, c'est différent, parce que mon point de vue est tératologique: c'est de l'horreur" (Deleuze, *Deux régimes*, 130). Later, in the same essay, he writes: "There is nothing alive in their work, but they will have fulfilled their function if they can occupy center stage long enough to give whatever is creative the kiss of death" (TRM, 147).

43 In the notes to "Immanence: A Life," the editor of *Two Regimes of Madness*, David Lapoujade, suggests that the essay represented Deleuze's effort to return to a concept, immanence, which he felt had been insufficiently elaborated (TRM, 416).

44 Having said this, I must admit: a number of contemporary thinkers have forcefully and persuasively argued, to the contrary, that Deleuze's philosophy acquires its consistency in light of his quasi-phenomenological enterprise. See especially Hughes, *Deleuze and the Genesis of Representation*. Also see my review of Hughes's text, written with Abe Geil, in *Notre Dame Philosophical Review* at http://ndpr.nd.edu/review.cfm?id = 19407.

45 Each plane or domain consists of a relation to something that cannot be understood, grasped, or thought, but at the same time, Deleuze and Guattari insist, without this relation, nonrelation or thought as such would not exist.

46 Gilles Deleuze, *The Fold: Leibniz and the Baroque*, trans. Tom Conley (Minneapolis: University of Minnesota Press, 1993), 76.

47 Hence, Deleuze treats chaos as a cosmological approximation ("the sum of all possibles" filtered through compossibility), a physical approximation ("depthless shadows" filtered though a prism of Nature), and a psychic approximation ("the sum of a possible perception" filtered through a differentiating perception) (Fold, 87).

48 James Williams, *Difference and Repetition: A Critical Introduction and Guide* (Edinburgh: Edinburgh University Press, 2003), 169.

49 Unlike the homogeneous field of equalities to which it gives rise, "intensity is itself differential, by itself a difference" (DR, 222).

50 Whence the great formula of *Difference and Repetition* that "difference is not diversity, but difference is that by which the given is given, that by which the given is given as diverse" (222).

51 Inasmuch as the engagement with chaos gives rise to an even more distressing struggle with opinion, Deleuze treats this inclination in the name of a number of different philosophers and in a number of different conceptual neighborhoods. But across these scattered discussions, and perhaps this leitmotiv, it is possible to discern the lineaments of a kind of cosmology that runs from the unfettered chaos of the universe to the evolutionary morphogenesis of *homo sapiens* to the natural history of morals and the production of a "regular and predictable animal" (Nietzsche)—the subject.

52 Flaxman, ed., *The Brain Is the Screen*, 367.

53 Deleuze refers to Prigogine and Stengers on several occasions, beginning in an interview on the subject of *A Thousand Plateaus* that he gave in 1980 (see Deleuze, *Negotiations 1972–1990*, 29), and concluding with his invocation of chaos theory in *WIP* (226).

54 Ilya Prigogine and Isabelle Stengers, *La Nouvelle Alliance* (Paris: Gallimard, 1986). Notably, this text was originally published in 1978.

55 It is important to emphasize that the "success" of physics, for Prigogine and Stengers, derives from its willingness to limit or even close off parts of the universe as opposed to seeing every system as invariably open.

56 Ilya Prigogine and Isabelle Stengers, *Order Out of Chaos* (New York: Bantam Books, 1984), 7.

57 Ibid., 49.

58 Ibid., 52.

59 Ibid., 60.

60 For a discussion of reversibility, see Ilya Prigogine, *The End of Certainty* (New York: Free Press, 1997), 12ff. As he explains, "the nineteenth century left us a double heritage: the laws of nature, such as Newton's law, which describes a time-reversible universe, and an evolutionary description associated with entropy" (17).

61 This is the fabulous conclusion to Poe's lesser-known detective story, "The Murder of Marie Roget." In effect, the remarkable chain of reason, which Dupin intuits, leads the narrator to affirm that there are no coincidences. See *The Complete Tales and Poems of Edgar Allan Poe*, 206.

62 Prigogine, *The End of Certainty*, 12. It may be useful to recall the first two laws of thermodynamics here. The first is the law of the conservation of energy, which maintains that while energy can be transferred and can change form, it can be neither created nor destroyed. The second law, the basis for irreversibility proper, states that in a closed system, the quality of energy degrades over time, which amounts to saying that entropy increases.

63 Ibid., 18.

64 Ibid., 54.

65 The paraphrase of a statement made in letters to Max Born. See *The Born–Einstein Letters*, trans. Irene Born (New York: Walker and Company, 1971), 146.

66 Stephen Hawking, *A Brief History of Time* (New York: Bantam, 1998), 63.

67 Stephen Hawking, "Gödel and the End of Physics," online lecture available at: http://www.hawking.org.uk/index.php/lectures/91.

68 Ibid.

69 Ibid.

70 Hesiod, *Theogony and Works and Days*, trans. M. L. West (New York: Filiquarian Publishing, LLC., 2007), 8. In effects, Hesiod produces a cosmology, an account of the cosmos that follows its generations and genealogies, but he also produces a cosmogony, an account of the origins of generation—of the emergence of something from next to nothing.

71 See, for instance, Lee Smollin's absolutely fantastic book *The Life of the Cosmos* (New York: Oxford University Press, 1999). In many respects, Smollin's conclusion as a physicist echo work being done in other fields, most especially evolutionary biology. Also see Stuart Kauffman, *At Home in the Universe,* as well as his earlier book, *The Origins of Order: Self-Organization and Selection in Evolution* (New York: Oxford University Press, 1993).

72 Prigogine and Stengers, *Order Out of Chaos*, 12.

73 We typically define "phase space," in mathematics, as a multidimensional space in which all possible states of a system are represented, such that every degree of freedom consists in an axis in the system. In *WIP* Deleuze says that "every concept therefore has a phase space, although not in the same way as science" (25). In terms of Deleuze's sense of complexity, see John Protevi's "Deleuze, Guattari, and Emergence" in *Paragraph: A Journal of Modern Critical Theory* 29, no. 2 (July 2006): 19–39, as well as Bonta and Protevi, *Deleuze and Geophilosophy*. Manuel Delanda has also written very clearly on the subject of phase space in *Intensive Science and Virtual Philosophy*. Also see Dorothea Olkowski's unique elaboration of chaos in the last chapter of *The Universal* (*In the Real of the Sensible*) (New York: Columbia University Press, 2007). Finally, see Elizabeth Grosz's *Chaos, Territory, Art: Deleuze and the Framing of the Earth* (New York: Columbia University Press, 2008).

74 Prigogine and Stengers, *Order Out of Chaos*, 162.

75 See Friedrich Nietzsche, *Daybreak: Thoughts on Prejudices of Morality*, ed. Maudemarie Clark and Brian Leiter (Cambridge: Cambridge University Press, 1997), 130. Also see Deleuze, *Nietzsche and Philosophy*, 26.

76 In full, the "rules" of the ideal game read as follows: "(1) There are no preexisting rules, each move (or throw) invents its own rules; it bears on its own rule. (2) Far from dividing and apportioning chance in a really distinct number of throws, all throws affirm chance and endlessly ramify it with each throw. (3) The throws therefore are not really numerically distinct. They are qualitatively distinct, but are the qualitative forms of a

single cast which is ontologically one. (4) Such a game—without rules, with neither winner nor loser, without responsibility, a game of innocence, a caucus-race, in which skill and chance are no longer distinguishable—seems to have no reality. Besides, it would amuse no one" (LS, 59).

77 Borges, *Collected Fictions*, 125. Borges provides a brief and frequently quoted example: "Fang, let us say, has a secret; a stranger knocks at his door; Fang decides to kill him. Naturally, there are various possible outcomes—Fang can kill the intruder, the intruder can kill Fang, they can both be killed, and so on."

78 Ibid.

79 Ibid.

80 Lecercle, *Deleuze and Language*, 16.

81 Ilya Prigogine, "The Networked Society," *Journal of World Systems Research* 6, no. 3 (Fall/Winter 2000): 895–96.

82 Erwin Schrödinger, *What Is Life? The Physical Aspect of the Living Cell* (Cambridge: Cambridge University Press, 1992), 3.

83 Ibid.

84 Ibid., 73.

85 Ibid., 69.

86 Hawking, *A Brief History of Time*, 190.

87 Prigogine, "The Networked Society," 895–96.

88 Ibid., 893–94.

89 Ibid., 895–96.

90 Ibid.

91 With the exception of his discussion of Foucault, Deleuze does not explicitly discuss biopower, though his considerations of control envision the new shape of contemporary biopolitics.

92 Broadly construed, we might say that the crisis about which Marx writes, and to which nineteenth-century liberalism responds, was posed in terms of labor (its abuse, its redress, its potential revolutionary efflorescence). But today, the problem is posed in terms of wealth, the accumulation of which has exposed markets to risk (cascading losses, bankruptcies, foreclosures, etc.).

93 Braudel, *Memory and the Mediterranean*, 222.

94 The question of capitalism in China, which leads to the more general questions of "Asiatic production" or "uneven development," is first broached by Deleuze and Guattari in *Anti-Oedipus*. Both there and then in *WIP* they tend to follow Fernand Braudel in suggesting that while the history of capitalism begins earlier than is typically dated by Marx's mature writings (Braudel effectively locates its initial organization in the great Italian market-cities of the fourteenth century, thereby following the writings of the younger Marx), this shift only serves to clarify the conditions (i.e., absence of transcendence) that permit the great syntheses of wealth and labor, which characterize capitalism as such. See the section "Savages, Barbarians and Civilized Men" in *Anti-Oedipus*

and the section "Towns and Cities" in Fernand Braudel, *The Structures of Everyday Life*, trans. Siân Reynolds (Berkeley: University of California Press, 1992).

95 Ibid., 190.

96 In fact, as Manuel Delanda has written, a number "of the inventions that Europeans used to colonize the world (the compass, gunpowder, paper money, the printing press) were of Chinese origin," but these technologies are invented within a profoundly territorialized, imperial formation that precluded the contingencies that made capitalism possible. Manuel Delanda, *1000 Years of Nonlinear History* (New York: Zone Books, 1997), 51.

97 See Karl Marx, *The Grundrisse: Foundations of the Critique of Political Economy*, trans. Marin Nicolaus (London: Penguin, 1993), 467–95.

98 Ibid. Braudel's sense of history, which Deleuze and Guattari affirm, can also be detected in more recent (and popular) global-historical accounts. Most notably, see Jared Diamond's *Guns, Germs, Steel: The Fates of Human Societies* (New York: W. W. Norton and Company, 2005).

99 Braudel, *Memory and the Mediterranean*, 192.

100 Ibid., 228.

101 Ibid., 244.

102 Ibid.

103 Ibid.

104 Ibid. As Braudel adds, "Cities with less in the way of advantages tended to look outwards," Braudel explains of ancient Greece. "Sooner or later they had to sail the sea, to 'marry it' as Venice did in a later age, to enter into conflict with those who stood in their way, and to sail to the ends of the earth" (230–31).

105 "The best illustration of a social institution that emerges spontaneously from the interaction of many decision makers is that of the precapitalist market, a collective entity arising from the decentralized interaction of many buyers and sellers, with no central 'decider' coordinating the whole process" (De Landa, *1000 Years of Nonlinear History*, 17).

106 Ibid., 87. Also see Braudel, *The Mediterranean in the Ancient World*. The innovation of the Greek world, which Braudel compares to that of the great Italian market cities of the fourteenth and fifteenth centuries, unleashed a sphere of "commerce" that encompassed not only goods but, also, ideas. "It was then that the network of Greek cities, both ancient and modern, really 'went live' " (216).

107 Ibid., 137.

108 To the question of whether Socrates establishes philosophy as a "free discussion among friends," Deleuze responds: "In fact, Socrates constantly made all discussion impossible, both in the short form of the contest of questions and answers and in the long form of rivalry between discourses" (WIP, 29).

109 See, for instance, Justin Wyatt, *High Concept: Movies and Marketing in Hollywood* (Austin: University of Texas Press, 1994).

110 No doubt the sense of an "epoch" on which Deleuze and Guattari draw (i.e., a point of chronology) is inflected by the related sense of "epoché" on which Husserl insists (i.e., a suspension or stoppage of historical judgment).

111 As Fredric Jameson writes in his recent book on science fiction, the most crippling aspect of intellectual existence today is "that the historic alternatives to capitalism have been proven unviable and impossible, and that no other socioeconomic system is conceivable, let alone practically available." See his *Archaeologies of the Future: The Desire Called Utopia and Other Science Fictions* (London: Verso, 2005), xii.

112 This suggestion was aired in a public lecture given at the University of North Carolina in 2005. Notably, White intended his diagnosis to reflect the current apotheosis of the social sciences, which rely for the most part on quantitative approaches and the concomitant diminishment of the humanities, which traditionally rely on more narrative means. But this division equally applies to the intellectual, since this figure, once firmly located in the human sciences and asserting his or her force in the name of humanism, has been increasingly supplanted by the expertise of the social scientists or "specialist."

113 See Foucault's interview, "Truth and Power," in *The Essential Works of Foucault*, vol. 3, 126.

114 See, for instance, Philip Sidney, *The Defense of Poesy Otherwise Known as an Apology for Poetry* (Ann Arbor: University of Michigan Press, 2009), line 600.

115 As Deleuze and Guattari say, "Utopia is not a good concept because even when opposed to History it is still subject to it and lodged within it as an ideal motivation" (WIP, 110).

116 Friedrich Nietzsche, "On the Utility and Liability of History for Life," in *Unfashionable Observations*, 57.

Coda

1 The distinction between *Chronos* and *Aion*, which Deleuze takes from the Stoics, is treated at length in Deleuze, *The Logic of Sense*. See, especially, the "Twenty-Third Series of the *Aion*."

2 Deleuze invokes this neologism, taken from the title of Samuel Butler's novel *Erehwon*, in *Difference and Repetition* (xxi), though it is in the context of *WIP* that it gains its most profound definition (100).

3 For a helpful accounting of these early texts, see Dosse's *Gilles Deleuze and Félix Guattari: Intersecting Lives*, 88–107.

4 Synthesis entails both reproduction and recognition insofar as we reproduce different parts of space, through time, and then go beyond this synthesis by virtue of relating the represented manifold to an object. In representation, the modulation of that which is represented is determined in accordance with the habit of the subject itself, a mobile milieu, which perpetuates itself in the proleptic synthesis of its own common and good sense. The subject of representation projects its own structure from one moment to the next as a "first repetition," namely, the continuity of its own abstract conditions, its habitas.

5 See Immanuel Kant, *Universal Natural History and Theory of the Heavens*, trans. Ian Johnston (Arlington, Va: Richer Resources Publications, 2008). While Kant's later or "critical" work seems to leave much of the analogical style of this book behind, his belief in extraterrestrials never wavers. In the *Critique of Pure Reason*, he writes: "If it were possible to settle by any sort of experience whether there are inhabitants of at least some of the planets that we see, I might well bet everything that I have on it. Hence I say that it is not merely an opinion but a strong belief . . . that there are inhabitants of other worlds" (A 825).

6 Nietzsche, "On Truth and Lying in a Non-Moral Sense" in *The Nietzsche Reader*, 120.

7 See "What Is Englishtenment?" in Immanuel Kant, *Political Writings*, ed. Hans Riess, trans. H. B. Nisbit (Cambridge: Cambridge University Press, 1991).

8 Ibid, 57.

9 Darko Suvin, *Metamorphoses of Science Fiction: On the Poetics and History of a Literary Genre* (New Haven: Yale University Press, 1979), 4.

10 In French, the passage reads: "et par là invoque en dernière instance une mystérieuse cohérence qui exclut la sienne propre, celle du monde et celle de Dieu" (Deleuze, *Différence et répétition*, 82).

11 See the second of Malebranche's *Dialogues on Metaphysics and Religion*, ed. Nicholas Jolley and David Scott (Cambridge: Cambridge University Press, 1997).

12 Note that in French *formation* also signifies education, training, and domestication.

13 This contention appears, perhaps most strikingly, in *Seminar XI: The Four Fundamental Concepts of Psychoanalysis*, 59.

14 The Greek word signifies both a sign and a tomb or dungeon: the signifier is mortifying.

15 See, for instance, Bill Brown's special issue of *Critical Inquiry* 28, no. 1, *Things* (Autumn 2001) and his essay therein, "Thing Theory" (1–22).

16 See Zourachbichvili's short piece, "Introduction inédite (2004): l'ontology et le transcendental," a new introduction written on the occasion of the republication of *Deleuze: Une philosophie de la evénément*. Both this new introduction and the book appear in a collection with Anne Sauvagnargues and Paola Marrati, *La philosophie de Deleuze* (Paris: Presses Universitaires de France, 2004), 7 (translation mine).

17 Ibid.

18 William Gibson, *Pattern Recognition* (New York: Berkeley Books, 2003), 58–59. In an interview, Gibson explained: "It just seemed to be happening—it was like the windshield kept getting closer and closer. The event horizon was getting closer [. . .] I have this conviction that the present is actually inexpressibly peculiar now, and that's the only thing that's worth dealing with. The volume of technological weirdness was being turned up all the time, but the world felt increasingly familiar." See Andrew Leonard, "Nodal Point: Interview with William Gibson." *Salon.com* (February 13, 2003). http://dir.salon.com/story/tech/books/2003/02/13/gibson/index.html. I am indebted to Al Miller for making this point.

19 The reference here is to Žižek, *The Sublime Object of Ideology*.

20 From Yeats's great poem "The Second Coming." See *The Collected Poems of W. B. Yeats*, ed. Richard J. Finneran (New York: Scribner, 1996), 187.

21 This neologism or play on words was coined by Lacan to describe the dimension of speech and the spoken (*dit*) which detours life into the signifying chain and thereby determines the subject. In a sense, as we have argued, Deleuze's response to psychoanalysis (especially, with Guattari, in the two volumes of *Capitalism and Schizophrenia*) consists in foreclosing this overcoding dimension (N-1). See the "Introduction" to *A Thousand Plateaus*.

22 *Mille plateaux*, 326.

23 *Philosophy and Truth: Selections from Nietzsche's Notebooks of the Early 1870s*, ed. Breazeale, 53.

INDEX

"a life," xx, 6, 241–43, 247, 253, 271, 309, 315–16. *See also* life

a priori, 186, 282, 297, 301; in Kant, 135, 196; Nietzsche's, 25–26, 73

Ab-grundung, 168, 174

adequation, 53, 182

aesthetics: and genealogy, 82; in Kant, xviii, 194–97, 297, 300; and modernism, 173, 183; in Nietzsche, 15, 23, 49, 50, 51, 52–54, 307, 329n4; in paranoia, 70; and representation, xx, 297, 300, 321; and transcendental empiricism, 300–301; and science fiction, 82, 297, 300–301, 306–7, 321–22. *See also* judgment, aesthetic

agôn, 107, 109–10, 112, 119, 130–31, 174, 278. *See also* rivalry

agonism: in ancient Greece, 16, 98, 110, 119–22, 129, 131–32, 174, 278–79, 355n79; of forces, 61, 78–79, 131–32, 179; and Heraclitus, 131–32; as a model for philosophy, 119–22, 129, 131–32, 174, 179, 278–79; and Nietzsche, 61, 78–79, 131–32. *See also* rivalry

agora, 100, 107–8

Aion, 20, 224, 293, 372n1. *See also* untimely

Alien (film), 321

Alliez, Eric, 348n1

Allison, David B., 334n30

Althusser, Louis, 59, 199, 250

America. *See* Anglo-America; United States of America

amphisbêtêsis, 136–50, 156–58. See also *agôn*; rivalry

anagnorisis, 150, 151, 353n53. *See also* recognition

analogy: between philosophy and literature, 3, 6, 332n8; in Plato, 144, 160

anamnêsis, 17, 123, 131, 136, 159, 169–70

anarchism, 11, 14, 175, 300

And, method of, 65, 198, 305

Anderson, Benedict, 202

Anderson, Perry, 14

anexactitude, xvii, 317, 331n19

Anglo-America: Deleuze's reception in, 11, 12, 38, 67, 175, 334n30

anthropocentrism, 83, 86–88

anthropology, 100, 102, 118, 148, 152, 174, 245

aphorism, xiii, 29; form of, 34–37; as machine, 23–24, 48; and the Outside, 35–37, 54, 60–61, 341n55; and Platonism, 61, 157

Apollon, Willy, 358n29

apperceptive unity, 41–42, 81, 194, 196.
   See also judgment, determinative

Arguments within English Marxism
   (Anderson, P.), 14

Aristophanes, 121, 349n11

Aristotle, 43, 50, 256, 337n20, 351n38;
   on division, 144–45, 352n42; and
   Platonism, 136–41

art: in ancient Greece, 92, 113, 136–37;
   and life 38, 65, 306–7; and the nomad,
   216; of philosophy, 30, 54; and philosophy and science, 49, 256–57, 258,
   261, 318–19, 356n1; in Platonism 133,
   140, 160–68, 354n66; in romanticism,
   90–94. *See also specific arts*

Artaud, Antonin, 7, 206

ascent, 143, 157, 350n16, 353n57. *See also*
   Platonic judgment

ascesis, 82, 233, 237, 310

assemblage, 198–99, 201, 232–34, 323;
   asignifying, 69; machinic, 69, 217,
   240, 323; of philosophy and literature,
   xx, 5, 185, 216–17. *See also* collective
   assemblage of enunciation

Athens: agonism in, 98, 110, 113, 119,
   131–32, 278; architecture in, 106;
   and autochthony, 101–14, 118, 120,
   152–55, 226; funeral orations (see
   epitaphios); geography of, 96–97, 98;
   modern invocation of, 280; political system (*see under* democracy);
   signular traits of (*see* indicies of
   philosophy)

au milieu, xvii, 13, 52, 340n43

Aubral, François, and Xavir Delacourt,
   367n41

Auden, W. H., 1

Auerbach, Erich, 150–51, 353n54

Aufhebung, 126, 323

Austen, Jane, 219–22, 361n71; *Emma*,
   221–22, 361n72

Austin, J. L., 200

author: in Foucault, 333n18; -function,
   203, 250–51, 333n18; the New Philosophers as, 250–52; and paternity,
   339n39; perversion of, 43–44, 65–66;
   and the state, 203, 228, 237; versus the
   writer, 4, 65–66, 216–17, 228

autocatalyis, 227, 272–73

autochthony: in Athens, 102–8, 109–10,
   111–14, 152–53, 226, 347n47, 349n8;
   as basis for philosophy, 16, 111–14,
   118–20, 152–55, 278–79; in German
   romanticism, 94; myth of, 10, 16, 81,
   101, 106

l'autrui. See Other

Badiou, Alain, 18, 64, 144, 175–80,
   352n47, 355n85, 355–56n91; *Deleuze:
   The Clamor of Being*, 14, 132,
   355nn88–89

bal(l)ade, 71

baroque, 9, 116, 268–69, 314

Barthes, Roland, 332n6, 365–66n30

Bataille, Georges, 14, 38, 330n17

Battlestar Galactica (television series),
   321

Baudrillard, Jean, 348–49n2, 361n81,
   365–66n30

beautiful, the, 52–54, 195, 297, 322–23

Beckett, Samuel, 205, 222

becoming, xvii–xviii, xx; of being, xviii,
   170–73, 226, 233–34, 304–5, 310–11,
   331n22; of Crusoe, 87, 89; Deleuze's
   13, 42, 52, 225–26, 239, 305, 318; as
   demonism, 226; in Heraclitus, 130; in
   Kafka, 212, 223–26, 232; of a life, xx, 6,

212, 223, 224–26, 239, 271, 304, 309; in May '68, 287–88; and Nitezsche, 44, 65, 239, 331n22, 339n39; as opposed to history, 94; in Platonism, 162, 169–71; of the schizo, 70, 342n65; and writing 3, 6–7, 18, 217, 20, 44, 62, 65, 212, 214, 217, 223–26, 232

becoming-animal, 177, 223–26, 337n14

becoming-imperceptible, 42, 171, 211–12, 217, 224, 234, 247, 293, 309

becoming-impersonal, 41–42, 212, 232–34, 241, 247,

becoming-literary, xx, 185

becoming-minor, 206, 208–9, 229–30

becoming-strange, 197, 209

becoming-woman, 43

beginning: 12, 46, 51–52, 74–75, 77, 78, 319; as a problem for philosophy, 62, 187. *See also* origin

Being: destruction of, 4, 31, 171–75, 302, 304–5, 310–11, 313–14, 331n22; in Husserl, 255; lack of, 214; in Platonism, 132, 133, 161, 165, 170, 171–75, 177–80, 351n32, 354n62; in the Presocratics, 132, 170, 177–78; of the sensible, 184, 297, 301, 317, 332n15; traditional concept of, xviii, 2, 28, 173, 304–5, 310–11, 313–14; and univocity, 177–78, 233–34, 362n92. *See also* nonbeing; ontology

Belinda (Edgeworth), 217

Benardete, Seth, 146, 159

Benveniste, Emile, 230–31, 362n85

Bergerson, Danille, 358n29

Bergson, Henri: and images, 296; influence on Deleuze, 12, 39, 116, 176, 245, 255; unassimilability of, 185–86

Between, method of. *See* And, method of; interval

Bildungsroman, 9, 237. *See also* novel

birth. *See* autochthony; *eugenia*

Blanchot, Maurice, xvii, 35, 224, 314, 330n17

Blood, Benjamin Paul: "The Anaesthetic Revelation," 300–301

body: determination of, 56–57, 200–201, 215, 283–84; in modernity, 59, 64; in old age, 239–41; paralysis of, 320–21; in Platonism, 123; -politic 104, 201–2, 284; and writing, 71, 198, 211–12, 219–20, 234, 242–43, 335n2

body without organs, 64, 88–89, 309, 310, 342n65

Bogue, Ronald, 210, 333n19, 356n1

Bonta, Mark, and John Protevi, 369n73

book, 55, 198–99, 214, apocalyptic, 302, 306, 314; form, 203, 208, 216; great, 204, 236, 332n9; and the New Philosophers, 248, 251, 252, 365n29; revolutionary, 55, 236

Borges, Jorge Luis, 146, 148, 268–70, 370n77; "Death and the Compass," 146, 148; "The Garden of the Forking Paths," 160, 269; "The Library of Babel," 10, 333–34n23

Bosquet, Joe, 243

Bourdieu, Pierre, 23

Boy and His Dog, A (film) 319

Boys from Brazil, The (film), 309

Bradbury, Ray, 299

brain, 239–40, 257–58, 315, 318

Braudel, Fernand; on ancient Greece, 96–99, 345–46nn35, 37, 39; on large-scale economic organization, 98, 104, 106, 272, 275–77, 370–71n94

Bréhier, Émile, 95

Brod, Max, 204–5, 239
Brown, Bill, 373n15
Bryden, Mary, 352n48
bureaucracy, 18–19, 58, 60, 191–94,
    202–4, 210, 226
Burney, Frances, 217–20; *Cecelia*, 217–18
Burroughs, William, 185, 201

cadre. *See* frame; screen
Canning, Peter, 344n14, 364n8
Cantin, Lucie, 358n29
capitalism, 273; as flows, 57, 63–64,
    342n65–66; geographic contingen-
    cies of, 273–80, 370–71n94, 371n96;
    and markets, 282, 283–84; Marx on,
    59; modern, 34, 57, 250, 372n111;
    and philosophy, 16–17, 274, 335n37;
    342n66; print, 202; and utopia, 290
Cecelia (Burney), 217–18
chance, 17, 41, 256, 264, 267–70, 288–89,
    291; in geneaology, 77; in the history
    of reason; 343n4; and the Idea, 135;
    in the ideal game, 369–70n76; versus
    fate, 95. *See also* chaos; contingency
Chaoids, 256–57, 318
chaos: daughters of, 256–57, 318; and
    history, 288; and myth, 81, 266; and
    philosophy, 11, 41, 20, 268–70, 288,
    300–301, 367n47, 368n53, 369n73; in
    Platonism, 132, 136, 146, 148, 175,
    183; and romanticism, 94; and sci-
    ence, 256–58, 260–63, 265–71
"chaosmos," 10, 184, 266. *See also* chaos
chaosophy, 261–62, 269
China, 275–77, 370–71n94
Césaire, Aimé, 230
Chernyshevsky, Nikolay, 285
children, 200–201, 209, 213
Chomsky, Noam, 199, 358n30

Christianity, 92–93, 129
Chronos, 20, 293, 372n1
cinema, xx–xxi, 314, 324, 331nn25–26;
    Hollywood, 282; and other arts, 2–3,
    216, 251; and people who are missing,
    227; world as meta-, 9, 296
citizen: Athenian, 104–10, 112–13,
    153–55, 247n60; subject as, 192
city-states: Italian, 96, 277–78, 346n39,
    371n106. *See* Athens; *polei*
Clausewitz, Carl von, 76
Close Encounters of the Third Kind (film),
    316–17
codes, 56–71; and capitalism, 57, 63; and
    earth, 84, 89; in Jameson, 68; and
    life, 56, 57; and literature, 202, 216;
    master, 61; and Nietzsche, 47, 58, 61;
    primtive, 57, 64; and the state, 61, 63.
    See also overcoding
cogitas cogitans, 186
cogito, 2, 4, 27
Cohn, Dorrit, 223
collective assemblage of enunciation:
    in communications society, 246;
    Deleuze's creation of, 19, 23, 190, 225–
    26, 232–34, 310, 363n96; in Fanon,
    230; as interpretation, 44, 225–26; in
    Kafka, 19, 190, 204, 207, 223, 228; in
    literature, 207, 215–19, 221
colonization, 276, 371n96; in ancient
    Greece, 15–16, 113, 278, 346n36–37
commentary: Deleuze's approach to
    Nietzsche, 13, 22–25, 38–39, 42–46, 73;
    Deleuze's approach to Plato, 115–16,
    136, 148, 177–80; Deleuze's method
    of (general), xiv, 17, 22, 37, 42–44, 115,
    151, 175–77, 224–25, 350n20. *See also*
    interpretation

common sense: in Descartes, 2, 187; and
geography, 84–85; and the image of
thought, 2, 184, 186–88, 259–60; in
Kant, 52–53, 185, 193–94; and opinion, 20, 37, 259–61; resistance to, xvi,
37, 53, 184, 293; and science, 261–62,
264; and science fiction, 296; in the
Sophist, 172; and the state-form,
192–94. *See also* good sense
communication, 255–56; age of, 11; and
control, 284–85, 308–9; as a discipline, 19, 245–46; and *doxa*, 183, 259;
philosophy as, 34, 251, 254, 279–81;
universal, 34, 238, 250, 259–60, 280,
282, 291
communications society, 11, 34, 238–39,
246–47, 249, 279–82, 308
communicative rationality, 34, 187, 280
competition. *See* agonism, rivalry
complexity. *See* chaos
composition. *See* plane of composition
"compossible," 269–70, 367n47
le concepteur. See idea man
conceptual persona, 41, 72–73, 184
connectivism: as Deleuze's imperative,
181, 184, 194, 226; horizontal model
of, 100; and language, 214–16; in
schizoanalysis, 65; against transcendence, 269, 310
conscience, xiv, 26, 56, 78, 82, 330n11
consciousness, 25–26, 35, 82, 227, 255;
debt and, 25, 56; history of, xiv, 80,
302; of Truth as a problem, 29–31
consistency: of Deleuze's philosophy,
9, 20–21, 367n44; in Gödel, 266; of
philosophy, 257. *See also* plane of
consistency
contemplation, 114, 253–55

contingency: and capitalism, 273–79,
371n96; in complexity, 267–69; and
encounter, 6; of geography, 15–17,
94–95, 106, 118, 276–79; of nature,
244; in Proust, 2, 6; and reception, xvi
contrapposto, 167. *See* sculpture; simulacrum
control society, xviii, 11, 57, 183, 246,
282–84, 308
Copernican "revolution," 87–88, 298
copy: Deleuze's critique of, 61, 116–17,
165–67, 168, 170–73, 310–14; in Plato,
17, 132–33, 142–43, 162–64, 348–49n2,
351n32; sophist as, 121, 173; without a
model, 117, 166, 173, 310–11, 313. *See
also* mimesis; simulacrum
cosmogony, 266, 369n70
cosmology: and complexity, 266, 270;
Deleuze's, 9, 367n47, 368n51; Greek,
130–31, 369n70
cosmos. *See* cosmology; universe
Cosmos (Gombrowicz), 6, 184
counter-philosophy, xvi, 47–48, 61
counter-utilization, 128, 156, 309, 351n26
creationism, xix, 23, 234–35
crible, 257–58
critique: and *Anti-Oedipus*, 68; in
Deleuze xviii; in Kant, 28, 75, 76, 187,
193–97, 255, 297–98, 322, 337n13;
of modernity, 55, 58–59, 60–61; in
Nietzsche, xiii, xvi, xviii, xix, 23–25, 27,
73–76, 78, 82–83, 337n13, 357n19; of
Truth, xiii, 28. *See also* geneaology
"crowned anarchy," 168, 178, 183, 268
Crusoe, myth of, 85–87

daughters of chaos, 256–57, 318
David (Michelangelo), 166–67
Davies, J. K., 348n70

de Romilly, Jacqueline, 349n8
death of the father, 45–46, 66, 69–70, 73, 165, 214, 343n80. *See also* foreclosure
death of God, 32, 45, 73, 88, 302–3, 355–56n91. *See also* God
Debray, Régis, 366–67n39
debt: Deleuze's, 9, 51, 73, 116, 245–46; economic, 229, 275; morality and, 25, 56–57
decisionism, 283, 308. *See also* control societies
decoding. *See* codes
Defoe, Daniel, 85–86, 217
dehors. See Outside
Delanda, Manuel, 84, 334–35n21, 369n73, 371n96
Deleuze, Gilles: and Foucault, 39, 286–7; friendship with Nietzsche, xvii, 13–14, 37–39, 46–47, 55, 335n3; friendship with Tournier, 86, 333n21; intellectual development, xvii, 9–10, 22–23, 37–39, 46–47, 61–62, 116, 334n34, 341n56; in old age, 239–40, 246–47, 252–53; and phenomenology, xvii, 58–59; reception of, 10, 11–14, 55, 66–69, 126, 132, 175–80, 228–29, 262, 281–82, 329n3, 354n88–89; shape of philosophy, 9–10
Deleuze, Gilles, and Félix Guattari, 364n20; on Marx, 273; and metaphor, 213–14; and the New Philosophers, 247–49; in old age, 239–40, 244; writing *Anti-Oedipus*, 55–56, 58, 61–62, 69, 175, 214, 341n56; writing *What Is Philosophy?* 239–40, 244, 245, 246–47, 253–54, 273. *See also* Guattari, Félix
Deleuze: The Clamor of Being (Badiou), 14, 132, 355nn88–89
democracy, 34, 189, 279–80, 299; in Athens, 90, 101, 106–7, 109–10, 112–14,

118, 120, 153, 155, 278 (see also *isonomia*; *metics*)
demonism, xv–xvi, 225–26
demos, 103, 106, 109–10, 279, 347n60
Demosthenes, 152
Derrida, Jacques, 7, 330n17, 332n6, 348n1; on friendship, 31, 337n20
Descartes, René, 2, 4, 187, 256, 356
Descombes, Vincent, 64, 335n3
desire: in *Anti-Oedipus*, 55, 57, 63, 66; in critiques of Deleuze, 14; desiring-machine, 66, 344n15; in psychoanalysis, 214
detective fiction, 295, 368n61
determinism, 263, 265–69
deterritorialization: in ancient Greece, 101–4, 111–13; capitalism and, 63, 273–75, 279, 342n64; and geneaology, 82; of the earth (*see under* earth); and language, 207–16, 224–26, 232; and Nietzsche, 15, 66, 74, 304; of philosophy, 15, 41, 63, 66, 88, 119, 154, 173, 174, 213, 237, 242, 290, 296, 302, 309, 310, 317, 320, 348–49n2; schizoanalysis and, 63, 70–71, 82, 344n15; and utopia, 289–90; and writing, xx, 19, 61, 66, 71, 188, 190, 208, 210–13, 224–26, 228, 232
Detienne, Marcel, 102–4, 107, 110, 113–14, 170, 174
dialectic: in *Anti-Oedipus*, 68–69; detection of in Deleuze, 67–68, 176; of enlightenment, xv; in French poststructuralism, 67–68; idealist, 116–17, 126, 322; materialist, 274; in phenomenology, 255; in Plato, 116–17, 127–29, 132–34, 136–50, 156–58, 160, 171–72, 349n12, 350n19, 351n39, 352–53n52, 354n58; of rivals (see *amphisbêtêsis*)

Diamond, Jared, 371n98
Dick, Philip K., 299
Dickens, Charles, 242–43
difference: in Aristotle, 139–40; in
complex systems, 288; Deleuze's
philosophy of, 115–16, 156–57,
176–80, 233–34, 241–42, 296, 301,
302, 304–5, 310–11, 313–14, 357n10;
and evaluation, xix, 79, 82, 124–25,
196, 340n43; and the event, 242; of
the Idea, 116–17, 137, 141, 156; and
intensity, 260, 368n49; ontology of,
233–34; and perception, 367n47; and
plane of immanence, 141, 242, 302,
304, 310, 311; in Plato, 122, 129–38,
141, 143–44, 150, 156–59, 162–63,
164, 170–71, 178–79, 311, 352–53n53;
and representation, 180, 259–60, 314;
sexual, 361n81; in Spinoza, 241–42,
304; and thermodynamics, 264–65
differenciation, 144, 178, 242, 260, 264,
355n89
differentiation, 79, 124–25, 141, 242, 251,
260, 271, 367n47
Diogenes Laertius, 139, 349n12,
351n37
Dionysus, 15, 25, 50, 93, 138
discipline, 81–82, 200, 283
discourse, 230, 362n85
discussion, 251–52
dividual, 284, 308
division: in Aristotle, 137–41, 144–46, 150,
352n42; and chance, 268, 369n76; in
Heraclitus, 130; in Plato, 117, 137–50,
156–57, 160, 162, 163, 171, 352–53n52;
sedentary, 226. See also *amphisbêtêsis*
Donne, John, 216
Dosse, François, 333n21, 334n34; 372n3;
on Deleuze's relationship with Guattari, 341n56, 364n20; on the New
Philosophers, 365n24, 365n26
Dostoyevsky, Fyodor, 188–89
doxa: and chaos, 257–61, 269–70; in the
Greek world, 114, 120, 134, 174–75,
355n79; in phenomenology ("intersubjectively"), 256; as precedent to
philosophy, 16, 101, 108, 110–11,
118–19, 154, 161–62, 174, 179–80,
278–79; as the problem of philosophy,
20, 183, 238, 254, 256, 282; and science, 262–63, 269
dramatization, method of, 80, 133–34,
141–42, 148
dualism: of appearance and essence,
77; in Deleuze, 67–68, 176, 355n88;
Deleuze's critique of, 251; of Idea and
image, 116–17, 133, 162; in Kant, 52,
116; of signifier and signified, 5

earth: born of (*see* autochthony); "deep
time" of, 97; deterritorialization of,
16, 81, 84–87, 88, 89–94, 99–100, 152,
154, 235, 273; and "geology of morals,"
89, 345n24; genealogy of, 80–81; in
German Romanticism, 92–94; in the
Greek world, 16, 81, 92–96, 99–109,
111–13, 118, 151–55, 266; and islands,
84–87; and Kant, 87–88, 298; and
Nietzsche, 71, 80–82, 84, 111; and the
Outside, 90, 92; and a people to come,
235–36; philosophy of (*see* geophilosophy); in schizoanalysis, 57, 63–64,
71, 87, 88, 344n15; and thinking, 15,
73, 89–90, 95–96, 100, 345n25
East, the, 95, 276; ancient empires of, 92,
97–99, 116, 118, 277
education, 200, 283; in ancient Greece,
120, 131, 154–55

ego, 303, 339n39

Eidê, 122, 132–33, 135–36, 183, 254–55; as species, 139. *See also* Idea

eidôla. *See* image

eidôla legomena, 167, 169

eikon, 164–65. *See also* image

Einstein, Albert, 264–65, 269

Eleatic Stranger. *See* Stranger (*Sophist*)

Eliot, T. S., 182

Emma (Austen), 221–22, 361n72

Empedocles, 102

encounter, 45, 111, 182–83, 298, 300; with chaos, 257–58; with Guattari, 9, 245; with the other person, 319–21; between philosopher and philosophy, 113; and the sign, 6–7, 182–84, 300, 317, 232

entropy, 264, 271, 321, 368n60, 368n62. *See also* thermodynamics

Entstehung, 74, 78, 305

enunciation: content of, 350n22; and *doxa*, 259; literary, 232; in the New Philosophers, 250–51; revolutionary, 207; subjects of, 200, 216, 218–19, 233, 363n96. *See also* collective assemblage of enunciation

episteme, 114, 161, 195, 283–84, 295–96

epistemology: in Aristotle, 137; and image of thought, 2; in Kant, 195; modern discipline of, 245, 304; and science, 262; and the state-form, 189; transformation of, 57, 246, 249, 283–86, 296, 330n20

epitaphios, 104, 106–7, 153–54, 169–70

equality, political, 16, 106–10, 118–19, 153–55, 278. See also *isonomia*

equilibrium, 242, 261–62, 265–67, 270–71, 273, 277; centers of, 70, 262; non-equilibrium, 261–62, 271

Erehwon, 293, 372n2. See also *outopos*

Eribon, Didier, 281

eris, 102, 109–10, 113, 130–31, 160, 278. *See also* agonism

essence: Deleuze's response to, 4, 35, 46, 126, 174–75, 340n43; and interpretation, 37; Nietzsche's critique of, 74, 77, 126; in Plato, 133–34, 142, 165, 174–75

eternal return, 296, 331n22

ethics, 244, 316; as discipline, 195, 238, 333n20; of the event, 249; of interpretation, 34

Eudoxus, 2, 186, 188

eugeneia, 104, 151. *See also* autochthony

eulogy. See *epitaphios*

eutopia, 289, 291. *See also* utopia

evaluation, xiii, xviii–xix, 76; in Deleuze, 307; of the earth, 84; and genealogy, xiii, xviii–xix, 76; Nietzsche's formulation, 56, 306–7; of the philosopher, 72; of Platonism, 124, 148, 157

event, 242–44, 246, 257, 267, 271, 272, 287–89, 291, 293; in free-indirect discourse, 218–19, 223; horizon, 135, 293, 373n18; May '68 as, 249–50, 286–89; multiple senses of, 79; in the New Philosophers, 248, 251

exterior. *See* Outside

fabulation. *See* powers of the false

face, 319–21, 323–24

faculty: *concordia facultatum*, 187, 259; of distribution, 259–60, 264; of imagination, 53, 194–96, 322–23; in Kant, 53, 186–87, 194–96, 322–23; of reason, 298, 302; and the state, 189, 192

faiblesse, 239–40, 296

false: and the arts, 5–6; claimant, 106, 127–28, 156–57, 354n58; demonization of, xiv–xv; friends of, 29; images, 121, 143, 171–72, 353n57; making (faire faux), xiii–xxi, 183–84, 316; versus truth, xiii, xviii, 114, 152, 183, 221, 282. *See also* powers of the false

family, 59–60, 63, 68, 206, 224, 299; and autochthony, 107, 155; in "The Metamorphosis," 223–24

Fanon, Frantz, 230

fascism, 366n33; and Nietzsche, 12–13, 33, 38, 46–47, 61, 65. *See also* nonfascist living

fate, 95, 244

Faye, Jean-Pierre, 112

Ferlinghetti, Lawrence, 231, 362n90

Feuerbach, Ludwig, 303

fiction, 4, 82–83, 269, 318; *epitaphios* as, 169; image of thought as, 192; philosophy and, 7–8, 197; and science (*see also* science fiction), 301–2, 307, 318; *A Thousand Plateaus* as, 1; transcendence as, 124

Flaubert, Gustave, 222

Flaxman, Gregory, 356n4

flows, 63–64, 69, 70, 71, 273, 306, 342n64, 342n66; in geophilosophy, 15–16, 84, 89, 277, 279; in Nietzsche, 36, 40

fold, 89–91, 303, 324; of the earth, 89–90, 92; in Foucault, 90–92, 303; of the future, 20

forces: active, 50–51, 52, 74, 124–26, 302; diabolical, 33, 234; in Heraclitus, 113, 130; in Nietzsche, 29, 33, 34–35, 36–40, 46–47, 51–54, 60–61, 65–66, 74–82, 92–93, 126, 130, 295, 303–4; and the Outside, 35–37, 40, 47, 54, 60–61, 71, 78, 90–91, 92, 294–95, 303,

309, 318–19, 324, 338n24; in physics, 265; of production, 89; reactive, 17, 32, 59, 61, 66, 80–82, 92–93, 118, 124–25, 130, 296, 343–44n7; ultimate or final, 34–35, 38, 47, 79; and utopia, 290

foreclosure, 46, 69, 73, 214–16, 232, 316, 355–56n91, 374n21

foreigners. See *metics*

Forms, 132, 183, 255. *See also* Idea

Forster, E. M., 181

Förster-Nietzsche, Elisabeth, 39, 338n29

Foucault, Michel: on the author, 333n18; on Deleuze, 126, 129, 350n21; diagram, 90–92, 200, 283, 349n5; on genealogy, 338n30, 344n12; histories, 196–97, 343n4; "Intellectuals and Power," 286; introduction to *Anti-Oedipus* (*see* nonfascist living); on Man-form, 303–4; and Nietzsche, xvii, 39, 58, 72, 73–74; "Nietzsche, Freud, Marx," 58; on Plato, 127; on truth, 350n22

foundation: in Aristotle, 144; and German philosophy, 94; in Greece, 113; in Nietzsche, 58, 74; of Platonism, 148–51, 157, 168, 352–53n52

fourth person singular. See *l'on*

frame, 35–36, 54, 235, 320–21, 341n55

Frank, Manfred, 175

free-indirect discourse, 40, 217–19, 221–24, 232–33

free-indirect philosophy, 217, 220, 224–26

freedom: and expression, 183; of old age, 244; in phase space, 369n73; in the theory of enlightenment, 299; and writing, 7, 226

Freudianism: in *Anti-Oedipus*, 63–64, 67–70; and modern critique, 58–61; and the modern subject, 303; as opposed to Nietzsche, 15, 23, 55–56, 64, 67–70. *See also* psychoanalysis

Friday (Tournier), 86–87

friendship, 26–27, 29–31, 41–43, 45–46, 279, 337n14. *See also under* Deleuze; *philia*

"On Friendship" (Montaigne), 31, 43

Frye, Northrup, 30

funeral oration. See *epitaphios*

future: Deleuze's philosophy of, 11, 20, 244, 292–96, 302–3, 306, 308, 315, 321–22, 337n21; evacuation of, 315; forces of/and the Outside, 20, 30, 33, 36, 37, 40, 60–61, 71; in Kant, 299; and Nietzsche's reception, xvi, 27, 30–33, 36–37, 40, 337–38n22, 362n82; predicting, 260, 266–67, 269; and science fiction, 292–96, 302–3, 315; and utopia, 285–86, 289–91

gaia, 81. *See also* geophilosophy

game, ideal, 267–68, 369–70n76

"The Garden of the Forking Paths" (Borges), 160, 269

game, ideal, 267–68, 369–70n76

geneaology, 72, 73–80, 82, 84, 87, 105, 338n30, 343n4, 344n12; scientific, 262–63

genius: in ancient Greece, 131; in Kant, 53–54; in Nietzsche, 44, 93; in romanticism, 93; sophist as, 161

genre, 185, 191–92, 295–302, 318

geography, 84, 86–87, 89, 94, 98; and myth, 103, 104

geology, 84, 89

geophilosophy, 15–16, 80–81, 101, 44–45n22; in ancient Greece, 95, 96, 98–103, 106, 108–10, 112–13, 118, 278; and capitalism, 273–74, 276, 278; and China, 275–76; and Foucault, 92, and Kant; 87–88, and Nietzsche, 73–80, 84

Gernet, Louis, 102, 123

Gibson, William, 315, 373n18

Glucksmann, André, 365n24, 365–66n30, 366nn36–37

God, 76, 135, 216, 263–64, 268–69, 296; judgment of, 115, 122, 206; as Truth, xiv, 28. *See also* death of God

Gödel, Kurt, 266, 318, 369n67

Goethe, Johann Wolfgang von, 92, 203, 358–59n35

Gombrowicz, Witold, 6, 184

good sense, 5, 20, 179, 259–60, 262, 264, 293,

good will, 2, 186–87. See also *Eudoxus*

Goodchild, Phlip, 363n3

Gorgias, 349n8, 354n69. *See also under* Plato, works of

gossip, 220–21, 252–53, 360–61n68

Greece, ancient: the arts in, 136–37, 167; *genoi* in, 80, 107; geography of, 97–98, 102–3, 111–12, 274–76, 345–46n35, 346n39, 371n104; city-states of (see *polei*); German reterritorialization of, 92–94; and Foucault, 90, 350n22; and myth, 80–81, 148–49, 225–26, 266; Nietzsche on, xiv, 30, 48–49, 76, 92–94; 130–31, 136–37, 339n39, 345n27; Sparta, 106, 349n8. *See also* Athens

Grosz, Elizabeth, 369n73

ground: deterritorialization of, xiv, xviii, 74, 79, 85–86, 92–93, 151–55, 345n24; of philosophy, xxiv, 2, 8,

92–94, 148–50, 172, 188, 290, 298, 313, 345n24, 352–53n52; in Platonism, 148–50, 156–57, 172, 352–53n52; in romanticism (Grund), 92–94

Grund, 144, 150, 157. See also *Abgrundung*

Guattari, Félix: 245, 364n19; influence on Deleuze, 38, 55, 213–14, 245, 306, 341n56. *See also* Deleuze, Gilles, and Félix Guattari

Haar, Michel, 337–38n22
Habermas, Jürgen, 34, 187, 280
Hallward, Peter, 177, 180
Hawking, Stephen, 265–66
health. See *faiblesse*
Hegel, Georg Wilhelm Friedrich, 14, 68, 117, 126, 183, 323; and Nietzsche, 45, 50, 335n3; three H's, xvii, 58
Heidegger, Martin, 14, 47, 88, 137, 323, 357n16; three H's, xvii, 58
Henri-Lévy, Bernard, 249, 251–52, 365n24, 365n27; 365–66n30
Heraclitus, 17, 102, 112–13, 129–32
Herkunft, 74–76, 78
hermenutics, 36–37, 67, 198, 199; Badiou's use of, 177; Heidegger on, 137; and minor literature, 228; and Nietzsche, 38; "of suscipcion," 199. *See also* interpretation
Herodotus, 105
Hesiod, 81, 130–31; *Theogony*, 266, 369n70
heterogenesis, 136, 198, 222, 226
Hibbard, Howard, 157
high principle. *See* ascent
Hippias, 160–61, 349n8. *See also under* Plato, works of

history: and becoming, 19, 37, 243, 288; in Braudel, 96–99, 275–77, 345n45, 370n94, 371n98, 371n106; and complexity, 272–75; of Deleuze's reception, 12; in Foucault, 283, 304, 338n30; and genealogy, 72–78, 83–84, 338n30, 368n51; and geography, 80, 83–84, 87, 96–98, 345n45, 370n94, 371n98, 371n106; literary, 19, 217; Lukács on, 342n69; of Nietzsche's reception, 33, 35, 37, 38–39, 66–67, 342n69; of philosophy, 22, 42–43, 58, 80, 120, 125, 225, 248, 254–55, 281, 342n69; and revolution, 288; and schizoanalysis, 65–66; of the sciences, 262–63; of theory, 14, 334n26; and utopia, 20, 284, 285, 289–91, 372n115. *See also* universal history
Hochquenhem, Guy, 365–66n30
Hölderlin, Friedrich, 7
Holland, Eugene, 343n79
Homer, 105, 136, 150–51, 353n54, 355n78. See also *Odyssey*
horizontal, 17, 99–101, 118, 122. *See also* plane of immanence
hors cadre. See offscreen; Outside
hospitality. See *meilcs*
Hughes, Robert, and Kathleen Ror Malone, 358n29
Hughs, Joe, 342n68, 367n44
human rights, 250, 279
human sciences, 245, 304, 372n112. *See also* social science
Hume, David, 22–23, 39, 43, 116, 176
Husserl, Edmund, 255; three H's, xvii, 58

"I think". *See* apperceptive unity; *cogito*
id, 62–63

Idea: in Heraclitus: 130–31; immanent, 135–36, 170, 174; in Kafka, 204; in Kant, 18, 135, 255, 322; marketplace of, 18–19, 34, 244, 246–48; and opinion, 258; in Platonism, 17, 114, 117, 119–23, 127–42, 143–44, 148–50, 152, 154, 156–58, 159, 161–67, 168, 170–74, 183–84, 239, 282, 350n14, 352n43; in pragmatism, 333n17; and the state-form, 192

idea man, 18, 246

ideal game, 267–68, 369–70n76

idiocy, 187–88

image: in Balzac, 364n6; in Bergson, 296; -book, 208; of the face, 320–21; in Kant, 322; in Platonism, 117, 121, 123, 128, 132–33, 142–43, 157–58, 161–71, 173–74, 351n32, 354n66, 355n79

image of thought, 1–4, 260–61, 298; Aristotelian versus Platonic, 138, 144; Deleuze's creation of a new, 6, 8, 35, 212; and *doxa*, 20, 182, 215, 256, 260–61, 282, 298; and literature 2–4, 6, 8, 212, 295, 332n8, 333n19; and Nietzsche, xvi; and the Outside, 35; and the state, 19, 192, 194; and style, 212, 295

immanence: 125, 241–42, 255–56; of the cosmos, 266; and evaluation, xviii–xix, 126, 129; in German philosophy, 94; and Ideas, 135; of language, 200, 204; and life, 241–42, 271, 330n8; and ontology, 304; in Platonism, 135, 141, 149; and politics, 204; in schizo-analysis, 69; and the simulacrum, xv; sociability, 16; and transcendence, 17, 94, 118–19, 122–23, 125, 215, 255–56, 329n5. *See also* plane of immanence

imperial state, 99–100, 118, 122–23, 125, 276–77, 278, 342n64; 346n39; 371n96

impersonal. *See* becoming-impersonal; free-indirect discourse

impossibility of writing, 4, 210–11, 227–28

Inception (film), 300

incompossible. *See* compossible

indicies of philosophy (*autochthony, doxa, philia*), 16, 101, 108, 110–11, 114, 118–19, 154, 174, 278

individual. *See* subject

inscription, 25, 56–58, 64, 70, 200, 239, 330n9, 341n58

intellectuals, 285–87, 365n29, 366n31, 366n34, 372n112

"Intellectuals and Power" (Deleuze and Foucault), 286

intensity: and the body without organs, 342n65; and the earth, 89–90; and the face, 320–21; in minor literature, 209–13, 222–23, 235, 363n2, 364n6; and ontogenesis, 135; and the proper name, 215; and the sign, 5, 182–83, 185; and science, 260, 264, 368n49; suppression of, 199, 260, 264, 302; and the writing of philosophy, 23, 35–37, 40–41, 51, 57–58, 60, 69, 71, 185, 213–14, 239–40, 302; zones of, 65

interiority: doubling of the state, 192–93, 203; evacuation of, 216; of a text 37, 54

interpretation, 29–30; of Deleuze's philosophy, 12, 68–70, 177–78, 342n75; Deleuze's procedures for, 29–30, 39–40, 42, 46; in genealogy, 76–79; and literature, 198, 221, 228, 363n2; of Nietzsche's philosophy, 23, 29–30, 33–36, 39–40, 46, 66–67, 84, 340n43. *See also* commentary; misinterpretation

interval, 242–43, 340n43, 363n4; and
Aion, 20; and the method of "And," 65,
198; as reflective judgment, 196. *See
also* heterogenesis
Invasion of the Body Snatchers , The
(film), 311–13
introduction, 62. *See also* beginning
island, 15, 84–85, 345–36n35. *See also*
Crusoe, myth of
isoi. See equality, political; *isonomia*
isonomia, 107–10, 113, 152–53, 278,
347–48nn60–61. *See also* equality,
political

James, William, 333n17
Jameson, Fredric, 67–70, 176, 295, 334n2,
372n11
Jauss, Hans Robert, 356n6
Joyce, James, 222; *Portrait of the Artist as
a Young Man*, 205–6
Judaism, 93, 209–11
judgment: and analogy, 3; to have done
with, 188, 206, 241, 213; in Kant, 52,
88, 193–97, 321–23; in Platonism, 114,
115, 122–23, 183; and the state-form,
192–94; and Truth, xi, 330n11
judgment, aesthetic, 52–53, 194–97,321–22
judgment, determinative, 182, 183–84,
194–97
judgment, reflective. *See* judgment,
aesthetic
jurisprudence, 134–35, 193, 195, 351n33.
See also law; *quid facti; quid juris*

Kafka, Franz, 197, 203–5, 211–13; 222–23,
228, 232; on Goethe, 203, 358–59n35;
and hope for philosophy, 18–19;
influence on Deleuze and Guattari,
4, 7, 184, 190, 197, 205, 222, 332n6;

Kafkaesque, 360n60; life of, 210–11;
metaphor in, 213; and Nietzsche, 207,
239, 363n2; and nonstyle, 364n6; on
writing "The Judgment," 235;
Kafka, Franz, works of: *The Castle*,
232; "A Hunger Artist," 211–12, 224;
"Josephine, the Mouse Singer,"
4; "The Judgment," 234–35; "The
Metamorphosis," 4, 206, 222–24; "In
the Penal Colony," 341n58, 363n2;
"A Report to an Academy," 4; *The
Trial*, 239
Kant, Immanuel: on aesthetics, 52–53;
Copernican turn, 87–88; critique
(*see under* critique); Deleuze's cri-
tique of, 52, 75, 116–17, 135, 357n19;
as Delezue's enemy, 43, 297; and
idealism, 126, 191, 255; and Leibniz,
351n33; and morality, 78; and sci-
ence fiction, 299, 301, 373n5; and
the subject, 88, 307; *See also specific
concepts*
Kant, Immanuel, works of: *Critique of
Judgment*, 52, 194–95, 332; *Critique of
Practical Reason*, 194; *Critique of Pure
Reason*, 88, 194–95, 297–98, 373n5;
"What Is Enlightenment?" 299
Kauffman, Eleanor, 330n17
Kauffman, Stuart, 330n8, 369n71
Kaufman, Philip, 312–13
Kaufmann, Walter, 38
Kerferd, G. B., 350n14
Kierkegaard, Søren, 4, 7, 190
Kirk, G. S., 351n28
Kleist, Heinrich von, 7
Klossowski, Pierre, xvii, 38, 330n17
Kofman, Sarah, xvii, 330n17
kthon, 81. See also geophilosophy

labyrinth, 10, 146, 148, 269–70

Lacan, Jacques: return to Freud, 59; and negation, 361n81; and *Nom-du-Père*, 45, 69–70, 214, 340n42, 343n80, 374n21; and psychosis, 69–70, in relation to Deleuze and Guattari, 69–70, 245, 364n19; 340n42; and the unconscious, 303, 374n21; in Žižek, 14, 362n91

Laclau, Ernesto, and Chantal Mouffe, 362n91

Lambert, Gregg, 329–30n7, 332n5, 334n26, 356n1

language, 197–219, 228–30; as compulsory system, 199–200, 228, 281, 358n27; contrived, 208–9, 359–60n49; as discourse, 230; image of 198, 202, 230; as indirect, 220; within language, 7–8, 40, 224, 232, 332n9, 364n6; paper, 210–11, 222; and the state-form, 189, 191; taking flight, 71; two dimensions of, 170–71. *See also* linguistics; pragmatics

Laplace, Pierre-Simon, 263–65, 269. *See also* physics

Lapoujade, David, 367n43

law: in Athens, 106–7, 109, 153–54, 347n60; of the book, 203; and codes, 58, 60, 191–92; and nature, 130–31, 153, 188, 241, 298, 368n60; in the New Philosophers, 250; and philosophy, 191–92, 302, 351n33; in Platonism, 124, 149; prohibiting images, 173; of science, 263, 265, 268, 288, 298, 368n60, 368n62. *See also* jurisprudence

Lawlor, Leonard, 348n1

Lawrence, D. H., 7

Lecercle, Jean-Jacques, 269–70, 358n23

left, 250, 286, 366n33

legislation, 53, 78, 188, 193, 195

Leibniz, Gottfried, 9, 43, 191, 256, 268–70, 296, 314, 351n33

Lenin, Vladimir Ilyich, 250, 285

Lévêque, Pierre, and Pierre Vidal-Naquet, 348n61

liberalism, 250, 279, 344n11, 370n92

"The Library of Babel" (Borges), 10, 333–34n23

life, xix, 6, 49–50, 56–57, 212, 223, 226, 239–44, 270–72, 306–9, 315–17, 329n4, 330n8, 345n25, 374n21; and art, 49; Greek, 100, 105, 110; and minor literature, 204–5, 206, 212, 224, 228, 331n24–45; nonorganic, 241, 271, 309. *See also* "a life"

lifestyle, 65, 212, 247, 308

line of flight: Deleuze's, xvii, 11, 35–37, 70–71, 172, 234–35, 238–39, 241, 244, 253, 291, 330n16; in "The Metamorphosis", 223–24; Nietzsche's, 35–37, 60–61; and style, 11, 20; in utopia, 291; and writing, 3, 7, 70–71, 185, 234–35

linguistics, 198–200, 230, 245, 358n23, 362n85, 364n19

literature: and athleticism, 240; Deleuze's engagement with, xx–xxi, 1–8, 10–11, 184–85, 232, 331n25, 356n1; as machine, xx, 198; national literature, 18–19, 202–4, 228; as philosophical model, 1–8, 18, 48, 54. *See also* minor literature

logos, 148–49, 354n69; *logos tomeus*, word knife, 144, 352–53n52

Loraux, Nicole, 81, 102, 104, 148, 152–53, 169, 335n35, 349n4, 349n8

Lukács, György, 67, 342n69

Luther, Martin, 202
Lyotard, Jean-François, 10, 237, 333n22
Lysias, 104–5

machine, 40, 44, 227, 244; art as, xx, 5, 19, 48, 184; desiring, 66, 344n15; as ghost, 271; science as, 300; simulacra as, 168. *See also* state machine; war machine; writing machine
macroscopic system, 271–73
Malebranche, Nicolas, 302
Mallarmé, Stéphane, 7
Malraux, André, 96
man: Aristotle on, 144–45, 352n42; Descartes on, 356–57n7; Feuerbach on, 303; Plato on, 139, 351n37
Man-form, 73, 81–82, 87–88, 296, 303–4, 330n9
manqué-à-être, 214. *See also* Lacan
Marchi, Dudley M., 337n19
marketing, 11, 19, 246, 248, 251, 279–80, 282–84, 365n27, 365–66n30, 371n109
marketplace of ideas, 19, 34, 238, 244. See also *agón*
Markov chain, 267
Marx, Karl, 85
Marxism: in *Anti-Oedipus*, 15, 55–56, 58–60, 64, 70, 273, 370n94; as complexity, 273–75; Deleuze's affirmation of, 273; and the dialectic, 117; French reception of, 33, 335n3; Jameson on, 67–68, 70; limits of, 23, 59–61, 66, 370n94; and the *New Philosophers*, 250, 366n34, 366n36
materialism, 9, 117–18, 132, 274
materialist psychiatry, 55, 69
Maxwell's demon, 264–65, 269. *See also* physics

May '68, 9, 14, 20, 38, 63, 249–50; as event, 286–88; "Intellectuals and Power," 286
mechanism. *See* physics
media (mass), 248, 251, 280, 284–85, 367n41
mediation, 68–69, 138, 140–41, 146, 150, 190, 352–53n52
Melville, Herman, xvii, 184, 206
Merleau-Ponty, Maurice, 335n3
Merz, 238, 291
metamorphosis, xviii, 3–4, 29, 32, 46, 52, 138, 162, 309, 357n17; and metaphor, 213–14, 234. *See also under* Kafka, Franz, works of
metaphor, 213–16, 218, 228, 234, 283, 316. *See also* paternal metaphor
metaphysical-moral, 61, 122, 129, 168, 173, 268, 299, 316; in Austen, 222; and genealogy, 76, 79; in Kant, 76, 88, 343n6; in Nietzsche, 25, 27, 28, 29, 83;
metaphysics, xiv, 28, 82, 151, 175, 298, 300; in Nietzsche, 49, 77; and the schizo, 344n15; in science fiction, 299
metics, 16, 104, 109, 112–13, 120, 154, 349n8
Michaux, Henri, 7, 240
Michelangelo, 166–67
micropolitics, 200, 202, 206
middle term. *See* mediation
middle. *See* *au milieu*
Miller, Henry, 7
Miller, Hillis J., 363–64n93
mimesis, 133, 146, 161–63, 168, 176–77, 203, 208. *See also* copy; *phantasm*; simulacrum
Mimesis (Auerbach), 150–51, 353n54
mimêtês. See mimesis

minor literature, 203–18, 222, 227–30, 232–35; as basis for philosophy, 18–19, 190, 214–15, 224–26, 233–34; critique of, 228–29; and fabulation, 4, 207, 216, 227, 234–36; and Joyce, 205–6; and Kafka, 4, 184, 203–5, 206, 207–8, 209–14, 222–24, 232, 234–35; as opposed to minor languages, 208–9

minor philosophy, 11–12, 19, 197, 207, 213–15, 235–36

"Minority Report" (Dick), 299

minorization, 184, 190, 199, 207–9, 229–30

misinterpretation, 29, 40, 69, 70, 79

missing. *See* people who are missing

mnemotechnics, 25, 55, 341n58. *See also* inscription

model: as basis of judgment, 133, 149–50, 156, 163–64; and copy, 61, 128, 163–66, 311–14, 348–49n2; dissolution of, xv, 61, 117, 128, 163–66, 172–73, 348–49n2; of language/linguistics, 198, 215, 358n30; of mathematics, 265; and recognition, 1, 183, 259, 298. *See also* image of thought; original

modernism, 8, 182–83, 222

modernity: and art, 173, 183, 198, 219, 222, 235, 307, 315; and critique, 55–62, 290–91, 311–14; in Foucault, 39, 82, 283; and philosophy, 32–33, 92, 125, 189, 198, 202, 238, 251, 335n37; and the New Philosophers, 248–51; in Nietzsche's philosophy, 32, 82; in relation to the ancients, 93, 274–80, 290, 335n37, 353n54; and representation, 248–51, 302, 311–14; and science, 262; tragic spirit 48, 50

molar, 15, 61, 68, 89, 256, 305

molecular, 68, 256, 305. *See also* difference

Montaigne, Michel de, 31, 43

morality: in Austen, 221–22; of enlightenment, 299; geology of, 89; in Kant, 29, 191, 343n6; Nietzsche's critique of, xv, 25–28, 56, 74–76, 78, 84, 191, 368n51; and sophistry, 164–65; of the state, 191, 197

More, Sir Thomas, 289

Mrs. Dalloway (Woolf), 218

multiplicity: assemblage as, 198, 217; in the diagram of power, 196; and interpretation, 78–79; in minor literature, 204; and n-1, 214, 232–33; in Nietzsche, 190; and *l'on*, 232–33, 310; in Platonism, 148; and the proper name, 215; sophistry and, 160; and unity, 8; and writing, 217

music, 38, 46, 50–51, 90, 93, 241; in "The Metamorphosis," 223

myth: American, 312; cosmos as, 266; Deleuze on, 149–51, 352–3n52; epitaphios as, 169–70; and German Romanticism, 92–93, 103–6; Greek, 81, 225–26; in human nature, 56; and logos, 148–49; modern, 85–86; and philosophy, 95, 102, 108, 159–60; of transcendence, 114, 123–25, 136 149–50, 154–60. *See also* autochthony

n-1, 214, 232–34. *See also* overcoding: dimension

Naas, Michael, 355n78

Nancy, Jean-Luc, 330n17, 332n6

narcissism, 15, 303, 308; in Athens, 104, 106, 153

narrative, 2, 151, 220–23, 237, 353n54; of the cosmos, 266; master, 284–85; and transcoding, 68, 342n75; wandering, 71

nation-state, 202, 279

nationalism, Greek, 103-6

nationalitarianisms, 75, 80

necessity, 6, 94, 244, 268, 273. *See also* contingency

negation: and affirmation, 8, 13, 239; of chaos, 257; in Deleuze's critique of transcendence, 176, 323; Nietzsche on friendship, 31; and nonbeing, 172, 290;and the people who are missing, 361n81; and utopia, 291

negative: and being, 172-73, 290-91; in Hegel, 323; in Jameson, 67; in Plato, 129-30, 172-73

Negri, Toni, 282

Negt, Oskar, 366n34

neoliberalism, 250, 282-83

neurosis, 57, 63, 71, 228, 298-99; universal, 59, 69

Never Let Me Go (film), 309

New Philosophers, 247-53, 280, 365n24-26, 365-66nn30-31, 366n33-34, 366-67n39, 367n41

Newton, Isaac, 263-65, 368n60. *See also* physics

Nietzsche, Friedrich: daimonic instinct: 25-27, 226; on friendship, 31; humor in, 239; on the Greeks (*see under* Greece, ancient); late career, 30, 332n11; nihilism in (*see under* nihilism); and operatic philosophy, 50-51; reception of, xvi-xvii, 12-15, 23, 32-33, 37-39, 46-47, 58-59, 64-65, 66-67, 73, 330n17, 331n18, 334n30, 335n3, 337-38n22, 342n69, 352n43; self-reflection, 48-49,

306-7; sister (*see* Förster-Nietzsche, Elisabeth)

Nietzsche, Friedrich, works of: "Attempt at Self-Criticism," 48-49, 50, 306-7; *Beyond Good and Evil*, 22, 26, 31, 84, 157, 295; *Birth of Tragedy*, 48-49, 50-51, 93, 306, 339n39, 345n27, 363n2; *On the Genealogy of Morals*, 25, 30, 56, 74-76, 83, 84, 330n9, 331n24, 341-42n59, 362n82; *Gay Science*, 303, 339n40; *Thus Spoke Zarathustra*, 48, 50, 58

nihilism: in Deleuze, xix, 59, 67, 83, 175, 237; in Nietzsche, xiv, xix, 32, 175, 249, 287, 291, 316

no-place. See *outopos*

Nom-du-Père, 45, 69-70, 214, 340n42

nom propre, 23-4, 335n2. *See also* proper name

nomadic: distribution, 10, 41-42, 168, 310; *nomos*, 175, 226; philosophy, 197; *sur place*, 212;

nomos, 144, 175, 184, 226, 348n6

non-equilibrium. *See* equilibrium

nonbeing, 10-11, 133, 172-73, 290, 313, 354n62. *See also* simulacrum

nonfascist living, 38, 189, 338n27

nonphilosophy, 2-3, 7, 12, 257, 293

nonstyle, 212-13, 240-41, 244, 247, 309, 360n59, 364n6. *See also* style

Notes from Underground (Dostoyevsky), 188-89

La Nouvelle Alliance (Prigogine and Stengers), 262, 368n54

novel: and Austen, 220-22; as Borges imagines, 269-70; future of, 295-96; history of, 217-18; philosophical, 1-3, 8-9, 357n12. *See also* philosophical novel

object: of an encounter, 6, 182–84,
319–20; in Kant, 53–54, 186–87,
194–96, 256, 322–23, 372n4;
Nietzsche's revision of, 35, 51,
53–54, 78, 340n43; partial, 184;
in Platonism, 133–34, 141, 161,
164–65, 167, 255, 350n22, 354n66;
and subject, 35, 86, 88, 89, 182–83,
186–87, 194–96, 198–99, 215,
224–25, 242, 255–56, 259, 320–23
Odyssey (Homer): philosophy as, 150,
153; scar incident, 150–51, 243,
353n53; suitors, 158–59
offscreen, 36, 54, 320–21, 323
old age, 238–40, 243–44, 253, 291
Olkowski, Dorothea, 369n73
Omega Man (film), 319
"Omnitudo," 178. *See also* One-All;
univocity
l'on, 231–34, 310, 339n34
One-All, 177–78, 180, 234, 310. *See also*
univocity
ontogenesis, 234, 257–58, 305
ontology: in Deleuze's philosophy,
174–75, 176, 178–80, 233–34, 302–5,
310–11, 355–56n91, 369–70n76; and
doxa, 174–75; and myth, 149–50; in
postwar French philosophy, 33. *See
also* being; nonbeing
opera, 50–51
opinion. See *doxa*
Order Out of Chaos (Prigogine and
Stengers), 262
order-words, xx, 199–201, 206, 233, 309,
358n24; and gossip, 221, 360–61n68;
in Prague German, 210
Organs without Bodies (Žižek), 14
origin, 73–79, 94–95, 102–3, 107, 260,
339n39, 344n12

original: and commentary, 38, 176; and
copy 116–17, 121, 128, 161, 163–65,
311–14, 348–49n2, 351n32. *See also*
model
orthodoxy, 59, 258–60, 280–81
Other, 73, 86–87, 89, 319–24
Our Mutual Friend (Dickens), 242–43
outopia, 289. *See also* utopia
outopos, 20, 285, 289, 293
Outside, 35–36, 37, 53–54, 257, 317–21;
and aesthetics, 3–54, 207, 239–40,
309, 317–21, 323–24; in *Anti-Oedipus*,
7; and chaos, 257; and the earth, 92,
98; and Foucault, 35, 90–92, 303; as
the future, 11, 20, 36, 37, 294–95,
309, 317–21; and Kafka, 207; and
Nietzsche, 33, 35–37, 40, 46–47, 60–61,
70, 207, 303, 341n55; and the other
person, 320–22, 323–24
overcoding, 68–70; dimension, 214, 216,
232, 374n21

painting, 54, 251, 334n24, 357n12; and
Platonism, 133, 163–66, 168
Pamela (Richardson), 217
paranoid, 66, 69–70. *See also* psychosis
Paris School, 102
Parmenides, 160, 172, 354n76
Parnet, Claire, 44, 212, 233, 335n2
pars destruens, par construens, xviii, 83,
235
Pascal, Blaise, 316
passage, 6–7, 223–24, 226, 239, 241, 267,
271, 317, as affect, 363n1; from I to he,
230, 232; from myth to reason, 149;
through Nietzsche, 73
paternal metaphor, 45–46, 61, 69–70,
214, 216, 232, 339n39. *See also* Lacan;
signifier

Pattern Recognition (Gibson), 315, 373n18

Patton, Paul, and John Protevi, 332n6

penser autrement. See think otherwise

people to come, 226–28, 230–33, 235

people who are missing, 215, 227, 231–32, 361n81

percept, 51, 183, 185

perception, 165–67, 255, 314, 316; "-image," 321; and represenatation, 254, 298; two kinds, 182. *See also* becoming-imperceptible

Perhaps, philosophers of the dangerous, 22, 26–27, 33

Pericles, 105, 112

Pessoa, Fernando, 7

Peters, F. E., 344n9

"Petition" (Auden), 1

phantasm, 164, 167–68. *See also* simulacrum

phenomenology, 255, 335n3, 367n44; three H's (Hegel, Husserl, Heidegger), xvii, 58

philia: in Athens, 16, 101, 107–11, 114, 278–79; and capitalism, 279; and Deleuze's style, 181. *See also* indicies of philosophy

philosophical novel, 1–3, 8–9, 48, 357n12

physics, 20, 262–65, 270–71, 368n55

plane of composition, 3, 5, 7

plane of consistency, 10, 270, 317–18, 334n25

plane of immanence: in ancient Greece, 17, 92, 98–99, 100–101, 108, 110, 113–14, 118–20, 122–23, 125, 141, 154–55, 274, 277–79, 335n37; Deleuze's population of, 18, 41, 72–73, 176, 267–68, 310 (*see also* conceptual persona); and *doxa*, 238, 254–55; and

the earth, 95, 99–100, 103, 152; and the emergence of modern philosophy, 274–75, 277–79, 335n37; as plane of consistency, 10, 270, 355–56n91; and science fiction, 302, 316–17; in Spinoza, 241–42; and utopia, 291; versus the plane of composition, 7. *See also* immanence

Planet of the Apes (film), 319, 321

Plato, 112, 127

Plato, works of: *Apology*, 336n10; *Euthydemus*, 127; *Gorgias*, 124, 127, 137, 349n11; *Hippias*, 121, 127; *Menexenus*, 101, 106–7, 109, 151, 153–54; *Parmenides*, 134, 354n62; *Phaedrus*, 115, 123, 142, 149, 156–57; *Philebus*, 134, 354n74; *Philosopher*, 159; *Protagoras*, 121, 127; *Republic*, 133, 134, 154–55, 161, 162, 165–66; *Sophist*, 17–18, 117, 127, 132, 134, 139–40, 144, 146, 156–65, 171–72, 174, 178–79, 351n35–36, 352n49, 354n76; *Statesman*, 142, 149, 156–57, 159; *Theaetetus*, 115, 159; *Timaeus*, 132

Platonism: history of, 102, 115, 119–20, 127, 148–49, 167, 254–55, 348–49n2, 349n11; neo-, 142; reception of, 14, 18, 126, 132, 137–38, 139–40, 176–80, 281, 348n1

Poe, Edgar Allan, 139–40; "Diddling," 351n37; "The Murder of Marie Roget," 263, 368n61

polei: and geography, 16, 98, 100, 106, 276–78; and geophilosophy, 100–101, 106–8, 109–13, 120, 131. *See also* Athens

Pollack, Jackson, 10, 334n24

Porphyrian Tree, 144–45

Portrait of the Artist as a Young Man
(Joyce), 205–6
postcolonialism, 206, 230. *See also* colonization
posthumanism, 15, 32, 309
postmodernism, 11, 67, 284–85, 348–49n2
poststructuralism, xvii, 361n81; and Nietzsche, 14, 32, 67, 333n18, 334n30, 335n5
Pound, Ezra, 8
power: bio-, 247, 274, 370n91; diagram of, 196–97; in Foucault, 197, 200, 283, 286, 349n5; history of, 283–85; and the intellectual, 286, 289, 308; of judgment, 194–95, 196; in Kant, 194–95, 196, 197, 322–24, 357n21; of language, 199–203, 206, 214, 229, 232, 234–36, 281, 358n30; and life, 239, 241; in the New Philosophers, 250, 365n24, 365n26; political, 193–94; of representation, 189; of sci-phi, 297; in the sublime, 323, 325; of utopia, 285, 289–90. *See also* will to power
powers of the false, xiii–xxi, 8, 11, 18, 29–30, 117, 168, 183, 239, 292, 295–96, 316; and the aphorism, 61; and the arts, 5–6, 18, 183–85, 204, 234–35, 295–96, 301; of being, 179; and interpretation, 29–30, 117; and Kant, 53; of a people, 234–35; and Plato, 18, 169; in Platonism, 18, 121, 169, 171–72, 180. *See also* false
pragmatics, 198–99, 201
pragmatism, 280, 333n17
Pre-Socratics, 123, 132, 135–36, 177. *See also* Heraclitus
present: resistance to, 37, 281, 285, 289
pretendre, 29, 142

Prigogine, Ilya, 270–72, 288, 368n60. *See also* Prigogine, Ilya, and Isabelle Stengers
Prigogine, Ilya, and Isabelle Stengers, 262–65, 266–6, 368n53, 368n55; *La Nouvelle Alliance*, 262, 368n54; *Order out of Chaos*, 262
Prince, Gerald, 360n62, 360n66
principle d'en haut. See ascent
prison, 196, 200, 213, 283–84
probability, 260–61, 263–64, 266–67, 269
proper name, 23–24, 215, 335n2
Protagoras, 137, 159, 349n8, 350n13
Protevi, John, 332n6, 369n73
Proust, Marcel, 332n6, 332n9, 360n59, 364n6; *A la recherche du temps perdu*, 2, 184
psychoanalysis, 55, 59–60, 63–64, 67–69, 81, 245, 362n91. See also Freudianism; Lacan
psychosis, 69–70, 343n81, 358n29
public sphere, 34, 279–80. See also *agora*
Pynchon, Thomas, 359–60n49

quid facti, 134, 183, 245
quid juris, 134, 183

Rancière, Jacques, 366–67n39
Rand, Ayn, 3
real: as basis for judgment, 114, 155, 162; claimant, 17, 114, 128, 143, 149; in Heraclitus, 130; in literature, 213, 216, 289; and the possible, 35, 321; in pragmatism, 333n17; sophist, 160, 165, 167, 168–70, 312; as unreal, 133, 157, 161, 165, 167, 171, 289, 300, 361; of the will to power, 80; world, xv, xviii, 114, 168, 169, 235, 289, 296

reality of the real, 24, 52, 71, 194, 242, 296, 300, 305, 307, 317, 321, 323

reason: Aristotelian versus Platonic, 139–40; contingent, 95, 275, 279; Foucault's history of, 343n4; in Kant, 76, 88, 192–95, 198, 298–99, 322–23, 343–44n6–7; in Platonism, 126, 138, 141, 145–46, 149, 158; reasonless, 2, 116, 305; sufficient, 268, 302–3

recognition, 182–84, 259, 298, 357n18.
See also *anagnorisis*

reflection, 182, 195, 203, 252, 254–55

religion, 63, 100, 118, 135, 191, 316. *See also* Christianity; wisdom: as religion

representation: in Aristotle, 137, 141; and common sense, 186, 189–90, 193, 258, 296, 297, 366n38, 372n4; Deleuze's transformation of, 52, 54, 57, 61, 117, 131, 134–35, 167, 173, 190, 197, 236, 234–35, 293, 296, 300–302, 311–14, 348–49n2; of the event, 288, 293; and Kant, 135, 193–94, 197, 255, 297–99, 322–23, 357n21; and literature, 1, 3, 183–84, 190, 197, 199, 219, 234, 236; and Nietzsche, 1, 52, 54, 57, 131, 157, 293, 319; in Plato, 125, 129–30, 134–35, 141, 144–45, 162, 167, 173; and psychcoanalysis, 45, 361n81; and science fiction, 296–300, 309, 311–15; and the state, 61, 189–90, 193, 197, 366n38; and "will to truth", xiv, xv. *See also* recognition

resistance, 61, 77; to the present, 37, 281, 285, 289

Rimbaud, Arthur, 7

rivalry: in ancient Greece, 92, 98, 131–32; in Athens, 16, 119–20, 131, 153; as basis for philosophy, 2, 6, 73, 92, 179–80, 278–81; in capitalism, 284;

and friendship, 16, 109–10; in Heraclitus, 92, 113, 131; in minor literature, 204; to philosophy, 2, 6, 19, 238–39, 245–46, 248, 281; in Platonism, 114, 115, 136–37, 142–43, 148, 159, 174–75, 238, 254, 278–80, 371n108; in the Odyssey, 159. See also *amphisbêtêsis*; *agôn*; friendship

Robertson, Ritchie, 359n36

Robinson Crusoe (Defoe), 85–86, 217

Romanticism, 50, 90, 92, 94, 106, 183, 208, 287, 307

Rosen, Stanley, 138, 158

Rossellini, Roberto, 196

Sallis, John, 350n17

schema. *See* sensory-motor schema

schematism, 41, 146, 184, 301, 322. See also Kant

Schiffer, Danielle Salvatore, 365n24

schizo, 63–65, 69–71; history, 66

schizoanalysis: and capitalism, 59–60, 63–64, 342n64; as extra-human, 82; Jameson's critique of, 67–68; and Nietzsche, 15, 55–58, 59, 65; as a response to May 1968, 249–50; versus psychoanalysis, 60–70, 214; and writing, xiv, 55–58, 64, 65, 71

schizophrenia. *See* pyschosis; schizophrenic

schizophrenic, 63–65, 69–71, 201–2

Schlegel, Karl Wilhelm Friedrich, 307

Schopenhauer, Arthur, 46, 93

Schrift, Alan, 14, 46, 334n30, 335n5

Schrödinger, Erwin, 270–71, 370n2

Schwab, Gabrielle, 332n6

sci-phi, 296–97, 300–304, 306–7, 309–11, 313–18, 324

science: and art and philosophy, 49, 256–57, 258, 261, 318–19, 356n1; and chaos, 261–63, 266–68, 270–72; gay 26–27, 76; and philosophy, 238, 261, 267–68, 306–7, 317, 321, 344n21; of the sensible, 6, 297, 301, 317; as the True World, xv. *See also* physics; *Wissenschaft*

science fiction: as diagnosis of the present, 315–16; and extinction, 82–83, 85, 311–12, 372n111; and Kant, 297, 99, 321–23; as a mode of philosophy, 20, 295–97, 300–302, 308–11, 316–19, 319–24; and the regime of representation, 298–300, 311–12

screen, 257–58

sculpture, 163, 165–66, 168

sedentary: *nomos*, xviii, 144, 175; organization, 3, 184, 191, 197, 204, 224, 275

selection: of forces and powers, xix, 50, 184; in Platonism, 142–43, 146–49, 154, 157, 171, 184; random, 267; in science, 262

sēma, 45, 303, 373n14

semblance. See *phantasma*; simulacrum

sensibilia, 18, 23, 35, 48, 51

sensory-motor schema, xx, 363n4

series: nomadic, 175; in the Platonic dialectic, 144–46; semi-aleatory, 267–69, 369–70n76; thermodynamic, 264

Serres, Michel, 331n19

Sidney, Philip, 372n11

Siegel, Don, 312

sign: and art, xx, 48, 356n4; as encounter, 182–83, 317; in science fiction, 300, 302, 317; as sensible aggregate, 5–6, 182–84; taxonomy of, xx. See also *sēma*

signifier: displacement of, xvii, 35, 54, 63, 69, 198, 204, 216, 245–46, 309, 315, 355n85; foreclosure of, 69, 214, 216; hidden, 222; master, 69, 204, 214, 245, 340n42, 362n91; of state, 213, 357n17; subject of, 198, 213; and the unconscious, 63, 214, 245, 340n42, 373n14

Simmel, Georg, 220

simulacrum, 117, 163–72, 310–11; according to Badiou, 178–79; in Baudrillard, 348–49n2; in contemporary theory, 129, 348–49n2; demise of, 19, 311–14; as method of overturning Platonism, 18, 61, 117, 127–29, 157, 172–75, 179–80, 348n1; in Nietzsche, 61, 157; Plato's reponse to, 127, 128, 142; and the power of the false, 10–11, 61;

Sleeper (film), 309

Smith, Daniel W., 352n45, n48, 353n57, 356n1

Smollin, Lee, 369n71

social science, 238, 245, 372n112. See also human sciences

society. *See* communications society; control society

socius: deterritorialization of, 16, 57, 63, 89, 273; primitive, 88; reterritorialization of, 57, 96

Socrates, 120–21, 124–25, 140, 158–60, 182, 280, 349n11, 350n19, 371n108; in *Gorgias*, 124–25; death of, 336n10; in *Menexenus*, 106–7, 109, 153–54, 170 (see also *epitaphios*); Nietzsche on, 25–26, 126, 128; in *Parmenides*, 354n62; in *Phaedrus*, 123; and Protagoras, 350n13; in the *Republic*, 133, 154–55, 162, 165–66

Solaris (film), 300

Solzhenitsyn, Alexandr, 366n33

sophist: Deleuze's procedures for, 10–11, 17–18, 122, 126–29, 131–36, 138, 165, 171–75, 176–80, 238, 254, 281, 354n58, 355n79; historical background for, 120–21, 127, 131–32, 169–70, 174, 349n8, 349n12, 350n13, 350n22; in Nietzsche, 131, 137, 157; Plato's battle against, 17, 116–17, 120–21, 124, 126–28, 131, 132–34, 137, 146–47, 156–67, 168–74, 183, 238, 254, 281, 350n14, 350n19, 350n22, 354n58. *See also under* Plato, works of

"A Sound of Thunder" (Bradbury), 299

Soviet Union, 229, 250, 359–60n49, 366n33

soyez sage, 26, 200

species, 138–42, 144–46, 233–34

speech act, 199–200, 221, 230, 358n24

Spinoza, Baruch, 9, 12, 22, 39, 43, 190, 241–42, 304, 335n2

Spivak, Gayatri Chakravorty, 251

Spivak, Gayatri Chakravorty, and Michael Ryan, 365n27

spoken image, 167, 169

Star Trek (television series), 299

state-apparatus book, 202–4, 216. *See also* book: great

state (form), 59–61, 189–93, 197; capitalist, 342n66, in Freud, 59–60; and literature, 202–3, 216, 228, 237; in Marx, 59–60. *See also* imperial state

state (physics), 263, 267–68

state machine, 61, 63, 200; "administrative" machine, 192, 197; capitalism, 273, 283, 342n64

Stengers, Isabelle. *See* Prigogine, Ilya, and Isabelle Stengers

Stivale, Charles, 332n5, 333n19, 363n2

Stranger (*Sophist*), 17–18, 156, 157, 158, 159–66, 168, 171–72, 178–79

stranger: in one's own language, 205, 207, 211; to oneself, 27, 81–82, 197; philosopher as, xiv, 16, 112–13, 317; in romanticism, 94. *See also metics*

structuralism, 5, 14, 63, 102, 245–46, 361n81. *See also* signifier

structure: ecomonic, 55; dissipative, 20, 267; linguistic, 63, 198–99, 209, 213, 245–46, 343n80

style: Deleuze's, xiii, xxi, 7–8, 10–13, 18–19, 20–21, 23–24, 34, 42, 56, 61–62, 177, 181, 185, 197, 213–14, 233–34, 237, 240–41, 247, 293–94, 300–301, 308–10, 314–15, 319, 323, 333n19, 341n56; Goethe's, 203, 358–59n35; Kafka's 18–19, 211–13, 222, 364n6; and life, xix, 69–70, 211–12, 240–41, 247, 307, 308–9, 315; neurotic, 308; Nietzsche's, xiii, xix, 13, 23–24, 28–29, 33–35, 47–48, 50–51, 54, 56, 58, 66, 306–7, 319; paranoid, 70; in philosophy, 35, 51, 186–87, 193, 294, 307; Plato's, 131, 141; as politics, 56, 226, 230, 234–36; "of psychosis," 69–70; and the state-form, 189–91

subject: of aesthetic judgment, 196; of control, 57, 246, 308; Deleueze's transformation of, 216, 224–25, 228, 233–34, 309, 319–20; of enunciation, 200, 216, 218–19, 224, 230, 233, 259; history of, 254–56; Kantian, 88, 307; Nietzschean, 65; and object, 35, 53, 86, 88–89, 182, 198, 215, 224, 242, 256; in relation to the earth, 87, 89; of representation, 189, 259, 298, 372n4; in romanticism, 94; of the signifier, sublime, the, 8, 70, 315, 319, 322–23, 356n4

substance, 77–78, 180, 144–45, 241–43, 256, 302–4, 329n5, 355–56n91
superior empiricism. *See* transcendental empiricism
sur place, 212, 295
suspicion, 59, 199; Nietzsche's, 26, 46, 226
Suvin, Darko, 373n9
syllogism, 139–41, 352n42
syntax: creation of a new, 208–10, 214–15, 314; and free-indirect discourse, 219; in minor literature, 203–14, 209–10, 309, 360n59; of philosophy, 8, 91, 214–15, 314; as politics, 230; in traditional linguistics, 199, 201
synthesis, 65–66, 79, 198, 260, 297–98, 352n43, 372n4; Deleuze's three syntheses, 65, 342n68
system, macroscopic, 271–73

Tarifa, Fatos, 365–66nn30–31
taste: and creation of concepts, 8, 50, 182, 215; good and bad, 221–22, 254; judgments of, 52, 195–96; in Nietzsche, 49–50, 124, 254; for opinion (*doxa*), 101, 279, 366–67n39; perverse, 23–24, 58–59
technology, 57, 206, 247, 283, 301, 309, 371n96, 373n18
territorialization, 57, 86, 88–89, 226
territory, 3, 103, 106, 118. *See also* imperial state
Theaetetus, 160, 162, 163–64, 354n63. *See also under* Plato, works of
theater, 2–3; "philosophical," 51. *See also* warrior theater
thermodynamics, 20, 262–65, 271, 277, 368n62
Theogony (Hesiod), 266, 369n70
They Live (film), 319

"think otherwise," xiv, 4, 26, 292, 296; and art, 5, 184–85; in *The Birth of Tragedy*, 49; and chaos, 258, 261; and utopia, 20
third person, 217–18, 222–23, 230–32
third world, 229–30
thought: in the age of communications, 238, 246–50, 52, 256–59, 284; in the city, 113; as combat, 17–18, 119; and the earth, 73, 80–81, 86–89, 95; in Foucault, 90–91; and friendship, 24–25, 41–42; in Heidegger, 47, 323; without an image, 1–2, 6, 9, 35–37, 47, 60–61, 85, 135, 182, 185–88 (*see also* Outside); and living, xix, 53–53, 240, 242; in Nietzsche, xx, 13–14, 24–25, 35–37, 47–48, 51–54, 56–58, 60–61, 68, 73, 80–81; partitioning of, 5, 257; in phenomenology, 255; as a problem, 4, 21, 47, 187, 356–57n7; and the schizo, 69–70, 73; and the state-form, 58, 189, 192–93; and writing, xv, 4, 6, 13, 19–20, 24–25, 35–37, 47–48, 51, 58, 60–61, 117, 295–96, 314–15. *See also* image of thought; think otherwise
Thucydides, 98, 103, 346n36
timai, 103, 225–26
time: and autochthony, 105, 169–70; and becoming, 36–37, 78, 242–43, 269, 293 (*see also* event); in Borges, 268–69; in the cinema, xx; and classical physics, 263, 269, 368n60; and complexity, 267–70; and *doxa*, 114, 260; geological, 73, 82, 89, 86, 97, 273, 303; and good sense, 259–60, 264; in Kant, 296–97; and marketing, 248, 253, 284; in Nietzsche, 27, 36–37, 78, 243, 291, 293–96, 303, 343n4; and physics, 265–66, 271; in Plato, 351n32, 372n4;

and science fiction, 293–96, 300;
and thermodynamics, 263–64, 269,
368n62; and utopia, 20, 264, 289–91;
and the virtual, 242–43, 269, 291, 293.
See also untimely

to mê on. See nonbeing

to on. See Being

Todd, Janet, 360n67

Tolstoy, Leo, 285

Tom Jones (Fielding), 217

topography, 100, 229. *See also* geography

topology, 9, 90–91, 229, 318; versus typology, 338n24

topos, 100, 106, 112–13, 285, 289;
aistêthos, 100; *noêtos,* 100, 108, 113,
136; versus *typos,* 112

Tournier, Michel, 185, 333n21; *Friday,*
86–87

transcendence: Christain, 92; conceptual
history, 254–56; of God, Man, and
World, 304, 329n5; in imperial forms,
99, 118, 123, 276–77; in Plato, 114,
115, 117–19, 122–26, 130, 134, 143,
154–57, 176, 238, 354n75; in Spinoza,
241, 304; and *Urdoxa,* 255, 269

transcendental empiricism, 194, 297,
300 302, 310, 315, 317

transcendental idealism, 76, 126, 193–94,
255, 297, 300–301

transcoding, 67–69. *See also* codes

transvaluation, xix, 20. *See also* geneaology

Tree, Porphyrian, 144–45

trinity of Marz, Nietzsche, Freud, 58–62

truth: creation of, xiv, xvi, xviii, 8, 11, 261,
316, 333n17; critique of, xiii–xx, 8,
27–31, 73–75, 79, 83, 117, 344n12; and
the intellectual, 286; and interpretation, 29–30, 36; in Leibniz, 261, 268;

masters of (in ancient Greece), 110,
121, 174; in Nietzsche, xiii–xx, 27–31,
73–79, 83; in Plato, 102, 122, 127–28,
155–57, 162–63, 168–69, 174, 350n14,
350n22; in pragmatism, 333n17; subject of, xv; and *Urdoxa,* 259; as value,
27–29. *See also* will to truth

2001: A Space Odyssey (film), 300

typology, 75, 125, 184, 338n24 . *See also*
topology

uncoding, 60–61, 64, 70. *See also* codes

unconscious: in Jameson, 67–68; in
psychoanalysis, 59, 63, 214, 303,
362n91; in schizoanalysis (machinic),
63

ungrounding, 151–55, 156–57, 172, 174,
179, 290, 313

United States of America, 70, 193, 272,
280, 312

universal: communication (*see under*
communication); in Kant, 88, 255,
297–98; knowledge, 188, 190, 259–60;
and language, 198–99, 209; -mind, 2;
in Plato, 114; and the schizo, 65; and
the state, 34, 192–93, 282; subject, 63,
188, 190, 259–60

universal history, 4, 16–17, 95, 273–74

universe: 262–66, 269, 271, 368n55,
368n60; in Bergson, 296; in Nietzsche,
83–84; in Plato, 351n32; and representation, 173, 259, 298–99

univocity, 178–80, 233–34, 310–11,
356n92

untimely: event as, 243; and the Outside,
78; philosophy as, 247, 293–94;
Nietzsche as, 27, 37, 61; utopia and,
20, 290–91, 293–94

Urdoxa, 20, 254, 256, 260, 262, 269, 282. *See also* image of thought; orthodoxy

Ursprung, 74–75, 78

Urstaat, 99–100, 276–77. *See also* imperial state

USSR. *See* Soviet Union

utopia, 11, 170, 203, 281, 284–91, 293, 372n115

value, xix, 25–28, 32–33, 76–79, 82–83, 226; in French philosophy of the 1950s, 33; traditional or "family", 299–300; use-value (of art), 133, 161; and utopia 286–87

Vernant, Jean-Pierre, 100, 102, 108–10, 119, 161–62, 174, 347–48n60–61

vertical, 17, 99, 118, 122. *See also* imperial state

Vidal-Naquet, Pierre, 102, 118, 148

virtual reality, 216, 242, 321

vis elastica, xvii, 241–42, 271, 364n7

vitalism: of Deleuze's philosophy, xvii, 241, 270, 309; and writing, 212, 222, 241, 357n12

Wagenbach, Klaus, 210

Wagner, Richard, 46, 50–51, 93

Wahl, Jean, xvii, 38

Wallerstein, Immaneul, 272–73

war machine, 76, 179, 213, 245

warrior theater, 109–10, 119–22, 125, 131; literary, 204

Weir, Peter, 152

West, the, 92, 95, 229, 276–77, 283, 308

White, Hayden, 286, 372n112

Whitehead, Alfred North, 292

Widder, Nathan, 178, 351n38

will to power, xiii, 39, 51–52, 74, 79–80, 82

will to truth, xiv, 30–31, 83, 125, 186–87, 329n4

Williams, James, 367n48

Williamson, George, 93

wisdom, 24–25, 27, 121, 238; philosopher as a friend to, 24, 119–20, 121; Platonic, 122, 123; as religion, 99–100, 118; unwise, 25, 26–27, 28, 29

Wissenschaft, xiv, 49–50, 307, 317

Woolf, Virginia, 222; *Mrs. Dalloway*, 218

world: ancient (*see* Greece, ancient), 15–16; before man, 96, 316–17; belief in, xv, 285–86, 306; conspiracy, 196; destruction of, 302–4, 306, 311, 313, 315, 329n5; external, 5, 35, 53, 324; fabulation of, xiv, xviii, 70, 85–86, 117, 223, 235–36, 290–91; internal, 35, 324; multiplicity of, 9–10; myth of, 132; in the New Philosophers, 250; in phenomenology, 255–56; possible, 9, 10, 20, 117, 268–70, 272, 290, 300, 320–21, 323; True, xiii–xv, xviii, 29, 83, 298, 330n11; without others, 73, 81–82, 86–87. See also third world

writing: and authorship, 216, 333n18; and becoming, 3–4, 6–7, 18, 70–71, 197, 206, 216, 224, 310, 317–18; Deleuze's, 7, 11, 13–14, 43, 55, 62–63, 70–72, 207, 224–26, 306, 310, 314–15, 317–18, 324, 331n19, 332n6; and the future, 295–96, 314–15, 317–18, 324; Kafka's, 19, 203–4, 206, 210–13, 224, 227, 235; and life, xx, 6–7, 45, 204, 211–12, 224; Nietzsche's, xiv–xv, 13–14, 33–35, 36–37, 46–48, 54, 56–61, 66–67; and philosophy, 3, 7, 10, 185–86, 197, 198, 214–15, 295–96, 318; and schizoanalysis, 55–63, 65–71; and the state, 198, 203–4, 206, 210,

228; and thinking, xv, 4, 6, 13, 19–20,
24–25, 35–37, 47–48, 51, 58, 60–61, 117,
295–96, 314–15, 317–18
writing machine, Deleuze's, 3, 19, 23–24,
61, 339n34; language as, 201–2,
358n30; and the literary machine,
185, 198, Nietzsche's, 15, 40, 48, 61;
and the subject, 65–66
Wyatt, Justin, 371n109

Xeno, 148, 243, 354n62, 354n76

Yeats, W. B., 374n20

Žižek, Slavoj, 176, 362n19, 373n19;
Organs without Bodies, 14
zone of indiscernibility, 40, 99, 218;
between philosophy and literature,
7, 185
Zourabichvili, François, 305, 343n82,
373n16
Zukunftsroman, 295. See also science
fiction

GREGORY FLAXMAN is associate professor of English and comparative literature and adjunct professor of communications at the University of North Carolina, Chapel Hill. He is editor of *The Brain Is the Screen: Deleuze and the Philosophy of Cinema* (Minnesota, 2000).